ORGANIZATIONAL
REALITY

Reports from the Firing Line

ORGANIZATIONAL REALITY

Reports from the Firing Line

edited by

PETER J. FROST
University of British Columbia

VANCE F. MITCHELL
University of British Columbia

WALTER R. NORD
Washington University

SCOTT, FORESMAN AND COMPANY
Glenview, Illinois
Dallas, Tex.   Oakland, N.J.   Palo Alto, Cal.   Tucker, Ga.   London, England

Organizational reality.

1. Organizational behavior—Addresses, essays,
lectures. I. Frost, Peter J. II. Mitchell,
Vance F. III. Nord, Walter R.
HD58.7.074 1982   658.4   81-21255
ISBN 0-673-16004-1   AACR2

*To
Nola,
Fran,
and
Ann*

ISBN: 0-673-16004-1

Copyright © 1982, 1977, Scott, Foresman and Company.

1 2 3 4 5 6-KPF-88 87 86 85 84 83 82

Contents

Preface

The enthusiasm with which the first edition of this book has been greeted by colleagues, students, and practicing managers in a variety of organizations far exceeded our initial expectations. The contrast between organizational life as presented in academic texts and the "reality" that emerges from the essentially non-academic literature from which our selections are drawn has provided a rich and flexible teaching tool. The regularity with which students read well beyond assigned material and drew on their additional reading for class discussions attests to their reception of the book. Practitioners have frequently commented to us that many of the readings describe "their" organizations.

In preparing this revision, over sixty percent of the selections in the first edition have been changed. In a number of instances, the selections we dropped were dated and have been replaced by more contemporary material. Other substitutions seemed to us more representative of the organizational reality we seek to present. The interest and stimulation we shared in preparing the first edition was experienced again in undertaking this revision. Once again, our contributions have been distributed equally throughout the book, and the ordering of names on the title page is simply a carry over of the random selection procedures followed in preparing the first edition.

No book is solely attributable to its authors and this book is no exception. Frances Mitchell did a great deal to make this revision possible by identifying and obtaining the numerous and often obscure permissions to reprint that were required. We owe a debt of gratitude to the many university and professional students in our courses whose reaction to the first edition guided this revision and served as a prod to our endeavor. We also thank the many astute and articulate students of organization whose reports comprise this book. Roger Holloway, our editor, was a continuing source of support and encouragement. Finally, our deep thanks to Susan Armstrong, Production Editor, and Jayne Cox, our Supervising Permissions Editor, who shepherded this book through with grace, good humor, and skill.

Peter J. Frost
Vance F. Mitchell
Walter R. Nord

Introduction

The introduction to the first edition of *Organizational Reality* began with the following four paragraphs.

"Suppose that you are a visitor to Earth from the distant planet Utopia. One of your assignments is to bring back printed materials to Utopian scholars who are attempting to understand what Earthlings call formal organizations. You have limited space so you must choose very carefully. One option you have is to bring back one or two of the leading textbooks on organizational behavior. Another option you have is to bring back selections from newspapers, business and general periodicals, and short stories and plays about life in organizations. Which would you choose to bring back?

"The picture that the Utopian scholars will develop from each of these sets of materials will most likely be very different. If you were to choose the textbooks, the scholars would most likely come to understand organizations as systems which are managed in a rational manner in pursuit of certain stated goals. They would be more than likely to conclude that organizations are staffed by people who are committed to achieve these objectives. Also, it is probable that the scholars would come to believe members of organizations are oriented towards cooperation and are sincerely concerned with each other's well being. Depending on the particular textbook you brought back, however, the scholars might conclude that organizations do not in fact operate in these ways, but that through the application of a certain set of procedures, techniques, philosophies, and so on, any organization which is not operating both rationally and cooperatively could be made to do so.

"By contrast, if you happened to take this book or some other collection of materials from periodicals, newspapers and other sources which have been less completely filtered by the academic mind, the picture of organizations the scholars derived would be quite different. They would be likely to decide that organizations are anything but rational, cooperative systems. They would conclude that members at all levels of the organization frequently pursue their own interests at the expense of others in the organization as well as at the expense of the achievement of the goals of a total organization. The scholars would see that organizations are frequently quite inhumane systems. Individuals experience intense stress from task demands as well as intense and often bitter conflict and rivalry with members of their own work group and with members of other work groups and organizations. One would also find that organizational participants often respond aggressively against these pressures and against whatever threatens their own interests. Furthermore, it is unlikely that the scholars would conclude that there is any discernible set of principles, techniques and philosophies which seems capable of turning most organizations into rational, cooperative systems. It is more likely that they would discover that various strategies of power, manipulation, human relations and 'all out war' are used, all having varying degrees of success in giving different organizational participants different degrees of influence in organizations.

"Most students in organizational behavior, introductory business and even management policy courses are exposed only to the first set of sources. In this book, we plan to provide a ready collection of the second set. We do not offer this collection as evidence that the normative views presented in most academic textbooks are totally irrelevant. In fact, we believe that the normative views are very relevant. However, it is ineffective to present them to students without complementary information about how organizations are experienced. Students readily discover that organizations as described in the textbooks are not the same as organizations they actually experience. Consequently, students and managers reject the 'whole package' of organizational behavior as 'soft,' theoretical or irrelevant without examining the potentially relevant materials. Many students take their courses in management and organizational behavior because they are required, but turn to accounting, finance, economics, information systems and even marketing when they seek to discover what organizations really are. Other students accept the text material while in school, but never find ways to translate it into action when they become managers."

These ideas provide a suitable introduction for this edition as well, since there appear to have been few changes either in the nature of organizations or in the description of organizations by academics. While a few anthologies similar to *Organizational Reality* have been published and more traditional anthologies on organizational behavior have begun to include a very few selections from non-traditional academic sources, for the most part textbooks in organizational behavior still fail to provide adequate descriptions of organizations as they are experienced by people.

Although the major thrust of this book remains the same, there are two reasons for publishing a revision at this time. First, many aspects of organizations are closely tied to current events; any book which attempts to deal with organizations as they are experienced will become dated very quickly. The dating does not seem to be due to the fact that old problems have disappeared but rather from either the appearance of new problems or the fact that old problems get discussed in somewhat different terms. The second, and most important, reason for this revision is that since we made our final decisions about what to include in the first edition a great amount of exciting and insightful material has been published. Moreover, we have become aware of several topics and a few excellent pieces that we wish we had included in the first edition. In short, our goal of providing a collection of materials that will introduce students to organizations as they are experienced has not changed. We do feel, however, that the updated edition provides a more stimulating, comprehensive collection for today's students.

Even though our basic purpose and approach remain the same, reactions of colleagues, students and other readers to the first edition have influenced our current positions in several ways. First, the number and intensity of the positive reactions we have received have strengthened our belief in the value of the perspective portrayed in this book. While we were not surprised by the favorable reactions of students, we have been particularly impressed by the fact that many of the most positive reactions have come from experienced managers who have reported seeing their organizations in a different and more informed way. In addition, we were made more aware of the somewhat arbitrary nature of our organization of the materials under the section headings we employed. This point was made quite well in Dr. Todd Jick's review of the first edition in the *Administrative Science Quarterly*, March, 1979. He observed that many of the presentations in the book are really holistic by themselves. Consequently, they

> ". . . do not subdivide into neat conceptual categories as textbooks and myopic journal articles would imply. Thus, it becomes an ill-fated effort to impose groupings among relatively holistic presentations." (p. 159)

Jick's criticism is a sound one. Many of the selections are rich; almost every one deals with at least several important issues. While we admit there is a certain arbitrariness in our grouping of the materials, we remain convinced that our message can be best communicated to students if the readings are organized in a framework which helps them to contrast these ideas with the ones they study in traditional textbooks and journals. Consequently we have retained the section organization, but have revised the section titles for the second edition.

One further change has taken place—in us. We have come to view organizations quite differently than we did as a result of our academic training. While we still feel that traditional academic approaches are worthwhile, we now see them more as one set of perspectives on the reality of the social processes we call organizations which needs to be complemented by other perspectives.

We do not propose that our collection of readings captures the "true" essence of organizations. We do suggest, however, that current management and organizational textbooks do not capture this essence either. Moreover, it may seem that the current collection provides a very distorted, biased picture of organizations. Undoubtedly there is some bias; we did not use a random selection procedure to determine which articles would be included. However, we did not systematically seek out muckrakers. We were amazed at how many other articles we could find which make very similar points to almost all the ones we have included. Therefore, we remain convinced that the contents of the book gives an accurate picture of many aspects of what people perceive to be the reality of organizations.

We ask the reader to pay careful attention to the sources of the articles included in this collection. Many of the selections come from what are normally considered mainstream business publications such as *Fortune* and the *Harvard Business Review*. Other selections come from fictional works, academic texts and journals, publications of organized labor, and several best selling books. Still, a number of selections were written by critics of organizations and individuals who are discontent with many elements of modern life. We believe these selections, taken together, provide a useful picture of a number of aspects of modern organizations.

Of course, the reader must ultimately determine for himself or herself how realistic the picture is. Unlike the interplanetary scholars, most readers of this book will have a number of alternative sources of information about organizations as they exist on earth. In addition to academic textbooks, they will have access to personal experiences and to the reactions of others who, willingly or not, have the quality of their lives thoroughly affected by their participation in modern organizations.

I

STAFFING

"Strip away the social proprieties and you are left with a primitive, ritualized confrontation, one which involves the mutual manipulation of firmly held self-interests."

—*Landau and Bailey*

During every working day, an intense struggle goes on in organizational settings. The focus of this struggle is the staffing decision — who gets into, moves in, and moves out of the organization. On one side is the organizational representative, typically a manager or administrator; on the other side is the individual, the job applicant or the candidate for promotion, transfer, or firing. The manager has at his or her disposal a wide range of tools, techniques, tactics, and devices, many of which have been revised and refined by behavioral scientists, and an insider's view of what the organization wants and intends from the staffing decision. These weapons provide the basis for the manager to probe and pry, to try to penetrate the protective armor of the individual on the other side of the decision equation. The weapons serve also to provide managers, if they wish, with protective cover so that they do not have to reveal a position unless by choice. A manager's tools include physical and psychological tests; tactics take the form of the panel interview, the business lunch, the appraisal interview, and the deep-end treatment. Devices managers use are the private secretary, as a buffer against intrusion, and the classification schemes themselves, which by defining people, jobs, roles, positions, and so forth, symbolize and shape what is within the organization's perspective and what is excluded.

The individual who wishes to gain entry to the organization, be promoted, move within, resign, or contest removal from the organization likewise has tools, techniques, tactics, and devices at his or her disposal. However, this protagonist in the struggle is not well served by behavioral scientists in any systematic sense. The applicants or contenders must make it on their own, drawing on personal resources, experience, a good deal of intuition, political savvy, and a smattering of survival or "how to" manuals written in the popular press. The objective for these individuals is to assess what the organization has to offer or has in store for them, while at the same time putting their best feet forward and protecting their self-esteem and self-interest.

We chose the articles in this section to display this battle and to point up and to dramatize certain features of the encounter. Taken as a whole, the articles provide an interesting spectrum of staffing issues. Getting past the receptionist to see the person who makes staffing decisions is a skill which Geoffrey Lalonde suggests requires firmness, a smile, and a certain amount of subterfuge. He recognizes the political nature of the struggle and identifies the role the receptionist plays in the process. In "What Every Woman Should Know" Landau and Bailey also recognize the politics of the staffing process. They identify several strategies imbedded in the selection interview at middle and senior levels of organizations and suggest ways to recognize and deal with these strategies. They note that the selection interview contains some traps to which women as job applicants are especially vulnerable.

The staffing contest typically involves parties of unequal power, and more often than not, it is the organization or its representative who holds the upper hand. Failure to manage this power differential with care and compassion may have unpleasant and undesirable consequences, particularly for the party in the low power position. "The Lab Rat" by Tom Wolfe illustrates the way in which individuals in the staffing process, in this case fighter pilots being considered for promotion to astronauts, can be humiliated, depersonalized, abused, and alienated by the experience. The article also shows that the individual's decision to fight back against organizational representatives can destroy his or her chances of being selected, especially if the targets are those who wield high power. "The Lab Rat" is a rich illustration of many other issues imbedded in the staffing process.

Failure to fight back can also damage the individual, as Sally Quinn found to her cost in her brief career with CBS in "We're Going to Make You a Star." In this case the struggle took on Kafkaesque proportions as neither side appeared to know which reality they were inhabiting. The emotional, psychological, and physical costs to individuals and, at times, the financial and effectiveness costs to organizations seem high when the staffing decision is either too loose or too programmed and depersonalized.

Staffing decisions need not proceed with the parties stumbling along in ignorance or behaving with arrogance and aggression. "Bob Six's Long Search for a Successor" by Rush Loving, Jr. reveals the anatomy of a promotion decision in which attention to tools, techniques, and tactics is blended with a concern for the self-esteem and dignity of all the parties and a time perspective for slowly evolving an acceptable outcome — something notably absent in the Sally Quinn story.

Ground rules for the staffing decision at senior levels of organizations appear to ensure sameness rather than to have encouraged diversity in outcomes in "Organization Men Still Run the Show" (Lynn Langway). Regardless of individual differences on a personal level, the staffing system, according to this article, appears to produce senior managers who are male, white, Republican, and Protestant with backgrounds in accounting or finance. It is interesting to note that Bob Six, after a complex and lengthy selection process, likewise chose a financial man as president. Bob Six rose to that same position having been characterized as an entrepreneur and an innovator, and he was not subjected to the same hurdles and evaluative encounters as those he managed. Perhaps the struggle at this level is too one-sided; that is, organizations respond positively only to a narrowly defined category of individual applicants. They fail to see that their imposed reality with its emphasis on reliability and consistency in choice of candidate type may discourage applications from or interest in other kinds of people who are needed for modern organizations to run effectively.

Perhaps the most painful of all staffing decisions is the firing of an employee. "The Art of Firing an Executive" by Judson Gooding once again exemplifies the struggle between the organization and the individual. Again, the decision can be reached with or without concern for the person who is to be released. Gooding discusses the guilt feelings that are aroused by having to fire an individual and points out the costs to both parties of failing to retain the dignity and self-esteem of the individual who is being fired.

Getting Past the Receptionist on the Phone or in Person

Geoffrey Lalonde

WHAT SEEMS DIFFICULT IS REALLY VERY EASY

Now we are going to show you how to get past a secretary/receptionist or administrative assistant in order to get right through to the boss.

The job of the receptionist or assistant is to screen everyone wanting to see the boss (ensuring that the boss's time is not wasted), and direct traffic to the right people.

You, as the job hunter, must get past the receptionist to see the boss. You don't want to be interviewed by the receptionist.

WHAT TO SAY

The most important thing to remember when you go into the room and see that receptionist is *smile* and *keep smiling*. (Refer to "Telephone Technique" for smiling!)

Remember, the job of the receptionist is to direct you to somebody else. Your job is to get to see the man who will help you with your career. Be convinced of the special contribution you can make to the organization. Make sure you are always in command of the situation. Be polite, but firm. Don't take no for an answer. Smile and move forward, assuming, as a matter of course, that you're going to get in.

Stand quite close to the reception desk. When a person stands a distance from the desk, it conveys an automatic subconscious impression that you do not think your business is really important enough to see the boss and that there really isn't much of a chance you will get in anyway.

So stand quite close to the reception desk, *smile,* and say:

"Good morning, may I see Mr. Jones (President, Manager, Executive)?"

When you say this, you're going to get a reply from her, such as:

"Do you have an appointment?" or "I'm sorry, he's busy." or "Why do you want to see him?" or "I'm sorry, you have to have an appointment." or "Mr. Jones always insists on knowing the nature of the business before seeing anyone." or "I'm sorry, he's busy this week."

Your response is:

"No, I don't have an appointment." or "It's personal. May I see Mr. Jones now?" or "It's personal. Could you tell him Geoffrey Lalonde is here to see him?" or "It's a personal matter. Could you tell him Geoffrey Lalonde is here to see him?"

The receptionist must make sure her boss doesn't spend time with a visitor she judges would be a waste of time. She may feel it would not be in his interest because it might be more appropriate for you to see another person. In each of the preceding questions the receptionist is doing the job that she is paid to do. You are likely to be a complete stranger to her. Part of the receptionist's training is to determine what your business is (what you want) and then send you to the appropriate person.

Don't be nervous if the receptionist questions you. *But don't tell her the purpose of your visit.* As soon as you tell her, she will be on the offensive and will fall back on her training. She'll send you to the Personnel Department — and you're dead!

Under no circumstances should you let the receptionist know what you want to talk to her boss about.

What will happen next? She may let you in by first calling her boss and getting a clearance. Then you're in.

She may not let you in and may give you a standard stall, "I'll have him/her call you." Your reply: "Thank you, I'd be happy to have him call, but could I make an appointment now? Could I see Mr. Jones at 3:00 P.M. this afternoon, or would 9:00 A.M. tomorrow morning be more convenient?"

Remember, she can only go so far. As long as you don't spill the beans and tell her the nature of your business, she will eventually have to pass you through to her boss.

The good secretary or receptionist has usually developed a considerable number of sneaky replies designed to trap you into stating your business.

She may come back with a legitimate response: "I'm sorry, Mr. Jones is busy. Would you care to see his assistant?"

Your come-back: "No, thank you. It's a personal matter. Would you tell him Geoffrey Lalonde was in to see him. I'll call him. When would be a good time? This afternoon at 2:00 P.M., or would 3:00 P.M. be more convenient?"

She may say, "I'm sorry, he's away in Nova Scotia until the end of the week."

Your come-back: "When would it be possible to set up a short meeting with him for ten minutes? Could I see him next Monday at 10:00 A.M., or would 11:00 A.M. be more convenient?"

She may say, "Sure. 10 o'clock. Could I tell him what it's about?"

Don't fall into the trap! This is a subtle trap to get you to tell her your business.

Simply reply: "Could you tell him it's a personal matter?" Then thank her and leave.

Remember, she is only doing the specialized screening job she was trained for. If she is unable to get the answer she wants from you, she has no alternative but to pass you on to her boss. That is exactly what you want.

Again remember, simply reply: "Could you tell him it's a personal matter?" Then thank her and leave.

HOW COMPLETE STRANGERS GOT IN TO SEE
THE MINISTER

In the three years I worked for C.M. Drury in Ottawa there were many strangers who got in to see him in spite of a large staff of assistants, executive secretaries, secretaries, and receptionists. These people called on the phone, or came in person without appointments. These people did not know him personally.

In our office on Parliament Hill, besides myself, there were two executive secretaries and the Minister's personal secretary. Among our many responsibilities was running interference on total strangers demanding to see the Minister. We were very successful in the vast majority of cases, giving prompt attention to the public by handling their problems personally, or referring them to other members of the staff of twenty-two, or to department officials. But regularly, week after week, strangers would get through us. How? By using the technique I have just outlined.

For example, a person would come in and ask to see the Minister. S/He would invariably run into the polite but formidable Edith Cornblatt, the Minister's personal secretary. If Edith didn't get to the bottom of the problem and was having trouble she would call me to help her or the visitor.

I would swing into high gear with "May I help you?" but, provided the visitor did not reveal his/her reason for wanting to see the Minister personally, there was absolutely nothing to be done but arrange an appointment.

Now, to put your mind at rest, let me tell you there were many other things which the visitor had in his/her favor. First of all, Edith might have felt the Minister could do with some public contact on that particular day. Second, sometimes Mr. Drury had a few free minutes because a meeting had finished early and would come through the door, speak to the visitor, ask if he could be of assistance, and invite the visitor in. Often the Minister would criticize our inability to spot a crank after a particularly onerous meeting — but still, week after week, we had to let through those who stuck to "It's personal."

What Every Woman Should Know
Here's how to cope with those tricky executive-level job interviews

Suzanne Landau and Geoffrey Bailey

Top job interviews are not often friendly. Neither are top-job interviewers, though they may appear to be on the surface. In fact, the higher up the business hierarchy you climb, the less likely you are to be interviewed (in the traditional sense of the word). You will engage in apparently genial and composed discussions whose outer informality disguises a scrupulous exercise in personal assessment. Strip

From the book *The Landau Strategy: How Working Women Win Top Jobs.* Published by Lester & Orpen Dennys Limited. Reproduced by permission.

away the social proprieties and you are left with a primitive, ritualized tribal confrontation, one which involved the mutual manipulation of firmly held self-interests. Be coldly realistic about this. Most men are. Keep in mind that the kind of person you have to persuade to hire you is a wily corporate pro. Competence will impress him, but not that much more than worldliness, self-assurance, and realism.

Think tough. At least during the last day or two before you start attending serious meetings. Have someone whose cynicism and business acumen you trust (you may even decide to use your genial neighborhood headhunter) go over your résumé and fire some hard questions at you. Get that person to play fast and loose with your accomplishments: attacking, probing, putting down. Keep in mind that somewhere out there, laying in wait for you, is a grizzled old pro who will rip your claims about yourself to shreds. Defend yourself against that possibility ahead of time, with a few dry runs.

Be prepared to:

- identify and discuss in detail the kinds of projects you worked on and what the precise consequences of your involvement were;
- justify your employment history, especially in terms of moving from one job to another, with carefully propounded reasons;
- express your career goals convincingly, preferably on the basis of a three-to-five-year timetable;
- rebut impertinent (and illegal) questions about marriage plans, intention to procreate, and domestic arrangements while you work.

Questions along these lines represent an unnecessary intrusion into your private life and are irrelevant to your professional preoccupations.

Say so.

Try to develop early insights about the person scheduled to interview you. Does your prospect receive you promptly? Lack of punctuality suggests one of four things: exceptional business (a good sign); a power-play mentality (a bad sign — power plays are for corporate infighting, not interviewing newcomers); disorganization or carelessness; or, finally, downright insecurity (disastrous). Observe the manner in which you are received: in person, or through a secretary. It's a surefire sign of a loser if an interviewer with an unprepossessing office feels the need to send a secretary out to fetch callers.

Bear in mind that an interview starts the moment your arrival is announced, not later when you cross the threshold of your prospect's office. It's astonishing (and more than a little frightening) to consider what some high-ranking people perceive as being significant personality indicators. One headhunter we interviewed talked at length about the pre-interview ploys he used to make early candidate assessments: the magazines people picked up (as an indication of their intellectual proclivities) and the chairs they chose.

Once inside your prospect's office, choose your seat carefully. Look for the second most powerful place to settle in (unless, of course, your choice is made for you) and slip into it gracefully.

Let your prospect lead. Especially during those vital early intuitive seconds of the meeting. Imagine that your prospect is a rather successful, professionally accomplished maiden aunt who, out of a distant interest in your personal development, has invited you for tea at her apartment. Behave towards your prospect as your aunt would almost certainly expect you to behave towards her: with a discreet mixture of controlled warmth and respect.

Pleasantries dealt with, go, urbanely, with the flow. That first transition, from the conversational to the professional, tells all. The range and variation of interview procedures women encounter are more complex and demanding than those met by men. Beyond having to deal with routine questions about background and technical ability, female candidates for particular job opportunities are frequently subjected to mild forms of harassment. Our research (and considerable personal experience) suggests that, broadly speaking, there are seven different kinds of interview, ranging from the routine fact-finding exercise right along to the business lunch. At least two of the interview formats we have isolated ("Big Daddy" and "Just a Gigolo") are, in our view, unique to women. The remainder are common to both sexes:

1. Down the line
2. Trick or treat
3. Big daddy
4. Just a gigolo
5. Menage à trois
6. Out to lunch
7. Only Cartesians need apply

Down the Line

The straightforward informational kind of interview, one that seemingly amounts to little more than a routine checking of your personal and professional background, is frequently misunderstood by women. Naively, they tend to believe that apparently honest, dispassionate-sounding questions deserve equally honest, dispassionate-sounding responses. But the politics of the recruitment process suggest that this kind of interview has to be treated not as an exercise in epistemology, but rather as an opportunity for some subtle showing-off.

"The secret with these routine interviews is to regard them as personality tests. Don't get bogged down with too much detail. Tell the interviewer accurately and snappily what he wants to hear — about yourself, your background, why you're interested in the job. Keep the delivery upbeat and fresh. The fact is that summarizing personal and career details in an interview is the easiest thing in the world to do. Okay. So recognize that. And put everything you've got into verbal presentation. But don't be cute."

Nancy Mayer knows what she's talking about. She works in the personnel department of a major Fifth Ave. retailer, interviewing hundreds of people a year in her job. She talks to women applying not only for secretarial and sales jobs but also for more senior positions in sales and general management. Many of her interviews are of the routine, fact-finding kind—exploring the when, what, and where of an employment history, prior to a candidate going forward to more detailed discussions with line managers.

"Very occasionally," Mayer told us, "I get to meet a young woman who turns me on during one of these exercises. Those that do turn me on—and remember I can do these interviews in my sleep—tend to have three characteristics in common. First, they're not afraid to be direct and warm. They look me in the eye and, believe it or not, they smile. Second, they're prepared to be humorous in the right places. I ask a routine question, they recognize it for what it is and respond with a sense of irony and fun about the thing. That's fine. It means they're alive, thinking. We don't hire people who appear to have just been lobotomized. Third, and this is very important, they take the trouble to give the impression that their job moves follow some kind of logic, that there's some kind of rhyme and reason to what they want to do. I can't stand it when women come to me and say, 'Gee, I just think it'll be a gas working here.' And some do say that, you know."

Think of the "Down the Line" interview as an opportunity to define and determine, quite apart from your basic occupational resources, a group of selling propositions about your character and personality that make you different from the competition. Since in the basic recruitment scheme of things women are still regarded as number twos, they have but one alternative: to try harder.

Trick or Treat

The principal difference between the "Down the Line" and the "Trick or Treat" interview is one of psychological and intellectual intensity. The former is, in principle anyway, "coastable." The latter is all sudden inclines, blind curves, and unexpected changes of pace. You are, at "Trick or Treat" time, on trial. The interviewer, though pleasant on the surface, will probe your background and experience with great resolution and incisiveness. If there is a chink in your armor he will pierce it and unless you maintain an impeccable facade, coolly watch you bleed.

During the "Trick or Treat" interview, your interviewer is quite likely to pick up on what you consider to be your finest and most clear-cut achievement, and belittle it. You may have been responsible for a $150,000 export deal or involved with a pivotal company economy or acquisition. No matter. "Trick or Treat" interviewers are more interested in personal or professional analysis than in any particular sense of self-worth their prey might have.

Your résumé is a thesis whose contents you are under an obligation to defend. The quality of your defense will determine, in the eyes of your questioner, the value of your professional achievements.

One woman we spoke to told us how the size of the budgets she was responsible for managing while working for a Canadian company operating out of Vancouver were ridiculed by a man interviewing her for a job in Los Angeles. Her response was cut and dried. She said, rightfully, that since markets in Canada were 10 times smaller than those in the United States, an intellectually honest appraisal of her performance by him would mean that every financial statement made in her résumé ought to be multiplied ten-fold.

Big Daddy

Big Daddy comes in two varieties: the paternalist and the soothsayer. Of interview encounters between the two, the latter is likely to be the most promising, for the soothsayer at least is capable of understanding you and your ambition on the only terms that count, those you have set for yourself. The paternalist sees you as an attractive stereotype, a fascinating version of the daughter he either has or has always wanted.

Much has been made of the role that certain kinds of sympathetic older men can play in the careers of young, ambitious women. The soothsayer (or rabbi, as he is sometimes referred to), identifiable by his honest enthusiasm for the energetic and intelligent efforts that you are evidently making to find yourself a job, is an interviewer whom it is least necessary for you to make a contrived effort to impress.

One woman we spoke to, working for a federal agency in Washington involved with developing financial aid programs for the Third World, observed that the secret with the soothsayer interview is that there is no secret. "Frankness and clarity of career intentions are what work in this kind of interview," she said. "Games, ploys, and stratagems are inappropriate. Just tell him what you've done and what you'd like to do. True to his nickname, he'll tell you whether your ambitions are realistic, and, if he takes to you, he'll also help you achieve them."

No such luck with the paternalist. In fact, of all the interview situations you encounter, the one involving him is least likely to bear fruit. It would be wonderful if we were able to recommend a list of stratagems that would enable a female interviewee to turn the tables on a dyed-in-the-wool male paternalist. But we can't — not quite. Paternalism, particularly towards women, is one of the most profoundly entrenched attitudes in corporate life. Like a debilitating disease, paternalism can only be treated by the sustained use of appropriate medication: first-class work presented unambiguously as your own. However, while this approach makes sense once you have a job, it is clearly irrelevant in a situation where you are trying to secure one.

One woman we interviewed (Elayne Bernay, research director of *Ms. Magazine)* was convinced that there is nothing you can do about overt paternalism in an interview situation. "We don't hire our children," she says bluntly. Another executive woman with whom we discussed the problem did have one recommendation. She advises that you unabashedly flatter your prospect into submission. "Tell him that the central reason why the job interests you is because of the opportunity to learn through the example and under the guidance of someone (namely him) whose reputation is of the highest order."

This statement puts your prospect in a double bind. He can only disagree with you at the risk of publicly diminishing his professional standing (and paternalists, rarely do that); or he can agree, in which case you have furnished him with a reason, over and above whatever hard qualifications support your candidacy, to take you more seriously than he did at the beginning of the meeting. Even if the paternalist sees through your soft soap, chances are that he will still be sufficiently impressed to offer you half-a-dozen referrals. If he doesn't, ask for them.

At this stage you have nothing to lose.

Just a Gigolo

The sexual harassment of women is extremely pervasive at all levels of working life. And there is no indication that it diminishes the higher up the socio-economic scale one goes. It becomes subtler perhaps but, according to at least two contemporary books on the subject *(The Secret Oppression: Sexual Harassment of Working Women* by Constance Backhouse and Leah Cohen, and *Sexual Shakedown: The Sexual Harassment of Women on the Job* by Lin Farley) no less prevalent.

While the male chauvinist is more likely to badger you once you've been hired—and you therefore have more to lose—he's by no means averse to pick-up attempts during job interviews. Since sexual harassment will probably take place in the privacy of an office, you have very fragile empirical grounds on which to lodge a complaint to the interviewer's superior, if you decide to do so. No Civil Rights Act can protect you from sexual innuendo expressed behind closed doors.

"Just a Gigolo" comes in all shapes and sizes. But if he has a single characteristic feature it is narcissism, a rabid self-love.

Any attempt at sexual harassment has to be handled sternly. The response, "My understanding is that this was intended to be a business meeting. I'm not prepared to respond to any questions or suggestions that bear on my personal life unless they are clearly relevant to the subject under discussion," is probably the most appropriate because:

- It serves notice that you take exception to his line of questioning;
- It is vague on the issue of whether or not the interviewer is deliberately testing you, therefore giving him an opportunity to backtrack;
- It gives the interviewer a chance to proceed on a civilized basis in a way that a straight "Listen, buster, this is a place of business not a singles' bar" does not;
- It works on men of all ages, from the pubescent stud to the middle-aged lecher.

A straightforward reprimand always beats moral indignation. It's more worldly, less ambiguous. Prissy people lack class. However, it's one thing to finesse a pass; it's another to work for the man who made it. Remember, you'll be seeing a lot of this man if he hires you.

Menage à Trois

It's two against one. Mr. X and Mr. Y. Mr. X asks the questions, Mr. Y sits there, watching, listening, and maybe taking notes. The atmosphere is formal, subdued, and almost alarmingly polite. It's like being back in the classroom.

The very artificiality of the situation is the reason why the "Menage à Trois" interview is the trickiest for a candidate to come through unscathed. The political chemistry of the meeting can very easily get confused, particularly if the relative status of your two interrogators has not been made plain. For some women, used to full-scale sales presentations that obliged them to address several people simultaneously, the "Menage à Trois" interview will present few problems. But for the rest, it can be downright terrifying.

And a terrified candidate, like a terrified actress, stands a better than average chance of flubbing her lines.

We spoke to one uncharacteristically hopeful and conscientious headhunter who spent a great deal of her time and energy preparing her candidates for interviews. We raised the issue of the two-against-one interview and asked if she had any advice to offer candidates, particularly women, confronted with such a situation.

"Absolutely," she says. "The two-on-one interview, as you call it, can be very unnerving and counterproductive, in my view. I have a couple of clients, though, who feel it to be a proper part of the recruitment procedure, and they do it frequently. They either double up a line manager with someone from personnel, or, if they have more than one opportunity available in different divisions, they may set the thing up between the two appropriate managers and cut out personnel altogether. I tell my candidate to try to do three things in these cases: (a) establish the relative seniority of the people doing the interview so you can at least have a crack at impressing the most powerful; (b) address your answers to both parties, switching your attention from one to the other, so that neither feels left out; and (c) try to create a discussion group atmosphere rather than that of a tribunal."

The headhunter went on to say that if the quieter of the two interviewers remains unresponsive, you have no alternative but to return to a straight question-and-answer session with the more talkative of the two. "But as least you've tried to get outside the straitjacket. And that shows determination, originality and strength of character, three very definite pluses."

Out to Lunch

There are three major tactical considerations for the job-related lunch: eat little, drink less, and stay alert to leading questions. An invitation to lunch is a further test, not a certificate of approval. While it suggests that your candidacy is being taken seriously (your prospects are prepared to invest some expenses in you), it certainly does not mean that you have been accepted and that further discussions are a formality.

In many ways the job-related lunch is the most demanding of all interview situations. Apart from being subjected to routine restaurant distractions (sudden outbursts of laughter, the clink of glasss), you are also obliged to juggle menus, cutlery, a napkin, the timing of your next mouthful.

The business lunch can be a trying affair, even for people who undertake it routinely. "Nevertheless," observed one former Hollywood agent we interviewed in Toronto, "there are rules. Believe me. I've breakfasted, brunched, and lunched my way into a zillion deals over the years and I know exactly what they are."

While our contact was not specifically concerned about discussing the problems associated with the job-related lunch, the observations she made are entirely appropriate to it:

- Order something simple or something you know. Don't use the lunch as a culinary experiment. Choose forkable food. An attempt to negotiate a bowl of spaghetti, for example, could be disastrous;
- Have no more than one drink. Order a white wine spritzer, something light anyway. Keep in mind, especially if you had no breakfast, that a drink unaccompanied by food will loosen your tongue faster than a drink consumed while eating;
- Don't equivocate when the time comes to order. Execute the task swiftly and surely. Stay away from the "shall I have this or shall I have that," syndrome;
- Don't forget that you're at a meeting where, coincidentally, food is being consumed. Your primary task is to concentrate on the conversation;
- Be as attentive to your smoking habits as you are to your drinking habits. Smoking is increasingly unfashionable these days. If you must smoke, at least ask the people with whom you are lunching whether or not they mind.

Only Cartesians Need Apply

We have all been subjected to the philosophical interview. Introduced towards the end of a series of preliminary discussions, or, perhaps, at the conclusion of a long, single conversation, the philosophical interview begins with the preamble: "Tell me. Now we've covered the basics about your job, let's talk about the future of (if it's your specialty) the synthetic rubber industry. Our problem is this. One of the major applications of our product is the prevention of soil erosion. But soil erosion is a topographical characteristic of Third World countries whose politics are, in general, erratic. What do you think our corporate policy should be?"

More than a few candidates have lost a job opportunity because they were unequal to the task of discussing long-term implications of their work. The response, "To be perfectly frank, I've never felt comfortable theorizing about the future of the synthetic rubber industry. Speculation is for academics or astrologers, not me," is rarely sufficient to turn the line of questioning away to more empirical ground. On the contrary, a declared reluctance to stargaze is the sign of a closed mind, of a parochial intellect.

Never go into a major job interview without being prepared for some tough exchanges about basic approaches, basic philosophies. And if you feel uncertain about your strengths in this area, bone up fast. Talk to colleagues, go to the library. Top job interviews rarely stop at technical qualifications. Being able to express a reasonably coherent overview of your subject can represent the difference between being passed over and being hired.

Concepts count.

In the Cartesian spirit of healthy skepticism and clarity of mind, we offer you a concluding checklist of five general questions you may be asked during your interviews. Since very few questions asked in interviews are entirely unambiguous, we have provided each one with a parenthetical translation:

Tell me a little bit about yourself. Translates to: How much trouble have you taken over your career? How well are you able to track your professional life?

Why do you want to leave your current employer? Translates to: What is the nature of your dissatisfactions and how rationally and coherently are you able to express them?

Tell me about your current job. Translates to: Give me a concisely expressed summary of your present responsibilities in a way that enables me to see how well your current work will have applications here.

What do you think of your current management? Translates to: To what extent are your present dissatisfactions likely to be duplicated here?

And finally, we list below working precepts to take with you to all your interviews:

- If there's a silence, don't fill it. Let the interviewer step in with a further question to which you can deliver a crisp, relevant answer;
- Never leave a weakness unqualified;
- Never leave a strength unsold.

The trouble with so many individuals involved in the recruitment process is that they have a natural, human aversion to rejecting people. This means that, unless brought firmly up against the issue, they will prefer prevarification to frankness. It's hard to look someone in the eye and tell her she is not going to make it. Far harder than a regretful telephone chat or, less upsetting still, than sending a tactful note.

The point of an interview is to proceed further. Better to provoke a turndown in a sequence of interviews by asking outright about your chances of success than to risk wasting time and energy pursuing the unpursuable.

One of your most formidable foes, at least during the interview stage of your campaign, is false hope. Your conviction that you have been outstandingly impressive in an interview is worthless without the interviewer's corresponding conviction that he wants to either continue the dialogue or make you an offer.

An offer closed is the job hunter's equivalent to a sale made.

We're Going to Make You a Star
Sally Quinn

The countdown: Dick Salant, president of CBS News, was beaming. Hughes Rudd was chuckling to himself and Sally Quinn was fending off questions about her sudden rise in TV news. The setting was a luncheon at "21" in New York and the guests included members of the press, who were given an opportunity to meet and chat with the CBS correspondents who will go on the air next Monday. Salant was saying he'd love to switch the time of the *CBS Morning News* show from 7 A.M. to 8 A.M. but he'd run into opposition from the fans of *Captain Kangaroo*. "I know because I raised all my children on *Captain Kangaroo*." If the new team is a success, Salant said naturally he'd take credit for the show, but if the show bombs he said he's going to find someone to point the finger at. Who dreamed up Rudd and Quinn? he was asked. "That was Lee Townsend." Townsend, the executive producer, however, modestly disclaimed credit. "It was a group effort," he told Eye, *Women's Wear Daily*, Tuesday, July 21, 1973 . . .

When Gordon and I first discussed the job I told him I had grave reservations about his choice. I reminded him that I was controversial, opinionated, flip, open and had no intention of changing. Was he sure this was what he wanted on television? Did they really want me to say what came to my mind during the ad libs, and would they not try to turn me into a bland, opinionless, dull-but-safe marshmallow? And I wondered aloud whether, if we were supposed to be journalists, we could maintain any kind of objectivity and still express controversial opinions—or any opinions, for that matter.

"Paley wants controversy," Gordon had said. "And so does Salant. You can get away with much, much more at that hour than you ever could on the *Evening News*."

I had doubts and so did a lot of people I talked to, but I figured CBS knew what it wanted.

I also pointed out to Gordon that I had a rather unconventional life style. I had been living on weekends with Warren, I explained, and if I moved to New York I would move in with him. I would also be talking about him openly and freely in interviews. I saw nothing wrong with it, and I had no intention of hiding the fact.

I think Gordon gulped a little at that one, but he gamely said that was just fine, I could say anything I wanted to. After all, CBS was not hiring me because or in spite of my personal life.

On Friday morning, June 22nd, the first piece about me appeared in *The Washington Post*. The head ran "SHOWDOWN AT SUNRISE," and it carried pictures of me and Barbara opposite each other. I wasn't too crazy about that. It created an atmosphere of rivalry I would have preferred to avoid. But my editors laughingly pointed out that I was now a public personality and had no say in the matter. They also pointed out that it was clearly the right angle for the story. They were right.

TV critic John Carmody had written, "Although a number of her candid interviews had attracted CBS's attention, it was, ironically enough, her appearance on Miss Walters' *Not for Women Only* TV program that whetted the network's interest." He quoted Salant as saying that the format of the revamped show would "have no relationship to the *Today* Show" and would "retain the integrity of the basic news show." But also as predicting that "*Today* is ripe to be taken."

Stuart Shulberg, the producer of the *Today* Show, was quoted: "We welcome fresh competition. *Today* has led the morning field for so long that we could run the risk of growing too fat, smug, and sassy. This will speed up the pace, sharpen our competitive spirit, and provide the kind of honest competition we need and relish. May the best program win."

Barbara Walters was quoted: "The only thing I can say as a woman in broadcasting is that I welcome any new member to the fold. . . . I have respect and friendship for Sally. I know her very well. And I applaud both her and CBS for a very smart choice."

And Sally Quinn said: "Barbara is a great friend of mine and one of the most professional people I've ever known. As far as competing with each other, we covered the Shah's celebration in the desert of Iran together last year and stayed in the same dormitory. That's like being in combat together, and I imagine this will be a somewhat similar situation."

And we were off. . . .

Monday, rehearsals began. Thank God. Now they were going to roll it all out for us, lay it on, let us in on all the fabulous plans for the first week of shows. And it was about time. I had begun to have doubts, but I knew that they would disappear as soon as we got to the studio and saw what they had for us.

We were to arrive at 6 A.M. to start getting the feel of getting up early. We would watch the *Morning News,* then go into a simulation of what our anchor booth was going to look like (it wasn't nearly ready) and tape a news broadcast. We were to write it from the same wires and newspapers that John Hart had used earlier.

Lee Townsend was jittery. Townsend, the most even-tempered man I know, was also as irritated as I had ever seen him. He had been against the promo tour (though he didn't object violently enough) because he felt we could have better used our time rehearsing. His objections had been overridden by Blackrock, which — who? I never got the pronoun straight — had insisted that it was necessary. So Townsend was nervous and angry because we had been away and virtually co-opted by the PR department, and because it was then clear to him that we didn't have a super-duper razzle-dazzle show to put on the air in a week's time. And no real studio to rehearse in.

He had reason to be more than nervous, and we did exactly what we had done for the pilot except at greater length. We wrote a little news and a few lead-ins to film pieces, and Hughes wrote an essay. I couldn't think of anything that morning, and besides, I'm not an essayist. I'm a reporter and interviewer. Hughes would do essays, which he did marvelously, and I would do what I did best.

In front of the camera, they outfitted me with an ear-piece on a wire, called a Telex, which enables them to talk to you from the control room. They handed us mikes, rolled our copy onto the TeleProm-Ters, and away we went. It was a disaster. There were two cameras and I didn't know which one to look at. The stage manager waved his hands around, but I hadn't a clue what he was trying to tell me. I was fumbling my words and couldn't read the prompters. They were shouting in my ear through the Telex to do this and do that, and three minutes here and twenty seconds there, and ad lib here. The ad libs were always by surprise, and I would fumble around trying to think of something clever to say about a film piece we had just seen. It might have been a bloody plane crash or a dairy farm. It BOMBED, and I was shell-shocked by the time it was over. Suddenly I *knew* this was the way it was going to be. There was nothing I could do about it. It was too late to get out of it.

I was even more upset when everyone came out of the control booth and said it was just fine and all it needed was a little smoothing out and we would be just great by the end of the week. No mention of any guests for interviews, no mention of any special film pieces that would lend themselves to interesting, informative ad libs and, most frightening of all, no mention of anything I should do to improve myself. I realized fully for the first time that I didn't know anything, and I panicked.

As we were filing down the stairs to the *Morning News* section, Jim Ganser, one of the producers, caught up with me. He was to be the only one at CBS who really tried to help me.

"Try to punch your words a little more," he sort of whispered out of the side of his mouth, as though he didn't want anyone to hear.

I fell on him. "What? How? What do you mean?" I said desperately. "Tell me, for God's sake. Tell me what I'm doing wrong."

And he told me. "You're wrong to expect anyone to give any help or guidance of any kind. You're a big star now, and people figure if you're a big star you must know what you're doing. Nobody's going to stick his neck out to help you."

I went to the ladies' room and threw up. But I had to hurry. Hughes and I were the "big stars" of a large press luncheon at the "21" Club, and we were late. . . .

We finally got into our own studio on Friday, and we rehearsed there Friday and Saturday. Nothing went right. Friday morning after John Hart's last show someone came into the Cronkites, where we were working, and said that the staff of the *Morning News* was having a farewell party for John and the old producer. I hadn't really seen John to talk to him. I like and respect him a great deal, but we had been so busy working the lobster shift (that's the night shift in newspapers) that we just hadn't had a chance to see each other.

"Oh, great, I'll go up and tell John goodbye," I said, jumping up from my chair.

"I wouldn't if I were you," someone said. "There's a great deal of hostility up there toward the new team. And the atmosphere upstairs is more like a wake than a party. I think you had better forget it."

That was the first I had heard of resentment or hostility on the home team front. It worried me because, except for Townsend, Hughes and me, the "team" was the same. There had been no staff changes. I had found that curious. If they had really wanted a whole new format, with more entertainment and a lighter mood, I thought that they would surely have tried to bring in some people who were more in the show-biz line. The *Morning News* staff was very good. But they were hard-news oriented, and Gordon had said the idea was to take on the *Today* Show.

That morning when I went in to get my makeup done for the rehearsals my hair was a mess. While I was upstairs, the woman who was doing my makeup said her friend Edith, the hairdresser for *Edge of Night,* was right down the hall and maybe she would roll my hair up on the hot rollers for me. She called Edith, and a round-faced woman in her late fifties, with reddish hair, big, wide innocent eyes, a very strong New York accent, and dyed-to-match pants, vest, blouse, and shoes, came rushing in. Edith said she would be delighted. She had the lightest, most soothing touch, and the whole time she did my hair she told me how great I looked and how terrific I was going to be on the air and that she was honored to do my hair. Then she asked who my official hairdresser was.

"Hairdresser? I don't have a hairdresser." Both women were stunned. "You have to have a hairdresser," they chimed. "Every woman on television has one. You can't just go on with your hair like this every morning."

Edith asked me if she could be my hairdresser and said she was sure that if I asked they would let me have one. I told Lee and Sandy Socolow about it and they both went blank. Nobody had given my hair a thought. They okayed it right away, but it indicates how little thought went into the planning for the first woman network anchor. Edith was a godsend. She not only took care of my hair, she took care of my ego.

After the rehearsal on Saturday, I was about to leave. No interviews were lined up for me for the following week. The big interview for Monday was with Patrick Buchanan, the President's speech writer, and that would be out of Washington. I had no idea what film pieces were going to be used. They weren't sure.

I was so depressed and scared that I didn't really care. I wanted to go somewhere and hide. As we were leaving (Sunday was a free day) Lee Townsend gave me a big smile and said, in a way I couldn't decide was joking or not, "Let me know if you have any good ideas tomorrow for the show."

Sunday was the worst day of my life. I thought about ways to disappear where no one would hear from me for years and would think I had been kidnapped by some freak. I considered the possibility of having plastic surgery so I would never be recognized as Sally Quinn. I fantasized about going on the broadcast and saying, "Good morning, I'm Sally Quinn and we are not prepared to do this show and I don't know what I'm doing up here." I thought seriously about calling Salant and Manning and telling them. I came close to quitting.

The water pipes broke in our apartment and I had to go to a friend's place on West End Avenue to wash my hair.

When I got out of the shower, I put on a large white robe that was hanging on the door. I came out of the bathroom draped in that robe and I said to Warren, who had been babysitting me all day, "I really feel like one of those ancient Aztec virgins who has been chosen to be sacrificed on top of the temple of the gods. All the other virgins are wildly jealous of her because she has this fabulous honor bestowed on her. What they don't know is that she doesn't want her heart cut out with a knife anytime by anyone. It hurts."

I went to bed at 5 P.M. It was bright and sunny outside, and I could hear the children playing on Riverside Drive and happy couples walking and chatting and laughing as they strolled in Riverside Park.

"I will never be happy again," I thought. "My life is over."

I never went to sleep. We had been coming in around 4 or 5 in the morning that week, but it wasn't proper preparation for coming in at 1:30. The alarm went off at 1:00 A.M. Warren was waiting to walk me to my limousine, which arrived promptly at 1:30 A.M. It was like being escorted in a golden carriage to the guillotine.

I didn't feel too hot. I figured it must be because I hadn't slept. I slipped into the gloamings of the enormous black car and we glided over to Hughes' apartment, the Apthorpe, a few blocks away on West End Avenue. He hadn't slept either. We didn't say a word. A few minutes later we arrived at the studio and went directly back to the *Morning News* area and into the Bullpen.

In front of each of us was a pile of news wire stories, the first edition of *The New York Times* and the *Daily News*. Bob Siller, the copy editor, was there and so was Dave Horowitz, one of the assistant producers. They would make up the "line-up." The line-up was a sheet on which the show was blocked out minute-by-minute. Taking all the film pieces and counting their time, they would, along with Hughes and me and Lee Townsend, decide what the top news stories were and allot a certain amount of time to each, from forty-five seconds to a minute, and then block out time for commercials (we had only network commercials for the first six weeks) and station breaks. They would leave about a minute and a half for Hughes' essay, and what was left — roughly five minutes — would be allotted for "ad libs."

While this was going on, Hughes and I read the papers and the wires to get an idea of what stories we wanted to use. When we had finished, about 3 or 3:30, Bob and Dave came back with the line-up designating which one of us would write which stories and which lead-ins to film pieces. If the film piece was ready, Hughes and I would try to take a look at it so that we could write a clearer lead-in; if not, there was generally some kind of script. Often the film piece wasn't ready. Horowitz and Siller, with our advice or without, would figure out which film piece seemed like the best topic for conversation and block in a certain amount of time for ad libs after those pieces. There was some freedom to move around, but not much. Everything we were to say we typed out on our enormous typewriters.

We had two writers who were to do the weather, sports and late-breaking news. Hughes was to read all the sports. We had tried to divide it, but I didn't understand sports and kept fumbling and breaking up in the middle of the report. Hughes hated it too, but it wasn't quite as ridiculous when he did it.

By the time Hughes and I would have read everything thoroughly, discussed camera angles with Bob Quinn, our director, who came in about 4, written all our news items, lead-ins and station and commercial breaks, had something to eat at our desks (it was called "lunch" and usually came from the CBS cafeteria, known appropriately and without affection as "the Bay of Pigs"), it would be about 6 A.M. — time for Edith and Rickey, the makeup person, to arrive and get us ready.

At around 3:30 I had started to break out in a cold sweat and I became weak and dizzy and slightly nauseated. I couldn't concentrate on what I was writing. Finally I went into Townsend's office and passed out. I tried to get up about 4 A.M. and write, but I stayed at my typewriter for about twenty minutes and then went back to Townsend's office and passed out again. I thought it was probably because I was tired and nervous, but by then my throat was so sore and I was coughing so badly that I could barely talk. I had shivers and had to be wrapped up in a blanket.

Everyone piled into Townsend's office and stared at me in horror. "Do you think you can do it?" Lee asked, terrified.

"I just don't know, Lee." I didn't.

I think at that point I was more scared not to go on than to go on.

"I'll try. I'll really try. But I can't talk. And I'm so dizzy. Is there any way I could get a vitamin B shot or something to give me quick energy?"

By then it was 5:30 in the morning and I was so sick I couldn't breathe. I kept trying to sit up and I would just fall right down. I couldn't tell whether the beads of perspiration on my head were from temperature or desperation. Finally Townsend said that they had to get me to a hospital. Somebody had a car and they carried me out to the front of the building, stuffed me in the car, and drove two blocks away to Roosevelt Hospital to the emergency room. A young doctor took me back to examine me and take my temperature. I had a temperature of 102 and he said he thought I might have pneumonia. I was coughing so badly that my body was racked. "You don't understand," I practically screamed. "I'm making my television debut in an hour."

"So I've heard," he smirked.

"Well, I can't possibly go on like this. Can't you give me a vitamin B shot or something? Anything."

He said that in my condition a vitamin B shot wouldn't do any good. The only thing he could do for me was to give me a throat spray that would stop me from coughing for a few hours. But he suggested that I get to a doctor immediately afterward for proper medication.

"Anything else I could give you now," he said, "would knock you out." Oh, how I wished . . .

He left the room and came back a few minutes later with the most enormous syringe I have ever seen, with a needle a mile long.

"Forget it," I said, backing away from him.

"Don't get hysterical," he said, laughing, "This is a throat spray. I'm not going to stick the needle in you."

He stuck the needle in my mouth and sprayed a gooey liquid, which coated the inside of my throat.

Lee grabbed me, back we went into the car, and we screeched off around the corner and back to CBS as though we were bank robbers getting away.

It was a little before 6:30. Edith and Rickey were frantic, and Hughes looked as though all his blood had drained out of him. Edith rolled my hair while Rickey sponged some makeup on me. I lay down while all this was going on. The hot rollers stayed in too long and I looked like Shirley Temple when my hair was combed out. There was nothing we could do about the frizz. At about ten minutes to seven they finished on me. I was still so weak and dizzy that I could barely move, and all I can remember is a large fuzz of Warren leaning over me asking if I was all right, Townsend in a frenzy, and Hughes pulling himself together as he walked into my dressing room. "Hughes —" I tried to smile — "get me off this horse immediately." Hughes tried to smile, too, but he wasn't very convincing. "Don't worry," he growled, "you'll make it, kid."

I tried to say thank you, but the throat spray had a numbing effect, like Novocain, and I couldn't feel whether my tongue was touching the roof of my mouth or whether I was forming my words properly.

"You look beautiful, darling, just beautiful. You'll be wonderful, I know you will," Edith was murmuring.

I looked in the mirror. I was hideous. My hair was frizzy, the granny glasses looked wrong, and the only thing I owned that wasn't blue (I hadn't had time to shop that week) was a yellow battle jacket that made me look like a dyke.

"Well," I thought, "there's no way anybody is going to accuse me of being a sex bomb this morning."

Somebody shoved a pile of telegrams in my face and I tried to read.

They were all amiable, from close friends and family, but it was upsetting me. "Oh, God," I thought, "if only they knew how terrible I'm going to be."

They were screaming for me to get into the studio and I ran in, got behind the desk, had my mike adjusted, and somebody handed me my Telex, which I stuck in my ear.

"One minute," yelled the floor manager.

My mouth was dry. No possibility of talking. I looked at Hughes. He was looking at me as though we were copilots and I had just been shot. He tried to smile. I tried to smile back.

"Thirty seconds," said the floor manager.

I looked straight outside the glass partition to the newsroom and saw everyone staring.

"Five seconds," the floor manager said.

For a fleeting moment I thought maybe I would wake up and find out this wasn't happening.

An arm went out to me and a finger pointed. I gazed at the Tele-PromTer.

"Good morning," I read, "I'm Sally Quinn. . . ."

I don't remember much else about that hour. I was propped up with several pillows because I was so weak and dizzy that I couldn't sit up by myself.

I coughed a lot. I remember a swirl of sweltering bright lights, moving cameras, different noises and shouts in my ear through the Telex — "Turn to Camera 2, thirty seconds to ad-lib, five seconds till commercial, ten seconds more of interview" — hand signals, desperate and self-delirious mumblings . . . and then it was over. And when it was over I felt completely numb. Nothing. . . .

When I walked back into my office there were three bouquets. One was from Charlotte Curtis, then editor of *The New York Times'* Family, Food, Fashions and Furnishings, now editor of the op-ed page of *The Times* and probably the woman I admire most in journalism. One from Vic Gold, former press secretary of former Vice President Spiro T. Agnew and now a columnist. And one from Connie Tremulis of "Flowers by Connie," Rockford, Illinois.

I still have their cards.

Everybody was talking at once and saying what a great show it had been and how did I ever get through it, and, boy, what a terrific start we had gotten off to, and how terrible the *Today* Show was outdoors in front of Rockefeller Center. I don't remember seeing Hughes. I remember Lee Townsend taking me by the hand and leading me outside to a taxi. I put my head back on the seat and stared out the window as we went whizzing up Central Park West. It was a beautiful day. I thought about all the people walking along the street and bicycling in the park and about how happy they looked. I thought how odd it was that my work day was over and it was only 8, and that that was going to be my life from now on. And how depressing it was. I did not think about the show. It had not happened. Nor did Lee mention it. . . .

During the first week, I had not seen or heard from Gordon. I debated whether or not to call him or leave a message, but then I figured if he wanted to see me he would have come back or sent a note. I will never understand why, after the first show, he didn't come screaming back to the *Morning News* and fire everybody, or put Hughes on with straight news, tell the world I had terminal pneumonia, and send me away to some hideaway studio in Connecticut with his trustiest producers and cameramen to work me over.

As far as I knew, nobody had seen or heard from Gordon. I waited each day for him to ask me into his office and explain gently that I needed some kind of training; that they were going to change the format, get a new set and a jazzy producer, set me up with taped interviews, get me out of reading the news, get me voice lessons, make me put on contact lenses, and demand that I grow my hair longer and cut out the ad libs.

Nothing.

The broadcast Monday was uneventful, including my first live television interview. It was — I still have a hard time believing this was the best person CBS could think of for my TV interview debut — the designer Emilio Pucci. I discovered that he was branching out from lingerie into sheets and men's wear.

Hughes did not participate. He wasn't all that anxious to, didn't particularly like to do interviews, and I'm sure he didn't have all that much to talk to Pucci about anyway, except the fact that they were both World War II pilots.

I called Gordon and left a message after the show. I was told he was out. Gordon soon became for me a Major Major Major figure from *Catch-22.* Hard to reach. . . .

My health all along had not been good. I still felt dizzy and nauseated in the early mornings, and I was constantly exhausted though there wasn't anything wrong with me as far as anyone could see.

There was, however, a major cosmetic problem.

For the first time since I was seventeen years old, I was developing acne. And it was getting bad. Rickey switched to an allergenic makeup, but it didn't help. The makeup and the bright lights must be doing it, I decided. I should have my face cleaned.

I remembered that a classmate of mine from Smith had a mother who ran an Institute of Cosmetology on East 62nd Street, which I occasionally read about in *Vogue* or *Harper's Bazaar*. Her name was Vera Falvy, and she was a Hungarian with the most beautiful complexion I had ever seen.

Mme. Falvy examined my face carefully and asked about my eating habits, health, and life style. She knew I was on TV but had no idea of the hours or the pressure. She felt the breakout was caused by emotional tension. I would need regular treatment. We made another appointment and she gave me a special lotion which I was to use under, or preferably instead of, makeup.

Altogether I visited Madame six times, and the bills ran close to $300. She did her best, but the tensions kept building and my face got worse. My complexion has never been the same. I have scars on my face to show for those horrible months. . . .

That week I got a call from Barbara Howar. We chatted for a bit and Barbara, who had had her own TV shows, gave me a few pointers. She told me that I was coming along really well and shouldn't worry. Then she said, "Why don't you look at the right camera when the show is closing each day? Half the time the camera zooms out to the newsroom while you're looking straight ahead into the camera in the studio, and whenever the camera is in the studio you're looking across at the newsroom. You've got to keep your eye on the red light."

"Red light?"

"For God's sake," she screamed, "hasn't anyone told you about the red light?"

"No," I said. "What about it?"

"There's a light on the side of the camera," she said, "and when it goes on red it means that camera is on you and that's where you're supposed to look."

"Oh, no," I moaned. "No wonder. I saw that light flash on and off but I didn't know what it meant." . . .

Thanksgiving was the next day, and we never had holidays off. It was the tenth anniversary of Kennedy's assassination. When I looked at the line-up that morning, I saw that the only scheduled interview was one I had done several weeks earlier with a woman who had written a diabetic cookbook.

I couldn't believe it. Hughes complained to no avail. That seemed like the final straw. On the tenth anniversary of a president's death we were to do a mediocre (at best) taped interview with a diabetic-cookbook writer. There was no hope for any of us, or that broadcast.

Without staff meetings, there was still no coordination. Things hadn't gotten better. Usually, we didn't know who the guest was to be until we came on the program, and half the time it was someone neither of us was interested in or wanted to interview. We wrote lists of suggestions and notes, but nothing ever came of them. It is not that the people on the staff were incompetent, but just that there was zero direction, that morale was low, and that there was no coordination.

We had a rule about not accepting guests if they'd already been on the *Today* Show, and they had the same rule about our show. What that meant was that we hardly ever got any of the good people because the *Today* Show had a much larger audience and no publisher would allow his author on our show unless he couldn't get him or her on the *Today* Show.

I thought that was dumb. I thought we should take people who'd been on the other show, then try to do a better, or a different kind of interview. We were in a no-win situation.

Another problem I kept hearing about third-hand from my friends was that some of them had talked their publishers into letting them go on our program because they were friends, and then for some odd reason they were rejected. This happened to Art Buchwald and Teddy White. There would be some vague explanation; but usually there were about three people involved in setting up the interviews, and often they weren't there when I was, so I couldn't find out. It was a mini-example of the total method of functioning at CBS. It was exasperating and, in the end, useless to try to do anything about anything.

The broadcast was beginning to take on a slight death smell. I had to get out. . . .

I've often asked myself how CBS could have made so many mistakes, how they could have let me go on the air with no experience.

Part of my despair during that terrible time had stemmed from trying to fathom where I had gone wrong. The thing is, nobody really yet understands the medium. Television isn't even fifty years old. Shows go on and off every month, people are hired and fired ruthlessly, because nobody knows what will work and what won't. They don't know what terrible vibes a great-looking or -talking person may give out over the air or what good vibes a clod may transmit. So they don't want to make decisions — especially long-term ones. Therefore nobody does. It's what Sander Vanocur calls the "how-about?" school. Somebody said, "How-about-Sally-Quinn?" and there was a generalized mumble, and that was it. They hired me and nobody ever did anything about it again. Mainly because they didn't know what to do.

So much money is at stake — millions and millions of dollars in advertisements — that those who make mistakes cost their company a lot of money. If they do that too often they lose their jobs. On newspapers everything doesn't ride on one story or one series but on the long run. Everyone in television is basically motivated by fear.

And television news is run by the network. It is not really autonomous. Those in charge of entertainment have ultimate charge over the news programs. CBS News has a buffer between the management and the news division: Richard Salant. In fact, that is his primary function. He is a lawyer, not a newsman, and he is able to negotiate the vast differences of approach between the news side and Blackrock and to work out acceptable compromises. . . .

Thursday of the first week, Small asked me to come down to his office. Gordon was sitting there. I was surprised, to say the least. He hadn't told me he was coming down. He asked where I would be later in the day. He said he would call.

He called around 3:30 and asked if I could have a drink with him. I suggested he have a drink with Ben [Bradley, *Washington Post*] and me, since they were old friends.

He hedged. Then he said he could get a hotel room and stay over if I wanted him to. We could have dinner. I suggested we all have dinner. He hesitated. I couldn't figure out what he wanted. "Well, Gordon," I said finally, "what do you want?"

He mumbled something about dinner for the two of us and how he could get a hotel room. I said I thought it would be more fun with the three of us. He blew up. . . .

"Gordon," I said quietly, "I'm going to quit CBS. I'll try to be out in about six weeks. But I've got to find a job first. Just get Small to let me stay in Washington until then. I can't — won't go back to the anchor job. But I don't want to just quit and have it look like I was a total loss. I want to have a great job to go to. Will you do that much for me? Just hold them off for a while?"

He looked relieved. "I'll do it," he promised.

We walked in silence to the Watergate Terrace Restaurant and made polite conversation through dinner. Nobody ate anything. I ordered gazpacho but I couldn't swallow it. As we were leaving I asked Gordon what I had been longing to ask him since we went on the air.

"Gordon, why did you do it? Why did you hire me and then throw me on the air like that with no training? Why did you do it to me?"

"What if I had told you we wanted to make you the anchor on the *Morning News* but that you'd have to have about three to six months' training on one of our local stations first. Would you have done it?"

"Of course not."

"That's why." . . .

The morning after I quit, Hughes signed me off: "Sally Quinn is leaving CBS News for *The New York Times* — not necessarily sadder, but certainly wiser. And we hope she's happier there than she was here. For one thing, the help over there don't have to get up as early as they do here."

I thought it was touching and funny in Hughes' own gruff way.

Later that morning Richard called to say that Don Hamilton, Director of Business Affairs, wanted that day to be my last day. I pointed out that I had two film pieces to finish and that I intended to work two more weeks, that I had two further weeks of vacation coming to me, and that therefore they could count me on the payroll for another month. I wasn't to start at *The Times* until March 18.

Richard said Hamilton wouldn't buy that. I told Richard that I would call Salant or Bill Paley if I had to, and give interviews about what a cheap crumby outfit CBS was if I heard another word on the subject. Just get me the four weeks' pay. I didn't care how he did it.

Richard understood that I meant it. A half hour later he called back and said, "It's all set."

It still made me chuckle, though, that such a huge corporation would be so unbelievably cheap, especially under the circumstances. But I don't know why I was surprised, after what I had been through.

Saturday, I got a letter from Dick Salant.

Dear Sally,

In case you missed the AP story, I am attaching it. It quotes me absolutely correctly.

I am terribly sorry that things did not work out as we all expected and hoped. The fault, I honestly believe, was ours — mine.

In any event, best wishes for every sort of satisfaction and happiness. And if you can bear it, do drop in so I can say goodbye and good luck.

All the best,

Dick Salant

The AP story was enclosed. It said: "CBS News President Richard Salant said Thursday that CBS would not hold her to her contract. Asked if he considered Miss Quinn's move a slap at CBS, Salant said, 'No, not at all. She doesn't owe us a thing. We owe her a lot. And we damn near ruined her by making a mistake and pushing her too far too fast.'"

On February 7 Gordon Manning was fired from his job as news director. He was given a job as "vice president and assistant to the president of CBS News."

Gordon had been news director for nine years. His ten years were up in June and he was to receive a pension. That's why he was given that job, to hold him over so he could get his pension. He was fifty-seven in June, 1974. Somehow Gordon managed to redeem himself, partly by landing Solzhenitsyn for Walter Cronkite to interview. He stayed on after June and became a producer for the public affairs division of CBS News.

Bill Small was given Gordon's job. Sandy Socolow was given the Washington bureau. The day the change was announced Small was in Gordon's office.

Reached there, he said he was completely surprised by the promotion. "I've only been at this desk for six hours," he said. "I'm just trying to find out where the men's room is and where they keep the key to the liquor cabinet."

On February 28 Lee Townsend was fired. They had no ready title for him to assume. He was later assigned to the investigative unit. The new *Morning News* producer was the Rome bureau manager, Joseph Dembo.

The Lab Rat

Tom Wolfe

Pete Conrad, being an alumnus of Princeton and the Philadelphia Main Line, had the standard E.S.A. charm and command of the proprieties. E.S.A. was 1950s Princeton club code for "Eastern Socially Attractive." E.S.A. qualities served a man well in the Navy, where refinement in the officer ranks was still valued. Yet Conrad remained, at bottom, the Hickory Kid. He had the same combination of party manners and Our Gang scrappiness that his wife, Jane, had found attractive when she met him six years before. Now, in 1959, at the age of twenty-eight, Conrad was still just as wirily built, five feet six and barely 140 pounds, still practically towheaded, and he had the same high-pitched nasal voice, the same collegiate cackle when he laughed, and the same Big Weekend grin that revealed the gap between his two front teeth. Nevertheless, people gave him room. There was an old-fashioned Huck Finn hickory-stick don't-cross-that-line-or-I'll-crawl-you streak in him. Unlike a lot of pilots, he tended to say exactly what was on his mind when aroused. He couldn't stand being trifled with. Consequently he seldom was.

That was Conrad. Add the normal self-esteem of the healthy young fighter jock making his way up the mighty ziggurat . . . and the lab rat's revolt was probably in the cards from the beginning.

The survivors of Group 20's *bad string* had just completed their flight-test training when the orders arrived. Conrad received them, and so did Wally Schirra and Jim Lovell. "Shaky" Lovell — he was stuck with the nickname Conrad had given him — had finished first in the training class. The orders were marked "top secret." That already had half the base talking, of course. There was nothing like issuing top-secret orders for a whole batch of officers in the same outfit to make the grapevine start lunging about like a live wire. They were supposed to report to a certain room at the Pentagon disguised as civilians.

So on the appointed Monday morning, February 2, Conrad, along with Schirra and Lovell, arrives at the Pentagon and presents his orders and files into a room with thirty-four other young men, most of them with crew cuts and all of them with lean lineless faces and suntans and the unmistakable cocky rolling gait of fighter jocks, not to mention the pathetic-looking civilian suits and the enormous wristwatches. The wristwatches had about two thousand calibrations on them and dials for recording everything short of the sound of enemy guns. These terrific wristwatches were practically fraternal insignia among the pilots. Thirty-odd young souls wearing Robert Hall clothes that cost about a fourth as much as their watches: in the year 1959 this just had to be a bunch of military pilots trying to disguise themselves as civilians.

Once inside the room, the boys realized that they were part of a secret gathering of military test pilots from all over the country. That was rather righteous stuff. Two of the highest ranking engineers of the National Aeronautics and Space Administration, Abe Silverstein and George Low, started briefing them. They had been brought to Washington, they were told, because NASA needed volunteers for suborbital and orbital flights above the earth's atmosphere in Project Mercury. The project had the highest national priority, comparable to that of a crash program in wartime. NASA intended to put astronauts into space by mid-1960, fifteen months from now.

A pilot could tell, if he listened carefully to the briefing, that an astronaut on a Project Mercury flight would do none of the things that comprised *flying* a ship: he would not take it aloft, control its flight, or land it. In short, he would be a passenger. The propulsion, guidance, and landing would all be determined automatically, by the ground. Yet the slender engineer, Low, went out of his way to show that the astronaut would exercise some forms of control. He would have "attitude control," for example. In fact, this meant only that the astronaut could make the capsule yaw, pitch, or roll by means of little hydrogen-peroxide thrusters, just as you could rock a seat on a Ferris wheel but couldn't change its orbit or direction in the slightest. But when a capsule was put into earth orbit, said Low, controlling the attitude would be essential for bringing the capsule back in through the atmosphere. Otherwise, the vehicle would burn up, and the as- tronaut with it. If the automatic control system malfunctioned, then the astronaut would have to take over on the manual or the fly-by- wire. In the fly-by-wire system the apparatus of the automatic system could be commandeered by the astronaut for manual control. The as- tronaut might also have to override the automatic system, in the case of a malfunction, to fire the retrorockets to reduce the capsule's speed and bring it out of orbit. *Retrofire! Fly-by-wire!* It was as if you really would be flying the thing. The stocky engineer, Silverstein, told them that obviously the Mercury flights might be hazardous. The first men to go into space would be running considerable risk. Therefore, the astronauts would be chosen on a strictly volunteer basis; and if a man did not volunteer, that fact would not be entered on his record or held against him in any way.

The message had a particular ring to it; but coming, as it did, from a civilian, it took a while for it to register.

Conrad and the rest of the Pax River contingent were staying at the Marriott motel near the Pentagon, and after dinner they got together in one of the rooms and had a long discussion. Schirra was there, and Lovell, and Alan Shepard, a veteran test pilot who had recently been reassigned from Pax River to a staff position in Norfolk, and a few others. What they talked about was not space travel, the future of the galaxy, or even the problems of riding a rocket into earth orbit. No, they talked about a rather more urgent matter: what this Project Mer- cury might do to your Navy career.

There were some obvious problems. One, Project Mercury was a civilian program; two, NASA had not yet developed the rockets or the capsule to carry it out; three, it involved no flying, at least not in the sense a pilot used that word. The Mercury capsule was not a ship but a can. Not only did it involve no *flying*, there wasn't even a win- dow to look out of. There wasn't even a hatch you could egress from like a man; it would take a crew of swabbos with lug wrenches to get you out of the thing. It was a *can*. Suppose you volunteered and got tied up in the project for two or three years, and then the whole thing fizzled? That was entirely possible, because this rocket-and-capsule system was novel and had a lot of Rube Goldberg stuff in it. Any test pilot who had ever been to the Society of Experimental Test Pilots convention, to one of those sessions where they show movies of Great Ideas that never made it out of the test stage, would know what he meant . . . the Sea Dart, a ten-ton jet fighter that was supposed to take off and land on water skis (up on the screen it keeps hopping up out of the waves, like a rock skipping across a pond, and the audience roars with laughter) . . . the single-engine plane, with a 25-foot propeller, that was propped up on its tail to take off vertically, like a hummingbird (it hangs in the air, suspended at forty feet, tail down, its engine churning furiously, not realizing that it has turned from an airplane into a cockeyed helicopter, and the audience roars with laughter) . . . In the history of flight these well-meant farces took place all the time. And where would you be then? You would be three years behind in flight test. You would be three years off the line in the general jockeying for promotion. You would be giving up whatever brownie points you had built up over the past four or five years.

From the beginning George Low and others in the NASA hierarchy had been afraid that the pilots would react in precisely this way. As a result, they were amazed. They had briefed thirty-five test pilots on Monday, February 2, Conrad, Schirra, Lovell, and Alan Shepard among them, and another thirty-four the following Monday; and of the total of sixty-nine, fifty-six volunteered to become astronauts. They now had so many volunteers they didn't even call in the remaining forty-one men who fit the profile. Why bother? They already had fifty-six grossly overqualified volunteers. Not only that, the men seemed so gung-ho about the project, they figured they could get by with seven astronauts instead of twelve.

Pete Conrad had ended up volunteering, and so had Jim Lovell. In fact, every man who had been in that room at the motel had volunteered, including Wally Schirra, who had been the most dubious of all. And why? That was a good question. Despite all the pondering, all the discussions, all the career-wrestling, all the toting up of pros and cons, none of them could give you a clear-cut answer. The matter had not been decided by sheer logic. Somehow, in that briefing in the inner room at the Pentagon, Silverstein and Low had hit every button just right. It was as if they possessed a blueprint of the way the fighter jock was wired.

"The highest national priority" . . . "hazardous undertaking" . . .

"strictly volunteer" . . . so hazardous that "if you don't volunteer, it won't be held against you" . . . And they had all gotten the signal, subliminally, in the solar plexus. They were being presented with the Cold War version of *the dangerous mission.* One of the maxims that was drilled into all career officers went: *Never refuse a combat assignment.* Moreover, there was the business of "the first men to go into space." *The first men to go into space.* Well . . . suppose it happened just that way? The rocket aces at Edwards, from their eminence, might be able to look down upon the whole scheme. But within the souls of the rest of the fighter jocks who came to the Pentagon was triggered a motivation that overrode all strictly logical career considerations: I must not get . . . *left behind.*

That feeling was magnified by the public reaction. No sooner had the first group of men been briefed than the news that NASA was looking for Mercury astronauts made its way into the press. From the beginning the reporters and broadcasters dealt with the subject in tones of awe. It was the awe that one has of an impending death-defying stunt. The question of whether an astronaut was a pilot or a mere guinea pig never entered into it for a moment, so far as the press was concerned. "Are they really looking for somebody to go into space on top of a rocket?" That was the question and the only one that seemed to matter. To almost anyone who had followed NASA's efforts on television, the odds against the successful launch of an American into space seemed absolutely dreadful. For four-teen months now the Eisenhower Administration had adopted the strategy of openly publicizing its attempts to catch up with the Rus-sians — and so people were being treated to the sight of the rock-ets at Cape Canaveral either blowing up on the launch pad in the most ignominious, if briefly hilarious, fashion or else heading off on crazy trajectories, toward downtown Orlando instead of outer space, in which case they had to be blown up by remote control. Well, not all of them, of course, for the United States had succeeded in putting up some small satellites, mere "oranges," as Nikita Khrushchev liked to put it, in his cruel colorful farmboy way, as compared to the 1,000-pound Sputniks the mighty Integral was sending around the earth loaded with dogs and other experiment-al animals. But the only obvious American talent was for blow-ing up. They had many names, these rockets, Atlas, Navaho, Little Joe, Jupiter, but they all blew up.

When Pete talked to Jane about Project Mercury, she was all for it! If he wanted to volunteer, then he should by all means do so. The thought of Pete riding a NASA rocket did not fill her with horror. On the contrary. Although she never quite put it this way to Pete, she felt that anything would be better, safer, saner than for him to continue flying high-performance jet fighters for the Navy. At the very least, astronaut training would take him away from that. As for rocket flights themselves, how could they possibly be any more dangerous than flying every day at Pax River? What rocket pilot's wife had ever been to more funerals than the wives of Group 20?

Albuquerque, home of the Lovelace Clinic, was a dirty red sod-hut tortilla highway desert city that was remarkably short on charm, despite the Mexican touch here and there. But career officers were used to dreary real estate. That was what they inhabited in America, especially if they were fliers. No, it was Lovelace itself that began to get everybody's back up. Lovelace was a fairly new private diagnostic clinic, somewhat like the Mayo Clinic, doing "aerospace-medical" work for the government, among other things. Lovelace had been founded by Randy Lovelace — W. Randolph Lovelace II — who had served along with Crossfield and Flickinger on the committee on "human factors" in space flight. The chief of the medical staff at Lovelace was a recently retired general of the Air Force medical corps, Dr. A. H. Schwichtenberg. He was General Schwichtenberg to everybody at Lovelace. The operation took itself very seriously. The candidates for astronaut would be given their physical testing here. Then they would go to Wright-Patterson Air Force Base in Dayton for psychological and stress testing. It was all very hush-hush. Conrad went to Lovelace in a group of only six men, once more in their ill-fitting mufti and terrific watches, apparently so that they would blend in with the clinic's civilian patients. They had been warned that the tests at Lovelace and Wright-Patterson would be more exacting and strenuous than any they had ever taken. It was not the tests *per se*, however, that made every self-respecting fighter jock, early in the game, begin to hate Lovelace.

Military pilots were veterans of physical examinations, but in addition to all the usual components of "the complete physical," the Lovelace doctors had devised a series of novel tests involving straps, tubes, hoses, and needles. They would put a strap around your head, clamp some sort of instrument over your eyes — and then stick a hose in your ear and pump cold water into your ear canal. It would make your eyeballs flutter. It was an unpleasant, disorienting sensation, although not painful. If you wanted to know what it was all about, the Lovelace doctors and technicians, in their uncompromising white smocks, indicated that you really didn't need to know, and that was that.

What really made Conrad feel that something *eccentric* was going on here, however, was the business of the electrode in the thumb muscle. They brought him into a room and strapped his hand down to a table, palm up. Then they brought out an ugly-looking needle attached to an electrical wire. Conrad didn't like needles in the first place, and this one looked like a monster. *Hannh?* — they drove the needle into the big muscle at the base of his thumb. It hurt like a bastard. Conrad looked up as if to say, "What the hell's going on?" But they weren't even looking at him. They were looking — at the meter. The wire from the needle led to what looked like a doorbell. They pushed the buzzer. Conrad looked down, and his hand — his own goddamned hand! — was balling up into a fist and springing open and balling up into a fist and springing open and balling up into a fist and springing open and balling up into a fist and springing open at an absolutely furious rate, faster than he could have ever made it do so on its own, and there seemed to be nothing that he, with his own mind and his own central nervous system, could do to stop his own hand or even slow it down. The Lovelace doctors in their white smocks, with their reflectors on their heads, were having a hell of a time for themselves . . . with *his* hand . . . They were reading the meter and scribbling away on their clipboards at a jolly rate.

Afterward Conrad said, "What was that for?"

A doctor looked up, distractedly, as if Conrad were interrupting an important train of thought.

"I'm afraid there's no simple way to explain it to you," he said. "There's nothing for you to worry about."

It was then that it began to dawn on Conrad, first as a feeling rather than as a fully formed thought: "Lab rats."

It went on like that. The White Smocks gave each of them a test tube and said they wanted a sperm count. *What do you mean?* Place your sperm in the tube. *How?* Through ejaculation. *Just like that?* Masturbation is the customary procedure. *What!* The best results seem to be obtained through fantasization, accompanied by masturbation, followed by ejaculation. *Where, f'r chrissake?* Use the bathroom. A couple of the boys said things such as, "Well, okay, I'll do it if you'll send a nurse in with me — to help me along if I get stuck." The White Smocks looked at them as if they were schoolboys making obscene noises. This got the pilots' back up, and a couple of them refused, flat out. But by and by they gave in, and so now you had the ennobling prospect of half a dozen test pilots padding off one by one to the head in their skivvies to jack off for the Lovelace Clinic, Project Mercury, and America's battle for the heavens. Sperm counts were supposed to determine the density and motility of the sperm. What this had to do with a man's fitness to fly on top of a rocket or anywhere else was incomprehensible. Conrad began to get the feeling that it wasn't just him and his brother lab rats who didn't know what was going on. He now had the suspicion that the Reflector Heads didn't know, either. They had somehow gotten *carte blanche* to try out any goddamned thing they could think up — and that was what they were doing, whether there was any logic to it or not.

Each candidate was to deliver two stool specimens to the Lovelace laboratory in Dixie cups, and days were going by and Conrad had been unable to egest even one, and the staff kept getting after him about it. Finally he managed to produce a single bolus, a mean hard little ball no more than an inch in diameter and shot through with some kind of seeds, whole seeds, undigested. Then he remembered. The first night in Albuquerque he had gone to a Mexican restaurant and eaten a lot of jalapeño peppers. They were jalapeño seeds. Even in the turd world this was a pretty miserable-looking *object*. So Conrad tied a red ribbon around the goddamned thing, with a bow and all, and put it in the Dixie cup and delivered it to the lab. Curious about the ribbons that flopped out over the lip of the cup, the technicians all peered in. Conrad broke into his full cackle of mirth, much the way Wally might have. No one was swept up in the joke, however. The Lovelace staffers looked at the beribboned bolus, and then they looked at Conrad . . . as if he were a bug on the windshield of the pace car of medical progress.

One of the tests at Lovelace was an examination of the prostate gland. There was nothing exotic about this, of course; it was a standard part of the complete physical for men. The doctor puts a rubber sleeve on a finger and slips the finger up the subject's rectum and presses the prostate, looking for signs of swelling, infection, and so on. But several men in Conrad's group had come back from the prostate examination gasping with pain and calling the doctor a sadistic little pervert and worse. He had prodded the prostate with such force a couple of them had passed blood.

Conrad goes into the room, and sure enough, the man reams him so hard the pain brings him to his knees.

"What the hell!—"

Conrad comes up swinging, but an orderly, a huge monster, immediately grabs him, and Conrad can't move. The doctor looks at him blankly, as if he's a vet and Conrad's a barking dog.

The probings of the bowels seemed to be endless, full proctosigmoidoscope examinations, the works. These things were never pleasant; in fact, they were a bit humiliating, involving, as they did, various things being shoved up your tail. The Lovelace Clinic specialty seemed to be the exacting of maximum indignity from each procedure. The pilots had never run into anything like this before. Not only that, before each ream-out you had to report to the clinic at seven o'clock in the morning and give yourself an enema. *Up yours!* seemed to be the motto of the Lovelace Clinic—and they even made you do it to yourself. So Conrad reports at seven one morning and gives himself the enema. He's supposed to undergo a lower gastrointestinal tract examination that morning. In the so-called lower G.I. examination, barium is pumped into the subject's bowels; then a little hose with a balloon on the end of it is inserted in the rectum, and the balloon is inflated, blocking the canal to keep the barium from forcing its way out before the radiologist can complete his examination. After the examination, like everyone who has ever been through the procedure, Conrad now feels as if there are eighty-five pounds of barium in his intestines and they are about to explode. The Smocks inform him that there is no john on this floor. He's supposed to pick up the tube that is coming out of his rectum and follow an orderly, who will lead him to a john two floors below. On the tube there is a clamp, and he can release the clamp, deflating the balloon, at the proper time. *It's unbelievable!* To try to walk, with this explosive load sloshing about in your pelvic saddle, is agony. Nevertheless, Conrad picks up the tube and follows the orderly. Conrad has on only the standard bed patient's tunic, the angel robes, open up the back. The tube leading out of his tail to the balloon gizmo is so short that he has to hunch over to about two feet off the floor to carry it in front of him. His tail is now, as the saying goes, flapping in the breeze, with a tube coming out of it. The orderly has on red cowboy boots. Conrad is intensely aware of that fact, because he is now hunched over so far that his eyes hit the orderly at about calf level. He's hunched over, with his tail in the breeze, scuttling like a crab after a pair of red cowboy boots. Out into a corridor they go, an ordinary public corridor, the full-moon hunchback and the red cowbow boots, amid men, women, children, nurses, nuns, the lot. The red cowboy boots are beginning to trot along like mad. The orderly is no fool. He's been through this before. He's been through the whole disaster. He's seen the explosions. Time is of the essence. There's a hunchback stick of dynamite behind him. To Conrad it becomes more incredible every step of the way. They actually have to go down an elevator — full of sane people — and do their crazy tango through another public hallway — agog with normal human beings — before finally reaching the goddamned john.

Later that day Conrad received, once more, instructions to report to the clinic at seven the next morning to give himself an enema. The next thing the people in the administrative office of the clinic knew, a small but enraged young man was storming into the office of General Schwichtenberg himself, waving a great flaccid flamingo-pink enema bag and hose like some sort of obese whip. As he waved it, it gurgled.

The enema bag came slamming down on the general's desk. It landed with a tremendous *plop* and then began gurgling and sighing.

"General Schwichtenberg," said Conrad, "you're looking at a man who has given himself his last enema. If you want enemas from me, from now on you can come get 'em yourself. You can take this bag and give it to a nurse and send her over—"

"Just you—"

"—and let her do the honors. I've given myself my last enema. Either things shape up around here, or I ship out."

The general stared at the great flamingo bag, which lay there heaving and wheezing on his desk, and then he stared at Conrad. The general seemed appalled . . . All the same it wouldn't do anybody any good, least of all the Lovelace Clinic, if one of the candidates pulled out, firing broadsides at the operation. The general started trying to mollify this vision of enema rage.

"Now, Lieutenant," he said, "I know this hasn't been pleasant. This is probably the toughest examination you'll ever have to go through in your life, but as you know, it's for a project of utmost importance. The project needs men like yourself. You have a compact build, and every pound saved in Project Mercury can be critical."

And so forth and so on. He kept spraying Conrad's fire.

"All the same, General, I've given myself my last enema."

Word of the Enema Bag Showdown spread rapidly among the other candidates, and they were delighted to hear about it. Practically all of them had wanted to do something of the sort. It wasn't just that the testing procedures were unpleasant; the entire atmosphere of the testing constituted an affront. There was something . . . decidedly *out of joint* about it. Pilots and doctors were natural enemies, of course, at least as pilots saw it. The flight surgeon was pretty much kept *in his place* in the service. His only real purpose was to tend to pilots and keep 'em flying. He was an attendant to the pilots' vital stuff. In fact, flight surgeons were encouraged to fly backseat with fighter pilots from time to time, so as to understand what stresses and righteous stuff the job entailed. Regardless of how much he thought of himself, no flight surgeon dared position himself *above* the pilots in his squadron in the way he conducted himself before them: i.e., it was hard for him to be a consummate panjandrum, the way the typical civilian doctor was.

But at Lovelace, in the testing for Project Mercury, the natural order was turned upside down. These people not only did not treat them as righteous pilots, they did not treat them as pilots of any sort. They never even alluded to the fact that they were pilots. An irksome thought was beginning to intrude. In the competition for *astronaut* the kind of stuff you were made of as a *pilot* didn't count for a goddamned thing. They were looking for a certain type of animal who registered bingo on the meter. You wouldn't win this competition in the air. If you won it, it would be right here on the examination table in the land of the rubber tubes.

Yes, the boys were delighted when Conrad finally told off General Schwichtenberg. Attaboy, Pete! At the same time, they were quite content to let the credit for the Lab Rat Revolt fall to Conrad and to him alone.

At Wright-Patterson Air Force Base, where they went for the psychological and stress testing, the air of secrecy was even more pronounced than at Lovelace. At Wright-Patterson they went through the testing in groups of eight. They were billeted off to themselves at the BOQ, the Bachelor Officers Quarters. If they had to call for anything on the base, they were not to refer to themselves by name. Instead, each of them had a number, Conrad was "Number 7." If he needed a car to take him from one place to another, to keep an appointment, he was supposed to ring up the car pool and say only: "This is Number Seven. I need a car . . ."

The testing, on the other hand, seemed — at first — more like what a self-respecting fighter jock might expect. They gave the candidate an oxygen mask and a partial-pressure suit and put him in an air-pressure chamber and reduced the pressure until an altitude of 65,000 feet was simulated. It made one feel as if his entire body were being squeezed by thongs, and he had to force his breath out in order to bring new oxygen into his lungs. Part of the stress was in the fact that they didn't tell him how long he had to stay there. They put each man in a small, pitch-black, windowless, soundproofed room — a "sensory deprivation chamber" — and locked the door, again without telling him how long he would have to stay there. It turned out to be three hours. They strapped each man into a huge human milkshake apparatus that vibrated the body at tremendous amplitudes and bombarded it with high-energy sound, some of it at excruciating frequencies. They put each man at the console of a machine called "the idiot box." It was like a simulator or a trainer. There were fourteen different signals that the candidate was supposed to respond to in different ways by pressing buttons or throwing switches; but the lights began lighting up so fast no human being could possibly keep up with them. This appeared to be not only a test of reaction times but of perseverance or ability to cope with frustration.

No, there was nothing wrong with tests of this sort. Nevertheless, the atmosphere around them was a bit . . . *off*. Psychiatrists were running the show at Wright-Patterson. Every inch of the way there were psychiatrists and psychologists standing over you taking notes and giving you little jot'em'n'dot'em tests. Before they put you in the Human Milkshake, some functionary in a white smock would present you with a series of numbered dots on a piece of paper on a clipboard and you were supposed to take a pencil and connect the dots so that the numbers beside them added up to certain sums. Then when you got out of the machine, the White Smock character would give you the same test again, presumably to see if the physical experience had impaired your ability to calculate. And that was all right, too. But they also had people staring at the candidate the whole time and taking notes. They took notes in little spiral notebooks. Every gesture you made, every tic, twitch, smile, stare, frown, every time you rubbed your nose—there was some White Smock standing by jotting it down in a notebook.

One of the most assiduous of the monitors was a psychologist, a woman named Dr. Gladys J. Loring—as Conrad could tell from the nameplate on her smock. Gladys J. Loring was beginning to annoy him intensely. Every time he turned around she seemed to be standing there staring at him, without a word, staring at him with utter White Smock detachment, as if he were a frog, a rabbit, a rat, a gerbil, a guinea pig, or some other lab animal, scribbling furiously in her notebook. For days she had been watching him, and they had never even been introduced. One day Conrad suddenly looked her straight in the eye and said: "Gladys! What . . . are . . . you . . . writing . . . in . . . your . . . notebook!"

Dr. Gladys J. Loring looked at him as if he were a flatworm. All she did was make another notation of the specimen's behavior in her notebook.

To fighter jocks it was bad enough to have doctors of any sort as your final judges. To find psychologists and psychiatrists positioned above you in this manner was irritating in the extreme. Military pilots, almost to a man, perceived psychiatry as a pseudo-science. They regarded the military psychiatrist as the modern and unusually batbrained version of the chaplain. But the shrink could be dealt with. You just turned on the charm—lit up the halo of the right stuff—and did some prudent lying.

In the interviews for this job of "astronaut," as in other situations, the psychiatrists would get on the subject of the hazards of the assignment, the unknowns, the potentially high risk, and then gauge the candidate's reaction. As all heads-up pilots knew, this called for "second-convolution" thinking. It was a mistake to say anything along the lines of: *Oh, I rather enjoy risks, I enjoy hanging my hide out over the edge, day in and day out, for that is what makes me superior to other men.* The psychiatrists always interpreted that as a reckless love of danger, an irrational impulse asociated with the late-Freudian concept of "the death wish." The proper response — heard more than once during that week at Wright-Patterson — was to say: "Oh, I don't regard Project Mercury as a particularly high-risk proposition, certainly not compared to the routine test work I've been doing for [the Air Force, the Navy, the Marines]. Since this project has a high national priority, I'm sure that the safety precautions will be far more thorough and reliable than they were on something like the [F–100F, F–102, F–104, F–4B], when I had *that one* in the test stage." (Very slight smile and roll of the eyeballs.) Beautiful stuff! This showed that you were a rational test pilot, as concerned about safety as any sensible professional . . . while at the same time getting across the idea that you had been routinely risking your life and were so used to it, had such righteous stuff, that riding a rocket seemed like a vacation by comparison. That created the Halo Effect. Offhand allusions to derring-do would have the psychiatrists looking at you with big wide eyes, like little boys.

Conrad knew all this as well as the rest of them. He knew exactly how the prudent officer should deal with these people. It was hard not to know. Every night the boys got together in the BOQ and regaled each other with stories of how they had lied their heads off or otherwise diligently subverted the inquiries of the shrinks. Conrad's problem was that somewhere along the way the Hickory Kid always took over and had to add *a wink or two* for good measure.

In one test the interviewer gave each candidate a blank sheet of paper and asked him to study it and describe what he saw in it. There was no one right response in this sort of test, because it was designed to force the candidate to free-associate in order to see where his mind wandered. The test-wise pilot knew that the main thing was to stay on dry land and not go swimming. As they described with some relish later on in the BOQ, quite a few studied the sheet of paper and then looked the interviewer in the eye and said, "All I see is a blank sheet of paper." This was not a "correct" answer, since the shrinks probably made note of "inhibited imaginative capacity" or some goddamned thing, but neither did it get you in trouble. One man said, "I see a field of snow." Well, you might get away with that, as long as you didn't go any further . . . as long as you did not thereupon start ruminating about freezing to death or getting lost in the snow and running into bears or something of that sort. But Conrad . . . well, the man is sitting across the table from Conrad and gives him the sheet of paper and asks him to study it and tell him what he sees. Conrad stares at the piece of paper and then looks up at the man and says in a wary tone, as if he fears a trick: "But it's upside down."

This so startles the man, he actually leans across the table and looks at this absolutely blank sheet of paper to see if it's true — and only after he is draped across the table does he realize that he has been had. He looks at Conrad and smiles a smile of about 33 degrees Fahrenheit.

This was *not* the way to produce the Halo Effect.

In another test they showed the candidates pictures of people in various situations and asked them to make up stories about them.

One of the pictures they showed Conrad was a piece of American Scene Okie Realism, apparently from the Depression years. You could see a poor sunken hookwormy sharecropper in bib overalls trying to push a rusty plow through some eroded ground that was more gully than topsoil, aided by a mule with all his ribs showing, while off to one side the man's sallow hollow-socketed pellagra-ravaged wife with a swollen eight-month belly covered by a dress made from a fertilizer sack leans up against their shack to catch her breath or else to prop up the side wall. Conrad looks at the picture and says, "Well, you can tell that this man is a nature lover. He not only tills the soil, he appreciates the scenery, as you can tell by the way he is looking off towards the mountains, the better to observe the way the pale blue of the range in the distance harmonizes with the purple haze of the hills near his beloved homestead"—and on and on in this fashion until, at long last, it dawns on the interviewer that this wiry wiseacre who chatters away with a gap between his front teeth . . . is sending him up, him and his whole test.

This did not create the Halo Effect, either.

Oh, Conrad was rolling now. He was beginning to have a good time. But he had one piece of unfinished business. That night he called up the car pool.

"This is Number Seven," he said. "Number Seven needs a car to go to the PX."

The next day, after the heat-chamber test, in which he spent three hours shut up in a cubicle heated to 130 degrees, Conrad was rubbing the sweat off the end of his nose when he looked up — and sure enough, Dr. Gladys J. Loring was right there, making note of the event in her spiral notebook with a ballpoint pen. Conrad reached into the pocket of his pants . . . and came up with a spiral notebook and a ballpoint pen just like hers.

"Gladys!" he said. She looked up. She was startled. Conrad started scribbling in his notebook and then looked at her again. "Aha! You touched your ear, Gladys! We call that inhibition of the exhibitionism!" More scribbling in the notebook. "Oh-oh! Lowering of the eyes, Gladys! Repressed hypertrophy of the latency! I'm sorry, but it has to go in the report!"

Word of how the flatworm turned . . . how the lab rat had risen up . . . how Pavlov's dog rang Pavlov's bell and took notes on it . . . oh, word of all this circulated quickly, too, and everyone, from Number 1 to Number 8, was quite delighted. There was no indication, however, then or later, that Dr. Gladys Loring was amused in the slightest.

Conrad was back home in North Town Creek, back at Pax River, when the letter from NASA arrived. He knew he had not played it very smoothly during the testing. He had compared notes with Wally Schirra, and it turned out that when Wally's group had gone through Lovelace, they had been just as ticked off at the way the place was run as Conrad and his group had been. Wally had even led his own little rebellion when they wanted their goddamned stool samples. One afternoon they had told Wally and the boys to avoid all highly seasoned food that evening, because they wanted to take stool samples the next day. So the whole group headed off to the Mexican section of Albuquerque, and they had picked out the rankest-looking restaurant they could find and fired up their innards with every red-mad dish they had ever heard of and hosed it down with plenty of good cheap rank Mexican beer. The jalapeño peppers had even gotten into the act! One of the boys had discovered a bowl of jalapeño pepper sauce on the table, a fiery reddish-brown concoction, and had poured it into a Dixie cup and presented it to the lab technicians as if he had a ferocious case of diarrhea — and he laughed his head off when the first sultry cloud of jalapeño aroma nearly wiped them out. But that was as far as he went — the lab technician level. He let the good General Schwichtenberg remain reserved and serene. That was the way Wally himself would have done it. He always knew where the outside of the envelope was, even when it came to pranks.

No, Conrad knew he had poked a few unfortunate holes in the old envelope . . . Still, he had spoken his mind before and it had never hurt him. His career in the Navy had gone up on a steady curve. He had never been left behind. So he opened the letter.

From the very first line he knew the rest. The letter noted that he had been among the finalists in the selection process and said he was to be commended for that. Alas, it went on, he had not been one of the seven chosen for the assignment, but NASA and one & all were grateful to him for volunteering and so forth and so on.

Well, there it was, your classic Dear John letter. Even though in his detached moments he realized that he had perhaps screwed the pooch here and there, it was hard to believe. He had been left behind. This was something that had never happened to him in the nearly six years he had been moving up the great invisible ziggurat.

A couple of days later he found out that Wally had made it. Wally was one of the seven. So was Alan Shepard, who had also been in that room at the Marriott.

Well, what the hell. Wally himself had given them all a lot of pretty sound reasons why a man shouldn't feel to goddamned unlucky if he *didn't* get involved in this Rube Goldberg *capsule* business. It was probably all for the best. Project Mercury was a civilian enterprise and slightly wacky when you got right down to it. They hadn't even chosen *pilots*, f'r chrissake. Jim Lovell had been ranked number one in

Group 20 at Pax River, and he hadn't been chosen, either. They had all been lab rats from beginning to end. It was a good thing someone had set the record straight . . .

Still! It was incredible! He had been . . . *left behind!*

Not too long afterward, Conrad was told that across the master sheet on top of his file at Wright-Patterson had been written: "Not suitable for long-duration flight."

The Seattle Times, 23 May 1976.

Marines accepted unfit men, says ex-recruiter

Knight News Service

DETROIT — Marine Corps recruiters in the Detroit area successfully arranged for the induction of men they knew were mentally and physically unfit, military records indicate.

They were motivated by strict monthly recruiting quotas set at Marine headquarters in Washington and passed down to local stations, sources say.

Copies of daily reports from January 19, 1973, to May 1, 1974, indicate that recruiters repeatedly changed the names of some unqualified candidates when they failed intelligence tests or medical examinations. Then, under another name, the candidate would be sent back to the examining station for retesting.

Bob Six's Long Search for a Successor

Rush Loving Jr.

During his tenure as chief executive, the head of a large corporation makes decisions that shape the lives of thousands. He decides whether people are hired, promoted, or fired. His policies may generate profits in the millions, or bring about huge losses. But no decision

---

is more critical to the future of the enterprise than his selection of a successor. That decision is irrevocable, like the writing of a will bequeathing all corporate powers to a sole survivor.

When the chief executive is the man who built the company, he can be racked by great emotion. Some pioneers have chosen their successors well. But at least three founders of major U.S. airlines have chosen unwisely. At United, at Pan Am, and at American, the successors of Pat Patterson, Juan Trippe, and C. R. Smith foundered and were eventually removed by the directors.

This hard fact has haunted one of the last of the airline pioneers, Robert F. Six, head of Continental Air Lines, who presented a plan for his own succession to the company's board last month. Six was determined that what had happened at United, Pan Am, and American would not happen at Continental, and to ensure that it would not, he spent eight years seeking the right man. The search was as thoughtful and incisive as it was deliberate. Its length and depth were especially surprising, because it was conducted personally by Six himself, a man who has acquired a reputation as a hip-shooter.

THE DROPOUT WHO MADE GOOD

As it happens, that reputation is undeserved, but it has been fostered by Six's colorful past. Fifteen years ago, Six literally did shoot from the hip. Traveling around Colorado with a group of quick-draw artists, he gave exhibitions with handguns, hitting a bull's-eye in a fraction of a second.

As a businessman, he talks bluntly and moves fast. The men he has been able to choose among in selecting a successor all know more about running an airline than he did when he became president thirty-seven years ago. "I just started off and learned the hard way," he says. "There wasn't any criteria for it."

A six-foot-four-inch outdoorsman, son of a doctor in Stockton, California, Six was a high-school dropout who worked as a factory hand and a merchant seaman (retaining a vocabulary to match). He got hooked on airplanes in the Twenties, and barnstormed throughout California for two years. He tried to become an airline pilot, but because he had already made three crash landings, he was turned away.

Finally, in 1936, Six borrowed $90,000 from his father-in-law and bought into Varney Air Transport Inc., a tiny El Paso mail-plane operator. First as operations manager, then as president, Six built Varney into the present-day Continental. Today his airline flies 22,657 miles of routes from Miami and Chicago to the West Coast and Hawaii.

ADMIRATION FROM THE FRIENDLY SKIES

Continental bears the vivid imprint of Six's flamboyant personality. He has an instinct for what the customers want, and he has sold the airline so well that some passengers revere it with the ardor of a cult. Many Westerners will fly no airliners but Six's golden-tailed 727s and DC-10s. Edward E. Carlson, chairman of United Air Lines, Continental's biggest and toughest competitor, says: "Continental is a great success story, and Continental is Bob Six. What the public perceives of Continental is Bob Six's imagination, personality, and willingness to do the unusual."

Six has played on the fact that Continental is a little company battling competitors who are mammoth and impersonal (Continental's operating revenues of $457 million were only one-fifth of United's last year). By casting his company in the role of David, Six has created a remarkable esprit de corps and a feisty and innovative operating style. Says Joseph A. Daley, Six's vice president for public relations and one of Continental's brightest marketing minds: "We've got to be different. Six is operating a delicatessen next to a supermarket. We've got to carry the bagels and the Danish beer and deliver." Among other things, Continental delivered the first hot meals and wide seats in coach, the first economy class, and a management representative on every airplane to take care of passengers' problems.

AN EBENEZER SCROOGE WITH CHARM

Continental's compactness makes the airline relatively easy to manage. Everyone seems to know everyone else. All flight crews based in Los Angeles check in at the operations room on the second floor of the company's general offices, where they frequently run into Continental's senior officers, and even the c.e.o. himself. Six insists that the officers take their lunch in the company cafeteria, where everyone from Six on down rubs elbows with mechanics, secretaries, and pilots. "Here the officers are human beings," says one Continental newcomer. "In some companies they go out to '21' and you never see them."

Six has instilled quality and consistency in the airline by treating his employees with the affection of a father while applying the tough discipline of a Puritan schoolmaster. At the same time, he has kept the company from bankruptcy by watching costs like an Ebenezer Scrooge reincarnate.

He charms his people into putting out for Continental, largely by knowing as many as he can personally. While clipping a twenty-five-year pin on a terminal supervisor, Six interrupted the proceedings to recall how the man had been first officer on a DC-3 that had iced up one night over Lubbock, Texas. The event took place more than two decades ago.

By touring the system and prowling the hallways at headquarters with a cold eye for detail, Six keeps acquainted with just about every facet of his company. He knows that there's been a low-pressure area over the Pacific for the past week, or that the cargo business is up from San Antonio to Alaska, or that National flies its DC-10s at lower cost than Continental.

And wherever he goes, Six reminds his people that what they do reflects on them, because *they* are Continental. When he finds that the airline is falling below his standards of quality, he is outraged — and the quality soon goes up. On a recent flight to Houston, he noticed that the tenderloin steaks were being served wrapped in strips of bacon that were nearly raw. Six asked the hostess if the dinners were being prepared this way for all flights.

"I haven't seen that on your airplanes before, sir," she said.

"What do you mean, my airplanes? This is *your* airplane!" he roared.

When Six returned to Los Angeles, he ordered the bacon taken off and the savings used to buy bigger steaks.

Although Continental has always been highly leveraged and sparse with cash, it has managed to report a profit every year but one since Six became president. The company has one of the lowest records of customer complaints in the industry. Its on-time performance last year was second (to Western) among all the nation's trunk lines. And on six of its nine most competitive routes, Continental fills more seats per plane than its competitors.

ADVICE FROM A HEADHUNTER

To find a man who can sustain that record is a difficult task. In the early Sixties, Six thought he had such a man in Harding Lawrence, Continental's executive vice president manager. Six planned to retire in 1972, when he would reach sixty-five, and he intended to promote Lawrence to president, but Lawrence quit in 1964 to run Braniff. Lawrence's departure left Six with no really qualified, well-identified successor, and in 1967 he asked the advice of Henry O. Golightly, president of Golightly & Co. International Inc., a New York consulting firm.

Golightly, fifty-nine, is a soft spoken, urbane man-about-town (Truman Capote, who was living next to Golightly's summer house on Long Island when he wrote *Breakfast at Tiffany's*, named the story's main character, Holly Golightly, after him). Golightly has been Six's chief outside confidant for more than a decade, consulting mostly on marketing and organizational problems and helping to set up new operations. He also is Continental's headhunter; many of the airline's top executives were hired on his recommendation.

Six and Golightly agreed to set up a secret program to determine whether there were any qualified candidates inside Continental. Six was looking for candidates whose aptitudes fit the company's own management needs and goals. He set August, 1970, as a deadline: if no inside candidates turned up by then he would have to search outside.

THE BLACK BOOKS IN THE SAFE

On April 21, 1967, Golightly sent Six a twenty-three-page outline of their plan. Using the outline as a guide, R. Randall Irwin, Golightly's expert on selecting and evaluating executives, interviewed every officer in Continental's top management who showed any measure of presidential potential. To keep their intentions secret, the interviews were conducted under cover of "a special program for assisting in the developing of executives."

By the end of June, Golightly and Irwin had singled out and pro-filed nine vice presidents, including former White House Press Secretary Pierre Salinger, who was then vice president, international (he later quit to return to politics). Each profile was ten to twelve pages long and included an appraisal by Irwin and an independent evaluation by Golightly, who knew each man personally. They bound each report in a black cover and sent them to Six. The black books described each man's character, background, education, management experience, and personal aspirations.

They also provided an insight into each officer's home life, sports, social graces, and his wife, including comments on whether she would be an asset if he became president. They even explored his relationship with his children and how well he had raised them.

At the same time, Irwin wrote Six a confidential letter telling him that out of the nine, he and Golightly had selected four potential candidates. "We are greatly impressed with their caliber," Irwin wrote. "They all have high intelligence; are highly motivated; and are completely dedicated to Continental." After reading the nine black books, marking key phrases with a red-felt-tipped pen, and putting the books away in his office safe, Six told Golightly he readily concurred with their conclusions.

A GAME OF MULTIPLE CHOICE

By both their positions in the company and the initials of their last names, the four candidates composed the A, B, C, and D of Continental Air Lines.

Richard M. Adams, now fifty-six, senior vice president, operating and technical services, is a quiet engineer who enjoys good music and photography. The son of a New Jersey patent attorney, Adams has a warmth and an air of ability that have won him a staunch following among his subordinates. He moved over from Pan Am in 1962 to head Continental's maintenance division. Six soon moved Adams up, putting him in charge of flight operations as well as maintenance. Under him Continental has achieved the best records in the industry for aircraft utilization and jet safety.

Charles A. Bucks, forty-seven, senior vice president, marketing, quit college after World War II to become a baggage handler in his home town of Lubbock at an airline that was later acquired by Continental. Showing a natural talent for salesmanship, he rapidly moved up through the marketing division until, at thirty-four, he became the air-transport industry's youngest vice president. (United now has a president ten years his junior, a fact that galls Bucks no little.)

Bucks has been the brain behind some of Continental's most outlandish marketing gimmicks. In 1959, to promote flights from Chicago, he dropped a helicopter onto Wrigley Field in the middle of a game and had a crew of midgets "kidnap" the Cubs' centerfielder. Six-foot-four, silver-maned, handsome, and an outdoorsman like Six, Bucks is second only to Six in popularity among Continental's rank and file. "Mr. Bucks knows he's a sex symbol," says a hostess on the ramp at Burbank, adding emphatically: "And he has the right to know it."

G. Edward Cotter, fifty-seven, is senior vice president, legal and diversification, and the company secretary. Disarmingly frank and ambitious, cool and well ordered, Cotter was born in the China mission field, the son of an Episcopal minister. He worked for a New York law firm and was secretary of Freeport Sulphur Co. before taking over Continental's legal division in 1965. Cotter has an extraordinary conceptual grasp of such broad issues as the airline's needs for long-term growth. And he articulates these ideas with the self-confidence and orderly flow of a seasoned barrister. "I'm a goddam good lawyer," he says. "I'm a very capable guy and this company is goddam lucky to have me."

Cotter has indeed been valuable to Continental, though most employees are unaware of his achievements. Yet everyone is aware of another fact of Cotter's life: he is Six's brother-in-law. His sister, actress Audrey Meadows, has been married to Six for fourteen years.

Alexander Damm, fifty-nine, senior vice president and general manager, is Continental's moneyman. Damm (rhymes with palm) came from TWA in 1959 to bolster the company's lackluster financial division. He installed tight budget controls and a monthly head count that allows Six to veto the most minute addition to the payroll. Damm and Six are opposites in personality and complement one another, but they have never forged a close personal bond.

Born in Nebraska, the son of a Burlington railroad roundhouse foreman, Damm is a serious, no-nonsense taskmaster. He lives by the memo, often to Six's exasperation, and insists that written communication is the best way for an executive to keep informed. Nevertheless, Damm's rigid system of controls has kept Continental out of the red. Like many good general managers, he is not well liked by employees, largely because over the years he has had to execute the austerity programs that have laid off hundreds of men and women.

Six watched each man's performance for two years. Then, in August, 1969, Golightly and Irwin presented him with an updated profile of each man. They also uncovered a fifth candidate, Dominic P. Renda, who had come to Continental eighteen months earlier as senior vice president, international. Renda, sixty-one, a tall, swarthy man who is married to a former Miss Maryland, had been senior vice president, legal, of Western Air Lines. At this point, Golightly told Six that Damm, Renda, and Adams — in that order — were the best qualified candidates, and that in an emergency Continental could turn to any one of them as a new president.

A TIME FOR GROOMING

So far as the other candidates were concerned, Cotter had shown surprising growth in the two years, tightening his grasp of the airline business and toning down his competitive spirit, though he was sometimes still abrasive. Bucks, however, was a real comer. Golightly told Six that, for the long haul, Bucks was probably the strongest presidential prospect in the entire industry. But Golightly and Six calculated that he would require five to eight more years of grooming.

For all their strengths, each of the five candidates needed more experience. Accordingly, Six decided to put off his retirement until 1976, when he would be sixty-nine. Meanwhile, he decided to broaden the younger men's duties and see how they developed. "It's been great fun," he says proudly. "I enjoy watching these guys come up."

Bucks, for instance, had headed only the sales end of the marketing division. Six exposed him to the rigors of top-level decision making by placing him in charge of the entire division. To expand Cotter's responsibilities beyond legal affairs and into operations, Six put him in charge of a small chain of hotels in the Pacific and Continental Air Services, a contract carrier serving the government and private companies in Southeast Asia.

As Six watched eagerly through the early 1970s, each of the candidates made noticeable progress. Bucks became a practiced witness at regulatory hearings and drew on his native traits of showmanship to strengthen his following among employees around the Continental system. When the women's liberation movement attacked Continental's ad slogan—"We Really Move Our Tail For You!"—Bucks turned the dispute to his advantage by getting on a TV talk show and, waving a copy of the ad in front of the camera, stealing the show—and valuable publicity.

Under Cotter's guidance, Continental Air Services outperformed its competitor, Air America, the Central Intelligence Agency's own air-transport arm. Cotter, the missionary's son, even showed a hidden marketing flair. When he opened a new hotel on Saipan for the Japanese tourist trade, he flew in three Shinto priests to bless the place.

SAVED FROM THE MONEY EATERS

Gaining experience as general manager, Damm extended his knowledge beyond his financial specialty and into operations. He became a tough inspector, and he soon recognized the untapped potential of air cargo, pestering Six and Bucks for a better, more comprehensive and competitive freight program.

Damm also was turning into a hard bargainer. As head of a Continental negotiating team, he used eleventh-hour brinksmanship to win very favorable contracts for new airplanes from McDonnell Douglas and Boeing. And while his demeanor remained very serious, he was becoming more relaxed with people.

But the most important accomplishment during the early Seventies belonged to Adams, who persuaded Damm and Six to go against all the sacrosanct dogma of the industry and sell off Continental's brand-new fleet of four 747s. Indisputably the most popular airplane now flying, the 747 can also be a money eater. While it carries twice as many passengers as the DC-10, it costs more than four times as much to maintain. By eliminating the 747, Adams saved $2 million a year in training costs alone. By substituting more of the smaller DC-10s, Continental was able to offer passengers additional flights to its destinations. Now the Continental fleet has only two basic airplane types—the 727 and the DC-10—instead of six.

FIGHTING OVER "NICKEL-AND-DIME STUFF"

With one notable exception, the five candidates worked well together, even though it was slowly dawning on all of them that they were in a race for the top. Any temptations to jockey for position were dampened by the knowledge that Six disliked office politics. The race did affect Six's relationship with Bucks, however. Since both men shared a fondness for the outdoors, they had gone off together over the years on week-long hunting trips. But, as the search for a president continued, their close companionship set off rumors that Six had anointed Bucks his heir. When Six heard the rumors, he abruptly ended their camaraderie. Unfortunately, he never explained why, and Bucks, who regards Six as something of a father, felt hurt afterwards. He believed he must have inadvertently done something that annoyed the boss.

The one major friction among the contenders was between Cotter and Renda, both lawyers and men of strong personality. "He's very amiable," Cotter says of Renda. "A lot of people like him. I didn't like him personally. We were not compatible." The two barraged Six with a cross fire of memos, each disputing the other on some minor matter. "It was all nickel-and-dime stuff," says Six, who talked to both men and tried to make peace. Finally Six lost patience and told them he wasn't having any more to do with their bickering, but the memos kept coming in. The fight ended in 1972, when Renda left Continental to go back to Western as its executive vice president.

By May of last year, Six was beginning to realize that even though the four remaining contenders had developed, not one of them had perfected all the attributes he wanted in his successor. Adams understood financing as well as operations, but he was short on marketing expertise. Long a staff man, Cotter still lacked experience as a line officer. Damm had little of Cotter's conceptual ability, but he had developed an eye for detail and a general knowledge of marketing, operations, and scheduling. Bucks had been so busy untangling the structural intricacies of the marketing division and selling seats on Continental's highly competitive new runs to Hawaii that he still lacked experience in finance and route planning. Besides, Six complained, Bucks was too reluctant to fire those subordinates who failed to measure up, declaring in exasperation: "Jesus, Charlie, you're the Billy Graham of the air-transport industry!"

A RETURN TO THE GOOD OLD WAYS

Since there was no single candidate with all the qualifications, Six decided to select a team of two successors. In the near term, he would move from president to chairman, a post that was vacant. One candidate would become vice chairman and another would be named president and chief operating officer. A year later, when Six stepped down, the best man would become chief executive.

To prepare for the final selection, Six and Golightly agreed they should compile an accurate measurement of the candidates' traits and have each man prepare an analysis of himself, though that would obviously be subject to some bias. "You'd do a perfect self-evaluation," said Golightly. "I'd write a glowing one," Six declared, grinning. "S —! It'd be half wrong." By last February all the evaluations were in, and Six put them away with the black books in his safe.

In the middle of last winter, Bucks's standing was enhanced by one further event. A number of rulings by the Civil Aeronautics Board had restricted Continental's use of some highly promotional sales gimmicks. Bucks's employees in the marketing division felt so hamstrung that they lost some of their enthusiasm, and the airline's distinctive individualism and feistiness was beginning to evaporate. For a year and a half, Six had been agitating for a return to the good old ways, and Bucks had picked up the call. The CAB had ordered Continental either to take the popular cocktail lounges out of its DC-10s or to charge extra for them. Continental had taken the ruling to court and, last December, the board was ordered to reconsider.

Even before the legal dust had settled, Bucks sold Six on a strategy to restore the airline's old-time pizzazz. Continental would reinstall the lounges and, going a step further, would put in electronic Ping-Pong games, show free movies — old newsreels, cartoons, and Saturday afternoon serials — and sell hot dogs, hot beef sandwiches, and Coors beer. The entire venture would cost $546,000, but Bucks estimated it would generate more than $1.3 million in extra revenues this year alone. If there had been any questions about Bucks's ability to burnish Continental's image, the new lounges swept those doubts away.

HE DIDN'T WANT PATSIES

Early this year, Six organized a selection committee including himself and three outside directors — Jay A. Pritzker, a Chicago investor whose family controls Hyatt Corp. and Cerro; Thomas D. Finney Jr., a Washington lawyer who is a partner of former Defense Secretary Clark Clifford; and David J. Mahoney, chairman and president of Norton Simon, Inc., a former Continental director who is now one of its two advisory directors (the other is Audrey Six). Six chose the outsiders with care because, as he later explained, "I didn't want a patsy f— committee." He was to get what he bargained for. The three men were to have a major impact on the final selection.

Six wanted to stick with his decision to name a vice chairman and a president, but now he worried about the two losers. He believed all four candidates would be valuable assets to any airline, and other carriers obviously shared that belief. In recent months Damm had been mentioned for the general manager's post of Pan Am, and Bucks had rejected the top marketing job at American. Six wanted to keep his team together, and to do that he planned to restructure the company's upper echelons and give the losing candidates additional powers.

Golightly urged Six to make his selection by using a scoring grid the consultant had set up for American Airlines:

TRAITS	MAXIMUM POINTS
Leadership	30
Technical ability	
airline experience	30
nonairline experience	15
Performance	20
Growth potential	10
Age:	
over 55	5
45-55	10
40-45	8
under 40	5

Though Golightly pressed the suggestion, Six rejected it. "Each of these guys I personally hired," he explained. "I just can't do it that way. My heart's not in it."

Six decided that his criteria had to be based on which man could best fulfill the particular goals and future needs of Continental. Now that the company had bought and financed its new airplanes, knowledge of operations and financing would be of secondary importance for the intermediate future. The company's main challenge would be to maintain its marketing edge and sustain its esprit de corps, while wringing as near perfect a performance as possible from the crews and terminal workers.

The unions had become more militant in recent years, and dealing with them would require personal leadership and insight into the art of handling people. While Damm had more general experience and Adams knew how to deal with flight crews, in Six's mind the candidate who fitted all those requirements best was Bucks.

But Six was also aware that Continental faced a serious and less noticeable challenge stemming from its own expansion. If the airline grew much larger, it might become impersonal and difficult for one or two men to control, a problem that had overwhelmed other airlines and railroads. Only one of the four candidates grasped the strategies needed to deal with this problem. That man was Cotter.

AUDREY KEEPS HER MOUTH SHUT

By late February the tension was gnawing at Six. Normally he can keep up with three conversations at once, but when Audrey broke the evening's silence to chat about some domestic subject, Six would answer absent-mindedly with a comment about the airline. Cotter's being his brother-in-law nagged at him terribly, perhaps more than he realized.

Except for attending traditional Christmas Eve family get-togethers, Six had made it a point to avoid seeing Cotter socially. For the past year Audrey had not discussed the four candidates with Six, knowing that he was aware of her preferences. "I'm not going to jeopardize anybody's chances by opening my big mouth," she told a friend. But once or twice she did pass on her observations to Golightly, who steadfastly refrained from repeating them to Six.

The candidates had their own opinions about who ought to get Six's job. Cotter believed himself both capable and worthy of it. "I have good judgment," he told a visitor one afternoon. "There are all sorts of extremely able people, fine sales types, accounting people. But they lack the basic element called common sense."

For his part, Damm had never doubted that his position as general manager put him next in line, but neither could he believe he would actually get the promotion. Adams and Bucks, on the other hand, took a rather unpretentious stance. Although both harbored the desire to run a major airline, they believed Damm to be the best choice. They were loyal to a senior executive who had worked hard and contributed greatly to the company's success.

Early this spring, Six privately reached his own decision. He favored Cotter as vice chairman because he understood the concepts needed to run an expanding company. He wanted Damm to be president and chief operating officer because of his vast experience in finance and administration. Six left open the decision as to which of the two would become chief executive upon his own retirement.

The trouble with the choices was that neither man was particularly popular with rank-and-file employees. When asked his opinion of Cotter, for instance, a passenger-service supervisor in Phoenix replied: "Cotter? He's in charge of ramp facilities, isn't he?" But Six believed he could persuade Continental employees that his decision was the right one. "I've been selling these kids all my life," he said. "There's no reason I can't sell them on this."

Six planned to reveal his decision to the selection committee, which had agreed to meet on April 2 in New York. He decided to send each member copies of the candidates' self-analyses, his own critique of these, and an outline of each man's career drawn up by Golightly. In order to avoid any possible leaks, Six flew from Los Angeles on March 23 to Continental's former headquarters at Denver's Stapleton field, where he still keeps an office. The following day he dictated his own critiques to a trusted former secretary, Judy L. Lawrence, who once worked for the FBI and holds a government security clearance. She typed copies for each committee member, and a little after five o'clock, Six stuffed the self-analyses and his critiques into three manila envelopes. Miss Lawrence handed the extra carbons and her stenographer's notebook over to Six and watched as he tore out her notes. He then drove to his apartment near downtown Denver and burned the notes in the kitchen sink.

"IF YOU GOT RUN OVER TOMORROW"

The committee (Six, Pritzker, Finney, and Mahoney) gathered at the Waldorf Towers at 6:30 on the evening of April 2, a Wednesday, in the living room of Suite 31-H, a warm and tasteful private apartment that Norton Simon Inc. keeps for private meetings and important visitors. Six sipped a vodka and Fresca, and the others, except for the teetotaling Mahoney, nursed scotches while they spread their papers on the carpet in front of their chairs and began talking. It soon became obvious that the outside members had studied the evaluations and come to some strong conclusions.

The committee seemed impressed by the fact that the evaluations and Six's critiques had shown incontrovertibly that none of the four candidates was totally equipped for the top job at Continental. Finney suggested that Six should postpone his retirement, and Mahoney asked him if he would extend his contract for two additional years. This proposition surprised Six, but the idea of remaining until he could bring Continental's earnings—and its stock price—closer to the levels the company had enjoyed in the mid-1960s greatly appealed to him. "Under today's conditions and with the stock options I've got," he replied, "the answer is yes."

Now that he was staying on, the Cotter-Damm tandem appointment he had in mind no longer made any sense. What Continental now needed was a president and a chief operating officer who could take over if something happened to Six. Mahoney asked: "Who would you name today if you got run over tomorrow?" Surprisingly, Six had not considered the question, but he did not hesitate in replying. The committee unanimously agreed that Al Damm would be recommended to the full board as president and chief operating officer after the annual meeting in Denver on May 7.

But Damm could not be expected to run the company for long. He will be sixty-two in 1978, when Six is to step down. With that in mind, the committee set about selecting a long-term heir. As one member said later: "Our discussion was not in the context of three years; our discussion was in the context of the next fifteen years." Nearly three hours later they came to a unanimous agreement and pledged themselves to secrecy. Some of the matters they had discussed were not to appear in the minutes of their meeting and not to be reported to the full board.

NO ONE TO TALK TO

A week or so after the meeting, Mahoney called to ask sympathetically if Six had told Audrey about his decision. The answer was no. That was the worst part, not being able to talk about it. One day he had happened to sit with Bucks at lunch in the company cafeteria. "Charlie," he said, "I'm going to have to have lunch with all you fellows. I don't want to show any favorites in the cafeteria." And in the next few days he ate with Damm, Adams, and Cotter.

As May approached, Six found it harder to sleep; he woke up night after night, thinking about the decision. There still was no one to talk to about it. By this time, Mahoney was in Paris, Pritzker was involved with a troublesome acquisition, Finney was busy with his law practice, and Golightly was in London.

On the weekend before the annual meeting, Six flew to Denver, and the candidates followed a few days later. They seemed relaxed enough. Bucks sat up most of the night before the meeting playing poker. Six was asleep by 10:30 and slept well, waking only to get a drink of water and let out the dog.

The next morning Six presided over a rather uneventful annual meeting in the ballroom of the Brown Palace Hotel. After a brief luncheon he and the board filed into a small paneled meeting room on the hotel's second floor. The pine shutters were drawn against the noise of passing cars below, and a coffeepot and soft drinks were spread on a table along one wall.

After spending thirty minutes on routine business, Six excused the four candidates, who were all members of the board, and launched into his report. When he finished, Finney began reading the minutes of the Waldorf meeting. As Finney droned on, smoke from Six's cigar curled into the air and the green cloth that covered the board table began to be blanketed by a clutter of papers and empty Fresca bottles. At one point Six got up and walked out the door. "I'm just going to the boys' room, nothing big," he told two of the candidates who were waiting outside with Golightly and a half dozen vice presidents.

Without much discussion, the board voted unanimously to accept the committee's recommendations. Out in the hallway, the executives had formed a pool on how long the board would take to reach a decision. After one hour and thirty-eight minutes, Six ushered the candidates back in and Golightly pocketed $8 in winnings. Cotter pulled back his shoulders and stiffened as he walked into the room; Adams and Bucks were relaxed, but Damm was so tense he steadily avoided looking Six in the eyes. Six opened up with a bit of lightness, saying: "Sit down. I've got bad news. You guys are not going to like it. You're not rid of me yet." Damm could not seem to manage a smile. Then Six told them the board's decision: Damm was to be president, the others were elected executive vice presidents with added responsibilities, and all were named to a new profit-planning committee, which would give them experience in making top-level financial decisions. Damm was so shocked and happy he could hardly find words.

WHAT THE BOARD DIDN'T KNOW

The selection committee is to continue until 1978, when it will formally choose a new chief executive. As Six explained the executives' additional duties, it was obvious that Bucks was well in the lead. He acquired control of scheduling, which Six considers the most important function of an airline executive. Essential to maintaining a competitive edge, good scheduling requires an ability to sniff out trends and plan capacity well in advance of the market.

But what Six did not tell either the candidates or the board was that the committee already had its eye on Bucks, as that committee member said, "in the context of the next fifteen years." For one thing, at forty-seven, Bucks is by far the youngest candidate. And during the Waldorf meeting, Mahoney, joined at times by Pritzker, had urged that the top job ultimately go to a line officer. Mahoney sprinkled his argument with examples of successful line executives who had been promoted at Norton Simon, and after thirty minutes of discussion, Six was convinced. Cotter, a staff man, was virtually eliminated from contention. Adams, a line officer like Bucks, remains a backup candidate, should Bucks stumble.

Much to Six's relief, Audrey declared at the board meeting that the decision was a good one. And even Cotter seemed content. "We're a team," he told the board. "We're going to make it work together."

[EDITORS' NOTE: In January, 1980 it was noted in *Air Transport World* that A. L. Feldman, president of Frontier Airlines, had been appointed president and chief executive officer of Continental Airlines. Bob Six was to remain as chairman until retirement in 1982. The current president, Alexander Damm, was to serve as vice-chairman until his retirement in July, 1980.

On Sunday night, August 9th, 1981, Alvin Feldman, Chairman and Chief Executive of Continental Airlines, was found shot to death in his Los Angeles office, an apparent suicide. He is replaced by George Warde who joined Continental as president on August 1st.

Feldman was apparently despondent over the death of his wife from cancer and the likelihood that his attempts to prevent the takeover of Continental by Texas International Airlines would fail. A group of 9 banks had withdrawn a multimillion dollar loan they had initially pledged to Continental's employee stock ownership plan. Employees are continuing their efforts to stop the takeover and to pursue their own goal of control of the airline.]

Organization Men Still Run the Show

Lynn Langway

The successful American businessman is aggressive, ambitious and willing to move anywhere for a shot at the top, right? Wrong, according to a provocative study by one of the world's largest executive recruiters, Korn/Ferry International.

In a survey of 3,600 senior-level executives (excluding presidents) working at several hundred of the nation's largest companies, Korn/Ferry found corporate society surprisingly immobile. The average senior vice president has worked for the same company for nearly twenty years. Most say they aspire to no higher job, don't expect to move, and would jump to another firm only for increased responsibility, rather than for more money or a chance to be more creative. On average, the executives surveyed have moved only three times in their career, yet earn more than $100,000 a year. "Patience is a virtue in the business world," says chairman Lester Korn.

In contrast to the findings of such books as "The Gamesman," the top vice presidents studied are rather conventional men with little flair. The composite exec is a 53-year-old white male, born in a medium-size Midwestern city, educated at a large public university, where he worked to pay about half his college expenses — and obtained an M.B.A. from a private school like Harvard. He is a registered Republican, a moderate drinker, a Protestant, and the father of three children; his mother did not work outside the home, nor does his wife. He began in accounting or finance and still believes that to be the fast track; he rates "hard work" rather than exceptional intelligence or creativity as his key to success.

Disturbing Profile

The survey was done to help identify future chief executives. But the researchers admit their dismay at the profile that emerges, particularly the dominance of accountants near the top of the corporate pyramid. In the past, business leaders often specialized in marketing, engineering and production — backgrounds that encourage innovation. According to the survey, however, these are the very skills that today's rising executives dismiss as "not of much value in enhancing one's progress." The result, says Korn, is that corporate America may be becoming "a nation of accountants or financial wizards."

The findings worry Korn. "They mean that the innovator and entrepreneur is not going to run the company," he says. He believes that companies may become less creative, less likely to tackle new markets and more willing to grow through acquisitions or mergers instead. "One wonders where our ideas for new products, services and management techniques will come from," the study concludes.

The Wall Street Journal, 18 November 1980.

Many Bosses Already Have Decided Who Successors Will Be and Why

By FRANK ALLEN

Staff Reporter of The Wall Street Journal

Speculation about likely heirs to the top jobs in corporate America may be mostly academic.

Two-thirds of the chief executives of the largest U.S. companies say they already have a clear idea who their successors will be. Half of these executives say they believe their top subordinates share that knowledge.

But the smaller the company, the less certain the chief executive is likely to be about a successor. And the smaller the company, the shorter the list of prospects the incumbent chief considers capable of doing his job.

What sort of person should a successor be? "Someone in our image," says the head of a medium-sized company in the West. "A person sensitive to the needs of his people who can motivate and lead by example. A hard worker who takes time to have fun with his employees."

The Art of Firing an Executive

Judson Gooding

Of all the corporate chores performed by executives, the most painful is firing other executives. The process appears to be getting more painful every year—and also more commonplace. It is sinking in on some executives, at least, that an ability to fire one's colleagues

Reprinted from material originally appearing in the October 1972 issue of *Fortune* Magazine by special permission; © 1972 Time, Inc. Research associate: Ann Hengstenberg.

properly is an important job qualification these days.

It is, of course, the fact that they *are* one's colleagues that makes the whole process so painful. Firing production workers or low-level white-collars is unpleasant enough; but generally those who make the decisions are shielded from direct contact with the victims. Those who decide that an executive colleague must get the ax are often obliged to wield it personally.

It is principally because of the "democratization" of American business that this process is becoming more traumatic every year. When the boss was a remote figure in an authoritarian corporate world, his concerns about the executives who worked under him were presumably minimal. He did not deal with them on a first-name basis; he probably didn't drink with them or belong to the same country club they did; his wife certainly wasn't a friend of their wives. But in the modern corporation, increasingly dominated by humanist values and a democratic ethic, webs of personal relationships are spun endlessly. It becomes harder all the time to view one's colleagues as just names on the table of organization — which means, among other things, that it becomes harder all the time to fire them.

Firing of executives seems to be increasing, despite all the attendant traumas, because of an intensifying pressure for profits. All data about frequency of firings are necessarily rather soft, but it is clear that during the 1969–1970 recession, when many large corporations found themselves under greater profit pressure than ever, executive firings soared, apparently to levels far higher than those of past economic downturns. E. A. Butler, who runs a management-consulting firm in New York, and who has spent more than twenty years talking to out-of-work executives and corporate personnel men, is persuaded that this wave of firing represented more than a cyclical phenomenon — that it also reflected a growing commitment to the kind of performance that would come down to the bottom line. Even in the present strong economy, Butler says, "the quickness to fire is much greater than it used to be."

The traumas accompanying executive firings have had a considerable influence on the way companies talk about the process. There is a strong tradition — it seems to be especially powerful when executives at the highest level are involved — requiring that public announcements characterize departures as resignations. Henry Ford's slam-bang firing of Semon Knudsen in 1969, only twenty months after he was hired as president of the Ford Motor Co., was one of the very few instances in recent times in which it was perfectly clear that the president had been fired. A far more typical scenario was the one enacted at General Foods last April.

Arthur E. Larkin, Jr., who had been president of General Foods since 1966, announced in April that he was taking early retirement at fifty-five—ten years before the company's mandatory retirement age. His departure came just after General Foods had taken a $46,800,000 write-down, most of it related to the Burger Chef fast-food operation, whose expansion Larkin had backed. C. W. Cook, the company's chairman and chief executive, who had originally hired Larkin and worked closely with him over the years, says of the reasons for the retirement that "a basic difference in management philosophy became more evident."

As a result of this difference, Cook recommended to the board that he himself "resume operating responsibility." At this point, as Cook describes the sequence, Larkin "saw that the only thing to do was to leave. He told me this, and I agreed." His request for early retirement was accepted at a meeting of the board of directors, and the retirement was noted in the General Foods annual report in one succinct sentence. Larkin himself insists that the retirement was voluntary and says that it was for "personal reasons."

Sweetening the terms of the separation is one obvious way of easing the pain associated with firings, and most large companies have gone pretty far along that road. Many corporate managements that resisted early-retirement plans because of their expense have discovered that they have at least made it a lot easier to fire executives: announcements of resignations have become more plausible and the job loss has become less painful to the executives involved. Pearl Meyer, vice president for research at Handy Associates, a management-consulting and recruiting firm, has observed that "companies nowadays are willing to pay liberally for the privilege of getting rid of people."

The blow can also be softened by getting another company to recruit the executive who is to be fired, and then, when it's clear that he has a job offer, lowering the boom. If the victim is reasonably astute, he may manage to resign before the bad news is actually delivered. Variations of this tactic now seem to be fairly widespread. Louis F. Polk Jr., a former president of Metro-Goldwyn-Mayer (he was fired in 1969), says that, as a result, "some people are afraid they're getting the ax when the headhunters come after them."

SAVING FACE IN CHICAGO

One rather special opportunity to eliminate people with a minimum of anguish arises when the company itself is planning to move its offices. Donald A. Petrie, a former Lazard Frères investment banker (he is now serving as treasurer of the Democratic National Committee), is something of an authority on this situation: at different times

in his career he has been a senior executive of both Hertz and Avis
—both of which moved their headquarters from one city to another.

In each case there was a compelling reason for the move, but the
opportunity to get rid of unproductive executives and staff members
was exploited to the full. "A move is a time to bring your organization
up to date," Petrie says. In the case of Hertz, "we had 525 persons in
Chicago, and we moved 125. We said to persons we were willing to
lose, 'We're moving to New York, and you ought to think about
whether you ought to go.' We asked questions like 'Do you want to
uproot your family?' and 'Is New York the kind of place you want to
live?' and 'Does it make sense to move away just three years before
retirement?'"

Just about everyone seems to have got the message. Petrie recalls:
"Of the 125 we wanted to keep, only three decided to stay in Chicago,
and of the 400 who remained, only seven had wanted to make the
move. They had a perfect out—the person who stays saves face. He
can say, 'I'm a Chicagoan, I don't want to move to New York.'" When
a company uses a move this way, Petrie says, "you do an enormous
amount for the people, because they never had to tell their wives or
their kids they were fired — the company just moved away. Some
never even admitted it to themselves."

Some of these employees benefited in still another way. When
other companies heard that Hertz was moving, they began raiding it.
"Most people love to steal executives," Petrie says, "so we allowed
anyone who wanted it the delectable pleasure of stealing those of our
people who were not making the move. They took thirty this way—
of whom we had wanted to keep two."

THE DOUBLE-TALK PROBLEM

There is certainly every reason for anyone firing an executive to
do whatever is possible to ease the pain, and in public statements a
certain amount of double-talk about "resignation" can be appropriate. Unfortunately, a good many executives also resort to double-
talk in their private sessions with men who are being fired — leaving the victims in a state of confusion about where they stand with
the company.

A man may be deemed fired when he gets a message telling him
that he must leave — that he has no choice about the matter. The
message may be verbal and explicit. It may conceivably be nonverbal
but still unmistakable—e.g., when an executive returns from vacation
and finds that he has no office or secretary and can't get an appointment with his boss. The elder Henry Ford occasionally had his staff
members' furniture moved out of their offices overnight.

But the message should at least be clear, and the most agonizing firings of all are those in which it isn't. Something happens — e.g., a sudden exclusion from key committees — to suggest that the executive is under a cloud. Yet the underlying message remains ambiguous: Is the man being told that he can stay, with his status somewhat reduced, or is he being told that his time is limited and that he'd better start looking for another job? Or is top management itself indecisive about the executive's future?

Personnel men and consultants who've thought a lot about the process generally agree that the ambiguous message is the cardinal sin of executive firing. Anyone who is being fired is entitled to be told clearly what's going on. Efforts to avoid telling him serve to prolong and maximize his anguish; and, for that matter, they are apt to make things harder in the long run for the senior executive who can't bring himself to deliver a clear message. Yet it is apparent that many otherwise sophisticated companies continue to fire executives the hard way.

The details are indeed harrowing. Consultants who have watched the process many times at many companies cite this typical sequence: Executives suddenly find that they've been taken off the circulation list for office memos, so that they are uninformed in meetings and liable to make fools of themselves. Then they're cut off from the meetings. Later their secretaries may be taken away, they are moved to smaller offices, and their expense accounts suddenly become the object of searching questions. Some companies have office areas known as Siberia, where executives getting the treatment are herded together.

A FEELING OF GUILT

The ultimate irony about these long, agonizing firings is that they're typically perpetrated by executives who are fearful of "hurting" a colleague. Dr. Harry Levinson, the psychologist and author, formerly a Distinguished Visiting Professor at Harvard Business School who has written several books about executive stress, says that many executives obliged to fire a colleague are overpowered by feelings of guilt. The feelings may lead them to evade the issue by keeping the message ambiguous. Alternatively, Levinson says, some executives react against their feelings and behave impulsively, even angrily, like a small boy who becomes enraged at others when he feels he has done something wrong himself. "Suddenly, without warning, they tell the man to clear out his desk, and they add 'or we'll send someone to do it for you.'"

Sometimes the senior executives will remain offstage themselves but arrange for firings to be carried out by underlings. One former executive at Metromedia, a victim of a major purge there several years ago, contends that Chairman John Kluge operated through subordinates, "somehow managing to avoid running into formerly close colleagues who were getting the ax, although some of them had helped him start the company and had been allies for ten or twenty years." The general manager of one major Metromedia-owned local station was summarily fired by a headquarters executive who had never liked him. The executive flew into town, marched into the general manager's office, and announced: "You're through." He demanded and got the keys to the manager's company car and his credit cards, snapped the credit cards in half, pocketed the keys, turned around, and left.

Sudden, brutal firings can have calamitous consequences. Not long ago, an executive of a large diversified corporation in western New York state was having lunch in a restaurant frequented by executives of a company that was being acquired by his own in a merger. He spotted a department manager, walked over to the man's table, and told him, without any preliminaries, that he was being fired. The department manager stood up, suddenly white-faced, clutched at his chest, then fell down and died of a heart attack.

Less brutal, but more unscrupulous, is an approach in which companies force executives out by getting their medical departments to overstate any problems the men may have. Dr. Walter Menninger, senior staff psychiatrist at the Menninger Foundation, says that he has received reports of this practice at a number of companies. "Management will try to get the medical department to provide a basis for early retirement. They do it to avoid the discomfort of firing." The managements in question can often cite some ailment that is real enough; after all, plenty of executives do suffer from high blood pressure or various psychosomatic ailments. Nevertheless, Menninger reports, "company physicians we've spoken to are very troubled by these attempts to use executives' medical status as grounds for retirement. It's a cop-out — the physicians feel they're being used as a tool to solve what should really be an executive's problem."

THE IMPORTANCE OF TELLING WHY

Despite the numerous inept firings in American business, there is no real mystery or disagreement about how the job should be done. The basic requirements are simple: the executive being fired must be told plainly that he is leaving the company and must also be told why. It is important to tell him why in a way that allows him to preserve his self-esteem and to explain to himself and his friends and family, particularly his wife, why this has happened to him. But the need for tact should not be allowed to obscure the realities about an inadequate performance. A. Edward Miller, president of Downe Publishing, who has fired a fair number of executives in his time (he has also been publisher of *McCall's* magazine and a consultant to Curtis Publishing Co.), says, "Most people I've fired have become better friends, because I've always told *why*. When he walks out the door, he knows why it happened." Alfred J. Seaman, president of the SSC&B advertising agency, says, "There is no one way to do it—much depends on the circumstances—but if I think firm criticism of the man will do any good, I'll tell him pretty bluntly what was going wrong."

Just about everyone agrees that it is an unacceptable evasion to blame the firing on vague authorities higher up, or on the board of directors ("I really can't go into what the board said, Bill, it has to stay confidential"). The evasion allows the man doing the firing to avoid taking any responsibility, but it deprives the victim of information he may need for success in his next job. It is also likely to leave him feeling angry and frustrated over his inability to find out just *why* his career is being deflected.

It is also generally agreed that, whenever possible, the firing should be performed by the executive's direct superior. (The man who is being dismissed should, however, be allowed to talk with a higher-up if he wants to.) Delegating the job to someone who doesn't know the situation in detail is not fair to the man being fired; at the same time it gives him an opportunity to muddy the issue by developing arguments about the merits of the case that the executive charged with firing him may not know how to answer.

In addition to being told clearly that he's leaving, and why, an executive who's being fired is entitled to know about a number of other matters that are, inevitably, of some concern to him. One matter simply involves the way any announcement of his departure will be made, and to what the departure will be attributed. He will certainly want to know how much time he's got and whether, in the interim, he can use an office to arrange to have telephone messages taken, and in general conduct his job hunt with the advantage of appearing to be employed.

SPECIALISTS IN FIRING

At some companies the executive who's doing the firing is able to tell the victim that the company can offer him the service of one of the handful of organizations specializing in "outplacement." Some of these organizations offer a kind of "full-line" firing service, which takes care of everything except the session at which the bad news is actually delivered. They counsel management on what severance arrangements are appropriate and work to help the executive find a satisfactory new job.

One of these services, called THINC., is a New York-based company that has seen its list of clients grow from three to more than a hundred companies or divisions since 1969. Thomas Hubbard, its president, says, "We consult with the company before the notices are given, to help it avoid making expensive mistakes. When they tell the man he's fired, they also tell him he will get the use of our services. This helps him at a difficult moment, and shows him he is not just being thrown out — that the company cares."

A CHANCE TO VENTILATE

The THINC. consultant meets with the man right after he has got the word, sometimes in the next room. This gives the departing executive a chance to "ventilate," as Hubbard describes the process — i.e., to get things off his chest that, if blurted out, might hurt his relationship with the company he's leaving — and also hurt him in his job hunt. The consultant helps him to avoid making serious mistakes, such as setting up interviews with job prospects before he is prepared for them. "Most mistakes in job hunting are made in the first seventy-two hours after the man is fired," Hubbard says.

One of THINC.'s major assignments in recent years was its effort in 1971 for New York's Bankers Trust Co., where sixty officers and 350 other staff members were laid off to cut costs. The bank offered THINC.'s services to all the employees involved. All forty of the executives who actively sought jobs with THINC.'s assistance were placed, according to Peter Gurney, the bank's vice president for personnel.

Richard Gleason is the proprietor of another major outplacement firm, Man-Marketing Services, Inc., of Chicago. The firm began counseling job seekers in 1954. Man-Marketing prepares résumés, provides tailor-made mailing lists, teaches the applicant how to plan for job interviews, advises on salary negotiations, counsels on follow-ups after interviews, and helps the job hunter decide which offer represents the best opportunity. Gleason's client companies include Borg-Warner Corp., for which he relocated eight executives in 1970, Mead Corp., Maremont Corp., and Jos. Schlitz Brewing Co.

A CASE FOR DEADLINES

The outplacement firms say that they can often save a lot of money for companies by simply talking them out of giving fired executives overgenerous flat settlements — a full year's pay being common. Instead, the firms may suggest that the man be kept on full salary while he conducts his job search, with a specific deadline. This arrangement motivates the fired executive to make a vigorous search and also can save the company thousands of dollars on any one separation.

Another substitute for heavy severance is putting the fired executive on a partial-pay contract basis. A contract provides a graceful exit for the executive and keeps his knowledge and contacts available if needed. An additional, sometimes critical, advantage is that it may ensure a degree of loyalty to the company and minimize the danger that secrets will be divulged. That danger is occasionally a very serious matter. Not long ago a major shopping-center developer abruptly fired the executive who had been in charge of site development and leasing. The firing took place at about the time an important rental prospect was agreeing to occupy the biggest single store in a large mid-western center; his agreement was considered crucial to the leasing of other stores. The executive who had been fired, angry at his summary treatment, proceeded to tell the client about a number of shortcomings in the facilities, some of which constituted violations of the leasing agreement. It cost $250,000 to fix up the facilities. The head of the company observed later, "That was the most expensive severance settlement I've ever had to pay."

2
BECOMING A MANAGER

"The competition of managers vying for recognition and position creates little trust and that means little human contact or concern."

—Robert Schrank

Much of the conventional wisdom suggests that the gateway to a career in business or government increasingly is found through graduation from a business school. Therein one gains a level of competence in an assortment of analytical skills and an understanding of financial, regulatory, and market institutions.

These neatly compartmented skills and bits of knowledge, leavened with some understanding of human behavior and management principles, entitle the reasonably diligent individual to a passport that more and more often takes the form of an MBA.

The passport in turn promises access to the ranks of management. There, once admitted, the innovative, hardworking individual can hope to find a challenging and rewarding life. The fortunate few may even end up as one of the movers and shakers with the material means to enjoy the good things our society can provide.

This scenario, of course, is greatly oversimplified. There are hazards along the way and many writers argue that the costs associated with the prize are far too high. Few organizational behaviorists or management scholars have addressed this question. Indeed, most texts assume that the rewards outweigh the costs if only one manages one's life appropriately. Pacing oneself and maintaining a well-rounded life perspective are, after all, matters for individual determination.

Yet evidence abounds of individuals whose failure to maintain a healthy perspective leads them to shallow or even tragic consequences. As Alvin Toffler and other contemporary observers have noted, the incidence of crippling imbalance in people's lives has risen alarmingly. Self-help books, seminars, and institutes dedicated to aiding us to find ourselves, to become "whole beings," have proliferated.

The casualty rate is high. In "A Body With Many Heads," Cohen shows us the tragic consequences to which the competitive struggle in a business school can lead. (In Section 8, The Compulsion to Perform, we see other illustrations of emotional dysfunction.) The situation Cohen describes is extreme, but every business school experiences its annual quota of students who crack up physically and/or emotionally in their overzealous pursuit of the passport to management.

The receipt of the passport is only the first step in the competitive struggle. Gwen Kinkead reports the formidable odds facing young managers and the expectations, values, and life styles of a selected group who have opted to get "On a Fast Track to the Good Life." Most of the young fast-trackers Kinkead quotes are in staff functions or service industries such as banking. In "Management" Schrank looks at managers from a different perspective. As a production manager with a background as a blue-collar worker and union organizer, he finds managers and engineers much less interesting.

Finally, the selection by J. Patrick Wright from "On a Clear Day You Can See General Motors" discusses some of the less talked about but equally crucial behaviors managers must exhibit. Our conversations with managers in other industries persuades us that these required demonstrations of "loyalty" are by no means unique to General Motors.

The theme of competition runs through all these selections. Cohen's MBA students, Kinkead's young managers, Schrank's engineers, and Wright's GM executives all compete, all chase the elusive grail of success. And for each group, success is defined as leading the pack or, at least, staying with the front runners. Further, each author illuminates a different aspect of the costs of becoming a manager.

Each article, however, invites us to examine at least one broader social issue. Cohen raises his question directly, pointing out the waste of human potential associated with unbridled competition. Schrank notes a single-minded isolation from living things among his managers that tended to negate human concerns at the workplace. He contrasts this with the warm companionship he experienced as a blue-collar worker. Need this be so?

Kinkead's younger generation reflects a shallow materialism and fuzziness of broader values that makes us ask, "How typical?" The excerpt from Wright's book points up the importance of corporate stereotypes and leaves us asking, just how much does ability really count?

A Body with Many Heads

Peter Cohen

April 8: The scene was all too familiar. First the police and then the dean and then, a couple of hours later — when people were having dinner — the little black wagon came. There were two men in the

From *The Gospel According to the Harvard Business School* by Peter Cohen. Copyright © 1973 by Peter Cohen. Reprinted by permission of Doubleday & Company, Inc.

wagon with a two-wheeled cart—the kind used to move heavy crates up and down staircases—they took the cart into one of the wings of the dorm, and when they came out, there was this thing strapped to the cart. Something the size and shape of a bag of golf clubs, only taller maybe—wrapped in dark tarpaulin.

They moved it quickly, and one of the men jumped and opened the rear of the wagon and they swung the cart around and lifted it in. The wagon was plain black, with no markings, and it drove away in a hurry.

That's how James Hinman left his first year at the Harvard Business School—dead of poison.

This is the third guy now, leaving like that, without knowing, without caring, where he is going to be five or a hundred or a couple of thousand years from now.

God knows how many times you have been told that competition is the American way and the only way; how you have heard it from lecterns and pulpits, and how you have almost come to believe it. And then you see a little cart wheel away what could have been a lifetime of laughter and tenderness and bright ideas. Suddenly you see the problems of it, the cost, and you wonder whether there *really* is no other way.

Because, when you come down to it, all competition is, is behavior. A piece of behavior that builds on the need of individuals to be faster, cleverer, richer than the next guy. And, undeniably, this need to be unequal is of great value to society. Because one way of getting things done is to get everybody to outdo each other.

So society encourages that kind of behavior by reward structures where the guy who ends up fastest or smartest gets everything, the others nothing. Suddenly it forgets that people have needs other than wanting to be unequal. That some groups and types of people, that everybody at certain times in his life, want very much to be *like*, not unlike, other types or groups of people. That progress doesn't just depend on people setting new and higher standards, but that, just as often, progress is a matter of attaining existing standards consistently.

Everybody forgets that despite its undeniable advantages competition is a wasteful process. That every winner comes at the cost of a hundred, a thousand, a hundred thousand losers. And that one ought to consider the cost of it, before one starts advocating indiscriminate competition.

And this is where the American society is at; it talks of *competition* as if it had never heard the word "cooperation." It refuses to see that too much pressure doesn't move people; it kills them. Instead, everybody pushes and pushes each other, and they call the other a lazy bastard, if one of them happens to break down.

No, Coach—winning isn't everything. It's only a thing.

On a Fast Track to the Good Life

Today's twenty-five-year-old business beginners know what they want and are uninhibited about demanding it

Gwen Kinkead

A quarter of a century ago, in the age of Ike, *Fortune* interviewed a large sampling of young men starting out in business and found them to be an optimistic, tractable, incurious lot, dedicated to family and community service. (See "The Confident Twenty-Five-Year-Olds," *Fortune*, February, 1955.) This year, repeating the exercise, *Fortune* selected eighty-two twenty-five-year-olds from all over the U.S. and talked with them at length about their views of business and the world at large. Like the 1955 sample, the new one was chosen unscientifically, although we made an effort to find young people who had shown promise of becoming high-level managers or entrepreneurs. All the people interviewed — this time they included women — are or will be twenty-five some time this year. The results show that the adjective "confident" still applies; indeed, the confidence borders on brashness. These new heirs of the nation's product want a lot more of everything than the Eisenhower generation, and they plan to get what they want — both the tangibles and the intangibles — by driving hard and fast up the career path.

The going is apt to be arduous. Because they had the tough luck to be born in 1955, smack in the middle of the postwar baby boom, today's twenty-fives face more competition for advancement in the corporate hierarchy than any generation in business history. Their progress will be impeded, if not blocked, by the many managers now in their mid-thirties who were born at the beginning of the boom and, more indirectly, by older executives who are choosing to retire later. And behind the twenty-fives bulks a horde of younger challengers born between 1956 and 1964, a span that included several peak years of the baby boom. The squeeze from fore and aft can only worsen when this class eventually vies for the few top positions at the apex of the hierarchy.

Yet, while the statistics portend a Hobbesian all-against-all future struggle, the realities are not nearly so grim. The prospective managers *Fortune* interviewed will progress more quickly into upper-income brackets — which start at about $29,000 per household today — than most of their predecessors would have dreamed possible.

"On a Fast Track to the Good Life" by Gwen Kinkead, abridged and reprinted from *Fortune*, April 7, 1980. © 1980 Time Inc. Reprinted by permission.

Single twenty-five-year-olds in the group are already earning a median of $20,000, well above the median U.S. family income, estimated at around $17,040. And those remarkable statistics pale beside another: the median income of twenty married couples in the sample is $37,250. (Twenty-four of the eighty-two are married, but in four cases only one spouse works.) In other words, most of them are already well into the upper-income bracket. As more of this group marry and achieve higher salaries, they will constitute a new "superclass." Whether all this conjugal earning power will compensate for what the demographics warn will be thwarted career ambitions remains to be seen.

All indicators suggest that it won't. Almost without exception these twenty-five-year-olds are careerists, in the sense that they measure their self-worth according to the accomplishment of their professional goals. There is nothing new or unusual about this: some twenty-five-year-olds have probably always viewed their lives this way. What is unusual is that it surfaces as the overriding characteristic of the entire group of promising young business people. They put their jobs ahead of most other diversions and commitments — including marriage, which many are in no hurry for, and children, which some claim they'll never want.

As careerists, they will not be content to get ahead in conventional ways at the inexorable steady-does-it pace of their 1955 predecessors. Impatient for recognition, they associate putting in time with stagnation. These pragmatic strategists have deliberately planned their career moves far in advance and are making a beeline to attain them. At their best, the twenty-fives are extremely hardworking, disciplined, and motivated, scornful of handouts or mooching off the system. At their worst, they are handicapped by tunnel vision. Immersed in their work, single-mindedly chasing their objectives, they ignore what doesn't blend or harmonize with their purposefully limited landscape. They view work and life as a series of "trade-offs" rather than compromises; for each opportunity surrendered, they demand an equal benefit in return. This is the only sensible approach, they argue, when you are confronted by an unprecedented number of obstacles: the worst U.S. inflation in modern history, a perverse demographic fate, and an economic and political future suddenly imperiled by a renewed cold war. To that list of hazards should be added the twenty-fives' own exalted standards. To them, being second best is anathema.

During their college years, the twenty-fives got a frightening whiff of economic trouble, first during the 1973 oil embargo and then in the 1974–75 economic slough. Some whom *Fortune* interviewed say this squelched their notions of pursuing graduate studies that would have led them into careers in education. They turned practical quickly and chose instead to shoot for business careers and the greater economic security that goes with them. So lining up jobs became this group's top priority while they were undergraduates. "It was a time when students worried that someone—the government, the poor, the Russians—would snatch the American dream away from them," recalls Washington lawyer Deena Rabinowicz, one of the few non-business professionals in the *Fortune* sample.

Overwhelmingly the twenty-fives treated their college education as precareer, almost vocational, training. Nearly all of them went into technical and practical majors such as accounting, engineering, and business administration; few in the sample have degrees in the liberal arts. Armed with business-research publications such as Moody's and Standard & Poor's, the shrewdest among them studied prospective employers' profit records and growth potential, and checked into such things as corporations' reputations for internal promotions and the average age of upper management.

The group seems drawn to business not only for the big money, but also for the authority and reputations they envision winning in the competition. For them, competition is nearly reflexive. Fully aware that the baby boom made them a dime a dozen, they set about very early competing to get into nursery school; then they fought for summer jobs and admission to college and, more recently, into M.B.A. programs. Lest they forget that they weren't the only candidate for each sought-after opening, their teachers, parents, and Scout leaders drilled them in the demographic facts of life. Gail Rodin, an I.B.M. systems engineer in Norwalk, Connecticut, remembers being admonished: "You have to excel, you have to be marketable; the competition is fierce and you have to be better." Moving up through the ranks according to their job performance suits these twenty-fives just fine. Indeed, after years of being sorted, classed, and graded upon their accomplishments, they relish such external, objective tests of progress as business provides.

They also believe that business offers the fastest means of gratifying their frankly materialistic requirements. Deferred success, the traditional basis of the work ethic, holds little appeal. Having contracted what few realize is a virulent case of "rising expectations," complicated by a disdain for forbearance, they expect to enjoy immediately a relatively high level of material comfort. They formed their norms of comfortable living during their youth in the seemingly endless prosperity of the Sixties. Too young to have been "flower children"—they were fifteen at the time of the U.S. invasion of Cambodia—they mocked their older siblings' anti-establishment aversion to making money. The economic jolts of the Seventies simply fanned their determination to waste no time building nest eggs. Terry Michel, a management trainee at Connecticut General Life Insurance Co., echoes the consensus: "I knew business would reward me in direct proportion to what I achieved," she says. "I like to spend money. I didn't feel like giving up any luxuries. I grew up with lots of land, private school, horses, dogs, a car at sixteen." To a stranger from another generation, they sometimes seem a grabby bunch.

Today's twenty-fives are phenomenally confident of their native abilities, maybe more so than any previous group of business beginners. Having got this far against the statistical odds—past college and (in some cases) several promotions — they figure they're not just lucky, they're good. Superior to their peers, maybe star material. Conditioned to competition, confirmed in their talent, they aim high without fear of overreaching. The eager minority in the 1955 group that refused to recognize career limitations has swollen, in 1980, into an overwhelming majority. Most of them, including Chemical Bank account officer Susan C. Coogan, aspire to reach the top, perhaps as early as age forty-five. "I see no reason why I can't go as far as I want," Coogan asserts. "I'd love to be chairman of a top-ranked bank." She adds, only half in jest, "My father is only senior vice president of his *Fortune* 500 company. I'm going to be chairman."

It seems that, almost on principle, this class vaunts its ambitions. Why bother with goals, they ask, if you don't shoot for the top? They're optimistic about getting there too. They suggest, rightly, that they're among the best-educated and best-qualified recruits ever to join industry. And their success to date in their present jobs serves to justify and perpetuate their sturdy, and occasionally arrogant, self-assurance.

If pluck, positive thinking, and ambition were all that were needed in the race ahead, many of the twenty-fives, men and women alike, might be sitting pretty in boardrooms thirty years hence. But the numerical odds augur many losers and few winners. How do the twenty-fives intend to handle the odds? Just three or four years into the work force (one or two if they acquired M.B.A.'s), even *they* admit they don't know all the answers. But characteristically, they outline several strategies that, with a few variations, cropped up in interviews all across the country. These, they trust, will favor them in the final reckoning with a glimpse of light at the end of the tunnel.

The most popular plan is to jump the gun on the race. By starting on a fast track, and then accelerating, they aim to rocket through the baby-boom congestion by age thirty-five. They would then be able to compete with a smaller batch of older aspiring executives for the few upper-level positions available. The root conviction bracing this strategy is, as they chorus, "the cream always rises"; it's just a matter of speeding up the separation.

The key tactic in this strategy is, one way or another, to keep moving. Shorter stints in each slot on the way up will maintain the momentum. This, in turn, involves putting in long hours and *demanding* more responsibility. The twenty-fives are emboldened to be so assertive by a generally dim regard for their present superiors. "I know managers so inept and incompetent," declares one, speaking of his company's upper echelon, "that there's no way in hell they should be managers. Maybe they're the best of a disastrous bunch." With varying degrees of invective, the twenty-fives describe their superiors as so much deadwood. Such porous ranks should yield easily to the assault from below.

One of the more articulate exponents of the "cream rises faster" theory is Jim Curtis, assistant product manager for Chivas Regal at Joseph E. Seagram & Sons in New York. Curtis joined Seagram's first management-training program two years ago from Dartmouth's Amos Tuck School of Business. After eight months of comprehensive training, he got his first big break during his debut as an assistant product manager for several cordials in the General Wine & Spirits division. Curtis recalls, "I knew I wouldn't be too efficient at first, so I thought I'd make up for it by working the job to death." Those long hours, frequently lasting until 10:00 P.M., inspired a product manager to give Curtis a plum: the job of assisting in the test-marketing of Von Konig, a new German liquor being unveiled with considerable fanfare. It was, says Curtis, "the best job for anyone my age and in my department."

Curtis now earns roughly $24,500, and where he'll go from here, he says, will depend partly on luck and vacancies. But he'd like to advance in a year or two from product manager toward strategic planning or new-product development, and emerge ten years from now as a group product manager. That position, Curtis figures, commands a salary of roughly $60,000 to $70,000. From there, Curtis thinks he would be by age forty within sight of an executive vice presidency in a division at headquarters, where he estimates salaries run about $150,000.

Following this track could be an ordeal, Curtis concedes. In rapid-fire delivery, as though the time to forge ahead were literally expiring, Curtis acknowledges the demographic pressure on his age group: "If I'd been born fifteen years earlier, the supply of qualified individuals with my background and training would have been relatively limited. Success would have been more a question of supply and demand, because anyone with dedication and ability couldn't be easily replaced —whereas I'll need all that dedication and ability just to stay even in the future. And I'll need to do more to rise. That's why I want to get a quick start, and be competing in fifteen years with fifty-year-olds up there where it's not so crowded."

Curtis counts on the aerodynamics of his resolution and stamina to keep him aloft and moving forward. With the energetic abandon typical of the twenty-fives, he rejoices, "I'm naturally suited for the race. I have intelligence (and the test scores to prove it). My energy and willingness to work hard seem to exceed most of my contemporaries'. That's really going to be my ace."

Shining early and surging onto the fast track entail at the very least getting noticed. What spooks this generation the most is anonymity, getting lost in the shuffle, or blurring into faceless organizational hirelings. Accordingly, the twenty-fives have polished up an old standby offense that's propelled them forward in the past — the art of self-promotion. They're firm believers in the virtue of tooting your own horn. Yet, even while they practice tireless, sophisticated self-merchandising, they denounce the infighting that often accompanies it. They hope the politics of advancement won't require "stepping on anyone else" or "backstabbing" — sins they associate with their parents' business generation. The twenty-fives are the clean squad: they want to deserve what they earn and to get ahead in a straightforward, aboveboard fashion.

Still, the interviews also revealed that this generation of go-getters is skeptical that outstanding performance will be a sufficient condition for success. Even if you outdo your peers, they say, promotions might occur too slowly to propel you past the pack. Or, if promotions are brisk, your raises might lag behind inflation, leaving you trailing behind economically if not professionally

A solution, and a key tactic that came up in the interviews, is to job-hop regularly. Some twenty-fives contend that job-hopping *always* pays, no matter how well you're doing where you are. As Kevan Full, a work management analyst with Teachers Insurance & Annuity Association, puts it, "Switching jobs looks good on résumés. It shows restlessness and ambition. I'm not going to stay with a company just because I love it." This group's advocacy of job-hopping is an outright rejection of corporate loyalty. Blind loyalty to an employer is something they think their parents suffered because they were scared into dead-end jobs by memories of the Depression and by the need to support large families. Many twenty-fives believe that yearly job searches are the only way to ensure that income and rank keep rising.

Most of them are too pragmatic to allow their names to be attached to these sentiments in print. But few would argue with this line of reasoning from a young administrator at a national network whose last nimble job hop nearly doubled his salary: "I can't plan on being in any one job with certainty for more than a year at a time. First, I'm too young to worry about finding some company to stay in for the next thirty years and, second, no one can count on his salary rising according to how good he is anymore. With the present 7 percent guidelines and 18 percent inflation, you just stand still no matter how remarkable your performance."

This generation rightly senses that in some large, old-guard companies which honor seniority, their tactics, and their eagerness, could count against them. If that happens, they will bail out into fast-growing, smaller companies thin in upper management. To ensure their marketability, the twenty-fives without M.B.A.'s (a majority of those interviewed) are hurrying back to night school to get them. Worries about marketability have turned this group into congenital scale-watchers who tote up their chances of promotion, weigh their salaries against the going market rate, and never, never do anything that won't enhance their records. Few lament the meretriciousness that results from scale-watching; they perceive with deadly earnestness that only the fittest will survive the final judgment.

While the women in the group are generally hell-bent to climb the tallest corporate peaks, a significant proportion of the men are planning to leave corporate life when they are in their thirties to start their own businesses. Some, like Boston investment banker Reuben Richards, who is with a division of Moseley, Hallgarten, Estabrook & Weeden, may turn entrepreneur even sooner. "I've gone as far as I can without being a vice president. But there aren't any v.p.'s here under thirty-five. I don't see sticking around till 1990 for the next step because by then I'd like to run my own very successful company." In part, it is the fear of being checkmated on the corporate ladder that has prompted twenty-five-year-olds to think of venturing out on their own. Economist Paul Samuelson, in a different context, has described their predicament ingeniously. Standing on tiptoe is a solution for one person viewing a parade, he says, and even for several people, but it is hardly a solution for an entire crowd.

The entrepreneurial approach also appeals to the twenty-fives for other reasons. It betokens savvy financial aggressiveness, more money than corporate success permits, and the freedom to control one's own destiny. In unison they assert they'd work harder if they ran their own businesses because work would then be "more like a hobby." Some have already picked out their prospective partners and are investing to accumulate the necessary seed capital. In this respect, Dwight Billingsly, a utilities consultant in a Washington, D.C., firm, strikes a common chord: "I plan to set up my own business, be independent, report to no one," he says. "Though I have more money now than I ever thought possible, I'd like all the money in the world, and to own a major-league baseball or football team." His reasoning: "Athletic teams provide immediate gratification — they either win or lose."

This generation's insistence upon gratification and the freedom to choose between a number of different careers involves a dramatic change in the definition of self-interest and work incentives. In essence, they are seeking from work what their predecessors sought more from their private lives, i.e., "self-actualization" (roughly translated as fulfilling one's potential). Greg Niedermeyer, a tax analyst with Evans Products in Portland, Oregon, illustrates the shift in perspective: "I can't just work for a living — that's a chore," he emphasizes. "If a company doesn't satisfy me by challenging me, or if I don't basically receive from it what it gets from me, I'm not willing to do it. I've got to enjoy my work, be stimulated by it, or I'll leave it."

Almost all the twenty-fives claim money isn't the main inducement in their jobs. But it's hard to take them seriously, because their requisite standard of living isn't cheap. The Good Life is defined as being free to follow their impulses, and above all, never worrying about money. Bradley Rotter, who earns $50,000 trading interest-rate futures in Chicago, says, "I don't want money to constrict what I can or cannot do; I'd like in the future to have the latitude to do what I want when I want." A version of this refrain appeared in most of the interviews. What's striking about it, of course, is not only that the twenty-fives want so much, but that they seem so cocksure about getting it.

The twenty-fives have concrete notions of what it is they are after. They envision a very private home life in the country — not the suburbs. They are fond of three-bedroom homes located on several wooded acres — convenient to their jobs, to boot. Rather than Mercedes and minks, they want small cars and goose-down coats. They don't hanker for memberships in clubs without athletic facilities. But they are unabashed materialists who crave the latest labor-saving and electronic hardware, along with frequent entertainment and travel. In their righteous aversion to conventional status symbols, they seem unaware that they're on their way to creating their own. Even the antimaterialistic minority among them equate well-being with the spending power to buy "experience" — vacations, chiefly.

Actually, most of this group already enjoy a great deal of material comfort. By any standard their lives are extremely carefree. The married couples own their homes or condominiums, and most of the unmarried men and women can afford to live alone. Even a few singles, like Merrill Lynch bond trader John Rhett in Atlanta, have purchased homes. Rhett finds his monthly mortgage payments "very nice for a very comfortable house." He adds, "Right now I've almost no monetary restraints. I can't buy a 100-foot yacht, but I can vacation in Europe or Tahiti."

To improve their present standards of living, those interviewed expect to make between $35,000 and $70,000 in ten years and, eventually, between $80,000 and $250,000. (All the aspirations were expressed in 1980 dollars.) Only a few modest souls aim for less than $60,000 and middle-management ranks — and the engineer with Pacific Power & Light who declared, "I don't care if I'm ungodly rich or dirt poor so long as I'm happy," stands alone. Couples will probably be able to afford high-class consumption even if they lose to the demographics and miss out on executiveships: these young men and women expect fo find career-minded spouses. "We'd have so much in common," they say.

But it's a safe bet they won't be regulars in the maternity wards. Despite the flexibility two-income marriages permit, scarcely any twenty-fives have children at present. Most of those who doubt they'll ever be parents say they can't spare the time. Explains Edward Beam, a planning officer at Chicago Northern Trust Co.: "I love kids, but I don't want any. I'm too selfish to give what's necessary to raise them properly. Eventually, I'd resent their taking me away from other interests, just as I'd be upset that I wasn't devoting enough attention to them."

Those who do want children want only two, and are postponing them till their early thirties. By then, they seem to think, there will be less disruption to careers, marriages, budgets, and free time. Some members of this generation actually believe children can be made convenient. Once you've got the prerequisites for minimal confusion, the right-size house, live-in child care, and plenty of income — *then* you have babies. Some already view owning a home (and having two incomes to cover the mortgage) as more desirable than having children. Later the choice may be between having children and an even higher standard of living — or greater job mobility.

Like many other women in her generation, Laurie Graves, an engineer at Northrop in Hawthorne, California, will not discount her career goals or sacrifice her standard of living to have children now. Graves and her thirty-year-old husband together earn $60,000. They expect to have a family in five years or so, once "we're financially secure enough to afford good child care so I can continue to work." Graves adds, "We want to make sure my career is well established, that we have all the material things we want, that our bills are caught up so we don't fight over what little money we'll have to raise a family on. With our life-style, we can't afford good child care now and all the things we like." Among these pleasures she mentions "skiing in the mountains, entertaining around the pool at home, houseboating on Lake Powell in Utah, and weekend waterskiing in the Baja peninsula in Mexico, where we own a small house with three couples." By 1985, the Graveses think they could be making $120,000, enough for both children and amusements. (The new house overlooking the ocean might have to wait.)

Behind this generation's ambivalence toward children also towers a great fear of ruined marriages. The men read the climbing divorce rate as a cautionary tale against repeating the sins of their fathers and neglecting family; the women as counsel not to compromise their career ambitions. The men are nagged remorselessly by the tension between surpassing ambition and worry about the possible toll on their children and marriages. They don't know where to draw the line between work and home life or if in the future they'll be willing to. Some of the women seem a new breed entirely—they may stay single or decide against children so they can have jobs that require them to travel a great deal, or so they can relocate repeatedly without a hitch.

The unending debate over what price success also centers on leisure time. Twenty-fives fear being so consumed by work that they aren't "well rounded." The urge to be well rounded, however, seems to be postponable to the indeterminate future: their outside interests at present congregate around sports, socializing with friends, and reading innumerable magazines.

The twenty-fives consider themselves selfish in some respects, but "not in a negative way." Far more than the group in 1955, they equate survival and satisfaction with individual initiative, nabbing a piece of the action and looking out for yourself. Even though they don't feel obligated to help others, they don't wish to hurt anyone either. Few devote time to public service or volunteer work or express concerns about social problems. Organized religion, favored by the 1955 group as a social and family adhesive, appears too proscriptive or irrelevant to today's secular twenty-fives. The majority call themselves agnostic or privately spiritual. In the South, however, active participation in church and community activities still counts for much.

As far as business's efforts to ameliorate social problems and to improve the ethics of its own operations, virtually all twenty-fives are cheerfully satisfied with the recent record. They credit this performance to government safety regulations, consumer demands, and the corporations' own awakened sense of responsibility. Nearly all are far more agitated about the general health of the free-enterprise system. In their view, the system suffers from a bad press, nitpicking government control, and diminished incentive for investment. They favor a return to a laissez-faire economy and cuts in government spending and social-welfare programs. In the long run, they're optimistic that the capitalistic system will survive the century with few structural changes, largely because they can conceive of no better alternative to it. The twenty-fives calmly consider the energy crisis within reach of technological solution by 1990. For the most part, they are resigned to the prospect of economic turbulence for the next five years, but after that they see a gradually expanding economy that will keep the general standard of living growing.

Politically these twenty-fives share with their counterparts of 1955 a distrust of ideological convictions and a middle-of-the-road alignment — though the 1980 group increasingly veers conservative. . . . As a generation they distrust most politicians and are more apathetic than active, and yet they yearn for the day when a unity of purpose will sweep the nation and galvanize the public into rallying behind a forceful president. In their confused and dispirited frustration with politics and their longing for a patriotic awakening, the twenty-fives precisely mirror the mood of the country.

Toward the world at large, the twenty-fives seem just to have waked up. Recent international crises in Iran and Afghanistan register with unwelcome force on a group that has never been particularly aware of international developments. To most of them, Vietnam was a once-removed war that ocurred on television. They escaped being drafted — the volunteer army was created the year they turned eighteen — and say they opposed the war on pragmatic grounds (it was fought poorly.) Later, in the Seventies, their noses hovered too close to the grindstone to sense much beyond their immediate problems. But the recent crises have jarred them; they wonder whether the world order is permanently unstable and where that leaves them. Yet they don't worry too much, or think too clearly, about these things. This leads them to temporize.

Their muddled international outlook shows up most clearly in their attitudes toward Communism. Most have no quarrel with Communism per se — it's just another form of government and thought. Completely unaware of the contradictions, they say that only Communism's repression of democratic liberties repels them. They're inclined to tolerate it as an ideological system and let the Communist nations do what they want in their spheres of influence. On the other hand, they perceive the Soviet Union to be an inherently expansionist power, the principal threat to international stability. Yet they are not prepared to "pay any price, bear any burden" to defend democracy overseas, as President Kennedy asked when they were six years old. They say they would oppose fighting for principles such as honor and freedom and would examine the circumstances of each international fracas before supporting U.S. troop involvement. Most twenty-fives are fuzzy about where they would stand and fight.

These inconsistent views derive in part from the group's historical innocence. History is anything but a nightmare from which they are trying to awake. In discussing Afghanistan, for example, a good many showed they were ignorant of the 1956 Russian invasion of Hungary or the 1968 takeover of Czechoslovakia.

In their lifetimes they anticipate that the U.S. will clash with the Soviet Union using proxy forces in conventional warfare. They doubt the superpowers will war head-on in the Middle East, or anywhere else, because they credit world leaders with too much rationality to risk nuclear holocaust. And they adhere to the terribly human fallacy that if it does happen, the bombs will miss *them*. As one twenty-five-year-old ventured, "You just dive into the subways and don't get involved."

In short, they have the self-confidence that they will prevail, regardless of outside circumstances. After all, their ability to survive has been proved again and again in the "battle of the bulge." Like Lisa Carbaugh, a buyer with Litton Industries in Los Angeles, they evaluate life as essentially "cyclical"—it will have its ups and downs. But Carbaugh also speaks for her generation when she offers this summation: "I hate to say faith, but I have this feeling that whatever happens, I'll make the best of it."

Management

Robert Schrank

I went to a fancy Madison Avenue employment agency, and within a few days I was on a new job as a foreman in the machine-building and maintenance division of a small retail data-processing company. After spending so many years fighting the bosses and their managers, becoming part of management proved to be more traumatic than I had expected.

I began to relax into being the foreman by spending a lot of time talking to the employees, listening to their beefs and suggestions. In the main, their suggestions were strictly work-related—the grinders are inaccurate, the spindle on the Number 4 miller is off, the light over the jig borer is insufficient, and so on. Then I spent sleepless nights asking myself, What will I do if the company tells me to do something to the employees that I find I cannot do? I said to myself, You're part of management now. You have to learn to play the role.

But what if that role turns out to be a bastard? I will just tell them they can shove the job they know where. On and on the paranoia grew until things proved not to be as bad as I had feared. Once again, the anticipation was far worse than the fact.

I began to remember the things workers beefed about when I was a union officer. Now I was determined to pay attention to the conditions of work. After all, I rationalized, even the socialist brotherhood in any form had to have some kind of supervision. I kept asking myself: Could I supervise others without myself becoming a mechanical robot?

There were about forty-five men, almost all skilled workers, in the department. There was no union. My first efforts were to become familiar with the work as well as to straighten out job order systems and establish cost centers and parts inventory. The plant manager was pleased with what I was doing. "You're doing a great job, Bob, keep it up." Now, I thought, I can start paying attention to working conditions.

I started by improving the ventilation, cleaning up the toilets, building an eating area, getting the windows washed; generally making the physical surroundings more pleasant. The employees loved it; and with no urging on my part, production began to increase. I had become an instant success, yet I did not have to do anything as a foreman that I considered antithetical to the interests of the workers, whom I now called employees. My paranoia was decreasing. I was beginning to enjoy being in management. I would learn in time that as a supervisor I used McGregor's model Y, the humane, participative, open management style. What I had fought so hard as a union organizer was what McGregor called management X, the traditional, authoritarian style.

Most behavioral scientists concerned with workplace issues have so little understanding of the part that unions play in alleviating working conditions that it is no wonder union leaders become frustrated: They find practically no recognition in the behavioral science workplace literature of the role of the labor movement in humanizing work. Without the work of the unions, it is hard for me to see how American business and industry could even consider the next steps toward autonomy, participation, and codetermination.

My relations with the men in the department were easy-going. I would walk around checking on the work, doing quality control and at the same time kidding about the difficult jobs, sports, politics, and sex in about that order. Thinking back, second only to being competent as a toolmaker machinist, the most important management quality I would say I had was a good sense of humor. The work itself I sort of knew by rote, and I could get answers, too, by consulting others. That was never of any earth-shaking importance to me, so I would joke about what had to be done. The men would sort of laugh, yet they rushed to meet schedules. That turned out to make me look good.

I told each man when we finished a job how he had done in terms of both quality and time. We joked a lot about how long it takes to get things right. Humans seem to have an almost limitless ability to solve mechanical problems and at the same time show an enormous inability to understand how to live with themselves and each other. I began to see the function of humor as a way of acknowledging the absurdity of the human condition in the face of this apparent contradiction.

I began to attend engineering expositions and conventions, meeting many men whose lives revolve around the design and development of machines. I remember a dullness about them, as though the gray of the steel had entered their souls. Compared to plumbers or my old union friends, they seemed like a drab lot. An old saying suggests that "dull people find dumb work." Well, I don't think so, because I too felt a certain lifelessness growing in me. The machines themselves seemed to be making ceaseless demands for the improvement of their efficiency, and their demands were draining my life energy. I had started to carry a small pocket notebook with me to jot down little ideas for improving or redesigning machines. It was a constant challenge to keep them from wearing out and at the same time make them do more for less.

There was something new in that engineering experience that I only recently have come to understand. It involves the nature of conflict in work. Working with machines has conflicts and tasks that involve objects and materials, all of which are inanimate. People are used as the instruments of the objects or machines. Engineers deal in the main with these inanimate things, whose only resistance is in the limits of their physical nature. They lose the human, living, dynamic element in work. Over time I found engineering work comfortable and absorbing, but my only challenges were excessive friction, unstable raw materials, tighter machine tolerances. I was becoming a very neutral person whom I was gradually getting to dislike. For someone who had tasted the excitement of human conflict in the unions and national politics, there was not much romance in developing a better rack and pinion mechanism for a high-speed press.

In contrast, the issues in the labor movement almost never were concerned with objects. They were the problems of people, of their working conditions, pay, and benefits. Union work also required me to take a stand, one that might be unpopular with management, and at times with the members. In the very neutral, alienated world of engineers there is a sense of being above or beyond the conflict issues, a sort of technological person. I found engineers reserved, expressing little or no curiosity outside of their engineering specialty. Compared with the openness of the average shop worker, their interest in sex, for instance, was a hidden, secretive business.

I was attending an engineering convention in Chicago, and because my company did considerable business with a major electrical manufacturer, I was assigned a lovely female friend to keep me company, if not warm, in the windy city. Helene, who had been "Helen" back in Des Moines, was a model-type — tall, skinny, and shining from an endless round of soaps and lotions. She had been trained in charm. We went to dinner, and for most of the evening I plied her with questions about her job. "I am hired as a bridge to customers like you, in order to further expose the potential buyer to our product line." I fantasized: Helene and I go to my room. We get into bed. We are about to go to it when out comes the newest high-speed gear box sample. "You were saying . . ."

"We are hired to give understanding to the customer."

"Do you go to bed with all the customers?"

"The decision is up to us. Now you must understand we don't *have* to. After all, we're not just call girls, but if we desire to, we can."

"Is your pay scaled to going to bed with a customer?"

"No, we get a flat rate a day during the convention, but if you want to be called back, you have to build a reputation for being friendly."

"How many conventions do you do a year, and what kinds?"

"Oh, maybe fifteen or twenty of all kinds: pharmaceutical companies are great, with doctors; then there are engineers, dentists, printing companies, truckers, political meetings." Helene was really enjoying the interview. She laughed. "I draw the line on morticians. Darned if I am going to have some undertaker work me over. No siree. Every job has to have its limits."

"How do you like this engineering crowd?"

"They're OK. Most of them are not like you. They don't talk much, and they're very secretive, so you have to meet them in their rooms, and they don't want you to know their names. They seem to be scared. I don't know of what. Now you take truckers. They're tough, they could care less, and they are great spenders."

My efforts on behalf of the company were rewarded by promotions, first to chief plant engineer and then to division engineer responsible for three plants. As the demands of the job increased, I found myself increasingly committing more of my life to the company. To the envy of other managing engineers, I began to be consulted by the vice president in charge of production at the head office of the corporation. I was now mixing with the corporate executives, traveling first class, eating at 21 Club with three corporate vice presidents to discuss the Swedish operation. Good food, fine wine, the best cigars — I felt big, contented, and sure I had made it. After all, the labor movement didn't want me, so why should I feel guilty about sitting here in the 21 Club making it? I thought Bertolt Brecht was stupid. Am I supporting corporate oppression if I share in the power, or can I use my position to humanize existing institutions? An irresolvable contradiction, or a paradox. Why be a man when I can be a success? Listen, Bertolt, class status is so damned insidious. You think that a little socialist shit can affect the intoxication of being accepted into the higher reaches of the corporate world. You're nuts. I was moving up, and, by God, I liked it.

Though sometimes deeply buried in our unconscious, the drive upward is everlastingly present. Being summoned to an audience with king, pope, president, secretary general, or prime minister gives us a heightened sense of importance, power, status, no matter how cynical we feel toward an institution. Even if I did not actually hold the power, just being in its presence was heady stuff. Antiestablishment people (we used to call them "radicals") suffer a heavy ambivalence.

I was now working for corporate headquarters. I found myself becoming more involved, absorbed, single-minded, with an excitement for equipment deadlines and new ideas that created in me a general sense of euphoria. Yet there was a difference between this kind of work and the labor movement. What was it? Slowly I was missing the old companionship, the wonderful conversation of all my friends in screw machines, turret lathes, and the machine shops. The management world was a circumspect one full of innuendo, nuance, correct dress, and carefully choreographed behavior. The result was little or no spontaneity, no feelings, no physical contact. All this meant zero sensuality. I was beginning to miss walking with my arm on another guy's shoulder at a union meeting. Doubts began to take root about whether I could make it as a corporate executive.

One winter night in a fine old Boston restaurant, the corporate boys from Yale and Groton, having belted down a few too many martinis, kept asking about life on the outside, the plant, the union, sex. I had a growing feeling that I was being spied on by a bunch of Harvard Business School voyeurs who seemed to sense something missing from their lives but were not sure what. I was missing something too. A short time later the vice president in charge of production, having learned that I was "getting antsy," said to me, "Schrank, you are too smart to lose; if it is the last thing I do, I am going to shoehorn you into this corporation."

I was going to college at night, having been urged to do so by the company, when they learned that I had no school beyond the eighth grade. "You're corporate material, but you will have to get a degree." College was a real growth experience, and it was reinforcing my distaste of corporate managing. I was on my way out.

Some doubts have grown in me about engineers and managers. The first has to do with management's ability to manage, and the second has to do with behavioral science notions about work, motivation, and job satisfaction. In my days as a union official, there was a fantasy that corporations were homogeneous, single-headed, efficient monsters systematically exploiting workers. Talk about being convinced by one's own propaganda! Institutions and professions now appear to me as tribal groups defending their turf—territoriality: their secrets, sacred bundles, and their leaders and tribal councils. When I moved from the union tribe to the corporate tribe, I learned some of their secrets. They were fumbling around pretty much like the rest of us, yet they were better able to conceal it through public relations, with its handouts, image building, color slide and sound shows. Then there is always the secrecy that is called up to "protect us from our competition" or from other tribes, but this is usually baloney since it is more often used to hide mistakes from the world at large.

The loss of perspective on their lives, the lack of joy in their work, seemed so natural for the engineers. Yet I became very involved in what I was doing, even though it made no social sense. It was so absorbing that it caused me to lose interest in a world of feelings and sensuality. Was it sublimation? I would doubt it. Maybe it happens because the work is with metals or plastics, usually to close tolerances in measurement or composition or both. The thing—the object, the task, the gear, cam, housing, nuts, bolts, timer—engulfs and dominates one's life until an obsession like building a better zipper takes over all thought and no one thinks to ask what was wrong with the button. The pressure of corporate life to come up with new products makes managers and engineers fearful if they do not constantly create and innovate. This makes for individual competition resulting in a lonely crowd. Productivity for engineers does not indicate the quantity of work produced but rather what new ideas or improvements they have generated. The pressure to come up with solutions to problems sends at least some competent engineers off into dealing or specializing.

I think that engineers and managers would rate considerably higher on the alienation scale than most unionized workers. The competition of managers vying for recognition and position creates little trust, and that means little human contact or concern. The corporation I worked for was liberal and easy-going, but even there the higher up the totem pole you climbed, the faster they went for your jugular. Life in the corporation tended to be isolated and cold, with some fucking, no love, and little sharing of sexual fantasies. It all reminded me of Wilhelm Reich's *Listen Little Man*: "Security is more important to you, even if it costs you your spine of life."

The gentility and civility of engineers and managers seemed to make them less sensuous, robust, and less aware of the organic qualities of life. They often struck me as being without affect because of their preoccupation with a large inanimate object or some minute, trivial part of it. It is the syndrome of overspecialization that Mumford talks about in *The Pentagon of Power*, when one becomes so highly specialized in the head of the pin that in time one no longer knows what the rest of the pin looks like, or worse, what it is used for. And there I was, totally involved in the feed mechanisms of continuous-web letterpresses.

Was this group of managers and engineers more satisfied with their jobs than plumbers or machinists? In general I would say yes, but I would add that most of these men were so completely and exclusively focused on the "head of the pin" that they had given very little thought to what they were doing, why they were doing it, and at what cost to themselves. In the recent NASA layoffs, some aerospace engineers had been forced into new careers. In an interview with one of them who opened a hot dog stand, he said he had suddenly discovered—guess what—that there was more to life than Wernher Von Braun's "bigger and better rockets." "I love owning my own business, but more important, I am my own boss."

Managers and engineers tend to lose their concern about people because of their total preoccupation with "the product." In my case, feed mechanisms, the product, took over most of my psychic energy. Such narrow frames of reference have an impact on how managers and engineers view other people. Preoccupied and obsessed with the product line, they can begin to view people, or the workers, as obstacles to reaching their objectives.

In the whole production matrix, people are probably the most frustrating for managers since they constitute the most difficult variable to control and predict. No matter how predictable society tries to make its members through its various socializing mechanisms, people continue to give managers the most trouble. Managers are always complaining about "those workers." "If only they would do what we tell them or learn to follow instructions, we would surpass all our quotas." It is this obsession with the product and the consequent neglect of human needs that could fill case-history books with stories of management's insensitivity to workers. This insensitivity is often turned around and explained as a "lack of worker motivation." Workers become strangers to many managers and are seen only as an extension of a piece of machinery in which a capital investment has been made. This leads to the engineering dream of eliminating the "human element" in production.

A good illustration of this phenomenon came up in a union negotiation. Sitting around the huge conference table in the mahogany-paneled conference room during an intensive collective bargaining session with the Republic Steel Corporation, the company was reciting a litany of how much production time is lost as a result of lateness, extended coffee breaks, lunch time beyond the bell, and early quitting. The whole discussion seemed kind of absurd, so I kept encouraging the industrial engineers to give us the data on what the lost-time factor added up to. Out came the slide rules as the figures multiplied upward. "The company has 5,000 employees in this division. Estimated loss on starting time seven minutes; on two coffee breaks, twelve minutes; and quitting ten minutes early. That makes a total of 2,400 hours a day." The company was very impressed with these figures. After all, they were clear evidence of the cost of malingering.

I said, "I would like to have a recess." It was agreed. The company representatives left the room, and the union committee remained. I asked the committee members how many times the average worker went to the toilet during the workday to pee or shit, and how long did each function take. After some bickering back and forth, we agreed on three times: two short and one long, the short about seven minutes, including travel and smoke, and the long about fourteen minutes. We calculated an average of twenty-eight or thirty minutes per employee lost a day in the toilet. I asked the committee if they would permit me to bargain away at least some of that time, or in other words, if we could reduce the toilet time in exchange, let's say, for a couple more holidays. Everyone appreciated the absurdity of this, but they were happy to join the dramatic fantasy that would reveal the production engineers' thought processes.

When the company representatives returned to the bargaining table, I put forth our propositions, in the course of which the absurdity of it all seemed to carry me away. "We are not only willing to reduce defecation time, but we have recently become aware of a pill that taken each morning, would assure the employer of no defecation on company time." Noticing on the other side of the table the industrial engineers all playing with their slide rules, the committee members almost blew it with their giggling.

Charles Hunsteter, chief of production engineering, a pudgy fellow with thin strands of hair plastered to his sweaty forehead, announced, "You think it's funny. Well, 1,166 hours a day at $5.00 per hour labor and overhead cost, $5,830 a day times 250 workdays a year: $1.500 million a year." The figures so excited him that he said, "Schrank, I don't know if you're kidding or serious, or what. But the fact is this could change our entire competitive position, and I would hope you would give our company first crack at it." Well, the poor committee members thought they would bust. The company attorney, a little more reality-oriented, was embarrassed by the joke and changed the subject. On the way out the door at the end of the session, Charlie said, "Schrank, you may be kidding, but this could be an extremely useful tool in production scheduling."

That incident epitomizes a particular kind of industrial engineering management viewpoint that I am amazed to find still prevails in some manufacturing companies. How to perfect a completely programmed person to eliminate the human element from technology continues to influence the thinking of at least some behavioral scientists and industrial engineers concerned with productivity and worker motivation.

How fulfilling is engineering and managing in terms of Maslow's higher-order needs of autonomy, creativity, and self-actualization? Blue-collar malaise is explained by some social scientists as caused by an absence of opportunities for autonomy, decision making, creativity, and self-actualization. I have often wondered to what extent these elements were present in the work life of engineers and managers. And though it may be true in some cases that persons of this rank in organizations have more opportunity to be creative and make the decisions related to their work, nowhere in the literature is an even more important question raised, that of the *purpose* of their creativity. What is it used for? In its most extreme form, the question of how one's creative energies are used is what confronted the atomic physicists when asked to perfect the bomb. What tends to get lost from Maslow's schema and its application to the workplace is the moral issue that asks: What does my creativity create? What is the impact of my self-actualization beyond me?

When I was busy increasing the speed and feed accuracy of high-speed web presses, it caused an isolation from living things that tended to negate the human concerns at the workplace. Relationships were important to me in terms of how they complemented my machine. I became caught in the treadmill of making better widgets, forgetting what I had learned many times as a union official when workers would say, "Listen, Schrank, I don't give a fuck for the junk we make here. I am here to make money so I can get my kicks outside of this dump." That often repeated basic philosophy of work stirred my subconscious as I wondered, How much did I really care about increasing the speed and efficiency of high-speed dumbwaiters?

Compared to managers and engineers, blue-collar workers seem more able to shed their work concerns at the end of the day. Workers are more concerned with security and pay than the product. Managers and engineers are concerned with upmanship. To get there, they must efficiently deliver a product. Different jobs create very different kinds of anxieties. Workers' concerns have most to do with security, wages, hours, and working conditions, but these tend to be group concerns that create a common bond. Manager-engineers tend to be primarily preoccupied with their own performance as a way of getting ahead—getting ahead of someone else—and thus produce a highly competitive, individualistic, nongroup life.

I believe blue-collar workers are able to shed their workplace anxieties more easily than managers because of less responsibility as well as a deeper resignation to their situation. Since Karl Marx, much of the literature on work alienation has had to do with blue-collar workers, but I experienced them as far less alienated than managers or engineers. Workers at least had each other. I have a hunch that some of the literature on blue-collar alienation written by behavioral scientists is more often an expression of their own malaise and alienation than that of the workers. The longer I was in the world of managers, the more I missed my union buddies, their ribald spirit, our singing together, their sensuousness, their sexuality. By comparison, managers were a deadhead lot who had traded humor and sensuality for the role-playing Kabuki world of the corporate headquarters. I have met more people having fun as clowns on one plant floor than in all the very many corporate headquarters I have gone in and out of.

Engineers, managers, or behavioral scientists, with their compulsive, competitive preoccupation with "making it," tend to see this as a paradigm for all workers. But many workers are not interested in "making it" in a career of power and responsibility, or even in increasing their autonomy and creativity. Some blue-collar workers prefer to make bowling the center of their lives. That may be a greater demonstration of autonomy and creativity than building a better high-speed gear box.

The Wall Street Journal, 15 June 1981.

Many Black Managers Hope to Enter Ranks Of Top Management

Trying to Be a 'Team Player'

By ROBERT S. GREENBERGER

Staff Reporter of The Wall Street Journal

Fleming Golden, a 34-year-old black manufacturing manager at International Business Machines Corp., recalls the incident that helped teach him how to climb the corporate ladder.

It happened in 1976, when he was with IBM's corporate staff in Armonk, N.Y. "I was always a flashy dresser," he says. "I had lots of orange and green suits. Then one day, an older, white guy took me aside and said, 'Hey, don't get offended, but it's about those suits you wear. They just don't blend in at IBM.'"

So Mr. Golden switched to pin stripes. "One day my boss mentioned that he liked the suit I was wearing. I got the message."

Mr. Golden understood that the message was less about his clothes than about the delicate line that he must walk between being black, or different, and being perceived as a "team player" in a white corporate culture. Having reached middle management by his technical skills, he learned that the selection for top management is more subjective.

Since then, "I've shown in a lot of ways that I function as a member of the team. I've established enough contacts so that I'll achieve my goals," he says confidently.

Loyalty—Team Play—The System

J. Patrick Wright

"Goddamnit! I served my time picking up my bosses at the airport. Now you guys are going to do this for me." —Pete Estes to John De Lorean.

Choosing among executives for promotion is a difficult task at best, but one which is vital to the success of a business. If two people vying for the same job are equal in talent and performance, and one is a friend, I will most likely choose the friend. That's human nature. If the other, however, is obviously more accomplished than my friend, the job would go to him or her. The point is that merit always surpasses friendship in matters that pertain to business promotion. This was not always the case in General Motors. But it is a practice I tried to follow closely because ultimately it is the best practice for the good of the corporation.

A classic test of this precept occurred when I was running the Pontiac Division. There was a guy in our marketing organization who was personally offensive to me. Whenever he got near me he just bugged the hell out of me. He was a blowhard and a name dropper, two traits which I find especially unlikeable.

At the same time, however, he was doing a helluva job for the Pontiac Division. Every job we gave him, he did to perfection. And every time he did, I'd ask, "How the hell can a guy I can't stand be doing such a good job?" But he continued to perform, and the reports I got from his superiors corroborated my observations about his work. So I promoted him several times in the four years I ran Pontiac. It was hard to do, but his performance demanded it. After promoting him I would just stay the hell away from him.

I cite this extreme example because as I grew in General Motors it became apparent that objective criteria were not always used to evaluate an executive's performance. Many times the work record of a man who was promoted was far inferior to the records of others around him who were not promoted. It was quite obvious that something different than job performance was being used to rate these men.

That something different was a very subjective criterion which encompassed style, appearance, personality and, most importantly, personal loyalty to the man (or men) who was the promoter, and to the

Abridged and reprinted from *On A Clear Day You Can See General Motors* by J. Patrick Wright, published by Wright Enterprises © 1979. Reproduced by permission.

system which brought this all about. There were rules of this fraternity of management at GM. Those pledges willing to obey the rules were promoted. In the vernacular, they were the company's "team players." Those who didn't fit into the mold of a manager, who didn't adhere to the rules because they thought they were silly, generally weren't promoted. "He's not a team player," was the frequent, and many times only, objection to an executive in line for promotion. It didn't mean he was doing a poor job. It meant he didn't fit neatly into a stereotype of style, appearance and manner. He didn't display blind loyalty to the system of management, to the man or men doing the promoting. He rocked the boat. He took unpopular stands on products or policy which contradicted the prevailing attitude of top management.

At General Motors, good appearance meant conservative dress. In my very first meeting as a GM employee in 1956 at Pontiac, half the session was taken up in discussion about some vice-president downtown at headquarters who was sent home that morning for wearing a brown suit. Only blue or black suits were tolerated then. I remember thinking that was silly. But in those days I followed the rules closely.

Style and personality in the corporate mold means simply that a GM executive is a low-profile executive. What is to be most memorable about the corporation today is the letters G and M, and not the people behind the letters. A General Motors man rarely says anything in public that adds the least bit of color or personality to those letters G and M. He identifies his success with the corporate success. And that success is measured in dollars earned per share. This system is best documented in its results.

The GM chairman annually is one of the least recognized businessmen in America. General Motors in the U.S. is almost twice the size of Ford Motor Company and yet the spokesman for the industry is Henry Ford II, chairman of Ford Motor Co. Former Ford President Lee A. Iacocca, who now is president of Chrysler Corporation, is better recognized than either of GM's top officers, Chairman Murphy or President Estes. Among GM's upper management today there is not a memorable one in the bunch. They want it that way. Even though GM in the past has produced some of the most memorable men in American business history — Billy Durant, Pierre S. du Pont and Alfred P. Sloan, Jr., William S. (Big Bill) Knudsen (Bunkie's father), and C.F. (Boss) Kettering—no one individual is permited to stand out in the corporation today. When one does, he is rebuked, ordered to disappear into the wallpaper. . . .

If your appearance, style and personality were consistent with the corporate stereotype, you were well on your way to being a "loyal" employee. But loyalty demanded more. If often demanded personal fealty, actual subservience to the boss. You learned loyalty as you learned the business. Loyalty was talked about openly. It was part of team play. Pete Estes often talked about the need for "loyalty to your boss." He demanded it. He got it.

My introduction to "loyalty" was as assistant chief engineer at Pontiac. The division was staging a "ride and drive" program in San Francisco. "Ride and drive" programs were common to the engineering departments of GM. They were test sessions set up around the country for top engineers and divisional brass to drive and grade a fleet of cars for performance, durability, handling, gasoline mileage. We'd test competitors' cars, too. In this case, we were testing Pontiacs with a newly designed carburetor. There were about ten engineers in San Francisco for the four-day test.

I was showering in a motel near San Francisco International Airport the morning of the first day out there when the bathroom door flew open practically taking the hinges off in one jerk. I was shocked by the noise and I threw open the shower curtain and saw Estes who was chief engineer at Pontiac and my boss. The spitting image of Tennessee Ernie Ford, Estes was usually happy and pleasant. This time, however, he was red-faced and mad. "Why the hell wasn't someone out to meet me at the airport this morning? You knew I was coming, but nobody was there. Goddamnit, I served my time picking up my bosses at the airport. Now you guys are going to do this for me," he barked.

The thought had never even crossed my mind until then. I figured we were just supposed to get out to the West Coast on our own and be on time for the ride and drive session. I quickly became aware, however, that the pecking order at GM, as at many major U.S. companies, demanded that inferiors on the corporate ladder cater to their superiors. It was called "brown-nosing" a professor in college, KMA-ing (kiss-my-assing) when it was done by a supplier to a customer, and "loyalty" when it was done inside GM. As a rule, bosses were to be met at the airports by their charges. The bigger the boss at General Motors, the bigger the retinue waiting at the airport terminal. A chief engineer required a show of at least one assistant engineer and maybe a local plant official. A divisional general manager commanded more. If he traveled to St. Louis to give a speech, waiting for him at the airport would be the local plant manager, the head of the regional and zone sales offices and the local public relations guy. Traveling with him would be at least one executive from home, usually his public relations director. These men would pick him up, carry his bags, pay his hotel and meal bills and chauffeur him around night and day.

The greatest shows of force were reserved for the chairman of the board. On a trip he would often take several top executives with him, even if they had no worthwhile purpose in accompanying him. When he got to his destination, it would seem as if half of the area's GM employees were there to greet him — local sales managers of the car divisions, top plant people, chauffeurs. It was expected and demanded. . . .

The practice of fawning over the boss gave birth to all kinds of ridiculous practices. One was the use of a secret network in the corporation to find out the likes, dislikes and idiosyncrasies of the boss. The information was usually passed on from one secretary to another. It was used by underlings to please their superiors. Display their loyalty. If the chairman liked Chivas Regal served in a hubcap, there would be a bar full of it and a dozen wheel-covers waiting in his hotel room wherever he traveled. His favorite scotch would be the only scotch served at a dealer reception. If the boss liked to read murder mysteries before retiring, there'd be a veritable library of murder mysteries when he walked through the doors to his suite.

This network of intelligence served up information which provided the most outlandish example of "loyalty" that I have ever heard of inside General Motors or out. And I heard it several times. It involved a Chevrolet sales official at a rather low level of management for this feat extraordinaire. It showed how deep in GM management the loyalty system ran.

In preparing for the sales official's trip to this particular city, the Chevrolet zone sales people learned from Detroit that the boss liked to have a refrigerator full of cold beer, sandwiches, and fruit in his room to snack on at night before going to bed. They lined up a suite in one of the city's better hotels, rented a refrigerator and ordered the food and beer. However, the door to the suite was too small to accommodate the icebox. The hotel apparently nixed a plan to rip out the door and part of the adjoining wall. So the quick-thinking zone sales people hired a crane and operator, put them on the roof of the hotel, knocked out a set of windows in the suite, and lowered and shoved the refrigerator into the room through this gaping hole.

That night the Chevrolet executive wolfed down cold-cut sandwiches, beer and fresh fruit, no doubt thinking, "What a great bunch of people we have in this zone." The next day he was off to another city and most likely another refrigerator, while back in the city of his departure the zone people were once again dismantling hotel windows and removing the refrigerator by crane. It was the most expensive midnight snack ever eaten by a GM executive.

While loyal employees attended the boss's personal needs with care and dispatch, they attended his corporate decisions with unwavering support, even if they thought the decisions were wrong. This was business loyalty. It not only capitalized on a natural inclination to support the man at the top. It made it mandatory.

This practice as I knew it flourished under Frederic G. Donner, who was chairman of the board of General Motors from 1958 to 1967. Short, stocky, with a stern face, Donner had all the emotion of a pancake.

He was cold and calculating in his approach to business. To Donner business came ahead of anything else. And business to him meant business his way. He would rarely tolerate views opposed to his. He refused to rediscuss previous decisions, even in the light of new information. "We already decided that!" he would snap. And that was the end of any attempt to reopen old business.

With such closed-mindedness at the top, a guiding precept of management soon developed. "Thou shalt not contradict the boss." Ideas in this kind of a system flowed from the top down, and not in the reverse direction. The man on top, whether he was a plant manager, department head or divisional general manager, was the final word. Each executive in turn supported the decisions of his boss right up the ladder. The chairman, of course, in this system had the final say on everything unless he parcelled out power to those around him. In Donner's case he was the unquestioned authority on financial matters. He would tolerate opposing views on product matters and usually gave authority for such matters to the president. But even in this area if he felt very keenly about a product decision, his way was the way the corporation went. The sovereignty of the president in product matters was generally as unchallenged as was Donner's overall authority, because the president got his power from Donner. What Donner and his men thought and supported became what the company thought and supported. Their attitudes were the prevailing attitudes. The system stayed on even though Donner retired in 1967. When I pushed for a program for drastically reducing the weight and size of all General Motors cars in 1969–1970, I sporadically had president Ed Cole's support. When I did, the program was red hot. When I didn't, it died.

This system quickly shut top management off from the real world because it surrounded itself in many cases with "yes" men. There soon became no real vehicle for adequate outside input. Lower executives, eager to please the boss and rise up the corporate ladder, worked hard to learn what he wanted or how he thought on a particular subject. They then either fed the boss exactly what he wanted to know, or they modified their own proposals to suit his preferences.

Original ideas were often sacrificed in deference to what the boss wanted. Committee meetings no longer were forums for open discourse, but rather either soliloquies by the top man, or conversations between a few top men with the rest of the meeting looking on. In

Fourteenth Floor meetings, often only three people, Cole, Gerstenberg, and Murphy, would have anything substantial to say, even
though there were 14 or 15 executives present. The rest of the team
would remain silent, speaking only when spoken to. When they did
offer a comment, in many cases it was just to paraphrase what had
already been said by one of the top guys.

Terrell was the master of the paraphrase, although he was by no
means the only practitioner. He often parrotted the views of Chairman Gerstenberg with unabashed rapidity. So often did he do this
that the practice became a joke. Divisional general managers and their
staffs entertained each other over lunch with various impressions of
Terrell paraphrasing Gerstenberg in an Administrative Committee
meeting. The dialogue would go something like this:

> *Gerstenberg:* "Goddamnit. We can not afford any new models
> next year because of the cost of this federally mandated equipment.
> There is no goddamn money left for styling changes. That's the
> biggest problem we face."
>
> *Terrell,* after waiting about 10 minutes: "Dick, goddamnit. We've
> just got to face up to the fact that our number one problem is the
> cost of this federally mandated equipment. This stuff costs so much
> that we just don't have any money left for styling our new cars.
> That's our biggest problem."
>
> *Gerstenberg:* "You're goddamn right, Dick. That's a good point."

It was humorous to witness and replay at lunch, but it was sad to
realize that executives could build credibility in this way. Top managers were sitting back in their chairs saying: "What a helluva hard-
charging, decisive guy this is."

Terrell was by no means alone. Many Fourteenth Floor executives
operated in similar ways. What they did to the Donners, Roches,
Gerstenbergs, and Coles of the corporation, the divisional general
managers often did to them. Simply regurgitated to the boss his own
ideas. These lower managers were identified as the young turks of the
corporation. They were loyal employees. They knew exactly where
the power resided at the top. They were more than willing to play up
to that power and rise in the company in the process. When the boss
said "jump," they never asked "why," only "how high."

A system which puts emphasis on form, style and unwavering
support for the decisions of the boss almost always loses its perspective about an executive's business competence. Even if the man in
power is a competent businessman, but adheres to the system, the
chances of his successors' being equally competent are reduced because they are graded not on how they perform as businessmen but
on how they perform as system-men. Once they get into power, they

don't tamper with the system which promoted them. So a built-in method of perpetuating an imperfect management system is established. This is what I feel has happened at General Motors. Not that every executive in an important position is incompetent. There are very many fine and talented men in GM management today. Nevertheless, top management has some less than competent executives who may be good system-men but poor managers of people and trustees of the corporation. And the system which promoted them is so firmly entrenched that it most likely will continue to promote mediocrity to the Fourteenth Floor, often stifling the progress of more talented executives.

Not only is the system perpetuating itself, but in the act of perpetuating itself the system has fostered several destructive practices which are harmful to executive morale. They developed from the psychological need, as I see it, of less competent managers to affirm in their own minds a logical right to their positions, even though the basis for their promotions was illogical by any business-performance standard. Once in a position of power, a manager who was promoted by the system is insecure because, consciously or not, he knows that it was something other than his ability to manage and his knowledge of the business that put him in his position. He knows that he is one step or more past his Peter Principle equivalent. He thus looks for methods and defense mechanisms to ward off threats to his power base.

Donner, as far as I know, had unassailable credentials as a sound financial mind. He was a product of the Alfred P. Sloan-Donaldson Brown (a financial expert in the early days of GM) school of thought on financial control, which not only guides General Motors but also a whole host of American businesses. He was not a knowledgeable product man. Finance men aren't and usually can't expect to be. But Donner, as chairman, wanted to affirm for all that he was the boss. He went about this through a system of calculated promotions of "loyal" employees and management by intimidation.

From him developed what I call "promotion of the unobvious choice." This means promoting someone who was not regarded as a contender for the post. Doing so not only puts "your man" in position, but it earns for you his undying loyalty because he owes his corporate life to you. The "unobvious choice" is a devoted follower of the system who has nothing noteworthy in his background to mark him as a promotable executive. He often is surrounded by team players who are more qualified for the promotion.

A study of the past ten years of General Motors top executives and an examination of their business biographies makes it obvious that some men with undistinguished business careers moved to the top and in many cases occupy positions of power within the corporation today. An understanding of their benefactors makes their ascension more explicable. In many cases, they were "unobvious choices." If the question were asked, "Would a man of these qualifications be chosen from outside the company for this post?" the answer would always be a resounding, "No!"

Donner himself was not an "unobvious choice," but as far as I know, he was the first major GM executive to promote an "unobvious choice." It happened in 1958. Harlow Curtice was then president and chief executive officer and about to retire. Red Curtice was warm, flamboyant, exciting, and as strong a product man as GM has ever known. Though he occasionally acted with a heavy hand, he had the compensating balance of being right most of the time. As chief executive officer he was the top corporate official. It was widely assumed in the corporation that his successor would be either Cliff Goad or Bud Goodman, two competent and strong executive vice-presidents.

The board was meeting in New York on a hot August day in 1958 to announce the successor not only to Curtice but also to Chairman Albert P. Bradley. I had been at Pontiac only about two years. But I was in a suite in the Book-Cadillac Hotel in downtown Detroit with a bunch of Pontiac people: Bunkie Knudsen, the divisional general manager; Pete Estes, chief engineer; Bob Emerick, the Public Relations director; and one or two other people. We were anxiously awaiting a call from New York. The phone rang and Bunkie picked it up. Suddenly his face dropped like frosting melting off a cake. He put the phone down and said: "Jack Gordon is the new president."

No one expected that. Even though John F. Gordon was group executive for the Body and Assembly Operations, he wasn't considered a corporate heavyweight. Not alongside Goad and Goodman.

We also learned that Donner not only was named chairman, as expected, but also chief executive officer. It was obvious that this hard-nosed finance man was going to run General Motors in the post-Curtice era. And it was just as obvious that Gordon was his "unobvious choice" for president. From then on, promoting the "unobvious choice" became a method of management. It was practiced more on the operations side of the business than the financial side, because the operational side is vast, offering a greater field for promoting the "unobvious choice."

James M. Roche's selection as president to succeed Gordon was an "unobvious choice." He also succeeded Donner as chairman in 1967. A kindly, grandfatherly man, and a hard worker, Roche nevertheless did not have a particularly distinguished career in General Motors, although before his rise to power he served a stint as general manager of Cadillac and several top corporate posts. Unlike many around him, however, I think Roche had a great sense of the corporate responsibility. He was not able to get this theme pushed through the corporation, however, perhaps because he was not forceful enough. It was obvious that he, like everyone else, was dominated by Donner.

Under the Donner-Roche regime a combination of Donner's arrogance and Roche's willingness to go along with the boss led to two of the most embarrassing public relations blunders in the corporation's history. First, in 1965, Donner performed abominably before Senator Abraham Ribicoff's Subcommitte on Executive Reorganization. He refused to, or could not, answer the simplest of questions about GM's operations and financial performance. Second was the whole sordid episode in which the company tailed Ralph Nader. Roche apologized to Nader, the Congress, and the country for the incident, and GM paid $425,000 in damages in an out-of-court settlement with the consumer advocate.

Donner also promoted to the Fourteenth Floor an "unobvious choice" in Roger M. Kyes, whose accomplishments at Frigidaire and then GM Truck & Coach Division were lackluster. Kyes in turn brought along his "unobvious choice," Dick Terrell, whose whole GM career was spent in nonautomotive operations, first Electro-Motive Division and then Frigidaire Division. From Terrell came his "unobvious choice," Reuben R. Jensen from the Allison Division.

Not one of these three was a distinguished businessman or had a reputation in the corporation for exceptional management ability. . . .

Whether these "unobvious choices" were unrecognized as capable, astute businessmen was unimportant; they were well-recognized as hard team players, loyal to their bosses and the system which promoted them.

In watching the promotions of Kyes, Terrell, and Jensen while others who I felt were more competent were overlooked (I'd gladly name them were it not that such mention might ensure then anonymity in the corporation), the words of Mr. Sloan take on new significance: "I happen to be one of the old school who thinks that a knowledge of the business is essential to a successful organization." That is simply not the case today at GM.

There were and are men in positions of power at GM who do not know the business they are running. Many were not good businessmen in the areas with which they are familiar. "Promotion of the unobvious choice" has put some of them into their positions. Others simply played the loyalty system game so well they just moved up the corporate ladder every few years. What developed in some cases is "management by crony" which Sloan denounced as detrimental to a corporation. Among upper management of GM's operations there are not many proven, successful executives. There are some with potential who have not served sufficient time in the divisions to bring to the Fourteenth Floor the type of broad experience and confidence that only time and achievement can produce.

Insecure, an executive often resorts to defense mechanisms to affirm psychologically his position. Intimidation is a favorite tool, and once again the art of management by intimidation as I know it at GM began with Frederic Donner. He was the master intimidator and often reverted to gimmicks to show his power.

One time in an Administrative Committee meeting he asked the head of GM Truck & Coach Division:

"How many buses did you build last month?"

The executive replied: "Approximately three thousand" or a rounded figure like that. It was an approximation.

Donner scowled and snapped back something like: "Last month you built three thousand, one hundred and eighty-seven vehicles." Whatever the figure was, it was precise.

It was obvious to most of us in the meeting that Donner had just looked it up since the precise figure wasn't all that important. But the fact that he would rattle off the exact production figure in such an authoritarian, arrogant manner told us just one thing, that Donner was trying to make the point, "Look how I know this goddamn business, people! Look what a mind I have!"

The Donner memory game is not new to GM or American business. But it is a management cheap shot. It was used often inside GM's hallowed corporate walls but never with the devastating effect that it was used by Donner.

Very few men are gifted with a photographic memory. Pete Estes is one who is, and in this respect he is brilliant. He is one of the very few people I have ever met with such an amazing memory. He can remember what he had for lunch on this day a year ago. But in dealing with top GM executives, you could get the notion that the Fourteenth Floor had a corner on the memory market. This is because GM executives take copious notes of almost every conversation they have and often use them to give the impression that they know everything that was ever said or done in the company. In meetings I would see them taking notes. Other times, after casual conversations, they would hustle back to their offices to jot down what was said by whom and to whom.

Note-taking of itself is a good practice because it can provide an executive with instant references to refresh his memory about business matters and keep him on top of his job. I often take notes. But it becomes a bad practice when it is used to intimidate.

In a conversation I had one time with Jim Roche, when he was chairman, we were discussing something less than significant like the development of a new tooling process. I offered a thought on the matter and he replied something like: "Well now, wait a minute. We talked about that two years ago, and you said just the opposite of what you are saying now. Why has your position changed?"

He didn't have a note in front of him. "Holy Moses!" I thought. "I'm talking with a goddamn genius here." I couldn't remember what I had said two years previously and I was somewhat embarrassed. Later, I learned about Roche's habit of taking detailed notes on everything and referring to them later. He became mortal once again. . . .

Donner had his corporate imitators. Roger Kyes learned the art of intimidation at the master's knee. He didn't play the memory game, but he tried to intimidate executives by talking unceasingly about what a business brain he was. He often took up two-hour meetings in his office with nothing more than a lecture to captive divisional people about how he saved one division after another. He told me on several occasions that he knew more about the car business and my operations than I ever would.

On one occasion shortly after I took over Chevrolet, he pulled me into his office and said, "I have made a private study, and the whole problem with Chevrolet's inventory mess is centered on 50 parts classifications. Clear them up and you've solved Chevy's problems."

He said it with such authority that I figured we'd better get onto that problem first. I went to Chevy's manufacturing and purchasing people. "Kyes told me about his private study and that it revealed that the whole problem centers on 50 parts classifications. Let's identify them right away, and get it solved."

They answered, "If there was a study made, we sure as hell don't know of it." And neither did any of the managers on down the line right into the manufacturing plants. If Kyes made a study he didn't bother to talk to a single soul in Chevrolet.

My own analysis soon showed me that Chevrolet's inventory problems were a helluva lot more complicated and fundamental than the misclassification of 50 parts. Kyes just made up the solution to the problem and picked the number 50 right out of the air. He was trying to dazzle me; it didn't work, but it intimidated a lot of other GM executives.

Kyes, to my way of thinking, was the consummate corporate bully. A man unfortunately given frighteningly bad looks, he used his features to his advantage. He once referred to himself as "one mean, ugly sonofabitch." At six-feet four, he was an imposing figure of a man with a harsh and foggy voice and penetrating look that made executives wilt.

He was a hatchet man in the corporation and relished the job just as he relished a similar duty while he was assistant secretary of Defense in the Eisenhower Administration. His proudest moment, he would tell anyone, was when a *Look* magazine article called him "The hatchet man in the Defense Department." He cherished the role and played it to bravura performances. One of his duties was to tell has-been executives that they were going to take early retirement. He bullied more than a couple of men into taking early retirement. If one rebelled, he'd gather a case against the executive, break the results to him and then give him the option of being fired or taking early retirement. On one occasion, he built up a case against an executive charging that "he did not travel enough to keep in touch with his operations." Then Kyes turned around and charged another executive whose "time was at hand" with traveling too much. "You're never home minding the store," he told him. In some of these cases, it was publicly announced that this or that executive was taking early retirement for health reasons. The word around the corporation was, "When Kyes tells you that you're sick, you're sick."

He threatened me with firing often when I ran Pontiac and Chevrolet. The threats were made in private when he objected to something I did which wasn't the way he wanted it done. One time, though, he threatened me in public, and I fought back.

All of the divisions were ordered to cut back on personnel. We were given specific areas in which to cut back. Included in my order was the dismissal of a handful of test drivers for Chevrolet Engineering at the GM Tech Center. It seemed like a ridiculous directive because we would still have to have the testing done. But we would have to go outside of the company to get it done and end up spending a helluva lot more money. So I practiced that old corporate trick of foot dragging. I didn't fire the drivers. A review of the cutback program was being conducted at an Administrative Committee meeting. I was asked about the dismissal of the test drivers and answered something innocuous like: "I'm working on it."

Suddenly Kyes boomed back: "If you can't fire those goddamn guys, then we will get somebody who can. If you can't do it, you don't know how the hell to do your job."

The words stung like arrowheads. I was thoroughly embarrassed at the dressing down in front of my superiors and peers. I was livid and started to yell back at him but stopped short and held my peace. After the meeting I went straight to Ed Cole's presidential office and said: "If you don't get that ugly sonofabitch off my back, I'm going right into his office and pinch his head off."

"Jeez, John," Cole said leaping up from his desk. It was the most violent outbreak he'd seen amidst the almost churchlike quiet of the Fourteenth Floor. "Cool it. Relax. I'll speak to him."

But I couldn't cool it. So I stormed down the hall into Kyes office.

"You sonofabitch! If you embarrass me with a tirade like that again, I'll knock you on your ass. Right in front of everybody."

He turned white and rattled off something about wanting to impress me with the importance of his orders. That was the end of it. He never confronted me in such a manner again in public.

3

LEADERSHIP

"If some found him tiresome . . . they were nonetheless bedazzled by his vitality, guile, endurance, his powers of divination and ability to appeal to the core interests of other people."

—*Doris Kearns*

What makes a person an effective leader? How does the leadership process work? Do leaders really make a difference to organizational outcomes and to the lives and fortunes of people in the organization? Nobody seems to have definitive answers to these questions. Indeed, many behavioral scientists, after observing or being part of the innumerable studies, debates and theoretical formulations focused on leadership, have thrown up their hands and turned to other concepts in an effort to understand and explain organizational life. Yet the fascination and indeed preoccupation with leadership remains for researchers and practitioners alike. The search for effective leaders goes on. Training courses abound which promise the development of improved leadership ability and research money is still allocated to its study. Owners of unsuccessful organizations, such as some sports teams, regularly blame the managers and replace them with "better leaders." People continue to attach their hopes and hatreds to those chosen as leaders.

We do not have the answers to the questions posed at the beginning of this section. We do feel, however, that one approach to a better understanding of what leadership comprises is to take a much closer look at leaders in action in a variety of real-life organizational situations. We have chosen several articles for this section which graphically illustrate leaders in various organizations and which seem to capture a sense of what leadership looks like. The leaders described differ in many ways, but they appear uniformly to be purposive, dynamic, durable individuals. Frequently they are manipulative, creating and interpreting realities and moving people into those realities so as to accomplish their goals. They often are admired and respected by their followers, but sometimes are feared and even hated by these same followers. We suspect that most people will have encountered, worked for, competed with or even acted as individuals having some or all of these leadership characteristics.

Maccoby ("Managers") describes four types of managers, the careful craftsman, the aggressive jungle fighter, the cautious company man, and the competitive gamesman. He suggests that the new corporate top executive combines many of the traits of the gamesman and the company man. In many respects, the leaders depicted in this chapter reflect this combination, although the combination of qualities may be generalized. Maccoby's gamesman in "A Creative Gamesman" is fleshed out in an interesting piece on running a strategy meeting. Wakefield, the manager, wields his influence and power shrewdly. He works through his staff, harnesses the strengths of one of his chief assistants, Ray Shultz, to complement his own, and gives every indication of subtly stage-managing the meeting to accomplish his ends, not all of which are overt and product oriented.

Acquiring a base of power and influence to operate as a leader is not necessarily an assigned or a static event, as Kearns ("Campus Politico") shows in her analysis of Lyndon Johnson as a student. Johnson created a position of leadership through intelligent definition and use of a very low-level post in the college administrative hierarchy. Johnson's capacity to build a power base, to analyze people and situations, to enter into the perspectives of others and to turn the knowledge gained to his own advantage are well illustrated in Kearns's companion piece on Johnson, "The Politics of Seduction."

The exerpt from "Boss" by Royko provides interesting illustrations of tactics used by the late Mayor Richard Daley of Chicago to exert control over the decision-making process in city government and to maintain and increase the bases of his power's influence.

Like Johnson, Vince Lombardi ("Winning Is the Only Thing") apparently had an ability to understand and be sensitive to the needs and emotions of people. Lombardi was able to persuade and coerce others to stretch their efforts, to accomplish the goals he set for them. He frequently took risks in handling his players, pushing them to their limits of patience and self-control in some of his encounters with them. The Johnson, Daley, and Lombardi pieces bring into focus the issue of the costs of leadership. There appear to be costs to the leader, to the followers, to the organization and to the larger society. Daley's style and system of leadership did not survive him; no effective subordinates developed to succeed him. Johnson and Lombardi suffered physically from the rigors of their endeavors and, as Maccoby points out, the Watergate cover-up dramatically illustrated the disadvantages to individuals and to society of an unquestioning commitment to the creed of "Winning Is the Only Thing."

That leadership is a tough, demanding process, often with a roughness ignored by those who study it, is graphically illustrated in John Coleman's "Blue Collar Journal." Coleman, a college president on a year's sabbatical, describes his experiences as a pipelayer on a construction gang. Coleman captures the physical ardor of the work as well as its occasional boredom. Most interesting of all is his portrait of supervisor Gus Reed's leadership. Reed is a hard-swearing, tough, unyielding man who supervises closely and frequently leads by example. He is as competent or better than his workers. He is alert and suspicious, always on the lookout for faking and featherbedding by his subordinates which will undermine the quality of their performance, and quick to administer reprimands physically or verbally. He appears to command respect and loyalty and the roughness of his language and his manner seem to fit the demands of the situation. Like the other leaders in this chapter, he seems highly committed to his work and to his objectives.

Managers

Michael Maccoby

When I described the craftsman, jungle fighter, company man, and gamesman in *Spectrum*, the journal of the IEEE (the Institute of Electronic and Electrical Engineers), many managers wrote to say they recognized themselves, and understood organizational problems better.

Since then, managers in other kinds of companies and elite bureaucracies ranging from the civil service to the foreign service to universities have found that these types fit their worlds of work. . . . Here are brief introductions to each type.

1. *The craftsman.* The craftsman holds the traditional values of the productive-hoarding character — the work ethic, respect for people, concern for quality and thrift. When he talks about his work, his interest is in the *process* of making something; he enjoys building. He sees others, coworkers as well as superiors, in terms of whether they help or hinder him in doing a craftsmanlike job. Most of the craftsmen whom we interviewed are quiet, sincere, modest, and practical, although there is a difference between those who are more receptive and democratic versus those who are more authoritarian and intolerant. Although his virtues are admired by everyone, his self-containment and perfectionism do not allow him to lead a complex and changing organization. Rather than engaging and trying to master the system with the cooperation of others who share his values, he tends to do his own thing and go along, sometimes reluctantly, toward goals he does not share, enjoying whatever opportunities he finds for interesting work.

Some corporate scientists we interviewed are essentially craftsmen but there is a type of scientist who shares some of the craftsman's interest in knowledge and creating, but who is more of a prima donna, and is found exclusively in research labs. Although these scientists might be more at home in universities than in corporations, among them are some of the most independent contributors who work in corporations. Since so few are successful managers, and do

From *The Gamesman: The New Corporate Leaders* by Michael Maccoby. Copyright © 1976 by Michael Maccoby. Reprinted by permission of Simon & Schuster, a Division of Gulf & Western Corporation.

not reach the top levels of the technostructure, the "corporate scientist" type will be sketched only in passing.

Some of the most creative and gifted scientists whom we have seen in the corporate world are included in this type, together with the most unhappy misfits, resentful failures whose gifts do not measure up to their ambition. What most distinguishes the "scientists" from the craftsmen is their narcissism, their idolatry of their own knowledge, talents, and technology and their hunger for admiration. They are the corporate intellectuals and many are fascinated by esoteric issues (e.g., outer space or eternal life) only tangentially related to either corporate goals or social needs. In exaggerating their own importance, some of the scientists we interviewed belittled those who were more down to earth. Yet beneath their narcissism we found a receptive and dependent attachment to those in power, both corporate and state leaders, the "decision makers" who could support them and make their ideas into reality. A grandiose scientist does not trust the public to understand him, and it doesn't occur to him that the reason may be that he does not create things that benefit the public. He invents what is demanded by those who pay him — the corporation and the state. Both at home and at work, the grandiose scientist seeks a protected nest. He wants an admiring mother-wife to meet his needs in return for a chance to share in his glory, and he seeks patrons at work who will agree to similar symbiotic relationships.

2. *The jungle fighter.* The jungle fighter's goal is power. He experiences life and work as a jungle (not a game), where it is eat or be eaten, and the winners destroy the losers. A major part of his psychic resources is budgeted for his internal department of defense. Jungle fighters tend to see their peers in terms of accomplices or enemies and their subordinates as objects to be utilized. There are two subtypes of jungle fighters, lions and foxes. The lions are the conquerors who when successful may build an empire; the foxes make their nests in the corporate hierarchy and move ahead by stealth and politicking.

3. *The company man.* In the company man, we recognize the well-known organization man, or the functionary whose sense of identity is based on being part of the powerful, protective company. His strongest traits are his concern with the human side of the company, his interest in the feelings of the people around him and his commitment to maintain the organization's integrity. At his weakest, he is fearful and submissive, concerned with security even more than with success. The most creative company men sustain an atmosphere in their groups of cooperation, stimulation, and mutuality. The least creative find a little niche and satisfy themselves by feeling that somehow they share in the glory of the corporation.

4. *The gamesman.* The gamesman is the new man, and, really, the leading character in this study. His main interest is in challenge, competitive activity where he can prove himself a winner. Impatient with others who are slower and more cautious, he likes to take risks and to

motivate others to push themselves beyond their normal pace. He responds to work and life as a game. The contest hypes him up and he communicates his enthusiasm, thus energizing others. He enjoys new ideas, new techniques, fresh approaches and shortcuts. His talk and his thinking are terse, dynamic, sometimes playful and come in quick flashes. His main goal in life is to be a winner, and talking about himself invariably leads to discussion of his tactics and strategy in the corporate contest.

In the sixties, the gamesman went all out to win. In the seventies, both the country and the corporations are more skeptical about adventurism and glory-seeking. Some of the biggest companies have discovered that symbiosis with the military weakens their ability to compete in other markets. Watergate shamed those who flew the banner "Winning is not everything; it's the only thing," which in the sixties decorated corporate walls and desks. In the seventies, America no longer considers itself the land of unlimited abundance. Rising energy costs and international competition still call for competitive, risk-taking corporate gamesmen as leaders, but they have become more sober and realistic, more concerned with reducing costs than overwhelming the opposition with innovation.

The new corporate top executive combines many gamesman traits with aspects of the company man. He is a team player whose center is the corporation. He feels himself responsible for the functioning of a system, and in his mind, his career goals have merged with those of the corporation. Thus he thinks in terms of what is good for the company, hardly separating that from what is good for himself. He tends to be a worrier, constantly on the lookout for something that might go wrong. He is self-protective and sees people in terms of their use for the larger organization. He even uses himself in this way, fine-tuning his sensitivity. He has succeeded in submerging his ego and gaining strength from this exercise in self-control.

To function, the corporations need craftsmen, scientists, and company men (many could do without jungle fighters), but their future depends most of all on the gamesmen's capacity for mature development.

A Creative Gamesman

Michael Maccoby

It was instructive to follow Wakefield as he interacted with his subordinates at a monthly strategy meeting. The purposes of the meeting were "planning and communications." He was using these meetings

From *The Gamesman: The New Corporate Leaders* by Michael Maccoby. Copyright © 1976 by Michael Maccoby. Reprinted by permission of Simon & Schuster, a Division of Gulf & Western Corporation.

to develop a more open and friendly environment, where people could know and trust one another, and talk more openly about their mutual areas of interest. His innovation in this meeting had been to emphasize cooperative division-wide planning and to have every person there, especially those on the lower levels who might be involved in the area under discussion. Wakefield wanted everyone to feel a part of the project and to take more responsibility for its success.

This meeting lasted from 8:15 to noon. It started out with talk about a new product being developed, and it ended up with Wakefield spending forty-five minutes describing strategy for the division in the next few months. We will see the kind of atmosphere Wakefield creates in order to open up the craftsmen.*

Everyone arrived on time. Wakefield came in and sat in the row next to the back of the room by the wall. From there he could see everyone in the room, hear everyone without turning around, but he was kind of invisible to the others. He had purposely chosen one of his subordinates to be the nominal chairman of the meeting, while he was taking a role of being just like everyone else.

When Wakefield sat down, people became impatient, squirming around, looking at their watches, and looking significantly at him. Wakefield, however, was not apparently paying attention to anything. Finally, he said in a whisper to the person next to him, "Someone should tell George to get things started." People started looking at George. Then Wakefield said aloud, "Well, say, George, why don't we quit wasting time and get started with this thing?" This forced George, the nominal chairman, to take a publicly active role, but all the emotional influence as the initiator and controller of the meeting belonged to Wakefield, sitting in the back of the room.

The chairman was a rather tight, tough character. He began with a spiel about how he wanted to encourage open, frank discussion. Everyone should freely contribute. Everyone should speak up about his ideas. He didn't seem to mean a word of it. The meeting started like a lead balloon. Wakefield was obviously dissatisfied, and he clearly could have done it much better if he hadn't resolved to keep a low profile. Although every word that the chair said was precisely what he wanted, the phrases were lifeless. The meeting proceeded until the coffee break at 9:15 with the group leader for the new product presenting detailed technical analyses and market forecasts. The purpose was for all the related project managers to see how this new product affected them, and to offer their observations, criticisms, and

---

*The description of the meeting is from notes taken by Mac Greene.

advice. But the people seemed restless and bored. Even Wakefield started to read reports about the project under discussion rather than listening to the speaker.

At the coffee break, everyone sprang out of their chairs. People were complaining about the meeting. There seemed to be a resistance to the whole purpose of the meeting. They were being forced to co-operate and they did not know how to do it. People were shy about giving their comments publicly. They preferred talking to one another privately.

One of Wakefield's chief assistants is Ray Schultz, the type of gamesman who is tougher, pushier, less seductive and supportive than Wakefield. He is playful, often a joker, but also like a fanatical football coach who has to win. Even more than Wakefield, Schultz cannot stand a situation that is static, where there is no action. He is the one who told us with a straight face that the three people he most admired historically were Vince Lombardi, Jesus Christ, and Harry Truman. He liked Lombardi because of his high ideals, Jesus Christ because of his incredible ability to motivate people, and Harry Truman was an ordinary man with whom Schultz could identify because he had guts and was a winner. Schultz is the kind of person who says he likes to put effort into things only if he's going to win. He doesn't like people who whine and he doesn't want to baby them. He told us he saw himself as a gamesman with a strong streak of jungle fighter in him. As we shall see, Wakefield used Schultz to perform functions that he himself could not do.

At the coffee break, Schultz promised to open up this meeting by shaking people up. He said what was needed was some tough action.

It may have been this threat by Schultz that helped to make the meeting after the coffee break more active so that some people started to speak more freely about their strategies and goals and to compare their products with those of competitors.

In the transitional point in the discussion, when the conversation lagged for just a minute, Wakefield made a strong contribution. He summarized the discussion up to then, describing the key points that had been made and fitting what had been said into the general strategy, emphasizing what was most important for the future. This contribution was in fact a decision to make compromises and trade-offs to settle conflicts about functions and schedules so that the project could move toward a final development of the product, but it was disguised as a summary and a clarification. From that point on, Wakefield's clarification became the ground of further discussion, but all the focus was on what Wakefield had said and not on Wakefield personally. After this clarification, others joined in and there was a great deal of joking. Someone mentioned that someone else was get-ing a lot of good feedback. Wakefield leaned over to him and whispered gruffly, "I'll say," giving the impression that he was privy to some secret. Everyone laughed.

As people began to open up, they began to make optimistic estimates of the future. Another manager, authoritarian and controlling, served a function in the meeting of always throwing cold water when spirits rose too high. The group was starting to get very enthusiastic. They were seeing their product as a real innovation, very useful, technically excellent, with elegant design, reliable operation. Furthermore, it would beat out IBM and other companies that were working along the same line. But this man broke in, saying, "I don't see how you're going to approach estimates like that. Aren't you deceiving people with figures like that? That's approaching the reliability of the dead." Of course people jumped in to defend their estimates, but the effect of this kind of put-down was very useful. It forced everyone to be very careful and to stay close to the facts. It was a way of controlling a tendency to "specmanship," competing by promising unrealistic performance specifications. Lest this be too much of a downer, both Wakefield and Schultz came in with playful encouragement about how the new product would upset things within the corporation and make everyone reorient his thinking, since it would replace products already being used generally.

Wakefield began to flower out of his invisibility from the back of the room. He started making asides to various people, drawing them into the discussion, and maintaining a lively, low-key interchange with the public presentation at the front of the room. He particularly paid attention to the guys who were the most shy and uptight. By sitting at the back of the room, he was close to those people who normally sat at the back of the room so they would not be seen and so they could get out quickly. It was to many of these people that he directed some of his whispered asides and encouragements. In this way, he would succeed in getting some of these backbenchers into the discussion, referring to something they had once said to him or done that was relevant to the discussion at hand, and encouraging them to speak up.

Suddenly Schultz, who had been joking around, became a nononsense, hard-line businessman. This sudden transformation seemed to scare most people. "This schedule is too tight," he said. "There's not enough money to meet this schedule. Who made up this schedule? Who thinks we can make dates like that? The pipeline is clogged and you know that. [He was jabbing with his finger.] We're overcommitted now, and we don't know what the orders will be. It's impossible to schedule this. We can't tie ourselves to this schedule. It's not funded for this fiscal half. Who are we trying to fool with a schedule like that?"

Schultz sat back, his eyes flashing with a smug look that asked, What will you do about it now? Everyone seemed upset, as though their illusion had been shattered. But they pulled themselves together and agreed that they had to admit more flexibility into the schedule. Although Schultz pressed them to agree that their schedule was a complete fraud, they would not go that far. The project leader, who had started the meeting, repeated several times with a dazed look on his face, "Remember, we are serious about the project. Our assumptions could be vastly wrong, but we have to start somewhere. We are absolutely serious about this product."

The effect of this intervention, however, was to bring people down to earth. Like the earlier intervention, which had questioned reliability, this one questioned the whole idea that the product could be developed on an easy schedule, without pushing people to the utmost. The craftsmen had been brought out of their shells and now they were going to be challenged and motivated to step up the pace. Schultz pointed out to another manager, "You have on that chart that this other product is due in 1974. I want to change that to 1973. I don't want that kind of pressure removed from that project." Schultz kept on. He was warming up the meeting, keeping everyone off balance and under pressure. The craftsmen never opened their mouths again in the meeting. How did Wakefield respond? Before, he had been acting as a kind of gentle stimulator, but as Schultz took off, he became harder and fitted himself into Schultz's tempo. The tone of the meeting became cooler and more efficient. Wakefield joined Schultz in challenging all kinds of assumptions.

The project leader tried to reassert his original estimate. But the challenge was making him give way on certain points, and he and his subordinates had to promise to commit themselves to work even harder. If they failed to meet the new schedule now, it would be their fault. They would be responsible. They had been warned. Wakefield also came in to point out to the project leader that the production department had to depend on the estimates of completion and sales. If things were going to be as good as he was predicting, then they would have to commit production in the future. Was he willing to take responsibility for this too?

The result was a reaffirmation of the product's value, but everyone had been scared so completely that they were easier to push into line in terms of the overall divisional requirements for timing and production capacity. After Schultz had led the browbeating, Wakefield stepped in and offered solutions which at that point everyone would have to accept gratefully.

The group's spirits rose again. They felt they had a winner. Wakefield pointed out how they had solved a problem that their competitor had failed at. He turned to the project leader directly and said, "It's a good system and it's gonna go. It's a winner." Some-body near Wakefield raised a question and he slipped directly into a tête-à-tête.

The mood was becoming more playful. Schultz's next challenge was not so scary. He said, "The numbers are still too low."

"Come on, Ray," said one of the project group, "it's only another fifty K."

Schultz laughed. "Fifty K here, fifty K there. *All right! When you're hot, you're hot!*" Everyone laughed and felt flattered.

Wakefield, speaking almost to himself, mumbled, "Even if it triples to a hundred and fifty K, the return will be incredible."

People then began to joke about all the new applications the prod-uct might create. Someone raised the possibility of environmental problems. What would be the tolerances for heat, humidity, dust, etc.? But the response was mainly boyish. At this point, no one was going to take this kind of problem seriously in comparison to the problems of scheduling and money. Schultz asked, "Do you mean will it run in the furnace or out?" Another man asked, "Can you run it under water?" But it was the end of the meeting. Wakefield came up to the front of the room. He congratulated everyone. "This is going to continually turn on the customers. It's an excellent program. It's the most exciting project I've seen at this company for years. We're in motion.". . .

Then Wakefield got serious. It was necessary to come up with a three-year plan. They would have to soon present the progress report to the president of the company. Wakefield stated that in this presen-tation he wanted the young guys out in front doing the presentation. He said, "I will introduce the guys and talk about their potential and growth and so forth." In this way, one might say that Wakefield would be showing the president of the company not only his success with products, but also his success in bringing along and developing new people. He then went on to give a strategy of how to present new material to the president of the company so that he would be-come most excited. "We give him the hard stuff in the morning and the exciting stuff in the afternoon. I've seen him go to sleep in these meetings. They don't do it right. It really turns the guys off and it's a big down."

At the very end of the meeting Wakefield discussed his plans for continual meetings that would allow people in different projects to meet those in other projects, to have some cross-fertilization and ex-change of information. They needed also to have more interrelation-ship between development, marketing, and production.

After the meeting, Wakefield and Schultz discussed how it had gone. They felt the meeting had been only a partial success. The dis-cussion of the new product was not the main point. The real goal of the meeting had been to get the shy and uptight craftsmen to work better together. Only that way could schedules be met and morale be raised. They felt that the meeting was only partially successful in terms of this criterion, since most people had not opened up. The pace of the meeting had been slow and without real enthusiasm. Schultz's pushing got some people responding in terms of having to defend themselves and commit themselves to a tight schedule. But it would have been better if they had not needed this kind of heavy-handed approach. Both Wakefield and Schultz believed it would take another year to open up the people satisfactorily. This meeting only reinforced Wakefield's view that the people needed strong leadership in order to become more cooperative.

Later in the day Wakefield presided over a meeting of his three top managers, including Schultz, in which they were going to assign people to teams to learn from one another and interact more. They all enjoyed this assignment, wanting to create exciting combinations of people who needed to know one another better and to keep apart those who might cause too much conflict. At this meeting, the managers showed their knowledge of the different people under them in terms of their strengths and weaknesses. They referred to the process of team-making as "packing in the brains."

In watching Wakefield at work, one was struck by how he responded to the different needs of different people. If he was talking about a problem with an uptight and controlling person, he played to the man's style, letting him think that he completely controlled the situation, encouraging him to take control. If he was talking with another gamesman, the conversation was hip and playful, totally different. In each case, Wakefield did not tell anyone what to do, but tried to state the situation in such a way that the other would see the answer and consider it his own solution.

For example, a manager came to see Wakefield with a problem. The manager, George Smith, just out of business school, was tense. He looked rather like a lieutenant fresh out of West Point trying to prove himself and keep everything under control. He had a customer problem. The customer had just installed a computer system, something wasn't working just right, and he wanted the company to come and fix it. Wakefield asked about the specific details concerning the service difficulties. He then asked whether these difficulties were specifically stated in the contract as the responsibility of the company. Smith, following Wakefield's train of thought, then suggested that maybe the customer was trying to beat the company out of some free service. Wakefield emphatically agreed, since that was the point he was trying to make without saying it. He then told a story about how one of their key technical managers had ended up spending a great deal of time helping another customer solve all sorts of applications problems that the customer maintained came from some initial faulty design. But the other company used this information to develop its own products. Wakefield eventually had kicked these people out, and he was now in the process of establishing a policy that key design people could not work with customers, who were often competitors. He intimated to Smith that brilliant designers were perhaps a little too naïve and nice to know when they were being exploited. Smith responded immediately to this idea, which fit his own prejudices. He agreed with Wakefield that these key design people had to be protected from aggressive customers, and people like himself needed to do the protecting. By this time, Smith was thinking that he had all along been intending to take a strong stand controlling the designer-customer interface. In this way, by understanding Smith's strengths and weaknesses, Wakefield had brilliantly solved a problem and made a new loyal ally.

We remarked to Wakefield that in contrast to his stated value that people should make decisions by themselves, he seemed to be very directive and manipulative. Wakefield responded, "I have to do that. It's not the way I'd like to do it, but this place was in chaos two years ago, and it takes a lot of work developing a good organization. People can't stand not knowing anything about what they're supposed to be doing. People are a lot happier being told what to do."

We can see that Wakefield's character, his game orientation, his joy of life, enthusiasm, and dazzling brilliance all served to make him effective as a top-level manager motivating a group of sensitive, rather closed but competent craftsmen. But just as he used himself as a key tool in his work, so his character was being molded in the workplace. Those traits and abilities that served the work were being exercised and reinforced constantly. The questions we will consider now are: What has been the human cost of his work to Wakefield? What has been the result to his own well-being of the character-development process going on in him? And which are the traits and capacities that have been left underdeveloped?

Campus Politico

Doris Kearns

From the beginning at San Marcos College (later Southwestern Texas State Teachers College), Johnson set out to win the friendship and respect of those people who would assist his rise within the commu-

Abridged and adapted from "Lyndon Johnson and the American Dream" by Doris Kearns, as it appeared in *The Atlantic Monthly.* Copyright © 1976 by Doris Kearns. Reprinted by permission of Harper & Row, Publishers, Inc., and Andre Deutsch, Ltd., Publishers.

nity which composed San Marcos. Most obvious was the president of the college, Cecil Evans, whose favor would have a multiplier effect with the faculty and student body. But Johnson was not alone in the desire to have a special relationhip with Evans. "I knew," Johnson later said, "there was only one way to get to know Evans and that was to work for him directly." He became special assistant to the president's personal secretary.

As special assistant, Johnson's assigned job was simply to carry messages from the president to the department heads and occasionally to other faculty members. Johnson saw that the rather limited function of messenger had possibilities for expansion; for example, encouraging recipients of the messages to transmit their own communications through him. He occupied a desk in the president's outer office, where he took it upon himself to announce the arrival of visitors. These added services evolved from a helpful convenience into an aspect of the normal process of presidential business. The messenger had become an appointments secretary, and, in time, faculty members came to think of Johnson as a funnel to the president. Using a technique which was later to serve him in achieving mastery over the Congress, Johnson turned a rather insubstantial service into a process through which power was exercised. By redefining the process, he had given power to himself.

Evans eventually broadened Johnson's responsibilities to include handling his political correspondence and preparing his reports for the state agencies with jurisdiction over the college and its appropriations. The student was quick to explain that his father had been a member of the state legislature (from 1905 to 1909, and from 1918 to 1925), and Lyndon had often accompanied him to Austin where he had gained some familiarity with the workings of the legislature and the personalities of its leaders. This claim might have sounded almost ludicrous had it not come from someone who already must have seemed an inordinately political creature. Soon Johnson was accompanying Evans on his trips to the state capital in Austin, and, before long, Evans came to rely upon his young apprentice for political counsel. For Johnson was clearly at home in the state legislature; whether sitting in a committee room during hearings or standing on the floor talking with representatives, he could, in later reports to Evans, capture the mood of individual legislators and the legislative body with entertaining accuracy. The older man, on whose favor Johnson depended, now relied on him, or at least found him useful.

The world of San Marcos accommodated Lyndon Johnson's gifts. If some found him tiresome, and even his friends admitted that he was difficult, they were nonetheless bedazzled by his vitality, guile, and endurance, his powers of divination, and ability to appeal to the core interests of other people. In two years, he became a campus politician, a prizewinning debater, an honors student, and the editor of the college *Star*.

The Politics of Seduction

Doris Kearns

The authority that Johnson inherited as Senate Democratic majority leader had been rendered ineffective by the Senate's inner club. Johnson set about to change all that, and before long he had transformed the instruments at hand — the steering committee, which determined committee assignments, and a hitherto unimportant Democratic Policy Committee — into mechanisms of influence and patronage in his relations with his Democratic colleagues and of control in the scheduling of legislation.

From facts, gossip, observation—a multitude of disparate elements — he shaped a composite mental portrait of every senator: his strengths and his weaknesses; his place in the political spectrum; his aspirations in the Senate, and perhaps beyond the Senate; how far he could be pushed in what direction, and by what means; how he liked his liquor; how he felt about his wife and his family; and, most important, how he felt about himself. For Johnson understood that the most important decision each senator made, often obscurely, was what kind of senator he wanted to be; whether he wanted to be a national leader in education, a regional leader in civil rights, a social magnate in Washington, an agent of the oil industry, a wheel horse of the party, a President of the United States. Yet his entrepreneurial spirit encompassed not simply the satisfaction of present needs but the development of new and expanding ones. He would, for instance, explain to a senator that "although five other senators are clamoring for this one remaining seat on the congressional delegation to Tokyo, I just might be able to swing it for you since I know how much you really want it. . . . It'll be tough but let me see what I can do." The joys of visiting Tokyo may never have occurred to the senator, but he was unlikely to deny Johnson's description of his desire—after all, it might be interesting, a relaxing change, even fun; and perhaps some of the businesses in his state had expressed concern about Japanese competition. By creating consumer needs in this fashion, and by then defining the terms of their realization, Johnson was able to expand the base of benefits upon which power could be built.

Johnson's capacities for control and domination found their consummate manifestation during his private meetings with individual senators. Face to face, behind office doors, Johnson could strike a different pose, a different form of behavior and argument. He would try to make each senator feel that his support in some particular matter was the critical element that would affect the well-being of the nation, the Senate, and the party leader; and would also serve the practical and political interests of the senator. . . .

The arrangements that preceded a private meeting were elaborate indeed. A meeting with a colleague might seem like an accidental encounter in a Senate corridor, but Johnson was not a man who roamed through halls in aimless fashion; when he began to wander he knew who it was he would find.

After the coincidental encounter and casual greetings, Johnson would remember that he had something he would like to talk about. The two men would walk down the corridor, ride the elevator, and enter an office where they would begin their conversation with small talk over Scotch. As the conversation progressed, Johnson would display an overwhelming combination of praise, scorn, rage, and friendship. His voice would rise and fall, moving from the thunder of an orator to the whisper reminiscent of a lover inviting physical touch. Transitions were abrupt. He responded to hostility with a disconcerting glance of indignation; the next minute he would evoke a smile by the warmth of his expression and a playful brush of his hand. Variations in pitch, stress, and gesture reflected the importance which he attached to certain words. His appeal would abound with illustration, anecdote, and hyperbole. He knew how to make his listeners *see* things he was describing, make them tangible to the senses. And he knew how to sustain a sense of uninterrupted flow by parallel structure and a stream of conjunctions.

From his own insistent energy, Johnson would create an illusion that the outcome, and thus the responsibility, rested on the decision of this one senator; refusing to permit any implication of the reality they both knew (but which in this office began to seem increasingly more uncertain), that the decisions of many other senators would also affect the results.

Then too, Johnson was that rare American man who felt free to display intimacy with another man, through expressions of feeling and also in physical closeness. In an empty room he would stand or sit next to a man as if all that were available was a three-foot space. He could flatter men with sentiments of love and touch their bodies with gestures of affection. The intimacy was all the more excusable because it seemed genuine and without menace. Yet it was also the product of meticulous calculation. And it worked. To the ardor and the bearing of this extraordinary man, the ordinary senator would almost invariably succumb.

Johnson was often able to use the same behavior with the press as he did with his colleagues, dividing it into separate components, and carving out a special relationship with each of the reporters.

"You learn," he said, "that Stewart Alsop cares a lot about appearing to be an intellectual and a historian — he strives to match his brother's intellectual attainments—so whenever you talk to him, play down the gold cufflinks which you play up with *Time* magazine, and to him, emphasize your relationship with FDR and your roots in Texas, so much so that even when it doesn't fit the conversation you make sure to bring in maxims from your father and stories from the Old West. You learn that Evans and Novak love to traffic in backroom politics and political intrigue, so that when you're with them you make sure to bring in lots of details and colorful description of personality. You learn that Mary McGrory likes dominant personalities and Doris Fleeson cares only about issues, so that when you're with McGrory you come on strong and with Fleeson you make yourself sound like some impractical red-hot liberal."

Boss: Richard J. Daley of Chicago

Mike Royko

If there is a council meeting, everybody marches downstairs at a few minutes before ten. Bush and the department heads and personal aides form a proud parade. The meeting begins when the seat of the mayor's pants touches the council president's chair, placed beneath the great seal of the city of Chicago and above the heads of the aldermen, who sit in a semibowl auditorium.

It is his council, and in all the years it has never once defied him as a body. Keane manages it for him, and most of its members do what they are told. In other eras, the aldermen ran the city and plundered it. In his boyhood they were so constantly on the prowl that they were known as "the Gray Wolves." His council is known as "the Rubber Stamp."

He looks down at them, bestowing a nod or a benign smile on a few favorites, and they smile back gratefully. He seldom nods or smiles at the small minority of white and black independents.

The independents anger him more than the Republicans do, because they accuse him of racism, fascism, and of being a dictator. The Republicans bluster about loafing payrollers, crumbling gutters, inflated budgets — traditional, comfortable accusations that don't stir the blood.

That is what Keane is for. When the minority goes on the attack, Keane himself, or one of the administration aldermen he has groomed for the purpose, will rise and answer the criticism by shouting that the critic is a fool, a hypocrite, ignorant, and misguided. Until his death, one alderman could be expected to leap to his feet at every meeting and cry, "God bless our mayor, the greatest mayor in the world."

But sometimes Keane and his trained orators can't shout down the minority, so Daley has to do it himself. If provoked, he'll break into a rambling, ranting speech, waving his arms, shaking his fists, defending his judgment, defending his administration, always with the familiar "It is easy to criticize . . . to find fault . . . but where are your programs . . . where are your ideas . . ."

If that doesn't shut off the critics, he will declare them to be out of order, threaten to have the sergeant at arms force them into their seats, and invoke *Robert's Rules of Order*, which, in the heat of debate, he once described as "the greatest book ever written."

All else failing, he will look toward a glass booth above the spectator's balcony and make a gesture known only to the man in the booth who operates the sound system that controls the microphones on each alderman's desk. The man in the booth will touch a switch and the offending critic's microphone will go dead and stay dead until he sinks into his chair and closes his mouth.

The meetings are seldom peaceful and orderly. The slightest criticism touches off shrill rebuttal, leading to louder criticism and finally an embarrassingly wild and vicious free-for-all. It can't be true, because Daley is a man who speaks highly of law and order, but sometimes it appears that he enjoys the chaos, and he seldom moves to end it until it has raged out of control.

Every word of criticism must be answered, every complaint must be disproved, every insult must be returned in kind. He doesn't take anything from anybody. While Daley was mediating negotiations between white trade unions and black groups who wanted the unions to accept blacks, a young militant angrily rejected one of his suggestions and concluded, "Up your ass!" Daley leaped to his feet and answered, "And up yours too." Would John Lindsay have become so involved?

Independent aldermen have been known to come up with a good idea, such as providing food for the city's hungry, or starting day-care centers for children of ghetto women who want to work; Daley will acknowledge it, but in his own way. He'll let Keane appropriate the idea and rewrite and resubmit it as an administration measure. That way, the independent has the satisfaction of seeing his idea reach fruition and the administration has more glory. But most of the independents' proposals are sent to a special subcommittee that exists solely to allow their unwelcome ideas to die.

The council meetings seldom last beyond the lunch hour. Aldermen have much to do. Many are lawyers and have thriving practices, because Chicagoans know that a dumb lawyer who is an alderman can often perform greater legal miracles than a smart lawyer who isn't. . . .

The afternoon work moves with never a minute wasted. The engineers and planners come with their reports on public works projects. Something is always being built, concrete being poured, steel being riveted, contractors being enriched.

"When will it be completed?" he asks.

"Early February."

"It would be a good thing for the people if it could be completed by the end of October."

The engineers say it can be done, but it will mean putting on extra shifts, night work, overtime pay, a much higher cost than was planned.

"It would be a good thing for the people if it could be completed by the end of October."

Of course it would be a good thing for the people. It would also be a good thing for the Democratic candidates who are seeking election in early November to go out and cut a ribbon for a new expressway or a water filtration plant or, if nothing else is handy, another wing at the O'Hare terminal. What ribbons do their opponents cut?

The engineers and planners understand, and they set about getting it finished by October.

On a good afternoon, there will be no neighborhood organizations to see him, because if they get to Daley, it means they have been up the ladder of government and nobody has been able to solve their problem. And that usually means a conflict between the people and somebody else, such as a politician or a business, whom his aides don't want to ruffle. There are many things his department heads can't do. They can't cross swords with ward bosses or politically heavy businessmen. They can't make important decisions. Some can't even make petty decisions. He runs City Hall like a small family business and keeps everybody on a short rein. They do only that which they know is safe and that which he tells them to do. So many things that should logically be solved several rungs below finally come to him.

Because of this, he has many requests from neighborhood people. And when a group is admitted to his office, most of them nervous and wide-eyed, he knows who they are, their leaders, their strength in the community. They have already been checked out by somebody. He must know everything. He doesn't like to be surprised. Just as he knows the name of every new worker, he must know what is going on in the various city offices. If the head of the office doesn't tell him, he has somebody there who will. In the office of other elected officials, he has trusted persons who will keep him informed. Out in the neighborhoods his precinct captains are reporting to the ward committeemen, and they in turn are reporting to him.

His police department's intelligence-gathering division gets bigger and bigger, its network of infiltrators, informers, and spies creating massive files on dissenters, street gangs, political enemies, newsmen, radicals, liberals, and anybody else who might be working against him. If one of his aides or handpicked officeholders is shacking up with a woman, he will know it. And if that man is married and a Catholic, his political career will wither and die. That is the greatest sin of all. You can make money under the table and move ahead, but you are forbidden to make secretaries under the sheets. He has dumped several party members for violating his personal moral standards. If something is leaked to the press, the bigmouth will be tracked down and punished. Scandals aren't public scandals if you get there before your enemies do.

So when the people come in, he knows what they want and whether it is possible. Not that it means they will get it. That often depends on how they act.

He will come out from behind his desk all smiles and handshakes and charm. Then he returns to his chair and sits very straight, hands folded on his immaculate desk, serious and attentive. To one side will be somebody from the appropriate city department.

Now it's up to the group. If they are respectful, he will express sympathy, ask encouraging questions, and finally tell them that everything possible will be done. And after they leave, he may say, "Take care of it." With that command, the royal seal, anything is possible, anybody's toes can be stepped on.

But if they are pushy, antagonistic, demanding instead of imploring, or bold enough to be critical of him, to tell him how he should do his job, to blame him for their problem, he will rub his hands together, harder and harder. In a long, difficult meeting, his hands will get raw. His voice gets lower, softer, and the corners of his mouth will turn down. At this point, those who know him will back off. They know what's next. But the unfamiliar, the militant, will mistake his lowered voice and nervousness for weakness. Then he'll blow, and it comes in a frantic roar:

"I want *you* to tell *me* what to do. *You* come up with the answers. *You* come up with the program. Are we perfect? Are *you* perfect? We all make mistakes. We all have faults. It's easy to criticize. It's easy to find fault. But *you* tell me what to do. This problem is all over the city. We didn't create these problems. We don't want them. But we are doing what we can. *You* tell me how to solve them. *You* give me a program." All of which leaves the petitioners dumb, since most people don't walk around with urban programs in their pockets. It can also leave them right back where they started.

They leave and the favor seekers come in. Half of the people he sees want a favor. They plead for promotions, something for their sons, a chance to do some business with the city, to get somebody in City Hall off their backs, a chance to return from political exile, a boon. They won't get an answer right there and then. It will be considered and he'll let them know. Later, sometimes much later, when he has considered the alternatives and the benefits, word will get back to them. Yes or no. Success or failure. Life or death.

Some jobseekers come directly to him. Complete outsiders, meaning those with no family or political connections, will be sent to see their ward committeemen. That is protocol, and that is what he did to the tall young black man who came to see him a few years ago, bearing a letter from the governor of North Carolina, who wrote that the young black man was a rising political prospect in his state. Daley told him to see his ward committeeman, and if he did some precinct work, rang doorbells, hustled up some votes, there might be a government job for him. Maybe something like taking coins in a tollway booth. The Rev. Jesse Jackson, now the city's leading black civil rights leader, still hasn't stopped smarting over that.

Others come asking him to resolve a problem. He is the city's leading labor mediator and has prevented the kind of strikes that have crippled New York. His father was a union man, and he comes from a union neighborhood, and many of the union leaders were his boyhood friends. He knows what they want. And if it is in the city's treasury, they will get it. If it isn't there, he'll promise to find it. He has ended a teachers' strike by promising that the state legislature would find funds for them, which surprised the Republicans in Springfield, as well as put them on the spot. He is an effective mediator with the management side of labor disputes, because they respect his judgment, and because there are few industries that do not need some favors from City Hall. . . .

The Wall Street Journal, 18 July 1979.

The ITT Coup

Why Harold Geneen Got the Board to Strip Power From Hamilton

Old Chief Resented Moves Made by His Successor; An Ovation Was Decisive

By PRISCILLA S. MEYER

Staff Reporter of The Wall Street Journal

NEW YORK—By most accounts, Harold Geneen didn't want to go to the annual International Telephone & Telegraph Corp. barbecue in Brussels last month. So reluctant was the chairman and former chief executive of ITT to attend the event, an associate says, that "we dragged him there kicking and screaming."

The reason for Mr. Geneen's reluctance, ITT officials say, was that the company's European operations were in an uproar. "A revolt was brewing," one official says, because of layoffs and a streamlining of operations directed by Lyman C. Hamilton Jr., who was ITT's president and chief executive. Mr. Hamilton, on a business trip in Asia, didn't attend the barbecue.

"Mr. Geneen was trying to stay out of it," an associate says. But once prevailed upon to attend, the 69-year-old chairman not only went to Brussels but also spoke to the gathering, including 90-odd European and U.S. managers. The speech concerned ITT's "momentum." According to some in the audience, it was low-key and witty. And when it was over, everyone seems to agree, the managers rose in thunderous applause that lasted a full seven minutes.

Afterward, an associate says, Mr. Geneen "was completely silent." But some feel that the chairman saw the ovation as a mandate to snatch the company back from the hands of the man to whom he had passed the chief executive's mantle only 18 months before. Thus, these observers say, was sealed the fate of Mr. Hamilton, who was ousted by ITT's 20-member board last Wednesday—to the surprise of the general public and the financial community.

Winning Is the Only Thing

Jerry Kramer

FRANK GIFFORD: "I WAS ALWAYS
TRYING TO PLEASE HIM"

When Vince joined the New York Giants in 1954, he walked into a disaster area. Their defense was a shambles; their offense was worse. The year before, they had lost nine out of twelve games and had scored only 179 points, the fewest of any team in the league. Vince immediately molded a new offense and, in the process, created a superstar: Frank Gifford, a halfback who could run, block, pass and catch passes.

An All-American at the University of Southern California, Gifford had been used almost exclusively on defense in 1952, his rookie season. Under Vince, he became the most exciting offensive halfback in the National Football League. In each of the five years he played for Vince, Gifford was nominated for the Pro Bowl. In those five years, the Giants never had a losing record, never scored fewer than 246 points. . . .

In the spring of 1970, before we knew of Vince's illness, I sat down with Frank Gifford in his office at CBS. After thirteen seasons with the Giants, Frank is now a highly successful sportscaster, covering everything from the Masters to the Super Bowl. . . .

To be honest, very few of the guys liked him at first. For one thing, he had us running like we had never run before. But the main thing was that we resented a guy coming in from college and telling us what to do. And he was completely in charge. Jim Lee never interfered; he left the offense entirely to Vinny and the defense entirely to Tom Landry. As Jim Lee himself said many times, "I'm just here to take the roll and blow up the balls."

The first two or three weeks, we weren't too impressed by Vinny's Here's-how-we-did-it-at-St.-Cecilia-High-or-at-Army attitude. . . .

But it didn't take us long to realize that even though Vinny's approach to football was very basic — fundamentals: hit, block and tackle — he was somebody special. His enthusiasm, his spirit, was infectious. We really began to dig him when he started coming up to our rooms at night after he'd put in a new play during a chalk talk. I was rooming with Charlie, and Vinny'd come to our room, after putting in an off-tackle play, and say, "Well, what do you think? Will it work?" He was very honest. When he put in the power sweep, he'd ask, "Can the halfback get down and hold that defensive end and stop the penetration?" That was my job on one side and Alex Webster's on the other. We'd say, "Oh, sure, Coach, we can do it." And then he'd just drill the hell out of us.

I can remember sneaking out some nights after curfew in Oregon, and sometimes I'd come back in pretty late, and the lights would still be on in his room. I realized then the kind of work he was putting in. He had to be exhausted, but he never showed it. He'd be out on the field the next day, going full speed, driving himself every minute.

We never feared Vinny in New York. It wasn't like in Green Bay later, when he came in with you guys as a winner, as an established person. To us, he was just an assistant coach from Army and St. Cecilia High. There are maybe twelve or fifteen of us who were the core of the offense, and we were kind of a clique, and Vinny liked to hang around with us. He'd eat dinner with us on the road and laugh with us when we won and die with us when we lost. We used to tease him and raise hell with him. We'd hide his baseball cap, things like that, just to see him get his emotions worked up. When he was showing us films, we used to bait him, lead him on to the point where he'd smash a table or throw an eraser at the blackboard. He'd break two or three projectors a year when he got angry. . . .

He was always a great psychologist, great at analyzing individuals, knowing which players needed to be driven and which ones needed a friendly pat on the fanny. When he was with us, we had a few players who needed driving. One was Mel Triplett. Mel used to exasperate Vinny. He could've been a great player—he had a fantastic year in 1956 — but he never played up to his potential, except on certain occasions, like against the Cleveland Browns after they got Jimmy Brown. Mel always felt that he was better than Jimmy. You and I both know that he wasn't, but he was a fine football player.

Vinny used to ride Mel pretty good, especially in the movies. You know how he is with that projector. You could miss a block, and he'd never say a word sometimes, but he'd run the film back and forth, back and forth, till every guy in the room felt like he'd done something wrong. It was sort of like going to a revival meeting. A preacher will fire some buckshot out there, and everybody is going to feel it. Everybody is the guilty party.

Well, Mel used to think that Vinny was persecuting him something awful. All he really was trying to do was help Mel along. But one time he went a little too far with Mel, who was kind of a frightening guy when he got hot. Vinny kept running this one play back and forth, back and forth, back and forth — with Mel missing a block —

and about the eighth or tenth time, Mel said, loud and hard, "Move on with that projector."

You could have heard a pin drop. We all wondered what was going to happen. Mel had told the rest of us a few times what he intended to do to Mr. Lombardi someday. And Mel was the kind of guy who was emotional and might do just what he said he would. He was at the breaking point right then. Vince didn't say a word. He went on to the next play. He read Mel just right. They never did have a confrontation. I heard a lot of guys over the years say they were going to punch Vinny out at the end of the season, but no one ever did. You've got to end up loving a guy who can build a team, put it all together — and you share in the rewards. But Vinny walked a very dangerous line at times.

He ruled us all equally — with one exception. He loved Charlie Conerly. He never said a harsh word to Charlie. And, again, he was really getting the proper reading, because Charlie didn't need it. You couldn't fire Charlie up with a branding iron. But you couldn't cool him off, either. Charlie was his own person.

When Charlie used to throw a couple of interceptions or blow an automatic — which really fried Vinny — Vinny wouldn't say a word. He'd get on Don Heinrich — Don was our other quarterback, and he was a little younger and a little wilder than Charlie — but never to the point where he got totally angry. I think he has a special fondness for his quarterbacks. A quarterback is his own extension on the field. I think he looked at Bart Starr as Vinny Lombardi out there. I think he feels the same way about Sonny Jurgensen.

But the rest of us got equal treatment. I remember when he put in the nutcracker drill: A defensive lineman sets himself in between two big bags, and an offensive lineman tries to lead a ballcarrier through. Eveybody always used to say, "Oh, that poor offensive lineman." Nobody ever thought about the poor offensive back, who was just getting the hell knocked out of him. After an hour of banging heads, those defensive linemen were so hot and mad they didn't care what they did to you. Maybe you were a star, or thought you were a star, but you ran the nutcracker as often as the rookie trying to make the team. Vinny kept track of it, close track, and if you tried to get out of one run at it, his teeth'd be grinning at you, and he'd be yelling. "Get in here, get in here," and there'd be no way you could escape. . . .

And Vinny could put his finger on these elements in a personality. He knew exactly how to motivate. He knew just what buttons to push. You see, I didn't hide anything from him. I was always just as open as I could be with him, because I liked him so much. I know that after a while it got to the point where I was playing football for just one reason: I was always trying to please him. When we played a game, I could care less about the headlines on Monday. All I wanted was to be able to walk into the meeting Tuesday morning and have Vinny give me that big grin and pat me on the fanny and let me know that I was doing what he wanted me to do. A lot of our guys felt that way. We had guys who would run through a stadium wall for him— and then maybe cuss him in the next breath. . . .

I can remember very clearly the happiest I've ever seen Vinny. It wasn't after a game. It was in the middle of a week during the 1956 season. We'd gotten up over .500 in 1954 and 1955, but we hadn't finished first or second in our division. Then, in 1956, we won four of our first five games, and on a Wednesday—we were getting ready to play Pittsburgh—he called us all around him, the whole offense. He just couldn't restrain himself. He was bubbling. He was bursting with pride. "By God," he said, "we've really got something going." His eyes were shining. He just felt that we were going to win everything, and he knew it was his baby, and he had to tell us, and, of course, he was right. We did go on to win everything that year. . . .

People are always asking me what makes Vince Lombardi different from other coaches, and I've got one answer: He can get that extra ten percent out of an individual. Multiply ten percent times forty men on a team times fourteen games a season—and you're going to win. He proved that last year at Washington. That's not a talented team, and my God, they hadn't had a winning team since 1955. But he made them winners. He made them believe they could win. Sonny Jurgensen loved him. He had no right to succeed in Washington. There are twenty-six teams now, not twelve like there were when he went to Green Bay. It's a hell of a lot harder to find good ballplayers. You can't trade the way you used to; you can't draft the way you could. There just isn't the same material available for every team. And the quality of coaching has been upgraded throughout the league. And, still, he did it. Nobody else could've done it. There are four or five coaches that know as much strategically and tactically as Lombardi, but they don't get that extra ten percent.

Vinny believes in the Spartan life, the total self-sacrifice, and to succeed and reach the pinnacle that he has, you've got to be that way. You've got to have total dedication. The hours you put in on a job can't even be considered. The job is to be done, and if it takes a hundred hours, you give it a hundred hours. If it takes fifteen minutes, you give it fifteen minutes. I saw the movie *Patton*, and it was Vince Lombardi. The situation was different, but the thought was the same: We're here to do a job, and each and every one of us will put everything we've got into getting the job done. That was Vince. . . .

KYLE ROTE: "HE WAS SEARCHING FOR A RELATIONSHIP WITH US"

During Vince's years with the New York Giants, Kyle Rote was more than one of his stars: He was Vince's kind of ballplayer. Kyle had a bad left knee that forced him, after a few pro seasons, to forget about playing halfback, to give up the brilliant running and passing that had made him college football's most spectacular All-American in 1950. He became a flanker instead and, through hard work and despite his painful knee, made himself one of the finest receivers in the league.

You may find this hard to believe, but Vince Lombardi impressed me as a shy person when he first came to the Giants.

When I look back at those days now, I suppose that I mistook caution for shyness. Vinny was a perfectionist, and to his credit, I think he wanted to make sure his feet were on solid ground before he asserted himself. He was feeling his way until he was positive of what he was doing.

His previous experience had been limited to high school and college football, and in his first exhibition season with the pros, Vinny was rather careful in his dealings with the players, especially the older players. I don't mean he was timid, but I do think he was searching for a relationship with us that would make us both feel acceptable to each other. He was perceptive enough to sense that, because of the absence of any arena for physical give and take, it's often more difficult for a rookie coach to be accepted by the veterans than it is for a rookie player.

Some of us tested Vinny in his first few weeks. Charlie Conerly and I were not above trying to play as little as possible in the preseason games, and I can recall Vinny, during one exhibition, coming to Conerly and me on the sidelines and asking if we thought we'd like to get in a little work. "Maybe in a couple of more series, Coach," we replied.

What Vinny didn't realize—or, at least, what we thought he didn't realize — was that Charlie and I were trying to pick our spot. We knew that before the game was over, we'd have to go in, and we were studying the opposing team's rookie defensive backs, trying to find one with a weakness we could take advantage of.

Fortunately for Charlie and me, we were usually able to find what we were looking for, and when we felt our club was in good field position, we'd tell Vinny we were ready. In we'd go, and more times than not, we were able to complete a pass on the rookie we'd been watching.

I honestly think Vinny, at the beginning, held most of the older players in slight awe, and when we'd pull off a stunt like that, it enhanced his image of us.

Of course, that was only the first few weeks. After a while, Vinny would turn to us and say, "You and Charlie ready to go in now?"

"Give us just a few more downs," I'd say.

"Go in there now," he'd say.

The shyness or the cautiousness wore off quickly, and as Vinny began to realize that pro ball is actually a less complicated game than college ball — that the tactics and skills of the opposition are much more predictable—the Lombardi confidence began to emerge. And in direct ratio to the emergence of his confidence, our little "confidence game" submerged. . . .

One year, when we were training at Bear Mountain, New York, we lost most of our exhibition games, and Vinny decided that we were too tight. So just before our opening game, when Jim Lee Howell, our head coach, was off scouting or something, Vinny threw a beer blast for the whole team in the basement of the Bear Mountain Inn. We all loosened up, and we went on to win the Eastern championship.

Kyle's mention of the beer blast and of how much Vince enjoyed being with the Giant players made me think of how difficult it must have been for him to divorce himself from the players in Green Bay. I think he really would have liked to have been close to us—I think he felt, as I did, that the special appeal of football was the camaraderie among men with a common goal — but he knew he couldn't allow himself that luxury. To fulfill his commitment to victory, he had to go against his nature and stay aloof from us.

I remember how much he enjoyed Rookie Night, the one night when we all really relaxed together, when the rookies staged a show and made fun of training camp in general and of Vince in particular. They could be pretty rough in their caricatures, and they portrayed Vince as a dictator, and they ridiculed his manner and his physical appearance, and he sat and watched and laughed as heartily as anyone. It took a big man, and a strong man, to see himself through others' eyes, to see his foibles exposed and attacked, but Vince seemed to love it. He would have liked more opportunities to relax and laugh with his players, but he knew, in Green Bay, he couldn't be one of the boys anymore. He wasn't an assistant coach anymore. He had to be a leader.

WILLIE DAVIS: "HE MADE ME FEEL IMPORTANT"

When I first saw Willie Davis, with his big torso and his relatively slender legs—his "getaway sticks," we called them—I was skeptical about his reputation for speed. I challenged him to a race. We both got down in three-point stances, and someone yelled, "Go," and he jumped and just beat me. We did it again, and I jumped and just beat him. That was enough for me; I didn't race Willie anymore.

Willie broke into our starting lineup right away, and by 1962, he was an All-Pro defensive end. Willie made All-Pro five out of six years and, in 1966, became captain of our defensive team, by then the toughest defensive unit in pro football.

Football is a game of emotion, and what the old man excels at is motivation. I maintain that there are two driving forces in football, and one is anger, and the other is fear, and he capitalized on both of them. Either he got us so mad we wanted to prove something to him or we were fearful of being singled out as the one guy who didn't do the job.

In the first place, he worked so hard that I always felt the old man was really putting more into the game on a day-to-day basis than I was. I felt obligated to put something extra into it on Sunday; I had to, just to be even with him.

Another thing was the way he made you a believer. He told you what the other team was going to do, and he told you what you had to do to beat them, and invariably he was right. He made us believe that all we had to do was follow his theories on how to get ready for each game and we'd win.

I knew we were going to win every game we played. Even if we were behind by two touchdowns in the fourth quarter, I just believed that somehow we were going to pull it out. I didn't know exactly how or when, but I knew that sooner or later, we'd get the break we needed — the interception or the fumble or something. And the more important it was for us to win, the more certain I was we would win. . . .

Probably the best job I can remember of him motivating us was when we played the Los Angeles Rams the next-to-last game of 1967. We had already clinched our divisional title, and the game didn't mean anything to us, and he was worried about us just going through the motions. He was on us all week, and in the locker room before the game, he was trembling like a leaf. I could see his leg shaking. "I wish I didn't have to ask you boys to go out there today and do the job," he said. "I wish I could go out and do it myself. Boy, this is one game I'd really like to be playing in. This is a game that you're playing for your pride." He went on like that and he got me so worked up that if he hadn't opened that locker-room door quick, I was going to make a hole in it, I was so eager.

And we played a helluva game. We had nothing to gain, and the Rams were fighting for their lives, and they just did manage to beat us. They won by three points when they blocked a punt right near the end. . . .

You never could predict how he was going to act. The days you really expected him to go through the ceiling, he'd come in and be very soft. He'd say something like, "You're a better football team than you showed today." Or he'd blame himself and the other coaches for not preparing us properly. He'd never let us slip into a defeatist attitude. But then sometimes, when you figured you'd played pretty decent — maybe you'd lived up to what you thought he expected of you—he'd come in and drop the bomb on you. Like one time we beat Minnesota, and didn't play all that bad even though they scored a lot of points, and he walked into the locker room and said, "I'd like our front four to apologize to the rest of the team. You cheated on us today. You should apologize. You didn't play the kind of football you're capable of playing." His words kind of froze me. I felt awful.

One time, when we thought we'd played a good game, he started in on us, "Who the hell do you think you are? The Green Bay Packers? The Green Bay Nothings, that's who you are. You're only a good football team when you play well together. Individually, none of you could make up a team. You'd be nothing without me. I made you, mister."

How about the day we beat the Rams, 6–3, in Milwaukee in 1965? We'd broken a two-game losing streak, and we were all kind of happy and clowning around, and he came in and you saw his face and you knew nothing was funny anymore. He kicked a bench and hurt his foot, and he had to take something out on somebody, so he started challenging us. "Nobody wants to pay the price," he said. "I'm the only one here that's willing to pay the price. You guys don't care. You don't want to win."

We were stunned. Nobody knew what to do, and, finally, Forrest Gregg stood up and said, "My God, I want to win," and then somebody else said, "Yeah, I want to win," and pretty soon there were forty guys standing, all of us shouting, "I want to win." If we had played any football team in the world during the next two hours, we'd have beaten them by ten touchdowns. The old man had us feeling so ashamed and angry. That was his greatest asset: His ability to motivate people.

He never got me too upset personally. Of course, I had pretty thick skin by the time I got to Green Bay. Paul Brown had chewed on me so much in Cleveland that when I got to the Packers, Vince was a welcome sight. Vince and Paul Brown were similar in the way they could cut you with words and make you want to rise up to prove something to them.

I think Vince got on me sharp maybe twice in eight years. I remember once, after the Colts had been hooking me on the sweep, he ate me up, and Max McGee said "Well, I've seen everything: Vince got on Willie Davis."

Maybe he wasn't as tough on me as he was on some people, but I'll tell you, I hated to have him tell me I was fat. I hated to have him tell me I didn't have the desire anymore. He'd just say those things to the whole team — "You're all fat; you don't want to win anymore" — and I'd get so angry I couldn't wait till I got out on the field.

I guess maybe my worst days in football were the days I tried to negotiate my contracts with the old man. I'd get myself all worked up before I went in to see him. I'd drive up from my home in Chicago, and all the way, I'd keep building up my anger, telling myself I was going to draw a hard line and get just as much money as I deserved.

One year, I walked into his office feeling cocky, you know, "Roll out the cash, Jack, I got no time for small change." All he had to do was say one harsh word, and I was really going to let him have it. I never got a word in. Soon as he saw me, he jumped up and began hugging me and patting me and telling me, "Willie, Willie, Willie it's so great to see you. You're the best trade I ever made. You're a leader. We couldn't have won without you, Willie. You had a beautiful year. And, Willie, I need your help. You see, I've got this budget problem. . ."

He got me so off-balance, I started feeling sorry for him. He had me thinking, "Yeah, he's right, he's gotta save some money for the Kramers and the Greggs and the Jordans," and the next thing I knew, I was saying, "Yes, sir, that's fine with me," and I ended up signing for about half what I was going to demand. When I got out of that office and started driving back to Chicago, I was so mad at myself, I was about to drive off the highway.

The next year, finally, I got him. I went into his office and I said, "Coach, you're quite a guy. I got to be very frank, Coach, I just can't argue with you. You know, you just overwhelm me. So I've jotted down a few things I want to tell you." And I handed him a letter I'd written.

He started reading the letter — and I'd put a lot of stuff in it, like how I felt about the fans and what he'd done for me and how many years I had left — and, at first, he gave me that "heh . . . heh . . . heh" of his. Then, when he got around to how much money I wanted, he put his frown on me. He looked at me and said, "I can't argue with what you say here, Willie, but I can't pay you that much money."

"Well, coach," I said, "I really feel that way."

He thought it over a little and said, "I'll tell you what I'll give you," and named a figure not too much below what I was willing to settle for. "You'd be one of the highest-paid linemen in the whole league," he whispered, like he was afraid somebody might hear him.

"Look, Coach," I said, "I really thought hard about this, and I got to have a thousand dollars more than that. It's only a thousand dollars, but it's the difference between me driving back to Chicago today feeling real good and driving back to Chicago wanting to go head-on into somebody. It's really what I feel like I'm worth."

"If it's that important to you," he said, "you got it."

I felt good. I had my letter in my hand and started to walk out, and he said, "Hey, wait a minute. Let me have that letter. Let me keep it. I don't want you giving it to anybody else."

Blue Collar Journal: A College President's Sabbatical

John R. Coleman

The pipelayers were Stanley and Robert. I learned that by keeping my ears open and not because anyone told me their names. Robert was the weary-looking older man who had been asked if he was sober this morning. His work in the afternoon sun showed that he was a bull as a worker, sober or not. As a pipelayer, it was his job to get each length laid just right, with the joint to the next length suitably tight. That task often required straining on a long, heavy steel bar to push the pipe into place. The sweat on his brow and the dripping stream from his nose told their own story of a life of hard work. Robert talked little but worked very hard.

Stanley was the man who had got the stream of abuse when he first arrived in his girlfriend's car. That early-morning abuse was repeated by Gus over and over throughout the day. It was worst when Stanley was laying pipe with Robert, right under Gus's nose.

"Goddamnit, Stanley, I've just learned another thing you can't do —lay water pipe. If you'd stop fuckin' that pussy of yours and get some sleep, maybe you'd learn to do somethin'. You're the shittiest fucker I've had on this job."

With every pipe length, it was the same. "Goddamnit, Stanley, put some fuckin' muscle behind that bar and let's get some pipe laid."

In the end, Stanley got a rest of a sort when one particular length of pipe proved stubborn about linking up with the next.

"Goddamnit, Stanley, get out of that trench and take a fuckin' long rest. You'll never amount to nothin' nohow. Never will."

Stanley stood and watched, without a word or much change of expression on a handsome face. I was scared, imagining when I would feel Gus's wrath. I wouldn't be on the job long enough to be broken in as a pipelayer, but I felt sure there would be other situations where Gus would come down on me hard.

Gus hopped out of the backhoe's cab and into the ditch to take over the bar. By now, the red of his face was approaching that of the jacket he wore all day. But that pipe length didn't go in one bit better for him than it had for Stanley. How would he explain that?

"Goddamnit, Stanley, do you see what the fuck you've done? You've gone and got us all upset. You're a menace just by bein' around."

That's the way it went most of the afternoon.

Eventually I was ordered to shovel asphalt and clay with two men from the group of eight laborers hired from the contract agency in Atlanta. These men are the equivalent in manual occupations of the Kelly Girls in office work. I asked one of them how these agencies work.

"Simple. It's about the same way they buy and sell cows. You get there about five-thirty or six in the morning and sit on one of their bare benches until a call comes. The guy who runs it says, 'O.K., you —and you—and you.' He crowds the gangs for two or three jobs into the back of an old panel truck — no windows, no heat. Then some young punk drives us out to the jobs, drops us off, gets a receipt for us, and disappears. If he's any good, he finds out when to pick us up again. If he isn't, we just wait. We do what we're told for the day. Then it's back into the truck, except it smells more by then, and back to the hiring hall. We get paid each night—and if we're smart we get drunk right after. Same thing the next day. You never know what you'll be doing. And nobody gives a shit anyway."

He thought they were getting $1.50 an hour, but he wasn't sure. He had no idea what the agency got. Their shoveling showed the low pay, low esteem, and low morale in their work. With a new boss every day of their lives, they saw no gain in impressing any one of them with a burst of energy. Now that I was working beside two of them, I couldn't decide whether to slow down to their pace as a way of getting along with them or to keep up the morning's pace as a way of getting along with Gus. As a result, I think I went back and forth from slow to fast and puzzled everyone in turn.

No one had mentioned anything about quitting time. I assumed now that it would be 4:00, making this an eight-hour day. But that hour came and went without any signal from Gus. So did 5:00. My shovel was fully a part of me now, just like my legs and arms. Most of what we had to show for the day was already buried beneath the ground. The trench was gone and so was the pipe. Only the newly raked ground would tell a passerby that we had done a job there.

It was 6:00 when Gus called it a day.

"John, go in that truck with all that equipment. You might as well learn where all that shit goes at night."

Everything had a neat place in the trailer. There was no way of making a mistake in stowing it for the night.

Gus and Stanley were talking down the road at some length. Or rather Gus was talking. Only the four-letter words and the strong gestures carried as far as the trailer.

At last Gus came to me. "See you Monday. This wasn't our usual work. We don't often lay lines along the highway. Usually we're over in the swampy stuff. Someday soon you'll be up to your ass in mud. Seven-thirty Monday."

I took off my coveralls before I got in my car. They were muddy enough for one clean day.

Stanley was standing alone as I drove away. He had told me he rode home with Gus each night. I wondered what they talked about.

I had no zest for looking for a place for the night. I had read rooming-house ads in yesterday's paper, but they were all downtown. I'm lazy enough to prefer living near the job; more than five years of stepping out of the door of a fine old home and crossing two small fields beneath the trees on the way to my office have spoiled me for commuting. I had no idea tonight where rooms could be found in the suburbs, and I was too weary to try to find out.

I remembered passing a motel this morning that advertised rooms for "$8 a day." Compared with the prices I usually paid, that seemed a steal. It was only after I registered that I realized eight dollars represented almost three hours of labor today. But at least I could now have a bath, eat, and get into bed.

I ate at a diner nearby. Heavily. Potatoes and bread and even pie— items I don't usually buy. But tonight they seemed just right. The bill came to almost another hour of my work.

Last night I started this journal with a firm resolve to write something, no matter how brief, each day. Whatever strength I have now to keep so new a resolve comes from the knowledge that tomorrow is a day off.

Sunday, February 18

I slept almost nine hours without waking.

My back was stiff and sore. Only as the day went on did I think I might be able to use it again. I discovered muscles in my arms and legs that I had never known existed before. Two days ago I prided myself on walking fast and tall. Today I prided myself on walking at all.

The chambermaid who came in to clean told me her husband was as young as she was. "But he works outdoors on construction. It's hard work, and when he comes home all he wants to do is sleep." I told her I understood.

I have decided to stay on at this motel. Its nearness to the job and the joy of its bathtub at the end of the day are enough to persuade me to stay. I see that this means I am making only part of the transfer from my usual life to that of an hourly man. Still, it's a big change for me.

The cost bothers me, I admit. I have those two hundred dollars in traveler's checks, but I promised myself to put that amount back in my checking account at home out of my earnings on the road. To keep that pledge and to avoid having to call my oldest son for money, I have to live within what I earn and set some money aside.

I am assuming that yesterday is about what I can expect in the weeks ahead. With so long a work day, there must be overtime pay. That lets me relax a bit about eight dollars a day for the room and almost four dollars for food. I obviously can't cook in my room, but I can buy cold meats, bread, fruit, and Cokes and make my lunches there. That leaves breakfast and dinner to buy. I have an assortment of clothes that should carry me through two months with ease. I have what I wore yesterday, an old pair of jeans, a denim jacket that I think belongs to my second son, Paul, a couple of work shirts from hiking trips, and two pairs of boots. Since there is so little I have to buy, I should be able to meet the budget with ease. This may be a small amount in comparison with what I usually spend — but it's a great deal more than many Americans see in a week. Whatever I learn now about the world of work, I can't pretend I'm learning what it's like to live at the bottom of the heap.

Monday, February 19

We worked from 7:30, a little before sunrise, until 7:00, a little after sunset. My car lights were on when I drove to work, and they were on when I drove home. Saturday had apparently been a short day.

I was on one job the entire day. A different part of Gus's crew took over extending the water line on which we had worked on Saturday. I was put on the opposite side of the road with a small gang that was to lay sewer pipe. The trenches now were deeper, about nine feet as against five for the water line. They were carefully sloped so that gravity could guide the sewage's flow.

Gus acted as craneman and exhorter for the job. He oversaw everything that we did, never stopped prodding us on, still managed to keep his eyes on the rest of his men on the site, and had time left over for brief fisticuffs with a passing truck driver who complained that one of our trucks blocked the road. I would never have considered getting into a fight with Gus; the truck driver probably wished he hadn't thought of it either.

We had two men laying the heavy clay pipes in the ditch. One was Robert, the stolid, steady man I had watched lay pipe before. With him was Langston, a taller, much younger, lighter-skinned black. His every movement was swift and free, and he furnished a line of reveries and gags that kept pace with the work he did. His worn and faded denims would have been the envy of our well-to-do students. Robert and Langston seemed to have little in common but their race, yet they worked as a team in a way that showed they had done this together before.

I was on top of the trench. My sole job was to shovel dirt back into the ditch to give a first covering to the pipe before a tractor operator came along and finished burying the line — though I never did figure out why it was necessary to do the hand job at all. The tractor did its work with such speed that it seemed idle for me to be messing around with that first layer of dirt. I had heard someone on Saturday say that Robert had been a pipelayer longer than anyone else on the job, so I asked him at one point why I was doing what I did.

"That's just the way we do it," he explained.

I don't suppose I could have done the job much better even if I had learned what it was about. It's just not something that can be done badly or well. Slow and fast were the only options open to me.

There is a lot of time for counting on a job like that. I kept track of the shovel loads of dirt needed to bury each of six lengths of pipe and averaged them out to ninety or so. We buried over one hundred lengths — nine thousand shovelfuls for the day.

I tried different techniques for doing the job. Left hand on top of the shovel. Right hand on top. Swing to the left. Swing to the right. When any lifting at all seemed too much for my arms, I tried just pushing whatever dirt lay near the ditch's edge into the hole. There wasn't enough dirt there to make much difference, so it was back to lifting again.

Eleven solid hours of it, broken only by lunch, two trips to the canteen truck for milk and the toilet for relief, and an occasional stint pushing new pipe lengths into the pit for Robert and Langston to lay.

I quickly found that I couldn't lift the clay pipe lengths alone. I had seen a worker named Braden do it easily when the pipes were laid along the embankment this morning. Braden was a white ex-Marine and so powerfully built that he almost seemed a match for Gus. It didn't surprise me that he could swing those pipes to his shoulder and down again without a crash. But when a much smaller man, Carl, filled in for a while for Gus on the backhoe and then swung a pipe length onto his shoulder with almost the same ease, I felt underprivileged.

Gus saw me try to lift one of the lengths, fail, and have to push it across the ground to the ditch's edge.

"Better hit the Wheaties, John," he called.

"Give me a week," I replied. But I knew that might not be enough.

At one point in handling the pipe, I smashed the watch on my arm. Then I understood why I was the only one who seemed to know the time before that. Watches and pipeline work don't mix.

After that I tried to tell the time by the sun. My shadow took forever to lengthen on the dirt pile where I worked. It was as if time stopped just because the watch I inherited from my father had stopped. We had seen fleets of trucks go out early in the morning from the electric utility down the road. I kept watching for them to return for the night. Eventually they came in, stirring up clouds of dust that blew in our faces. That meant our quitting time too shouldn't be far away — but it was. The sun clung stubbornly to its place in the sky. There were trees at the far edge of the field, and I waited for the sun to edge closer to their tops and kept myself from looking up from the dirt for, say, two full pipe lengths. When I did look up, I couldn't see that the trees and the sun were one bit closer together.

The men on the utility trucks must be home, showered, and beered by now, I thought. Maybe I chose the wrong job.

At last the sun gave up and yielded to the trees. Once it did, darkness came with merciful swiftness. We put the last tools away by the light from the trailer.

Stanley told me with a smile in one break that Gus was always after his ass. The abuse seemed to roll off him. I wondered how. Two days on the job told me I couldn't take that treatment. I needed some bit of encouragement.

Gus finally made the day for me in the last minutes, as we were cleaning up in the semidarkness. "John, clean away that shit around the hydrant. Please."

Please.

I'd have done it with my toothbrush.

Tuesday, February 20

I count. My name went on a time card today.

Gus had to ask my last name in order to put it on. Last names are almost unknown here. I think Goddamnit is Stanley's other name, but beyond that Gus is the only man whose full name I know.

The boss told me that my first job this morning was important in determining whether or not the water line would eventually pass its pressure tests. I spent an hour putting rubber rings in the flanges of the eight-inch and six-inch pipe lengths. Each ring had to fit perfectly, and there was to be no dirt at all in the seal. To get the pipe ends clean took a cloth and a lot of blowing. The blowing had the effect of transferring most of the reddish brown dust from the pipe end to my face, but I felt almost semiskilled for that hour. The feeling disappeared later in the day when I saw the pipes deringed and cleaned all over again because of the dirt they gathered as they bumped along the ground on their way to the trench for laying.

For most of the day, Stanley, Langston, and I were a pipelaying crew under the direction of the project engineer. Dick is the only college man here; he's a Cornell civil engineer. Where everyone else seems to fit in with the pipes, machinery, mud, and tools of the trade, he just doesn't look quite right. He has a gentleness and a quizzical look that would go better at Haverford than it does here. Even his few obscenities seem out of place. Most of the time Dick works the transit and sets up the laser beam used in getting the sewer line straight and properly sloped. Today he operated the backhoe too, but with more determination than style.

The work seemed easy by comparison to the trench shoveling. And there was time for fun. The kidding that went back and forth among the four of us flowed easily from our work together. I was happy working with each of these men; I thought they enjoyed the day too. I even thought that we were making good headway. We had laid over eight hundred feet of sewer by sunset.

Then Gus called us into the trailer at checkout time. The entire crew was there to hear him. He proceeded to lay us low.

"You call eight hundred feet in a fuckin' day a good job? Why, Ronnie and me and two colored fellows from the part-time agency once laid nineteen hundred feet in one day. And once when Robert was so drunk I had to grab him by the fuckin' seat of the pants to keep him from fallin' in the ditch, we laid twice *that* much. You ask Robert."

Robert said nothing. He didn't even smile, although I think he heard.

"The trouble with you guys is you're all ironheads. You don't think. You use your muscles and your feet when you should use your heads. Use the machines. Let them do the fuckin' work. But use them right. Get the fuckin' cable from the machines straight up and down when you're tryin' to place pipe or you're wastin' your fuckin' time.

And my fuckin' money too. I get two dollars a foot for layin' that pipe. You laid eight hundred feet. How do we make money that way? The damn machine alone is worth forty dollars an hour.

"It all comes down to the supervisor. Dick, you did a shit of a job with this crew. How can you boast about it?"

"I didn't," was Dick's quiet reply.

"You've got to plan ahead, Dick. You're always thinkin' an hour or two behind where you're workin'. I'm an hour or two ahead. That's the difference between a hundred-dollar-a-week man and a thousand-dollar-a-week man."

And on, and on.

Gus's lungs match his muscles; he seemingly cannot tire. Yet, strangely, he didn't seem all that angry as he dressed us down. It was disconcerting, too, that his sons, about nine and seven, climbed all over his shoulders while he talked. They grinned. We didn't.

"And who the hell moved that stake to make it look as if you had come to the end of the line? I know damn well it doesn't belong there —and you guys ain't finished by twenty feet or more. Who's the shit that tried that trick?"

We had all seen it moved. But no one squealed.

When I got back to my room, I rather liked what I saw in the mirror. Two days outdoors in the Georgia sun had given me a healthier tan than I had ever had before. It was reddish brown and remarkably even. Unfortunately, almost all of it came off in the bathtub or on the towel.

Wednesday, February 21

I was happy driving to work this morning. The muscles were no longer as sore as before, I knew some of the men I'd be working with for the day, and I felt that I was beginning to fit in with the crew. At the diner where I had breakfast once again, I felt that I was fully a part of the blue-collar world. Two gas station attendants, a schoolbus driver, and the short-order cook knew mine was a familiar face and said hello. I was proud of the fact that I would probably work more hours and use up more physical energy that day than most of the others with whom I ate eggs and toast.

Whatever pride I felt lasted through the morning, even though there was not much work to do. This particular project is almost complete. We will soon move to a site somewhere southwest of the city. What remains to be done here is mainly cleaning up. I spent the morning, therefore, raking the dirt on a slope beneath which our sewer lay. It is part of Gus's contract that the land is left clean and level after the pipes are laid. The sun was warm on the slope. I made more of the raking than was necessary, perhaps, but it did fill the time while Gus was away. I was content.

I had time too to watch the cars that raced by all morning on I-285. Many of the drivers in them were salesmen, I felt sure. I found myself feeling sorry for them and imagining that some of them would surely be happier raking on the slope rather than rushing to make the same sales pitch again. I jump in my thinking from the conceit that no one is quite like me to the bigger conceit that everyone is just like me. This morning I was at that latter point. I was sure I had found a rhythm in my life that men and women in those cars must envy. My job didn't have much status or pay, but it had a sense of immediate utility and also of peace.

The afternoon killed that feeling completely. We did nothing. Almost six hours of nothing. That turned out to be harder than anything I had yet done, even though we were being paid. Back in my job at Haverford, there never was a time without work to do. Sometimes what I did may have been make-work and inefficient, but, when worse came to worst and I wanted to avoid digging into one of the piles of unfinished work on my desk, I could always turn to the latest report from the American Council on Education and persuade myself that I needed to read it — or I could stare out the window in such a way that, if one of my secretaries caught me at it, she would be kind enough to assume I was planning another speech.

But this afternoon there was no escape from doing nothing. Almost everyone except Al and me seemed to be off somewhere doing something. Not us. We stood, first on one foot, then on the other. We tried the north side of the road, then the south. We stood right where Gus, who was in the trailer's office a good part of the time, could see us. Then we got out of his sight. Any small task that Gus gave us came as a relief. We did it with zeal. We even did it over again when that was possible.

Even conversation didn't work as it had in the morning. There's only so much you can say on the subject of boredom before it gets boring in turn. I looked at the cars racing by on I-285 now and thought a salesman's job wouldn't be such a bad deal after all. At least there would always be something to do.

I think it bothered Gus that he couldn't think of anything for us to do at this site. He is never still himself and likes motion all around him. But today he was stumped.

At one point he sent me with the company's mechanic on a one-hour trip on a truck. I was useless on the errand, but I was out of the way.

We had loaded six pipe lengths, a couple of valves, and numerous fittings onto the truck. They were the last loose pieces of sewer or water line left on the site. Our job now was to take them back to the county's water and sewer department to get credit for them. One large water valve had a missing cap, and I learned from the mechanic that the valve was worth about $250 complete but was of little value without the cap. He hoped for our company's sake that the receiving man in the county yard wouldn't notice it until it was too late.

That man spotted it at once. He stood with his hands jammed deep into the pockets of the county's uniform tan coveralls and looked straight at the mechanic.

"We can't take it. It won't pass."

I was impressed that he saw it so fast. My eyes were much slower. I missed seeing the size of the bill that the mechanic drew from his pocket. All I saw was one hand fly out to receive it and the bill go deep into the county's coveralls.

"Well, maybe we can fix it up."

That was the high point of my day.

As I waited for the papers acknowledging receipt of the parts to be filled out, I got talking with a laborer on a similar mission for another sewer company. He appeared to be thirty years of age. My mouth fell open when he told me he used to be in sales work but had shifted to this job three months ago. "I couldn't take the pressure there any more," he said. "I'm happy as hell now." I almost asked him what college he was president of.

We hadn't talked more than a minute or so when he asked me how much money I made. It has been a long time since anyone other than one of my children or the Internal Revenue Service asked me that. I told him. He said he was making $3.75 an hour, a dollar more than I was. He didn't seem pitying or even contemptuous toward me. He just seemed to take it for granted that this was the way labor markets worked. Some people got a good rate, and others got a poor one for doing exactly the same job. It occurred to me that this man knew what some of our labor economics texts still have not learned about the world of work. . . .

Thursday, March 1

We wallowed in mud which was just about as deep as Gus had told me it would be that first day. A shovelful of it made a sucking sound as it pulled away from the ground and thick, black water oozed in to fill the space left behind. It was the kind of mud that boys always hope to find and that their fathers always hope to avoid. But the work still moved along nicely. We came to the last pipe length. It was too long by a few feet. All that had to be done was to start up the saw and make the one cut of the day. We tried it. The engine was out of gas.

That left us with a problem. We had forgotten to bring the gas can. Just then Gus came along. The time required for someone to go back to the trailer to get the gas gave Gus ample time to discourse at length on just how stupid we were. It was quite a colorful talk.

He was down on everybody today. His invective is endless. There are no shadings between what he says when we have made a major error and when we've been just a little bit stupid. Only the length of what he says tells whether it's a big deal or not.

Dick caught its fullest force at the day's end. Under his direction, we moved out of the swamp to bury a twenty-four-inch storm pipe under what would be one of the developer's major roads. It was the biggest pipe I had worked on, and I felt I was in the big league now. We were within half an hour of being finished with the job of laying the pipe and connecting it to the huge pre-cast concrete blocks that marked both edges of the road and the intake and outlet for the drain. We had followed stakes put there by the developer's engineers in placing the headwalls and pipes. Gus then appeared. One look was all he needed to know that we were wrong.

"You're goin' to have the fuckin' headwall in the middle of the fuckin' road. Use your mother-fuckin' head, you shits."

"But, Gus, we're just doing what the stakes said to do."

"I don't give a damn what the stakes say. Look, you can see where the fuckin' road is goin' on this side. And you can see where it's fuckin' well goin' on the other side. How in shit is it going to bend around to miss your goddamn headwalls?"

"But the engineers put the stakes . . ."

"Fuck the engineers. It fuckin' well ain't right. Use your goddamn eyes."

That was just the warmup. It was followed by speculation on Dick's parentage and the quality of education given engineers in college these days. This was the longest of his speeches to date. I never found out whether Gus was really right. It hardly mattered, anyway. So far as we were concerned, if Gus said the stakes were wrong, they were wrong.

Dick is a man one has to like. The six of us on his crew were solidly united behind him, not because we were so sure he was right but because he was our man at this point. He was the one who sweated it out while we tried to maneuver that monstrous pipe into place. But our support was of no use to him now. We stood silent and embarrassed until the boss was done.

Gus hadn't really exhausted his theme when he had to stop. A county safety inspector came by and, after looking over the crew, took Gus aside for a chat. When Gus returned, he was a little milder in his tone. But not much.

"Startin' Monday, everyone wears the hard hat I gave you. Every fuckin' one of you. And, Stanley, you either cut that goddamn long hair or you put it up in a net, do you hear?"

Stanley heard. But he didn't like what he heard. "I ain't wearin' no net."

"Suit yourself. It's the net or the hair. I don't give a shit which you choose. We're goin' to be safe. This is a fuckin' hard-hat job, just like I been tellin' you."

We were silent in the back of the truck as we rode back to the trailer tonight. Only Carl, the backhoe operator, could find the right words. He spoke without anger or blame. He simply stated the facts.

"One good thing about Gus," he said, "is that he's always right—even when he's wrong."

Friday, March 2

This was my last day here.

It was to have been the second to the last. I had told Gus earlier that I had to get back to Philadelphia and would be quitting tomorrow. But it rained, a soft, steady rain beginning in late morning, so we were sent home at 1:00—that is, the newer men such as Al and I were sent home, while the veterans were kept busy on make-work jobs for the afternoon. The forecast is for more rain tomorrow. Gus has decided there's no more work this week.

We were laying a twelve-inch clay sewer pipe in a fifteen-foot trench along the main highway. This was not only the deepest trench we had seen, it was also far and away the heaviest pipe I had been asked to lift. It took two of us—and one was Braden, the ex-Marine, so that alone is like having two men there—to lift each length into the bobcat tractor's bucket to get it to the trench. I knew in those morning hours exactly what "straining one's gut out" meant. If ever there was a time to get a hernia, this was it. It helped me to see that Braden was straining too. That was brutal work by any man's test. I'm frankly proud that I did as well as I did.

These were good men to work with. In my days with them, I never saw any of them stand idle while someone else was straining on a job; there are different skill levels and rates of pay, of course, but the men all share in the loads.

Even as I left, Gus was yelling about something in the rain. That seemed the right way to end.

Braden asked me this morning, "Have you ever worked for a swearing fucker like Gus?"

I admitted that I hadn't. I could have added too that I'd do it again.

Saturday, March 3   *Charlotte, North Carolina*

A free day that I hadn't counted on until yesterday.

The weather was wet enough to prove Gus right again. We couldn't have worked. I have to be in Philadelphia by Monday, but I didn't want to go home yet. It would be too tempting to get caught up in campus affairs if I stayed at my house more than one night. So I drove part of the way home, found another eight-dollar motel, and settled in to read.

Placed somewhere between Atlanta and Haverford, I find my thoughts running easily to contrasts between Gus Reed's leadership style and my own. If someone had told me about Gus before I made that first telephone call two weeks ago, I might never have called him at all. That would have been too bad.

There's not much of his remarkable style I could copy back on the campus even if I wanted to. Suppose I singled out some academic department at a faculty meeting and delivered my thoughts as Gus did. "You're the shittiest bunch of professors I ever saw. You call what you're doing good teaching? Why, I fucking well recall when I handled classes twice the size of yours and still gave every goddamn student more fucking attention than you bastards do. You don't amount to nothing and never will."

After a period of silence, a few of the faculty would say, "Let's talk this matter out." The peacemakers among them would suggest that we refer "the president's concern" to a standing committee. One or two professors, once they saw that everyone else was shocked, would predictably take the other side and utter words they'd gag over at any other time: "I think the president's right." But most of the faculty would simply agree that it was time to have me committed to the state hospital, which fortunately is only a few blocks away.

No, I couldn't use Gus's style. But it sure would be interesting to try.

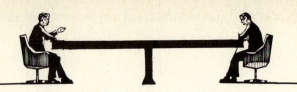

4

MAKING IT

"They might mess with him once, but no one messed with Walter Cronkite a second time."

—David Halberstam

"Making it" is a long-standing concern. Whereas in earlier times it seems that hard work was associated with making it (i.e., succeeding), more recently the notion of making it has taken on a somewhat different connotation. As Daniel Rodgers observed in his excellent book, *The History of the Work Ethic,* the notion that hard work leads to success appears increasingly to be more of a myth than a fact. As organizations have become larger and more impersonal it appears that more than hard work and competence at one's work tasks are required to make it. While competence and diligence are still relevant, it seems that often the appearance of competence is less strongly correlated with actual performance than managers frequently assume. So many things combine to determine the results of one's efforts that attributions of success or failure to individual persons, while still made, seem tenuous. Moreover, given the fact that these attributions are often difficult to support with documentation, appearances (and the manipulation of appearances) often play an important role in determining an individual's success. Under these conditions success is a judgment call.

The contrast between this view of making it and the more traditional view is well illustrated by a story related by Karl Weick. It seems that three umpires were discussing their job of calling balls and strikes. One umpire said, "I calls them as they is." A second umpire said, "I calls them as I sees them." The third umpire observed, "They ain't nothin' till I calls them." In this view, making it is seen as having strong elements of subjectivity, arbitrariness, and even invention of facts.

Furthermore, our revised view of making it suggests that many of the elements which contribute to a person being judged successful involve social, political, and personal attributes which may have little to do with the technical aspects of one's work, but in actuality contribute a great deal both to a person's ability to get things done and to being called successful. Finally, as the readings in this chapter suggest, making it for many people has a more basic component than being successful: making it often means merely surviving!

The selections in this section deal with how people make it in organizations. The first piece is taken from Culbert and McDonough's award-winning book, *The Invisible War.* This selection describes how people in organizations pursue their own interests simultaneously with achieving success in the organization via the process of alignment. Culbert and McDonough view alignment as the key process for understanding what organizations are about; unfortunately we did not have the space to reprint other important ideas from their book. We urge the reader to consult other chapters in their book — especially chapters 6 – 8, in which they describe the survival tactics of framing, fragmenting, and playing it both ways.

"Managing Your Boss" (Gabarro and Kotter) explores another issue which many managers confess has been a major key to their success or failure in organizations. Often subordinates wait passively for their superiors to define their mutual relationship. This article points out how subordinates can play more active roles.

The next four articles reveal a number of skills which people use both to survive and to succeed in organizations. Terkel's interview with Diane Wilson points out a somewhat different set of techniques for managing one's boss. Halberstam's account of the career of Walter Cronkite reveals how a combination of elements contributed to Cronkite's success. Some of these elements are clearly congruent with the traditional view of how to make it; however, much of Cronkite's success reflected his ability to manage power relationships within CBS. Schrank's description of life in the furniture factory and Dalton's account of the ratebuster reveal a series of events which surrounded the ability of individuals to survive and to succeed. Finally, Vice Admiral Stockdale's review of parts of his career reveals the importance of personal values in making it — succeeding and surviving.

The Invisible War: Pursuing Self-Interest at Work

Samuel A. Culbert and John J. McDonough

Each time people enter a new work situation they engage in the implicit process of *aligning* personal values, interests, and skills with what they perceive to be the task requirements of their job. They seek an orientation that maximizes self-pursuits and organizational contribution. *Alignment* is our term for the orientation that results from such

From *The Invisible War: Pursuing Self-Interest at Work* by Samuel A. Culbert and John J. McDonough. Copyright © 1980 John Wiley & Sons, Inc., Publishers. Reprinted by permission of John Wiley & Sons, Inc.

an effort, however implicitly this takes place. Once such an orientation has been evolved, it becomes a self-convenient lens through which all organizational happenings are viewed. That is, once people hit on an alignment — an orientation that lines self-interests up with the task-requirements of their jobs — this alignment serves to alert them to meanings they can use in promoting and supporting their personal and organizational endeavors, and to meanings put forth by others which threaten the credibility and relevance of what they are pursuing.

Not all alignments are effective. That is, the orientation some people use is too far removed either from the needs and obligations of their jobs or from expressing the inner themes that can make their jobs personally meaningful. We say an individual possesses an "effective" alignment when the orientation directing that person's actions and view of reality allows him or her to represent important self-interests while making a contribution to the organization. We say an individual lacks an effective alignment when important discrepancies exist between what that person inwardly values, endeavors to express, does well, and needs to do in order to satisfy what he or she perceives to be the task requirements of the job.

Now we can return to the questions raised at the beginning of this chapter.

Why do people with the same job perform their assignments so differently?

Easy, they have unique interests, values, and competencies to bootleg into their jobs at every opportunity.

Why do people with comparable organizational goals see the same situation differently and fight unyieldingly over which interpretation is correct?

Easy, while they may be striving to attain comparable organizational objectives, what they are striving to attain in their lives and careers is very different. This causes them to attend differently to each of the elements in a given situation. Finally,

What determines the specific way individuals decide to perform their jobs and how they interpret each situation?

Easy again, it's what we've termed alignment. People proceed with a job orientation that spontaneously spins out interpretations and meanings that serve the unique way they need reality constructed in order to be a "success." How individuals do a job and what they see are influenced by what they find personally interesting, by the concepts they can master and the skills they can peform with excellence, by the self-ideals and values they seek to attain, by their unique ideas of what constitutes career advancement, by what they believe will score on the checklist that others will use in evaluating their performance, and by what they genuinely believe the organization needs from someone in their role.

Few people are all that aware of their alignment. Even fewer are conscious of the fact that systematic biases permeate their view of the organizational world. And, almost no one understands that such biases play a major role in making organizations effective. All this is because most people work their alignment out implicitly and take its presence for granted until a change in the external scene, in other people's views of their effectiveness, or in their own sense of satisfaction show it to be obsolete. Then they can appreciate what they lost and strive for a new alignment that will again allow them to satisfy self-interests and personal pride while getting acclaim for doing a good job. For example, consider what happened to a middle manager named Pete who had a marvelous alignment until he got promoted and suddenly found himself faced with a serious gap between his own and the organization's definition of success.

Pete was one of twenty in his corporation who, some five years ago, agreed to take on a newly created mission, that of improving communications and managerial competence within his company. This function seemed right up Pete's alley. He'd attended sensitivity training sessions, had a reputation of being genuinely concerned with people, and was respected up and down the ranks for his leadership ability even though he had not burned up the track with his progress.

Pete saw the new assignment as a chance to bolster a lagging career. He had never been overly concerned with rising in the hierarchy, but his failure to take a fast track to the top was presenting him with daily redundancies that left him feeling somewhat stale. At forty-five he needed another challenge and this assignment held the potential to revitalize his career. Eagerly he accepted.

Pete threw himself into the new position. He enrolled in outside courses and hired skilled consultants to design training programs for the corporation's managers. Whenever possible he assisted the consultants and within a short time he understood their technology and was able to play a role in tailoring their inputs to the specific needs of his corporation. His learning continued and soon he was running programs on his own, involving personnel from each divisional level. Almost immediately his reputation as a man who genuinely cared was enhanced by widespread recognition of his competence in the management development technologies. And he was no soft touch either. He aggressively challenged managers on their "self-sealing" logics and constructed boat-rocking experiments to confront higher-ups with the demotivating and profit-eroding consequences of their autocratic styles.

Pete's involvements took an exciting turn with the advent of minority and women's consciousness. If the corporation's managers weren't racist, their de facto hiring and promotion policies were. This meant a greater volume of work and warranted an increase in the size of his staff. From a resource base that started with himself and a secretary, his department increased to two professionals, an administrative assistant, and two secretaries. Their operation hummed. They did career development counseling with secretaries. They got involved with the corporation's recruiters, both to encourage the hiring of blacks and females and to create programs that would support the new employees' progress in an essentially all white male management structure. They hired racial-awareness consultants to get managers in touch with their prejudices and help them work these out. And with this heightened workload, Pete even found time to continue his efforts in getting managers to identify areas in which their style intruded on the effectiveness of others.

Pete also had marvelous latitude in job definition which he exploited to match his interests and values. He enrolled in personal growth courses, attended conventions, joined professional associations, and on occasion even used the company plane. Because Pete identified both with the welfare of people and the productivity of the corporation and was concerned that his work produce tangible outcomes, his indulgences were hardly noticed — rather they were seen as part of his power. The people on his staff looked up to him and nondefensively brought him their toughest problems for coaching and support. His credibility with people lower in the hierarchy provided him a position of influence with those at the highest corporate levels. And, delightfully for Pete, his reputation among blacks and women was impeccable.

Within a couple of years Pete had worked out an ideal *alignment*. He had a way of engaging each constituency that allowed them to see how his actions related to results they valued. There seemed to be a 99 percent overlap between his personal definition of success and the missions and responsibilities assigned to him, and no one in the company could perform them better.

The other nineteen managers receiving the same charter as Pete, but working elsewhere in the corporation, didn't fare nearly as well. Perhaps lack of know-how, perhaps enculturation in the corporation's way of doing things, or perhaps a different tolerance for conflict had made them reluctant to aggressively challenge higher-ups. With time, to a greater or lesser degree, their roles degenerated to those of commiserator and management "go-for." They always seemed to be on the defensive, trying to prove themselves rather than challenging others to be more excellent. Their weakness and low-keyed tactics made Pete's strength and accomplishments look all the more potent.

Eventually those sitting in upper corporate echelons took notice of the overall situation and decided that Pete was the role model of what they were trying to achieve. They approached Pete with an offer of a promotion if he would agree to supervise and train the other nineteen managers. Pete's first reaction was to accept, but something held him back. At the time, he didn't understand his hesitancy, so he merely used it to negotiate a sweeter deal. He would not take responsibility for the others, there were too many bad habits to overcome. But he would step up a level in his current territory and accept overall responsibility for recruitment, career planning, minority advancement, and improved managerial functioning.

Pete's promotion put him on the same level with other line managers. He became a regular member of the management team and now directly supervised three managers who were responsible for about forty professional employees and oversaw the hiring of outside consultants.

Unfortunately, at this point, his alignment fell apart and his work life became filled with aggravation. *First,* his former associates began treating him like their boss, which he was, and this severely undermined his ability to coach and openly suggest. Now his suggestions were heard as orders and his inadvertent questions were received as well-thought-out criticisms.

Next, his relationships with blacks and women went to pot. His elevation in the hierarchy caused him to be seen as manager rather than human rights worker and he was treated to rounds of Mau-Mauing and confrontations, as what formerly had been received as his in-group remarks were interpreted as racial and sexist slurs.

Next, Pete found that the added amount of time his new job required for supervision, staff meetings, and report writing reduced the time available for the internal consulting role he prized.

On top of everything else, a "screw-up" in another division involving a racial-awareness consultant set off a reactionary wave up to an executive vice-president who responded by ordering sharp cutbacks in the use of outside consultants. For Pete, this had the personal effect of cutting off sources of his support and learning and the task effect of withdrawing the quality resources needed to keep his operation competently stationed and challenging to the status quo.

To top these disappointments, after about three months in the new job, Pete's boss called him in for a coaching session where he received word that his new peers were concerned that he was hurting his career by appearing to be such a deviant and advocate for minorities. Pete returned to his office screaming, "What the hell is going on here, these are the same jokers who wanted me promoted because I *was* such a deviant?!"

This was the last straw. Not only were his former constituents treating him like one of the "other guys" but the "other guys" were claiming that he was too much of a deviant for them.

From our perspective Pete was caught without either a personally effective or an organizationally successful alignment. His personal viewpoint wasn't registering anywhere. Nowhere was he actively shaping reality. His alignment had become obsolete. He was in the same position his nineteen former counterparts had found themselves in when they were charged with a mission to which they could not personally relate and thus could not confidently assert an articulate point of view.

Incidentally, and no pun intended, this is not a case of the "Peter Principle." We know Pete and he's anything but a person who had been promoted above his level of competence. We believe it is just a matter of time before Pete constructs a new alignment, one that allows him to use his new job for personal expression and to further the missions he values. But until he gets realigned, the self-deliberations entailed in trying to match self-interests with what seems to be required by his job will provide him with many lonely hours of unhappiness and frustration.

Pete's story was chosen because it illustrates the active dimension of the orienting process we call alignment. It shows the importance of an individual's commitment to inner values. That Pete could succeed, both inwardly and outwardly, where nineteen others could not is a tribute to his success in finding a good match between his personal needs and interests and what he saw as needed by the job. He had an effective alignment. The nineteen others lacked an effective alignment and most of them became either *cynics* or *careerists*. The cynics converged on alignments that subordinated the organization's needs to their own interests and values. They saw management's view as constraints to be navigated around, not perspectives to be joined and possibly learned from. Conversely, the careerists adopted alignments that subordinated their personal interests and values to what they thought would score on the organization checklist. They ground out workshop after workshop, training event after training event, but without the conversations and conflicts that could budge the status quo.

The concept of alignment, and Pete's story, provides support for most people's contention that repackaging themselves to fit a particular job or role does not constitute a sell-out to the job, although to an outsider their compromises frequently appear fatal. As Pete's situation illustrates, people need to shift alignments when they change jobs or experience a new set of external demands, even though their interests, skills and values remain the same. While self-interests remain relatively constant, the form in which they are pursued and expressed must shift. How often we've seen people criticize the way their boss operates only to themselves embody much of the same behavior as they shift alignments upon moving up to the boss's level in the organization.

In summary, we see the concept of alignment as a key addition to how people should be thinking about organizations. There's a level of organization residing within each individual that explains how that person does his or her job and views external organization events. If there's an external organization that determines how groups of people relate in doing work together then there's an *internal organization*, far more encompassing than an individual's personality, that determines how individuals within groups transact their business and work for the greater institutional good. Moreover, despite their lack of prominence in how people present themselves, self-interests are a dominant factor in determining what gets produced in the name of organizationally required product and how what is produced is received. And you don't need the skills of a psychoanalyst to understand these self-interests. You merely need to comprehend what an individual is trying to express personally and achieve in his or her career, and what he or she perceives as making a valuable contribution to the job. At every point personal needs and organization goals impact on one another, and it's always up in the air whether the needs of the job or the interests of the individual will swamp the other or whether a synergy of interests will evolve.

Thus *alignment* is our term for the highly personal orientation one takes to the job that must be known before we can comprehend the meaning and intent of someone's actions. Sometimes people do different things for the same reason. Sometimes people do the same things for different reasons. Without knowing people's alignment, taking their actions on face value — even those with a direct connection to bottom-line product — leads to erroneous conclusions. The only way to comprehend what people are about is to know what they are trying to express and achieve personally and what assumptions they are making about the organizational avenues for doing so.

At this point we provide a guide to comprehending the personal side of an individual's orientation to the job. It's a set of questions which, when thoughtfully answered, provide a new perspective on why an individual does his or her job the way he or she does it, and why that person views organization events in a particular way. Add in the task requisites of the job, as the individual sees them, and you've got that person's alignment. Incidentally, we've had marvelous results using an abbreviated list of these questions as preparation for team-building meetings at which a boss and his or her subordinates get together for a long session to discuss opportunities for improving their work-group's effectiveness. Twenty to forty minutes each, around the group, and the edge comes off many premeeting criticisms. Instead of being programmed to fault one another for inadequacy, the discussion takes a constructive turn as participants contrast the fit between an individual's needs and talents with what participants see as the task requisites of that person's job.

The questions we use in seeking to understand the self-interest side of an individual's alignment fall into three categories: personal, career, and organizational. Specifically we ask questions drawn from, but not limited to, the following list.

SELF-INTEREST QUESTIONS

Personal

What are you trying to prove to yourself and, very importantly, why?

What are you trying to prove to others? Give an instance that illustrates why and how.

What style of life are you trying to maintain or achieve? (Does this entail a change in income? geography? family size? etc.)

Name the people who have played significant roles in your life and say what those roles were.

What dimensions would you like to add to your personal life and why?

What motto would you like to have carved on your tombstone and how do you want to be remembered by the people who are close to you?

Career

What profession do you want to wind up in? (If you are an engineer and you say "management," tell why. If you are not in that profession, say how you plan to get into it.)

How did you, or will you, develop competency in that profession?

What do you want to accomplish in that profession?

What honor or monument would you like to have symbolize your success in that profession? Say why it would constitute a personal hallmark.

Organizational

What has been your image in your organization and what would you like it to be?

Describe a bum-rap or overly simplistic category others have used in describing you and tell either why you are different now or why their statement was simplistic or too categorical.

What is the next lesson you need to learn and what are your plans for doing so?

What would you like to be doing two to five years out?*

What would you like to be doing ten years out?*

While we encourage people to share perspectives generated by these questions with work associates whom they trust, we do not recommend that they reveal specific instances in which self-interests played a role in determining one of their organizational actions. We don't because we fear that others, however well-intentioned, will inadvertently misuse such candor later on. What we advocate is that each individual simply provide associates a more valid context for viewing his or her goals and accomplishments. . . .

CONCLUSION

It's appropriate that we've saved our favorite story for the end. It's a story about a manager who embodies the best of both the subjective and the rational approaches to leadership and for us is a symbol that it can be done. This manager is able to go toe to toe with hard-boiled characters like Charlie and at the same time remain sensitive to the contributions made by leaders like Fred.** He's a manager who searches for ways of relating to the uniqueness of those reporting to him while he shuns calling "objective" that which he sees as arbitrary and a matter of personal convenience.

The manager we have in mind demonstrated the effectiveness of much that we are advocating in three distinct settings: industry, education, and public service. First, he fought his way through the highly competitive world of consumer products where he became chairman of the board of one of the nation's largest and most successful conglomerates. Next, in the educational field, he became the dean of a large and prestigious professional school, instituting changes that brought national recognition to that institution. And most recently he was the President's choice to head a world-renowned agency and this appointment brought instant acclamation from the Senate Hearings Committee. All this took place before his forty-seventh birthday!

In our view the key to this manager's success lies in his ability to see the connection between personal effectiveness and organizational efficiency. To him, these are highly related issues. He believes that organizations exist to serve people, not the other way around, and he constantly searches to understand what people are trying to achieve in the way of personal meaning and career success. Nevertheless, his style is one which frequently gets misinterpreted as soft and permissive leadership and does not produce an easy route to universal love and appreciation. His understanding of personal projects allows him to penetrate many of the facades people construct, and this makes him the target of behind-the-scenes ambivalence and face-to-face suspicion. Let's examine his impact more closely.

In the first place, he resists spending the bulk of his energies responding to problems defined by others as "crises." This orientation allows him to take tough stands with respect to the succession of "crises" any top administrator faces, and which, if passed down through the organization, can make it impossible for anyone to align self-interests with the task requirements of their job in a way that's constructive for the institution. In the short run his "nonresponsiveness" makes him vulnerable to the charge that he is not on top of a situation. In the long run, however, he frees himself and the people in his organization from the oppressive burden of always responding to someone else's fire drill.

We certainly don't want to mislead you into thinking that our hero, or any other leader, could emerge from each of these settings totally unscarred. To the contrary, on his way to the board chairmanship he spent more than three years going eyeball to eyeball with a manager whose style was the antithesis of his own and whose subordinates consider him to be "the biggest prick you're ever going to find in a chief executive's office." When our leader realized that he was going to be locked in mortal combat for as long as he stayed with the conglomerate, he began to look around. That's when he got into education. Some say things got too hot for him to handle. In our minds his decision revealed that he saw more to life than surviving corporate death struggles.

It's interesting to contrast the subordinates who value his leadership style with those who don't. Those who see flexibility in the construction of their own alignments generally appreciate his style. But he causes fits among those with careerist and martyr mentalities. These people are confused by his respect for the personal side of their alignments. They mistake his sensitivity to what is personally mean- ingful to them as agreement with their self-beneficial formulations of what the organization needs to do. Consequently they experience small betrayals when learning of a decision he takes after surveying their perspective. What they don't understand is that our hero seri- ously considers competing perspectives prior to making a decision and that his integration is almost always original, with even the people who influenced him the most finding themselves unable to identify their input in what he prints out. But for those with open- ended questions, his print-outs are almost always educational. By fac- toring out what he added, they deduce what this leader sees as the limitations in their formulations.

For almost everyone, his style is disarming. His searching respect for the subjective side of an individual's participation is responded to as a warm and irresistible invitation to tell all. This makes it quite difficult to fragment. Knowing that he knows their subjective interests causes most people to tell their whole story — either out of a fear of looking stupid or one of getting caught telling a half-truth. In subtle ways this leader conveys the message that he's not there simply to serve the self-indulgent needs of individuals but to provide another perspective on what the organization needs and to challenge people to find a more synergistic means of relating their needs to organiza- tion product. And he's been able to do this and still score on the traditional checklist.

In many ways this leader is bigger than life; certainly his ac- complishments surpass what most of us are externally striving to achieve. Today's society seems to worship external success, yet each of us knows that we're up to so much more. Our hero often strikes us as a very lonely man and we can't help but think that a major part of what appears to be a self-imposed solitude derives from an under- standing that, in today's world, his accomplishments are valued for reasons which bear little resemblance to what he sets out to do. But help should be on the way. We believe the evaluation categories which convey illusions of objectivity and overemphasize externals will gradually change. And as more people demonstrate an enhanced ap- preciation for the subjective involvements that everyone brings to or- ganization life, this leader, together with the rest of us, will have an easier time being himself and gaining recognition for just that.

NOTES

*Think of "doing" in terms of a specific assignment (job, position, status) and specify it in terms of a specific role (player, coach, expert) and how you would like to be performing it.

**Charlie and Fred are characters introduced earlier in the book from which this excerpt is taken. — Eds.

Managing Your Boss

John J. Gabarro and John P. Kotter

To many the phrase *managing your boss* may sound unusual or suspicious. Because of the traditional top-down emphasis in organizations, it is not obvious why you need to manage relationships upward — unless, of course, you would do so for personal or political reasons. But in using the expression *managing your boss*, we are not referring to political maneuvering or apple polishing. Rather we are using the term to mean the process of consciously working with your superior to obtain the best possible results for you, your boss, and the company.

Recent studies suggest that effective managers take time and effort to manage not only relationships with their subordinates but also those with their bosses.[1] These studies show as well that this aspect of management, essential though it is to survival and advancement, is sometimes ignored by otherwise talented and aggressive managers. Indeed, some managers who actively and effectively supervise subordinates, products, markets, and technologies, nevertheless assume an almost passively reactive stance vis-à-vis their bosses. Such a stance practically always hurts these managers and their companies.

If you doubt the importance of managing your relationship with your boss or how difficult it is to do so effectively, consider for a moment the following sad but telling story:

Frank Gibbons was an acknowledged manufacturing genius in his industry and, by any profitability standard, a very effective executive. In 1973, his strengths propelled him into the position of vice president of manufacturing for the second largest and most profitable company in its industry. Gibbons was not, however, a good manager of people. He knew this, as did others in his company and his industry. Recognizing this weakness, the president made sure that those who reported to Gibbons were good at working with people and could compensate for his limitations. The arrangement worked well.

In 1975, Philip Bonnevie was promoted into a position reporting to Gibbons. In keeping with the previous pattern, the president selected Bonnevie because he had an excellent track record and a reputation

---

for being good with people. In making that selection, however, the president neglected to notice that, in his rapid rise through the organization, Bonnevie himself had never reported to anyone who was poor at managing subordinates. Bonnevie had always had good-to-excellent bosses. He had never been forced to manage a relationship with a difficult boss. In retrospect, Bonnevie admits he had never thought that managing his boss was a part of his job.

Fourteen months after he started working for Gibbons, Bonnevie was fired. During that same quarter, the company reported a net loss for the first time in seven years. Many of those who were close to these events say that they don't really understand what happened. This much is known, however: while the company was bringing out a major new product — a process that required its sales, engineering, and manufacturing groups to coordinate their decisions very carefully — a whole series of misunderstandings and bad feelings developed between Gibbons and Bonnevie.

For example, Bonnevie claims Gibbons was aware of and had accepted Bonnevie's decision to use a new type of machinery to make the new product; Gibbons swears he did not. Furthermore, Gibbons claims he made it clear to Bonnevie that introduction of the product was too important to the company in the short run to take any major risks.

As a result of such misunderstandings, planning went awry: a new manufacturing plant was built that could not produce the new product designed by engineering, in the volume desired by sales, at a cost agreed on by the executive committee. Gibbons blamed Bonnevie for the mistake. Bonnevie blamed Gibbons.

Of course, one could argue that the problem here was caused by Gibbons's inability to manage his subordinates. But one can make just as strong a case that the problem was related to Bonnevie's inability to manage his boss. Remember, Gibbons was not having difficulty with any other subordinates. Moreover, given the personal price paid by Bonnevie (being fired and having his reputation within the industry severely tarnished), there was little consolation in saying the problem was that Gibbons was poor at managing subordinates. Everyone already knew that.

We believe that the situation could have turned out differently had Bonnevie been more adept at understanding Gibbons and at managing his relationship with him. In this case, an inability to manage upward was unusually costly. The company lost $2 to $5 million, and Bonnevie's career was, at least temporarily, disrupted. Many less costly cases like this probably occur regularly in all major corporations, and the cumulative effect can be very destructive.

MISREADING THE
BOSS-SUBORDINATE RELATIONSHIP

People often dismiss stories like the one we just related as being merely cases of personality conflict. Because two people can on occasion be psychologically or temperamentally incapable of working together, this can be an apt description. But more often, we have found, a personality conflict is only a part of the problem—sometimes a very small part.

Bonnevie did not just have a different personality from Gibbons, he also made or had unrealistic assumptions and expectations about the very nature of boss-subordinate relationships. Specifically, he did not recognize that his relationship to Gibbons involved *mutual dependence* between two *fallible* human beings. Failing to recognize this, a manager typically either avoids trying to manage his or her relationship with a boss or manages it ineffectively.

Some people behave as if their bosses were not very dependent on them. They fail to see how much the boss needs their help and cooperation to do his or her job effectively. These people refuse to acknowledge that the boss can be severely hurt by their actions and needs cooperation, dependability, and honesty from them.

Some see themselves as not very dependent on their bosses. They gloss over how much help and information they need from the boss in order to perform their own jobs well. This superficial view is particularly damaging when a manager's job and decisions affect other parts of the organization, as was the case in Bonnevie's situation. A manager's immediate boss can play a critical role in linking the manager to the rest of the organization, in making sure the manager's priorities are consistent with organizational needs, and in securing the resources the manager needs to perform well. Yet some managers need to see themselves as practically self-sufficient, as not needing the critical information and resources a boss can supply.

Many managers, like Bonnevie, assume that the boss will magically know what information or help their subordinates need and provide it to them. Certainly, some bosses do an excellent job of caring for their subordinates in this way, but for a manager to expect that from all bosses is dangerously unrealistic. A more reasonable expectation for managers to have is that modest help will be forthcoming. After all, bosses are only human. Most really effective managers accept this fact and assume primary responsibility for their own careers and development. They make a point of seeking the information and help they need to do a job instead of waiting for their bosses to provide it.

In light of the foregoing, it seems to us that managing a situation of mutual dependence among fallible human beings requires the following:

- That you have a good understanding of the other person and yourself, especially regarding strengths, weaknesses, work styles, and needs.
- That you use this information to develop and manage a healthy working relationship — one which is compatible with both persons' work styles and assets, is characterized by mutual expectations, and meets the most critical needs of the other person. And that is essentially what we have found highly effective managers doing.

UNDERSTANDING THE BOSS & YOURSELF

Managing your boss requires that you gain an understanding of both the boss and his context as well as your own situation and needs. All managers do this to some degree, but many are not thorough enough.

The Boss's World

At a minimum, you need to appreciate your boss's goals and pressures, his or her strengths and weaknesses. What are your boss's organizational and personal objectives, and what are the pressures on him, especially those from his boss and others at his level? What are your boss's long suits and blind spots? What is his or her preferred style of working? Does he or she like to get information through memos, formal meetings, or phone calls? Does your boss thrive on conflict or try to minimize it?

Without this information, a manager is flying blind when dealing with his boss, and unnecessary conflicts, misunderstandings, and problems are inevitable.

Goals and Pressures.   In one situation we studied, a top-notch marketing manager with a superior performance record was hired into a company as a vice president "to straighten out the marketing and sales problems." The company, which was having financial difficulties, had been recently acquired by a larger corporation. The president was eager to turn it around and gave the new marketing vice president free rein—at least initially. Based on his previous experience, the new vice president correctly diagnosed that greater market share was needed and that strong product management was required to bring that about. As a result, he made a number of pricing decisions aimed at increasing high-volume business.

When margins declined and the financial situation did not improve, however, the president increased pressure on the new vice president. Believing that the situation would eventually correct itself as the company gained back market share, the vice president resisted the pressure.

When by the second quarter margins and profits had still failed to improve, the president took direct control over all pricing decisions and put all items on a set level of margin, regardless of volume. The new vice president began to find himself shut out by the president, and their relationship deteriorated. In fact, the vice president found the president's behavior bizarre. Unfortunately, the president's new pricing scheme also failed to increase margins, and by the fourth quarter both the president and the vice president were fired.

What the new vice president had not known until it was too late was that improving marketing and sales had been only *one* of the president's goals. His most immediate goal had been to make the company more profitable — quickly.

Nor had the new vice president known that his boss was invested in this short-term priority for personal as well as business reasons. The president had been a strong advocate of the acquisition within the parent company, and his personal credibility was at stake.

The vice president made three basic errors. He took information supplied to him at face value, he made assumptions in areas where he had no information, and — most damaging — he never actively tried to clarify what his boss's objectives were. As a result, he ended up taking actions that were actually at odds with the president's priorities and objectives.

Managers who work effectively with their bosses do not behave this way. They seek out information about the boss's goals and problems and pressures. They are alert for opportunities to question the boss and others around him to test their assumptions. They pay attention to clues in the boss's behavior. Although it is imperative they do this when they begin working with a new boss, effective managers also do this on an ongoing basis because they recognize that priorities and concerns change.

Strengths, Weaknesses and Work Style.   Being sensitive to a boss's work style can be crucial, especially when the boss is new. For example, a new president who was organized and formal in his approach replaced a man who was informal and intuitive. The new president worked best when he had written reports. He also preferred formal meetings with set agendas.

One of his division managers realized this need and worked with the new president to identify the kinds and frequency of information and reports the president wanted. This manager also made a point of sending background information and brief agendas for their discussions. He found that with this type of preparation their meetings were very useful. Moreover, he found that with adequate preparation his new boss was even more effective at brainstorming problems than his more informal and intuitive predecessor had been.

In contrast, another division manager never fully understood how the new boss's work style differed from that of his predecessor. To the degree that he did sense it, he experienced it as too much control. As a result, he seldom sent the new president the background information he needed, and the president never felt fully prepared for meetings with the manager. In fact, the president spent much of his time when they met trying to get information that he felt he should have had before his arrival. The boss experienced these meetings as frustrating and inefficient, and the subordinate often found himself thrown off guard by the questions that the president asked. Ultimately, this division manager resigned.

The difference between the two division managers just described was not so much one of ability or even adaptability. Rather, the difference was that one of the men was more sensitive to his boss's work style than the other and to the implications of his boss's needs.

You and Your Needs

The boss is only one-half of the relationship. You are the other half, as well as the part over which you have more direct control. Developing an effective working relationship requires, then, that you know your own needs, strengths and weaknesses, and personal style.

Your Own Style.   You are not going to change either your basic personality structure or that of your boss. But you can become aware of what it is about you that impedes or facilitates working with your boss and, with that awareness, take actions that make the relationship more effective.

For example, in one case we observed, a manager and his superior ran into problems whenever they disagreed. The boss's typical response was to harden his position and overstate it. The manager's reaction was then to raise the ante and intensify the forcefulness of his argument. In doing this, he channeled his anger into sharpening his attacks on the logical fallacies in his boss's assumptions. His boss in turn would become even more adamant about holding his original position. Predictably, this escalating cycle resulted in the subordinate avoiding whenever possible any topic of potential conflict with his boss.

In discussing this problem with his peers, the manager discovered that his reaction to the boss was typical of how he generally reacted to counterarguments — but with a difference. His response would overwhelm his peers, but not his boss. Because his attempts to discuss this problem with his boss were unsuccessful, he concluded that the only way to change the situation was to deal with his own instinctive reactions. Whenever the two reached an impasse, he would check his own impatience and suggest that they break up and think about it before getting together again. Usually when they renewed their discussion, they had digested their differences and were more able to work them through.

Gaining this level of self-awareness and acting on it are difficult but not impossible. For example, by reflecting over his past experiences, a young manager learned that he was not very good at dealing with difficult and emotional issues where people were involved. Because he disliked those issues and realized that his instinctive responses to them were seldom very good, he developed a habit of touching base with his boss whenever such a problem arose. Their discussions always surfaced ideas and approaches the manager had not considered. In many cases, they also identified specific actions the boss could take to help.

Dependence on Authority Figures.   Although a superior-subordinate relationship is one of mutual dependence, it is also one in which the subordinate is typically more dependent on the boss than the other way around. This dependence inevitably results in the subordinate feeling a certain degree of frustration, sometimes anger, when his actions or options are constrained by his boss's decisions. This is a normal part of life and occurs in the best of relationships. The way in which a manager handles these frustrations largely depends on his or her predisposition toward dependence on authority figures.

Some people's instinctive reaction under these circumstances is to resent the boss's authority and to rebel against the boss's decisions. Sometimes a person will escalate a conflict beyond what is appropriate. Seeing the boss almost as an institutional enemy, this type of manager will often, without being conscious of it, fight with the boss just for the sake of fighting. His reactions to being constrained are usually strong and sometimes impulsive. He sees the boss as someone who, by virtue of his role, is a hindrance to progress, an obstacle to be circumvented or at best tolerated.

Psychologists call this pattern of reactions counterdependent behavior. Although a counterdependent person is difficult for most superiors to manage and usually has a history of strained relationships with superiors, this sort of manager is apt to have even more trouble with a boss who tends to be directive or authoritarian. When the manager acts on his or her negative feelings, often in subtle and nonverbal ways, the boss sometimes *does* become the enemy. Sensing the subordinate's latent hostility, the boss will lose trust in the subordinate or his judgment and behave less openly.

Paradoxically, a manager with this type of predisposition is often a good manager of his own people. He will often go out of his way to get support for them and will not hesitate to go to bat for them.

At the other extreme are managers who swallow their anger and behave in a very compliant fashion when the boss makes what they know to be a poor decision. These managers will agree with the boss even when a disagreement might be welcome or when the boss would easily alter his decision if given more information. Because they bear no relationship to the specific situation at hand, their responses are as much an overreaction as those of counterdependent managers. Instead of seeing the boss as an enemy, these people deny their anger — the other extreme — and tend to see the boss as if he or she were an all-wise parent who should know best, should take responsibility for their careers, train them in all they need to know, and protect them from overly ambitious peers.

Both counterdependence and overdependence lead managers to hold unrealistic views of what a boss is. Both views ignore that most bosses, like everyone else, are imperfect and fallible. They don't have unlimited time, encyclopedic knowledge, or extrasensory perception; nor are they evil enemies. They have their own pressures and concerns that are sometimes at odds with the wishes of the subordinate —and often for good reason.

Altering predispositions toward authority, especially at the extremes, is almost impossible without intensive psychotherapy (psychoanalytic theory and research suggest that such predispositions are deeply rooted in a person's personality and upbringing). However, an awareness of these extremes and the range between them can be very useful in understanding where your own predispositions fall and what the implications are for how you tend to behave in relation to your boss.

If you believe, on the one hand, that you have some tendencies toward counterdependence, you can understand and even predict what your reactions and overreactions are likely to be. If, on the other hand, you believe you have some tendencies toward overdependence, you might question the extent to which your overcompliance or inability to confront real differences may be making both you and your boss less effective.

DEVELOPING & MANAGING THE RELATIONSHIP

With a clear understanding of both your boss and yourself, you can — usually — establish a way of working together that fits both of you, that is characterized by unambiguous mutual expectations, and that helps both of you to be more productive and effective. We have already outlined a few things such a relationship consists of, which are itemized in the [accompanying table], and here are a few more.

Compatible Work Styles

Above all else, a good working relationship with a boss accommodates differences in work style. For example, in one situation we studied, a manager (who had a relatively good relationship with his superior) realized that during meetings his boss would often become inattentive and sometimes brusque. The subordinate's own style tended to be discursive and exploratory. He would often digress from the topic at hand to deal with background factors, alternative approaches, and so forth. His boss, instead, preferred to discuss problems with a minimum of background detail and became impatient and distracted whenever his subordinate digressed from the immediate issue.

Recognizing this difference in style, the manager became terser and more direct during meetings with his boss. To help himself do this, before meetings with the boss he would develop brief agendas that he used as a guide. Whenever he felt that a digression was needed, he explained why. This small shift in his own style made these meetings more effective and far less frustrating for them both.

Subordinates can adjust their styles in response to their bosses' preferred method for receiving information. Peter Drucker divides bosses into "listeners" and "readers." Some bosses like to get information in report form so that they can read and study it. Others work better with information and reports presented in person so that they can ask questions. As Drucker points out, the implications are obvious. If your boss is a listener, you brief him in person, *then* follow it up with a memo. If your boss is a reader, you cover important items or proposals in a memo or report, *then* discuss them with him.

Other adjustments can be made according to a boss's decision-making style. Some bosses prefer to be involved in decisions and problems as they arise. These are high-involvement managers who like to keep their hands on the pulse of the operation. Usually their needs (and your own) are best satisfied if you touch base with them on an ad hoc basis. A boss who has a need to be involved will become involved one way or another, so there are advantages to including him at your initiative. Other bosses prefer to delegate — they don't want to be involved. They expect you to come to them with major problems and inform them of important changes.

Creating a compatible relationship also involves drawing on each other's strengths and making up for each other's weaknesses. Because he knew that his boss — the vice president of engineering — was not very good at monitoring his employees' problems, one manager we studied made a point of doing it himself. The stakes were high: the engineers and technicians were all union members, the company worked on a customer-contract basis, and the company had recently experienced a serious strike.

The manager worked closely with his boss, the scheduling department, and the personnel office to ensure that potential problems were avoided. He also developed an informal arrangement through which his boss would review with him any proposed changes in personnel or assignment policies before taking action. The boss valued his advice and credited his subordinate for improving both the performance of the division and the labor-management climate.

Mutual Expectations

The subordinate who passively assumes that he or she knows what the boss expects is in for trouble. Of course, some superiors will spell out their expectations very explicitly and in great detail. But most do not. And although many corporations have systems that provide a basis for communicating expectations (such as formal planning processes, career planning reviews, and performance appraisal reviews), these systems never work perfectly. Also, between these formal reviews expectations invariably change.

Ultimately, the burden falls on the subordinate to find out what the boss's expectations are. These expectations can be both broad (regarding, for example, what kinds of problems the boss wishes to be informed about and when) as well as very specific (regarding such things as when a particular project should be completed and what kinds of information the boss needs in the interim).

Getting a boss who tends to be vague or nonexplicit to express his expectations can be difficult. But effective managers find ways to get that information. Some will draft a detailed memo covering key aspects of their work and then send it to their bosses for approval. They then follow this up with a face-to-face discussion in which they go over each item in the memo. This discussion often surfaces virtually all of the boss's relevant expectations.

Other effective managers will deal with an inexplicit boss by initiating an ongoing series of informal discussions about "good management" and "our objectives." Still others find useful information more indirectly through those who used to work for the boss and through the formal planning systems in which the boss makes commitments to his superior. Which approach you choose, of course, should depend on your understanding of your boss's style.

Developing a workable set of mutual expectations also requires that you communicate your own expectations to the boss, find out if they are realistic, and influence the boss to accept the ones that are important to you. Being able to influence the boss to value your expectations can be particularly important if the boss is an overachiever. Such a boss will often set unrealistically high standards that need to be brought into line with reality.

Managing the Relationship with Your Boss

Make sure you understand your boss and his context, including:

His goals and objectives

The pressures on him

His strengths, weaknesses, blind spots

His preferred work style

Assess yourself and your needs, including:

Your own strengths and weaknesses

Your personal style

Your predisposition toward dependence on authority figures

Develop and maintain a relationship that:

Fits both your needs and styles

Is characterized by mutual expectations

Keeps your boss informed

Is based on dependability and honesty

Selectively uses your boss's time and resources

A Flow of Information

How much information a boss needs about what a subordinate is doing will vary significantly depending on the boss's style, the situation he is in, and the confidence he has in the subordinate. But it is not uncommon for a boss to need more information than the subordinate would naturally supply or for the subordinate to think the boss knows more than he really does. Effective managers recognize that they probably underestimate what the boss needs to know and make sure they find ways to keep him informed through a process that fits his style.

Managing the flow of information upward is particularly difficult if the boss does not like to hear about problems. Although many would deny it, bosses often give off signals that they want to hear only good news. They show great displeasure — usually nonverbally — when someone tells them about a problem. Ignoring individual achievement, they may even evaluate more favorably subordinates who do not bring problems to them.

Nevertheless — for the good of the organization, boss, and subordinate — a superior needs to hear about failures as well as successes. Some subordinates deal with a good-news-only boss by finding indirect ways to get the necessary information to him, such as a management information system in which there is no messenger to be killed. Others see to it that potential problems, whether in the form of good surprises or bad news, are communicated immediately.

Dependability and Honesty

Few things are more disabling to a boss than a subordinate on whom he cannot depend, whose work he cannot trust. Almost no one is intentionally undependable, but many managers are inadvertently so because of oversight or uncertainty about the boss's priorities. A commitment to an optimistic delivery date may please a superior in the short term but be a source of displeasure if not honored. It's difficult for a boss to rely on a subordinate who repeatedly slips deadlines. As one president put it (describing a subordinate): "When he's great, he's terrific, but I can't depend on him. I'd rather he be more consistent even if he delivered fewer peak successes — at least I could rely on him."

Nor are many managers intentionally dishonest with their bosses. But it is so easy to shade the truth a bit and play down concerns. Current concerns often become future surprise problems. It's almost impossible for bosses to work effectively if they cannot rely on a fairly accurate reading from their subordinates. Because it undermines credibility, dishonesty is perhaps the most troubling trait a subordinate can have. Without a basic level of trust in a subordinate's word, a boss feels he has to check all of a subordinate's decisions, which makes it difficult to delegate.

Good Use of Time and Resources

Your boss is probably as limited in his store of time, energy, and influence as you are. Every request you make of him uses up some of these resources. For this reason, common sense suggests drawing on these resources with some selectivity. This may sound obvious, but it is surprising how many managers use up their boss's time (and some of their own credibility) over relatively trivial issues.

In one instance, a vice president went to great lengths to get his boss to fire a meddlesome secretary in another department. His boss had to use considerable effort and influence to do it. Understandably, the head of the other department was not pleased. Later, when the vice president wanted to tackle other more important problems that required changes in the scheduling and control practices of the other department, he ran into trouble. He had used up many of his own as well as his boss's blue chips on the relatively trivial issue of getting the secretary fired, thereby making it difficult for him and his boss to meet more important goals.

WHOSE JOB IS IT?

No doubt, some subordinates will resent that on top of all their other duties, they also need to take time and energy to manage their relationships with their bosses. Such managers fail to realize the importance of this activity and how it can simplify their jobs by eliminating potentially severe problems. Effective managers recognize that this part of their work is legitimate. Seeing themselves as ultimately responsible for what they achieve in an organization, they know they need to establish and manage relationships with everyone on whom they are dependent, and that includes the boss.

NOTE

1. See, for example, John J. Gabarro, "Socialization at the Top: How CEOs and Their Subordinates Develop Interpersonal Contracts," *Organizational Dynamics*, Winter 1979; and John P. Kotter, *Power in Management*, AMACOM, 1979.

The Wall Street Journal, 16 June 1981.

> BIG DEAL: Being tall may help you get ahead. A survey of 156 chief executives at major companies found that 56% ranged from six feet to six feet, seven inches tall. Only 3% were under five feet, seven inches, says Howard-Sloan Legal Search, a recruiter. The executives' average weight was 184 pounds.

Diane Wilson

Studs Terkel

You wish there was a better system. A lot of money is held up and the grantees want to know why they can't get it. Sometimes they call and get the run-around on the phone. I never do that. I tell the truth. If they don't have any money left, they don't have it. No, I'm not disturbed any more. If I was just starting on this job, I probably would. But the older I get, I realize it's a farce. You just get used to it. It's a job. I get my paycheck—that's it. It's all political anyway.

A lot of times the grantee comes down to our audit department for aid. They're not treated as human beings. Sometimes they have to wait, wait, wait — for no reason. The grantee doesn't know it's for no reason. He thinks he's getting somewhere and he really isn't.

They send him from floor to floor and from person to person, it's just around and around he goes. Sometimes he leaves, he hasn't accomplished anything. I don't know why this is so. You can see 'em waiting — so long. Sometimes it has to do with color. Whoever is the boss. If you're in the minority group, you can tell by their actions. A lot of times they don't realize that you know, but this has happened to you.

So this person was standing out there. He had come to offer something. He was from out of state. The secretary told this boss he had someone waiting. He also had someone in the office. He could've waited on the grantee and got him on his way quick. But he closed the door in the young man's face and the young man stood there. That went on for about forty-five minutes. The secretary got tired of seein' the man standin' there, so she said, could she help him? Was it somethin' he just wanted to give the man? He told her yes. She took it, so he wouldn't stand there. That was all he was gonna do, give it to him. I thought this was awfully rude. This boss does this quite often. I don't know if he does it on purpose. I know if it's an Indian or a black or a Latin he does this.

Life is a funny thing. We had this boss come in from Internal Revenue. He wanted to be very, very strict. He used to have meetings every Friday — about people comin' in late, people leavin' early, people abusin' lunch time. Everyone was used to this relaxed attitude. You kind of went overtime. No one bothered you. The old boss went along. You did your work.

Every Friday, everyone would sit there and listen to this man. And we'd all go out and do the same thing again. Next Friday he'd have another meeting and he would tell us the same thing. (Laughs.) We'd all go out and do the same thing again. (Laughs.) He would try to talk to one and see what they'd say about the other. But we'd been working all together for quite a while. You know how the game is played. Tomorrow you might need a favor. So nobody would say anything. If he'd want to find out what time someone came in, who's gonna tell 'em? He'd want to find out where someone was, we'd always say, "They're at the Xerox." Just anywhere. He couldn't get through. Now, lo and behold! We can't find *him* anywhere. He's got into this nice, relaxed atmosphere . . . (Laughs.) He leaves early, he takes long lunch hours. We've converted him. (Laughs.)

After my grievances and my fighting, I'm a processing clerk. Never a typist no more or anything like that. (Laughs.) I started working here in 1969. There was an emergency and they all wanted to work overtime. So I made arrangements at home, 'cause I have to catch a later train. Our supervisor's black. All of us are black. We'll help her get it out so there won't be any back drag on this. Okay, so we all worked overtime and made a good showing.

Then they just didn't want to give us the promotion which was due us anyhow. They just don't want to give you anything. The personnel man, all of them, they show you why you don't deserve a promotion. The boss, the one we converted — he came on board, as they call it, after we sweated to meet the deadline. So he didn't know what we did. But he told us we didn't deserve it. That stayed with me forever. I won't be bothered with him ever again.

But our grievance man was very good. He stayed right on the case. We filed a civil rights complaint. Otherwise we woulda never got the promotion. They don't want anybody coming in investigating for race. They said, "Oh, it's not that." But you sit around and see white women do nothin' and get promotions. Here we're working and they say you don't deserve it. The black men are just as hard on us as the white man. Harder. They get angry with you because you started a lot of trouble. The way I feel about it, I'm gonna give 'em all the trouble I can.

Our boss is black, the one that told us we didn't deserve it. (Laughs.) And our union man fighting for us, sittin' there, punchin' away, is white. (Laughs.) We finally got up to the deputy director and he was the one — the white man — that finally went ahead and gave us the promotion. (Laughs.) So we went from grade 4 clerk-typist to grade 5 processing clerk.

We had another boss, he would walk around and he wouldn't want to see you idle at all. Sometimes you're gonna have a lag in your work, you're all caught up. This had gotten on his nerves. We got our promotion and we weren't continually busy. Any time they see black women idle, that irks 'em. I'm talkin' about black men as well as whites. They want you to work continuously.

One day I'd gotten a call to go to his office and do some typing. He's given me all this handwritten script. I don't know to this day what all that stuff was. I asked him, "Why was I picked for this job?" He said his secretary was out and he needs this done by noon. I said, "I'm no longer a clerk-typist and you yourself said for me to get it out of my mind. Are you trying to get me confused? Anyway, I can't read this stuff." He tells me he'll read it. I said, "Okay, I'll write it out as you read it." There's his hand going all over the script, busy. He doesn't know what he's readin', I could tell. I know why he's doing it. He just wants to see me busy.

So we finished the first long sheet. He wants to continue. I said, "No, I can only do one sheet at a time. I'll go over and type this up."

So what I did, I would type a paragraph and wait five or ten minutes. I made sure I made all the mistakes I could. It's amazing, when you want to make mistakes, you really can't. So I just put Ko-rect-type paper over this yellow sheet. I fixed it up real pretty. I wouldn't stay on the margins. He told me himself I was no longer a clerk-typist.

I took him back this first sheet and, of course, I had left out a line or two. I told him it made me nervous to have this typed by a certain time, and I didn't have time to proofread it, "but I'm ready for you to read the other sheet to me." He started to proofread. I deliberately misspelled some words. Oh, I did it up beautifully. (Laughs.) He got the dictionary out and he looked up the words for me. I took it back and crossed out the words and squeezed the new ones in there. He started on the next sheet. I did the same thing all over again. There were four sheets. He proofread them all. Oh, he looked so serious! All this time he's spendin' just to keep me busy, see? Well, I didn't finish it by noon.

I'm just gonna see what he does if I don't finish it on time. Oh, it was imperative! I knew the world's not gonna change that quickly. It was nice outside. If it gets to be a problem, I'll go home. It's a beautiful day, the heck with it. So twelve-thirty comes and the work just looks awful. (Laughs.) I typed on all the lines, I continued it anywhere. One of the girls comes over, she says, "You're goin' off the line." I said, "Oh, be quiet. I know what I'm doin'. (Laughs.) Just go away." (Laughs.) I put the four sheets together. I never saw anything as horrible in my life. (Laughs.)

I decided I'd write him a note. "Dear Mr. Roberts: You've been so much help. You proofread, you look up words for your secretary. It must be marvelous working for you. I hope this has met with your approval. Please call on me again." I never heard from him. (A long laugh.)

These other people, they work, work, work, work and nothing comes of it. They're the ones that catch hell. The ones that come in every day on time, do the job, and try to keep up with everybody else. A timekeeper, a skinny little black woman. She's fanatic about time. She would argue with you if you were late or something. She's been working for the government twenty-five years and she hadn't gotten a promotion, 'cause she's not a fighter.

She has never reported sick. Some days I won't come. If it's bad outside, heavy snow, a storm, I won't go. You go the next day. The work's gonna be there. She thinks my attitude is just terrible. She's always runnin', acts like she's scared of everybody. She was off *one* day. She had a dental appointment. Oh, did the boss raise hell! Oh, my goodness! He never argues with me.

The boss whose typing I messed up lost his secretary. She got promoted. They told this old timekeeper she's to be his secretary-assistant. Oh, she's in her glory. No more money or anything and she's doing two jobs all day long. She's rushin' and runnin' all the time, all day. She's a nervous wreck. And when she asked him to write her up for an award, he refused. That's *her* reward for being so faithful, obedient.

Oh, we love it when the bosses go to those long meetings, those important conferences. (Laughs.) We just leave in a group and go for a show. We don't care. When we get back, they roll their eyes. They know they better not say anything, 'cause they've done nothing when we've been gone anyhow. We do the work that we have to do. The old timekeeper, she sits and knits all that time, always busy.

I've been readin'. Everything I could on China, ever since he made that visit. Tryin' to see how people live and the ideas. It changed me a lot. I don't see any need for work you don't enjoy. I like the way the Indians lived. They moved from season to season. They didn't pay taxes. Everybody had enough. I don't think a few should control everything. I don't think it's right that women lay down and bear sons and then you have a few rich people that tell your sons they have to go and die for their country. They're not dying for their country. They're dying for the few to stay on top. I don't think that's necessary. I'm just tired of this type of thing. I just think we ought to be just human.

Walter Cronkite at CBS

David Halberstam

The 1952 Democratic convention was important in part because it brought a new face to the American people, a face that would be known in television history. The CBS team going to Chicago knew that it was going to be on the air live for endless hours and it needed someone to hold the broadcast together. The word for that in the trade, but not yet in the popular vernacular, was anchorman. Murrow himself, still at the peak of his influence, was not much interested. Nor were many of his colleagues. Walter Cronkite, however, was. Walter Cronkite was not one of the Murrow Boys. Cronkite in 1952 was perhaps the one rising star within the company who was outside the Murrow clique. There was a time in London during the war when he might have made the connection with Murrow. He was a United Press correspondent in London and a very good one. He was, in the eyes of Harrison Salisbury, the man then running the UP bureau and an exceptionally good judge of talent, the best on his beat. . . .

He finished the war with UP and there was no doubt of his excellence; the brass there thought highly of him and he was awarded, as a sign of his success, the Moscow bureau. Those were days of minimal creature comforts in Moscow, and he and his wife, Betsy, were warned that they had to bring everything to Moscow, which they did, and on the day they departed someone mentioned to Betsy Cronkite that she would do well to buy a lot of golf balls since there were none available in Moscow, which she immediately rushed out and did, buying hundreds and hundreds of them; an exceptional supply, considering that (a) Walter Cronkite did not play golf and (b) there were no golf courses at all in the Soviet Union. Moscow in 1946 was not very great fun, nor for that matter was United Press; the Russians were fast discontinuing their policy of limited friendship to brotherly Western correspondents, revoking the marginal privileges that had once existed; in addition, the financial generosity of United Press, which was always somewhat limited, seemed to diminish. The UP car was of antique proportions and did not run, and when, during one of the worst winters of recent Russian history, Cronkite asked for permission to buy a new car since even the Russians were complaining about the condition of his vehicle, his superiors suggested that he get a bicycle.

Things like that often undermine a correspondent's confidence and Cronkite quickly asked to be brought out of Moscow. He came home to America for a year with a promise that he would soon return to Europe as the number-one man on the entire Continent. His salary was then a hundred and twenty-five dollars a week, and, with family obligations growing, he asked for more. The UP executives assured him, probably accurately, that he was already the highest-paid man on the staff. Which was fine except he still wanted more; yes, he said, he loved United Press, which he truly did, he loved scooping people and getting the story straight and clean and fast with no frills — even years later, reminiscing, there is a kind of love in his voice talking about the old UP days, how much he loved UP, how he liked the feel of dirt in his hands, he was not at home with a lot of commentary — but love or no, there had to be some money. So Earl Johnson, his superior, said that he thought it was time that he and Walter had a little talk, since Cronkite apparently did not understand the economic basis of United Press, an economic attitude which was legendary among most journalists and secret only to Cronkite. "No, I guess I don't understand it," Cronkite said, and so Johnson explained: "We take the best and the most eager young men we can find and we train them and we pay them very little and we give them a lot of room and then when they get very good they go elsewhere."

"Are you asking me to go somewhere else?" Cronkite asked.

"No, no," said Johnson, though adding that a hundred and twenty-five dollars a week is a lot of money for us, though probably not for you.

So Cronkite returned to Kansas City, whence he came, on a kind of extended leave, and while he was there he saw an old friend named Karl Koerper, who was a big local civic booster and the head of KMBC, which was a CBS affiliate. And Cronkite, who was disturbed by what he had found in Kansas City, told Koerper at lunch that Kansas City seemed to have died, there was no spirit and excitement any more. What had happened? Then he answered his own question, it was the death of the Kansas City *Journal*. You get monopoly journalism, he said, and something goes out of a city, a sense of excitement and competition. When newspaper competition dies, something dies with it. Kansas City is a duller town now, Cronkite said.

"What do you mean?" Koerper asked.

"It's your fault," Cronkite continued. "You radio guys cut the advertising dollars so much that you drove the newspapers out but you haven't replaced them. You have no news staff."

"We certainly do — we have eight men," said Koerper proudly.

"Do you know how many reporters the Kansas City *Star* has?" Cronkite asked.

"But that's their principal business," Koerper answered.

"There!" said Cronkite, seizing on it. "That's the answer!" So the upshot of the conversation was that Walter Cronkite was hired in 1948 by Karl Koerper to work as Washington correspondent for his station and a series of other Kansas and Missouri stations, which was the beginning of Walter Cronkite's career as a broadcaster. He was thirty-one years old, he was from the world of print, and more, he was from the highly specialized, fiercely competitive world of wire-service print. But he went to Washington; his salary was $250 a week and he was working for a string of midwestern radio stations. Somehow in the snobbery and pecking order of American journalism there was something slightly demeaning about seeing Walter Cronkite, who had been a big man during the war, hustling around Washington as a radio man for a bunch of small midwestern stations, although Cronkite did not find it demeaning since he liked the excitement of Washington and since he intended to return soon to Kansas City as general manager of the station.

He worked in Washington for about a year and a half, not entirely satisfied, but not all that restless, and then the Korean War broke out and he got a phone call from Ed Murrow asking whether he might be willing to go to Korea and cover the war for CBS. Would he? Well, Murrow better believe that he would, it was the kind of assignment he loved and wanted, it was exactly where he wanted to be. There was, Murrow said, no great problem with KMBC since it was a CBS affiliate and that type of thing would be easily straightened out. In the meantime, Cronkite should get himself ready to go overseas again. But there was some delay because one of his children was about to be born. Then in the middle of all this, the freeze on ownership of stations ended and CBS bought WTOP, which had been a locally owned Washington station, wanting it as a major outlet in the Washington area, a kind of political flagship. The station television news director asked Cronkite to do the Korean story every night, and inquired what he needed in the way of graphics, which turned out to be chalk and a blackboard. Everyone else was trying to make things more complicated and Cronkite, typically, was trying to make them more simple. He worked so hard in preparation for it, backgrounding himself, going to the Pentagon to develop independent sources, that his mastery and control of the subject were absolutely unique. He simply worked harder than everyone else, and in a profession as embryonic as television news, peopled as it frequently was in those days by pretty boys, he was an immediate success. He had that special quality that television demands, that audiences sense, and that is somehow intangible — he had *weight*, he projected a kind of authority. The people in the station knew that he was stronger and more professional than anyone else around and very soon he was asked to do the Korean War story twice a day, and then, very soon after that, the entire news show, and then two news shows a day. He was an immediate hit, a very good professional reporter on a new medium, and he soon began to do network feeds from Washington back to the network news show in New York. Korea began to slip away as an assignment.

Among those most aware of Cronkite's talents was Sig Mickelson, who was then in charge of television news at CBS. He was in effect the head of the stepchild section of CBS News, trying to build up television, but doing it very much against the grain, since in comparison with Murrow he had no bureaucratic muscle, and since all the stars of the News Department were in the Murrow group. Mickelson was quietly strengthening the rest of the News Department. He had known Cronkite in earlier incarnations and from the start he had seen Cronkite as the man around whom he could build the future television staff. As the 1952 convention approached, radio was still bigger than television, although the convention itself would help tip the balance in favor of television. The Mickelson group wanted a full-time correspondent who would sit there all day long and all night long and hold the coverage together, not get tired, and have great control over his material. Mickelson asked for Murrow, Sevareid, or Collingwood, the big radio stars. But the radio people told Mickelson to get lost. Instead, negotiating through Hubbell Robinson, they offered a list of reporters who were ostensibly second-stringers. On the list was precisely the name that Mickelson wanted, that of Walter Cronkite.

The Murrow group had never really considered Cronkite one of them and there was a certain snobbery about it all; Cronkite was somehow different from the others; it was not just that they had been stars longer than he, they were of a different cast and a different type and it would be crucial in the difference between television news reporting and radio news reporting. Cronkite was then, and he remained some twenty-five years later, almost consciously a nonsophisticate, and he is even now, much as he was then, right out of the Midwest, and there was a touch of *The Front Page* to him, he was almost joyously what he had always been, a lot of gee whiz, it was all new and fresh even when surely he had seen much of it before, and it was as if he took delight in not having been changed externally by all that he had seen. He was above all *of* the wire services — get it fast and get it straight and make it understandable and do not agonize over the larger questions that it raises. The Murrow men — Sevareid, Howard Smith, Collingwood, Shirer, Schoenbrun — were notoriously cerebral and had been picked for that reason; they had been encouraged to think and analyze, not just to run as sprinters. They had dined with the great and mighty of Europe and they had entered the great salons and taken on the mannerisms of those salons; they were, whether they wanted to be or not (and most of them wanted to be), sophisticates. If they had once worked for organizations like UP, they were glad to have that behind them and they did not romanticize those years. Sevareid, for example, came from Velva, North Dakota, which was smaller than St. Joseph, Missouri, where Cronkite came from, but Sevareid had left Velva behind long ago and there was a part of Cronkite which had never left St. Joe, and which he quite consciously projected.

Cronkite had come to the 1952 convention knowing that it was his big chance. He had come thoroughly prepared, he knew the weight of each delegation and he was able to bind the coverage together at all times. He was, in a field very short on professionalism, incredibly professional, and in a job that required great durability, he was the ultimate durable man. By the end of the first day, in the early morning, the other people in the control booth just looked at each other, they knew they had a winner, and a new dimension of importance for television; they knew it even more the next day when some of the Murrow people began to drift around to let the television staff know they were, well, available for assignment. Cronkite himself had little immediate sense of it, he was so obsessed by the action in front of

him that he had no awareness of the growing reaction to his performance. It was true that people kept coming up and congratulating
him on his work and it was true that there seemed to be a new attitude on the part of his colleagues, but he still did not realize what
had happened. On the last morning of the convention, when it was
all over, he went for an early-morning walk with Sig Mickelson along
Michigan Avenue. Mickelson said that his life was going to change,
he was going to want to renegotiate his contract and he would need a
lot more money.

"Do you have an agent?" Mickelson asked.

"No," said Cronkite.

"Well, you better get one," Mickelson said. "You're going to need
one."

"No, I won't," Cronkite said.

"Yes, you will," Mickelson said. . . .

Sig Mickelson and some of the other news executives had been
looking to replace Doug Edwards as the anchorman of the evening
news as early as the mid-fifties. Edwards was the original CBS anchorman, he had been given the job during the embryonic days of
television. He had been fine standing off the "Camel News Caravan"
of NBC's John Cameron Swayze ("Let's hopscotch the world"), but
the rise of Huntley-Brinkley was a serious challenge. Edwards did not
project the kind of weight that Mickelson and the others wanted, he
simply did not seem strong and solid enough a personality to anchor
a new modern news show. Douglas Edwards might close the evening
news by saying, "And that's the way it is," but people might not
necessarily believe that that was the way it was. . . . The job was the
most prestigious that CBS had, but it was also not a commentator's
job, television was simply too powerful for that kind of personal freedom. For the correspondents in their regular nightly appearances
were an interesting combination, part wire-service men (in terms of
the narrow spectrum of personal expression and the brevity of their
reports) and part superstar, known to the entire country, as recognizable on a presidential campaign and often as sought out by the public
as many candidates themselves. But the power was so great and the
time on camera so limited that the reporters themselves often seemed
underemployed. They were often serious and intelligent and sophisticated, and they seemed more knowledgeable than their nightly reports. The difference between the insight of the CBS reporting team
on a brief spot on the news program and its performance at a national
convention or during a Watergate special seemed enormous. Even a
half-hour show was like trying to put *The New York Times* on a postage
stamp, and there was a standing insider's joke at CBS that if Moses
came down from the mountain the evening news lead would be:

"Moses today came down from the mountain with the Ten Commandments, the two most important of which are . . ."

Sevareid and Collingwood might be the disciples of Murrow, and Cronkite might be the outsider who had never crashed the insider's club, but his style was now more compatible with what the show needed. His roots were in the wire service, he was the embodiment of the wire-service man sprung to life, speed, simplicity, scoop, a ten-minute beat; Hildy Johnson with his shirt sleeves rolled up. He came through to his friends and to his listeners alike as straight, clear, and simple, more interested in hard news than analysis; the viewers could more readily picture Walter Cronkite jumping into a car to cover a ten-alarm fire than they could visualize him doing cerebral commentary on a great summit meeting in Geneva. From his earliest days he was one of the hungriest reporters around, wildly competitive, no one was going to beat Walter Cronkite on a story, and as he grew older and more successful, the marvel of it was that he never changed, the wild fires still burned. . . .

In addition, he had enormous physical strength and durability. Iron pants, as they say in the trade. He could sit there all night under great stress and constant pressure and never wear down, never blow it. And he never seemed bored by it all, even when it was in fact boring. When both Blair Clark and Sig Mickelson recommended him for the job, the sheer durability, what they called the farm boy in him, was a key factor. He was the workhorse. After all, the qualities of an anchorman were not necessarily those of brilliance, he had to synthesize others. There were those who felt that Sevareid had simply priced himself out of the market intellectually. Eric was too interested in analysis and opinion and thus not an entirely believable transmission belt for straight information. He was an intellectual, he wrote serious articles in serious magazines, and yet he wanted to be an anchorman as well, and there were those who thought this a contradiction in terms. When he found out that Cronkite was getting the job he was furious. "After all I've done for the company," he protested to Blair Clark.

The casting of Cronkite was perfect. He looked like Middle America, there was nothing slick about his looks (he was the son of a dentist in St. Joe, Missouri, and his accent was midwestern). He was from the heartland, and people from the Midwest are considered trustworthy, they are of the soil rather than of the sidewalks, and in American mythology the soil teaches real values and the sidewalks teach shortcuts. Though he had been a foreign correspondent and a very good one, in his television incarnation he had been definitively American, in those less combative, less divisive days of the late fifties and early sixties; Good Guy American. He had covered conventions, which were very American, and space shots, which were big stories where no one became very angry. When there was an Eisenhower special to do, Walter did it; he was seen with Eisenhower, and that too was reassuring. Ike and Walter got along, shared values, it spoke well for both of them. (Among those not comforted was John F. Kennedy, who, shortly after his election to the presidency in 1960, took CBS producer Don Hewitt aside. "Walter Cronkite's a Republican, isn't he?" Kennedy asked. No, said Hewitt, he didn't think so. "He's a Republican," said Kennedy, "I know he's a Republican." Again Hewitt said he didn't think so, and indeed he suspected that Cronkite had voted for Eisenhower over Stevenson and Kennedy over Nixon. "He's always with Eisenhower," insisted Kennedy. "Always having his picture taken with Eisenhower and going somewhere with him.")

Cronkite was careful not to be controversial, disciplining himself severely against giving vent to his own personal opinions and prejudices, and this would be an asset for CBS in the decade to come. He represented in a real way the American center, and he was acutely aware when he went against it. To him editorializing was going against the government. He had little awareness, nor did his employers want him to, of the editorializing which he did automatically by unconsciously going along with the government's position. He was never precipitous. His wire-service background gave him a very strong innate sense of the limits to which a correspondent should go, a sense that blended perfectly with what management now deemed to be the role of the anchorman and the news show itself. He represented a certain breed and he was by far the best of the breed. He was wise and decent enough to be uneasy with his power, and the restraints the job required were built into him. And so he was chosen to anchor the half-hour news show — a mass figure who held centrist attitudes for a mass audience.

He became an institution. His influence, if not his power, rivaled that of Presidents. . . .

Robert Kintner had brought NBC News alive, and in doing so strengthened the entire network. He was a driving, difficult man with a great instinct for excellence and a great feel for what television was, for the excitement it could project, *and* he knew that the quickest and the cheapest way to create excitement was through an expanded news organization. The news organization could be the sinews of the network, could hold it together, and a great news organization would make a reputation for NBC and thus for Bob Kintner as well. He loved the sheer electricity of news, and he delighted in instant specials (in 1964 when Lyndon Johnson had a heavy cold there were constant bulletins throughout the day about Lyndon's health, interrupting the NBC programming schedule and blowing up the cold to massive proportions). In addition, he had come up with the Huntley-Brinkley team, which was an almost perfect anchor: Huntley, from Montana, Cronkitelike in his rock steadiness; David Brinkley, from North Carolina, the tart, slightly rebellious younger brother who could by deft tonal inflection imply a disbelief and an irreverence that the medium with its inherent overseriousness badly needed. Backing them was a team of fine floor reporters. In 1956 NBC had challenged CBS's supremacy for the first time; 1956 was the Huntley-Brinkley Democratic convention and as it went on, hour after hour, much too long, journalistic overkill, ultimately picking the same two candidates who had run in 1952, it had become a fine showcase for Brinkley's dry humor.

The sudden surge in the NBC ratings had subsequently scared CBS, indeed terrified the news executives, and Don Hewitt, the CBS producer, had panicked and had gone to Mickelson and suggested teaming Cronkite, who was then doing the anchor, with Murrow. The two big guns of CBS against the upstarts of NBC. A sure winner on paper. Ruth and Gehrig on the same team. It was a disaster. They were both the same man, playing the same role—two avunculars for the price of one. They did not play to each other or against each other as Huntley and Brinkley did. The chemistry was bad: Cronkite liked to work alone, and Murrow was not a good ad-libber.

By 1960 Huntley-Brinkley was number one in the ratings. For the first time, Paley, who loved to be number one, took notice and began to complain to his news executives — not about content but about ratings. Kintner loved it; he ordered the NBC people to close the nightly news with a statement saying that this news program had the largest audience in the world. Bill Paley was Number Two! It grated on him terribly, but not so terribly that he would change the sched-ules of the five CBS-owned and -operated—O and O—stations (the five stations the FCC allowed each network to own outright, and in-deed the richest source of network income) and put the Cronkite news on at 7 P.M. instead of 6:30, when it was then showing. NBC, of course, was showing Huntley-Brinkley at 7 on its O and O stations. Seven was the better hour, more people were at home then. The pleas of the CBS News Division that they be allowed to broadcast at seven, too, fell on deaf ears. It was a galling problem for the news people, it taught them how little muscle and prestige they really had in the company. Paley was adamant. Somewhere deep in the bowels of CBS, the news people were sure, there was a very smart accountant who was beating them on this issue.

It was in general a bad time for CBS News. The reason was simple: the rest of CBS was so successful, so dominant under Aubrey, that any interference with entertainment by public affairs lost money, real money; NBC, by contrast, not only was fielding an excellent news team at the peak of its ability, it was weaker in programming and had less to lose by emphasizing news, by interrupting programs, by promoting its apparent love of public affairs. Every NBC program seemed to bear some reminder that the way to watch the 1964 conventions was with Huntley-Brinkley. . . .

In 1964 NBC's success was awesome. A debacle for CBS. At one point in San Francisco NBC seemed to have submerged the entire opposition. Kintner, of course, loved it. He had a booth of his own with a special telephone to call his subordinates — it rang on their desks when he picked it up. Julian Goodman was in charge of listening on the phone, but at one point Goodman was out of the room and the job of handling Kintner and his phone fell to a producer named Shad Northshield. The phone rang.

"Northshield," said Northshield.

"The news ratings we've got are eighty-six," said Kintner's gravelly voice.

"That's great," said Northshield.

Kintner hung up immediately. A second later the phone rang again.

"Did you get that straight — eighty-six percent?" Kintner said, and hung up.

Seconds later the phone rang again.

"It seems to me that you could give me more of a reaction," Kintner said.

"Well, what do you want, a hundred percent?" asked Northshield.

"Yes," said Kintner. Bang went the phone. . . .

The difference between the NBC and the CBS coverage of the convention was not great; NBC was in command with a good team, and CBS with a younger floor team and a highly frenetic new level of executive leadership was less experienced. But there were not that many stories missed, because there were not that many stories to miss. The real difference was in the ratings, and it was an immense difference. Someone would have to pay. Long, long afterward, Walter Cronkite was still bothered, not just by the fact that he had been scapegoated, but because his superiors, in their discussion of what had gone wrong, never mentioned the coverage itself. He for one did not think that the coverage was very good, he thought that he hadn't done a particularly good job. But no one, when the crunch came, ever mentioned his weaknesses. And no one, certainly, thought of blaming the people who had failed to support the news program, Aubrey and Paley.

Paley had seemed irritable and restless at the Republican convention, and when Friendly and Bill Leonard, his deputy, returned to New York, that small media capital where everyone was talking only about NBC's triumph, they found his irritability had hardened. Paley now wanted drastic and immediate changes in the convention team, he was not about to remain number two. Friendly and Leonard tried to explain the performance in San Francisco, they pointed out that this was a young team, that time was now on their side, and that besides it was simply too late to change the team for the Democratic convention. They had compromised themselves slightly in their talks with Paley by mentioning innocently that Cronkite had talked a little too much during the convention. They realized their mistake immediately. Paley had seized on the comment: Yes, Cronkite was talking too much. Suddenly it was clear to them that Cronkite was going to be the fall guy, as far as Paley was concerned. Why was Cronkite on the air so much? Why did he dominate the others? Why did he talk too much? He had to go. There would be a new anchor. Paley and Stanton — usually it was Stanton who brought down the word from the corporate level but this time Paley was there as well—asked what changes the News Department was recommending. This was an ominous word, *recommending*. Friendly and Leonard said they planned to do nothing. Do you recommend, said Paley, that we get rid of Cronkite? Absolutely not, said Friendly. Then Paley told them to come back with specific recommendations in a few days. The corporation, it seemed, was about to confront the News Department. Friendly and Leonard met with Ernie Leiser, who was Cronkite's producer, and after much soul searching they recommended that it was impractical to do anything about the convention team. NBC was going to dominate at Atlantic City as it had in San Francisco and there was nothing that could be done about it. The best thing was simply to take your lumps and plan for the future.

It was not what Paley wanted to hear. This time the suggestion was a little less of a suggestion, more of a command. Come back and bring with you the names of the correspondents with whom you intend to replace Cronkite. Now they were meeting almost every day. At the next session Friendly and Leonard were still trying to hold the line, but Paley now had his own suggestion. Mudd. This terrific young correspondent Roger Mudd. Mudd, he said, was a born anchorman. (Which was perhaps true, particularly for a team that had been beaten by David Brinkley, for there was a touch of Brinkley in Roger Mudd, he was intelligent and wry and slightly irreverent, he seemed not to be overwhelmed by the gravity of occasions which, as a matter of fact, were rarely grave.) And now Paley became enthusiastic, there was nothing like this young fellow Mudd, he was terrific. And, with Mudd, said Paley, how about Bob Trout? If Mudd was young and from the world of television, Trout was senior and a word man, Trout could really describe things. Trout, of course, was a famous radio man who could go on for hours with lingering descriptions of events. A Mudd-Trout anchor, that was Paley's idea. The great thing about being Bill Paley, thought one of his aides, was that he could put the hook to Cronkite for Mudd-Trout, and then a few months later, when Mudd-Trout had failed, he could wonder aloud why he had allowed Friendly and Leonard to force such a weak team upon him.

In all this there was no talk of substance, no talk of missed coverage or of bad reporting, it was all of image and ratings. Friendly found himself caught between his ambition and his News Department, and what bothered friends of his in those days, as he talked his dilemma out, was that he seemed or at least half seemed to accept management's right to make nonnews judgments on news questions. A sacred line was being crossed without protest. Telling Dick Salant, his predecessor on the job, of the pressure and of the case Paley was building against Cronkite, Friendly said he did not know what to do. He just did not know which way to go. Salant answered: Fred, is it just ratings or is there a professional case against Cronkite? And Friendly answered, inadequately, that it was their candy store, that it all belonged to Paley. Knowing that he was being ordered to fire Cronkite, Friendly warned Paley that Cronkite would not stand for it and would quit if he lost his anchor, and Friendly was shocked by Paley's response: "Good, I hope he does." Finally Friendly gave in. It was a shocking failure, a classic example of what serious journalists had always feared about television, that the show-biz part would ultimately dominate the serious part. Among CBS working reporters Friendly's decision was not accepted; two years later, when Friendly resigned over the CBS failure to televise the Fulbright hearings, most members of his own staff thought he had chosen the wrong issue at the wrong time, that the real issue had been the yanking of Cronkite.

Friendly and Leonard flew out to California to break the news to Cronkite, who was vacationing. There was some talk of the possibility of a Mudd-Cronkite anchor, but Cronkite, a wildly proud man, wanted no part of it, he did not want to share his role with Mudd, and he knew CBS did not want him in the booth. Cronkite in his hour of crisis behaved very well. He did not dump on the company. He was properly loyal. Privately, talking with friends, he protected the company and the institution of television, saying that as a newspaper had a right to change editors if it wanted to, so too did a network have a right to change anchors. Then he held a public news conference and said yes, he thought the company had a right to change anchormen. No, he was not going to worry about it. He did not complain, nor did he agree to the suggestion of the CBS PR man who asked him to pose by a television set for an ad that was to say: *Even Walter Cronkite Listens to Mudd-Trout;* his loyalty to CBS did not extend to fatuousness. At Atlantic City he happened, by chance, to enter an elevator that contained Bob Kintner of NBC. Reporters spotted them coming out and thereupon wrote that Cronkite was going to NBC, a rumor that helped him in his next CBS contract negotiations. All in all it could have been worse for him; he was buttressed by an inner and quite valid suspicion that a Mudd-Trout was likely to be an endangered species.

When Friendly returned from his trip to California, he called Stanton to let him know that the preeminent figure of television had been separated from his most important job, and Stanton had said (it made Friendly feel like a sinister character in a Shakespeare play—yes, the deed has been done, sire), "Good, the chairman will be delighted." Mudd-Trout duly appeared. They were a total failure. NBC routed CBS even more dramatically at Atlantic City (some Cronkite fans going over to NBC in anger), and there was one moment during the convention (which, of course, was not a convention so much as it was a coronation) that remained engraved on the minds of the two news teams. It was the night that Johnson was to accept the nomination. Sander Vanocur of NBC had known Johnson and knew his style, and what he was likely to be feeling like, so he positioned himself near the entrance and waited and waited, guessing that Johnson at this moment might just be in a expansive mood, and then Johnson appeared and Vanocur popped up and had him. Yes, Johnson was in a marvelous, rich, anecdotal mood and — perhaps because Vanocur was regarded as a Kennedy man, what better way to vanquish the ghosts — he had gone on and on. With no one from CBS there at all. It was a marvelous exclusive and Kintner ran it and ran it all night, and when the CBS people saw it come over they were appalled. There was no one near at hand and so Bill Leonard, who was the head of the election unit and not a reporter at all, put on an electronic backpack and went rushing over, panting, and Vanocur, his exclusive done and by now running on the air for the third time, a great scoop in a scoopless convention, turned with a small smile of comfortable charity (which might later have cost him a job at CBS) and said to the President of the United States, "Mr. President, you know Bill Leonard of CBS — he's a good man." Victory at Atlantic City. The end of the Mudd-Trout.

Friendly had worked hard to keep Cronkite from quitting outright to persuade him to stay with the evening news. Cronkite did stay, and that fall CBS put together a magnificent election unit that ran far ahead of NBC up through election eve and that gave CBS the major share of the ratings. Cronkite was, of course, immediately rehabilitated; at the same time, the Huntley-Brinkley format was slipping, it had played for eight years and that was, given the insatiable greed of television, a very long time. The Cronkite show, aided by what was to be exceptional coverage of the Vietnam War by a team of talented young reporters, regained its prestige. But there are two footnotes to the tensions of the 1964 convention.

The first deals with the question of being number one. Paley had wanted to be number one without paying the price, while Friendly and the others had argued for the change in evening time slots that would allow Cronkite to come in at the better hour. But Paley had never listened. Then the dismal ratings of San Francisco stirred him, and one night during the convention, when all the indicators were absolutely terrible, Frank Stanton flew from New York to San Francisco and gathered Leiser, Friendly, and Leonard for dinner. He had, he said, some very good news. And so with that marvelous delicacy which marks the way things are done in corporations (no admission that perhaps the News Department was right and that Paley had changed his mind — chairmen do not change their minds), Stanton said that if Friendly called the people at the local stations in New York and Philadelphia he might be able to argue them into letting Cronkite come on at seven o'clock. So Friendly made the calls, and lo and behold, his marvelous persuasive powers worked and Cronkite got just enough of a boost from the time change to regain his rating.

The second footnote deals with the man himself. For the Walter Cronkite who came back to work was a somewhat different man from the one he had been before being humiliated in public. As the next few years passed and he became even more the dominant figure of the industry, his pride intensified. In 1968 during the Democratic convention the delegates were voting on the peace plank. And suddenly, as sometimes happens at conventions, Cronkite and everyone else started using — overusing — a single word to refer to a situation. The word this time was *erosion*, which had obviously replaced *slippage*, the last convention's word. The vote came to Alabama and Cronkite mentioned that there was an erosion of two votes. He was broadcasting live and suddenly someone passed him a scribbled note: "Tell Walter not to use the word 'erosion'!" Cronkite, without missing a beat in the commentary, answered with his own note: "Who says?" Back came another note: "Stanton." Suddenly it was as if there were fire coming out of Cronkite's nostrils, and even as he continued the delegate count he wrote one more note: "I quit." So someone handed a note to pass to the brass saying: "Walter quits." And this was passed back and even as it was being passed back Cronkite was standing up and taking off his headset and reaching for his jacket. It was an electric moment. And suddenly someone was yelling, "For God's sake tell him to get back down there, don't let him leave. They're not trying to censor him. They just don't like the word 'erosion.'" So he sat down, and continued his broadcast. They might mess with him once, but no one messed with Walter Cronkite a second time.

Furniture Factory

Robert Schrank

It was 1932 and we were in the depths of the depression. If you were lucky enough to find a job, it was usually through a friend, and that was how I got my first full-time job in a Brooklyn factory that made frames for upholstered furniture. I was fifteen years old and lived in the Bronx, traveling on the subway for an hour and fifteen minutes each way, every day, six days a week for twelve dollars. I considered myself to be the luckiest boy in the world to get that job. When Mr. Miller, the owner of the Miller Parlor Frame Company, interviewed me and agreed to hire me, he made it quite clear that he was doing a favor for a mutual friend and did not really care much about giving me a job.

Like most small factory offices, Mr. Miller's was cluttered with catalogs, samples of materials, some small tools, a rolltop desk with a large blotter pad worn through the corners. The whole place was in a sawdust fog with a persistent cover of dust over everything. Mr. Miller was a short fat man who chewed cigars and sort of drooled as he talked to me. He sat on the edge of his big oak swivel chair. I had a feeling he might slip off anytime. He never looked at me as we spoke. He made it clear that he was annoyed at people asking favors, saying that he did not like people who were "always trying to get something out of me."

The sour smell of the oak sawdust comes back to fill my nose as I recall the furniture factory. It is a smell I always welcomed until I had to live in it eight hours a day. There were days, especially when it was damp or raining, when the wood smell was so strong you could not eat your lunch. Next to the smell I remember getting to the factory and back as being an awful drag. But the New York subway that I rode to and from work for many years had two marked positive effects on me. First, I felt part of a general condition that nobody seemed to like. I was part of a group and we were all in the same fix, busting our asses to get to work in the morning and home at night. While I felt unhappy, it was made easier through the traditional "misery loves company," and there was plenty of that. And second, if I had a lucky day, there was the chance of seeing or being pressed up against some sweet-smelling, young, pretty thing who would get me all excited. Sometimes I tried a pickup, but it usually did not work because the situation was too public. With each person rigidly contained, it was surprising if anyone tried to move out of his shell. Everyone in the train would be staring to see what would develop. Almost nothing did.

To be at the furniture factory in Brooklyn by 8 A.M., I would leave my house in the Bronx by 6:30 A.M. While it was always a bad trip it became less so in the long spring days of the year as contrasted with December, when I most hated getting up in the dark. It was very important to be very quiet as I would feel my way around our old frame house, so as not to wake people who had another thirty or forty minutes to sleep. I would sleepily make a sandwich for lunch, preferably from a leftover or just bologna, grab a cup of coffee — always with one eye on the clock—and run for the station. Luckily, we lived at the end of a subway line, and in the morning I was usually able to get a corner seat in the train. The corner seat was good for sleeping because I could rest against the train wall and not have the embarrassment of falling asleep on the person sitting next to me. It meant being able to sleep the hour-long trip to Brooklyn, and it was critical to set my "inner clock" so it would wake me up at the Morgan Avenue station in Brooklyn. If it failed or was a little late, which sometimes happened, panic would ensue, as I usually would wake up just as the train was pulling out of Morgan Avenue. I would make a quick, unsuccessful dash for the door, and people would try to help by grabbing at the door. Then I would burn with anger for being late and maybe losing the job. When I would end up past my stop, I would have to make a fast decision to either spend another nickel and go back or go on to a double station where I could race down the steps to the other side of the tracks and catch a train going the other way without paying an additional fare.

The trip home from work on the New York subway in the evening rush hour is an experience most difficult to describe. The train, packed full of people, hurtles into a station. The doors slide open. There is always an illusion that someone may be getting out. That never seems to happen while a mass of people begin to push their way in. All strangers, we are not packed like sardines in a can, as is often suggested; the packing of sardines is an orderly process. The rush hour subway is more like a garbage compacter that just squeezes trash and rubbish into a dense mass and then hurtles it at very high speeds through a small underground tube. Unlike the morning, at night when I was exhausted from the day's work I never was able to get a seat, and that meant standing on my dog-tired feet for more than an hour and trying not to lean on the person next to me, an almost impossible thing to do. . . .

As I walked from the subway in the morning I could smell the furniture factory a block away. It was a powerful smell; as I said, I loved that oak at first. It was a perfume from the woods: a combination of skunk, mushrooms, and honeysuckle blended to a musk, a sweet contrast to the steel-and-oil stink of the subway. Yet, by the end of a day's work, the factory, its smells, its noise, its tedium all became so terribly tiresome and exhausting that leaving every day was an act of liberation.

The factory was a five-story loft building about half a city block long. The making of the furniture frames began on the bottom floor where the rough cuts were made from huge pieces of lumber. As the cut wood moved along from floor to floor, it was formed, shaped, carved, dowled, sanded, and finally assembled on the top floor into completed frames. The machines in the plant included table saws, band saws, planers, carving machines, routers, drills, hydraulic presses, all run by 125 machine operators who were almost all European immigrants. My job was to keep the operators supplied with material, moving the finished stuff to the assembly floor, a sort of human conveyor. When I wasn't moving pieces around, I was supposed to clean up, which meant bagging sawdust into burlap bags. Sometimes the foreman would come and say, "Hey, kid, how would you like to run the dowling machine?" At first I thought that was a real break, a chance to get on a machine and become an operator. I told him enthusiastically, "Yeah, that would be great." I would sit in front of this little machine, pick up a predrilled piece, hold it to the machine, which would push two glued dowels into the holes. I soon found that I preferred moving parts around the plant and cleaning up to sitting at that machine all day, picking up a piece of wood from one pile, locating the holes at the dowel feeder that pushed in two preglued dowels, then dropping it on the other side. The machine had a sort of gallump, gallump rhythm that made me sleepy and started me watching the clock, the worst thing you can do in a factory. It would begin to get to me, and I would just sit and stare at the machine, the clock, the machine, the clock.

Those first few weeks in that factory were an agony of never-ending time. The damn clock just never moved, and over and over again I became convinced that it had stopped. Gradually, life in the furniture factory boiled down to waiting for the four work breaks: coffee, lunch hour, coffee, and quitting time. When the machines stopped, it was only in their sudden silence that I became aware of their deafening whine. It was almost impossible to hear each other talk while they were running, and all we were able to do was to scream essential information at one another.

The breaks were the best times of the day, for I could become intoxicated listening to the older men talk of rough, tough things in the big world out there. Being accepted was a slow process, and I was just happy to be allowed to listen. When I had been there for a couple of weeks, Mike the Polack said, "Hey, kid, meet in the shit house for talk." I was making it all right.

The coffee- and lunch-break talks centered around the family, sports, politics, and sex, in about that order. The immigrants from Middle Europe, and especially the Jews, were the most political. Most of them seemed to believe that politicians were crooks and that's how it is. The Jews talked the least about sex and the Italians the most. Luigi would endlessly bait Max (who would soon be my friend), saying that what he needed most was "a good woman who make you forget all dat political shit." There were a whole variety of newspapers published in New York at that time and one way workers had of figuring out each other's politics, interests, and habits was by the papers they read.

Max Teitelbaum would say to me, "See Louie over there. You can tell he's just a dummy, he reads that *Daily Mirror.* It fills his head with garbage so he can't tink about vot is *really* happening in the vorld." Arguing strongly in the defense of Franklin Roosevelt, probably too strongly, Mike the Polack told me with his finger waving close to my nose, "Listen, kid, vot I tink and vot I do is my business, and nobody, no politician or union or smart-ass kid like you is gonna butt into dat. You got it? Don't forget it!"

As people began to trust me, I was slowly making friends. Their trust was expressed in small ways, like when Luigi called me over to his workbench, held up a picture of Jean Harlow for me to look at as he shook his big head of black hair, all the time contemplating the picture together with me, and said, "Now, whaddya tink, boy?" . . . Then he said, "OK, kid, you gotta work hard and learn something. See all those poor bastards out there outa work. Watch out or you could be one of dem." Luigi was a wood-carver who made the models for the multiple-spindle carving machine and was probably the only real craftsman in the place.

One day as I distributed work in process to the operators and picked up their finished stuff, I received one of my first lessons in the fundamentals of working that I would relearn again and again in almost every job I have had: How to work less hard in order to make the task easier.

Max Teitelbaum, a band saw operator just a few years out of Krakow, Poland, a slightly built man with sort of Mickey Mouse ears, twinkling eyes, and a wry smile, would upbraid me repeatedly with such passing comments as, "You are a dummy," or "You're not stupid, so what's da matter vit you?" Finally one day he stopped his machine, turned to me, and said, "Look, come over here. I vant to talk vit you. Vy you are using your back instead your head? Max Teitelbaum's first rule is: Don't carry nuttin' you could put a veel under. It's a good ting you wasn't helpin' mit der pyramids — you vould get crushed under the stones."

I said, "But Max, if the hand truck is on the third floor and I'm on the fifth, I can't go all the way down there just for that."

"You see," he said, "you are a dummy. Vy you can't go down dere? Huh, vy not? You tell me!"

"Well," I said, "it would take a lot of time — "

He cut me off. "You see, you are vorrying about da wrong tings, like da boss. Is he vorrying about you? Like da Tzar vorried about Max Teitelbaum. Listen, kid, you vorry about you because no von else vill. Understand? You vill get nuttin' for vorking harder den more vork. Now ven you even don't understand someting, you come and ask Max. OK?" Max became my friend, adviser, and critic.

By the end of my first weeks in the factory I began to feel as if I was crushed under stones. My body helped me to understand what Max was saying. I would come home from work on Saturday afternoon and go to bed expecting to go out later that night with a girl friend. For some weeks when I lay down on Saturday I did not try, nor was I able, to move my body from bed until some time on Sunday. The whole thing just throbbed with fatigue: arms, shoulders, legs, and back were in fierce competition for which hurt the most. I began to learn what Max meant by "Always put a veel under it and don't do more than you have to."

My third or fourth week at the factory found me earnestly launched in my quest for holding the job but doing less work — or working less hard. This was immediately recognized and hailed by the men with "Now you're gettin' smart, kid. Stop bustin' your ass and only do what you have to do. You don't get any more money for bustin' your hump and you might put some other poor bastard outa a job." Remember this was the depression. Most workers, while aware of the preciousness of their jobs, felt that doing more work than necessary could be putting someone else, even yourself, out of a job. "Only do what you have to" became a rule not only to save your own neck but to make sure you were not depriving some other soul like yourself from getting a job.

In the next few weeks, I was to be taught a second important lesson about working. One day while picking up sawdust, I began to "find" pieces in the sawdust or behind a woodpile or under a machine. The first few times, with great delight, I would announce to the operator, "Hey, look what I found!" I should have figured something was wrong by the lack of any similar enthusiasm from the operator. Sam was a generally quiet Midwesterner who never seemed to raise his voice much, but now when I showed him my finished-work discovery behind his milling machine he shouted, "Who the fuck asked you to be a detective? Keep your silly ass out from behind my machine; I'll tell you what to pick up. So don't go being a big brown-nosing hero around here."

Wow, I sure never expected that. Confused, troubled, almost in tears, not knowing what to do or where to go, I went to the toilet to hide my hurt and just sat down on an open bowl and thought what the hell am I doing in this goddamned place anyway? I lit a cigarette and began pacing up and down in front of the three stalls, puffing away at my Camel. I thought, What the hell should I do? This job is terrible, the men are pissed off at me. I hate the place, why don't I just quit? Well, it's a job and you get paid, I said to myself, so take it easy.

While I'm pacing and puffing, Sam comes in, saying, "Lissen, kid, don't get sore. I was just trying to set you straight. Let me tell you what it's all about. The guys around, that is the machine operators, agree on how much we are gonna turn out, and that's what the boss gets, no more, no less. Now sometimes any one of us might just fall behind a little, so we always keep some finished stuff hidden away just in case." The more he talked, the more I really began to feel like the enemy. I tried to apologize, but he just went on. "Look, kid, the boss always wants more and he doesn't give a shit if we die giving it to him, so we [it was that "we" that seemed to retrieve my soul back into the community; my tears just went away] agree on how much we're going to give him — no more, no less. You see, kid, if you keep running around, moving the stuff too fast, the boss will get wise about what's going on." Sam put his arm on my shoulder. (My God! I was one of them! I love Sam and the place. I am in!) "So look," he says, "your job is to figure out how to move and work no faster than we turn the stuff out. Get it? OK? You'll get it." I said, "Yes, of course, I understand everything." I was being initiated into the secrets of a work tribe, and I loved it.

I was beginning to learn the second work lesson that would be taught me many times over in a variety of different jobs: Don't do more work than is absolutely necessary. Years later I would read about how people in the Hawthorne works of Western Electric would "bank work" and use it when they fell behind or just wanted to take it easy. I have seen a lot of work banking, especially in machine shops. In some way I have felt that banking work was the workers' response to the stopwatches of industrial engineers. It is an interesting sort of game of hide the work now, take it out later. In another plant, would you believe we banked propellor shafts for Liberty ships!

I learned most of the rules, written and unwritten, about the furniture factory, but I never got to like the job. After I had been there six or seven months, the Furniture Workers Union began an organizing drive. I hated the furniture factory, the noise, the dust, and the travel, so I, too, quickly signed a union card. I was just as quickly out on my ass. It was a good way to go, since my radical friends considered me a hero of sorts, having been victimized for the cause. The first time I ever considered suicide in my life was in that furniture factory as I would stare at the clock and think to myself, "If I have to spend my life in this hellhole, I would rather end it." Well, of course, I didn't; and as I look back, it was not the worst place I worked, but I was young and unwilling to relinquish childhood.

The Ratebuster: The Case of the Saleswoman*

Melville Dalton

THE SALESWOMAN

Of the six people in the boys' department only the head was male, and he made sales only occasionally. Two of the women were high sellers—Mrs. White and Mrs. Brown. Mrs. White was fifty-nine years old, large physically and somewhat taciturn. She had worked at Lassiters for fourteen years. Mrs. Brown was a small active person, thirty-two, and had been with the store for eight years. Masters told me that when she started in the store she was much taken with Mrs. White and copied and improved upon Mrs. White's selling techniques. Then, too, Mrs. Brown had the insights that came from close personal experience in outfitting her son. Over a period of several months they developed a rivalry. For the last six years or so, according to Masters [Mike Masters, head of the boys' department], they

From Melville Dalton, "The Ratebuster: The Case of the Saleswoman," in *Varieties of Work Experience: The Social Control of Occupational Groups and Roles,* by P. L. Stewart and M. G. Cantor, eds., pp. 206–214. Copyright 1974 by Schenkman Publishing Co., Inc. Reprinted by permission.

were coldly polite to each other when it was necessary to speak. Masters regarded existence of this hostility as one of his major problems. His professed ideal was that the women should all be circulating among the customers, busy all the time and cordial to each other.

The other three salesgirls were Mrs. Bonomo, thirty-five, a quiet amenable person, in the department for four years; Mrs. Selby, forty-eight, an employee for five years, who took things as they came without being much disturbed — though judging from her behavior and remarks she made, she disliked Mrs. White much more than she did Mrs. Brown. Mrs. Dawson, at twenty-two, was the youngest member of the department. She had dubbed Mrs. Brown and Mrs. White "sales hogs." She had worked there less than two years. She liked Mrs. Brown despite the epithet she had given her. Mrs. Dawson had two years of college, the most schooling in the department.

The saleswomen received from $1.75 to $2.25 per hour, depending on how long they had been in the department. Records of sales (dollar-volume) for the department were kept for the past year and varied from month to month. These records established the quota for the current year. Once this was equaled, the women started drawing commission pay at the rate of five percent. Commission was paid separately once a month.

Before describing the selling tactics of Mrs. Brown and Mrs. White, the ratebuster types, it is instructive to note the average daily sales established over a six-month period[1] by the five saleswomen. Mrs. Brown with $227 average daily sales is over twice as much as Mrs. Dawson and Mrs. Selby, nearly twice as much as Mrs. Bonomo, and $74 more than the second ratebuster, Mrs. White. Masters assured me that Mrs. White had slowed up noticeably in her selling over the last two years, but in terms of dollar sales and her constant challenge to Mrs. Brown she should still be classified as a ratebuster, or a ratebuster in decline.

Saleswomen	Average Daily Dollar Sales
Mrs. Brown	227
Mrs. White	153
Mrs. Bonomo	119
Mrs. Selby	110
Mrs. Dawson	101

Lassiters had an employee credit union. Masters had access to the complete membership, which was seventy-six. He gave me *rank only* of the five saleswomen based on the individual amounts deposited in the credit union. (He was so shocked when I requested the total savings of each of the saleswomen that I gladly accepted the partial data.) Mrs. White stood third in the store, and Mrs. Brown was fourth. Mrs.

Selby ranked forty-ninth and Mrs. Bonomo was sixty-sixth. Mrs. Dawson was not a member. These data alone do not tell much, but they do indicate that Mrs. White and Mrs. Brown were among the top investors, and that commission was important in their behavior.

RATEBUSTER TACTICS

Mrs. Brown apparently had more personal relations with customers than anyone in the boys' department. She learned from Masters when specially priced merchandise was coming in. She telephoned customers she knew well and made arrangements to lay away items of given size and style that were scheduled to go on sale. When she had filled these private orders there was little of the merchandise left for the general public when the official sale day arrived. These sales by telephone constituted about fifteen percent of her total sales. Relatively new customers who bought heavily a time or two she filed in her retentive memory and took steps to acquaint them with her special services.

Among her repeat buyers was a working woman with four sons who treated their clothing roughly. Every six weeks this woman came in to buy nearly complete outfits for the boys. This included shirts, underwear, socks and blue jeans, which amounted to what the sales force called a "big ticket" of about $120.

Mrs. Brown had another woman customer who did not believe in having the younger boys of her five sons wear the older boys' outgrown clothing. She did not come in much oftener than once a year to buy complete outfits, usually just before Easter, which could run to two hundred dollars or more. Mrs. Brown acted as though she had an exclusive right[2] to these customers, and several others that she knew who had only two sons. When Mrs. Brown expected these people she would skip her lunch hour for fear she might miss them, or ask Masters to make the sale and ring it up on her cash drawer in case the woman came when she was out to lunch. He was glad to do this. When business was very good, whether she expected specific customers or not, she ignored the coffee breaks (ten minutes each morning and afternoon) and the lunch hour, leaving the selling floor only long enough to eat a sandwich in the dressing room.

She also had a practical monopoly on sales for boys on welfare. These boys had to be presented by an agent of the welfare organization the first time they did business with the store. Masters turned the welfare customer over to Mrs. Brown and forever afterwards[3] she made the sales. In some cases the welfare officer brought the boy, or boys, with their only clothes on their backs, to buy a complete outfit with extra socks, handkerchiefs and underwear. (Shoes were not sold in the boys' department.) In any case, Mrs. Brown took care of the sales then and afterwards.

Mrs. Brown's housekeeping area was just inside the entrance from the parking lot. She watched this approach closely. When she was not busy, or was talking to the other members of the department, she could break off instantly — even when she was telling a joke — and move toward the door. If she did not recognize the person she formed some judgment on him based on the affluence of his dress and his bearing. If the customer had a boy along, she judged whether he would be hard to fit. In her own words, she had a theory that "the kids who are tall and skinny or short and fat are hard to fit."[4] Thus she made quick appraisals of everybody who moved toward the department. If she approached a customer and learned that he was not as promising as he looked, she often brought the person to one of the other saleswomen and presented him with a statement of what he wanted as though — according to the women — she was giving them an assured sale. She made no revealing comment on the matter, but she seemed at the same time to be putting a restraint on her rivals.

Mrs. Brown's most galling behavior to the group was her practice of getting sale claims on as many prospective buyers as possible. She thus deprived the other saleswomen of a chance at the buyers. For instance, as she was serving one person, she would see another coming through the door — which she nearly always faced even when busiest. Quickly she would lay a number of items before the first person with the promise to be back in a moment, then hurry to capture the second customer. If the situation were right, she might get her claim on three or four buyers while two or more of the saleswomen were reduced to maintaining the show cases, and setting things in order so as not to appear idle. Mrs. Brown was able to do this because her own housekeeping and stocking area (assigned by Masters) lay between the entrance to the store and the other sections of the boys' department. Only Mrs. White would challenge her by intercepting a patron. The rivalry between them never came to a visible break. As noted earlier some of the other saleswomen resented Mrs. Brown's behavior and privately called her a "sales hog." She was not called that by Mrs. Bonomo and Mrs. Selby who thought — as they said — that Mrs. Brown in action was a "show in itself."

A standard device was used by Mrs. Brown, for ends not intended, with the understanding and collaboration of Masters. On very slack days she frequently left the store shortly after one or two o'clock to do "comparative shopping," that is, to compare the selling prices of items that Lassiters sold with the prices that other local stores charged for the same or similar items. Sometimes Mrs. Brown actually did this, but often she would attend a matinee, or go home to catch up with her housework, or just take a nap. (Her time card was punched out by Masters at the official quitting time.) In any case, to the favorable implications of "comparative shopping," the further obvious inference was made that her absense from the store allowed the other salesgirls to make more commission. (Actually, business was so slow on some days, because of weather, etc., that it was not possible for any of the saleswomen to earn bonus pay.)

Mrs. Brown's conduct may suggest total indifference to the group. But possibly because she was a female in our society, she was not as nonconformist as the grim ratebusters in industry. Some of these could work for years without exchange of words with people, only a few feet away, that they knew hated them. To a degree Mrs. Brown was concerned about her group. Every week or so she would buy a two-pound box of choice chocolates from a candy store near Lassiters and bring it in to share with the group. She could have bought a less expensive grade of candy at Lassiters. Sharing of the candy was almost certainly calculated (she ate little of it herself) but it appeared spontaneous and was received without hesitation. The saleswomen could not direct an unqualified hostility toward her.

She had another uncommon practice which made her stand apart from all of Lassiters' employees. Despite her determined assault on the commission system she did not use her right to a discount on items that she might buy for herself or members of her family. She took her fifteen-year-old son to a local independent department store to buy his clothes. She vigorously declared that "I don't want anything that [Lassiters] has." She was emphatic to the group—and implicitly condemned them—that she did not want to participate in the common practice of getting legal price reductions in addition to the regular employee discount by buying items at the end of a season. For example, an assortment of women's purses would be delivered to the selling floor. This was the "beginning of the season" for that batch of purses. The saleswomen with friends in the purse department would look at the display and select ones that appealed to them. These were laid away until the "end of the season" when they could be bought at the sale price which was further reduced by the regular discount. Mrs. Brown would have nothing to do with such items. She clearly did not want it said that she was taking advantage of her job.

A likely interpretation is that she sensed she was rejected and widely critized for her methods and high bonus pay. She feared that some envious salesperson would report any borderline activity on her part to top management. Her own explanation implied that her esthetic taste could not be satisfied by the merchandise at Lassiters. In effect she downgraded the status of the store. As part of this complex she also implied that she was morally somewhat above the group. Also she may have been posing to hide her possible guilt feelings about her treatment of the group.

Although the aim of this paper is not to deal with morale problems, it was glaringly clear that Masters damaged group feeling by routing welfare customers to Mrs. Brown, and by ringing up some of his sales on her cash drawer. His tacit approval of her behavior discouraged the other saleswomen from attempting to control her.

NOTES

*The names of the individuals in this case and the department store (Lassiters) are fictional. The incidents described took place in the boys' department of Lassiters. The saleswomen in the department were all on commission.

As Dalton observed in a portion of this article which was omitted here, it is common for members of work groups who are on a commission or other system of incentive payments to avoid showing each other up. In other words, there are informal standards about what members of the group perceive to be a reasonable amount of work. Individuals who produce significantly above this level are often called "ratebusters" or "grabbers" by social scientists. Members of the work group often apply less complimentary labels and even sanctions to individuals who violate the output norms. At Lassiters, ratebusters were called "sales hogs" by their peers. — Eds.

1. Masters gave me these figures based on average of 44 hours a week and including the back-to-school buying months of August and September 1969.

2. Probably she was encouraged by the customers to think that way; certainly some customers waited for her to be free to serve them.

3. The other saleswomen knew about this and resented it. Grateful to Masters for allowing me to observe and talk with the saleswomen, I naturally did not ask him why there was no sharing of such sales among his force. I inquired, but there was no voiced conception of a "day's work" among the saleswomen. This general practice of informal rewarding is not uncommon in industry, where it is sometimes done even with the knowledge and cooperation of individual officers of the union. (Lassiters was not unionized.)

4. Alteration of coats and trousers was done free by the store's tailor. But measuring and marking and the extra trying on were time-consuming. In the extreme cases this was futuile. In any case Mrs. Brown avoided customers with "odd size" boys unless she knew them to be liberal buyers and worth her time.

The World of Epictetus

Reflections on survival and leadership

Vice Admiral James Bond Stockdale, USN

*The author was the senior naval service prisoner of war and leader of
American covert resistance in North Vietnamese prisons from 1965 to 1973.
He was awarded the Congressional Medal of Honor and is currently a
senior research fellow at the Hoover Institution at Stanford University. An
award for "inspirational leadership" has been established in his name by
the Navy for commanding officers below the grade of captain who are serving in command of fleet operational ships, submarines, or aviation squad-
rons.*

In 1965 I was a forty-one-year-old commander, the senior pilot of Air
Wing 16, flying combat missions in the area just south of Hanoi from
the aircraft carrier *Oriskany.* By September of that year I had grown
quite accustomed to briefing dozens of pilots and leading them on
daily air strikes; I had flown nearly 200 missions myself and knew the
countryside of North Vietnam like the back of my hand. On the ninth
of that month I led about thirty-five airplanes to the Thanh Hoa
Bridge, just west of that city. That bridge was tough; we had been
bouncing 500-pounders off it for weeks.

The September 9 raid held special meaning for *Oriskany* pilots because of a special bomb load we had improvised; we were going in
with our biggest, the 2000-pounders, hung not only on our attack
planes but on our F-8 fighter-bombers as well. This increase in
bridge-busting capability came from the innovative brain of a major
flying with my Marine fighter squadron. He had figured out how we
could jury-rig some switches, hang the big bombs, pump out some of
the fuel to stay within takeoff weight limits, and then top off our
tanks from our airborne refuelers while en route to the target. Although the pilot had to throw several switches in sequence to get rid
of his bombs, a procedure requiring above-average cockpit agility, we
routinely operated on the premise that all pilots of Air Wing 16 were
above average. I test-flew the new load on a mission, thought it over,
and approved it; that's the way we did business.

Our spirit was up. That morning, the *Oriskany* Air Wing was finally
going to drop the bridge that was becoming a North Vietnamese
symbol of resistance. You can imagine our dismay when we crossed
the coast and the weather scout I had sent on ahead radioed back that
ceiling and visibility were zero-zero in the bridge area. In the tiny

cockpit of my A-4 at the front of the pack, I pushed the button on the throttle, spoke into the radio mike in my oxygen mask, and told the formation to split up and proceed in pairs to the secondary targets I had specified in my contingency briefing. What a letdown.

The adrenaline stopped flowing as my wingman and I broke left and down and started sauntering along toward our "milk run" target: boxcars on a railroad siding between Vinh and Thanh Hoa, where the flak was light. Descending through 10,000 feet, I unsnapped my oxygen mask and let it dangle, giving my pinched face a rest—no reason to stay uncomfortable on this run.

As I glided toward that easy target, I'm sure I felt totally self-satisfied. I had the top combat job that a Navy commander can hold and I was in tune with my environment. I was confident—I knew airplanes and flying inside out. I was comfortable with the people I worked with and I knew the trade so well that I often improvised variations in accepted procedures and encouraged others to do so under my watchful eye. I was on top. I thought I had found every key to success and had no doubt that my Academy and test-pilot schooling had provided me with everything I needed in life.

I passed down the middle of those boxcars and smiled as I saw the results of my instinctive timing. A neat pattern—perfection. I was just pulling out of my dive low to the ground when I heard a noise I hadn't expected—the *boom boom boom* of a 57-millimeter gun—and then I saw it just behind my wingtip. I was hit—all the red lights came on, my control system was going out—and I could barely keep that plane from flying into the ground while I got that damned oxygen mask up to my mouth so I could tell my wingman that I was about to eject. What rotten luck. And on a "milk run"!

The descent in the chute was quiet except for occasional rifle shots from the streets below. My mind was clear, and I said to myself, "five years." I knew we were making a mess of the war in Southeast Asia, but I didn't think it would last longer than that; I was also naive about the resources I would need in order to survive a lengthy period of captivity.

The Durants have said that culture is a thin and fragile veneer that superimposes itself on mankind. For the first time I was on my own, without the veneer. I was to spend years searching through and refining my bag of memories, looking for useful tools, things of value. The values were there, but they were all mixed up with technology, bureaucracy, and expediency, and had to be brought up into the open.

Education should take care to illuminate values, not bury them amongst the trivia. Are our students getting the message that without personal integrity intellectual skills are worthless?

Integrity is one of those words which many people keep in that desk drawer labeled "too hard." It's not a topic for the dinner table or the cocktail party. You can't buy or sell it. When supported with education, a person's integrity can give him something to rely on when his perspective seems to blur, when rules and principles seem to waver, and when he's faced with hard choices of right or wrong. It's something to keep him on the right track, something to keep him afloat when he's drowning; if only for practical reasons, it is an attribute that should be kept at the very top of a young person's consciousness.

The importance of the latter point is highlighted in prison camps, where everyday human nature, stripped bare, can be studied under a magnifying glass in accelerated time. Lessons spotlighted and absorbed in that laboratory sharpen one's eye for their abstruse but highly relevant applications in the "real time" world of now.

In the five years since I've been out of prison, I've participated several times in the process of selecting senior naval officers for promotion or important command assignments. I doubt that the experience is significantly different from that of executives who sit on "selection boards" in any large hierarchy. The system must be formal, objective, and fair; if you've seen one, you've probably seen them all. Navy selection board proceedings go something like this.

The first time you know the identity of the other members of the board is when you walk into a boardroom at eight o'clock on an appointed morning. The first order of business is to stand, raise your right hand, put your left hand on the Bible, and swear to make the best judgment you can, on the basis of merit, without prejudice. You're sworn to confidentiality regarding all board members' remarks during the proceedings. Board members are chosen for their experience and understanding; they often have knowledge of the particular individuals under consideration. They must feel free to speak their minds. They read and grade dozens of dossiers, and each candidate is discussed extensively. At voting time, a member casts his vote by selecting and pushing a "percent confidence" button, visible only to himself, on a console attached to his chair. When the last member pushes his button, a totalizer displays the numerical average "confidence" of the board. No one knows who voted what.

I'm always impressed by the fact that every effort is made to be fair to the candidate. Some are clearly out, some are clearly in; the borderline cases are the tough ones. You go over and over those in the "middle pile" and usually you vote and revote until late at night. In all the boards I've sat on, no inference or statement in a "jacket" is as sure to portend a low confidence score on the vote as evidence of a lack of directness or rectitude of a candidate in his dealings with others. Any hint of moral turpitude really turns people off. When the crunch comes, they prefer to work with forthright plodders rather than with devious geniuses. I don't believe that this preference is unique to the military. In any hierarchy where people's fates are decided by committees or boards, those who lose credibility with their peers and who cause their superiors to doubt their directness, honesty, or integrity are dead. Recovery isn't possible.

The linkage of men's ethics, reputations, and fates can be studied in even more vivid detail in prison camp. In that brutally controlled environment a perceptive enemy can get his hooks into the slightest chink in a man's ethical armor and accelerate his downfall. Given the right opening, the right moral weakness, a certain susceptibility on the part of the prisoner, a clever extortionist can drive his victim into a downhill slide that will ruin his image, self-respect, and life in a very short time.

There are some uncharted aspects to this, some traits of susceptibility which I don't think psychologists yet have words for. I am thinking of the tragedy that can befall a person who has such a need for love or attention that he will sell his soul for it. I use tragedy with the rigorous definition Aristotle applied to it: the story of a good man with a flaw who comes to an unjustified bad end. This is a rather delicate point and one that I want to emphasize. We had very very few collaborators in prison, and comparatively few Aristotelian tragedies, but the story and fate of one of these good men with a flaw might be instructive.

He was handsome, smart, articulate, and smooth. He was almost sincere. He was obsessed with success. When the going got tough, he decided expediency was preferable to principle.

This man was a classical opportunist. He befriended and worked for the enemy to the detriment of his fellow Americans. He made a tacit deal; moreover, he accepted favors (a violation of the code of conduct). In time, out of fear and shame, he withdrew; we could not get him to communicate with the American prisoner organization.

I couldn't learn what made the man tick. One of my best friends in prison, one of the wisest persons I have ever known, had once been in a squadron with this fellow. In prisoners' code I tapped a question to my philosophical friend: "What in the world is going on with that fink?"

"You're going to be surprised at what I have to say," he meticulously tapped back. "In a squadron he pushes himself forward and dominates the scene. He's a continual fountain of information. He's the person everybody relies on for inside dope. He works like mad;

often flies more hops than others. It drives him crazy if he's not liked. He tends to grovel and ingratiate himself before others. I didn't realize he was really pathetic until I was sitting around with him and his wife one night when he was spinning his yarns of delusions of grandeur, telling of his great successes and his pending ascension to the top. His wife knew him better than anybody else; she shook her head with genuine sympathy and said to him: 'Gee, you're just a phony.' "

In prison, this man had somehow reached the point where he was willing to sell his soul just to satisfy this need, this immaturity. The only way he could get the attention that he demanded from authority was to grovel and ingratiate himself before the enemy. As a soldier he was a miserable failure, but he had not crossed the boundary of willful treason; he was not written off as an irrevocable loss, as were the two patent collaborators with whom the Vietnamese soon arranged that he live.

As we American POWs built our civilization, and wrote our own laws (which we leaders obliged all to memorize), we also codified certain principles which formed the backbone of our policies and attitudes. I codified the principles of compassion, rehabilitation, and forgiveness with the slogan: "It is neither American nor Christian to nag a repentant sinner to his grave." (Some didn't like it, thought it seemed soft on finks.) And so, we really gave this man a chance. Over time, our efforts worked. After five years of self-indulgence he got himself together and started to communicate with the prisoner organization. I sent the message "Are you on the team or not?"; he replied, "Yes," and came back. He told the Vietnamese that he didn't want to play their dirty games anymore. He wanted to get away from those willful collaborators and he came back and he was accepted, after a fashion.

I wish that were the end of the story. Although he came back, joined us, and even became a leader of sorts, he never totally won himself back. No matter how forgiving we were, he was conscious that many resented him—not so much because he was weak but because he had broken what we might call a gentleman's code. In all of those years when he, a senior officer, had willingly participated in making tape recordings of anti-American material, he had deeply offended the sensibilities of the American prisoners who were forced to listen to him. To most of us it wasn't the rhetoric of the war or the goodness or the badness of this or that issue that counted. The object of our highest value was the well-being of our fellow prisoners. He had broken that code and hurt some of those people. Some thought that as an informer he had indirectly hurt them physically. I don't believe that. What indisputably hurt them was his not having the sensitivity to realize the damage his opportunistic conduct would do to the morale of a bunch of Middle American guys with Middle American attitudes which they naturally cherished. He should have known that in those solitary cells where his tapes were piped were idealistic, direct, patriotic fellows who would be crushed and embarrassed to have him, a senior man in excellent physical shape, so obviously not under torture, telling the world that the war was wrong. Even if he believed what he said, which he did not, he should have had the common decency to keep his mouth shut. You can sit and think anything you want, but when you insensitively cut down those who want to love and help you, you cross a line. He seemed to sense that he could never truly be one of us.

And yet he was likable—particularly back in civilization after release—when tension was off, and making a deal did not seem so important. He exuded charm and "hail fellow" sophistication. He wanted so to be liked by all those men he had once discarded in his search for new friends, new deals, new fields to conquer in Hanoi. The tragedy of his life was obvious to us all. Tears were shed by some of his old prison mates when he was killed in an accident that strongly resembled suicide some months later. The Greek drama had run its course. He was right out of Aristotle's book, a good man with a flaw who had come to an unjustified bad end. The flaw was insecurity: the need to ingratiate himself, the need for love and adulation at any price.

He reminded me of Paul Newman in *The Hustler.* Newman couldn't stand success. He knew how to make a deal. He was handsome, he was smart, he was attractive to everybody; but he had to have adulation, and therein lay the seed of tragedy. Playing high-stakes pool against old Minnesota Fats (Jackie Gleason), Newman was well in the lead, and getting more full of himself by the hour. George C. Scott, the pool bettor, whispered to his partner: "I'm going to keep betting on Minnesota Fats; this other guy [Newman] is a born loser—he's all skill and no character." And he was right, a born loser—I think that's the message.

How can we educate to avoid these casualties? Can we by means of education prevent this kind of tragedy? What we prisoners were in was a one-way leverage game in which the other side had all the mechanical advantage. I suppose you could say that we all live in a leverage world to some degree; we all experience people trying to use us in one way or another. The difference in Hanoi was the degradation of the ends (to be used as propaganda agents of an enemy, or as informers on your fellow Americans), and the power of the means (total environmental control including solitary confinement, restraint by means of leg-irons and handcuffs, and torture). Extortionists always go down the same track: the imposition of guilt and fear for having disobeyed their rules, followed in turn by punishment, apology, confession, and atonement (their payoff). Our captors would go to great lengths to get a man to compromise his own code, even if only slightly, and then they would hold that in their bag, and the next time get him to go a little further.

Some people are psychologically, if not physically, at home in extortion environments. They are tough people who instinctively avoid getting sucked into the undertows. They never kid themselves or their friends; if they miss the mark they admit it. But there's another category of person who gets tripped up. He makes a small compromise, perhaps rationalizes it, and then makes another one; and then he gets depressed, full of shame, lonesome, loses his willpower and self-respect, and comes to a tragic end. Somewhere along the line he realizes that he has turned a corner that he didn't mean to turn. All too late he realizes that he has been worshiping the wrong gods and discovers the wisdom of the ages: life is not fair.

In sorting out the story after our release, we found that most of us had come to combat constant mental and physical pressure in much the same way. We discovered that when a person is alone in a cell and sees the door open only once or twice a day for a bowl of soup, he realizes after a period of weeks in isolation and darkness that he has to build some sort of ritual into his life if he wants to avoid becoming an animal. Ritual fills a need in a hard life and it's easy to see how formal church ritual grew. For almost all of us, this ritual was built around prayer, exercise, and clandestine communication. The prayers I said during those days were prayers of quality with ideas of substance. We found that over the course of time our minds had a tremendous capacity for invention and introspection, but had the weakness of being an integral part of our bodies. I remembered Descartes and how in his philosophy he separated mind and body. One time I cursed my body for the way it decayed my mind. I had decided that I would become a Gandhi. I would have to be carried around on a pallet and in that state I could not be used by my captors for propaganda purposes. After about ten days of fasting, I found that I had become so depressed that soon I would risk going into interrogation ready to spill my guts just looking for a friend. I tapped to the guy next door and I said, "Gosh, how I wish Descartes could have been right, but he's wrong." He was a little slow to reply; I reviewed Descartes's deduction with him and explained how I had discovered that body and mind are inseparable.

On the positive side, I discovered the tremendous file-cabinet volume of the human mind. You can memorize an incredible amount of material and you can draw the past out of your memory with remarkable recall by easing slowly toward the event you seek and not crowding the mind too closely. You'll try to remember who was at your birthday party when you were five years old, and you can get it, but only after months of effort. You can break the locks and find the answers, but you need time and solitude to learn how to use this marvelous device in your head which is the greatest computer on earth.

Of course many of the things we recalled from the past were utterly useless as sources of strength or practicality. For instance, events brought back from cocktail parties or insincere social contacts were almost repugnant because of their emptiness, their utter lack of value. More often than not, the locks worth picking had been on old schoolroom doors. School days can be thought of as a time when one is filling the important stacks of one's memory library. For me, the golden doors were labeled history and the classics. The historical perspective which enabled a man to take himself away from all the agitation, not necessarily to see a rosy lining, but to see the real nature of the situation he faced, was truly a thing of value.

Here's how this historical perspective helped me see the reality of my own situation and thus cope better with it. I learned from a Vietnamese prisoner that the same cells we occupied had in years before been lived in by many of the leaders of the Hanoi government. From my history lessons I recalled that when metropolitan France permitted communists in the government in 1936, the communists who occupied cells in Vietnam were set free. I marveled at the cycle of history, all within my memory, which prompted Hitler's rise in Germany, then led to the rise of the Popular Front in France, and finally vacated this cell of mine halfway around the world ("Perhaps Pham Van Dong lived here"). I came to understand what tough people these were. I was willing to fight them to the death, but I grew to realize that hatred was an indulgence, a very inefficient emotion. I remember thinking, "If you were committed to beating the dealer in a gambling casino, would *hating* him help your game?" In a pidgin English propaganda book the guard gave me, speeches by these old communists about their prison experiences stressed how they learned to beat down the enemy by being united. It seemed comforting to know that we were united against the communist administration of Hoa Lo prison just as the Vietnamese communists had united against the French administration of Hoa Lo in the thirties. Prisoners are prisoners, and there's only one way to beat administrations. We resolved to do it better in the sixties than they had in the thirties. You don't base system-beating on any thought of political idealism; you do it as a competitive thing, as an expression of self-respect.

Education in the classics teaches you that all organizations since the beginning of time have used the power of guilt; that cycles are repetitive; and that this is the way of the world. It's a naive person who comes in and says, "Let's see, what's good and what's bad?" That's a quagmire. You can get out of that quagmire only by recalling how wise men before you accommodated the same dilemmas. And I believe a good classical education and an understanding of history can best determine the rules you should live by. They also give you the power to analyze reasons for these rules and guide you as to how to apply them to your own situation. In a broader sense, all my education helped me. Naval Academy discipline and body contact sports helped me. But the education which I found myself using most was what I got in graduate school. The messages of history and philosophy I used were simple.

The first one is this business about life not being fair. That is a very important lesson and I learned it from a wonderful man named Philip Rhinelander. As a lieutenant commander in the Navy studying political science at Stanford University in 1961, I went over to philosophy corner one day and an older gentleman said, "Can I help you?" I said, "Yes, I'd like to take some courses in philosophy." I told him I'd been in college for six years and had never had a course in philosophy. He couldn't believe it. I told him that I was a naval officer and he said, "Well, I used to be in the Navy. Sit down." Philip Rhinelander became a great influence in my life.

He had been a Harvard lawyer and had pleaded cases before the Supreme Court and then gone to war as a reserve officer. When he came back he took his doctorate at Harvard. He was also a music composer, had been director of general education at Harvard, dean of the School of Humanities and Sciences at Stanford, and by the time I met him had by choice returned to teaching in the classroom. He said, "The course I'm teaching is my personal two-term favorite—The Problems of Good and Evil—and we're starting our second term." He said the message of his course was from the Book of Job. The number one problem in this world is that people are not able to accommodate the lesson in the book.

He recounted the story of Job. It starts out by establishing that Job was the most honorable of men. Then he lost all his goods. He also lost his reputation, which is what really hurt. His wife was badgering him to admit his sins, but he knew he had made no errors. He was not a patient man and demanded to speak to the Lord. When the Lord appeared in the whirlwind, he said, "Now, Job, you have to shape up! Life is not fair." That's my interpretation and that's the way the book ended for hundreds of years. I agree with those of the opinion that the happy ending was spliced on many years later. If you read it, you'll note that the meter changes. People couldn't live with the original message. Here was a good man who came to unexplained grief, and the Lord told him: "That's the way it is. Don't challenge me. This is my world and you either live in it as I designed it or get out."

This was a great comfort to me in prison. It answered the question "Why me?" It cast aside any thoughts of being punished for past actions. Sometimes I shared the message with fellow prisoners as I tapped through the walls to them, but I learned to be selective. It's a strong message which upsets some people.

Rhinelander also passed on to me another piece of classical information which I found of great value. On the day of our last session together he said, "You're a military man, let me give you a book to remember me by. It's a book of military ethics." He handed it to me, and I bade him goodbye with great emotion. I took the book home and that night started to read it. It was the *Enchiridion* of the philosopher Epictetus, his "manual" for the Roman field soldier.

As I began to read, I thought to myself in disbelief, "Does Rhinelander think I'm going to draw lessons for my life from this thing? I'm a fighter pilot. I'm a technical man. I'm a test pilot. I know how to get people to do technical work. I play golf; I drink martinis. I know how to get ahead in my profession. And what does he hand me? A book that says in part, 'It's better to die in hunger, exempt from guilt and fear, than to live in affluence and with perturbation.' " I remembered this later in prison because perturbation was what I was living with. When I ejected from the airplane on that September morn in 1965, I had left the land of technology. I had entered the world of Epictetus, and it's a world that few of us, whether we know it or not, are ever far away from.

In Palo Alto, I had read this book, not with contentment, but with annoyance. Statement after statement: "Men are disturbed not by things, but by the view that they take of them." "Do not be concerned with things which are beyond your power." "Demand not that events should happen as you wish, but wish them to happen as they do happen and you will go on well." This is stoicism. It's not the last word, but it's a viewpoint that comes in handy in many circumstances, and it surely did for me. Particularly this line: "Lameness is an impediment to the body but not to the will." That was significant for me because I wasn't able to stand up and support myself on my badly broken leg for the first couple of years I was in solitary confinement.

Other statements of Epictetus took on added meaning in the light of extortions which often began with our captors' callous pleas: "If you are just reasonable with us we will compensate you. You get your meals, you get to sleep, you won't be pestered, you might even get a cellmate." The catch was that by being "reasonable with us" our enemies meant being their informers, their propagandists. The old stoic had said, "If I can get the things I need with the preservation of my honor and fidelity and self-respect, show me the way and I will get them. But, if you require me to lose my own proper good, that you may gain what is no good, consider how unreasonable and foolish you are." To love our fellow prisoners was within our power. To betray, to propagandize, to disillusion conscientious and patriotic shipmates and destroy their morale so that they in turn would be destroyed was to lose one's proper good.

What attributes serve you well in the extortion environment? We learned there, above all else, that the best defense is to keep your conscience clean. When we did something we were ashamed of, and our captors realized we were ashamed of it, we were in trouble. A little white lie is where extortion and ultimately blackmail start. In 1965, I was crippled and I was alone. I realized that they had all the power. I couldn't see how I was ever going to get out with my honor and self-respect. The one thing I came to realize was that if you don't lose integrity you can't be had and you can't be hurt. Compromises multiply and build up when you're working against a skilled extortionist or a good manipulator. You can't be had if you don't take that first shortcut, or "meet them halfway," as they say, or look for that tacit "deal," or make that first compromise.

Bob North, a political science professor at Stanford, taught me a course called Comparative Marxist Thought. This was not an anticommunist course. It was the study of dogma and thought patterns. We read no criticisms of Marxism, only primary sources. All year we read the works of Marx and Lenin. In Hanoi, I understood more about Marxist theory than my interrogator did. I was able to say to that interrogator, "That's not what Lenin said; you're a deviationist."

One of the things North talked about was brainwashing. A psychologist who studied the Korean prisoner situation, which somewhat paralleled ours, concluded that three categories of prisoners were involved there. The first was the redneck Marine sergeant from Tennessee who had an eighth-grade education. He would get in that interrogation room and they would say that the Spanish-American War was started by the bomb within the *Maine*, which might be true, and he would answer, "B.S." They would show him something about racial unrest in Detroit. "B.S." There was no way they could get to him; his mind was made up. He was a straight guy, red, white, and blue, and everything else was B.S.! He didn't give it a second thought. Not much of a historian, perhaps, but a good security risk.

In the next category were the sophisticates. They were the fellows who could be told these same things about the horrors of American history and our social problems, but had heard it all before, knew both sides of every story, and thought we were on the right track. They weren't ashamed that we had robber barons at a certain time of our history; they were aware of the skeletons in most civilizations' closets. They could not be emotionally involved and so they were good security risks.

The ones who were in trouble were the high school graduates who had enough sense to pick up the innuendo, and yet not enough education to accommodate it properly. Not many of them fell, but most of the men that got entangled started from that background.

The psychologist's point is possibly oversimplistic, but I think his message has some validity. A little knowledge is a dangerous thing.

Generally speaking, I think education is a tremendous defense; the broader, the better. After I was shot down my wife, Sybil, found a clipping glued in the front of my collegiate dictionary: "Education is an ornament in prosperity and a refuge in adversity." She certainly agrees with me on that. Most of us prisoners found that the so-called practical academic exercises in how to do things, which I'm told are proliferating, were useless. I'm not saying that we should base education on training people to be in prison, but I am saying that in stress situations, the fundamentals, the hard-core classical subjects, are what serve best.

Theatrics also helped sustain me. My mother had been a drama coach when I was young and I was in many of her plays. In prison I learned how to manufacture a personality and live it, crawl into it, and hold that role without deviation. During interrogations, I'd check the responses I got to different kinds of behavior. They'd get worried when I did things irrationally. And so, every so often, I would play that "irrational" role and come completely unglued. When I could tell that pressure to make a public exhibition of me was building, I'd stand up, tip the table over, attempt to throw the chair through the window, and say, "No way. Goddammit! I'm not doing that! Now, come over here and fight!" This was a risky ploy, because if they thought you were acting, they would slam you into the ropes and make you scream in pain like a baby. You could watch their faces and read their minds. They had expected me to behave like a stoic. But a man would be a fool to make their job easy by being conventional and predictable. I could feel the tide turn in my favor at that magic moment when their anger turned to pleading: "Calm down, now calm down." The payoff would come when they decided that the risk of my going haywire in front of some touring American professor on a "fact-finding" mission was too great. More important, they had reason to believe that I would tell the truth—namely, that I had been in solitary confinement for four years and tortured fifteen times—without fear of future consequences. So theatrical training proved helpful to me.

Can you educate for leadership? I think you can, but the communists would probably say no. One day in an argument with an interrogator, I said, "You are so proud of being a party member, what are the criteria?" He said in a flurry of anger, "There are only four: you have to be seventeen years old, you have to be selfless, you have to be smart enough to understand the theory, and you've got to be a person who innately influences others." He stressed that fourth one. I think psychologists would say that leadership is innate, and there is truth in that. But, I also think you can learn some leadership traits that naturally accrue from a good education: compassion is a necessity for leaders, as are spontaneity, bravery, self-discipline, honesty, and above all, integrity.

I remember being disappointed about a month after I was back when one of my young friends, a prison mate, came running up after a reunion at the Naval Academy. He said with glee, "This is really great, you won't believe how this country has advanced. They've practically done away with plebe year at the Academy, and they've got computers in the basement of Bancroft Hall." I thought, "My God, if there was anything that helped us get through those eight years, it was plebe year, and if anything screwed up that war, it was computers!"

5

BEING DIFFERENT

"They know that I am bound to run into prejudice; yet no one lifts a finger when I am treated unfairly. Do they expect a person to be stupid enough to come right out and say, 'Get out, blackie; we don't want your type here?' "

—*Edward W. Jones, Jr.*

People and the organizations they create often act as if they are threatened by sources of uncertainty. Consequently, they often find it difficult to cope with stimuli that differ in salient ways from the stimuli they assume to be normal. Some of the symptoms of these difficulties take the form of perceptual errors as stereotypes and perceptual defenses.

Of course, perceptual activity is only one way people and organizations use to attempt to restore certainty when confronted by stimuli that are "different." Often they attempt to create environments that are free of difference. In organizations these attempts can be seen in selection processes which screen out people who, because they are different, are not fully trusted. (For example, see Tom Wolfe's "The Lab Rat" in Section I and J. Patrick Wright's treatment of loyalty in Section 2.) Similarly, attempts to eliminate differences can be seen in interpersonal situations. People put pressures on group members who pose a threat to the certainty that can be derived from group norms and the feeling of consensus. (See, for example, Dalton's paper on the ratebuster in Section 4 and Janis's paper on "groupthink" in Section 7.) Moreover, it is clear that powerful groups and individuals use a number of coercive mechanisms to discourage and control deviant behavior. (See, for example, O'Day's discussion of intimidation rituals and Vaughn's paper, "The Management Monopoly," both in Section 6.)

Some limitations on differences in behavior can be justified as necessary for efficient operation of an organization—after all, one of the major advantages of formal organizations is their ability to make the behavior of individuals highly predictable. However, it is well known that often the reduction of differences among organization members can cause the organization to stagnate by eliminating the diversity needed to cope with complex changing environments. In short, many of the tactics that people and organizations employ to cope with people and other stimuli that are "different" can be described as neurotic—they are motivated to reduce anxiety and lead to dysfunctional outcomes.

The rational design of organizations would provide for optimal levels of being different. However, the treatment of differences in organizations is seldom that rational. Often valuable human resources are underutilized. The costs of this underutilization are borne by the organization and the individuals who are "different." Moreover, the rather inhumane processes by which those who are "different" are treated often cause considerable stress.

The selections in this section focus on the experience of "being different." In particular they call attention to some of the dimensions in which organizational members differ and examine how the presence of people who are perceived as different affects the "different" as well as those who are "not different."

What is so startling and ironic about the people who are "different" is how many of them there are! People who are "different" include those at the bottom of the socioeconomic ladder, blacks and other minorities, women, the aged, and homosexuals. In the first selection, "Life at the Bottom" (Lieberman and Goolrick), the experiences of three workers are reviewed to reveal a side of organization life which, although real to a large number of people, is seldom found in modern textbooks.

Most of the remaining articles deal with issues that have received far more attention. Edward Jones provides an excellent example of how being of a different race can result in a complex, stressful set of relationships. Similarly, Bernstein's account of the experiences of Mary Cunningham shows a somewhat different, but equally complex and stressful set of consequences which resulted from the rapid progress of a competent woman. The article by Ann Sagi reveals some other sides of the plight of women in organizations—particularly those who are confined to low-level jobs and those who work outside the home but feel pressure to perform their traditional roles in the home.

Two papers deal with aging and should be read together. In "Fighting Off Old Age" John Leo summarizes some of our current knowledge about the physiology of the aging process; Bernard Lefkowitz's article makes a case for one of the most radical ways one can be different in our society—deciding not to work for an organization.

"Institutional Bigotry" raises yet another dimension along which people are different—sexual preference. While the policy of the Air Force may be an extreme one, Leonard Matlovich's experience of being discriminated against because he was known to be homosexual is by no means uncommon.

The final paper, "Two Women, Three Men on a Raft," by Robert Schrank, provides a stimulating capstone to this section. What subtle domination occurred on the river and with what consequences? Why did the raft flip over? The feedback processes he describes could apply equally well to all the situations raised in this section, as well as to many situations that are not covered (e.g., the employment of the physically handicapped). Overall, the experience of being "different" and of dealing with people who are "different" presents troublesome problems that have a major impact on how people experience life in organizations.

Life at the Bottom, alias the Minimum Wage

Paul Lieberman and Chester Goolrick

Hardworking people like Clifford Giles, Buddy Lane, and Daisy Stripling are among the estimated 9 million American workers who get paid below or just at the federal minimum wage level. Some of these workers are covered by the federal Fair Labor Standards Act, some are not.

But in either case, they are not earning very much money. In 1977, the average full-time male worker in the U.S. earned almost $17,000, and the average woman earned $9,353. In 1979, a worker being paid the federal minimum wage could earn $6,032 by working 40 hours a week for 52 weeks; the poverty level for a family of four in 1979 was $6,700.

But even the annual figure of $6,032 as the income for a minimum wage earner can be misleadingly high. Many workers who receive only the minimum wage, or even less, do not work a full 40-hour week, 52 weeks a year, because of the limited or unpredictable availability of work. A man who loads tobacco bales onto trucks gets paid when there are bales to load. There may not be any bales on a given day, and the worker is not paid for the time he must spend waiting to find this out.

Many other workers earning the minimum wage or less have a somewhat opposite situation: there is no upper limit to the time they might have to put in on the job. Although their pay is fixed to reflect a 40-hour, five-day week, in actuality they are expected to be available almost day or night, seven days a week, 52 weeks a year. This may come about in cases where employers find it convenient to provide housing for their employees adjacent to the work place, as when poultry workers are settled in houses perhaps only yards from the chicken sheds they are hired to look after.

Underemployment and, conversely, lack of time off are not the only potential drawbacks accompanying certain low-paying jobs. Some workers find their pay falling below the minimum guaranteed wage because of deductions their employers feel justified in taking

Abridged from the AFL-CIO *American Federationist* (February, 1981), pp. 13–18, whose article was excerpted from a series of articles in the *Atlanta Constitution* written by Paul Lieberman and Chester Goolrick and entitled, "The Underpaid and Under-Protected."

from their paychecks. Other workers may be entitled to the minimum wage but accept less, having no idea a federal minimum wage law applies to their work. And where workers are aware they are not being paid what the law provides, they are often reluctant to complain; they fear gaining a reputation as a troublemaker, or they wish to be loyal to an employer they may have known all their lives.

And finally some workers are simply outside the umbrella of the federal law and must accept whatever pay is offered them. While they may still be covered by a state minimum wage law, such pay is not likely to be a living wage.

What is life like for these underpaid, often overworked wage earners? What is their daily routine like? What do they expect from their work and from their employers, and what do they expect to give?

When their places of work are visited and observed, and details are recorded, vivid pictures emerge in which the generalities of low pay, long hours, or unpredictably fluctuating income take on particular meaning in the lives of individuals who are at or near the bottom of the economic system. These workers appear to have few choices; they not only take what they can get in the way of work and pay, but often must accept extra tasks and conditions arbitrarily imposed by their employers. Indeed, for certain workers employer-provided living arrangements lead to an association between employee and employer reminiscent in some ways of supposedly long-dead economic systems: feudalism and slavery.

But there is another side to this story. Some of these same people in America's lowest-paid groups express, directly or indirectly, considerable satisfaction with their lives. They appear to go about their work and their lives without reflecting at all upon their situation or seeing it as something to be changed or even deplored. They may even extol the independence of their working lives, as some did in interviews with the *Atlanta Constitution*.

TURPENTINE MAN

After a grueling day of gathering pine gum, turpentine worker Clifford Giles uncomplainingly tosses hay until nightfall to supplement his pay. If there is one job many men resist at almost all costs, it is turpentining. Experts on the turpentining industry say the people who are willing to do the work are mostly those who "like the woods," or simply don't know anything else. Still, there is admiration for the men who are proficient at collecting the gum.

Clifford Giles is a turpentine man. He works in pine woods in the deep South, collecting gum from the trees. Using a dipping iron, he scoops the sticky gum from tin cups attached to each tree, filling a large bucket he carries from tree to tree. When the bucket is full, he empties it into one of several large metal barrels that wait on a mule-drawn wooden cart. Each barrel weighs about 435 pounds when full, and on an average day Giles may fill two of them.

For every barrel Giles fills he is paid $8. At the turpentine distillery, the boss will receive about $80 per barrel, an amount Giles may make in an average week. In a very good week, working from 7 A.M. until 3 or 4 P.M., Monday through Friday, Giles may fill 13 barrels and thus make as much as $104.

The work is hard. On a hot midsummer day, Clifford Giles has to slosh through swamp water and fight off thorny bush, mosquitoes and horseflies, and an occasional rattlesnake. Sweat will pour from his body; his gummy, wet clothes will become like a second skin.

Giles is the son and the grandson of turpentine men, black laborers working in an industry that has changed little in a hundred years, with its hand labor, mule-drawn carts, and company-provided living arrangements. Although their operation is covered by the Fair Labor Standards Act, the minimum wage means little to Giles and his co-workers, who live in the turpentine "quarters" of a tiny southern town and are trucked daily to and from the pine forests by the company foreman.

The quarters, hidden from the main street of the town, are a cluster of faded, ramshackle clapboard shacks where Giles and 15 other workers and their families live. The shacks, like the turpentining rights, are leased to the turpentine company by the landowners; the laborers pay the company no rent.

Showing only traces of their original red paint, the shacks have tin roofs and one or two chimneys. Fireplaces supply the heat in winter. Covered porches in varying states of decay are in front of the shacks. On some porches, junk—automobile tires and rims, boxes, old chairs—leaves little room for sitting.

A wooden, tin-roofed outhouse is behind each shack. The outhouse behind Clifford Giles' four-room shack is overrun with maggots. Several small pigs root around one shack, and scrawny dogs have free run of the entire quarters.

On weekday mornings the company foreman drives his truck through the quarters at dawn, swinging through once to wake the workers with his horn, then a second time to pick them up. Carrying lunch, water jugs, and other supplies, the men climb into the back of the truck and bounce over the route to the edge of the woods, where they transfer to mule carts and slowly penetrate deeper among the trees.

On a summer day, Clifford Giles will probably be working in 90-degree heat by late morning. Swamp water will flow from his boots through holes cut into them for just that purpose. He will take one break, at noon, from his steady progress from tree to tree. Finally, at 3 or 4 P.M., he will drive the barrel-laden mule cart out of the woods, and feed and settle the animals in their corral. It may be 5 or 6 o'clock when the truck brings him and his coworkers back to the quarters. He may have filled two 435-pound barrels and earned $16 for the grueling labor.

Part of the $16 will go for deductions the boss figures in, deductions for water and electricity, perhaps for money advanced, perhaps for other services. Giles does not compute his deductions himself: "The boss adds it up." Nor does Giles add up and record his hours worked. It's barrels, not hours, that count; most turpentine men have only a vague notion of how much time they put in on the job.

Thirteen barrels, or $104 a week—before deductions—is a good week for a hard-working turpentine veteran. There are many weeks when the pay is considerably less. One group of turpentine men has estimated that during a busy summer season they were earning an average of $70 a week.

The work is relatively solitary and silent. "Chippers" and "pullers" go off to an assigned section of woods to prepare the trees by scraping off bark. Giles, as a "dipper," works alone or in a two-man team. With vast numbers of trees to work, turpentine men often see none of their colleagues, except possibly during a lunch break. When the men do meet in the woods, exchanges are apt to be complaints about the scarcity of gum in the tin cups—which means a scarcity of earnings—or gossip about the previous weekend. There is rarely any complaining about pay or working conditions, or any talk about finding better jobs.

While the men work, the foreman monitors their progress on horseback. It's slow and exhausting in stifling summer weather. But if it rains, there is no work, and thus no pay, at all.

Most of the men are anxious to work. Only one worker in Clifford Giles' group expresses open dissatisfaction with the system, and urges a new worker to "get your money and save it up and get the hell out. 'Cause you ain't going to make nuthin' here." The rest of the experienced turpentine men consider the complainer a misfit; many believe he doesn't really want to work, and he is criticized for getting food stamps. When Clifford Giles is asked about food stamps, he says, "Yeah, I could get them free stamps, but I ain't got time to go sign up. I'm too busy workin'."

Indeed, Giles seems to be. When he returns from a full day in the woods, he and several other men take a short break, then head out for several hours of loading hay for a farmer in town.

But if it's Friday, there won't be any evening work. On Friday afternoon, it's payday, and a sense of quickening anticipation is evident as the men quit the trees earlier than usual. They must have time to load the barrels for transport to the distillery and return the mules from their five-day stay in the woods, where they spend the night in their corral, to an old wooden stable next to the quarters. A $10 fine can be incurred for hurrying the hard-working mules, so the drive back is slow and long.

When the stable is finally reached, the men spend an hour caring for the animals and the wagons. Some men begin washing up, someone goes for liquor, the first drinking begins, and men line up on the porch of the pay house. On one Friday, the foreman starts, then stops, the pay process, announcing that men are needed to get the boss's truck out of some mud. When nobody volunteers, the boss emerges from the pay house to make it clear that no more wages will be paid out until the truck is freed. Five men leave to work on the truck, and when they return the boss starts paying again. One by one, the workers go into the pay house, advancing according to the foreman's repeated invitation, "Anybody who's out here, go on in."

The top dipper for this week filled 13 barrels and earned $104. Clifford Giles had a bad week: $56. Two other dippers earned $72 and $40.

POULTRY WORK

Poultry worker Buddy Lane speaks matter-of-factly about no days off for several years. A whole family working for the normal salary of one person is not uncommon on some chicken farms. The family is provided with a house close to the chicken sheds. In return for the family's labor, the head of the household receives a single weekly salary, typically between $100 and $125.

David Babb, his wife Sandy, and their three children lived and worked on a poultry farm for 14 months. As a result of their experience, the five members of the Babb family filed suit against the farm, alleging that its employment practices had violated the federal minimum wage law.

It was David Babb who was hired as "flock tender." He accepted the job with enthusiasm because a small, wood-frame house near the chicken shed, where they tended the layers and collected the eggs, was provided for him and his family. Babb says the man who hired him had made it clear that both husband and wife would have to work in the six chicken sheds to pick up the eggs laid by 15,000 chickens every day. The pay would be $100 a week, with a week's vacation sometime during the year. For the Babbs, the house and the opportunity to work together made the seven-day work week appear acceptable.

For the first three months, Sandy and David Babb spent three hours together every morning, and perhaps another three or four hours in the afternoon, making their way through the row of long, low chicken sheds a short downhill distance from their house. On a typical day, they might pick up some 12,000 freshly laid eggs and place them into cartons to be taken to the packer. There were other responsibilities, like checking on the layers' feed, and David Babb would make repairs on the house during the evenings.

David Babb says he was asked after these first three months by one of his two bosses if Sandy could pick up the eggs alone. The boss wanted David to do some odd jobs around the farm, for which David would receive the minimum wage on an hourly basis. The arrangement seemed fine to the Babbs: Sandy was glad to be working, and the extra money David would be making—sometimes as much as $90 a week—was welcome in a time of rising prices.

Although Babb recalls that the boss's original instructions had called for the three Babb children to stay away from the chicken house, the children started helping Sandy collect eggs. David would also help Sandy when there were no odd jobs. It did not occur to the Babbs to question their work arrangements or the pay.

It took the near loss of Sandy's left hand to make it plain that while her labor was useful to the poultry farm operators, as a worker entitled to compensation she was nonexistent in their eyes.

Sandy Babb's left hand got caught in an automatic feeder one day while she was making her rounds. The children heard her screams and got someone to turn off the machine. She was rushed to a hospital where doctors were able to save her hand. But they said that nerve damage would prevent her from using her hand for a long time. Since she was left-handed, Sandy faced considerable disability.

Sandy's hospital bill came to $1,680, her doctor's bill was $825, and ongoing therapy was $171 for every three days of treatment. But the poultry farm's insurance company refused to pay for anything. Since Sandy had never been placed on the payroll, as far as the insurance company was concerned she had never worked at all. It didn't matter that some days she was the sole "flock tender."

It was David Babb, the poultry farm operator said, "who signed the workers' compensation card. He was the one who was hired." The operator said he knew that poultry workers often had family members or even friends help them in the sheds, but he implied that the practice was beyond the control of the employer. He said Sandy Babb was not supposed to work in the sheds at all.

After the accident and the insurance company's refusal to pay, an angry David Babb packed up his family and left the chicken farm. Wondering how they would pay the medical bills, the Babbs began wondering too about the entire arrangement under which at times the whole family was working for David Babb's regular salary plus earnings for odd jobs. The family finally filed suit in federal court alleging that their bosses "were in a position to know and did, in fact, know" that each of the family members were working. The suit asked that Babb be paid $23,000 "as difference paid to his family and minimum wages." The Babbs had hoped that the suit would at least win them a settlement covering the medical bills.

Several months after the accident, with a new job and living with his family in a trailer—it was the house on the poultry farm that had made the poultry work especially attractive—David Babb had allowed his initial anger to subside somewhat. He said, "I've learned my lesson. There should be a written contract and everything should have been clearly understood from the first."

And he suggested another lesson from the job he had held for 14 months: "As long as there are people who will work, there will be some cotton pickin' turkey who will work for next to nothing."

MOTEL MAID

Motel maids comprise one of the nation's largest, and most visible, groups of underpaid workers. Thousands of women are paid less than the federal minimum wage—sometimes legally, sometimes illegally—to clean rooms in motels and hotels across America. One of them, Daisy Stripling, is proud of her long years of nearly unbroken service at a tourist inn, years for which she got little more than $1 an hour.

Daisy Stripling has been working at the Almar Tourist Inn for more than 15 years. The inn is more a boarding house, really, located about five miles from a southern coastal city. Miss Stripling walks there every morning, perhaps wearing a polyester dress over a pair of trousers and sporting a brown paper bag as headgear, to clean some of the inn's 10 rooms and do whatever else Mrs. Willie Shurling, the proprietor, has in mind.

After 15 years, Miss Stripling does the job almost automatically, without instruction. She resents it when Mrs. Shurling tells her what to do. She works hard, if slowly, and she gets paid very little for her work.

On one particular day, she can be seen keeping careful watch over a pile of leaves she is burning in the yard. The day before, she says, she worked from 10 until 5, and was given $3.50 for the day. She adds that "it seems like I should make more than that."

But since the Almar Tourist Inn grosses far less than $250,000 a year, Daisy Stripling is not covered by the Fair Labor Standards Act. Neither does she have any of the job protections, benefits, retirement plans, paid sick days, and vacations that millions of Americans routinely expect from their employers.

One summer day recently, Mrs. Shurling dismissed Miss Stripling after the maid apparently failed to heed warnings not to come to work accompanied by some dogs that were becoming nuisances around the inn. When a reporter gathering material for a newspaper story learned of the opening at Mrs. Shurling's establishment, she took the maid's job and worked there for three days.

Riding to work on an early-morning bus filled with maids headed for their own jobs in motels and private homes, the reporter found that most of the workers would not discuss their wages. But one woman said she made $10 a day for about six hours' work, and another said $7 a day. Mrs. Shurling at the Almar Tourist Inn was offering the new maid $1.25 an hour.

Mrs. Shurling greeted her new employee pleasantly at 7:30 A.M. on the first day and started her cleaning a bathroom, checking her progress periodically. After an hour, the maid was next assigned to a bedroom to wash and polish walls, woodwork, and baseboards, and vacuum the rug. Continuing under Mrs. Shurling's instructions, she cleaned out the closet and polished the floor and furniture. Before lunch, she moved on to vacuum the main living room and put a load of Mrs. Shurling's clothes into the washer in the laundry.

Mrs. Shurling then provided a light lunch, for which the maid took 20 minutes. In the afternoon she was asked to pick pole beans in the garden, then to wash dishes and fold laundry.

The maid began her second and third days in the back yard, picking up pears that dropped overnight from the pear tree. She would later carry the fruit to the house of Mrs. Shurling's sister for preserving. When the yard work was finished on the second day, the maid cleaned three of the rented rooms, finishing her tasks at 5 P.M.

On the third day, after picking up pears, the maid spent an hour clearing debris from an empty trailer lot in back of the inn. Next she scoured garbage cans and washed windows. Then beds had to be stripped and remade, and the sheets machine-washed and dried. Emptying trash baskets and changing towels completed the morning. After a few minutes for another light lunch provided by Mrs. Shurling, the maid swept and scrubbed floors, cleaned the kitchen, and watered plants.

Mrs. Shurling was friendly as she prepared to pay the new employee at the end of the third day. "That's about 25 hours, isn't it?" she asked, stating the time on the job correctly. Mrs. Shurling paid the maid $30 for the three days, $20 in cash and $10 by check because, she said, she didn't have change "for another $20."

One day shortly thereafter Daisy Stripling reappeared at the Almar Tourist Inn, and Mrs. Shurling took her back. Later Mrs. Shurling willingly discussed her longtime maid's good qualities but refused to say what she paid her. Mrs. Shurling said she and Miss Stripling get along pretty well; she gives Miss Stripling lunch, and they "talk about things." Together, the 70-year-old employer and her employee are able to maintain the tourist inn in a condition suitable for boarders. As Mrs. Shurling talks about their arrangement, Miss Stripling rakes leaves and watches them burn in the bright autumn air. It is not known how much this day's work will pay her. Yesterday's work paid, according to Miss Stripling, about 50 cents an hour.

What It's Like to Be a Black Manager

Edward W. Jones, Jr.

THE JOB OFFER

My story begins when I happened to bump into a recruiter who was talking to a friend of mine. On gathering that I was a college senior, the recruiter asked whether I had considered his company as an employer. I responded, "Are you kidding me—you don't have any black managers, do you?" He replied, "No, but that's why I'm here."

I did well in a subsequent interview procedure, and received an invitation for a company tour. Still skeptical, I accepted, feeling that I had nothing to lose. During a lunch discussion concerning the contemplated job and its requirements, I experienced my first reminder that I was black. After a strained silence, one of the executives at our table looked at me, smiled, and said, "Why is it that everyone likes Roy Campanella, but so many people dislike Jackie Robinson?"

I knew that this man was trying to be pleasant; yet I felt nothing but disgust at what seemed a ridiculous deterioration in the level of conversation. Here was the beginning of the games that I expected but dreaded playing. The question was demeaning and an insult to my intelligence. It was merely a rephrasing of the familiar patronizing comment, "One of my best friends is a negro." Most blacks recognize this type of statement as a thinly veiled attempt to hide bias. After all, if a person, is unbiased, why does he make such a point of trying to prove it?

In the fragment of time between the question and my response, the tension within me grew. Were these people serious about a job offer? If so, what did they expect from me? I had no desire to be the corporate black in a glass office, but I did not wish to be abrasive or ungracious if the company was sincere about its desire to have an integrated organization.

There was no way to resolve these kinds of questions at that moment, so I gathered up my courage and replied, "Roy Campanella is a great baseball player. But off the field he is not an overwhelming intellectual challenge to anyone. Jackie Robinson is great both on and off the baseball field. He is very intelligent and therefore more of a threat than Roy Campanella. In fact, I'm sure that if he wanted to, he could out-perform you in your job."

There was a stunned silence around the table, and from that point on until I arrived back at the employment office, I was sure that I had ended any chances of receiving a job offer.

I was wrong. I subsequently received an outstanding salary offer from the recruiter. But I had no intention of being this company's showcase black and asked seriously, "Why do you want me to work for you? Because of my ability or because you need a black?" I was reassured that ability was the "only" criterion, and one month later, after much introspection, I accepted the offer.

INITIAL EXPOSURE

I entered the first formal training phase, in which I was the only black trainee in a department of over 8,000 employees. During this period, my tension increased as I was repeatedly called on to be the in-house expert on anything pertaining to civil rights. I was proud to be black and had many opinions about civil rights, but I did not feel qualified to give "the" black opinion. I developed the feeling that I was considered a black first and an individual second by many of the people I came into contact with. This feeling was exacerbated by the curious executive visitors to the training class who had to be introduced to everyone except me. Everyone knew my name, and I constantly had the feeling of being on stage.

The next phase of training was intended to prepare trainees for supervisory responsibilities. The tension of the trainee group had risen somewhat because of the loss of several trainees and the increased challenges facing us. In my own case, an increasing fear of failure began to impact on the other tensions that I felt from being "a speck of pepper in a sea of salt." The result of these tensions was that I began behaving with an air of bravado. I wasn't outwardly concerned or afraid, but I was inwardly terrified. This phase of training was also completed satisfactorily, at least in an official sense.

At the conclusion of the training, I received a "yes, but" type of appraisal. For example: "Mr. Jones doesn't take notes and seems to have trouble using the reference material, but he seems to be able to recall the material." This is the type of appraisal that says you've done satisfactorily, yet leaves a negative or dubious impression. I questioned the subjective inputs but dropped the matter without any vehement objections.

Prior to embarking on my first management assignment, I resolved to learn from this appraisal and to use more tact and talk less. These resolutions were re-emphasized by my adviser, who was an executive with responsibility for giving me counsel and acting as a sounding board. He also suggested that I relax my handshake and speak more softly.

ON THE JOB

A warm welcome awaited me in the office where I was to complete my first assignment as a supervisor. I looked forward to going to work because I felt that subjectivity in appraisals would now be replaced by objectivity. Here was a situation in which I would either meet or fail to meet clearly defined numerical objectives.

There were no serious problems for three weeks, and I started to relax and just worry about the job. But then I had a conflict in my schedule. An urgent matter had to be taken care of in the office at the same time that I had an appointment elsewhere. I wrote a note to a supervisor who worked for another manager, asking him if he would be kind enough to follow up on the matter in the office for me.

I chose that particular supervisor because he had given me an embarrassingly warm welcome to the office and insisted that I "just ask" if there was anything at all that he could do to help me. I relied on the impersonality of the note because he was out on a coffee break and I had to leave immediately. The note was short and tactfully worded, and ended by giving my advance "thanks" for the requested help. Moreover, the office norms encouraged supervisory cooperation, so the fact that we worked under different managers did not seem to be a problem.

When I returned to the office, the manager I worked for called me in. He was visibly irritated. I sat down and he said, "Ed, you're rocking the boat." He stated that the supervisor I had asked for help had complained directly to the area manager that I was ordering him around and said he wasn't about to take any nonsense from a "new kid" in the office.

In a very calm voice, I explained what I had done and why I had done it. I then asked my manager, "What did I do wrong?" He looked at me and said, "I don't know, but whatever it is cut it out. Stop rocking the boat." When I asked why the note wasn't produced to verify my statements, he said that it "wasn't available."

I left my manager's office totally perplexed. How could I correct my behavior if I didn't know what was wrong with it? I resolved that I had no choice except to be totally self-reliant, since one thing was obvious: what I had taken at face value as friendliness was potentially a fatal trap.

The feelings aroused in this incident were indicative of those I was to maintain for some time. While I felt a need for closeness, the only option open to me was self-reliance. I felt that my manager should support and defend me, but it was obvious that he was not willing to take such a stance. Worst of all, however, was my feeling of disappointment and the ensuing confusion due to my lack of guidance. I felt that if my manager was not willing to protect and defend me, he had an increased responsibility to give me guidance on how to avoid future explosions of a similar nature.

For some months I worked in that office without any additional explosions, although I was continually admonished not to "rock the boat." During a luncheon with the area manager one day, I remember, he said, "Ed, I've never seen a guy try so hard. If we tell you to tie your tie to the right, you sure try to do it. But why can't you be like Joe [another trainee the area manager supervised]? He doesn't seem to be having any problems."

The Appraisal Incident

I directed my energies and frustrations into my work, and my supervisory section improved in every measured area of performance until it led the unit. At the end of my first six months on the job, I was slated to go on active duty to fulfill my military requirements as a lieutenant in the Army. Shortly before I left, my manager stated, "Ed, you've done a tremendous job. You write your own appraisal." I wrote the appraisal, but was told to rewrite it because "it's not good enough." I rewrote the appraisal four times before he was satisfied that I was not being too modest. As I indicated earlier, I had resolved to be as unabrasive as possible, and, even though I had met or exceeded all my objectives, I was trying not to be pompous in critiquing my own performance.

Finally, on my next to last day on the job, my manager said, "Ed, this is a fine appraisal. I don't have time to get it typed before you go, but I'll submit this appraisal just as you have written it." With that, I went into the service, feeling that, finally, I had solved my problems.

Six months later, I took several days' leave from the Army to spend Christmas in the city with my family. On the afternoon of the day before Christmas, I decided to visit the personnel executive who had originally given me encouragement. So, wearing my officer's uniform, I stopped by his office.

After exchanging greetings and making small talk, I asked him if he had seen my appraisal. He answered, "yes," but when his face failed to reflect the look of satisfaction that I expected, I asked him if I could see it. The appraisal had been changed from the one that I had originally written to another "yes, but" appraisal. The numerical results said that I had met or exceeded all objectives, but under the section entitled "Development Program" the following paragraph had been inserted:

"Mr. Jones's biggest problem has been overcoming his own impulsiveness. He has on occasion, early in his tour, jumped too fast with the result that he has incurred some resentment. In these cases his objectives have been good, but his method has ruffled feathers."

I asked the personnel executive to interpret my overall rating. He answered, "Well, we can run the business with people with that rating." I then asked him to explain the various ratings possible, and it became clear that I had received the lowest acceptable rating that wouldn't require the company to fire me. I could not see how this could be, since I had exceeded all my objectives. I explained how I had written my own appraisal and that this appraisal had been rewritten. The personnel officer could not offer an explanation; he recommended that I speak to my old area manager, who had had the responsibility to review and approve my appraisal, and ask him why I had been treated in that manner.

A Bleak Christmas

I tried to sort things out on my way to see my former area manager. My head was spinning, and I was disgusted. The appraisal was not just unfair—it was overtly dishonest. I thought of standing up in righteous indignation and appealing to higher authority in the company, but I had always resisted calling attention to my blackness by asking for special concessions and wanted to avoid creating a conflict situation if at all possible. While the 15-minute walk in the cold air calmed my anger, I still hadn't decided what I was going to do when I arrived at the area manager's office.

I walked into a scene that is typical of Christmas Eve in an office. People were everywhere, and discarded gift wrappings filled the wastebaskets. The area manager still had on the red Santa Claus suit. I looked around at the scene of merriment and decided that this was a poor time to "rock the boat."

The area manager greeted me warmly, exclaimed how great I looked, and offered to buy me a drink on his way home. I accepted, and with a feeling of disgust and disappointment, toasted to a Merry Christmas. I knew then that this situation was hopeless and there was little to be gained by raising a stink while we were alone. I had been naive, and there was no way to prove that the appraisal had been changed.

I was a very lonely fellow that Christmas Eve. My feelings of a lack of closeness, support, and protection were renewed and amplified. It became obvious that no matter how much I achieved, how hard I worked, or how many personal adjustments I made, this system was trying to reject me.

I didn't know which way to turn, whom to trust, or who would be willing to listen. The personnel executive had told me to expect prejudice, but when he saw that I was being treated unfairly, he sent me off on my own.

"What do they expect?" I thought. "They know that I am bound to run into prejudice; yet no one lifts a finger when I am treated unfairly. Do they expect a person to be stupid enough to come right out and say, 'Get out, blackie; we don't want your type here'? This surely wouldn't happen—such overt behavior would endanger the offending person's career."

After the Christmas Eve incident, I went off to finish the remaining time in the Army. During that period, I tossed my work problems around in my mind, trying to find the right approach. The only answer I came up with was to stand fast, do my best, ask for no special favors, and refuse to quit voluntarily.

NEW CHALLENGES

When I returned to the company, I was assigned as a supervisor in another area for five or six weeks, to do the same work as I had been doing prior to my departure for the military service. At the end of this uneventful refamiliarization period, I was reassigned as a manager in an area that had poor performance and was recognized as being one of the most difficult in the company. The fact that I would be responsible for one of three "manager units" in the area was exciting, and I looked forward to this new challenge.

I walked into my new area manager's office with a smile and an extended hand, anxious to start off on the right foot and do a good job. After shaking hands, my new boss invited me to sit down while he told me about the job. He began by saying, "I hope you don't, but I am pretty sure you are going to fall flat on your face. When you do, my job is to kick you in the butt so hard that they'll have to take us both to the hospital."

I was shocked and angry. In the first place, my pride as a man said you don't have to take that kind of talk from anyone. I fought the temptation to say something like, "If you even raise your foot, you may well go to the hospital to have it put in a cast."

As I held back the anger, he continued, "I don't know anything about your previous performance, and I don't intend to try to find out. I'm going to evaluate you strictly on your performance for me."

The red lights went on in my mind. This guy was making too much of an issue about his lack of knowledge concerning my previous performance. Whom was he trying to kid? He had heard rumors and read my personnel records. I was starting off with two strikes against me. I looked at him and said, "I'll do my best."

More Appraisal Troubles

The area's results failed to improve, and John, the area manager, was replaced by a new boss, Ralph. Two weeks after Ralph arrived, he called me on the intercom and said, "Ed, John has your appraisal ready. Go down to see him in his new office. Don't worry about it; we'll talk when you get back." Ralph's words and tone of foreboding made me brace for the worst.

John ushered me into his office and began by telling me that I had been his worst problem. He then proceeded to read a list of every disagreement involving me that he was aware of. These ranged from corrective actions with clerks to resource-allocation discussions with my fellow managers. It was a strange appraisal session. John wound up crossing out half of the examples cited as I rebutted his statements. At the end of the appraisal, he turned and said, "I've tried to be fair, Ed. I've tried not to be vindictive. But if someone were to ask how you're doing, I would have to say you've got room for improvement."

Discussions with Ralph, my new boss, followed as soon as I returned to my office. He advised me not to worry, that we would work out any problems. I told him that this was fine, but I also pointed out the subjectivity and dishonesty reflected in previous and current appraisals and the circumstances surrounding them.

I was bitter that a person who had just been relieved for ineffectiveness could be allowed to have such a resounding impact on my chances in the company. My predecessor had been promoted; I had improved on his results; but here I was, back in questionable status again.

The Turning Point

About six weeks later, Ralph called me in and said, "Ed, I hope you make it on the job. But what are you going to do if you don't?"

At that moment, I felt as if the hands on the clock of life had reached 11:59. Time was running out very rapidly on me, and I saw myself against a wall, with my new boss about to deliver the coup de grâce. I felt that he was an honest and very capable person, but that circumstances had combined to give him the role of executioner. It seemed from his question that he was in the process of either wrestling with his own conscience or testing me to see how much resistance, if any, I would put up when he delivered the fatal blow. After all, while I had not made an issue of my ill treatment thus far in my career, no matter how unjustly I felt I had been dealt with, he was smart enough to realize that this option was still open to me.

I looked at Ralph and any thought about trying to please him went out of my mind. Sitting up straight in my chair, I met his relaxed smile with a very stern face. "Why do you care what I do if I don't make it?" I asked coldly.

"I care about you as a person," he replied.

"It's not your job to be concerned about me as a person," I said. "Your job is to evaluate my performance results. But since you've asked, it will be rough if I am fired, because I have a family and responsibilities. However, that's not your concern. You make your decision; and when you do, I'll make my decision." With that statement I returned to my office.

Several weeks after this discussion, a vice president came around to the office to discuss objectives and job philosophy with the managers. I noted at the time that while he only spent 15 or 20 minutes with the other managers, he spent over an hour talking with me. After this visit, Ralph and I had numerous daily discussions. Then Ralph called me into his office to tell me he had written a new appraisal with an improved rating. I was thrilled. I was going to make it. Later, he told me that he was writing another appraisal, stating I not only would make it but also had promotional potential.

After Ralph had changed the first appraisal, my tensions began to decrease and my effectiveness began to increase proportionately. The looser and more confident I became, the more rapidly the results improved. My assignment under Ralph became very fulfilling, and one of the best years I've spent in the company ensued. Other assignments followed, each more challenging than the previous, and each was handled satisfactorily.

Things the B-School Never Taught

Peter W. Bernstein

Mary Cunningham was a hot topic at Bendix long before that late September day when Bill Agee stood before more than 600 employees and denied that her advancement had anything to do with "a personal relationship that we have." Clearly, Cunningham's rise at Bendix was meteoric. She joined the company in June of last year as executive assistant to Agee, after a three-hour interview in New York at the Waldorf-Astoria. ("A meeting of kindred spirits," she says.)

This June, a year later, Agee gave her added responsibilities and a bigger title—vice president for corporate and public affairs. Three months after that came the promotion to vice president for strategic planning, touching off the uproar that culminated in Cunningham's resignation last week.

Agee's judgment that a public discussion of the matter would clear the air could not have been more wrong. His comments to the employees set off an avalanche of press coverage, and Mary Cunningham instantly became a minor celebrity. Top corporate executives in the U.S. have been accused of almost everything imaginable except having romances with one another. Now that the inevitable has finally happened, the business world is atwitter.

Is It Anyone's Business?

Underneath the prurient speculation are more serious questions that touch on some of the thorniest issues of the day. Is Cunningham being unfairly victimized by a society suspicious that attractive women advance on their wiles, not their wits? Is any 29-year-old fresh from business school, no matter how smart, qualified to be the chief planning executive of a multibillion-dollar corporation in the throes of a major restructuring? Are the personal lives of Agee and Cunningham—or any other corporate officials—anybody's business? Finally, once such an embarrassing controversy surfaces, how should a corporation deal with it?

The woman at the center of the storm is as complex and as controversial as the issues swirling around her. "My whole life has been unusual," she says. Her upbringing certainly was. The fourth of five children, she grew up in Hanover, New Hampshire. Her parents divorced when she was five, and she was raised by her mother and Monsignor William Nolan, then the curate of the local church and now the Catholic chaplain at Dartmouth College. "That was another platonic relationship the world didn't understand," she says, comparing her relationship with Bill Agee to her mother's with Father Bill. When she was 6, she says, she took an I.Q. test that indicated she was a genius. Her score: over 160.

Her life took another unusual twist during her senior year at Wellesley College when she met Howard R. Gray Jr., a black man 11 years her senior who was then attending Harvard Business School. Within a year they were married. "It was not a typical relationship," Cunningham said recently. "We were much more focused on the message we were sending to society than our marriage." Husband and wife both worked in New York for four years—she was first a paralegal and then a junior officer at Chase Manhattan Bank for three years. The marriage started breaking up when they began commuting after Mary entered Harvard Business School in 1977. They are now separated, and she is seeking an annulment.

Cunningham gets mixed reviews from her business-school classmates. Her precise and professional manner impressed some of them. "With many people it takes some time to develop confidence in their competence, but not with Mary," remembers one woman who worked with her at the Women's Student Association. "From the beginning, you knew she could get the job done." But she also inspired jealousy and did not win many friends. Several of her classmates describe her as a "teacher's pet type," both calculating and manipulative. She left behind an excellent academic record, as she had at Wellesley, and took away a vocabulary of business-school jargon that can numb the ears.

Inside Bendix, gossip about the relationship between Cunningham and Agee began to reach a crescendo after her June promotion, and all sorts of things helped keep the noise level up. A TV camera focusing on former President Gerald Ford at the Republican National Convention happened to find Agee and Cunningham sitting next to him. Some Bendix people suggested that Agee was less accessible than he had once been, and Cunningham's growing influence with him did not help to allay suspicions. She has called herself his "alter ego" and "most trusted confidante"; he says she is his "best friend." Then in August, Agee and his wife of 23 years got a divorce so quickly it surprised even top officials at Bendix.

What was one to think? Here were two young, attractive, unattached people working together, traveling together, even staying in the same two-bedroom suite at the Waldorf Towers. They *had* to be having an affair—and that would explain Cunningham's sprint up the ranks.

"There is no affair"

However indisputable the logic, it wasn't true — or so Agee told Bendix's top management and the executive committee of the board in separate, and discreet, meetings a couple of weeks before the press got wind of the story. Cunningham, who also appeared at the two meetings, offered to resign, but argued that doing so would appear to corroborate the rumors and set the terrible precedent that rumors can dictate policy. Besides, she added, her resignation would serve notice to young people, especially young women, that they cannot achieve positions of responsibility rapidly. But it was Agee who provided a crucial piece of information. "I told them there was no romantic involvement between us," he says. Oddly, however, he didn't stop there. "The moment this becomes a romantic relationship," he recalls adding, "you will be the first to know." So far, he has had nothing more to say. And Cunningham recently said flatly, "The fact of the matter is there is no affair."

Agee has never confronted the question head-on in public. At the employee assembly that sparked the publicity, he predictably defended Cunningham's rapid promotions as "totally justified," and described her contribution to Bendix as "outstanding." Yet he hardly dispelled the notion that Cunningham's rise might have been due to cronyism. "It is true," Agee told the employees, "that we are very, very close friends, and she's a very close friend of my family."

His failure to repeat the disclaimer he had privately given top management might have been deliberate. Agee would later argue that the personal life of any employee, from the chairman of the board to an assembly-line worker, was nobody else's businesss. "In the future," Agee said, "I do not believe that I owe the management committee, the board, or external audiences a discussion or explanation of any aspects of my personal life unless I am accused of breaking the law." Henry Ford II, and before him Benjamin Disraeli, had already said it more succinctly: "Never complain, never explain."

Cunningham's actions after the publicity erupted can't have won over many skeptics. When the calls from the national press began on a Thursday, she let it be known she would make a "major" announcement the next day. Then she confided to a couple of journalists that she would resign, an "irreversible" decision. About an hour later, fearing her resignation would confirm the innuendos, she told the reporters to scratch the "irreversible." By the following morning, she had decided not to make any statement—and not to resign.

A Half-Baked Solution

Over the weekend, she decided to ask the compensation committee for an "immediate but temporary leave of absence." This half-baked solution was a setup designed to elicit a vote of confidence from the directors. And though she got it the following Monday when the committee unanimously rejected her request, she continued to waver between resignation and staying on. When the full board met last week, the directors had reached a consensus that all the publicity had impaired Cunningham's effectiveness. Cunningham, who had come to the same conclusion, then resigned. She says she has already had a lot of job offers.

The issue might never have arisen if Cunningham and Agee, but especially Agee, had behaved in a way that avoided the appearance of any impropriety. Several Bendix directors and executives—while accepting that there was no romance and happy with Cunningham's performance—argued that she ought to resign, just to get rid of the problem. Both Agee and Cunningham initially resisted that suggestion, although resistance had its risks—particularly for Agee, whose own position may have been jeopardized. He doesn't think so. "Short term, people will say there has been a modest hurt," he says now in assessing the damage. "But I never felt in serious jeopardy."

As more women win senior corporate jobs, romantic ties between top executives are bound to develop. How they, and their companies, should handle the situation presents some bewildering questions. In some ways, the problems can be the same whether the romance is real or imagined. "It's not like dealing with spark plugs," one of Bendix's operating executives remarked in the midst of the Agee-Cunningham flap. Adds Cunningham: "There are certainly no Harvard Business School cases on how to deal with this." Maybe nowadays there should be.

What the Working Woman Needs Is a Wife

Ann Sagi

"Every working woman needs a wife," says a University of Maryland professor. "Imagine going home from work and having a drink ready or dinner ready. Or, when you go on a business trip, someone to pack for you, and even better, someone to unpack and do your laundry when you get home."

Because executives work under constant, intolerable stress, large corporations spend millions to help managers cope with the rigors of running the company.

But it's not the executives who need help, says Dale Masi of the University of Maryland School of Social Work. It's secretaries.

A secretary—generally a woman—pounding a typewriter and scribbling in a steno pad is subjected to much more pressure than her higher-salaried boss, Masi says. The boss often is responsible for her stress. He uses her as an escape valve for his tension.

Secretarial pressure often leads to mental and physical damage, alcohol and drug abuse, Masi said, and it can be deadly.

A U.S. federal government ranking of the 10 most stressful occupations rates secretary second, below coal miners and construction workers. Office managers and foremen are ranked lower. The ranking is based on death rates and admissions records at hospitals and mental health facilities.

Masi, who works for the U.S. department of health and human services through the University of Maryland, said secretarial strain is

"What the Working Woman Needs Is a Wife," as it appeared in the *Vancouver Sun* (Canada), April 24, 1981. Reprinted by permission of United Press International.

manifested by a greater risk of heart disease, abuse of legal drugs, alcoholism and mental illness, most often in the form of depression.

She said the rate of coronary disease among clerical workers is double that of all other working women.

Stress among women office workers is more acute than other "pink collar," low-paying occupations—cashiers, nurses and waitresses—for several reasons, Masi said.

One is the disparity between the amount of responsibility and autonomy. Secretaries very often have more knowledge of the nuts-and-bolts operation of the firm than their bosses, but seldom have the authority to make or implement decisions.

Other factors are lack of opportunity for advancement and boredom, particularly for secretaries with college degrees who entered the field because they couldn't decide on a career.

"Secretaries are underemployed, especially college grads who didn't know what to major in. You work for years as a secretary and all of a sudden, you wonder if there isn't something more, something better. You ask, 'Where do I go from here?' " Masi said.

Feeling that their contribution to the firm is minimal, or completely ignored, enhances low self-esteem and heightens frustration.

Another factor among all women workers, but particularly secretaries, is lack of sleep caused by trying to excel at two jobs—one at home and one outside.

"The biggest social change of the past decade is the number of women working outside the home," Masi said. "One reason is because they want to, but in a great number of cases, the economy pushed them into the work force to keep their families going."

Trying to stretch a meagre pay cheque also exacerbates stress, particularly for divorced women and single parents, whom Masi called the fastest growing poverty group. They bear the double burden of child care and job.

Married women don't fare much better, Masi said, because they are saddled with *hausfrau* responsibilities after they cover their typewriters for the day. Working women often feel guilty if they can't handle both jobs properly, she added.

On-the-job stress has boosted the number of secretaries abusing legal drugs and alcohol. Masi said women workers are "almost matching" men addicted to alcohol, with one woman alcoholic for every four males.

Masi said companies can save money by implementing programs to alleviate secretarial stress.

"People with personal problems don't operate at peak efficiency. Lateness, absence, hangovers, poor decision-making, a lot of lost time—if companies can do something to get people functioning, it's very cost-effective."

She said women employees should present their needs and concerns to their male supervisors "and put their heads together to solve these problems. After all, these men are fathers of daughters who might become secretaries one day."

Companies should institute employment counseling for secretaries who want to move up the career ladder, she said. They should also involve clerical workers in decision-making, hold workshops on how to handle stress, set up in-house day care and offer flex time to let secretaries schedule their work days around family needs.

Institutional Bigotry

Roger Wilkins

A Federal court in the District of Columbia recently ordered the Air Force to reinstate Leonard P. Matlovich, a former sergeant who was dismissed five years ago because he admitted that he was a homosexual. Though it is on a narrower and more technical ground than I would have liked, I am delighted by the judge's decision.

Leonard Matlovich was a superb airman. He was a decorated Vietnam veteran whose service ratings were always excellent. There was nothing in Sergeant Matlovich's behavior in the service to single him out from anybody else except that he did his job far better than most people in the Air Force did theirs. But his spirit bothered him. He wasn't being honest with the world about himself. Part of his identity as a human being was his homosexuality. But he was hiding it, pretending it didn't exist, pretending he was something other than what he was. He was behaving as if he was ashamed of what he was and that made him ashamed of himself.

So he did a courageous thing: He announced his homosexuality. And the Air Force promptly threw this distinguished airman out of the service. The Air Force had a regulation prohibiting the retention of homosexuals in the service unless "the most unusual circumstances exist." The judge said the Air Force had engaged in "perverse behavior" in being unable to explain its policy, and ordered Matlovich reinstated.

I met Matlovich and another homosexual airman back when they were both fighting their original expulsions from the Air Force. The other airman, Skip Keith, was a mechanic trained to work on C-5A engines. He loved his work and had been judged to be good at it, but when he felt he had enough of hiding part of himself from the world, he too was tossed out of the Air Force.

I am not surprised that the Air Force could not explain its position clearly. Shortly after I met Matlovich and Keith, I had lunch with a group of journalists and an Air Force lieutenant general. During the course of the lunch, I asked the general why the Air Force tossed homosexuals out on their ears. He practically choked on his food. The best I could get from him was that when he was flying he wanted a wing man he could rely on. He couldn't answer why gay airmen would be more unreliable than anybody else. He just got more incoherent.

The general was black. If I had closed my eyes and changed his words a little bit, I could have imagined that tirade coming from a white general in 1940 trying to explain why the Army couldn't be integrated. Institutional bigotry in any form stinks, and men like Len Matlovich and Skip Keith are heroes to have stood up to it.

Chicago Tribune 9 March 1979.

Male nurses battle prejudice

By JACK MABLEY

One of the most blatant examples of sexual discrimination is in nursing, male nurses say.

A male nurse is a man in a woman's world. The trial he faces are as real as those of the woman in business who gets pinched at the water cooler instead of seated in the board room.

Male nurses often are not allowed to care for female patients, although the doctors are men. Male nurses endure snide remarks at work and in their social life. Their opportunities are reduced significantly.

There are somewhere between 26,000 and 52,000 males among the nation's 1.3 million nurses.

Some of these men—some succesful, others not—were interviewed. Luther Christman is dean of the nursing school at Rush-Presbyterian-St. Luke's Medical Center in Chicago.

"My career has been very mixed," he said. "There's been either a lot of positive support or automatic rejection.

"I compare it to the way the National Organization for Women says men discriminate against women.

"Whoever's in power doesn't want to share.

"It's economic fear, the same thing that makes men chauvinists...A man has to be two or three times as good to get recognition. It's the same thing blacks complain about. Even if you are very competent, there's a reluctance to accept you.

"I've had to take a great many remarks, almost entirely from women nurses, comments like "You're only successful because you're a man, not because you're any good."

Fighting Off Old Age

A theory that exercise and positive thinking really work

John Leo

Ronald Reagan, say gerontologists, may do for old age what Henry VIII did for divorce. Not that the new President, who turned 70 last week, is about to lavish money on septuagenarian lobbyists, the Gray Panthers or age researchers. Those researchers, in fact, consider themselves prime targets for Reagan's budget cutting. The gerontologists, rather, think Reagan may actually help retard the rate of aging among senior citizens simply by remaining active and competent. Reason: after decades of work in the field, researchers have concluded that warding off old age is in large part a matter of self-image, positive thinking and staying active. Says Jack Botwinick, a psychologist and the author of *Aging and Behavior:* "There's a general feeling that people could have a self-fulfilling prophecy of decline. By keeping active they'll hang on longer."

Part of the problem, say the researchers, is the chilling power that certain numbers have come to possess: to many Americans, 65 means used up; 70 or 75 means ready for death. Yet today's 65-year-olds can expect to live 16 more years. In sports too, numbers have some of the same paralyzing power. A baseball player is considered old at 35, a basketball guard at 30. Athletic skills clearly erode with time just as everyday physical capabilities inevitably decline after, say, 65, but some researchers think that even in sports aging is nearly as much mental as physical. A baseball star, knowing that most players are washed up at 35 or 36, begins to expect a decline and helps produce it by a lack of concentration. Yet highly motivated athletes can keep their skills longer. Philadelphia Phillies First Baseman Pete Rose, who will be 40 in April, is still going strong. Quarterback George Blanda played pro football at age 48, and at age 52, Gordie Howe played pro hockey on the same team as his two sons.

Dr. James Fries of the Stanford University Medical Center talks of shifting the "markers" of age in much the same way that Rose talks about rejuvenating himself each spring: exercise plus an upbeat attitude equal success. At Stanford's arthritis clinic, says Fries, "I tell patients to exercise—use it or lose it. 'Run, not rest' is the new advice of the cardiologist."

Most progress in medicine, Fries maintains, has come from exchanging acute medical problems for chronic ones. For instance, people who might once have died from diseases such as smallpox and tuberculosis now live long enouh to develop chronic ailments like atherosclerosis and emphysema. Since we are running out of acute problems to "exchange," Fries says, the job of medical researchers is to keep the steady decay of organs at a low level, and the task of everybody is to work at postponing or reducing the severity of their chronic problems — giving up smoking to delay emphysema, for example, or treating hypertension to delay problems with the arteries. Regular checkups are necessary to detect early signs of disease, and exercise is crucial. "The body is now felt to rust out rather than wear out," says Fries. Every organ has a reserve capacity that declines gradually. "If loss of reserve function represents aging in some sense, then exercising an organ presents a strategy for modifying the aging process."

That includes the brain. Fries thinks that memory loss can be successfully resisted by memory-training techniques and that mental agility in old age comes from giving the brain regular workouts. "You can't fight the trend entirely," he says, "but within the envelope of human potential, you can greatly slow that progress toward the end." Estimates are that 10% of Americans over age 65 show some signs of senility. According to a task force sponsored by the National Institute on Aging, some of this deterioration — perhaps 10% or 20% — can be cured if caught early enough. Says K. Warner Schaie, director of the Gerontology Research Institute at the University of Southern California: "We find that people who have been very active and involved in life tend to maintain their intellectual functions."

Senile dementia, a degenerative organic brain disorder, of which a major type is Alzheimer's disease, is not much affected by positive thinking, but some doctors think that quicker treatment may cut the rate of the disorder. Psychologist Botwinick, coinvestigator in a study of the early stages of senility, says families waste too much time fretting and trying to cope before calling in a doctor. "By the time a doctor sees an Alzheimer's patient, that patient is pretty far along. Getting to him early may make a big difference."

Genetics, socioeconomic status and luck all help determine who will live to a ripe old age. So does education, according to one theory. Sociologist George Maddox, director of the Center for the Study of Aging and Human Development at Duke University, argues that education "is associated with the notion of taking hold of the future in a special way, and it leads people to organize their lives differently." If that theory is correct, then rising national levels of education may mean that tomorrow's elderly will have an easier time of it than today's.

One of the elderly who fit the gerontologist's prescription of peppy indomitability is Al Beatty, 87, a retired railroad man living alone in a trailer in the Riviera Mobile Park in Scottsdale, Ariz. Beatty is legally blind and partially deaf, but he manages to keep a full daily schedule, dances whenever he can, and about four years ago started to teach a workshop in personal development to the elderly at the Scottsdale Senior Center. "It's the ones who don't conform to the stereotype of the elderly who live the longest," says Rosemary Perry, director of Beatty's center. Though she has not read about Dr. Fries's ideas, she manages to express them well enough: "You may have a chronic illness and have to get to bed earlier. But it's not the end of the world. It's just a slowdown."

Life Without Work

Bernard Lefkowitz

One night, ten years ago, my father was complaining about his job. After 40 years of selling women's hats on the same street in Manhattan, the pay was still lousy, his boss didn't give a damn about him and nobody bought hats anymore. I had heard it all many times and had never known what to do except listen silently. That night, I wanted to say something because I knew time was running out, that every morning he had to put a nitroglycerin tablet under his tongue to make it up the subway steps with his sample case. So I offered him some money and suggested he take time off to relax and perhaps think about another job. Secretly, I hoped to coax him into early retirement.

"I can't quit," he said.

"Why not?" I asked, impatiently.

"Because I'd miss it," he said.

About a year later, he died. For a long time after his death, I wondered what kept him working when he knew he was dying. I understand now that it was the sense of community, and his position as a tribal elder in it, that drew him to The Street even when his heart was failing.

As a kid I'd sometimes go with my father when he went out selling, and he had always seemed happiest when he was shmoozing—

shmoozing about politics or sex or the price of felt with the counter-
man at the luncheonette, the black woman who sewed the hat bodies
at the back of the shop, the kid who ran the boutique in the East
Village and hit him up for a contribution to the Abbie Hoffman bail
fund. He cared for the people who populated his work world.

Patterns

In his life, work was a seamless cloth that stretched from his childhood to his death at the age of 64. Today, the pattern of work in
America is much more uneven and irregular, a patchwork of frequent
shifts in jobs and even occupations. In a two-year national study supported by the Ford Foundation, I interviewed more than 100 men and
women who had stopped working for a minimum of two years. Almost all of them were in their 30s, 40s and early 50s. The point of the
study was to find out how their lives had been affected by their dis-
engagement from work and how they reassessed their position in society from their vantage point outside the factory gates.

In one sense they were all conventional. They had begun their
working lives with high hopes and swelling ambition. Like my father,
they had proceeded along a traditional path; first you found a job,
then you married, raised a family, achieved a measure of economic
security and earned the respect of your colleagues and neighbors.

Now they had veered off onto uncharted ground. At first I thought
that their most difficult adjustment would involve finding the money
to survive and filling up the time that had been occupied by their
work. But most of the people made the transition without great
trauma. They put together a basic economic package which consisted
of government assistance, contributions from family members who
had not worked before and some bartering of goods and services.
When they couldn't meet a mortgage payment, they sometimes took
a temporary off-the-books job or rented out a room. Generally they
seemed to be living almost as well as when they were drawing a
salary.

Unlike the Depression-era image of the man who crumbles when
he doesn't have a job, these people found plenty to do. When they
were working they had daydreamed about other interests and en-
thusiasms. Quitting gave them the chance to live out their day-
dreams. The aeronautics engineer who was laid off by Boeing in 1971
after twenty years on the job never went back to work. Instead, he
builds magnificent, high-power electronic telescopes in his basement.
The government economist who was never quite certain of the purpose of the programs he was analyzing does not doubt his purpose
today; it is to take moving, richly evocative photographs of the people
who live in his neighborhood in Boston.

At work, my father had found a community that recognized and respected both his craft and his qualities of character. This was not so for these people: they had doubted the value and meaning of their labor. Test a new jet engine, add a new wrinkle to a state tax plan — they woke up in the morning asking themselves the fatal question: what difference does it make?

On the corporate organization chart, their positions were called slots and after a while they had begun to think of themselves as slots. If they quit or died tomorrow, somebody else would fill in the slot. The common theme, which surfaced again and again in their histories, was the need to find a new social connection — to reassert control over their lives, to gain some sense of freedom. As the economist-turned-photographer told me, "I worked to buy fine cognac and I bought fine cognac to keep working. Now the cognac's gone, but I understand what I'm doing and why I'm doing it."

Some were brilliantly successful in their pursuit of personal efficacy and community. I remember with great fondness the Yale architect who became the unofficial mayor of a houseboat community in California. He hasn't worked for fifteen years but nothing that affects his constituency escapes his scrutiny. There were also the woman who sold her farm and devoted herself to rescuing a bankrupt cooperative of black farmers, and the former keypunch operator who led a campaign to force state legislators to disclose their private sources of income. But they were in the minority. Most of the people I spoke to wanted to rejoin the intimate circle they felt they had neglected in their years of work. They are represented by the pilot who grounded himself because he realized he had become a stranger to his teen-age daughters.

An Alternative

The difference between them and my father was their belief that they were *entitled* to freedom and independence. For my father, who grew up in a cold-water tenement and suffered through the Depression, independence — especially independence from work — was a luxury and certainly not a right. In my father's time, a family breadwinner who left his job would be condemned by everyone as a bum. The people I interviewed came largely from middle-class backgrounds. They were educated, self-assured, articulate and, with a few exceptions, white. They were sure they could talk themselves back into a job if need be. And that belief licensed them to explore an alternative to the American idea of success.

My father was born too early. It makes me sad that he could never exorcise the demons—those economic and social anxieties that always haunted him. I'm not saying he would have died happy and fulfilled if he had been secure enough to investigate the world beyond work. But I believe he would have come closer.

Two Women, Three Men on a Raft

What Really Happened to Raft No. 4 on an Outward Bound Trip down the Rogue River?

Robert Schrank

One afternoon in June, I left the cloistered halls of the Ford Foundation and within 36 hours found myself standing on the pebbled banks of the Rogue River in Oregon with three other uncertain souls who had embarked on a week of "survival training" sponsored by Outward Bound. It was a cloudy, cold day, and as we pumped up our rubber raft and contemplated the Rogue, we also wondered about each other.

Before embarking on a Greyhound for the raft launching site, we had gathered the night before at the Medford Holiday Inn. That night, the Outward Bound staff had distributed individual camping gear and waterproof sleeping/storage bags to the 20 of us, almost all novices, and had given us a short briefing on the perils of going down the Rogue River on a raft.

As they explained the nature of the trip, the Outward Bound staffers reminded me of seasoned military men or safari leaders about to take a group of know-nothings into a world of lurking danger. Their talk was a kind of machismo jargon about "swells," rattlers, safety lines, portages, and pitons. Because they had known and conquered the dangers, it seemed they could talk of such things with assurance. This kind of "man talk" called to a primitive ear in us novices, and we began to perceive the grave dangers out there as evils to be overcome. In our minds, we planned to meet "Big Foot" the very next day, and we were secretly thrilled at the prospect.

If the Outward Bound staff briefing was designed to put us at ease, its effect, if anything, was the opposite. Hearing the detailed outline of what would be expected of us increased our anxiety. "You will work in teams as assigned to your raft," said Bill Boyd, the Northwest Outward Bound director, "and you will be responsible for running your raft, setting up camp each night, cooking every fourth meal for the whole gang, and taking care of all your personal needs."

The staff divided the 20 of us into four groups, each of which would remain together for the week on the raft. How we were grouped was never explained, but of the five rafts on the river, No. 4 was the only one that ended up with two women and three men.

One of the men was a member of the Outward Bound staff, a counselor and guide who was considerably younger than his four charges.

The four of us on Raft No. 4 were all in our middle fifties. Each of us had experienced some modicum of success in his or her life, and Outward Bound had invited each of us in the hope that after a week of living on the Rogue River we would go back from that trip as Outward Bound supporters and promoters.

Outward Bound exists because of the surprising fact that during World War II fewer younger men survived being torpedoed on the Murmansk, Russia convoy run than older men. Dr. Kurt Hahn, C.B.E., an emigrant German educator living in England, had observed that the older men did things to help themselves survive, such as collecting rain water for drinking, building shelters in the lifeboats, catching and eating raw fish, and learning to care for each other.

Dr. Hahn found that many of the younger seamen, by contrast, tended to sit and wait for somebody to come and rescue them. If no one came, which was often the case, they died just sitting there. Dr. Hahn felt that these seamen must have lacked a certain self-confidence or an awareness that they could take action that would result in survival, and founded Outward Bound to help young people learn that they can take charge of their own survival and lives.

The worldwide organization has been operating in the United States for 14 years; its 35,000 graduates attest to its popularity. During this time, however, Outward Bound has evolved into more of a learning institution than a survival training organization. It now operates under a variety of different notions, one of them being that industrial man has lost and should regain the art of living with nature. The organization believes that the wilderness can teach people about themselves by providing a different backdrop against which they can gain insight into their day-to-day behavior.

This article is about what happened to two women and three men on a raft for a week on the Rogue River in Oregon.

ON THE RIVER

Like most of the other 19 people on the trip, at the outset I had little or no idea of what to expect. I had participated in a few human growth encounter workshops, so I was prepared for, although again surprised at, how willingly people seem to accept the authority of a completely unknown group leader. Most people seem able to participate in all kinds of strange and, in many instances, new behaviors with no knowledge regarding the possible outcomes. This group was no exception. All of us had some notion of Outward Bound, but we knew nothing about each other, or our raft leader John, or the Rogue River.

Even though their preembarkation talk was filled with the machismo jargon I mentioned, the staff did not describe what we might actually expect to happen, nor did they talk about the many other river trips they had been on. I suppose the staff leaders assumed that the best way for a group of people to learn about themselves and each other is to let the experience talk to them directly.

The two women assigned to Raft No. 4 were named Marlene and Helen. Marlene was a recently divorced mother of five kids from Washington, whom a number of us had observed in her pink bikini in the Holiday Inn pool when we had arrived. Most of us acknowledged that because of that build we would love to have her along. Marlene used to wear her red ski suit at night and talked a lot about times she'd spent on the slopes. A top-notch skier, she said she divorced her husband because she was tired of making believe he was a better skier than she was.

Helen, a big blonde woman with a fierce sense of humor and a divorced mother of two grown boys, was at the time of our trip the president of the Fund Center in Denver, a coordinating body for local foundations, as well as a political activist. She and I became each other's clowns, and one night at a campfire she leaned over and asked me, "Bobbie, is this just another plaything of the bored rich, or can we really learn something out here in this godforsaken wilderness?" I told her I wasn't sure but we ought to give it a chance, which we did.

One of the two other men was Bill, a very successful lawyer from Darien, Connecticut. He was the only one of the four passengers who was still happily married, since I too was divorced. Bill was a busy executive, but he managed to find time for hiking, skiing, and fishing. While Outward Bound took care of all our food requirements and most of our medical needs, Raft No. 4 had its own supply officer in Bill. His backpack was organized like a Civil War surgeon's field kit. He had all his changes of clothing scheduled, and when it rained, his extra plastic rainjacket kept me dry since mine leaked like a sieve. Though he and Marlene were obviously attracted to each other from the start, it was clear from his "happy family" talk that nothing was going to change, and it didn't.

The other man was John Rhoades, our heavily mustached, vigorous leader, in his early thirties, who saw himself as a teacher, educator, and trainer. As a progressive educator, John was over-dedicated to the notion that no one can learn from anyone else since learning is a singular, unique experience. At night John slept away from the rest of us under a very fancy Abercrombie and Fitch drop cloth which was made to be strung up in many different ways. Trying a new fancy pitch, John would say to Bill and me, "Be imaginative in how you pitch your tarpaulin." As we had nothing but pieces of plastic as tarpaulins, we would greet John's injunction with amused silence.

The men and women of Raft No. 4 were a warm, friendly, out-going bunch, each of whom helped create a nice supportive atmosphere.

When we arrived at the river, each was anxious to pitch in and do his or her part. The staff distributed the rafts, each of which had a small foot pump, and Bill and I, with instruction from John, proceeded to inflate ours. It was one of our first chores, and we did it with a machismo fervor that suggested either previous knowledge, or that it was man's work, or both. Marlene and Helen carried food bags, buckets, and ropes. It was a cold day, a gray mist hung over the towering Oregon pines, and I had a feeling that at least some of us, given a choice, would have opted for going back to the Holiday Inn. There was a lot of forced joking and kidding, with which we attempted to overcome some of our anxieties — we were whistling in the dark.

John gave each of us a Mae West-type life preserver and instructed us on how to use it. He told us, "You are not to go on the raft without it." Now with all of us bulging out of our Mae Wests, a Richter scale applied to anxiety would have registered eight or a full-scale break-down. Postponing the inevitable, we shivered, fussed, and helped each other get adjusted to our life jackets. The trip down the Rogue was beginning to have a serious quality.

The rafts we used were small, about 10 feet long and 4 feet wide. The passengers sit on the inflated outer tube with their feet on the inside. Everyone is very close together with little or no room to move around. Also, unlike a boat, a raft has no keel or rudder mechanism, which means that it tends to roll and bobble around on top of the water. Unless the occupants work as a team and use their paddles in close coordination, it is very difficult to control.

While we were still on shore, John perched himself in the helmsman position at the back of the raft and said, "OK, I am going to teach you how to navigate the Rogue. When I say 'right turn,' the two people on the left side of the raft are to paddle forward and the two on the right are to backpaddle. When I say 'left turn,' the two people on the right are to paddle forward and the two on the left are to backpaddle. When I say 'forward,' I want everyone digging that paddle in like his life depended on it, and when I say 'backpaddle,' everyone paddle backward. When I say 'hold,' all paddles out of the water. Now you got it, or should we go over it again?" We pushed the raft out over the beach pebbles and paddled out into the Rogue, which at this point seemed like a nice pond. John barked his commands, and the team did just fine in the quiet water.

John told us that we were Raft No. 4 of five rafts, and it was important to everyone's safety that each raft maintain its position so that we could make periodic personnel checks to make sure no one was missing. John gave the command "forward," and because No. 3 raft was already far ahead of us and out of sight, Marlene, Helen, Bill, and I paddled vigorously.

As we proceeded down the river, John announced, "Each of you will take turns at being the helmsman." After some comment by Helen, this term was quickly corrected to conform to the new non-discriminatory linguistics, as well as for the EEOC, to "helmsperson." John said that this person would be in charge of the raft — steering from the stern and issuing the commands.

As John talked, my mind drifted. I was suddenly overwhelmed by the grandeur and beauty of this great wilderness river road we were traveling. In awe of the hugeness of the trees, I did not hear nor respond to a command. John, a very earnest fellow, was somewhat annoyed at my daydreaming and upbraided me saying, "Look, we all have to concentrate on our job or we will be in trouble." And then he explained the nature of the rapids up ahead.

He told us how to recognize a rapid's tongue (entrance), how to avoid "sleepers" (hidden rocks), and then how to ride the "haystacks" (the choppy waves that form at the outlet of the rapids) as you come through the rapids. He said that the most important art we would learn would be how to chop our paddles into the waves as we rode the haystacks. Since a raft has no seat belts, or even seats for that matter, unless you chop down hard the rough water can bounce you right out of it.

As we paddled through the still calm waters, trying to catch up with Raft No. 3, Helen began to complain that she was already getting tired. "I'm just not used to pushing a paddle, but I'm damn good at pushing a pencil," she said. I too was beginning to feel the strain of the paddle, but rather than admit it, I just laughed saying, "Why this is nothing, Helen. You should canoe the St. John in Maine. That would teach you." Bill chimed in with "Yeah, this is nothing compared to climbing Pike's Peak."

As we moved down the river a faint distant roar broke the silence of the forest. And as we drew nearer to it, our excitement grew bigger. One might have thought that rather than a 4-foot rapids, Niagara Falls lay dead ahead. I was relieved when, some distance before the rapids, John told us to head for the bank where we would go ashore and study the rapids. As a team we would then decide what kind of a course to take through them.

We had been on the river for a few hours, and, as it would be many times during the trip, getting on dry land was a great relief. Life on a small rubber raft consists of sitting in ankle-deep cold water, anticpating a periodic refill over both the side of the raft and one's genitals. If there was not time to bail out, we would just sit in the cold water. And even if there were time we would still be soaking wet and cold from the hips down. Though this was our first chance to escape the cold water treatment, we quickly learned to look forward to such opportunities. The physical discomfort we felt together on the raft was overcoming our sense of being strangers; by the time we disembarked that first time, we were a band of fellow sufferers.

At that point on the river, the bank was very steep, so we had a tough climb up a high rock cliff to get a good look at the rapids. Just before the rapids, the river makes a sharp 90-degree bend creating an additional danger. The swiftly running river could pile the raft up on the bank or into a hidden rock. After considerable discussion, during which Bill and I tried to demonstrate to Helen and Marlene our previous if not superior knowledge of boating, we agreed on taking a left course into the tongue while at the same time trying to bear right to avoid being swept onto the bank.

Coming up and down the steep river bank Bill helped Marlene over the rocks, holding her elbow. A ways behind them Helen commented to me, "Honestly, Bob, Marlene isn't that helpless." As we climbed into the raft, Bill helped Marlene again, and I, smiling sheepishly, offered my arm to Helen. I said, holding the raft, "Well, if we go, we all go together, and may we all end up in the same hospital room." Sitting herself down, Helen said, "Who will notify next of kin since no one will be left." After they were seated, Bill and I huddled and agreed that if anything went wrong, he would look after Marlene and I would look after Helen.

Once back on the river, with John at the helm, we paddled into the rapid's tongue, where the raft picked up speed. Staying to the left but maintaining our right orientation, before we knew what had happened, we were roaring through the tongue, roller coasting through the haystacks, screaming with excitement. Flushed with our first real achievement, the raft awash with ice-cold water, we patted each other on the back on our first great success. While bailing out the raft we paid each other compliments and convinced ourselves that we could master the Rogue River.

But this was our first set of rapids, and while John assured us that we had done well, he also reminded us of the meaner rapids yet to come with such potent names as Mule Creek Canyon, Blossom Bar, Big Bend, Copper Canyon, and Grave Creek. My God, I thought, did we really have to go through all of those terrible places?

Life on the Rogue included many other things besides shooting rapids. We pitched tarpaulins every night, lugged supplies in and out of the raft, and became accustomed to the discomforts of having no running water and of being absolutely frozen after sitting in cold water for a whole day. Nothing cements a group together like collective misery, and the people of Raft No. 4 had a *real* concern for each other as mutually suffering humans.

Each raft carried a watertight supply bag of sleeping bags and personal clothing. The bag was strapped to the front of the raft and had to be carried to and fro every morning and night. When we tied up at our first campsite, Marlene and Helen each took an end and started to carry the bag from the raft up the bank. Bill ran after them yelling, "Hey, hold it. That's too heavy for you," and grabbed the bag. Throwing it over his shoulder, he said, "You shouldn't try to do that heavy stuff." Marlene smiled and said, "Bill, anytime, be my guest." Helen, who was a little annoyed, commented sarcastically, "Well, it's great to have these big, strong men around now, ain't it though?"

When we came off the raft at night, most everybody instantly undressed to put on dry clothes, caring not one fig for a leaf or modesty. But even though on the surface it looked as though the physical sex differences had disappeared, the emergency nature of things exerted a different pressure, forcing each of us to "do what you know best."

Bill and I, for example, would pitch the tarpaulins each night and haul water, while Marlene and Helen would make the beds, clean the ground, and arrange the sleeping bags. Our mutual concern was evident; it was a beautiful experience of caring for one's fellow sisters and brothers, and I loved it.

After pitching our plastic tarpaulins (which were not much bigger than queen-size beds) as protection against the rain, the four of us would wiggle into our sleeping bags for the night. The first night Helen said she thought we were "four wonderful people gone batty sleeping on the hard cold ground when they could all be in soft feather beds." We laughed and helped each other zip up, arranged sweaters as pillows, and made sure we were all protected. Raft No. 4 was a real team.

During the days, I was beginning to learn some basics about rafts and rapids. Once the raft starts down the river and enters a swiftly moving rapid, the helmsperson must give and the crew respond to commands in quick succession in order to avoid hidden rocks, suck holes, boulders, and other obstacles, which can either flip the raft over or pull it under, bouncing it back like a ball.

As we approached the second rapids, we again went ashore to "look over our approach." It was a bad situation as the rapids planed out over a very rocky riverbed. Helen suggested that we let John take the raft through while we watch. "Now, Bob," she said, "do we really care about this damn river? I don't care if we can squeak through these rocks or not. Hit your head on them or something and you could really get hurt." Bill, John, and I cheered us on.

When I became helmsperson, I discovered quickly how difficult it is to steer a raft. The helmsperson can have some effect on the direction in which the raft goes, and because Bill and I had some boating experience, we were at least familiar with the idea of using the paddle as a rudder. Neither Helen nor Marlene seemed to understand how to use a paddle that way, nor did they have the experience.

When one of the two women on our raft, more so Marlene than Helen, was the helmsperson, she would chant, "I can't do it; I can't do it." Each time they cried out neither Bill nor I would answer right away, but we would eventually try to convince them that they could. Typically, Marlene would say, "I don't know right from left. One of you guys do it; you're so much better."

At Copper Canyon we needed a "hard right" command. With Marlene at the helm, we got a "hard left" instead. Bill and I looked at each other in utter disgust.

He asked Marlene, "What's the matter, honey?"

She said, "I don't know right from left. You be the helmsperson."

He said, "Why don't we write on the back of your hands 'right' and 'left'?"

Bill was kidding, but the next thing I knew, they were doing it.

Helen was mad and said to me, "Is it really necesary to make a baby out of her?"

"No," I said, "of course not. But she really doesn't know right from left."

As Marlene would say, "I can't do it," Bill and I would say, "Of course you can do it. It's easy; you're doing just fine." All the time we were speaking, we were thinking, "Ye gods! When is she going to give up?" Each time either Marlene or Helen would be helmsperson, we'd have the same conversation; each time Bill's and my reassurances would be more and more halfhearted. Before long we weren't responding at all.

As the days wore on, Bill and I proceeded subtly but surely to take charge. The teamwork was unraveling. When we approached a tongue, if either Marlene or Helen were helmsperson, Bill and I would look at each other, and with very slight headshakes and grimaces we would indicate agreement that things were not going well at all. Once we had established that things were not going well, we then felt free to take our own corrective measures, such as trying to steer the raft from our forward paddle positions, an almost imposible thing to do. Not only is running the raft from the front not at all helpful to the person at the helm, but also if the helmsperson is not aware of the counterforces, the raft can easily turn around like a carousel. The unaware helmsperson is then totally out of control. When that would happen, Marlene would say, "I just don't know what's wrong with me," and Helen would echo, "I don't know what's wrong with me either." Bill's and my disgust would mount.

Eventually, John became fed up with the inability of the bunch on Raft No. 4 to work together, which was mainly a result, he said, of the two "captains" in the front. As a last resort he ordered each one of us to give a single command that he or she would shout as needed. My command was "hold," Bill's command was "left," Marlene's was "right," and Helen's was "backpaddle." John's teaching objective was to get the four of us working together, or else. Needless to say, "or else" prevailed.

On the fifth day, Marlene was helmsperson. Bill and I were in the bow, silently anxious. Even voluble Helen was silent as the raft approached a fast-moving chute. At that time only a clear, concise, direct command and a rapid response would be of any use at all.

Instead of a "hard right" command, we had no command. Marlene froze, the raft slid up on a big boulder, and in an instant we flipped over like a flapjack on a griddle. The current was swift and swept the five of us away in different directions. As I splashed around in the cold water, cursing that "goddamned dumb Marlene," I spotted Bill nearby. The two of us began together to look for Marlene and Helen, whom we found each grappling with paddles and gear they'd grabbed as the raft had gone over. We assured each other we were OK and expressed relief at finding each other.

Cold, wet, and shivering uncontrollably, we made our way out of the river. To warm us and to keep us moving, John chased us around the bank to get wood for a fire. He stuffed us with candies and other sweets to give us energy. As we stood around the fire, chilled and wet, unable to stop shaking, we talked about what had happened, and why.

There was mutiny in the air now and a consensus emerged. The four of us were furious at John and blamed him for our predicament. John retreated, but finally we were agreed that we would not have any more of this kind of thing. Regardless of John's wishes, anyone who did not want to be helmsperson could simply pass. Marlene was certain that she wanted no part of being at the helm, and Helen, though less sure, was happy to say, "Yeah, I just want to stay dry. Let you guys take the helm."

After becoming somewhat dry, sober, and a bit remorseful, the crew of Raft No. 4 returned to the river to resume our run down the Rogue. We had lost our No. 4 position, the other rafts having run past us. John was helmsperson. Helen and Marlene were settled into the backpaddle seats. Bill and I, miffed over our mishap, felt self-conscious and fell silent thinking of the inevitable joshing we'd receive from the other rafts.

We slowly overcame the tensions of our crisis, and as the trip came to an end, we were friends again; the fifth day was forgotten. As we climbed out of the raft for the last time, Marlene said, "Well, the next raft trip I take, it will be as a passenger and not as a crew member."

That last night on the Rogue, we celebrated with a big party. The women dressed up in improvised bangles and baubles. I was the maître d', and none of us thought much about what really had happened on Raft No. 4.

6

CONTROL AND RESISTANCE

"Rather than bringing formal charges against an employee, an agency may choose to use the threat of charges to force his retirement or resignation."

— Robert Vaughn

The struggle for control of people's behavior and their efforts to evade it have been noted throughout recorded history in virtually every organizational setting. Managerial theorists and behavioral scientists of virtually every persuasion have written volumes on how to control, but resistance and evasion continue under even the most harsh and coercive circumstances. In most contemporary organizations, attempts to control behavior must be more subtle than in the past, but then so are many of the techniques subordinates use to frustrate the wishes of their superiors. Much of the waste and bad blood that result seem to us to be directly attributable to the short-sightedness of management, subterfuge, organizational politics and attempts at exploitation that we have noted elsewhere in this book.

The articles in this section describe several of the less publicized systems organizations have evolved to control the behavior of their members and, as a counterpoint, techniques employees use to counter attempts at control.

In "Intimidation Rituals: Reactions to Reform" O'Day describes a series of actions commonly taken by officials in organizations to nullify grievances presented by subordinates that are accompanied by proposals for their solution. While O'Day is describing behavior in contemporary organizations, it is worth noting that these actions evolved and were formalized by the church and military several hundred years ago as means of dealing with deviant or charismatic individuals who threatened the established order.

Robert Vaughn's "The Management Monopoly" describes in part how these same rituals are used with only minor variations by the U.S. Civil Service to deal with employees who would rock the boat. They are used often, as

Vaughn points out, through selective application of procedures that were established initially to protect the rights of the very individuals who are unfairly manipulated.

"Hamburgerology at Hamburger U." by Max Boas and Steve Chain tells us how organizational psychology is used by McDonald's to equip their managers with the behavioral skills that will enable them to manipulate their teen-age employees.

These articles illustrate but a few of the control systems in everyday use in organizations. Management textbooks describe many of these but fail to note the many instances where they are either deliberately misused to exploit or are used so clumsily as to be easily subverted by lower-level employees.

When we think of employee resistance to control, tactics such as collective bargaining, strikes, and the slowdown usually come first to mind. Indeed, these tactics are most visible. While our focus is not on the field of industrial relations, we have included the anonymous poem "Harmony" in recognition of those individuals who elect deliberate restriction of output as a means of redressing inequities they perceive.

Informally organized resistance to management by groups of workers is the subject of Watson's "Counter-Planning on the Shop Floor." Although the workers' efforts meet with varying degrees of success, it is interesting to note the motivations prompting the several forms of resistance that are described. The reader should compare this account with the excerpt from Arthur Hailey's *Wheels* in Section 8.

In another story drawn from the plant floor, Barrett's "Señor Payroll" is an amusing account of how a group of Mexican stokers foiled the best efforts at bureaucratic control of their work habits by the company's head office.

Thus far our illustrations have all been drawn from the bottom of the organizational ladder. But, of course, resistance occurs at almost every level in some form or other. Salespeople resist filing activity reports; department heads resist intrusions of their territory by their peers; clerks resist duties they see as demeaning (see "Diane Wilson" in Section 4); and the heads of operating divisions resist encroachment of their discretion by corporate headquarters (see "The Vega" in Section 10). The tactics used vary widely. But our last selection, James Thurber's humorous story, "The Catbird Seat," contains a very real warning of what may be encountered by managers who attempt to introduce change that lower-level employees see as threatening.

Intimidation Rituals: Reactions to Reform

Rory O'Day

The reaction of authority in social systems to the reform initiatives of a subordinate is viewed as a series of intimidation rituals. These rituals divide into two major phases, each involving two distinct steps. The first

Reproduced by special permission from *The Journal of Applied Behavioral Science*, "Intimidation Rituals: Reactions to Reform," by Rory O'Day, Vol. 10, No. 3, pp. 373–386. Copyright, 1974, NTL Institute.

phase, Indirect Intimidation, *includes the rituals of* nullification *and* isolation; *the second*, Direct Intimidation, *the rituals of* defamation *and* expulsion. *Why these rituals for protest-suppression in organizations are powerful tools in the hands of the middle manager is discussed. Attention is also given to various images projected by the organizational reformer and reasons for resistance to reform from within an organization.*

This paper characterizes the reactions of superiors in social systems to a reform-minded subordinate as a series of intimidation rituals. Each successive "ritual of control" represents an escalation in the efforts of authority to discourage an individual (and those who may support him or her) from continuing to seek reform.

MIDDLE MANAGEMENT'S MECHANISM OF CONTROL

The rituals of intimidation satisfy the two primary concerns of authorities confronted by a subordinate who appears not only able to articulate the grievances of a significant number of other system members but also capable of proposing solutions to them. Their first concern is, of course, to control the reformer so that he does not succeed in recruiting support. Their other concern is to exercise this control in ways that absolve them of any wrongdoing in the matter. The individual in question must be controlled in such a way that he neither continues to be an effective spokesman nor becomes a martyr. When superiors are confronted with a reform-minded subordinate, they want his silence or his absence, whichever is easier to achieve. The "authorities" must also preserve their carefully managed image of reasonableness, and would prefer that the reformer leave voluntarily rather than be removed officially.

For purposes of illustration, this presentation will describe intimidation rituals used by various organizations in the service of protest-suppression, for organizational authorities prefer to *intimidate* a reform-minded individual rather than commit organizational energy to the structural and personnel changes required to transform a "nonconforming enclave" into a legitimate subunit.[1] It is further suggested that an organization undergoes major changes that incorporate and accommodate a group of dissidents only when the intimidation rituals do not succeed in silencing the individuals who constitute the "leading edges" of the reform movement.

In the discussion that follows, I will be concerned primarily with the reformer who emerges from the lower hierarchy in an organization and challenges the *middle hierarchy*. A reformer threatens middle management in three distinctly different ways. The first threat is a function of the validity of his accusations about the inadequacy of specific actions of middle-level members and his suggestions for correcting them. If the reformer is correct, those in the middle will fear that those at the top will punish them when they discover the truth. The second threat comes from the moral challenge presented by such a reformer, for his demand for action will reveal the strength or weakness of middle management's commitment to the organization. And thirdly, the reformer's challenge may indicate to people at the top that middle management is unable to maintain order in its own jurisdiction. To protect their interests, middle-level bureaucrats therefore feel their only defense against reform-minded subordinates is intimidation.[2]

The rituals of intimidation involve two phases: *Indirect Intimidation,* which has two steps, *nullification* and *isolation;* and *Direct Intimidation,* which also comprises two steps, *defamation* and *expulsion.*

PHASE I: INDIRECT INTIMIDATION

Step 1: Nullification

When a reformer first approaches his immediate superiors, they will assure him that his accusations or suggestions are invalid — the result of misunderstandings and misperceptions on his part. His superiors, in this phase, hope that the reformer will be so awed by authority that he will simply take their word that his initiative is based on error. If, however, the reformer insists, his superiors will often agree to conduct an ''investigation.'' The results of such an investigation will convince the reformer that his accusations are groundless and that his suggestions for enhancing organizational effectiveness or revising organizational goals have been duly noted by the appropriate authorities.

Bureaucratic justification for this response usually rests on the argument that this method copes with the system's ''crackpots'' and ''hot-heads,'' discouraging them from disturbing the smooth, routine functioning of the organization with their crazy ideas and their personal feuds. But middle management also uses these rituals of nullification to handle a potentially explosive (for them and others in the organization) situation quickly and quietly, in order to prevent unfavorable publicity, maintain the organization's state of pluralistic ignorance, and prevent the development of a sympathetic and concerned audience for the reformer's ideas. The explicit message is: ''You don't know what you're talking about, but thank you anyway for telling us. We'll certainly look into the matter for you.'' Members of the middle hierarchy then proceed to cover up whatever embarrassing (for them) truth exists in the reformer's arguments.

The protest-absorption power of the ritual of nullification derives from an element inherent in bureaucracies: the always-attractive opportunity to avoid personal responsibility for one's actions. Thus, if people attempt reform at all, they generally do not proceed beyond the first ritual, which is a process designed to quash the reformer and allow his superiors to reaffirm the collective wisdom of the organization, while clearing their consciences of wrongdoing. Nullification even gets the would-be reformer off the hook — and he may remain grateful to the organization for this added convenience. This shedding of personal responsibility allows the reformer and the authorities alike to compromise in the belief that although it might not be a perfect organizational world, it is nevertheless a self-correcting one.

Repeated exposure to the nullification ritual (the "beating your head against the wall" phenomenon) is expected to convince any sane organizational member that a reformist voice or presence is unwelcome. He is expected to take the hint and stop pestering his superiors with his misguided opinions. Gestures of generosity on the part of the middle hierarchy are not unusual if he decides to leave the organization — and such concern is usually expressed by offering to help the individual find employment opportunities elsewhere.

Step 2: Isolation

If the reformer persists in his efforts, middle management will separate him from his peers, subordinates, and superiors, thereby softening his impact on the organization and making it extremely difficult for him to mobilize any support for his position.

Middle managers argue that these procedures represent the exercise of their rights of office in the service of protecting the organization. But these attempts to isolate the reformer can also be seen as a show of force, as a way of reassuring their own superiors (if they are paying attention), their subordinates, and perhaps themselves that they can maintain order in their own jurisdiction.

Attempts at isolating the reformer include closing his communication links, restricting his freedom of movement, and reducing his allocation of organization resources. If these do not neutralize the reformer, he will be transferred to a less visible position in the organization. In these rituals, the bureaucratic message is: "If you insist on talking about things which you do not understand, then we will have to prevent you from bothering other people with your nonsense."

Systematic unresponsiveness to a reformer's criticism and suggestions is a particularly interesting form of isolation. This lack of response is meant to convince the reformer of the invalidity of his position; but if he presses his right to be heard, it may be used to create a feeling of such impotence that the reformer overreacts in order to elicit a response from his superiors. This overreaction may then be used to demonstrate the reformer's psychological imperfections.

When subjected to organizational isolation, most people come to see the error of their ways or the handwriting on the wall. When an individual learns that there is still time to mend his ways, he usually steps back in line and becomes a silent participant in the organization. When he realizes his career in the organization is at a standstill, he may decide to leave as gracefully as possible while he can still leave under his own steam. Middle managers closest to him then often offer him assistance in finding a new job, with the assurance that *"we only want what is best for you."*

Most forms of isolation are designed to persuade the reformer of the futility of trying to initiate change until such time as he is instructed by his superiors to concern himself with change. The reformer practically guarantees his defeat if he reacts to systematic organizational unresponsiveness by confronting his superiors in ways that violate policy or law. The temptation to confront administrative unresponsiveness in dramatic and often self-defeating ways stems in large part from the intense frustration induced by the reformer's belief that systematic unresponsiveness violates his basic rights of freedom of expression and carries with it the implication that he is personally ineffectual (Turner, 1973). Administrative unresponsiveness to what the reformer believes are crucial issues both for himself and for the organization may be sufficiently frustrating to compel him to act, however rashly, in order to clarify the situation. From the administration's point of view, this can be seen as "flushing the rebels out into the open," "giving them enough rope to hang themselves," or, more formally, deviance-heresy conversion (Harshbarger, 1973).

PHASE II: DIRECT INTIMIDATION

Step 3: Defamation

Should the reformer refuse to remain silent, and instead mobilizes support for his position, middle management will begin to impugn his character and his motives. "When legitimate techniques fail—the middle hierarchy might resort to illegitimate or non-legitimate ones" (Leeds, 1964, p. 126). Middle managers will often distort events or even fabricate instances of misconduct in order to intimidate not only the reformer but also those who would listen to or believe him.

Defamation attempts to cut the reformer off from a potentially sympathetic following by attributing his attempts at reform to questionable motives, underlying psychopathology, or gross incompetence. This three-pronged attack is meant to blackmail the reformer into submission and to transform a sympathetic following into a mistrustful crowd of onlookers or an angry mob that feels resentful at having been deceived by the reformer.

From the vantage point of the reformer, the Kafkaesque or Alice-in-Wonderland quality of the rituals of intimidation becomes particularly evident at this time. The reformer finds himself faced with charges which only he and his accusers know are either false or irrelevant in relation to the value of his reform initiatives. The reformer is in a double bind. His superiors will use their offices and positions of trust and responsibility to create the impression in the minds of others in the organization that their accusations of incompetence, self-interest, or psychopathology are true. If the reformer continues in the face of these accusations, he risks being viewed as power-hungry or irrational. If he allows himself to be intimidated by the threat of lies, he allows his superiors to win by default.

One tactic of the superior is to accuse the reformer of acting out his Oedipal conflicts. Such a personalization of a subordinate's reform efforts (especially a younger subordinate) permits his superior to present himself as a harassed "father" faced with a troubled "son," and blocks any examination of his conduct that might reveal provocation on his part. In this way the bureaucrat hopes to persuade others in the organization to respond to the reformer as a sick person in need of therapy or as a child in need of nurturing — a stance that allows him to take on the role of "good father" in relation to other subordinates and to the reformer, if and when the latter capitulates and admits his need for help and guidance.

Rituals of defamation are undertaken by superiors in order to focus attention away from themselves and onto the reformer. The superiors hope that by casting enough doubt on the motives, intentions, and personality of the reformer, enough people in the organization will think that "where there is smoke, there must be fire." The message of this ritual is: "Don't listen to him (his message) because you can't trust a person like him."

Like the rituals of nullification and isolation, the ritual of defamation is both an end in itself and a preliminary to the final ritual of expulsion. The superiors hope by threatening to destroy the reformer's reputation and his character, he will retreat into silence and passivity or leave the organization for greener pastures; if, however, the reformer continues his efforts, his superiors have laid the groundwork for his expulsion.

If the ritual of defamation is undertaken, its target is usually indeed a reformer and not simply a nonconformist or a deviant. His superiors would not need to engage in public tactics of intimidation if there were no substance to his challenge. It is precisely the validity of his reform initiatives that leads his superiors to attempt to destroy his credibility. If this destruction of the reformer's credibility with his peers, subordinates, and top management is effectively conducted, others in the organization will desert his cause and he can be dismissed easily as an undesirable member of the intact organizational team.

Step 4: Expulsion

When neither nullification, isolation, nor defamation can silence the reformer or force his "voluntary withdrawal" from the organization, the middle hierarchy seeks an official decision for his dismissal.

If successful, at least three aims may be achieved thereby. Obviously, by expelling the reformer, his superiors will cut him off from any actual or potential following and weaken any opposition to their authority. An official dismissal also serves as a warning to other budding reformers that middle management has the necessary power and authority to expel troublemakers. Finally, the act of expulsion—a verdict of unfitness — supports the contention that the reformer is an immoral or irrational person.

Of course, the middle hierarchy would prefer the reformer to withdraw voluntarily. Managers want to avoid the public and formal proceedings that often accompany an official request for dismissal of an employee, for the accuser (superior) can often then be scrutinized as carefully as the accused, if the accused person wishes to avail himself of the opportunity. The expulsion ritual involves the formal submission of evidence, the keeping of records, the establishment of independent investigative bodies, and the right of cross-examination, which all function to threaten the image of managers as reasonable, honest, and hardworking servants of the organization. Formal dismissal proceedings are also avoided by middle management because in some fundamental sense they imply that the organization has failed and that they, in particular, have shown themselves unable to maintain order.

THE RITUAL CYCLE ABSORBS AND DESTROYS

Indirect Intimidation attempts to absorb the accusations and suggestions of the reformer, first by depriving him of effectiveness or validity, then by treating him as if he were an "invisible person." The object here is to define the reformer as "harmless." It also attempts to absorb protest by psychologically and physically exhausting the reformer so that he comes to doubt his own experience of reality, his abilities to accomplish the task he sets for himself, and its significance. The authorities hope that the reformer will come to believe the task he has set for himself is humanly impossible and that his fatigue and confusion are the result of his inability to accept human nature for what it is. Short of this, they hope that the reformer will come to feel so inadequate that he will be grateful for continued employment by the organization, in any capacity. ("You're welcome to stay aboard as long as you don't rock the boat.")

Direct Intimidation attempts to destroy protest through destruction of the *character* of the reformer (defamation) or, if necessary, of his *position* in the organization (expulsion). Direct Intimidation represents middle management's active attempt to destroy the reformer as a source of legitimate grievances and suggestions and to terrorize, if necessary, other organizational members. Successful rituals of defamation create a "bad" person, enabling the "good" organization to close ranks once again and benefit from the curative properties of solidarity when he is cast out of the system. In this sense, the ritual destruction of the person (Garfinkel, 1956) necessarily precedes the destruction of his place in the organization.

In sum, Figure 1 portrays the specific cycles of intimidation rituals. Cycle 1 is most preferred by all organizations, while Cycle 4 is the least preferred. Cycle 2 is preferred to Cycle 3.

FIGURE 1.

Cycles of Intimidation Rituals

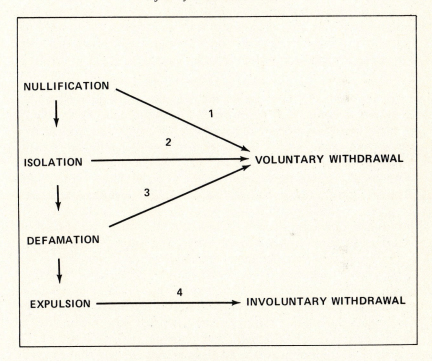

THE REFORMER IMAGE

Throughout this discussion, the individual subjected to the rituals of intimidation has been referred to as the *reformer*, a generic term for any organizational member who resorts to voice rather than to avoidance when faced with what *he* regards as a situation of organizational deterioration or imperfection. Voice is defined as

. . . any attempt at all to change, rather than escape from, an objectionable state of affairs, whether through individual or collective petition to the management directly in charge, through appeal to a higher authority with the intention of forcing a change in management, or through various types of actions and protests, including those that are meant to mobilize public opinion (Hirschman, 1970, p. 30).

Therefore, in the sense in which it is being used here, "reformer" includes the various meanings contained in such labels as "internal muckraker" or "pure whistle-blower" (Peters & Branch, 1972), "innovator in innovation-resisting organizations" (Shepard, 1969), "crusader for corporate responsibility" (Heilbroner, 1972), "nonconforming individual" (Etzioni, 1961; Leeds, 1964), and "heretic" (Harshbarger, 1973); but it is not intended to include the various meanings inherent in the term "organizational change agent."[3] Thus *reformer* refers to any member who acts, in any way and for any reason, to alter the structure and functioning of the organization, when he has *not* been formally delegated authority to institute change.

Why Intimidation Works

From this definition we can see that it is the organization which has the power to define the "reformer" as such, and attaches the stigma to many a well-meaning individual who does not see himself in a protest role. It is often the case that a potential reformer initially thinks of himself or herself only as a hard-working and loyal member of the organization who is simply trying to make things "better" and wishes to be "understood" by busy but well-meaning superiors. However, by the time authorities begin the rituals of defamation, the most naive individual usually realizes that, at least in the eyes of his superiors, he poses a threat to the established order (Herbert, 1972).

The inside reformer is vulnerable to all the intimidation rituals that his particular organization has at its disposal. The reformer outside an organization is usually vulnerable only to the rituals of nullification, isolation (in the form of systematic unresponsiveness), and defamation, unless the organization he is challenging is able to pressure the parent organization into doing the intimidating for it (McCarry, 1972).

Authorities in formal organizations are rarely directly challenged by subordinates. As in the Hans Christian Andersen tale, most individuals do not presume to stand in public judgment of their organizational superiors. Belief in the wisdom and power of the people at the top serves to keep most individuals silent about their grievances concerning the status quo and their ideas (if they have any) for enhancing organizational effectiveness or revising organizational goals. Subordinates do not generally demand, as part of their organizational contractual arrangements, the power to hold their superiors accountable for actions in direct and continuing ways. So intimidation rituals are held to be a last resort — reserved for organizational members who resist, for whatever reason, the usual mechanisms of social control (Millham, Bullock, & Cherrett, 1972).

In their discussion of the obstacles to whistle-blowing, Peters and Branch (1972) include the "loyal-member-of-the-team" trap, the feeling that "going public" is unseemly and embarrassing, and the fear of current and future job vulnerability. Thompson (1968) and Peters and Branch (1972) also refer to the subconscious accommodative device of the "effectiveness trap," an organizational argument that permits its members to avoid conflict on an immediate issue in order to ensure "effectiveness" on some more important issue, at some future time. The curator mentality and emotional detachment generated by the bureaucratic role; the tendency to resort to wishful thinking that organizational deterioration and the consequences of bad policy must soon stop simply because they cannot go on; and the fear that one disagrees with a particular exercise of power only because one is too weak to handle it further contribute to inaction on the part of most "loyal" organizational members (Thompson, 1968).

Reformer as Bad Guy
In point of fact, the protest-absorbing and protest-destroying power of intimidation rituals derives, in large measure, from their infrequent use by organizations. Conversely, if more members were willing to turn their various dissatisfactions into reformist activities, intimidation rituals would lose much of their power.

To understand the effectiveness of organizational intimidation one must examine the reasons why peers and subordinates usually fail to support the reformer, withdraw support, or even actively resist his efforts. Their passive or active resistance may indicate an increased desire or struggle for an organization's scarce resources (material benefits or status, power or prestige — or even dependency). It may also indicate that they perceive themselves as cast in an unfavorable light by the reformer's enthusiasm and heightened activities in pursuing present or changed organizational goals. Members of the organization may secretly believe that the reformer's efforts will be successful, and fear its implication for their position in the organization. If the reformer is successful in convincing top management to investigate the organizational "engine," many may fear that close scrutiny of the performance of the parts will find them wanting. On the other hand, on the outside chance that the reformer manages to seize the reins of power, peers and subordinates may fear that if they do not match his zeal in pursuing new as well as old organizational goals he will turn them out of their present positions.

It frequently seems that practically everyone except the reformer has a personal stake in preserving the complicated fantasy of the organization, even though conditions in the organization are in fact unsatisfying to all but a few elite members. Bion (1959) has described a similar situation in therapy groups where members engage in a variety of neurotic attempts to resist and discourage changing the structure and

functioning of a group that is obviously less than fully satisfying. It seems likely, then, that subordinates in an organization
actively or passively resist a peer's reform initiatives because the pain
of the status quo is less intense than their fear of the unknown.

In general, the reformer finds himself initially with little or no support because there is an implicit acceptance of the bureaucratic order
in our society (Wilcox, 1968) and because most people find it difficult
and improper to question the actions of authority (Milgram, 1965; Peters & Branch, 1972). There is also the well-ingrained reflex of flight in
the face of crisis and change, which has characterized North American society since its colonial days (Hartz, 1955; Hirschman, 1970;
Slater, 1970).

Most organizational members do not support the reformer at all, or
they desert him at the first opportunity because they believe he will
lose in his struggle with institutional authority — and they want to be
on the winning side. Moreover, as Walzer (1969) has pointed out,
most people accept nondemocratic organizational conditions on the
basis of the argument of tacit consent and withhold or withdraw support from the reformer, saying that he is free to go someplace else if
he does not like it where he is.

Peers and subordinates may also resist a reformer because they
suspect that he is committing the unforgivable sin of pride (Slater,
1963). They may come to believe that in taking it upon himself to
judge the organization and its leaders he is acting in a self-righteous
manner (Peters & Branch, 1972). Those who wish to desert the reformer on this ground often use as supporting data the reformer's
persistent efforts in the face of the rituals of defamation.

Since the reformer's departure is usually associated with an immediate reduction or elimination of overt conflict, which in turn re-
lieves tension in the organization, members can wrap themselves in
the organizational blanket and tell themselves that he was the source
of the problem all along. When the emotional ruckus dies down, most
members therefore experience a heightened commitment to the organization and return to their jobs with a renewed vigor. For those
organizational members who continue to harbor some doubt about
the reformer's guilt, the fear of retaliation against "sympathizers"
usually dampens their enthusiasm for the reformer's cause and sup-
presses all but ritualistic expressions of concern for his plight.

SEIZE THE DAY

It is not possible here to do more than raise the issue of whether
one should attempt to change organizations from within or whether
one should create alternative organizations. Large formal organizations are going to be with us for a long time to come (Heilbroner,

1972), and their members are going to have to devise ways to make them more democratic, because there really is no place to run to anymore.

The serious reformer should be prepared to take advantage of organizational crises. He must learn how to recognize, expose, and make concrete those administratively designed arrangements that do not satisfactorily resolve critical problems. For it is in a time of crisis that an organization is open to solutions to the basic problem of survival. Organizational members will be eager to adopt new structures that promise to relieve the uncertainty and anxiety generated by a crisis (Shepard, 1969). If the organization has become weak internally, if it contains corruption and indolence at various levels, if the organization is beset by energy-consuming external pressures, and if the organizational elite lack the resources or the will to initiate changes essential for organizational survival, then the organization might well be ready for successful reform from within (Leeds, 1964). Such an organization might not be capable of successfully administering the intimidation rituals.

Internal organizational reform is a difficult process. The cause of reform as well as constructive revolution cannot be served by deluding ourselves as to the ease of restructuring human society (Heilbroner, 1972; Schon, 1973). The reformer's life is not an easy one. But neither need he feel doomed from the start by the inevitability of the success of intimidation rituals mobilized against him.

NOTES

1. "Nonconforming enclave" refers to the existence of a number of organizational members who, through collective effort, ". . . could potentially divert organization resources from their current commitments, undermine organizational effectiveness, or form a front capable of capturing control of the organization" (Leeds, 1964, p. 155).

2. In a related context, Etzioni (1961, p. 241) asserts, "Once deviant charisma has manifested itself, despite . . . elaborate preventive mechanisms, counter-processes are set into motion. These are of two kinds: those which attempt to eliminate the deviant charisma; and those which seek to limit its effect."

3. It is possible, however, that an organizational change agent might find himself undergoing the rituals of intimidation if he insists that effective action be taken on his proposals for change, particularly if such action would threaten certain organizational power arrangements.

REFERENCES

Bion, W. R. *Experiences in Groups.* New York: Basic Books, 1959.

Etzioni, A. *A Comparative Analysis of Complex Organizations.* New York: The Free Press, 1961.

Garfinkel, H. "Conditions of Successful Degradation Ceremonies," *American Journal of Sociology*, 1956, *61*, 420–424.

Harshbarger, D. "The Individual and the Social Order: Notes on the Management of Heresy and Deviance in Complex Organizations," *Human Relations*, 1973, *26*, 251–269.

Hartz, L. *The Liberal Tradition in America*. New York: Harcourt, Brace and World, 1955.

Heilbroner, R. L. *In the Name of Profit*. New York: Doubleday, 1972.

Herbert, A. *Soldier*. New York: Holt, Rinehart and Winston, 1972.

Hirschman, A. O. *Exit, Voice, and Loyalty*. Cambridge, Mass.: Harvard University Press, 1970.

Leeds, R. "The Absorption of Protest: A Working Paper," in W. W. Cooper, H. J. Leavitt, and M. W. Shelly, II (Eds.), *New Perspectives in Organization Research*. New York: Wiley, 1964.

McCarry, C. *Citizen Nader*. New York: Saturday Review Press, 1972.

Millham, S., Bullock, R., and Cherrett, P. "Social Control in Organizations," *The British Journal of Sociology*, 1972, *23*, 406–421.

Peters, C., and Branch, T. *Blowing the Whistle: Dissent in the Public Interest*. New York: Praeger, 1972.

Schon, D. S. *Beyond the Stable State*. New York: Norton, 1973.

Shepard, H. A. "Innovation-resisting and Innovation-producing Organizations," in W. G. Bennis, K. D. Benne, and R. Chin (Eds.), *The Planning of Change*, Rev. ed. New York: Holt, Rinehart and Winston, 1969. Pp. 519–525.

Slater, P. E. "On Social Regression," *American Sociological Review*, 1963, *29*, 339–364.

Slater, P. E. *The Pursuit of Loneliness*. Boston: Beacon Press, 1970.

Thompson, J. C. "How Could Vietnam Happen? An Autopsy," *Atlantic Monthly*, April 1968, *221* (4), 47–53.

Turner, R. H. "Unresponsiveness as a Social Sanction," *Sociometry*, 1973, *36*, 1–19.

Walzer, M. "Corporate Responsibility and Civil Disobedience," *Dissent*, Sept.–Oct., 1969, pp. 395–406.

Wilcox, H. G. "The Cultural Trait of Hierarchy in Middle Class Children," *Public Administration Review*, 1968, *28*, 222–235.

The Management Monopoly

Robert Vaughn

After Ralph Nader announced that the Public Interest Research Group would be mounting a study of the Civil Service Commission, hundreds of federal employees were heard from. The complaints seemed to indicate not simply individual dislocations, but structural faults in the ways in which employees are disciplined.

The civil servant finds himself in an unpleasant position in which his relationship with his agency is marked by a lack of substantive rights. It is a relationship between superior and subordinate in which the superior has many opportunities to make discretionary judgments of considerable importance to the subordinate. The exercise of legal rights in such a relationship is often difficult and restrained.

Few organizations stress superior-subordinate relationships more than the federal government. Status differentiations are made clear by the general service (GS) ratings. The GS scale establishes the rate of pay for employees in the federal service. As of January 1974 salaries range from approximately $5,000 for a GS-1 to $40,000 for a GS-18 with several years of service. The system provides precise differentiation between grades one through eighteen and ten salary step levels within each. (As one indication of status, lower-grade employees are given small metal desks while higher-grade employees receive larger wooden desks. Even space is an indication of station; a GS-5 is allowed 60 square feet of work space while a GS-15 supervisory employee is allotted 225 square feet.)

All communication is made through layers of intermediaries. Each employee must be given performance and appraisal ratings for purposes of retention and promotion. Such appraisals are always made by superiors, and the goodwill of one's supervisor therefore becomes paramount. The work environment may be made friendly or hostile, open or repressive, tolerable or intolerable by the superior, who is equipped with a finely honed and calibrated set of sanctions to be used against subordinates. The granting of leave and the assignment of duties may be effective tools of discipline in the hands of the superior. We found that employee after employee believed that an agency could "get" any employee. Some of the personnel officers with whom we spoke believed that it was always possible "to remove an irritant." Several methods are available by which agencies may remove or restrain a troublesome employee.

Adapted and reprinted by permission from *The Spoiled System* by Robert Vaughn, copyright © 1975 by the Center for Study of Responsive Law. Reprinted by permission of Charterhouse Books, Publishers.

THE DIRECT APPROACH

One of the myths surrounding federal employment is that it is difficult or impossible to remove a federal employee. Initial restraints upon removals — the reluctance of managers to confront employees and the time and effort required to build a case — may cause a manager to reassess what would be an arbitrary decision, but these restraints may not serve the purpose for which they are intended; they may discourage management from removing a marginal employee who, while inconvenient, poses no real threat to the perpetuation of the status quo within the agency, but they do not prevent moving against outspoken or unorthodox employees who do pose a threat.

In actuality, a removal is easy if one takes the proper procedural steps, and even procedural safeguards against unfair use of removal mechanisms are susceptible to manipulation. (One personnel director noted, "Thirty days notice is required for a dismissal, but no notice is required for a suspension. We give the removal notice and a thirty-day suspension notice at the same time.")

Finding grounds presents little difficulty for motivated management. If the difficulty of building a case against an employee is too great, or if the agency does not want to risk the review of the grounds of removal, other methods, are available. When it is not possible to build a case on nonperformance, management has the discretion of selective enforcement of regulations.[1] Consider, for example, that almost all federal employees occasionally violate the thirty-minute lunch rule; indeed, many employees regularly take an hour. But management can select employees to be punished for this violation. Similarly, many employees are late for work and escape with impunity, yet lateness can be selected as grounds for dismissal.

LOVE IT OR LEAVE IT

Rather than bringing formal charges against an employee, an agency may choose to use the threat of charges to force his retirement or resignation.[2] Even when the threatened charges are improper or not clearly supportable, an employee may be tempted to capitulate. If he fights and loses, he has a dismissal on his record and loses his pension and insurance rights. If he feels that his appeal will not be evaluated fairly, he may decide to resign. The legal process appears lengthy and, if there is a possibility that the case may be appealed ultimately in court, expensive, during which time the employee is out of a job and the psychological pressures on him are great.

Some officials argue that the opportunity to resign or retire is an act of mercy to protect an employee's record. Such protestations, however, are belied by the behavior of many agencies. Rather than ending the matter, many an employee has found that his resignation only began a new ordeal. The resignation that goes into his personnel folder, to be referred to by potential employers, is marked "resigned under charges of dismissal." (Bernard Rosen indicated that this practice is no longer tolerated, but nothing prevents management from providing this information when consulted by potential employers.)[3]

LOST IN A RIF

When an agency is required by budget restraints or by reorganization to reduce its staff, it follows a process known as a Reduction in Force (RIF). A dismissal by RIF carries with it no stigma of nonperformance or inadequate performance, for it is the job that is being eliminated, and not the jobholder. Management can and does use RIFs to rid itself of employees against whom dismissal actions would not be sustained.

In theory, who will lose his job in a RIF is based on objective principles that center on retention ratings. (Retention ratings are based in large part upon length of service; veterans receive special consideration, and additional retention points are given to employees who have received awards for superior service.) An employee's right to challenge a RIF is limited to questions of whether his retention rating has been properly computed, whether his job was in the proper category, whether he has been placed in the proper competitive area, and whether certain procedural requirements have been followed. An employee whose job is abolished in a RIF may take over the job of another employee in the same competitive category, who then loses his job instead. While this "bumping" is done on the basis of retention points, management has considerable discretion in establishing the competitive categories. Thus, an employee with several years of service and with high performance ratings may find himself in a category where his seniority and performance count for little.

One of the more famous examples of RIFing was that of Ernest Fitzgerald. Mr. Fitzgerald, an air force civilian employee who exposed before the joint Economic Committee in the fall of 1968 a $2.5 billion cost overrun on the C-5A transport plane, was shortly thereafter removed in a Reduction in Force, which the air force described as an "economy move." His retention rights were mooted because he was the only man in his competitive category — his was the one job abolished and no similar jobs existed in which he might exercise his retention rights. An air force memorandum of January 6, 1969, suggested a RIF as one of three ways to get rid of Fitzgerald.

Fitzgerald appealed to the Civil Service Commission. After court action, he won in 1972 the right to an open hearing. The Commission's Appeals Examining Office recently ordered Fitzgerald's reinstatement. However, the Commission failed to find that Fitzgerald's dismissal was in retaliation for his congressional testimony but was rather the result of an "adversary relationship" which had been allowed to develop between Fitzgerald and the Air Force. Fitzgerald commented that he made the appeals system work only because he had received approximately $200,000 in donated legal services from the American Civil Liberties Union to wage his lengthy battle.

Reduction in force can prove an effective tool to silence troublesome employees as the following case shows:

Oscar Hoffman, a government inspector of pipe welds on combat ships being built for the navy, troubled his superiors by finding a great many defects. When he resisted pressure to ease up, he was threatened with a reprimand. When he filed a grievance against this threat, he was reprimanded and transferred shortly from Seattle to Tacoma, Washington, where he was RIFed in 1970 soon after his arrival. (Accidents involving faulty welds have occurred since on some of the ships about which Mr. Hoffman had expressed concern. Although his superior has been promoted, Mr. Hoffman has been unable to secure another job as a government inspector.)

Those who appeal RIF actions are not notably successful. In 1970, 62,720 Reductions in Force occurred. In 1971, 2,241 RIF appeals were processed at the Commission's first appellate level. The appellant was defeated in 90 percent of the actions. Statistics do not indicate precisely how many of the remainder were reversed on grounds of faulty procedure, but the Commission's ultimate appeals level, its Board of Appeals and Review, processed 1,147 RIF appeals in 1971.

The examples of Fitzgerald and Hoffman do not begin to exhaust the possibilities inherent in RIFing. An employee may, for example, be downgraded to a position soon to be abolished; an employee may be RIFed on the basis of lack of work, and a temporary employee hired soon after; an employee may find that employees he might "bump" have been placed in special training programs where they are not subject to RIF. A variant of RIFing gets the employee down to get him out—to exercise bumping rights he may have to accept a reduction in grade or a reassignment. In 1970, 25,890 employees were downgraded and 17,350 were reassigned through reductions in force. Management has considerable discretion in determining what positions will be offered an employee who is RIFed, and many employees will leave rather than accept the offered job. Such rejection ends all rights that the employee has to appeal the RIF. Of course, demotion or reassignment may itself be an effective sanction, even if the employee does not leave.

EXILED TO SIBERIA

Some agencies have a Siberia — an unpleasant or professionally unproductive duty station, to which rebellious employees may be reassigned. Faced with Siberia, an employee may, of course, resign, but even if he accepts exile, he is effectively removed from the position in which he caused difficulty.

Reassignments may be either to a different geographical location or to a different division within the agency. Since the decision to reassign is considered to be a management prerogative, an employee may have difficulty proving that the reassignment is unnecessary or retaliatory.[4] Because an employee must accept reassignment in order to file a grievance challenging reassignment, he may have to go through the trouble and expense of relocating his family before he can begin his appeal.[5]

"You'd be surprised how many resignations we had when people discovered they had been reassigned to Anchorage," said one former Federal Aeronautics Administration official. A Colorado-stationed research scientist for the Agricultural Research Service who expressed concern about consultants for private industry using laboratory facilities found himself exiled to Alabama. H. Battle Hale, the Department of Agriculture official who questioned the propriety of the activities of Billy Sol Estes, was sent to Louisiana for a nonexistent "key job" before he was eventually reassigned to Kansas City. What is exile for a New Yorker is, of course, not necessarily exile for a Texan. Management is, however, able to tailor the geographical Siberia to the individual. In 1970, 1,960 employees were separated for refusal to relocate geographically.

But it is hardly necessary to send an employee far away to convince him to resign. For many government employees a rewarding and stimulating job assignment is important, and transfer to an agency dumping ground creates, particularly for a professional, great pressure to resign or retire. (Within the Federal Trade Commission, for example, the Division of Wools and Textiles functions as Siberia.)

In regulatory areas, these reassignments directly affect the consumer, since they either incline an aggressive employee to resign or, by discouraging aggressive behavior, they weaken an entire regulatory program. The consumer's "cops on the beat," such as meat and poultry inspectors, are particularly susceptible to this type of harassment.[6]

But perhaps the best example of the use of Siberia to leave the consumer out in the cold is found in a case within the Food and Drug Administration.

Crucial to the FDA's ability to protect the consumer from unsafe or inadequately tested prescription drugs are the medical officers within its Bureau of New Drugs. The medical officer must determine whether clinical trials of new drugs on animals are adequate to justify tests on man. Based on his evaluation of their safety and effectiveness, he must determine whether new drugs should be marketed and whether proposed labeling contains truthful claims and adequate directions. The history of John O. Nestor, M.D., board-certified in pediatrics and board-eligible in cardiology, shows that it is often the most diligent civil servant who is marked for Siberia.

In 1961, Dr. Nestor was enjoying a lucrative practice as a pediatric cardiologist in Arlington, Virginia. In the same year that the FDA was excusing its ineffectiveness before the Kefauver Committee by pleading an inability to attract specialists, Dr. Nestor, who himself had been the victim of an adverse drug reaction because of a faulty label warning, volunteered to work part time for the FDA. When the FDA indicated it would not accept part-time work, Dr. Nestor agreed to give up the greater part of his practice in order to work full time for the FDA.

Immediately after joining, Dr. Nestor attacked his job with a dedication and intensity that should, although it does not, characterize all those who hold a public trust. He was responsible for the withdrawal from the market of Entoquel, a White Laboratories product for the systematic treatment of diarrhea, after he uncovered erroneous test data submitted to the FDA. Dr. Bennet A. Robin, who had submitted the data and who had "tested" approximately forty-five drugs for twenty-two firms, pleaded no contest to charges of submitting erroneous reports. Dr. Nestor was instrumental in helping to block the marketing here of Thalidomide, a drug that caused hundreds of deformed babies in Europe. He was also responsible for the withdrawal from the market of MER/29, a cholesterol-lowering drug that posed a significant risk of producing cataracts in patients, while having doubtful therapeutic efficacy. Three officials of Richardson-Merrill, the manufacturers of MER/29, after pleading no contest to charges of withholding information concerning the drug, were placed on probation.

In the wake of the MER/29 scandal, Dr. Nestor raised issues of general FDA policy before congressional committees and in the form of memoranda to FDA officials. In March 1963, testifying before Senator Hubert Humphrey's Subcommittee on Reorganization, Dr. Nestor criticized the fact that there was "no internal appraisal to determine how a drug was allowed to clear New Drug Procedures."

Rather than being rewarded for his record of public service, Dr. Nestor's tenure at the FDA has been one of trial. At one point, when he questioned a supervisor about not having received a pay increase, he was asked, "Why are you acting the way you are acting?" After a session with the grand jury investigating the MER/29 incident, Dr.

Nestor returned to find his office empty; without consulting him the FDA had reassigned Dr. Nestor to the Surveillance Division of the Bureau of Medicine, an undesirable post. This was not to be the last undesirable reassignment Dr. Nestor would receive. In 1965 he was transferred to the Case Review Branch of the Division of Medical Review, which collects evidence for prosecution. Some eighteen months later, as the result of White House inquiries, Dr. Nestor was returned to the Bureau of New Drugs.

On June 11, 1970, Dr. Nestor directed a special memorandum to Charles Edwards, commissioner of the Food and Drug Administration, warning him of the risks involved in existing FDA testing procedures. Although Dr. Henry Simmons, director of the Bureau of New Drugs, did not approve of this communication, Dr. Nestor used the FDA Critical Problem Report System, ostensibly established to cut red tape in communicating with top officials. In July, Dr. Nestor again wrote Commissioner Edwards discussing the morality and ethics of human experimentation encouraged by the FDA and reiterating the gravity of the situation.

Early in the week of August 17, 1970, Dr. Nestor was called into the office of Dr. Marian Finkel, the deputy director of the Bureau of New Drugs, and asked if he would be interested in working in the Division of Drug Advertising. Dr. Nestor responded that he was not at all interested and left, believing the matter closed. On September 1, 1970, however, Dr. Nestor was informed that he was being transferred to the Division of Drug Advertising.[7] He had not been consulted prior to the decision and it was not until September 4 that he learned from Commissioner Edwards that he would be detailed to the division for only four months. The detail placed Dr. Nestor, a GS-15, under the supervision of a GS-14 whom he had formerly supervised. Dr. Nestor believed that the action was a retaliatory one, motivated by his use of the Critical Problem Report System and by a desire to remove him from the sensitive drug applications with which he was dealing. He feared that he would be placed on other undesirable details when this one was completed or would eventually be reassigned from the bureau entirely. Dr. J. Marion Bryant, a fellow medical officer, commented in 1970 on Dr. Nestor's reassignment. "A large segment of the medical officers, including myself, are of the opinion that it *is* retaliatory and intended to silence Dr. Nestor."

Articles by Morton Mintz in the *Washington Post* of September 7, 1970, and by Reginald W. Rhein in *U.S. Medicine* of September 15, 1970, and continuing congressional inquiry and support for Dr. Nestor may have aided his return to the Cardiopulmonary-Renal Division of the Bureau of New Drugs. Once back, he proceeded to pursue his responsibilities with his customary zeal. Along with several other doctors, including Dr. John W. Winkler, acting division director, Dr. Nestor had turned the Cardiopulmonary-Renal Division into one of the most effective units within the bureau, an effectiveness that distressed the drug industry, and, apparently, the hierarchy of the FDA.

On March 14, 1972, Dr. Nestor was called to the office of Dr. Henry Simmons, director of the Bureau of New Drugs, and told that he was being reassigned to the Bureau of Compliance — effective in six days. Neither Dr. Nestor nor his supervisor had been consulted about the reassignment. When asked the reason for the transfer, Dr. Simmons answered that Dr. Nestor had done such a good job with other investigations that the Bureau of Compliance wanted him to work on Laetrile, an anticancer drug. Dr. Nestor pointed out that he was not a cancer specialist and that one drug investigation hardly justified a reassignment, since he could work on loan for that. The reassignment, furthermore, would be to a nonspecialist position and would remove Dr. Nestor from important current drug investigations. Dr. Nestor became more concerned about the reassignment when he spoke the next day with the director of the Bureau of Compliance. The director told of a conversation with Dr. Simmons the week before in which Dr. Simmons said that he intended to move Dr. Nestor, and asked if he could be used in the Bureau of Compliance. The director had responded by saying there were some problems, such as Laetrile, on which Dr. Nestor could work.

Dr. Nestor filed a formal grievance with the FDA and an appeal with the Civil Service Commission, contending that his assignment to a general medical position not requiring a specialty was an improper reduction in rank. According to him, much of the work he had been assigned could be handled by "a competent first year medical student."

Dr. Nestor had been reviewing an application for the proposed new use of a cholesterol-lowering drug, which had been reviewed previously and approved for use in human investigation by Dr. Finkel. At the time of his transfer he was raising serious questions about the adequacy of the previous tests. He was also raising embarrassing questions about the propriety of the FDA's use of medical consultants to review drug applications who had tested or were testing drugs for private industry.

Dr. Nestor's formal grievance to the Food and Drug Administration was ultimately denied. Today, Dr. Nestor remains in the Office of Compliance. His assignments have become more substantive and, as he put it, "There is always something a concerned individual can find to do."

Not all reassignments, of course, are punitive or coercive, but present policies provide management with a means to suppress and punish dissidents that poses dangers for the effective enforcement of regulatory programs.[8]

THE DEEP FREEZE

Sometimes an instant Siberia can be created without moving the objectionable employee at all. Separation from contact with other employees, physical isolation, and boredom are part of the deep freeze treatment.

One GS-13 employee in the Department of Agriculture was assigned nothing but the task of organizing departmental beauty contests. A GS-9 employee in the Department of Labor was deprived of a telephone and given no work assignment for several weeks. At first he found the resemblance to solitary confinement amusing, but after a while the lack of anything to do became distressing. He began to bring magazines to work with him, a diversion that was ended when a supervisor told him that he was not allowed to read magazines while working. When the employee had the temerity to ask what he was to be working at, his supervisor responded, "What you are assigned." This technique is particularly useful when the employee has violated no regulation.

The deep freeze is also particularly valuable when an employee has been complaining about agency malfeasance, and it appears that an attempt to remove the employee would lead to uncovering the mess. A scientist who worked for the National Institutes of Health complained about the safety of vaccines and found himself placed under "house arrest." First, his secretary was reassigned and not replaced. Then his phone was removed. Eventually, he was moved into an isolated office, the physical access to which was monitored by the agency.

The technique is not always so severe. Often an employee will simply be denied information about what happens to his work or whether his memoranda are accepted or rewritten. One high-ranking HEW employee described these practices as "being sent to Coventry." Rather than a deep freeze, a merely chilly reception is provided. Many employees simply do not like the cold and resign.

FORCED ACCULTURATION

It is important to keep in mind that dismissal is not only a means to get people out, but a means to keep people in line.

Probationary employees — those who will be appointed to or who have served for less than a year in career civil service positions — are particularly vulnerable to manipulation. If the employee is being removed for unsatisfactory performance, he need only be notified in writing of the effective date of his separation and the agency's very brief statement of his inadequacies. In 1970, 9,680 probationary employees were thus removed.

The probationary period can and does serve a valuable purpose, but the lack of standards and the lack of requirements for a meaningful statement of the reasons for removal means that removal can be made on emotion or caprice. Since almost any basis will support a removal, an employee must be very careful not only to perform adequately, but also to refrain from extensive criticism of the agency's performance. This procedure tends to breed timidity and to deny the agency the benefit of a fresh and unbiased perspective.

The histories of the immediate victims of unjustly applied sanctions — the psychologically and morally wounded, the economically and physically destroyed — do not tell all that needs to be told. The coal miner dead because of a failure to enforce safety regulations is a victim of the same lack of external accountability within the management structure of federal agencies. But even if unfair disciplinary actions had no impact beyond the affected personnel, the individual injustices themselves would require that the system of discipline be examined.

For every Ernest Fitzgerald — who had the intelligence and luck to marshal and direct his resources, who had the active support of congressmen, who survived the investigation of his personal life and the attempts to destroy his reputation — there are hundreds who have not survived. Of course, the employees who have chosen to resign rather than to be cast into the agency mold are those who find it easiest to get another job — the most able.

NOTES

1. Kenneth Culp Davis in *Discretionary Justice* indicates that selective enforcement of rules and regulations is widespread in the administrative process. Professor Davis gives an excellent example:

An Oakland ordinance, as interpreted officially by the district attorney, required holding every woman arrested for prostitution for eight days in jail for venereal testing. The ordinance conferred no discretionary power on the police. Even so, the police illegally assumed a discretionary power to be lenient to the girls who cooperated; only 38 percent of those arrested were held for venereal testing. One officer explained: "If a girl gives us a hard time . . . we'll put a hold on her. I guess we're actually supposed to put a hold on everybody so there's nothing wrong in putting a hold on her . . . but you know how it is, you get to know some of the girls, and you don't want to give them extra trouble." (1) The ordinance required holding every arrested woman, yet the police illegally assumed the power to be lenient. (2) The police converted the power to be lenient into an affirmative weapon: "if a girl gives us a hard time . . . we'll put a hold on her." (3) The innocent girl is more likely to resist and therefore less likely to cooperate and therefore more likely to be held. The discrimination seems clearly unjust. And the personal element as part of the motivation is even acknowledged: "You get to know some of the girls." (4) The usual specious reasoning that leniency for some is not unjust comes out with great clarity: "We're actually supposed to put a hold on everybody, so there's nothing wrong in putting a hold on her."

The dynamics of selective enforcement of personnel rules are quite similar. According to USDA regulations, for example, ready-to-cook products coming from meat and poultry plants are to be 100 percent free of processing errors. This standard, however, is not met in any poultry plant, and veterinarians who serve as inspectors-in-charge vary in the number of processing errors they allow. An inspector may, however, find himself faced with the charge that he is allowing excessive errors in the ready-to-cook product.

2. Commission regulations consider but fail to protect the employee effectively from the pressures that can be used to force resignation. F.P.M. Supplement S1-la(3) provides that an agency may give an employee a choice between leaving his position voluntarily or having the agency initiate formal action against him. "It is also proper for the agency in the course of the discussion to advise the employee which of the possible alternatives will be in his best interests. . . . However, if the agency uses deception, duress, time pressure, or intimidation to force him to choose a particular course of action, the action is involuntary."

3. F.P.M. Supplement S1-26c(i) provides that if, after an employee is influenced to separate voluntarily by his agency's assurance that the action will leave him with a clear record in his official personnel folder, the agency enters any unfavorable information on the separation form, the separation is faulty because the employee was deceived. An employee who accepts an agency offer to resign rather than face charges would be well advised to acquire letters of recommendation from his supervisors and the personnel officer *before* he submits his resignation.

4. Federal employees are asked on their employment applications about their willingness to change job locations after they are hired. This information is used, presumably, to evaluate the applicant for employment. If an employee is unwilling to accept geographical reassignments, this may well be a factor in deciding whether or not to hire. An employee who indicates his unwillingness to be reassigned on his application cannot be criticized, however, for feeling that the government has implicitly taken that to be a consideration of his employment. The Public Interest Research Group has received complaints indicating that employees who expressed an unwillingness to relocate on their job applications still face dismissal for refusing to do so.

5. In some agencies, employees are not necessarily faced with this Hobson's choice. For example, in the Department of Labor, Secretary's Order #2-62 provides that any proposed personnel action (transfer) which has been made the subject of a grievance shall not be taken pending settlement of the grievance. Such an action could be taken prior to the resolution of the grievance only if the Secretary determines that the action must be taken to prevent hazards to other employees, to preserve the reputation of the department, or for the best interests of the department.

6. This procedure is described in Harrison Wellford's *Sowing the Wind*, a Nader Task Force study of the Department of Agriculture published in 1972.

7. The FDA contended that the reassignment was to "beef up" the Division of Drug Advertising by placing an M.D. in it. This explanation, however, seemed somewhat bizarre — a recent reorganization of the Division of Drug Advertising specifically excluded medical personnel. (Both Commissioner Edwards and Elliot Richardson, then Secretary of Health, Education and Welfare, had justified the exclusion of physicians by emphasizing that the division could call on medical expertise within other divisions of the FDA.)

8. The federal courts rather than the Civil Service Commission have begun to restrict the ability of agencies to use reassignments to circumvent the appellate rights of an employee. A district court in Louisiana held that reassignments could not be used to force the resignation of an employee as an attempt to circumvent his appellate rights. *Motto* v. *G.S.A.*, 335 F. Supp. 694 (E.D. La. 1971).

Hamburgerology at Hamburger U.

Max Boas and Steve Chain

A bust of Ray Kroc stands in the richly carpeted lobby of Hamburger University, the back of the bronze head turned to the dark-tinted window and the reflecting pool outside. Between classes the lobby becomes the crossroad for students who gather in bunches, carrying their manuals like order books. At peak hours, the whole university takes on the look of a busy sales convention. The light from wheel-shaped chandeliers is subdued as the students mingle in a swirl of bold-colored sports jackets, patterned shirts, turtlenecks, blazers, suits and ties. They have come from all over the United States and they talk with the regional accents of Main Street America. They are in a hurry. For most, HU is the only hope for a career and possible job security. Well into the night they will cling to their manuals in the dormitory atmosphere of the Elk Grove Hyatt Chalet — "Survey. Question. Answer. Read and Hunt. Think It Over. Recite. Review. . . ."

The students cling to prescribed steps to take them through the maze of subjects that have grown in number as well as complexity. The Science grew up with the System, and the System today is no longer simply confined to the making and serving of a hamburger.

In the early years when classes were held in the "pit," it had been enough to know the fast-food fundamentals — Kroc's Trinity of Patty, Bun, and Secret Sauce. But today Hamburger Central is active in many areas of public life. It is busy in Washington, fighting for *sub*-minimum wages and against wage and price controls. It deals with municipal zoning and permit bodies, with courts, judges, and councilmen in virtually every American community, and it is engaged in a struggle with organized labor.

By 1973 union strife in the McDonald's stands had reached the point where Hamburger Central found it necessary to implement a comprehensive campaign. At HU this led to the hasty institution of a brand-new field of study concerned with the psychological methods of managing McDonald's vast work force, 90 percent of which consists of low-paid students and part-time teen-age workers. HU's addition to the curriculum dealt with "motivation" and "communication." The name of the course: Personnel I.

"We are at the point now," Dean Breitkreutz says proudly, "of developing our managers beyond the hamburger knowledge that they already have." Much of this development is in the hands of Dr. Leroy G. Cougle, known among the faculty as "Doc" Cougle, HU's only *real* Ph.D. and a *real* professor of Business Management at the University of Wisconsin.

Doc Cougle explains that Personnel I teaches that the manager's success will be primarily based on how he deals with the teen-agers working in the stand, but before he can "motivate" the "kids," he must have a positive image of himself. He must think of himself as being somebody very special because he works for a highly successful company that sells more hamburgers than any other in the world. He must think of himself as being able to determine his own life and achieve his goals. Personnel I was designed to indoctrinate this "positive" attitude throughout the ranks of hamburger management.

"The point is," says Doc Cougle, "I can't start motivating you as a subordinate until I have some decent feelings about myself. In other words, if I feel very negative about myself, that negativism will transmit that to you, and it is very difficult for me to treat you as a normal producing, achieving human being. If I think that I'm a no-goodnik, it becomes very difficult for me to deal with you in a very positive way. So the first thing I have to do is to start thinking positively about myself. The McDonald's managers do think positively about themselves. They're a part of the leaders of the industry, there's no question about that."

How positively HU students think of themselves is tested in Personnel I with one of Doc Cougle's sentence-completions in which members of the class are asked to finish the sentence "I am."

They usually respond with self-addressed tributes like "I am achieving" . . . "I am successful."

"They all come through very positive," says Doc Cougle, "because they do feel good about themselves; whereas if you were to ask that same question of a bunch of industrialists or the people running Burger King, it would be my guess that you would not get that almost unanimous agreement that 'I-am-something-very-positive.'"

Doc Cougle has been chiefly responsible for bringing Personnel I to

Hamburger U. He is thin, sandy-haired, with a sharp nose and quick, darting eyes. He likes to wear a tan sporty suede three-button jacket and new-looking desert boots. Besides teaching at the University of Wisconsin, he is also chief partner in Cougle and Associates, training and organizational development consultants of Waukegan, Illinois. Twice a month he travels down to Elk Grove Village to administer his "motivation and communication" course.

Doc Cougle believes in the open office and the open shop, and on the question of labor he functions as HU's primary teen-age theoretician. He has instituted the current rule among McDonald's management to no longer refer to the young hamburger workers as "kids" but as "people." Consequently, the increasingly bitter labor strife in the hamburger stands has been reduced to a "people" problem — a "failure to communicate and motivate," according to Doc Cougle. "I have never seen a union shop that deserves to be called a union shop," he says. He is pleased to confide that McDonald's, thanks to Personnel I, has unions "pretty well beaten down for now."

Among HU's more colorfully dressed faculty, Doc Cougle conveys the look of the solid academic, secure in the world of concept, abstraction, social engineering, and psychological tests. In his own low-key collegiate way he is not much different from the aspiring small businessmen and hamburger managers he teaches — a traveling salesman from academe with a sample book of attractive products: Fleischman's work in "leadership"; the "achievement orientation" of Argyris; Herzberg's "job enrichment principles" and "five basic motivators"; and last, but not least, the Transactional Analysis (T/A) techniques of Dr. Eric Berne and Dr. Richard Harris.

In 1973 T/A became the vogue at Hamburger U. Everybody, including the dean, carried a paperback copy of Dr. Harris's best-selling *I'm OK — You're OK*, a hybrid of Dr. Coué and Dale Carnegie, Billy Sunday and Sigmund Freud. Transactional Analysis had been founded by the late Dr. Eric Berne, who believed that people had been "programmed" from an early age; and he set forth the techniques by which the "program" could be switched and tinkered with, tuned and adjusted.

Dr. Berne proclaimed T/A as a form of self-therapy to achieve a positive life-style and material success. But corporate management, from Pan American to McDonald's, has found T/A useful in teaching supervisors the psychological techniques of handling their subordinates. One of the chief T/A techniques is called "stroking" — that is, giving signs of "recognition" and even "physical touch" in order to prompt other people's behavior and make them act in desired ways. An article in *Supervisory Management*, published by the American Management Association, recognized "stroking" as an effective "management tool." According to the article, a supervisor could use this technique in dealing with subordinates "in order to motivate, reward, or reprimand them."

Doc Cougle was instrumental in bringing T/A to Hamburger U. as part of the "management techniques." "Most of the people we have working for us," he explains, "are high school youngsters, male and female. They're adolescents and they're searching and they're looking, and one of the things they search for is their own identity."

Personnel I expounds the labor crisis and T/A resolves it. HU's eager corps of graduate hamburgerologists is encouraged to motivate crews "by trying to find out what the individual needs are and trying to deal with them." Says Doc Cougle, "If that need is for recognition, then try to give that individual crewman recognition. A slap on the back, just saying hello is sometimes enough."

Commencement exercises for the graduates are held in the East Room at Hamburger Central, where they are presented with parchment degrees to mark their passage into the System — the B.H. (Bachelor of Hamburgerology) and M.H. (Master of Hamburgerology); also the Golden Hat for the student voted most helpful to his classmates, the Archie Award for the top man in the class, and a Parker pen that flashes "Quality-Service-Cleanliness" when the plunger is pushed, for outstanding seminar students.

The following poem was composed by a machine-shop worker out of the fullness of his heart. It was discovered on the bulletin board of the shop in which he worked.

Harmony?

I am working with the feeling
That the company is stealing
Fifty pennies from my pocket every day;
But for every single pennie
They will lose ten times as many
By the speed that I'm producing, I dare say.
For it makes me so disgusted

Reprinted by permission from *Restriction of Output among Unorganized Workers* by Stanley B. Mathewson. Copyright © 1959 by Antioch University.

That my speed shall be adjusted
So that nevermore my brow will drip with sweat;
When they're in an awful hurry
Someone else can rush and worry
Till an increase in my wages do I get.

No malicious thoughts I harbor
For the butcher or the barber
Who get eighty cents an hour from the start.
Nearly three years I've been working
Like a fool, but now I'm shirking —
When I get what's fair, I'll always do my part.
Someone else can run their races
Till I'm on an equal basis
With the ones who learned the trade by mining coal.
Though I can do the work, it's funny
New Men can get the money
And I cannot get the same to save my soul.

Counter-Planning on the Shop Floor

Bill Watson

It is difficult to judge just when working-class practice at the point of production learned to bypass the union structure in dealing with its problems, and to substitute (in bits and pieces) a new organizational form. It was clear to me, with my year's stay in an auto motor plant (Detroit area, 1968), that the process had been long underway. What I find crucial to understand is that while sabotage and other forms of independent workers' activity had existed before (certainly in the late nineteenth century and with the Wobbly period), that which exists today is unique in that it follows mass unionism and is a definite response to the obsolescence of that social form. The building of a new form of organization today by workers is the outcome of attempts, here and there, to seize control of various aspects of production. These forms are beyond unionism; they are only secondarily concerned with the process of negotiation, while unionism made that

Reprinted from *Radical America*, May–June 1971 (38 Union Sq., Somerville, MA 02143) Reproduced by permission.

its central point. Just as the CIO was created as a form of struggle by workers, so, out of necessity, that form is being bypassed and destroyed now, and a new organizational form is being developed in its place. The following, then, is by implication a discussion of the self-differentiation of workers from the form of their own former making. The activities and the new relationships which I record here are glimpses of a new social form we are yet to see full-blown, perhaps American workers' councils.[1]

Planning and counter-planning are terms which flow from actual examples. The most flagrant case in my experience involved the sabotaging of a six-cylinder model. The model, intended as a large, fast "6", was hastily planned by the company, without any interest in the life or the precision of the motor. It ran rough with a very sloppy cam. The motor became an issue first with complaints emanating from the motor-test area along with dozens of suggestions for improving the motor and modifying its design (all ignored). From this level, activities eventually arose to counter-plan the production of the motor.

The interest in the motor had grown plant-wide. The general opinion among workers was that certain strategic modifications could be made in the assembly and that workers had suggestions which could well be utilized. This interest was flouted, and the contradictions of planning and producing poor quality, beginning as the stuff of jokes, eventually became a source of anger. In several localities of the plant organized acts of sabotage began. They began as acts of misassembling or even omitting parts on a larger-than-normal scale so that many motors would not pass inspection. Organization involved various deals between inspection and several assembly areas with mixed feelings and motives among those involved—some determined, some revengeful, some just participating for the fun of it. With an air of excitement, the thing pushed on.

Temporary deals unfolded between inspection and assembly and between assembly and trim, each with planned sabotage. Such things were done as neglecting to weld unmachined spots on motor heads; leaving out gaskets to create a loss of compression; putting in bad or wrong-size spark plugs; leaving bolts loose in the motor assembly; or, for example, assembling the plug wires in the wrong firing order so that the motor appeared to be off balance during inspection. Rejected motors accumulated.

In inspection, the systematic cracking of oil-filter pins, rocker-arm covers, or distributor caps with a blow from a timing wrench allowed the rejection of motors in cases in which no defect had been built in earlier along the line. In some cases, motors were simply rejected for their rough running.

There was a general atmosphere of hassling and arguing for several weeks as foremen and workers haggled over particular motors. The situation was tense, with no admission of sabotage by workers and a cautious fear of escalating it among management personnel.

Varying in degrees of intensity, these conflicts continued for several months. In the weeks just preceding a change-over period, a struggle against the V-8s (which will be discussed later) combined with the campaign against the "6s" to create a shortage of motors. At the same time management's headaches were increased by the absolute ultimate in auto-plant disasters — the discovery of a barrage of motors that had to be painstakingly removed from their bodies so that defects that had slipped through could be repaired.

Workers returning from a six-week change-over layoff discovered an interesting outcome of the previous conflict. The entire six-cylinder assembly and inspection operation had been moved away from the V-8s — undoubtedly at great cost — to an area at the other end of the plant where new workers were brought in to man it. In the most dramatic way, the necessity of taking the product out of the hands of laborers who insisted on planning the product became overwhelming. There was hardly a doubt in the minds of the men — in a plant teeming with discussion about the move for days — that the act had countered their activities.

A parallel situation arose in the weeks just preceding that year's changeover, when the company attempted to build the last V-8s using parts which had been rejected during the year. The hope of management was that the foundry could close early and that there would be minimal waste. The fact, however, was that the motors were running extremely rough; the crankshafts were particularly shoddy; and the pistons had been formerly rejected, mostly because of omitted oil holes or rough surfaces.

The first protest came from the motor-test area, where the motors were being rejected. It was quickly checked, however, by management, which sent down personnel to hound the inspectors and to insist on the acceptance of the motors. It was after this that a series of contacts, initiated by motor-test men, took place between areas during breaks and lunch periods. Planning at these innumerable meetings ultimately led to plantwide sabotage of the V-8s. As with the six-cylinder motor sabotage, the V-8s were defectively assembled or damaged en route so that they would be rejected. In addition to that, the inspectors agreed to reject something like three out of every four or five motors.

The result was stacks upon stacks of motors awaiting repair, piled up and down the aisles of the plant. This continued at an accelerating pace up to a night when the plant was forced to shut down, losing more than 10 hours of production time. At that point there were so many defective motors piled around the plant that it was almost impossible to move from one area to another.

The work force was sent home in this unusually climactic shutdown, while the inspectors were summoned to the head supervisor's office, where a long interrogation began. Without any confession of foul play from the men, the supervisor was forced into a tortuous display which obviously troubled even his senses, trying to tell the men they should not reject motors which were clearly of poor quality without actually being able to say that. With tongue in cheek, the inspectors thwarted his attempts by asserting again and again that their interests were as one with the company's in getting out the best possible product.

In both the case of the "6s" and the V-8s, there was an organized struggle for control over the planning of the product of labor; its manifestation through sabotage was only secondarily important. A distinct feature of this struggle is that its focus is not on negotiating a higher price at which wage labor is to be bought, but rather on making the working day more palatable. The use of sabotage in the instances cited above is a means of reaching out for control over one's own work. In the following we can see it extended as a means of controlling one's working "time."

The shutdown is radically different from the strike; its focus is on the actual working day. It is not, as popularly thought, a rare conflict. It is a regular occurrence, and, depending on the time of year, even an hourly occurrence. The time lost from these shutdowns poses a real threat to capital through both increased costs and loss of output. Most of these shutdowns are the result of planned sabotage by workers in certain areas, and often of plantwide organization.

The shutdown is nothing more than a device for controlling the rationalization of time by curtailing overtime planned by management. It is a regular device in the hot summer months. Sabotage is also exerted to shut down the process to gain extra time before lunch and, in some areas, to lengthen group breaks or allow friends to break at the same time. In the especially hot months of June and July, when the temperature rises to 115 degrees in the plant and remains there for hours, such sabotage is used to gain free time to sit with friends in front of a fan or simply away from the machinery.

A plantwide rotating sabotage program was planned in the summer to gain free time. At one meeting workers counted off numbers from 1 to 50 or more. Reportedly similar meetings took place in other areas. Each man took a period of about 20 minutes during the next two weeks, and when his period arrived he did something to sabotage the production process in his area, hopefully shutting down the entire line. No sooner would the management wheel in a crew to repair or correct the problem area than it would go off in another key area. Thus the entire plant usually sat out anywhere from 5 to 20 minutes of each hour for a number of weeks due to either a stopped line or a line passing by with no units on it. The techniques for this sabotage are many and varied, going well beyond my understanding in most areas.

The "sabotage of the rationalization of time" is not some foolery of men. In its own context it appears as nothing more than the forcing of more free time into existence; any worker would tell you as much. Yet as an activity which counteracts capital's prerogative of ordering labor's time, it is a profound organized effort by labor to undermine its own existence as "abstract labor power." The seizing of quantities of time for getting together with friends and the amusement of activities ranging from card games to reading or walking around the plant to see what other areas are doing is an important achievement for laborers. Not only does it demonstrate the feeling that much of the time should be organized by the workers themselves, but it also demonstrates an existing animosity toward the practice of constantly postponing all of one's desires and inclinations so the rational process of production can go on uninterrupted. The frequency of planned shutdowns in production increases as more opposition exists toward such rationalization of the workers' time.

What stands out in all this is the level of cooperative organization of workers in and between areas. While this organization is a reaction to the need for common action in getting the work done, relationships like these also function to carry out sabotage, to make collections, or even to organize games and contests which serve to turn the working day into an enjoyable event. Such was the case in the motor-test area.

The inspectors organized a rod-blowing contest which required the posting of lookouts at the entrances to the shop area and the making of deals with assembly, for example, to neglect the torquing of bolts on rods for a random number of motors so that there would be loose rods. When an inspector stepped up to a motor and felt the telltale knock in the water-pump wheel, he would scream out to clear the shop, the men abandoning their work and running behind boxes and benches. Then he would arc himself away from the stand and ram the throttle up to first 4,000 and then 5,000 rpm. The motor would knock, clank, and finally blur to a cracking halt with the rod blowing through the side of the oil pan and across the shop. The men would rise up from their cover, exploding with cheers, and another point would be chalked on the wall for that inspector. This particular contest went on for several weeks, resulting in more than 150 blown motors. No small amount of money was exchanged in bets over the contests.

In another case, what began as a couple of men's squirting each other on a hot day with the hoses on the test stands developed into a standing hose fight in the shop area which lasted several days. Most of the motors were either neglected or simply okayed so that the men were free for the fight, and in many cases they would destroy or dent a unit so that it could be quickly written up. The fight usually involved about 10 or 15 unused hoses, each with the water pressure of a fire hose. With streams of crossfire, shouting, laughing, and running about, there was hardly a man in the mood for doing his job. The shop area was regularly drenched from ceiling to floor, with every man completely soaked. Squirt guns, nozzles, and buckets were soon brought in, and the game took on the proportions of a brawl for hours on end. One man walked around with his wife's shower cap on for a few days to the amusement of the rest of the factory, which wasn't aware of what was happening in the test area.

The turning of the working day into an enjoyable activity becomes more of a necessary event as the loneliness and hardship of constant and rapid production becomes more oppressive. Part of the reality of concrete labor is that it is less and less able to see itself as merely an abstract means to some end, and more and more inclined to see its working day as a time in which the interaction of men should be an interesting and enjoyable thing. In this way the campaign against the six-cylinder motors does not differ from the rod-blowing contest or the hose fight: each is the expression of men who see their work as a practical concrete process and their relations as men as simple and spontaneous, to be structured as they see fit. Whether they should work together at full steam or with intermittent periods of diversity — or even cease working altogether — comes to be more and more a matter for their own decision. The evolution of these attitudes is, needless to say, a constant target for bureaucratic counter-insurgency.[2]

This constant conflict with the bureaucratic rationalization of time is expressed dramatically each day at quitting time. Most workers not on the main assembly line finish work, wash, and are ready to go a full four minutes ahead of the quitting siren. But with 30 or 40 white-shirt foremen on one side of the main aisle and 300 or 400 men on the other side, the men begin, en masse, to imitate the sound of the siren with their mouths, moving and then literally running over the foremen, stampeding for the punch clocks, punching out, and racing out of the plant as the actual siren finally blends into their voices.

With a feeling of release after hours of monotonous work, gangs of workers move out from the side aisles into the main aisles, pushing along, shouting, laughing, knocking each other around—heading for the fresh air on the outside. The women sometimes put their arms around the guards at the gates, flirting with them and drawing their attention away from the men who scurry from the plant with distributors, spark plugs, carburetors, even a head here and there under their coats — bursting with laughter as they move out into the cool night. Especially in the summers, the nights come alive at quitting time with the energy of release: the squealing of tires out of the parking lot, racing each other and dragging up and down the streets. Beer in coolers stored in trunks is not uncommon and leads to spontaneous parties, wrestling, brawling, and laughter that spills over into the parks and streets round the factory. There is that simple joy of hearing your voice loudly and clearly for the first time in 10 or 12 hours.

There is planning and counter-planning in the plant because there is clearly a situation of dual power. A regular phenomenon in the daily reality of the plant is the substitution of entirely different plans for carrying out particular jobs in place of the rational plans organized by management.

On the very casual level, these substitutions involve, for example, a complete alternative break system of workers whereby they create large chunks of free time for each other on a regular basis. This plan involves a voluntary rotation of alternately working long stretches and taking off long stretches. Jobs are illegally traded off, and men relieve each other for long periods to accomplish this. The smuggling of men through different areas of the plant to work with friends is yet another regular activity requiring no small amount of organization.

The substitution of alternative systems of executing work has its counterpart in areas of the plant which have become, strictly speaking, off limits to nonworkers; they are havens of the plant where men are not subject to external regulation. Usually they are bathrooms, most of which are built next to the ceiling with openings onto the roof. Chaise lounges, lawn chairs, cots, and the like have been smuggled into most of them. Sweepers, who move around the plant, frequently keep tabs on what is called "john time"; the men line up an hour here or there when they can take a turn in the fresh air of the roof or space out on a cot in one of the ripped-out stalls. The "off-limits" character of these areas is solid, as was demonstrated when a foreman, looking for a worker who had illegally arranged to leave his job, went into one of the workers' bathrooms. Reportedly he walked up the stairs into the room, and within seconds was knocked out the door, down the stairs, and onto his back on the floor. That particular incident involved two foremen and several workers and ended with the hospitalization of two participants with broken ribs and bruises.

The coexistence of two distinct sets of relations, two modes of work, and two power structures in the plant is evident to the worker who becomes part of any of the main plant areas. But that coexistence is the object of constant turmoil and strife; it is hardly an equilibrium when considered over time. It is a struggle of losing and gaining ground. The attempt to assert an alternative plan of action on the part of workers is a constant threat to management.

During the model changeover mentioned above, the management had scheduled an inventory which was to last six weeks. They held at work more than 50 men who otherwise would have been laid off with 90% of their pay. The immediate reaction to this was the self-organization of workers, who attempted to take the upper hand and finish the inventory in three or four days so they could have the remaining time off. Several men were trained in the elementary use of the counting scales while the hi-lo truck drivers set up an informal school to teach other men to use their vehicles. Others worked directly with experienced stock chasers and were soon running down part numbers and taking inventory of the counted stock. In several other ways the established plan of ranking and job classification was circumvented in order to slice through the required working time.

The response to this was peculiarly harsh. Management forced it to a halt, claiming that the legitimate channels of authority, training, and communication had been violated. Being certified as a truck driver, for example, required that a worker have a certain amount of seniority and complete a company training program. There was a great deal of heated exchange and conflict, but to no avail. Management was really determined to stop the workers from organizing their own work, even when it meant that the work would be finished quicker and, with the men quickly laid off, less would be advanced in wages.

The threat which this unleashing of energy in an alternative plan of action presented to the authority of the bureaucracy was evidently quite great. Management took a stand, and, with only a limited number of men involved in a nonproduction activity, retained its power to plan that particular event. For six weeks, then, the "rational" plan of work was executed—which meant that the labor force was watched over and directed in an orderly fashion by foremen and various other agents of social control. The work which men want to do together takes four days—at most a six-day week; the work which is forced on them, in the same amount, is monotonously dragged out for six weeks, with all the rational breaks and lunch periods which are deemed necessary for the laborers.

We end, then, more or less on the note on which we began: stressing a new social form of working-class struggle. The few examples here have been a mere glimpse of that form and hardly entitle us to fully comprehend it. But we can see that as a form it is applied to the actual working day itself and to the issues of planning and control which, in my view, make it distinctly postunionism as a practice. The use of sabotage as a method of struggling for control will increase as this form of struggle develops further, but this is merely the apparatus of movement. A crucial point to focus on is the differentiation of this new form of struggle from its former organization: mass unionism.

Within these new independent forms of workers' organization lies a foundation of social relations at the point of production which can potentially come forward to seize power in a crisis situation and give new direction to the society. I would urge, in closing, that our attention and work be focused on the investigating and reporting of the gradual emergence of this new mode of production out of the old. "Like a thief in the night" it advances relatively unnoticed.

NOTES

1. In this plant more than half the workers were either black or newly arrived Southern whites; that percentage may be as high as 75%. The remainder were mixed: whites of Northern origin, many Italians and Mexicans, and a small Hungarian and Polish segment. The women constituted from 5% to 10% of the work force and were generally black or Southern white. In the actions and organizations of workers which this paper describes, the most operative relationships were between blacks and Southern whites. Despite the prevalence of racist attitudes, which were a regular substance of interaction and even a source of open talk and joking, these two groups functioned together better than any other groups in the plant. Also in the events described women were no less active than men. Finally, there was a definite relationship between age and action. Younger workers were more willing to fight back and risk their positions than older workers. The workers from 18 to 35 were the most militantly antiunion and the most willing to go beyond the established channels in their work actions.

2. The overt expressions of the men themselves about their activity are closely tied to the actual work experience. There is little if any notion that the daily struggle in the plant has anything to do with the state or the society as a whole. Rather, it is seen as a struggle waged against an immobile bureaucracy in the company and against the labor establishment so as to improve working conditions. A kind of populist mentality is crucial here, particularly with the Southern whites who show an immediate dislike for all organizational authority and believe (like a religion) that the only way to get anything done well is to do it themselves. While workers clearly design activity to control the length of the working day, for example, these same men are unaware that the relationships and organization involved could also function to plan and control their own production. Yet it is not so important that workers so often miss the social significance of their activities; the vital point is not their consciousness, but what they actually do. Their activity smashes into the contradictions of productive relations and motivates the evolution of counter-structures in the plant.

Señor Payroll

William E. Barrett

Larry and I were Junior Engineers in the gas plant, which means that we were clerks. Anything that could be classified as paperwork came to the flat double desk across which we faced each other. The Main Office downtown sent us a bewildering array of orders and rules that were to be put into effect.

Junior Engineers were beneath the notice of everyone except the Mexican laborers at the plant. To them we were the visible form of a distant, unknowable paymaster. We were Señor Payroll.

Those Mexicans were great workmen: the aristocrats among them were the stokers, big men who worked Herculean eight-hour shifts in the fierce heat of the retorts. They scooped coal with huge shovels and hurled it with uncanny aim at tiny doors. The coal streamed out from the shovels like black water from a high pressure nozzle, and never missed the narrow opening. The stokers worked stripped to the waist, and there was pride and dignity in them. Few men could do such work, and they were the few.

The Company paid its men only twice a month, on the fifth and on the twentieth. To a Mexican, this was absurd. What man with money will make it last 15 days? If he hoarded money beyond the spending of three days, he was a miser — and when, Señor, did the blood of Spain flow in the veins of misers? Hence it was the custom for our stokers to appear every third or fourth day to draw the money due to them.

There was a certain elasticity in the Company rules, and Larry and I sent the necessary forms to the Main Office and received an "advance" against a man's paycheck. Then, one day, Downtown favored us with a memorandum:

"There have been too many abuses of the advance-against-wages privilege. Hereafter, no advance against wages will be made to any employee except in a case of genuine emergency."

We had no sooner posted the notice when in came stoker Juan Garcia. He asked for an advance. I pointed to the notice. He spelled it through slowly, then said, "What does this mean, this 'genuine emergency'?"

I explained to him patiently that the Company was kind and sympathetic, but that it was a great nuisance to have to pay wages every few days. If someone was ill or if money was urgently needed for some other good reason, then the Company would make an exception to the rule.

Juan Garcia turned his hat over and over slowly in his big hands. "I do not get my money?"

"Next payday, Juan. On the 20th."

He went out silently and I felt a little ashamed of myself. I looked across the desk at Larry. He avoided my eyes.

In the next hour two other stokers came in, looked at the notice, had it explained and walked solemnly out; then no more came. What we did not know was that Juan Garcia, Pete Mendoza and Francisco Gonzalez had spread the word and that every Mexican in the plant was explaining the order to every other Mexican. "To get the money now, the wife must be sick. There must be medicine for the baby."

The next morning Juan Garcia's wife was practically dying, Pete Mendoza's mother would hardly last the day, there was a veritable epidemic among children and, just for variety, there was one sick father. We always suspected that the old man was really sick; no Mexican would otherwise have thought of him. At any rate, nobody paid Larry and me to examine private lives; we made out our forms with an added line describing the "genuine emergency." Our people got paid.

That went on for a week. Then came a new order, curt and to the point: "Hereafter, employees will be paid ONLY on the fifth and the 20th of the month. No exceptions will be made except in the cases of employees leaving the service of the Company."

The notice went up on the board and we explained its significance gravely. "No, Juan Garcia, we cannot advance your wages. It is too bad about your wife and your cousins and your aunts, but there is a new rule."

Juan Garcia went out and thought it over. He thought out loud with Mendoza and Gonzalez and Ayala, then, in the morning, he was back. "I am quitting this company for different job. You pay me now?"

We argued that it was a good company and that it loved its employees like children, but in the end we paid off, because Juan Garcia quit. And so did Gonzalez, Mendoza, Obregon, Ayala and Ortez, the best stokers, men who could not be replaced.

Larry and I looked at each other; we knew what was coming in about three days. One of our duties was to sit on the hiring line early each morning, engaging transient workers for the handy gangs. Any man was accepted who could walk up and ask for a job without falling down. Never before had we been called upon to hire such skilled virtuosos as stokers for handy gang work, but we were called upon to hire them now.

The day foreman was wringing his hands and asking the Almighty if he was personally supposed to shovel this condemned coal, while there in a stolid, patient line were skilled men—Garcia, Mendoza and others — waiting to be hired. We hired them, of course. There was nothing else to do.

Every day we had a line of resigning stokers, and another line of stokers seeking work. Our paperwork became very complicated. At the Main Office they were jumping up and down. The procession of forms showing Juan Garcia's resigning and being hired over and over again was too much for them. Sometimes Downtown had Garcia on the payroll twice at the same time when someone down there was slow in entering a resignation. Our phone rang early and often.

Tolerantly and patiently we explained: "There's nothing we can do if a man wants to quit, and if there are stokers available when the plant needs stokers, we hire them."

Out of chaos, Downtown issued another order. I read it and whistled. Larry looked at it and said, "It is going to be very quiet around here."

The order read: "Hereafter, no employee who resigns may be re-hired within a period of 30 days."

Juan Garcia was due for another resignation, and when he came in we showed him the order and explained that standing in line the next day would do him no good if he resigned today. "Thirty days is a long time, Juan."

It was a grave matter and he took time to reflect on it. So did Gonzalez, Mendoza, Ayala and Ortez. Ultimately, however, they were all back—and all resigned.

We did our best to dissuade them and we were sad about the parting. This time it was for keeps and they shook hands with us solemnly. It was very nice knowing us. Larry and I looked at each other when they were gone and we both knew that neither of us had been pulling for Downtown to win this duel. It was a blue day.

In the morning, however, they were all back in line. With the utmost gravity, Juan Garcia informed me that he was a stoker looking for a job.

"No dice, Juan," I said. "Come back in 30 days. I warned you."

His eyes looked straight into mine without a flicker. "There is some mistake, Señor," he said. "I am Manuel Hernandez. I work as the stoker in Pueblo, in Santa Fe, in many places."

I stared back at him, remembering the sick wife and the babies without medicine, the mother-in-law in the hospital, the many resignations and the rehirings. I knew that there was a gas plant in Pueblo, and that there wasn't any in Santa Fe; but who was I to argue with a man about his own name? A stoker is a stoker.

So I hired him. I hired Gonzalez, too, who swore that his name was Carrera, and Ayala, who had shamelessly become Smith.

Three days later, the resigning started.

Within a week our payroll read like a history of Latin America. Everyone was on it: Lopez and Obregon, Villa, Diaz, Batista, Gomez, and even San Martin and Bolivar. Finally Larry and I, growing weary of staring at familiar faces and writing unfamiliar names, went to the Superintendent and told him the whole story. He tried not to grin, and said, "Damned nonsense!"

The next day the orders were taken down. We called our most prominent stokers into the office and pointed to the board. No rules any more.

"The next time we hire you *hombres*," Larry said grimly, "come in under the names you like best, because that's the way you are going to stay on the books."

They looked at us and they looked at the board; then for the first time in the long duel, their teeth flashed white. *"Si, Señores,"* they said.

And so it was.

The Catbird Seat

James Thurber

Mr. Martin bought the pack of Camels on Monday night in the most crowded cigar store on Broadway. It was theater time and seven or eight men were buying cigarettes. The clerk didn't even glance at Mr. Martin, who put the pack in his overcoat pocket and went out. If any of the staff at F & S had seen him buy the cigarettes, they would have been astonished, for it was generally known that Mr. Martin did not smoke, and never had. No one saw him.

It was just a week to the day since Mr. Martin had decided to rub out Mrs. Ulgine Barrows. The term "rub out" pleased him because it suggested nothing more than the correction of an error — in this case an error of Mr. Fitweiler. Mr. Martin had spent each night of the past week working out his plan and examining it. As he walked home now he went over it again. For the hundredth time he resented the element of imprecision, the margin of guesswork that entered into the business. The project as he had worked it out was casual and bold, the risks were considerable. Something might go wrong anywhere along the line. And therein lay the cunning of his scheme. No one would ever see in it the cautious, painstaking hand of Erwin Martin, head of the filing department of F & S, of whom Mr. Fitweiler had once said, "Man is fallible but Martin isn't." No one would see his hand, that is, unless it were caught in the act.

Sitting in his apartment, drinking a glass of milk, Mr. Martin reviewed his case against Mrs. Ulgine Barrows, as he had every night for seven nights. He began at the beginning. Her quacking voice and braying laugh had first profaned the halls of F & S on March 7, 1941 (Mr. Martin had a head for dates). Old Roberts, the personnel chief, had introduced her as the newly appointed special adviser to the president of the firm, Mr. Fitweiler. The woman had appalled Mr. Martin instantly, but he hadn't shown it. He had given her his dry hand, a look of studious concentration, and a faint smile. "Well," she had said, looking at the papers on his desk, "are you lifting the oxcart out of the ditch?" As Mr. Martin recalled that moment, over his milk, he squirmed slightly. He must keep his mind on her crimes as a special adviser, not on her peccadillos as a personality. This he found difficult to do, in spite of entering an objection and sustaining it. The faults of the woman as a woman kept chattering on in his mind like an unruly witness. She had, for almost two years now, baited him. In the halls, in the elevator, even in his own office, into which she romped now and then like a circus horse, she was constantly shouting these silly questions at him. "Are you lifting the oxcart out of the ditch? Are you tearing up the pea patch? Are you hollering down the rain barrel? Are you scraping around the bottom of the pickle barrel? Are you sitting in the catbird seat?"

It was Joey Hart, one of Mr. Martin's two assistants, who had explained what the gibberish meant. "She must be a Dodger fan," he had said. "Red Barber announces the Dodger games over the radio and he uses those expressions — picked 'em up down South." Joey had gone on to explain one or two. "Tearing up the pea patch" meant going on a rampage; "sitting in the catbird seat" meant sitting pretty, like a batter with three balls and no strikes on him. Mr. Martin dismissed all this with an effort. It had been annoying, it had driven him near to distraction, but he was too solid a man to be moved to murder by anything so childish. It was fortunate, he reflected as he passed on to the important charges against Mrs. Barrows, that he had stood up under it so well. He had maintained always an outward appearance of polite tolerance. "Why, I even believe you like the woman," Miss Paird, his other assistant, had once said to him. He had simply smiled.

A gavel rapped in Mr. Martin's mind and the case proper was resumed. Mrs. Ulgine Barrows stood charged with willful, blatant, and persistent attempts to destroy the efficiency and system of F & S. It was competent, material, and relevant to review her advent and rise to power. Mr. Martin had got the story from Miss Paird, who seemed always able to find things out. According to her, Mrs. Barrows had met Mr. Fitweiler at a party, where she had rescued him from the embraces of a powerfully built drunken man who had mistaken the president of F & S for a famous retired Middle Western football coach. She had led him to a sofa and somehow worked upon him a monstrous magic. The aging gentleman had jumped to the conclusion there and then that this was a woman of singular attainments, equipped to bring out the best in him and in the firm. A week later he had introduced her into F & S as his special adviser. On that day confusion got its foot in the door. After Miss Tyson, Mr. Brundage, and Mr. Bartlett had been fired and Mr. Munson had taken his hat and stalked out, mailing in his resignation later, old Roberts had been emboldened to speak to Mr. Fitweiler. He mentioned that Mr. Munson's department had been "a little disrupted" and hadn't they perhaps better resume the old system there? Mr. Fitweiler had said certainly not. He had the greatest faith in Mrs. Barrows' ideas. "They require a little seasoning, a little seasoning, is all," he had added. Mr. Roberts had given it up. Mr. Martin reviewed in detail all the changes wrought by Mrs. Barrows. She had begun chipping at the cornices of the firm's edifice and now she was swinging at the foundation stones with a pickaxe.

Mr. Martin came now, in his summing up, to the afternoon of Monday, November 2, 1942 — just one week ago. On that day, at 3 P.M., Mrs. Barrows had bounced into his office. "Boo!" she had yelled. "Are you scraping around the bottom of the pickle barrel?" Mr. Martin had looked at her from under his green eyeshade, saying nothing. She had begun to wander about the office, taking it in with her great, popping eyes. "Do you really need *all* these filing cabinets?" she had demanded suddenly. Mr. Martin's heart had jumped. "Each of these files," he had said, keeping his voice even, "plays an indispensable part in the system of F & S." She had brayed at him, "Well, don't tear up the pea patch!" and gone to the door. From there she had bawled, "But you sure have got a lot of fine scrap in here!" Mr. Martin could no longer doubt that the finger was on his beloved department. Her pickaxe was on the upswing, poised for the first blow. It had not come yet; he had received no blue memo from the enchanted Mr. Fitweiler bearing nonsensical instructions deriving from the obscene woman. But there was no doubt in Mr. Martin's mind that one would be forthcoming. He must act quickly. Already a precious week had gone by. Mr. Martin stood up in his living room, still holding his milk glass. "Gentlemen of the jury," he said to himself, "I demand the death penalty for this horrible person."

The next day Mr. Martin followed his routine, as usual. He polished his glasses more often and once sharpened an already sharp pencil, but not even Miss Paird noticed. Only once did he catch sight of his victim; she swept past him in the hall with a patronizing "Hi!" At five-thirty he walked home, as usual, and had a glass of milk, as usual. He had never drunk anything stronger in his life — unless you could count ginger ale. The late Sam Schlosser, the S of F & S, had praised Mr. Martin at a staff meeting several years before for his temperate habits. "Our most efficient worker neither drinks nor smokes," he had said. "The results speak for themselves." Mr. Fitweiler had sat by, nodding approval.

Mr. Martin was still thinking about that red-letter day as he walked over to the Schrafft's on Fifth Avenue near Forty-sixth Street. He got there, as he always did, at eight o'clock. He finished his dinner and the financial page of the *Sun* at a quarter to nine, as he always did. It was his custom after dinner to take a walk. This time he walked down Fifth Avenue at a casual pace. His gloved hands felt moist and warm, his forehead cold. He transferred the Camels from his overcoat to a jacket pocket. He wondered, as he did so, if they did not represent an unnecessary note of strain. Mrs. Barrows smoked only Luckies. It was his idea to puff a few puffs on a Camel (after the rubbing-out), stub it out in the ashtray holding her lipstick-stained Luckies, and thus drag a small red herring across the trail. Perhaps it was not a good idea. It would take time. He might even choke, too loudly.

Mr. Martin had never seen the house on West Twelfth Street where Mrs. Barrows lived, but he had a clear enough picture of it. Fortunately, she had bragged to everybody about her ducky first-floor apartment in the perfectly darling three-story red-brick. There would be no doorman or other attendants; just the tenants of the second and third floors. As he walked along, Mr. Martin realized that he would get there before nine-thirty. He had considered walking north on Fifth Avenue from Schrafft's to a point from which it would take him until ten o'clock to reach the house. At that hour people were less likely to be coming in or going out. But the procedure would have made an awkward loop in the straight thread of his casualness, and he had abandoned it. It was impossible to figure when people would be entering or leaving the house, anyway. There was a great risk at any hour. If he ran into anybody, he would simply have to place the rubbing-out of Ulgine Barrows in the inactive file forever. The same thing would hold true if there were someone in her apartment. In that case he would just say that he had been passing by, recognized her charming house and thought to drop in.

It was eighteen minutes after nine when Mr. Martin turned into Twelfth Street. A man passed him, and a man and a woman talking. There was no one within fifty paces when he came to the house, halfway down the block. He was up the steps and in the small vestibule in no time, pressing the bell under the card that said "Mrs. Ulgine Barrows." When the clicking in the lock started, he jumped forward against the door. He got inside fast, closing the door behind him. A bulb in a lantern hung from the hall ceiling on a chain seemed to give a monstrously bright light. There was nobody on the stair, which went up ahead of him along the left wall. A door opened down the hall in the wall on the right. He went toward it swiftly, on tiptoe.

"Well, for God's sake, look who's here!" bawled Mrs. Barrows, and her braying laugh rang out like the report of a shotgun. He rushed past her like a football tackle, bumping her. "Hey, quit shoving!" she said, closing the door behind them. They were in her living room, which seemed to Mr. Martin to be lighted by a hundred lamps. "What's after you?" she said. "You're as jumpy as a goat." He found he was unable to speak. His heart was wheezing in his throat. "I — yes," he finally brought out. She was jabbering and laughing as she started to help him off with his coat. "No, no," he said. "I'll put it here." He took it off and put it on a chair near the door. "Your hat and gloves, too," she said. "You're in a lady's house." He put his hat on top of the coat. Mrs. Barrows seemed larger than he had thought. He kept his gloves on. "I was passing by," he said. "I recognized — is there anyone here?" She laughed louder than ever. "No," she said, "we're all alone. You're as white as a sheet, you funny man. Whatever *has* come over you? I'll mix you a toddy." She started toward a door across the room. "Scotch-and-soda be all right? But say, you don't drink, do you?" She turned and gave him her amused look. Mr. Martin pulled himself together. "Scotch-and-soda will be all right," he heard himself say. He could hear her laughing in the kitchen.

Mr. Martin looked quickly around the living room for the weapon. He had counted on finding one there. There were andirons and a poker and something in a corner that looked like an Indian club. None of them would do. It couldn't be that way. He began to pace around. He came to a desk. On it lay a metal paper knife with an ornate handle. Would it be sharp enough? He reached for it and knocked over a small brass jar. Stamps spilled out of it and it fell to the floor with a clatter. "Hey," Mrs. Barrows yelled from the kitchen, "are you tearing up the pea patch?" Mr. Martin gave a strange laugh. Picking up the knife, he tried its point against his left wrist. It was blunt. It wouldn't do.

When Mrs. Barrows reappeared, carrying two highballs, Mr. Martin, standing there with his gloves on, became acutely conscious of the fantasy he had wrought. Cigarettes in his pocket, a drink prepared for him — it was all too grossly improbable. It was more than that; it was impossible. Somewhere in the back of his mind a vague idea stirred, sprouted. "For heaven's sake, take off those gloves," said Mrs. Barrows. "I always wear them in the house," said Mr. Martin. The idea began to bloom, strange and wonderful. She put the glasses on a coffee table in front of a sofa and sat on the sofa. "Come over here, you odd little man," she said. Mr. Martin went over and sat beside her. It was difficult getting a cigarette out of the pack of Camels, but he managed it. She held a match for him, laughing. "Well," she said, handing him his drink, "this is perfectly marvelous. You with a drink and a cigarette."

Mr. Martin puffed, not too awkwardly, and took a gulp of the highball. "I drink and smoke all the time," he said. He clinked his glass against hers. "Here's nuts to that old windbag, Fitweiler," he said, and gulped again. The stuff tasted awful, but he made no grimace. "Really, Mr. Martin," she said, her voice and posture changing, "you are insulting our employer." Mrs. Barrows was now all special adviser to the president. "I am preparing a bomb," said Mr. Martin, "which will blow the old goat higher than hell." He had only had a little of the drink, which was not strong. It couldn't be that. "Do you take dope or something?" Mrs. Barrows asked coldly. "Heroin," said Mr. Martin. "I'll be coked to the gills when I bump that old buzzard off." "Mr. Martin!" she shouted, getting to her feet. "That will be all of that. You must go at once." Mr. Martin took another swallow of his drink. He tapped his cigarette out in the ashtray and put the pack of Camels on the coffee table. Then he got up. She stood glaring at him. He walked over and put on his hat and coat. "Not a word about this," he said, and laid an index finger against his lips. All Mrs. Barrows could bring out was "Really!" Mr. Martin put his hand on the doorknob. "I'm sitting in the catbird seat," he said. He stuck his tongue out at her and left. Nobody saw him go.

Mr. Martin got to his apartment, walking, well before eleven. No one saw him go in. He had two glasses of milk after brushing his teeth, and he felt elated. It wasn't tipsiness, because he hadn't been tipsy. Anyway, the walk had worn off all effects of the whisky. He got in bed and read a magazine for a while. He was asleep before midnight.

Mr. Martin got to the office at eight-thirty the next morning, as usual. At a quarter to nine, Ulgine Barrows, who had never before arrived at work before ten, swept into his office. "I'm reporting to Mr. Fitweiler now!" she shouted. "If he turns you over to the police, it's no more than you deserve!" Mr. Martin gave her a look of shocked surprise. "I beg your pardon?" he said. Mrs. Barrows snorted and bounced out of the room, leaving Miss Paird and Joey Hart staring after her. "What's the matter with that old devil now?" asked Miss Paird. "I have no idea," said Mr. Martin, resuming his work. The other two looked at him and then at each other. Miss Paird got up and went out. She walked slowly past the closed door of Mr. Fitweiler's office. Mrs. Barrows was yelling inside, but she was not braying. Miss Paird could not hear what the woman was saying. She went back to her desk.

Forty-five minutes later, Mrs. Barrows left the president's office and went into her own, shutting the door. It wasn't until half an hour later that Mr. Fitweiler sent for Mr. Martin. The head of the filing department, neat, quiet, attentive, stood in front of the old man's desk. Mr. Fitweiler was pale and nervous. He took his glasses off and twiddled them. He made a small, bruffing sound in his throat. "Martin," he said, "you have been with us more than twenty years." "Twenty-two, sir," said Mr. Martin. "In that time," pursued the president, "your work and your—uh—manner have been exemplary." "I trust so, sir," said Mr. Martin. "I have understood, Martin," said Mr. Fitweiler, "that you have never taken a drink or smoked." "That is correct, sir," said Mr. Martin. "Ah, yes." Mr. Fitweiler polished his glasses. "You may describe what you did after leaving the office yesterday, Martin," he said. Mr. Martin allowed less than a second for his bewildered pause. "Certainly, sir," he said. "I walked home. Then I went to Schrafft's for dinner. Afterward I walked home again. I went to bed early, sir, and read a magazine for a while. I was asleep before eleven." "Ah, yes," said Mr. Fitweiler again. He was silent for a moment, searching for the proper words to say to the head of the filing department. "Mrs. Barrows," he said finally, "Mrs. Barrows has worked hard, Martin, very hard. It grieves me to report that she has suffered a severe breakdown. It has taken the form of a persecution complex accompanied by distressing hallucinations." "I am very sorry, sir," said Mr. Martin. "Mrs. Barrows is under the delusion," continued Mr. Fitweiler, "that you visited her last evening and behaved yourself in an—uh—unseemly manner." He raised his hand to silence Mr. Martin's little pained outcry. "It is the nature of these psychological diseases," Mr. Fitweiler said, "to fix upon the least likely and most innocent party as the—uh—source of persecution. These matters are not for the lay mind to grasp, Martin. I've just had my psychiatrist, Dr. Fitch, on the phone. He would not, of course, commit himself, but he made enough generalizations to substantiate my suspicions. I suggested to Mrs. Barrows when she had completed her — uh — story to me this morning, that she visit Dr. Fitch, for I suspected a condition at once. She flew, I regret to say, into a rage, and demanded — uh — requested that I call you on the carpet. You may not know, Martin, but Mrs. Barrows had planned a reorganization of your department — subject to my approval, of course, subject to my approval. This brought you, rather than anyone else, to her mind — but again that is a phenomenon for Dr. Fitch and not for us. So, Martin, I am afraid Mrs. Barrows' usefulness here is at an end." "I am dreadfully sorry, sir," said Mr. Martin.

It was at this point that the door to the office blew open with the suddenness of a gas-main explosion and Mrs. Barrows catapulted through it. "Is the little rat denying it?" she screamed. "He can't get away with that!" Mr Martin got up and moved discreetly to a point beside Mr. Fitweiler's chair. "You drank and smoked at my apartment," she bawled at Mr. Martin, "and you know it! You called Mr. Fitweiler an old windbag and said you were going to blow him up when you got coked to the gills on your heroin!" She stopped yelling to catch her breath and a new glint came into her popping eyes. "If you weren't such a drab, ordinary little man," she said, "I'd think you'd planned it all. Sticking your tongue out, saying you were sitting in the catbird seat, because you thought no one would believe me when I told it! My God, it's really too perfect!" She brayed loudly and hysterically, and the fury was on her again. She glared at Mr. Fitweiler. "Can't you see how he has tricked us, you old fool? Can't you see his little game?" But Mr. Fitweiler had been surreptitiously pressing all the buttons under the top of his desk and employees of F & S began pouring into the room. "Stockton," said Mr. Fitweiler, "you and Fishbein will take Mrs. Barrows to her home. Mrs. Powell, you will go with them." Stockton, who had played a little football in high school, blocked Mrs. Barrows as she made for Mr. Martin. It took him and Fishbein together to force her out of the door into the hall, crowded with stenographers and office boys. She was still screaming imprecations at Mr. Martin, tangled and contradictory imprecations. The hubbub finally died out down the corridor.

"I regret that this has happened," said Mr. Fitweiler. "I shall ask you to dismiss it from your mind, Martin." "Yes, sir," said Mr. Martin, anticipating his chief's "That will be all" by moving to the door. "I will dismiss it." He went out and shut the door, and his step was light and quick in the hall. When he entered his department he had slowed down to his customary gait, and he walked quietly across the room to the W20 file, wearing a look of studious concentration.

7

HIDDEN INFLUENCES

"Like the shields carried by knights of legend, the modern corporate building reeks with symbolism."

—Betty Harragan

Whether people in organizations are consciously aware of it or not, they are constantly exposed to subtle and in many cases decidedly complex influences which play a part in determining what they think, feel and do. Many of these hidden influences are consciously created by organizational participants to bolster their own positions, to maintain or to enhance the power and control they have over others. Examples abound in the readings we have selected in this chapter. Harragan ("Games Mother Never Taught You"), for example, describes a variety of status symbols in organizations and Korda ("Symbols of Power") discusses the choice, positioning, and behavioral impacts of offices and office furniture.

Some influences pervade an organization, reflecting its culture, and are so taken for granted that it becomes necessary to challenge or to contradict the culture quite dramatically to reveal their elements and interconnections. Harragan's provocative description of the immobilizing and discriminating effects on females of women's attire in organizations ("Women's Apparel Is a Badge of Servitude," in "Games Mother Never Taught You"), *Newsweek*'s article on the undermining effects on employees of sexual innuendos and jokes ("Abusing Sex at the Office"), and Janis's identification of the ingredients of groupthink, which numb people's critical faculties ("Symptoms of Groupthink among President Kennedy's Advisors"), all provide rich illustrations of complex patterns of covert influences embedded in organizational life. The wise individual, the organizational survivor, typically takes note of and learns to identify and to interpret these patterns and harnesses or at times even tries to change them.

Still other subtle influences appear to have unconscious origins, to stem from distortions in human relationships and attitudes. They emerge as systems that trap and tyrannize organizational members who fail to recognize them or are unable to resist them. Dabney ("Passions at Work") describes irrational authority systems of dominance and submission in organizations and provides a challenging interpretation of their origins and impact.

Humor is a particularly rich source of hidden influences on people's behavior and attitudes. It conveys messages and meanings coded in ways that allow listeners to be surprised, intrigued, or persuaded by information that they might otherwise resist, reject, or ignore. Humor also presents information about individuals and groups in a form that they find difficult to contest or refute. The damage done in this way cannot easily be repaired by denial or logical argument.

Albert Speer ("Inside the Third Reich") describes how Hitler's subordinates used humorous stories in which rivals were ridiculed to change his mind on important decisions. Speer indicates that Hitler was unaware of the subterfuge. The sexual innuendos and jokes in the *Newsweek* article mentioned earlier likewise damage the credibility of those individuals and groups who are the targets of the jokes in a similarly insidious way, so that they are not taken seriously as employees or managers with any real potential or influence in the organization. Humor also can be used to define situations, to signal pecking orders, to convey to workers in an acceptable form the extent and the limits of their control over difficult and dangerous tasks. These and other themes are delightfully displayed in Boland and Hoffman's description of "Humor in a Machine Shop." The new worker who fails to interpret such humor correctly risks isolation from the work group and perhaps even failure on the job.

The precise nature of hidden influences and their character and impact in organizations remains to be charted. Behavioral scientists are beginning to explore this perspective of organizational life. The articles we chose for this chapter reveal that close observers of the organizational scene detect a variety of influences which many managers and their employees would have little difficulty validating once identified, based on their own experiences and intuition — including dress codes, furniture, office location and layout, the language of organizations, jokes, policy statements containing embedded messages, and so on. How does one deal with these influences — harness, avoid, blunt, or alter them?

Each of the articles in the section contains suggestions for organizational participants to consider. However, the most comprehensive approach is outlined and illustrated in Culbert's "A General Strategy for Getting Out of Traps." Fundamental to his approach is the need to recognize that when one is in an organizational trap, the reasons for one's unhappiness and ineffective responses do not necessarily lie with oneself but are more likely to reside in the pattern of surrounding influences, which must be detected and made explicit, and then responded to in a coherent fashion.

The realities outlined in this section reflect a combative world. The organization is a setting in which it is wise to be wary. We think that it is important for people in organizations to pay careful attention to the subtleties of their settings. The articles also contain information that permits development of more humane organizations in which dignity and productivity can coexist. Examination and understanding of the hidden influences can enable managers to root out the more destructive effects. An office layout can be prepared with the conscious intention of relaxing tension and encouraging communication and joint problem solving; dress codes need not be discriminatory; groupthink can be avoided. While ignorance or manipulation of hidden influences may be common, they need not be inevitable responses to organizational life.

Games Mother Never Taught You

Betty Lehan Harragan

To awestruck sightseers in the land of the business hierarchy, the architectural grandeur is overpowering and impressive. Stately edifices dominate landscaped vistas of suburbia and mighty skyscrapers silhouette the profiles of major cities. Flowering gardens, soaring plazas, ample parking, vaulted lobbies, air conditioning, musical elevators, carpeted lounges, spacious dining rooms, and hundreds upon hundreds of linear offices bathed relentlessly in fluorescent brilliance dutifully impress gaping tourists.

But all this structural munificence does not divert the expert gamester who looks beyond the steel and concrete public visor of the corporate persona to identify the heraldic markings painted on the battle armor. Like the shields carried by knights of legend, the modern corporate building reeks with symbolism. Far from being a mere architectural wonder, every pane of glass, slab of marble, and foot of carpet performs a dual function in identifying the tournament site. The buildings are impersonal monuments to the power and wealth contained therein. Space itself, in both the exterior and interior layout, is weighted with abstract significance. Just as a heraldic seal reveals a great deal about the one using it, so spatial divisions reveal important information about the modern-day knights.

Today's business building, especially the corporate headquarters, is a physical representation of the hierarchical pyramid. It is the tangible game board. A walk through a large office, from floor to floor, is like threading a course through the hierarchy. Trappings of rank, position, and power are spread around the place like icons in a cathedral. They identify the important players and signal their positions in the game. Neophytes must grasp the design of the game board and learn the initial placement of the pieces before making any irreversible move.

Very often businesswomen approach the game of corporate gamemanship as if it were a throw of the dice which pits their future against pure chance, or luck. The real game for women more nearly resembles chess, in which one of the sixteen playing pieces is a strong female (the Queen) and the object of the game is to "check" the adverse King. Chess is an intellectual military exercise based on a combative attack against equally matched opposing fighting units. The descriptive play language of chess is indistinguishable from that of war "games" or football or business — lines of attack, defensive systems, infiltration, onslaught, sacrifice, control (territory or foes), power, weakness, strength, strategy, tactics, maneuver, surrender, challenge, conquer, win. Each pawn, rook, knight, bishop, queen, and king in the chess set is endowed with specific agility to move only in certain directions and for stipulated distances. Each piece is made clearly identifiable so that players and observers can watch the game progress and know exactly what moves have been made. Unlike cards, chess is a public game spread out for all to see.

So is corporate politics a public game. In business the so-called status symbols serve to identify the playing pieces and reveal their positions on the board. The masculine pecking system, regardless of the all-male activity, is replete with emblems and shared identity signals, many of which speak louder than words and obviate the need for verbal communication. If you've ever wondered why your boss pays inordinate attention to "silly" objects or personal privileges, very likely these are crucial business status symbols. Few of the customs and practices of business life are meaningless. They only look that way to women who have not learned the fundamentals of the game.

HOW TO TELL THE PLAYERS APART

Status symbols are two-way communications. If you can interpret them, they tell you where a coworker stands in the ranking system, and they tell others where you stand. For that reason, women cannot afford to ignore these ubiquitous symbols because each tiny accumulation of visible status is an increase in power or advancement. Indeed, as the game plays out, a woman often needs her power emblems more than a title or salary increase to effectively use any authority she acquires. It is difficult if not impossible for a pawn to behave like a bishop or queen if she doesn't have the mitre or crown that differentiates the chess pieces.

Most of the common status differentials can be perceived at even the lowest levels. As employees move up the hierarchical ladder, the emblems are gradually emblazoned with additional symbols or sophisticated refinements of the basic seal. Here are some of the categories of rank insignia which help you tell the players apart and prevent you from being bluffed by someone at your own level who tries to "pull rank" on you without justification. Conversely, a familiarity with the status symbols protects you from being duped by management if you are offered an empty promotion or promise which carries no visible authority emblem.

How You Are Paid
Not how much, *how.* Cash in a brown envelope indicates the lowest rank. A check thus becomes a status symbol, a sign of progress. If

the wage is figured on an hourly basis or a weekly basis (the nonexempt jobs which are subject to overtime beyond forty hours), it has a lower status than jobs which are exempt from overtime. I remember a junior writer who tried to lord it over her friends with a claim that she had been promoted to professional ranks. She lost all respect and admiration when it was discovered that she still filled out "the little green slips" which were required for weekly time sheets. She thought she was a "writer" because she was allowed to write; her shrewd coworkers knew she was still considered an hourly clerical worker by management because that's how she was paid. An annual salary paid out in the standard semimonthly equal installments is a symbol of the supervisory and professional ranks. Very high levels of management often have options to tailor payment methods to suit their own convenience. Many executives don't get a check at all; they have it sent directly to their banks and deposited to their personal accounts. Corporate officers almost all arrange to have big portions of their high salaries "deferred," that is, not paid to them until some later date or in some other form. It pays to keep an eye on how superiors receive and cash their salary checks. Incidentally, some executives send their secretaries to the bank with their checks; these secretaries are worth wooing if you're trying to collect salary data.

What Time You Report to Work

Flexibility in choosing one's own working hours is a clear mark of distinction. The lowest degree of status is reflected in punching a time clock or being "signed in" by an overseer, the sure tag of a manual or clerical job. The time-clock insignia also extends to lunch hours and coffee breaks which are strictly regimented to the prescribed minute. As one moves upward into supervisory and professional ranks, *it is taken for granted* that you have a degree of autonomy in fixing your work hours and lunch times or breaks. Women frequently don't seem to recognize that they have this status privilege, or else they are afraid to display it, and use it. I'm often jarred when I have lunch with an apparent "executive" woman who suddenly bolts her lunch and dashes away because she'll be "late" getting back to the office within an hour. This is the time-clock thinking, lowest-level clerical insignia. If her boss is what she's afraid of (as many have told me), she is being treated as a time-clock employee and allowing herself and her job to be thus degraded. No brownie points accrue to a game player who refuses to wear her status symbols. You establish rank privileges simply by taking advantage of work-hour freedom according to the local department pattern.

Freedom to determine your own working hours does not mean you work shorter hours or ignore the working timetable your boss adopts. Some women consider it wise to dovetail their hours with their boss's—so they are always in the office at the same time. Others work more independently and arrive at the hour most convenient to their personal schedule and vary lunch periods to suit personal or business commitments. One woman executive I know has remained at the same job level for twenty years although a more astute game-ster with her options would have progressed several steps. Her prob-lem is low-echelon thinking; she still acts like a time-clock secretary. Even though she travels on business regularly, she schedules her trips for one-day, eighteen-hour commutes and gets home after midnight to appear in the office before nine the next morning. Bedraggled and exhausted, she complains about her terrible schedule, but neither her subordinates nor her superiors have any sympathy; they've long since chalked her off as lacking management potential. Men who pro-gressed from a duplicate position scheduled their trips over two or three days each time; they knew better than to ignore status symbols. If you're uncertain about your status entitlement in time flexibility, watch what male colleagues and bosses do. Then go out and do likewise! Don't, for heaven's sake, complain about men who proudly display their ranking privileges and wonder why your hard work isn't appreciated after you've thrown away your own equality symbol.

Where You Eat

Not only when but where one eats is a status distinction. The low-est indication is being restricted to the premises as are many plant and factory workers. Freedom to leave the work premises (whether you do or not) is a step upward. Voluntary on-site lunching in large cor-porations is usually stamped with clear status distinctions. Lower-echelon workers go to the general cafeteria; middle-management dines in the executive lunchroom; and top officers eat in the private dining room. Senior executives can always drop into the general cafeteria if they want, but it takes a symbolic ID card to get into the executive dining halls. Anyone who is eligible to eat in the executive dining room but eschews the privilege to continue lunching with friends in the general cafeteria is pretty sure to be knocked out of the game very soon. If, for example, you had a boss who did that, you'd know it was time to look for a transfer or new job because you're stuck with a dead-head. See how attention to visible status emblems can tip you off?

In some companies even eating at your desk can reveal status. Did you get the food yourself from the friendly mobile vendor? Did a sec-retary order it from a good delicatessen and have it delivered? Was a complete hot-plate sent from the executive dining room? Or did you bring a sandwich from home in a brown paper bag?

Are you beginning to think all this is silly, like who cares? That's just it; nobody cares—if you're a woman. All your male colleagues and coworkers will ignore your eating habits as long as it keeps you out of their favorite rendezvous. They've already decided you belong with the brown-baggers (low-paid secretaries and clerks who bring their lunch), so it won't surprise them one bit to see you ally yourself with lower-status lunch groups. As an ambitious woman you have to care. It will never do for you to exclude yourself from the semisocial lunch and cocktail gatherings where more business is conducted, more information exchanged, and more contacts made than during the regular working hours. If you can't worm your way into a suitable lunch group, go to a movie or go shopping for a couple of hours, but definitely exercise your status prerogative.

The Mail You Get

Mail sorters, if they were so minded, could diagram the organizational chart by noting the incoming mail for various individuals and the routing pattern on memos. One of the first status symbols is an in-box on your desk. The next improvement is denoted by an out-box. Increasing status is determined by the style of the containers, utilitarian metal being at the lower end and hand-woven straw, hand-painted wood, or other elaborate designs being better. Perhaps because this symbol is so widely distributed, some statusy types dispense with this common denominator and have incoming correspondence neatly piled on the center of an empty desk (they probably have little of significance to do and hope their status symbols will carry them through to retirement).

More important than the box is the incoming contents. Daily deliveries of the *Wall Street Journal* and *New York Times* or regular copies of *Business Week, Fortune, Barron's, Forbes, U.S. News and World Report,* or economic newsletters are distinctive emblems. Company-paid subscriptions are status symbols in general, but the more management-oriented the publication, the higher the status rating, *Harvard Business Review* outranking the Gizmo trade journal by far.

Outgoing mail also has status value if your name is imprinted on the corporate letterhead, either by itself or as one of the partners or officers of a firm.

Your Working Location

In a factory, the operator at the end of the assembly line has more prestige than one near the beginning because the product is more valuable in its finished state. The principle of increasing value of work follows through to the top of the hierarchy where the office of the chief executive is obviously the ultimate in status and power and the choicest in location. Proximity to the power generator exudes status, with the office adjacent to the CEO being the most prestigious but the entire floor sharing in shadings of top rank. In a suburban complex with several buildings, the one with the executive offices is the power generator and a poor location there is superior to choice space in any lesser building. In short, physical locale is a status symbol, so the location of your office is one of the most telling emblems in revealing your rank in the hierarchy and your favor with the boss. It's an important piece in the game.

HOW SPACE CONFERS STATUS

The "executive floor" is known to most employees by virtue of the fact that they have never set foot on it. This is the true inner sanctum, and the power emanations are so strong that minor employees are afraid to get near. I've seen adult men literally shake in their boots at the prospect of answering a call to the executive floor. For those who are physically located "in the boondocks," "over in the boneyard," or "out in the sticks," (i.e., distant buildings or branch offices), a move to the headquarters city or building signifies a boom in status long before anyone knows if the shift was accompanied by a change in title or a better salary. Geographic and internal physical office moves can track an executive's path through the hierarchical labyrinth more clearly than a title change. A company may have hundreds of vice-presidents or divisional managers but the really important ones are distinguished from titular peers by that prime emblem of status—the office location.

Within the physical boundaries of every corporate department or operation much the same pattern of office locale identifies the ranking of subordinates and superiors. Most department layouts are square or rectangular. The corner offices, which are larger, brighter, and most secluded, are choice spots and the highest ranking executives naturally choose them. The remainder of the outside walls are customarily divided into small offices so that each has a window or a portion of plate glass. These are known universally as the "window offices" and have much higher status value than nonwindowed offices. Size is also an emblematic factor, so a large window office is more valuable than a small window office, but a small window office is superior to a much larger "interior" office.

The internal space in a typical office floor layout can be left wide open and filled with rows upon rows of desks (generally populated with clerical women). Here employees work in the wide-open area with no privacy and where they can be easily observed by the supervisors. Another solution is to partition the vast internal space with one or more rows of "interior" offices, each of which has walls to the ceiling and doors; these are real private offices but have no windows. The third alternative, and a highly favored one, is to erect movable partitions which enclose the desks of individuals in the interior sector.

These tin or plastic partitions are waist- or shoulder-high; they block the view of a person sitting at the enclosed desk but allow any passer-by to look over the top and see the occupant at work. These constructions are well known to all working women as cubicles. Status-wise, they are a step up from the wide-open clerical or secretarial pool pattern (often referred to as "paper factories"), but not as prestigious as a fully enclosed office which carries more symbolic value even if it must be shared with another. A "window" office is generally considered an "executive" or supervisory symbol.

SYMBOLIC MEANINGS OF WINDOWS AND WALLS

Since window offices can be roughly defined as officers' quarters, the position of rooms "weights" their relative values. Proximity to the corner offices carries the most weight, then comes view. An unobstructed view of the skyline or gardens is far more prestigious than a window on the ventilating shaft or one overlooking the parking lot or delivery entrance. An office located on the traffic lanes, one in the center arena of business activity, represents higher status than one hidden away in an isolated nook or placed near the non-status "public" areas, such as cloakrooms, bathrooms, lounges, elevators, or storerooms.

Offices in the middle of the outside walls, that is, those that are equidistant from either corner office, are least desirable because the occupant's connection to either corner power generator is weak, tenuous, and not immediately identifiable. Michael Korda, the best-selling folk etymologist of sophisticated male business mores, attributes this midcenter office weakness to a power dead spot. In his book *Power: How to Get It, How to Use It,* he asserts that power flows in a X-shaped pattern from each corner office to the one diagonally opposite. The center of the space (where the X-lines bisect) represents the point at which the authority of the corner person peters out. Under his theory, the center of the floor layout is equivalent to a power blackout area and outer offices parallel with the center of the room are thus located in power dead-spots.

I've seen office setups where enclaves of competing executives use the X theory to amass power. With their cronies and subordinates flanking them, they set up hostile camps in each of the corners. Newcomers or nonaligned workers invariably float to the nondescript center offices. In firms where several executives have equal rank, for instance partners in auditing, law, or brokerage firms, they can apportion the corner offices by a coin toss and the power flow runs as easily down the sides as across a diagonal. Even so, the central offices are less prestigious because ranking executives like to have their closest allies physically near them. Proximity to a superior is undoubtedly the best gauge of status within a team group. Watch carefully when offices get switched around. It means that status symbols are changing hands and the rank of the movers is being visibly altered although their titles and salaries are unchanged.

A lot of women may think this game of musical chairs with office locations is also silly and unnecessary. It may be, but the accretion of status symbols is very serious business to ambitious businessmen. They know that a display of status symbols means as much in the corporate hierarchy as a chest full of medals does to an ambitious officer in the military hierarchy. If women are to function equally in the action arena of business they must be able to decipher the code and demand the proper rank insignia for themselves as they progress haltingly up the corporate ladder. To disregard the value of preferred office location is tantamount to selecting a rhinestone ring over a diamond because the first one looked "prettier." Refusing to wear epaulets which identify your business rank because you don't appreciate the genuine value is a disastrous mistake.

DON'T GARBLE THE LOCALITY MESSAGE

Judging from my personal observations during the past five years that women have begun moving ahead in corporate jobs en masse, it seems safe to say that many have ignored the status code. Which is to say that they get a better title but they seldom get the visible emblems of rank. If you believe you are making progress on your job, count the number of times you have changed offices. A meaningful promotion almost mandates an office change; a token title and slight salary increase does not give you the necessary authority to handle the new job unless subordinates and outsiders see that you were issued the appropriate rank insignia.

By and large, women are oblivious to rank symbols because so few working women have *any* office privacy that a room of one's own is—in comparative *women's* terms — the ultimate achievement. As long as it's private and "workable," women are inclined to "accept" any office offered them and make the best of the disadvantages that inevitably appear. I know women who have sat in the same office for the past twenty years. I don't know any men in that category. In the industry circles I travel, men who are that immobile were fired or quit years ago.

If you had trouble . . . in diagramming your department's organization chart or evaluating your own advancement potential, try a different tack. Make a floor plan of the office layout and see who's sitting where. This floor plan will guide you in determining which of several people on the same job level are the more favored or powerful—they will have offices very near the top-ranked superior, or they will have established a power enclave of their own in one of the opposite corners. Then locate your own office in relation to these authority areas. You should get a pretty good idea of what your superiors think of you and your potential according to the office they assigned you. It may be more than adequate by your personal comfort standards, but if it doesn't translate into appropriate status according to the male heraldic seal, you are being symbolically downgraded or dead-ended.

ALWAYS COLLECT YOUR EARNED MEDALLIONS

Reluctance on management's part to dispense money in the form of raises is understandable because of manifest business concern but unwillingness to issue women their status insignia is propelled by pure male chauvinism. A female corporate politician must be alert to this subtle form of sex discrimination and take steps to alleviate it. Specifically, *ask* for and fight for your office emblem. Before making a final decision on a new job offer, ask to see the office that goes with the job. If you get a promotion, inquire immediately about the new office that you'll get. If you discover you have a lesser status office than your job indicates, ask for the next vacant office in the area you decide you belong in. Keep your eye on possible office vacancies and ask for a more desirable location before they put a newcomer (usually a man) in a higher status office than you have. Keep asking.

One woman I know who was an analyst in the research department of a large investment firm reacted instinctively and volubly when her company moved to elegant new offices in a beautiful skyscraper. She was the only woman in an all-male group and the covey of expensive industrial designers, office planners, and management consultants had settled her in a noisy isolated corner next to the coat room and elevator banks and off-kilter from the rest of the section. "I didn't know anything about office sites," she told me, "but I felt like I'd been slapped in the face. My intuition told me there was something seriously wrong and I refused to take the office. A young guy who had just arrived was settled in an office I liked, so I demanded that one on the basis of seniority. I loved the job, but I refused to appear at the office until I got the right accommodations. They put up a terrible fight, until I was mentally prepared to quit over the issue." Her determination paid off and she got the office space she selected. Later that year, one of the firm's partners brought his wife in to meet her, saying proudly, "I'd like you to meet the only woman in our research department." My friend pointed out that there was now another woman in research but he brushed that aside, saying, "I forget about her. I consider you our only woman because you are the only one who fought for your office!"

By contrast, a lawyer I know got a very good job in the corporate counsel's office of a huge industrial corporation. She's the only woman on the executive floor and since her first day's pro forma expense-account lunch with a few of the senior attorneys she has been totally ostracized by her colleagues. That was easily accomplished because her office (with a spectacular view from the top floor of a Manhattan skyscraper) is on a corridor on the opposite side of the building from the legal department. For all intents and purposes, she is physically as well as psychologically isolated from the counsel's team! Asked why she accepted that office she exclaimed, "Oh, it's beautiful! Carpets six inches thick, anything I request in the way of furniture and equipment, and that astronomical view. They originally apologized for it, saying nothing better was available, but I told them this was perfect. How much better could you get?" But when visiting executives from divisional offices and subsidiaries regularly take her for a temporary secretary, it's partly because she has no rank insignia, no team identification.

WATCH OUT FOR FEMALE GHETTOES

The retailing industry and fashion merchandising are typical of businesses where women predominate at lower levels and have moved upward in restricted areas to executive levels (a handful are getting close to the top). These industries are nevertheless dominated by male status symbols, and clever corporate politicians must analyze the patterns and play the game by classic standards. Many women who have "made it" through the twisted paths of historic blatant discrimination have had no opportunity to learn the game rules in entirety. They are particularly blind to status emblems or, to be more precise, they were furnished garbled emblems intended to ghetto-ize them and they now have difficulty unscrambling the hodge-podge.

I will be watching the progress of an executive friend who just began playing the corporate game in the retailing field. Helena has been floating on a relatively high plateau in specialty fashion retailing for the past several years. She's spent her entire career — close to twenty years — working with women colleagues whom she likes and admires. But once she was alerted to the broad ramifications of the corporate politics game, she recognized that her advancement opportunities were nonexistent in the retail complex where she was employed. She found a new job with a national consulting firm, using her expertise in fashion retailing as the wedge to negotiate a 50-percent salary increase. In her new firm all the employees and executives are women except for the vice-president in charge of merchandising, who is a man.

"After doing the same job for years, this offers an exciting new opportunity," she told me. "The company is dynamic, the vice-president, my boss, sounds very progressive, and the other women executives are tops in their fields, stimulating people to work with. Everything about the job seemed perfect—until I evaluated the status symbols, especially office location. I drew diagrams of the layout to analyze where my office was situated. The picture prompted me to reopen negotiations although I had accepted the job. I realized I'd be stalemated again if I didn't insist on the right office locale. I got it changed before I started."

Helena's analysis was perceptive gaming. The male vice-president had the most prestigious corner office. She had been assigned a large office next to the corner in the diagonally opposite area. All the women in that area were fashion specialists, too. Each of the corners held clusters of women experienced in various retail specialties. Helena is cognizant of the categorizing which restricts women executives to food, fashion, home furnishings, fabrics, domestics, cosmetics, accessories or whatever gave them their start. "When men start in ties, they don't end up tie specialists — they branch out to merchandising executives. When women start in dresses, they don't end up dress specialists — they're catalogued as high fashion, budget, sports, evening, lounge, or boutique. They are constricted by experience, not broadened to becoming merchandising generalists." This was the pattern she saw duplicated in the office layout at her new firm — women segregated according to narrow specialties. Since her goal was to break out of overspecialization, she perceived correctly that an office located in the midst of fashion specialists would lock her into the very trap she was escaping.

"I didn't explain *why* I wanted the particular office I chose; after all I'll be working closely with the fashion group at the beginning. But my career plan demands some proximity to the vice-president and a door on the traffic lane to his office. I'll use it for visibility and getting to know the types of merchandising clients who visit the V-P. I intend to move toward merchandising management, and my first successful game move was getting myself dissociated from all the specialty enclaves."

Office location is invested with good and poor status insignia. Office positioning has a direct relationship to job advancement. Certain office locales have high status value precisely because ambitious, aggressive people fight for them in order to get close to the central action area. Once again, watch how progressing men move closer and closer to higher superiors with every promotion. Careers and office insignia move in tandem.

WHEN STATUS EMBLEMS AND STEREOTYPES
COLLIDE, MOVE!

Not much is known yet about potential boomerang effects when classic male rank symbols are acquired by women. One danger area is already evident — the office adjacent to a male senior executive. Sex, sexism, and female stereotypes can rear up to cancel out all the job benefits and rank status that traditionally accrue to men who achieve this enviable geographic site, which frequently has the invisible logo "next in line for the top job." When a woman earns that status locale, the invisible logo shifts to "she's sleeping with her boss," or "she's a glorified secretary (who's sleeping with the guy)."

Over a lunch, a female officer of a subsidiary company of a financial corporation explained how her advancement was nearly jeopardized because she occupied the office adjacent to the president. "I'm not quite sure how I got assigned to the office since I was one of several vice-presidents who were eligible for it. Probably a misguided attempt to prove they didn't discriminate against women, a laugh considering I was the only woman executive in the entire firm at the time. Take it from me, token women are more to be pitied than censured; like the first child of nervous parents we suffer from the ignorance of our elders." At any rate, she occupied what male colleagues looked upon as the most enviable office in the company, but it slowly turned into nightmare alley for her. "I had an important and demanding job but I was interrupted constantly. Executives from our own company as well as all outside visitors marched straight into my office, left messages for me to relay to the president, explained their problems to me, or dropped in for idle chats if the president got an important private phone call during their appointment."

At first she tried directing the men to the private secretaries and assistants, but each day there were other strangers who made the same automatic assumption — that the woman closest to the top executive was naturally his private secretary or assistant. "I foresaw the end of the line in my career if I remained in that close proximity to the chief executive. I was becoming identified with him and his work, not my own operating responsibilities. My authority was rapidly eroding as I was stereotyped into an 'assistant' or 'helper' to the great man. I decided I *had* to get out of there and I'm absolutely positive I'd never be where I am today, a functioning administrator and top management, if I'd allowed the implied tie-up of superior male-subservient female to continue."

The educational aspect of her story was how she made her moves to solve the problem. She assayed all the male vice-presidents who were equally eligible for the office. From the group she picked the man she disliked the most and who returned the feeling with a vengeance. He was also the one most envious of her position and most blatant about his raw ambition and his disparagement of her qualifications. When she invited him to lunch with her, he was wary and hostile. "He almost choked to death on a piece of fish when I asked him if he'd like to trade offices. He couldn't believe anybody would be so stupid as to give up the ultimate status symbol, and it took a while to convince him I was serious. Once he saw that (swallowing my story that I really *liked* his office better for its afternoon sunshine!), he joined the conspiracy with me to get the trade approved without any flak." Between the two of them they arranged the transfer smoothly and she regained her independence as a line executive. Her male accomplice gained his most cherished desire. "He was in seventh heaven in that office and the superior rank symbol pushed him steadily ahead. My freedom from that office allowed me to grow and develop on my merits and demonstrated performance; we both benefited. Best of all, he turned from an enemy into an ally. He is one of my strongest supporters and advocates."

PORCELAIN INSIGNIA THAT WON'T FLUSH AWAY

Toilets seem to be the major obstacle to women's equality. If you don't think so, you haven't heard the nuttiest arguments against the Equal Rights Amendment (i.e., the ridiculous fear that public restrooms will be coed). Or you haven't been faced with employment problems which evolve from the superior status symbolism of urinals. The good news is that women aren't entirely alone trying to revamp this physical hallmark of sexual supremacy; management is a nervous wreck as working women demand equal facilities and senior executives in many institutions expend as much energy on the dilemma of bathrooms as they do on the next quarterly earnings' prediction. Porcelain status symbols are proving to be nonbiodegradable.

Some companies try to evade the entire subject. To this day, the J. Walter Thompson Company advertising agency refuses to recognize indelicate functions. Its dozens of bathrooms hide decorously behind plain unmarked doors and nary a disciminatory word such as "Men's" or "Women's" sullies its pristine halls or executive offices. Pity the new male client or supplier whose initial contact is a woman executive (if any); the prime executive-to-executive bond has evaporated into embarrassed agony.

Some companies treat the subject like a huge, salacious joke. They are apt to be institutions that have given urinals the most visible priority status. One of the country's largest utilities (hardly the only offender in this category) left no doubt where its sympathies lay by installing men's urinals in spacious rooms off the well-lit hall-ways. Women's facilities (patronized by vast majorities of the working population) were jammed into dingy, cramped quarters on the un-used stairway landings. Female complaints were dismissed cavalierly even though several women had been frightened or molested by ra-pacious public freaks who crept up the abandoned stairwell. The enraged women got together and organized a pee-in in the men's bath-rooms until their class status was upgraded and the bathrooms were switched.

Some companies are just plain scared as women edge closer and closer to a highly prized male status symbol — "the key to the execu-tive bathroom." One of the few women who arrived at this eminence insisted on her executive token and demanded her status key. She promptly ordered the sign changed from "Men" to "Executives." Every so often she pretends to use her key (of course she's the first and only women to collect this rank emblem) just to see what male executive comes bounding out of his office to "check if it's clear." Privately she admits to gleeful friends that she'd never really use it. "I'll never give up my privilege to use the ladies' room. For one thing, I hear all the juicy gossip that doesn't get on the grapevine, or I hear things before any of the men at my level. But most of all because I'm in a position to help other women. I can get to know women from several departments and keep an eye on the progress of those I admire. Already I've pulled one promising young wom-an into my department simply from meetings in the bathroom. I'm anticipating the day when the women's bathroom becomes just as powerful a focal point as the men's urinals when it comes to internal political manipulation."

The Queen in the chess set (in case you don't know) can move any number of clear spaces in *any* direction, backward, forward, side-ways, or diagonally. A lot of visible status symbols can be collected with that maneuverability.

WOMEN'S APPAREL IS A BADGE OF SERVITUDE

Men's clothing is not unique in assigning attributes to its wearers; women's clothing is historically symbolic, too. As far as I know, no contemporary feminist has researched the subject (no nonfeminist would care), but women who are moving into the male world of work must begin to pay attention to the symbolism of clothing.

Why are men's and women's clothes so different? Why, as a woman, do you wear what you wear? What is your conscious or sub-conscious motivation each morning as you dress for work? Why not just wear your bathrobe?

The phenomenon of sex differential in wearing apparel intrigued

Lawrence Langner, a prodigiously successful businessman who was also an erudite scholar, a popular playwright, and a perceptive social observer. His many-faceted talents led him to the theater where he founded the Theater Guild and the Shakespeare Festival at Stratford, Connecticut. The importance of costumes to theatrical productions and the social significance of costumes impelled him to study the meaning and psychology of clothing throughout history. In 1959 he published his remarkable psycho-history of clothing through the ages, *The Importance of Wearing Clothes* (New York: Hastings House). Several years before the current wave of feminism erupted, his studies led him to the following conclusion about the marked dissimilarity between men's and women's clothes:

> Contrary to established beliefs, the differentiation in clothing between men and women arose from the male's desire to assert superiority over the female and to hold her in his service. This he accomplished through the ages by means of special clothing which hampered or handicapped the female in her movements. Then men prohibited one sex from wearing the clothing of the other, in order to maintain this differentiation.

Langner traced his hypothesis as far back as Spanish Levant rock paintings, circa 10,000 B.C. and followed the evidence through subsequent ages, civilizations, and cultures. He found the primary purpose of women's dress throughout history was to prevent them from running away from their lords and masters. The ancient Chinese bound the feet of growing girls to hopelessly deform the adult woman's feet; African tribes weighted women's legs with up to fifty pounds of "beautifying" nonremovable brass coils or protruding metal disks; in Palestine women's ankles were connected with chains and tinkling bells; Moslems swathed women in heavy, opaque shrouds from head to toe; upper-class women in Venice and Spain had to be assisted by pages when they walked in their gorgeous gowns because of the fashionable chimpanies or stilts attached to their shoes — some as much as a yard high!

The only exception to foot crippling was found among nomadic tribes where women were forced to keep up with their men during the seasonal migrations. In these groups, the women were the beasts of burden, walking with the animals and loaded almost as heavily with household goods. They could walk but could not run far.

In Western societies the ubiquitous hobbling device for women has been skirts, usually accompanied by dysfunctional stilted shoes. Although skirt styles changed over time and in various societies, skirts of all kinds served to encumber women. Skirts that consisted of long robes reaching to or below the ankles hampered movement by entangling the legs in layers of heavy textiles. In more "modern" times straight fitted skirts effectively bound the knees or ankles together to impede free stride and enforce an awkward, staggering gait. Whatever the society, skirts for females were characterized by their impracticality, inefficiency, and uncomfortable designs. Not only walking but sitting, bending, stooping, and climbing were totally enjoined via "female" dress. Utility, comfort, ornamentation, or sexual attraction has nothing to do with why females wear skirts or other distinctively "female" articles of clothing. These garments were invented thousands of years ago by men to label females as dependents and to "keep them in their place." In consequence, "female" apparel carries a universal symbolism of servitude — the badge of subservience.

In contrast the exclusive male clothing in every society where women were constricted consisted of divided garments — trousers or knickerbockers — which permitted free, unrestricted movement while protecting the wearer's extremities. Men exerted superiority over women by laying exclusive claim to clothing which gives the greatest mobility, freedom for action, and self-protection.

At all times, from earliest societies, women were prohibited from wearing the clothing of males — and vice versa. The penalties for breaking the strict laws against transvestitism ("a morbid craving to dress in garments of the opposite sex") were (and are) severe. In Deuteronomy, the Old Testament thundered the "moral" imprecations which many women feel bound by even in the twentieth century. "A woman shall not wear that which pertaineth unto a man, neither shall a man put on a woman's garment."

Despite these savage laws and vicious punishments, women have periodically rebelled against their enforced clothing shackles, especially skirts. Early American feminists of the 1850s took up the issue of women's dress reform. Amelia Bloomer is the best known of the many who took to wearing short skirts or tunics over loose trousers gathered at the ankle. "Bloomers" became the derisive term for any divided skirt or knickerbocker dress. One optimistic feminist, Helen Marie Weber, told the Women's Rights Convention of 1850 in Worcester, Massachusetts that, "In ten years time male attire will be generally worn by women of most civilized countries." She was at least a hundred years off in her prediction; it has taken until the 1970s for women to dare to flout the age-old inventions of man to keep her inferior and immobile.

There are still corporations that issue edicts to keep women employees in their place by forbidding women to wear slacks or pants suits to work. Such a company policy is telling women employees that they are inferior beings whose only status in the corporate setup is to serve their male masters. The clothing symbolism says: "You have no mobility in this corporation." No woman who understands the significance of corporate status symbolism would be caught dead working for such a company. Displaying a blatant badge of servitude is no way to progress in the male corporate milieu, but that is exactly what "female" dress codes dictated by men set out to accomplish.

DRESSING FOR SUCCESS — FEMALE STYLE

Given all the historical, psychological, cultural, and social factors that impinge on the personal dress habits of women, there is, as yet, no clear-cut solution to the problem ambitious women must face in inventing a suitable costume for their business role. (Anything goes outside of business situations for both women and men; our concern is limited to work costumes.) Given my personal orientation in male business fashions, plus my lifelong abhorrence of "feminine" fashions, I am convinced that the most important consideration for women is the underlying symbolism of clothing. There is no question in my mind that many women are held back in their job progress because of their inattention to dress. Or rather, their introspective evaluation of what they wear. In business you are not dressing to express personal taste; you are dressing in a costume which should be designed to have an impact on your bosses and teammates. If your clothes don't convey the message that you are competent, able, ambitious, self-confident, reliable, and authoritative, nothing you say or do will overcome the negative signals emanating from your apparel.

My personal observations of women at work, plus my own experiences over many years, plus the opinions of increasingly succcessful women at work today are all I have to go on when proposing the following suggestions for guiding women toward a female business uniform style. I pass them along not as definitive rules but as the genesis of a practical, symbolic movement toward revitalizing women's perspective on "proper" attire for management executives, female.

Be Aware of the Uniform Concept

An amazing number of women dress wholly at variance with the "uniform" of their male associates. Your first prerequisite is to study the attire of men in your department or company. For instance, if the important men wear dark, conservative suits with white shirts and rep ties, you do not "fit in" if you are partial to busy prints, exuberant colors, extravagant hats, mod fashions, or lacy, frilly blouses. You may be a genius at that business but I guarantee you will never make it far up that hierarchical ladder. On the other hand, if you work for a go-go company where hard-driving male executives have adopted high-style Italian jeans, expensive leather boots, and suede jackets as a trend-setting uniform, you are an eyesore if you appear in inconspicuous navy knits with sedate pumps and a string of pearls. You may have exceptional talent but you will be "hidden away" far from the male executives in a dead-end service job, kept away from the gaming tables.

Keep an eye on the costumes of *superiors* to ascertain the "tone" or "look" that is voluntarily adopted by upward-moving men. Be very careful not to dress in conformity with lower-echelon jobs. If your company has a written secretarial dress code, executive women must *never* obey it. They will instantly ally themselves with the clerical ranks rather than executive or supervisory ranks. One woman told me how the point was accidentally brought to her attention, although she was thoroughly confused when the incident occurred.

She had continued to wear what she described as "attractive, feminine dresses" when she was promoted to her first true executive-level job. She did a certain amount of traveling and decided she could be more casual and comfortable on airplanes. One day she joined her boss at the airport wearing a navy pants suit. When her boss came toward her, he too was wearing a navy suit that looked almost identical. "I blushed in embarrassment," she said. "We looked like the Bobbsey Twins and all I could think of was how angry women get if somebody else has on the same dress. I think I was afraid that he'd be mad at me." But her boss didn't react that way at all! Quite the reverse; he approved of the way she was dressed although he never said a word. "I could sense a change in his attitude toward me. For the first time in two years he was relaxed and comfortable traveling with me. It was as if he finally accepted me as an executive with the firm and not some secretary he was forced to accompany. The only thing different about me was the clothes."

Dresses versus Suits

Instinctively for most of my working life I preferred two-piece women's suits to one-piece dresses. For reasons I couldn't explain there was a feeling of defenselessness or nakedness about dresses when all the men in the room wore jackets. When you think in terms of symbolism, it seems quite obvious that a man's jacket is his "mantle of authority." The first thing a man does when preparing for a business meeting or visiting his boss is to don his suit jacket. Many women executives unconsciously adopt the idea in their favored work clothing. Some wear dress costumes with a matching or contrasting jacket. Some wear sleeveless tunics which seem to serve the same purpose. Others use sweaters by wearing twin-sweater outfits or merely carrying a jacket sweater over their shoulders. The current fashion in "layered looks" is possibly a recognition of this authority-mantle concept. At any rate, a separate jacket or shoulder mantle of some nature (a shirt over a T-shirt or turtle-neck sweater has somewhat the same connotation) gives a feeling of strength and control to women's appearance.

A women who hopes to manage affairs, control subordinates, and exert authority must avoid any kind of dresses which portray her as weak or indecisive. Any taint of the "little girl" look is anathema — pinafores, ruffles, bows, cute prints, flouncy skirts, clinging fabrics, or distinctively "feminine" frills will contradict any effort to be viewed as forceful.

Skirt Suits versus Pants Suits

As far as I can see, there doesn't seem to be any difference whether a woman chooses skirts or pants to go with her jacketed costume as long as the skirt is appropriate for her daily activities. That means the skirt must be pleated or flared enough to allow a free stride. Walk around in your skirt before buying it to make sure you can get into a car, mount the bus steps, climb stairs, or get on the commuter train without looking awkward, ungainly, or inept. A clumsy or mincing gait suggests that such a person may be clumsy or inept in other ways.

Pay particular attention to the skirt when you sit down. Test it in a mirror and see if it rides up above your knees or otherwise disturbs men, who all have an innate impulse to look between your legs. Assume that you will be seated on an open stage or head table at some point in your business rounds, so check that the skirt will not force you to concentrate on pressing your knees together or otherwise protecting your genitals from male peeks. If the shoeshine man comes around and you don't dare put your foot up to join in the ritual because of your "immodesty," that skirt is no good as a work uniform. On the other hand, voluminous skirts which get caught in doors or overhang chairs are equally inappropriate. In short, if your skirt distracts your own attention and observers' attention from the business matter under discussion, it is not acceptable as a work uniform.

Pants suits are booming in popularity with women for good reason. Once a woman starts wearing pants suits she finds it very difficult to go back to skirts and dresses. Pants serve the same function for women as they do for men. They give absolute freedom of motion, allow you to sit, stand, run, or bend over without worrying about how much "shows" or adopting all the female contortions that impede physical movement. But pants suits alone don't add up to a team uniform. There are many other details to watch when adopting this once forbidden male apparel.

Attention to Fit

Many women think they look terrible in pants (and many do) because they don't know how pants should fit. They must fit perfectly, just as men's do (or should). Relatively few women can buy a pants suit without having one or both the pieces altered. Women's pants should have a fitted waistband (not an elastic stretch which fits everybody and nobody), and the creases must fall straight to the floor. If you have acquired a lifelong habit of walking in a typically female knock-kneed position, pants will not hang right. Watch men in jobs above you to see what length they wear their trousers and lengthen or shorten yours to conform. A "high-water" look (i.e., so short your socks show) has always been the sign of a hayseed.

Suit jackets, too, must fit perfectly. Men notice those things even if you don't. I vividly remember my initial encounter with a clothing executive when I first entered the men's fashion promotion field. I was wearing a good-looking tailored woman's suit which I thought was very appropriate. The first thing he did was grab my jacket at the back of the neckline and say, "This thing doesn't fit you at all! What kind of a tailor do you have? The collar should lie flat with no bulges. Also, that shoulder seam hangs over a half-inch too far." I had never thought about such "minor details," but I immediately found myself a men's tailor, and that dear little old man gave me invaluable lessons in how clothes should fit, and can be easily altered by an expert, preferably one who tailors men's suits, until they feel as comfortable as a second skin.

Watch Your Fabrics and Finishing

A big part of achieving the "uniform" look is matching the fabric and quality of male colleagues' clothes. If your boss wears $400 wool suits, you are nowhere near the "uniform" concept in a $69.95 suit of polyester. One woman executive told me that the first thing she did when getting a promotion to a managerial position was go to the bank and make a $1,000 loan which she immediately spent on clothes. She recognized that her previous limitation on clothing expenses made her look dowdy and unsuccessful. An appropriately expensive wardrobe is likely to be a better investment in your future than a college course in some technical subject. Try to match the price and quality of your superior's uniforms, but don't surpass them. "It is not nice," one corporate wife was told, "to outdress the president's wife." The same holds true for bona fide team members. Men are inclined to understand immediately that they match but never overshadow their boss's clothes.

Remember the Function of Uniforms

Whatever else they represent, executive clothes are first and foremost appropriate to the demands of the job duties. By quasi-military standards a uniform must appear as fresh, unwrinkled, and sharply creased at midnight as it did that morning although it was worn for a full day at the office, was drenched in a rain shower, traveled 5,000 miles by five modes of transportation, and had to be presentable for a late dinner and possibly a nightclub. Executive uniforms must be sturdy and versatile.

In this respect women executives' clothes must be equally versatile and adaptable to all business exigencies. If women travel with men, they must be able to take everything they need in hand luggage that can be carried on and off the plane, just as men do. The first truly great woman's commercial I've ever seen is one by United Airlines showing a woman executive deplaning in an efficient, self-confident manner, with the comment "The boss is on her way." To be so well organized and efficient she had to pay attention to the functionalism of her wardrobe. Fabrics that wrinkle, rumple, sag, or wilt have no place in a woman executive's wardrobe.

Pay Attention to Coordination of Parts

One well-dressed woman executive who flatly says, "Most women dress terribly," confines her shopping to a single shop where she gets the full attention of the owner each year when she buys her standard $1,000 worth of replacement clothes. "By giving all my business to one shop I can be sure that everything matches and parts can coordinate with other things. The shop owner orders the right color blouses or accessories so that all of my clothes are quite interchangeable. The new outfits always go with the previous year's leftovers because we select compatible fabrics, styles, or colors."

Colors Are Ambivalent

Most successful corporate businessmen find that dark blues, grays, pinstripes, and subtle plaids convey the symbol of authority most effectively. With women I do not believe the same effect is achieved. Women executives can probably exert a stronger impression with distinctive colors or patterns that men cannot get away with. Navy, black (let's raze the "little basic black dress"), dull grays, or very subdued solids do not impress me as symbols of strength in women's clothes. They smack too much of "blending with the wallpaper" and taking a back seat to the powerful men. No man could wear a red suit, for instance, but a woman dressed in the red color spectrum has a definite air of confidence and assurance. Any such powerful color must be counteracted with blended and softening blouses or scarves, but strong colors may be the one male dress qualm which women can interpret to their purposes. Women by their very nature are not "con-servative" in the business world. By their very presence they are breaking the establishment rule of no-females. Since women do have great fashion sense, the best way to judge is to examine yourself criti-cally in the mirror and ask, "What impression does this outfit convey to others?" You are after a "strong" and "self-assured" look, not a mousy, timid, unassertive impression. Whatever costume creates that impact is probably right as a business uniform.

Never Wear a Man's Tie

Never, never, never. A man's tie is a penis symbol. No woman with any self-respect wants to walk around advertising "I'm pretending I have a penis." It was this article of men's clothing above all else that probably created the stereotype of the butch lesbian look. (No self-respecting lesbian would ever make such a mistake today, either, even in the gay bars.)

Wear Shoes You Can Walk In

As we have seen, foot-crippling shoes have been a favorite method to keep women in their place. The day is centuries off when "serious" business can be delayed because an executive's feet hurt. Urban busi-nessmen do a lot of walking around city streets, and women execu-tives must be ready to join them and keep up with them.

Buy Clothes with Pockets

One manufacturing detail sets off women's clothes (even man-tailored clothes) from men's clothes — the lack of pockets. When I used to complain about this to buyers years ago, they insisted that women didn't want pockets because it would "spoil the fit" of their clothes, which presumably were supposed to be skintight over the torture-racks of girdles and padded bras. That's nonsense. Women's clothes don't have pockets because men like to reserve these essential and handy devices for themselves. I think women should insist that all their clothes have functional pockets, not cheap imitation flaps. No-pockets is an inferiority symbol.

Dump Your Burdensome Handbag

One favorite accessory of women deserves special mention — the ubiquitous carryall handbag. There's no denying that women need handbags to transport keys, money, checkbooks, glasses, makeup, cigarettes, credit cards, notebooks, and assorted sundries between home and office, but there are powerful reasons not to drag such an encumbrance all over a business office, especially to meetings. A purse or handbag is so uniquely a female article that it arouses a host of subconscious connotations among men. The typical male outfit contains an average of nine pockets, while women's clothes usually have none or no adequate ones, thereby forcing women to carry a hampering weight in the form of exterior hand baggage.

I once asked a woman track star if she practiced her running to beat traffic congestion during the day. "You can't," she said, "because of the handbag. It's impossible to run while carrying a purse in hand or on your shoulder — it slows your speed by half and throws you off balance." A woman vice-president in an all-male group says she's noticed that men "hate the sight of a woman settling a hand-bag under a conference table." Many bosses I've known in business consider it a sign of subservience to carry anything except vital busi-ness papers which they are entrusted to deliver to another execu-tive. The image of messenger, errand boy, or beast of burden is avoided as much as possible by men. Symbolically, women are the burden carriers.

Both the physical and psychological handicaps of a handbag were exposed to a skeptical member of my Womanschool class when she tested the principle during a business luncheon with three male exec-utives. "The difference was unbelievable," she reported. "I slipped a credit card and a few bills in my jacket pocket (and a comb and a lipstick, I must admit), but carried nothing in my hands or on my shoulder. We walked a couple of blocks to the restaurant and for the first time I kept apace with no trouble. I hadn't realized how often my big shoulder-bag bumped into people and forced me to zigzag or keep manipulating it. The men, whom I had lunched with a few times before, sensed something different but didn't know what it was. One said approvingly, 'You must have new shoes on today, I see you're keeping up with us.' At the restaurant I sat down freely and grace-fully without shoving chairs or tables around to accommodate a spot for my usual luggage. I didn't have to warn waiters not to trip over it nor divert my attention repeatedly to check that my bag wasn't stolen or something. I can't explain the sense of freedom and equality I felt. And somehow it was communicated to my male companions — as if I really *belonged* in an expensive restaurant having a business luncheon with coequal executives."

Be Careful about Uniquely Female Accessories

There's one cardinal rule: Don't wear anything that jingles, wig-gles, clanks, or glitters. Executive insignia are silent, understated and unobtrusive — never sexy.

Jewelry — Dangling earrings, charm bracelets, metal bangles, chain collections, novelty pins, or garish, attention-getting items that dis-tract listeners from what you are *saying* or *ordering* will dilute any woman's authority image. Take your cue from successful men in your organization. Their idea of jewelry will be reflected in their watches, possibly cufflinks, belt buckles, rings, and tie clasps. They seldom have a wardrobe of decorations; they stick to one or two favorites that look (and are) expensive, and wear them repeatedly. Never forget that money is the scorecard in this game so executive women's jewelry no longer acts as costume decoration but as a *symbol of success,* i.e. expensive and real, not junk. Women should probably limit themselves to one or two jewelry items at a time, such as a ring and a necklace. Neck jewelry indeed may become the female equivalent of men's ties so each piece should be selected with care and be what the jewelry trade calls an "important" design, one that stands alone as a distinctive, powerful emblem. The exception to expensive elegance is when you work for a company where the *men* wear extravagant jewelry; in that case your rule is probably "the funkier the better."

Perfume — Save it for after-work hours when it can perform its function of making you a desirable sex object. The lingering odor of the most expensive perfume is overpowering and headachey in the confines of a small office or closed conference room.

Makeup and Hairstyles — Women are no different than men in wanting to look their best when they are in the public eye, as they are at work. Just remember that your makeup and hairdo must hold up under all the exigencies of a business day without excessive attention. It goes without saying that all touch-ups, including lipstick, must be done in private. Naturalness, as opposed to painted artificiality, is the aim.

The development of a "superior" or "high status" uniform for female management executives must come from women themselves because men's reactions to female dress are highly suspect. Conscious and unconscious male attitudes toward women's dress will be skewed in the direction of reducing women to their traditional weak and dependent roles. A strong and authoritative costume is apt to be criticized by men when a woman wears it. That may be the best sign you're on the right track — if you can scare a pewter-gray pinstripe into a worried comment about your bright green velvet blazer, you've accomplished something. Men will seldom tell women their clothes are inadequate to their job; they'll gladly let women make the wrong moves in the game. Some male comments can be tip-offs.

- "I see you're wearing a dress today — you look so pretty." If a man says that to you at the staff meeting, never wear that outfit again. Any time you look "sweet" and "pretty," you are in trouble; some fast-moving gamester has just captured your pawn.
- "I don't remember what she said, but she sure has great tits." When I heard this male summation of a brilliant woman's contribution to a prestigious government-business conference, I had

visions of her in a neat brown-and-white print jersey V-neck dress which accentuated a generous bosom. I wasn't there; I don't know; but whatever she wore, it's obvious that her costume did more for her figure than it did for her career.

- "You have a good job. You ought to dress the part." If a man says that to you, adopt him as your mentor. He's the best business friend you've run across. It may sound like he's insulting your taste in clothes, but he's telling it like it is. He's trying to help you get ahead in business.

Symbols of Power

Michael Korda

Office furnishings have strong symbolic value. Take file cabinets — in themselves, they are meaningless. Most executives, in fact, place them out of sight, in their secretaries' offices or cubicles. Put a lock on the filing cabinet, however, and it becomes a power symbol, however unsightly and bulky. When you want to take a file out, you have to walk over to it and unlock it, the implication being that it contains material of great importance and confidentiality. Given a lock, the filing cabinet can become a central power symbol, well worth having in your own office, no matter how much space it takes up.

Furniture can tell one a great deal about the person. A *New York Times* reporter remarked of one tycoon that "Callers, supplicants and salesmen who make their way to [the chairman's] 42nd floor office get swallowed up and find themselves peering between their knees at him," helplessly sunk in deep, soft chairs. This is a fairly common power game, and can be observed in many offices. One young lady, job hunting, noted that almost every senior executive in the publishing business had a low sofa. "You go in," she said, "and they ask you to sit down on the sofa, which is about four feet lower than his desk chair, so he's looking down at you, and you're looking up from nowhere, with your ass practically on the floor and your knees up in the air. You couldn't arrange things better to make a person seem really unimportant."

This is not altogether true. There are more elaborate ways of making people feel unimportant. Harry Cohn, the tyrannical president of Columbia Pictures, designed his office in imitation of Mussolini's, a huge, elongated room with the desk at the far end, raised above floor level. "The portal to the position of power was a massive sound-proofed door which had no knob and no keyhole on the outside. It could only be opened by a buzzer operated from Cohn's or his secretary's desk . . . In later years Glenn Ford noted discoloration of the door jamb at mid-level; it had been soiled by the sweat of innumerable palms of those who had passed through to an audience with Harry Cohn."

This is a somewhat extreme example of power decoration, but even lesser power players will usually arrange their offices so that their visitors are obliged to sit in as much discomfort as possible. It is particularly helpful to make sure that all the ashtrays are just slightly out of reach so that visitors sitting in low chairs and unable to rise have to stretch awkwardly to dispose of their cigarette ash.

The disposition of furniture is a better indication of power than the furniture itself. Some offices run to luxurious decoration, others do not, but the scale of luxury is more likely to be dependent upon the management's whim than the occupant's status. At *Playboy's* Chicago headquarters, for instance, even the junior editors have "plush, cork-paneled hideaways, many equipped with soft chairs, stereo sets and stunning secretaries," an atmosphere of sybaritic luxury that emanates from Hugh Hefner's vision of himself, rather than from any power they may have.

Power lies in how you use what you have, not in the accouterments per se. All the leather and chrome in the world will not replace a truly well-thought-out power scheme. A large office is pointless unless it is arranged so that a visitor has to walk the length of it before getting to your desk, and it is valuable to put as many objects as possible in his path—coffee tables, chairs and sofas, for example—to hinder his progress. However small the office, it is important to have the visitor's chair facing toward you, so that you are separated by the width of your desk. This is a much better power position than one in which the visitor sits *next* to the desk, even though it may make access to your desk inconvenient for you. When a small office is very narrow (and most are) it is often useful to have the desk placed well forward in the room, thus minimizing the space available for the visitor, and increasing the area in which it is possible for you to retreat, at least psychologically. Thus, in a typical small office, the alternative desk/chair relationships would look like [those in the accompanying illustration.]

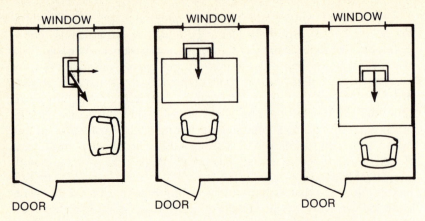

WINDOW   WINDOW   WINDOW

DOOR   DOOR   DOOR

Of these possibilities, number three is by far the strongest power position for the occupant. Behind his desk, he has left himself plenty of room, so that he isn't likely to feel that his back is against the wall when arguing with a caller or a colleague, while his visitor is tightly enclosed, with little psychological space and breathing room. In drawing number two, the visitor is placed in an aggressive position, having more space than the occupant, and being further forward in the room. In drawing number one, the occupant has no power position at all, and is obliged to turn to his right at an uncomfortable angle to talk to the visitor. Power, let it be remembered, moves in direct lines. (Attempts to do without desks altogether, though popular in the recording and the broadcasting businesses, have never caught on. The desk performs a useful social function in power terms that is hard to eliminate.)

In larger offices, power arrangements are more varied. Most people prefer to divide their offices into two separate sections, one containing a couch, which can be used for informal, semisocial discussions, where decisions do not actually have to be made, and the other containing the usual desk and chair, for "pressure situations" and confrontations, in which the whole object is to reach a firm decision. In entering such an office, it is therefore very important to notice in what area the occupant wishes you to take a seat. If you have come to negotiate a deal, and he moves toward the sofa, you can be fairly sure that he has decided to stall you; if he asks you to sit at his desk, you can be equally sure that he is ready for serious negotiation. At the same time, you can influence *him*. By firmly seating yourself at the desk, you make it clear that you want an answer; by sitting on the sofa, you demonstrate that you are not eager to conclude the deal. A certain tug-of-war is often evident when the two parties have different goals in mind, the "host" trying to push the visitor toward the sofa, with the plea that he will be "more comfortable" there, the visitor obstinately making his way toward the desk, or vice versa, of course.

334

Some people are past masters at this game. When he comes to my office, a well-known lawyer of my acquaintance always manages to sit on the sofa between me and the telephone on the end table when he wants to persuade me to do something I would just as soon not do. In the first place, he has trapped me in a semisocial position, by getting us both on the sofa; in the second place, he has effectively cut me off from the telephone, so that I can't be interrupted by a call. In this position, he has me at his mercy — we are seated side by side, at the same level, both facing the window and away from desk and telephone. When he wants to *sell* me on something, he sits on the chair in front of my desk, then gradually works it around until it's beside mine, so that he's moved to my side of the barrier, so to speak. There are several ways in which he assures himself of this position, the first being to put his portfolio, hat and coat on the sofa, so that we *can't* sit on it, the second being to plead mild deafness, so that he has an excuse to come to my side of the desk, which implies an invasion of my territory. An attempt to prevent his moving closer by buying an armchair so massive and heavy as to be practically immovable failed; he pleads a bad back and asks the secretary to find him a simple, straight chair, which he then places exactly where he wants it.

This subtle use of space can best be understood by seeing how the two different areas, the semisocial and the pressure, relate to each other spatially [as in the accompanying illustration.]

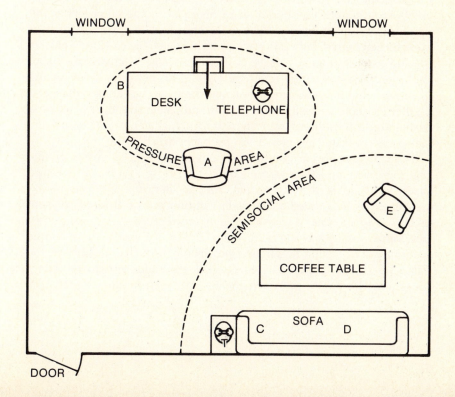

A typical office is divided into a "pressure area" and a "semisocial area." If the occupant is intent on serious business, he should try to place his visitor in position A, squarely facing the desk. If he wants to delay a decision or placate a visitor, he should try to place him in position D on sofa. An aggressive visitor will either move his chair to position B, or assume position C on sofa, forcing the occupant to sit at D, cut off by an intruder from his own telephone. Chair E is the weakest power position, and is reserved for unimportant third parties. Note that the coffee table separates one area from the other, and that the sofa should be as low as possible.

Still larger offices are sometimes divided into *three* areas, one end being set aside for a large conference table, with chairs around it. This is frequently the case with the offices of chairmen of the board, and is usually a sign that they want to maintain control over the board by holding its meetings on their own territory, rather than having them in a separate board room. As a general rule, boards that meet in an office a corner of which is used as a board meeting area have less power and autonomy than those that meet in a separate board room, and are to that extent less valuable to be on.

Boardroom tables, it should be noted, are almost never round, since it is necessary to have a very precise gradation of power, and above all, imperative that the most important person, usually the chairman, should sit at the end next to the window, with his back to it, while the second most important person, usually the president or chief executive officer, should sit to his right. If the latter sits at the opposite end of the table (playing "mother," so to speak, in dining-table terms) he not only has the sun in his eyes, but is almost always placing himself in an adversary position vis-à-vis the chairman, a sign that there is either a power struggle going on between them, or the likelihood that one will develop. If the chairman has an armchair and all the rest have straight chairs, it is an indication that the company is run along firm, authoritarian lines. If all the chairs are the same, the prospects for acquiring power are probably much better.

Even bathrooms can matter. It is obviously best to have a private bathroom in your office, second best to be close to a bathroom, and worst to be miles away from one. As one literary agent said, in explaining why he wanted a best-selling author moved from his present publisher to another, "He should have a nice office to come and visit, you know, someplace where he can sit down in a social way when he wants without feeling he's in an *office*. The bathroom should be in the same office, you know? If it's in the hall, it's a little less good. Where he is now, he has to go down the hall to wash his hands when he visits, it's not so nice."

Desks can tell us a great deal about people's power quotient. The objects most people place on their desks are not there by accident, after all, and usually give some clue to the power status of the occupant. One successful conglomerator was described as having "his desk peculiarly arranged—with a window at the back—so that outdoor light all but blinds the visitor while striking two polished glass paperweights on his desk, giving an impression that you have come under the scrutiny of two translucent orbs, that your thoughts are being read and your capabilities assayed in a second or two."

Desk sets—usually a pen and pencil set in a marble or onyx base—used to be potent power symbols, perhaps because of their phallic appearance, but they have been eclipsed, partly because of the popularity of the ubiquitous felt-tip marker pen, and mostly because too many people finally acquired a set. Framed diplomas are definitely out as power symbols, and so are stuffed fish, family photographs, children's paintings, mezotint engravings of Harvard Yard in 1889, all posters, Audubon prints (unless they're originals), 37mm. cannon shells converted into paperweights, anything made of plastic or lucite and ashtrays stolen from famous restaurants or hotels. Simplicity is the best way of suggesting power. It's also useful to maintain a certain amount of clutter, just enough to make it clear that you're busy, but not so much as to suggest you're a slob. A nice touch is to leave out two or three red folders marked "Confidential" and to push them out of sight once any visitor has noticed them. Stacks of magazines give a good impression, particularly if they have slips of paper inserted in them, as if for future reference. Care should be taken, however, to ensure that they aren't such magazines as *Playboy* or *Penthouse* — *Foreign Affairs* carries considerable prestige, *Psychology Today* suggests an interest in alternative life-styles, a large stack of *Fortune*s look very good, and *Forbes* gives the impression of a serious interest in money, never a bad thing. Television sets have become popular as power symbols, perhaps because the late Lyndon B. Johnson had three of them in his office (so he could see himself on all three channels at once). A television set in the office is supposed to connote a burning interest in current events and world affairs (nobody assumes the owner is watching reruns of *I Love Lucy* during office hours), and also implies that the occupant of the office works at odd and irregular hours, always a sign of power.

Indeed, semidomestic furnishings are very good power symbols, since they suggest the office is a kind of home away from home, not just a place in which one comes to work from nine to five on weekdays. Even people who go home religiously at five-thirty like to give the impression that they often stay to eight or nine at night, which explains the popularity of radios, clock radios, bars, small refrigerators, blenders, heating pads, exercise poles and Health-O-Matic scales, all of which I have seen in people's offices. Electric hot plates, on the other hand, are out, since they imply you haven't enough authority to send your secretary out for coffee.

A special category of office furnishing would have to be established for my friend Tim Hennessey, a successful sales executive who had a convertible sofa bed installed in his office. This was a doubly potent power symbol, since it suggested at once that he had to work late enough to spend the night in the office, and that his sexual successes with the office staff justified his having a sofa bed handy. To the best of my knowledge, it was never opened, but he acquired a valuable reputation as a hard worker and a daring cocksman, and became, overnight as it were, a legendary figure. Hennessey also had a lock fitted to his private telephone, a nice, small touch which certainly impressed many people, and a rheostat switch under his desk so that he could dim the lights, partly because he believed it would make it easier to carry out a seduction, partly because he liked to think he could persuade the more elderly executives that they were going blind by alternately dimming and brightening the lights during a meeting. He was also the first person in publishing to have three wall clocks, one for New York time, one for California time, and one for London time, suggesting an international scope to his job which was purely imaginary.

TIME POWER

Clocks and watches are in fact the ultimate power symbols; for time, in a very real sense, *is* power.

For people who make an hourly wage, time is money in a direct sense. Analysts, for example, inevitably see the day as being divided into so many hourly sessions (fifty-five minutes actually) at so much an hour. Freudian analysts tend to maintain a certain power over their patients by not having a clock visible — the patient knows when his hour is up when the analyst tells him it is, thus intensifying the analyst's control over the patient, who can hardly look at his watch and is therefore kept in suspense, unsure of how much time he has left to drag out a boring dream or compress a whole, rich life experience into a few minutes.

The greatest compliment a busy executive can pay to a visitor is to take off his watch ostentatiously and place it — face down — on the desk. It's a way of saying, "My time belongs to you, for as long as you need me." Alternatively, taking off your watch and placing it face *up* on your desk is a way of announcing that you're a busy man and can't spare much time for your visitor's business, that he'd better damn well state his case in a hurry and get out. I personally am such a taker-off and putter-on of wrist watches that I have to go into Cartier's at regular intervals to have my watchstrap retightened, and often manage to leave it behind on my desk, or even on someone else's (leaving it in somebody else's bed is, generally speaking, a dangerous thing to do and leads to bad scenes and divorces).

One executive I know has a huge outdoor pool clock with numbers 2 inches high on the wall, and a second hand that clicks to signify passing time. It is arranged so that it faces his visitor squarely, thus announcing that his time is more important than yours, and has the same effect on most people as the writing on the wall at Belshazzar's unfortunate feast ("God hath numbered thy kingdom, and finished it"). This somewhat oppressive effect can be reinforced by arranging to have his secretary come in at regular intervals to announce that he's running behind schedule, or that Edward Bennett Williams is waiting outside to see him, but the consummate time player shouldn't need anything so obvious as this to fluster a visitor and give him the terrible guilt of wasting a busy person's precious time.

Lawyers, who usually charge on the basis of time, have their own ways of establishing their importance. At the lowest level, they have clocks that face toward them, status being set by the kind of clock it is. A round, wedge-topped battery-operated clock that sits flat on the desk and is only visible to the lawyer himself seems to be this year's favorite, though I greatly admire one lawyer who has a complicated Swiss "Atmos" clock in a glass case on his desk with the dial facing him, leaving the client to become mesmerized by the restless swing of the brass pendulum and the endless clicking of the gears and wheels — without ever being able to see what time it is. At this stage of power, the lawyer wants to know how long the client has been there, but would just as soon the client didn't know. More important lawyers announce that their time is expensive by having the clock face the client, digital clocks being favored by corporation lawyers and ancient, noisy grandfather and railroad clocks by the more traditional old-line lawyers. The *most* important lawyers have no clocks at all, the implication being that everyone they see is on a retainer basis anyway, and if they're not, there's a secretary outside to keep the log. Divorce lawyers, who have to listen to endless personal *Angst* from their clients, like analysts, seem to have no clocks and often no watches either, though one lawyer I know wears a Mickey Mouse watch which he never winds, on the grounds that it makes him seem like a simple, unthreatening figure, rather than a symbol of authority or a husband.

Just as there are fashions in clocks, there are fashions in watches, which can tell you a good deal about the people who wear them. The West Coast watchpower symbol is to have the letters of your name painted on the dial instead of numbers though this only works when your name has twelve letters, like Ernest Lehman, the producer, unless you can abbreviate your first name, like Irving Mansfield, the late Jacqueline Susann's protean husband, whose watch reads "Irv Mansfield." This fashion does not seem to have made it to New York, where the status watch is still the old Cartier tank watch, with one of those Cartier hinged gold buckles that is almost invisible except to the connoisseur, who *knows*. On the whole though, watch wearers are divided into two basic categories: those who like watches that are impossible to read, either having no numbers or four almost invisible dots, and those who like the kind of watches astronauts, pilots and skindivers wear, with enormous luminous dials and bezel rings that allow you to compute how much air you have left or what GMT is, in case you need to know. One executive I know wears a watch that actually tells the time in London and New York simultaneously at the push of a button, but my own experience is that the less powerful the executive, the more intricate the watch. The lowest power rating goes to those who wear little miniature calendars on their watchbands, thus indicating both that they can't afford an automatic date-adjusting watch and that they need to be reminded what day it is. A complicated watch like a Rolex "Submariner" usually shows the wearer is prey to extreme time anxiety, and thus fairly far down the scale of power. More powerful executives wear watches that hardly even show the time, so thin are the hands and so obscure the marks on the face. People who are really secure in their power sometimes show it by not wearing watches at all, relying on the fact that nothing important can happen without them anyway.

Styles of wearing wristwatches are pretty limited — after all, we only have two wrists—but I have noticed that a good many men now wear their wrist watch on the *inside* of the left wrist, an affectation that puzzled me for some time. In my youth it was one of those mysterious British military customs, like a rolled-up handkerchief in one's right coat sleeve, and indicated membership in the professional officer caste. I think officers wore their watches on the inside wrist so that the luminous dial wouldn't be visible to the enemy at night, or possibly so that you could look at the time while keeping the reins of your horse in the left hand (most military affectations are cavalry inspired). None of these reasons seemed to me to apply to modern businessmen, who could hardly have been inculcated in the sartorial traditions of Sandhurst and Cranwell, but close observation has shown that this habit has its purpose in the modern world. A man with a watch on the inside of his left wrist can put his arm around a woman and kiss her while looking at his watch, which will then be facing him at about the level of her left ear, invisible to her. This custom can be observed in a great many midtown bars and restaurants at lunchtime, when men are making the difficult decision of whether to stay and suggest an afternoon in bed or go back to the office and answer their telephone calls. It is obviously callow to look at one's watch openly; still, at a certain point, say, one forty-five, or just about the time one is thinking of ordering coffee, it's necessary to know what time it is and move accordingly. An arm around the shoulder and a kiss will quickly establish whether a proposition is likely to succeed and simultaneously, if one's watch is in the correct position, whether one has time to follow through.

Time has its own rules, its own victories and defeats, its own symbols. In a city like New York, Chicago, or Los Angeles, you can see the losers every day at lunchtime, if you care to, sitting at restaurant tables (usually too near the entrance — winners sit as far away from the door as possible), glancing at their watches and trying to look as if they had all the time in the world or intended to eat alone. They are the people who arrived on time for a luncheon and are going to be kept waiting for at least half an hour because their guest or host is still on the telephone in his office while they're already on their fourth Rye-Krisp, and wishing they had brought a magazine along.

Lunches, of course, and meals in general, are very much connected to time concepts. The late M. Lincoln Schuster, for example, used to fit as many as four lunch dates into one day's lunch, arranging to meet several different people at the same restaurant, taking soup at one table, main course at the next, dessert at the third and coffee at the last. Had he been a drinker, he could no doubt have managed a cocktail at the beginning of the meal with a fifth person. To get through this kind of gastronomic relay race takes an iron digestive system or a total indifference to food. Still, it can be done, and allows one to have as many as twenty lunch dates in a five-day work week.

The power trick in lunch dates, apart from making sure that you're never kept waiting (even if this involves lurking in a telephone booth to watch the doorway of the restaurant), is winning the preliminary battle to fix the meeting at a time of your choosing, and in many businesses, particularly those in large cities, a great deal of the morning is spent in determining whether to meet at 12:30, 12:45 or 1:00; the point being that the person who proposes to win must not only establish the time but arrange to arrive last.

Whether in a restaurant or elsewhere, the most important aspect of the time game is making people wait, the most familiar example being the old one of not speaking on the telephone until the other person is already on the line, a power struggle which can occupy many otherwise unproductive minutes in a busy executive's day. "Buzz me when X is on the line," says the power player, while X is naturally telling *his* secretary to buzz him when Y is on the line. Some people play another form of this game by answering all their telephone calls themselves, asking the caller to wait "just one second," then putting everyone on hold, until they have three or four people backed up waiting to speak to them.

Those who play the power game seriously can never be free from the tyranny of time, and don't even want to be, since a tightly packed schedule not only gives them a sense of importance, but is a perfect excuse for not doing whatever it is they don't want to do. A full calendar is proof of power, and for this reason, the most powerful people prefer small calendars, which are easily filled up, and which give the impression of frenetic activity, particularly if one's writing is fairly large. One of the best power symbols is a desk diary that shows the whole week at a glance, with every available square inch of space filled in or crossed out. It provides visible evidence that one is busy — too busy to see someone who is anxious to discuss a complaint or a burdensome request. At the same time, one can confer a favor by crossing out an existing appointment and, in the current phrase, "penciling in" the name of someone who has requested an appointment. A close inspection of such diaries often reveals that a good many of the entries read "Gray suit at cleaners" or "Betsy's birthday — present?," but the effect from a distance is awe-inspiring.

Many executives stroll to work in a leisurely fashion, stopping to look in shop windows and pausing to glance at pretty girls, then, as soon as they pass through the revolving doors of their office buildings, gather themselves up in a kind of Groucho Marx crouch, as if they wanted to run but felt constrained to hold themselves down to a fast, breathless walk. By the time they reach their offices, they are moving at top speed, already giving dictation while they're struggling out of their topcoats. Men who could quite easily allow themselves a good hour to get to the airport for a flight will happily waste time until they have to leave in a dramatic rush, shouting out last-minute instructions as they run down the hall and pursued to the elevator by people with telephone messages and letters to be signed.

STANDING BY

Another excellent tactic is to allow half an hour for meetings that are sure to last at least an hour, so that the people who have to see you afterward are obliged to wait without knowing quite when they'll be called for. This is the familiar "stand by" game, in which people are warned to "stand by" for a meeting that was supposed to take place at 10 A.M. and probably won't begin until noon, or may even be postponed until next week. In the meantime, of course, they are more or less obliged to stay close to their phones, and may even have to cancel their lunch dates. The busier you can make yourself, the more you can impose your schedule on other people; the more you impose your schedule on other people, the more power you have. The definition of power, in fact, is that more people inconvenience themselves on your behalf than those on whose behalf you would inconvenience yourself. At the very summit of power — the President of the United States, for example — almost everybody will wait, go without lunch, "stand by" or give up dinner with a beautiful woman on your behalf. One doubts, for example, that everyone in the White House necessarily *wants* to rush through lunch in order to fly to Camp David in the Presidential helicopter at the last minute, canceling their weekend plans and their golf dates. But when power beckons, most people follow, at whatever cost to their comfort and private lives. The important thing is to keep moving and drag as many people along in your wake as possible.

A tight schedule is a guarantee of power, as anyone can tell from the description of David Rockefeller's departure from his office. "The man who runs the garage at the Chase Manhattan Bank Building has been keeping watch. When he saw David Rockefeller leave the Federal Reserve Bank of New York . . . he shouted, 'O.K., Chester!' No sooner has Chester pulled up the maroon Cadillac limousine than Mr. Rockefeller is into it (his aides are already waiting in the car, presumably having been sitting there for hours in the underground garage to be ready for the moment), and opening his scarlet folder marked 'For Immediate Action,' he proceeds to give his orders for the afternoon on the way to a waiting helicopter, its rotor blades already turning, which will carry him to a cocktail party in Albany."

One might well ask whether a cocktail party in Albany is worth this kind of mobilized effort, but worth it or not, the elements of time power are perfectly illustrated in Mr. Rockefeller's breathless rush to the helicopter, involving the time of the pilot, Chester, the chauffeur, the aides who have been waiting in the car, the garageman who gives Chester the warning, and presumably a host of other people at both ends of the journey, all of whom are at "stand by" for hours in order to convey one man to a party. David Rockefeller's power would hardly be emphasized if he had strolled out of his office with time to spare, whistled at a passing girl, bought himself a Hershey bar and a copy of *Penthouse* and left himself plenty of time to walk to the Wall Street heliport. The higher up one goes, the more valuable one's time must appear to be.

Closely allied with time is the ability to make other people perform the small demeaning tasks of life for you. Men do not necessarily ask their secretaries to get a cup of coffee for them because they are lazy, or because they are male chauvinists, or even because they don't know where the coffee machine is. Getting one's own coffee is a sign that one's time is not all that important, that it can be wasted on inconsequential personal chores. People who are power-conscious would rather sit at their desks with their eyes closed "thinking" than get up and go for their own coffee, or collect their own dry cleaning, or fetch their own mail. In extreme cases, they insulate themselves from *any* trivial task; as John Z. DeLorean, the flamboyant former general manager of General Motors' car and truck division, put it, "I don't think the heads of state of many countries come close. You travel like an oil sheik." G. M.'s senior executives travel in private jet aircraft, limousines carry them to and fro, teams of PR men fly in a day or two before their visits to ensure that everything is in order, and check the hotel suites "to make certain, among other things, that flowers are in place." One PR man, *Fortune* reported, found what seemed suspiciously like semen stains on a sofa in the suite reserved for the president of G. M., and spent the afternoon before the great man's arrival cleaning the furniture off with his handkerchief.

Not everyone can aspire to this kind of insulation from everyday life, but it represents the ultimate symbol of power in our culture, the notion that one has no time for mundane details and that one's comfort and convenience are the responsibility of other people.

In the words of one executive, "I've always somehow associated power with cleanliness, maybe because at heart we're all afraid of falling back into manual labor, of having to get our hands dirty, like our fathers or grandfathers. Right from the beginning, I've always noticed that powerful people *never seem to get dirty*. You take a rainy day in the city, when everyone arrives with wrinkled, wet trousers and wet shoes, powerful people appear magically with knife-edged creases and shiny, dry shoes. How do they do it? I don't know. I can't even imagine it, which is the reason, I suppose, that I'm down here on this floor, and they're up there. Do they change when they arrive at the office? Do they walk around sealed in plastic Baggies? Is it just that they don't have to take the subway or stand waiting for the Fifth Avenue bus in the rain? Who knows? But it's true — they have this magic gloss to them, they don't sweat, you don't see them coming in after a taxi has splashed muddy water all over them. I know, deep down in my rational mind, that it isn't altogether true, and that a lot of it has to do with limos and company planes and things like that, but for me, powerful people are forever defined as those who can walk to work without stepping in a puddle. When all is said and done it's like the old vaudeville routine about sex appeal — 'Some people got it, some people don't got it. I got it.'"

Abusing Sex at the Office

Aric Press with Emily F. Newhall in New York,
Jonathan Kirsch in Los Angeles,
Holly Morris in Atlanta,
Gloria Borger in Washington
and bureau reports.

It may be as subtle as a leer and a series of off-color jokes, or as direct as grabbing a woman's breast. It can be found in typing pools and factories, Army barracks and legislature suites, city rooms and college lecture halls. It is fundamentally a man's problem, an exercise of power almost analogous to rape, for which women pay with their jobs, and sometimes their health. It's as traditional as underpaying women — and now appears to be just as illegal. Sexual harassment, the boss's dirty little fringe benefit, has been dragged out of the closet.

Authorities can only guess how widespread sexual harassment on the job really is, but the number and nature of reported episodes form an ugly pattern. In Los Angeles, supermarket checker Hallie Edwards walked into a storeroom and found a manager exposing himself and groping for her breasts. After Edwards complained, the chain promoted her boss and transferred her. In Cambridge, Mass., college freshman Helene Sahadi York went to her Harvard professor's office looking for research help. She found an instructor determined to kiss her. In New York, typist Doreen Romano's boss offered her a raise if she would sleep with him. When she refused, he fired her. In each case, the women didn't ignore the incident. Edwards and Romano won out-of-court money settlements; York's professor received a university reprimand. "Men are learning that women are not going to take this kind of behavior," says Romano's lawyer, Michael Krinsky.

What women are learning is how to fight back. They've sued, won judicial condemnations of a boys-will-be-boys attitude and convinced at least a few corporations that harassment in the workplace will cost them money. Women have opened counseling centers in major cities and their appearances on television shows in places like Boston and Dallas have prompted enormous viewer response. They've lobbied state legislatures, and they're monitoring federal agencies' threats to lift government contracts from offending companies or, perhaps worse, tie up corporations in protracted equal-employment litigation. "Women are realizing that harassment is a form of discrimination — and it's not O.K.," says San Francisco lawyer Judith Kurtz.

The increase in complaints parallels the upsurge in the number of women working outside the home. "You now have an extraordinary number of women coming into the work force," says Eleanor Holmes Norton, head of the Equal Employment Opportunity Commission. "They are not nearly as inclined to keep these things to themselves these days." Although many have entered the professional ranks, women, as a class, are still largely segregated into "pink collar" jobs — clerks, typists, waitresses — and usually work for a man. Their supervisors often have complete control over raises, promotions and other working conditions, and some treat sexual favors as just another badge of rank. When women reach supervisory level, they sometimes make the same sort of sexual demands on men. "The basic motivation behind it is not sex, it's power," says Georgia State University Prof. Jacqueline Boles, who is preparing a major study on the issue. "Sexual harassment is a lot like rape."

Atmosphere

Still, sexual harassment remains difficult to define. Beyond the obvious lewd cases lies an uncharted area. What one woman may dismiss as innocent or manageable flirting may drive another to tranquilizers. In one study, women who felt sexually harassed reported suffering from headaches, nausea and sleeplessness. "Harassment is not limited to grabbing and pinching," says Karen Sauvigné, program director of Working Women's Institute in New York, which has developed legal strategies for harassment cases. "It's also the atmosphere loaded with sexual innuendoes and jokes." Unsought verbal intimacy, she adds, "makes you feel horrible." For instance, one Atlanta secretary quit her last job after her boss and three other men watched as she locked a long row of filing cabinets and called out, "Isn't she a cutie?" The woman says simply, "They strip you of your dignity."

It is difficult for the law to be clear when the definition of the action remains so elusive. No federal statute specifically bans sexual harassment. Only Wisconsin has identified harassment in its antidiscrimination law; another ten states are considering the matter. So far, enforcement has come mainly from the courts. During the last five years, several federal judges have ruled that if sexual harassment costs women jobs or benefits, it violates Title VII of the 1964 Civil Rights Act, which prohibits sex discrimination in employment. Judges have ordered corporations to pay for lost wages and attorneys' fees. "Employers realize that it costs money to allow sexual harassment," says Susan Blumenthal of the National Organization for Women's Legal Defense and Education Fund. "It's affecting them where they're most likely to change."

Even if they have legal recourse, however, victims have serious problems of proof. As in rape cases, women who bring complaints are often taunted with the suggestion that they invited the harassment. In hearings, one person's word against another's may not be enough. Sometimes, written evidence barely suffices. For more than a year, the boss of Cathy Peter, a 37-year-old secretary to a New Jersey school superintendent, repeatedly made passes at her. Because she needed the job, she did not complain. One day, he left a note on her desk describing the attributes of a good secretary. Among them: "neat appearance, slender in body and willing to go to bed with the boss, satisfaction guaranteed." Peter protested to the board of education, which dismissed her charges. Finally, Peter sued. The school board and the superintendent paid her a $14,000 settlement. The superintendent, who resigned after a similar incident with another woman, apologized in writing.

"War"

Under any circumstances, bringing a sexual-harassment lawsuit or complaint is emotionally demanding. "A woman has to realize she's declaring war," says Nadine Taub of Rutgers School of Law. Erin Sneed, an attorney for Women for Change, Inc., in Dallas, says, "When a woman comes to me with a good case, my advice is to get another job before you do anything, because you don't want to be blackballed." For Mary K. Heelan, who won a landmark Title VII suit against Johns-Manville, the battle grew very personal. Before the trial, lawyers for her former employer asked her to name all of her previous sexual partners. "It was a ploy to make me think about the awful things they could do to me in court," she says. "It gave me second thoughts."

The psychological drain can be particularly severe in a university. "There needs to be a relationship of trust and even intimacy between student and professor," says attorney Catherine A. MacKinnon, the author of "Sexual Harassment of Working Women" and a teacher at Yale. "Sexual harassment can destroy even the possibility of learning." Affairs between professors and students have long been the subject of campus jokes, but women aren't laughing anymore. Harvard, Yale and the University of California, Berkeley, are among the institutions where formal charges have been filed. A lawsuit alleging that a Yale political-science professor promised an "A" grade in return for sexual intercourse is now pending in Federal appeals court.

One result of the new look at sexual harassment is the discovery that women are not the only victims. John[1], 32, married and a father, wanted to enroll in a federally funded training program. A higher-ranking single woman offered to guarantee his admission if he would sleep with her. He did, two or three times, and she provided the promised recommendation. But their relationship had other costs. "She made it very obvious in the office," John says. "She'd come over and say things like, 'I'm looking forward to tonight'." Hal, 31, a married federal bureaucrat, found that his new boss kept inviting him into her office where she would close the door and load the conversation with sexual innuendoes. After two months, she offered to become his sponsor in exchange for sex. "She was so blatant," he says now after transferring to another agency, "I felt like it was a reversal of a '40s movie and I was Betty Grable."

Hollywood's "casting couch" for a long time symbolized the mixture of sex and power in the workplace. Unquestionably, some young women — and men — still try to make their careers with their perfect bodies, and randy producers use professional clout to take advantage of them. "But it's more the exception than the rule now," says Norma Connolly, head of the Women's Committee of the Screen Actors Guild. Hollywood has taken clear steps to curtail sexual harassment. The guild has a watch-dog morals committee and a clause in SAG's industry contract forbids producers to ask actresses to interview in the nude.

No one believes that legalities will eliminate sexual harassment. "To do so places an unfair and totally unrealistic burden on women to come forward in an extremely difficult situation," says the EEOC's Norton. She and others contend that the answer lies in prevention: employers should be educated to treat the workplace as a job and not as a singles bar. To encourage this, the EEOC is preparing guidelines for employers that are expected to parallel rules against racial discrimination. Says Norton, "You can't have one standard for racial epithets and another for sexual."

Favors

The Office of Federal Contract Compliance Programs has already circulated for comment its own rules for companies doing business with the government. The regulations would forbid company officials to base any personnel decisions on sexual favors. Firms that violate OFCCP guidelines may be stripped of sizable federal contracts. Many private employers have begun to get the message. Some have incorporated prohibitions against sexual harassment into equal-employment programs and have pledged to deal promptly with grievances. And last December, the federal Office of Personnel Management announced that the government itself would not condone sexual harassment.

For the moment, a woman's best response remains a firm, polite, nonthreatening, "No." That is particularly true for verbal harassment unconnected to professional favor. Even sensitive men, women say, often will engage in this kind of banter unaware that they are offensive. If the man persists, some feminists endorse the actions of a Colorado woman who tired of being patted on her rump. She wheeled around and purposefully grabbed her harasser by his genitals. He didn't bother her anymore.

NOTE

1. Men who recount such incidents feel too humiliated and "emasculated" to give their full names for publication.

Symptoms of Groupthink among President Kennedy's Advisers

Irving L. Janis

According to the groupthink hypothesis, members of any small cohesive group tend to maintain esprit de corps by unconsciously developing a number of shared illusions and related norms that interfere with critical thinking and reality testing. If the available accounts describe the deliberations accurately, typical illusions can be discerned among the members of the Kennedy team during the period when they were deciding whether to approve the CIA's invasion plan.

THE ILLUSION OF INVULNERABILITY

An important symptom of groupthink is the illusion of being invulnerable to the main dangers that might arise from a risky action in which the group is strongly tempted to engage. Essentially, the notion is that "If our leader and everyone else in our group decides that it is okay, the plan is bound to succeed. Even if it is quite risky, luck will be on our side." A sense of "unlimited confidence" was widespread among the "New Frontiersmen" as soon as they took over their high government posts, according to a Justice Department confidant, with whom Robert Kennedy discussed the secret CIA plan on the day it was launched:

> It seemed that, with John Kennedy leading us and with all the talent he had assembled, *nothing could stop us*. We believed that if we faced up to the nation's problems and applied bold, new ideas with common sense and hard work, we would overcome whatever challenged us.

That this attitude was shared by the members of the President's inner circle is indicated by Schlesinger's statement that the men around Kennedy had enormous confidence in his ability and luck: "Everything had broken right for him since 1956. He had won the nomination and the election against all the odds in the book. Everyone around him thought he had the Midas touch and could not lose." Kennedy and his principal advisers were sophisticated and skeptical men, but they were, nevertheless, "affected by the euphoria of the new day." During the first three months after he took office — despite growing concerns created by the emerging crisis in Southeast Asia, the gold drain, and the Cuban exiles who were awaiting the go-ahead signal to invade Cuba — the dominant mood in the White House, according to Schlesinger, was "buoyant optimism." It was centered on the "promise of hope" held out by the President: *"Euphoria reigned; we thought for a moment that the world was plastic and the future unlimited."*. . .

Once this euphoric phase takes hold, decision-making for everyday activities, as well as long-range planning, is likely to be seriously impaired. The members of a cohesive group become very reluctant to carry out the unpleasant task of critically assessing the limits of their power and the real losses that could arise if their luck does not hold. They tend to examine each risk in black and white terms. If it does not seem overwhelmingly dangerous, they are inclined simply to forget about it, instead of developing contingency plans in case it materializes. The group members know that no one among them is a superman, but they feel that somehow the group is a supergroup, capable of surmounting all risks that stand in the way of carrying out any desired course of action: "Nothing can stop us!" Athletic teams and military combat units may often benefit from members' enthusiastic confidence in the power and luck of their group. But policy-making committees usually do not. . . .

THE ILLUSION OF UNANIMITY

When a group of people who respect each other's opinions arrive at a unanimous view, each member is likely to feel that the belief must be true. This reliance on consensual validation tends to replace individual critical thinking and reality-testing, unless there are clear-cut disagreements among the members. The members of a face-to-face group often become inclined, without quite realizing it, to prevent latent disagreements from surfacing when they are about to initiate a risky course of action. The group leader and the members support each other, playing up the areas of convergence in their thinking, at the expense of fully exploring divergences that might disrupt the apparent unity of the group. Better to share a pleasant, balmy group atmosphere than to be battered in a storm.

This brings us to the second outstanding symptom of groupthink manifested by the Kennedy team—a shared illusion of unanimity. In the formal sessions dealing with the Cuban invasion plan, the group's consensus that the basic features of the CIA plan should be adopted was relatively free of disagreement.

According to Sorensen, "No strong voice of opposition was raised in any of the key meetings, and no realistic alternatives were presented." According to Schlesinger, "the massed and caparisoned authority of his senior officials in the realm of foreign policy and defense was unanimous for going ahead. . . . Had one senior adviser opposed the adventure, I believe that Kennedy would have canceled it. No one spoke against it."

Perhaps the most crucial of Schlesinger's observations is, "Our meetings took place in a *curious atmosphere of assumed consensus*." His additional comments clearly show that the assumed consensus was an illusion that could be maintained only because the major participants did not reveal their own reasoning or discuss their idiosyncratic assumptions and vague reservations. President Kennedy thought that prime consideration was being given to his prohibition of direct military intervention by the United States. He assumed that the operation had been pared down to a kind of unobtrusive infiltration that, if reported in the newspapers, would be buried in the inside pages. Rusk was certainly not on the same wavelength as the President, for at one point he suggested that it might be better to have the invaders fan out from the United States naval base at Guantánamo, rather than land at the Bay of Pigs, so they could readily retreat to the base if necessary. Implicit in his suggestion was a lack of concern about revealing United States military support as well as implicit distrust in the assumption made by the others about the ease of escaping from the Bay of Pigs. But discussion of Rusk's strange proposal was evidently dropped long before he was induced to reveal whatever vague misgivings he may have had about the Bay of Pigs plan. At meetings in the State Department, according to Roger Hilsman, who worked closely with him, "Rusk asked penetrating questions that frequently caused us to reexamine our position." But at the White House meetings Rusk said little except to offer gentle warnings about avoiding excesses.

As usually happens in cohesive groups, the members assumed that "silence gives consent." Kennedy and the others supposed that Rusk was in substantial agreement with what the CIA representatives were saying about the soundness of the invasion plan. But about one week before the invasion was scheduled, when Schlesinger told Rusk in private about his objections to the plan, Rusk, surprisingly, offered no arguments against Schlesinger's objections. He said that he had been wanting for some time to draw up a balance sheet of the pros and cons and that he was annoyed at the Joint Chiefs because "they are perfectly willing to put the President's head on the block, but they recoil at doing anything which might risk Guantánamo." At that late date, he evidently still preferred his suggestion to launch the invasion from the United States naval base in Cuba, even though doing so would violate President Kennedy's stricture against involving America's armed forces.

McNamara's assumptions about the invasion were quite different from both Rusk's and Kennedy's. McNamara thought that the main objective was to touch off a revolt of the Cuban people to overthrow Castro. The members of the group who knew something about Cuban politics and Castro's popular support must have had strong doubts about this assumption. Why did they fail to convey their misgivings at any of the meetings?

SUPPRESSION OF PERSONAL DOUBTS

The sense of group unity concerning the advisability of going ahead with the CIA's invasion plan appears to have been based on superficial appearances of complete concurrence, achieved at the cost of self-censorship of misgivings by several of the members. From post-mortem discussions with participants, Sorensen concluded that among the men in the State Department, as well as those on the White House staff, "doubts were entertained but never pressed, partly out of a fear of being labelled 'soft' or undaring in the eyes of their colleagues." Schlesinger was not at all hesitant about presenting his strong objections in a memorandum he gave to the President and the Secretary of State. But he became keenly aware of his tendency to suppress objections when he attended the White House meetings of the Kennedy team, with their atmosphere of assumed consensus:

> In the months after the Bay of Pigs I bitterly reproached myself
> for having kept so silent during those crucial discussions in the

Cabinet Room, though my feelings of guilt were tempered by the knowledge that a course of objection would have accomplished little save to *gain me a name as a nuisance*. I can only explain my failure to do more than raise a few timid questions by reporting that one's impulse to blow the whistle on this nonsense was simply undone by the *circumstances of the discussion*.

Whether or not his retrospective explanation includes all his real reasons for having remained silent, Schlesinger appears to have been quite aware of the need to refrain from saying anything that would create a nuisance by breaking down the assumed consensus.[1]

Participants in the White House meetings, like members of many other discussion groups, evidently felt reluctant to raise questions that might cast doubt on a plan that they thought was accepted by the consensus of the group, for fear of evoking disapproval from their associates. This type of fear is probably not the same as fear of losing one's effectiveness or damaging one's career. Many forthright men who are quite willing to speak their piece despite risks to their career become silent when faced with the possibility of losing the approval of fellow members of their primary work group. The discrepancy between Schlesinger's critical memoranda and his silent acquiescence during the meetings might be an example of this.

Schlesinger says that when the Cuban invasion plan was being presented to the group, "virile poses" were conveyed in the rhetoric used by the representatives of the CIA and the Joint Chiefs of Staff. He thought the State Department representatives and others responded by becoming anxious to show that they were not softheaded idealists but really were just as tough as the military men. Schlesinger's references to the "virile" stance of the militant advocates of the invasion plan suggest that the members of Kennedy's in-group may have been concerned about protecting the leader from being embarrassed by their voicing "unvirile" concerns about the high risks of the venture. . . .

SELF-APPOINTED MINDGUARDS

Among the well-known phenomena of group dynamics is the alacrity with which members of a cohesive in-group suppress deviational points of view by putting social pressure on any member who begins to express a view that deviates from the dominant beliefs of the group, to make sure that he will not disrupt the consensus of the group as a whole. This pressure often takes the form of urging the dissident member to remain silent if he cannot match up his own beliefs with those of the rest of the group. At least one dramatic instance of this type of pressure occurred a few days after President Kennedy had said, "we seem now destined to go ahead on a quasi-minimum basis." This was still several days before the final decision was made.

At a large birthday party for his wife, Robert Kennedy, who had been constantly informed about the Cuban invasion plan, took Schlesinger aside and asked him why he was opposed. The President's brother listened coldly and then said, "You might be right or you may be wrong, but the President has made his mind up. Don't push it any further. Now is the time for everyone to help him all they can." Here is another symptom of groupthink, displayed by a highly intelligent man whose ethical code committed him to freedom of dissent. What he was saying, in effect was, "You may well be right about the dangerous risks, but I don't give a damn about that; all of us should help our leader right now by not sounding any discordant notes that would interfere with the harmonious support he should have."

When Robert Kennedy told Schlesinger to lay off, he was functioning in a self-appointed role that I call being a "mindguard." Just as a bodyguard protects the President and other high officials from injurious physical assaults, a mindguard protects them from thoughts that might damage their confidence in the soundness of the policies to which they are committed or to which they are about to commit themselves.

At least one other member of the Kennedy team, Secretary of State Rusk, also effectively functioned as a mindguard, protecting the leader and the members from unwelcome ideas that might set them to thinking about unfavorable consequences of their preferred course of action and that might lead to dissension instead of a comfortable consensus. Undersecretary of State Chester Bowles, who had attended a White House meeting at which he was given no opportunity to express his dissenting views, decided not to continue to remain silent about such a vital matter. He prepared a strong memorandum for Secretary Rusk opposing the CIA plan and, keeping well within the prescribed bureaucratic channels, requested Rusk's permission to present his case to the President. Rusk told Bowles that there was no need for any concern, that the invasion plan would be dropped in favor of a quiet little guerrilla infiltration. Rusk may have believed this at the time, but at subsequent White House meetings he must soon have learned otherwise. Had Rusk transmitted the undersecretary's memorandum, the urgent warnings it contained might have reinforced Schlesinger's memorandum and jolted some of Kennedy's ingroup, if not Kennedy himself, to reconsider the decision. But Rusk kept Bowles's memorandum firmly buried in the State Department files.

Rusk may also have played a similar role in preventing Kennedy and the others from learning about the strong objections raised by Edward R. Murrow, whom the President had just appointed director of the United States Information Agency. In yet another instance, Rusk appears to have functioned as a dogged mindguard, protecting the group from the opposing ideas of a government official with access to information that could have enabled him to assess the political consequences of the Cuban invasion better than anyone present at the White House meetings could. As director of intelligence and research in the State Department, Roger Hilsman got wind of the invasion plan from his colleague Allen Dulles and strongly warned Secretary Rusk of the dangers. He asked Rusk for permission to allow the Cuban experts in his department to scrutinize thoroughly the assumptions relevant to their expertise. "I'm sorry," Rusk told him, "but I can't let you. This is being too tightly held." Rusk's reaction struck Hilsman as strange because all the relevant men in his department already had top security clearance. Hilsman assumed that Rusk turned down his urgent request because of pressure from Dulles and Bissel to adhere to the CIA's special security restrictions. But if so, why, when so much was at stake, did the Secretary of State fail to communicate to the President or to anyone else in the core group that his most trusted intelligence expert had grave doubts about the invasion plan and felt that it should be appraised by the Cuban specialists? As a result of Rusk's handling of Hilsman's request, the President and his advisers remained in the curious position, as Hilsman put it, of making an important political judgment without the benefit of advice from the government's most relevant intelligence experts. . . .

DOCILITY FOSTERED BY SUAVE LEADERSHIP

The group pressures that help to maintain a group's illusions are sometimes fostered by various leadership practices, some of which involve subtle ways of making it difficult for those who question the initial consensus to suggest alternatives and to raise critical issues. The group's agenda can readily be manipulated by a suave leader, often with the tacit approval of the members, so that there is simply no opportunity to discuss the drawbacks of a seemingly satisfactory plan of action. This is one of the conditions that fosters groupthink.

President Kennedy, as leader at the meetings in the White House, was probably more active than anyone else in raising skeptical questions; yet he seems to have encouraged the group's docility and uncritical acceptance of the defective arguments in favor of the CIA's plan. At each meeting, instead of opening up the agenda to permit a full airing of the opposing considerations, he allowed the CIA representatives to dominate the entire discussion. The President permitted them to refute immediately each tentative doubt that one of the others might express, instead of asking whether anyone else had the same doubt or wanted to pursue the implications of the new worrisome issue that had been raised.

Moreover, although the President went out of his way to bring to a crucial meeting an outsider who was an eloquent opponent of the invasion plan, his style of conducting the meeting presented no opportunity for discussion of the controversial issues that were raised. The visitor was Senator J. William Fulbright. The occasion was the climactic meeting of April 4, 1961, held at the State Department, at which the apparent consensus that had emerged in earlier meetings was seemingly confirmed by an open straw vote. The President invited Senator Fulbright after the Senator had made known his concern about newspaper stories forecasting a United States invasion of Cuba. At the meeting, Fulbright was given an opportunity to present his opposing views. In a "sensible and strong" speech Fulbright correctly predicted many of the damaging effects the invasion would have on United States foreign relations. The President did not open the floor to discussion of the questions raised in Fulbright's rousing speech. Instead, he returned to the procedure he had initiated earlier in the meeting; he asked each person around the table to state his final judgment and after Fulbright had taken his turn, he continued the straw vote around the table. McNamara said he approved the plan. Berle was also for it; his advice was to "let her rip." Mann, who had been on the fence, also spoke in favor of it.

Picking up a point mentioned by Berle, who had said he approved but did not insist on "a major production," President Kennedy changed the agenda by asking what could be done to make the infiltration more quiet. Following discussion of this question — quite remote from the fundamental moral and political issues raised by Senator Fulbright — the meeting ended. Schlesinger mentions that the meeting broke up before completion of the intended straw vote around the table. Thus, wittingly or unwittingly, the President conducted the meeting in such a way that not only was there no time to discuss the potential dangers to United States foreign relations raised by Senator Fulbright, but there was also no time to call upon Schlesinger, the one man present who the President knew strongly shared Senator Fulbright's misgivings.

Of course, one or more members of the group could have prevented this by-passing by suggesting that the group discuss Senator Fulbright's arguments and requesting that Schlesinger and the others who had not been called upon be given the opportunity to state their views. But no one made such a request.

The President's demand that each person, in turn, state his overall judgment, especially after having just heard an outsider oppose the group consensus, must have put the members on their mettle. These are exactly the conditions that most strongly foster docile conformity to a group's norms. After listening to an opinion leader (McNamara, for example) express his unequivocal acceptance, it becomes more difficult than ever for other members to state a different view. Open straw votes generally put pressure on each individual to agree with the apparent group consensus, as has been shown by well-known social psychological experiments.

A few days before the crucial meeting of April 4, another outsider who might have challenged some of the group's illusions attended one of the meetings but was never given the opportunity to speak his piece. At the earlier meeting, the outsider was the acting Secretary of State, Chester Bowles, attending in place of Secretary Rusk, who was abroad at a SEATO conference. Like Senator Fulbright, Bowles was incredulous and at times even "horrified" at the group's complacent acceptance of the CIA's invasion plans. However, President Kennedy had no idea what Bowles was thinking about the plan, and he probably felt that Bowles was there more in the role of a reporter to keep Rusk up to date on the deliberations than as a participant in the discussion. In any case, the President neglected to give the group the opportunity to hear the reactions of a fresh mind; he did not call upon Bowles at any time. Bowles sat through the meeting in complete silence. He felt he could not break with formal bureaucratic protocol, which prevents an undersecretary from volunteering his opinion unless directed to do so by his chief or by the President. Bowles behaved in the prescribed way and confined his protestations to a State Department memorandum addressed to Rusk, which, as we have seen, was not communicated to the President. . . .

During the Bay of Pigs planning sessions, President Kennedy, probably unwittingly, allowed the one-sided CIA memoranda to monopolize the attention of the group by failing to circulate opposing statements that might have stimulated an intensive discussion of the drawbacks and might therefore have revealed the illusory nature of the group's consensus. Although the President read and privately discussed the strongly opposing memoranda prepared by Schlesinger and Senator Fulbright, he never distributed them to the policy-makers whose critical judgment he was seeking. Kennedy also knew that Joseph Newman, a foreign correspondent who had just visited Cuba, had written a series of incisive articles that disagreed with forecasts concerning the ease of generating a revolt against Castro. But, although he invited Newman to the White House for a chat, he did not distribute Newman's impressive writings to the advisory group. . . .

THE TABOO AGAINST ANTAGONIZING VALUABLE NEW MEMBERS

It seems likely that one of the reasons the members of the core group accepted the President's restricted agenda and his extraordinarily indulgent treatment of the CIA representatives was that a kind of informal group norm had developed, producing a desire to avoid saying anything that could be construed as an attack on the CIA's plan. The group apparently accepted a kind of taboo against voicing damaging criticisms. This may have been another important factor contributing to the group's tendency to indulge in groupthink.

How could such a norm come into being? Why would President Kennedy give preferential treatment to the two CIA representatives? Why would Bundy, McNamara, Rusk, and the others on his team fail to challenge this preferential treatment and accept a taboo against voicing critical opposition? A few clues permit some conjectures to be made, although we have much less evidence to go on than for delineating the pattern of preferential treatment itself.

It seems that Allen Dulles and Richard Bissell, despite being holdovers from the Eisenhower administration, were not considered outsiders by the inner core of the Kennedy team. President Kennedy and his closest associates did not place these two men in the same category as the Joint Chiefs of Staff, who were seen as members of an outside military clique established during the earlier admin-istration, men whose primary loyalties belonged elsewhere and whose presence at the White House meetings was tolerated as a necessary requirement of governmental protocol. (Witness Secre-tary Rusk's unfriendly comments about the Joint Chiefs being more loyal to their military group in the Pentagon than to the Pres-ident, when he was conversing privately with fellow in-group mem-ber Schlesinger.) President Kennedy and those in his inner circle admired Dulles and Bissell, regarded them as valuable new mem-bers of the Kennedy team, and were pleased to have them on board. Everyone in the group was keenly aware of the fact that Bissell had been devoting his talents with great intensity for over a year to de-veloping the Cuban invasion project and that Dulles was also deeply committed to it. Whenever Bissell presented his arguments, "we all listened transfixed," Schlesinger informs us, "fascinated by the workings of this superbly clear, organized and articulate intelli-gence." Schlesinger reports that Bissell was regarded by the group as "a man of high character and remarkable intellectual gifts." In short, he was accepted as a highly prized member.

The sense of power of the core group was probably enhanced by the realization that the two potent bureaucrats who were in control of America's extensive intelligence network were affiliated with the Kennedy team. The core members of the team would certainly want to avoid antagonizing or alienating them. They would be inclined, therefore, to soft-pedal their criticisms of the CIA plan and perhaps even to suspend their critical judgment in evaluating it. . . .

The picture we get, therefore, is that the two CIA representatives, both highly esteemed men who had recently joined the Kennedy team, were presenting their "baby" to the rest of the team. As pro-tagonists, they had a big head start toward eliciting a favorable con-sensus. New in-group members would be listened to much more sympathetically and much less critically than outsiders representing an agency that might be trying to sell one of its own pet projects to the new President.

Hilsman, who also respected the two men, says that Dulles and Bissell "had become emotionally involved . . . so deeply involved in the development of the Cuban invasion plans that they were no longer able to see clearly or to judge soundly." He adds, "There was so deep a commitment, indeed, that there was an unconscious effort to confine consideration of the proposed operation to as small a number of people as possible, so as to avoid too harsh or thorough a scrutiny of the plans." If Hilsman is correct, it is reasonable to assume that the two men managed to convey to the other members of the Kennedy team their strong desire "to avoid too harsh or thorough a scrutiny. . . ."[2]

NOTES

1. Schlesinger's somewhat self-abasing confession about his failure to present his objections at the group meetings might be a symptom of persisting loyalty to the dead leader and to the group. He appears to be saying, in effect, "Don't put all the blame on President Kennedy or on the other leading members of our team." This theme is not apparent in other portions of Schlesinger's account of the Bay of Pigs fiasco, which level many serious criticisms against the Kennedy team and is far from a whitewash. Still, at present there is no way of knowing to what extent a protective attitude colors Schlesinger's description of how the CIA's invasion plan came to be accepted at the White House. The same problem arises, of course, for all accounts by pro-Kennedy authors, especially Sorensen (who has sought to gain political office on his record as a participant on the Kennedy team and his close personal ties with the Kennedy brothers). My only solution to the problem of subtle distortions and biased reporting is to take the position that *if* the facts reported by Schlesinger, Sorensen, and the other authors are essentially accurate, my analysis of the converging pattern of this "evidence" leads to the conclusion that the groupthink hypothesis helps to account for the deficiencies in the decision-making of the Kennedy team.

2. Bureaucratic political considerations might also have contributed to the group norm of trying to keep the two new members of the team happy. The President and his senior advisers may have realized that if they asked Dulles and Bissell too many embarrassing questions and appeared to be rejecting the work of their agency, the two chiefs of the CIA might be pushed in the direction of becoming allied with the military men in the Pentagon, who were already supporting them, rather than with the Kennedy team in the White House.

Another contributing factor might have been the President's personal receptivity to the idea of taking aggressive action against Castro. Although somewhat skeptical of the plan, Kennedy may have welcomed the opportunity to make good on his campaign pledge to aid the anti-Castro rebels. According to Sorensen, the opportunity to inflict a blow against Castro was especially appealing to the President: "He should never have permitted his own deep feeling against Castro (unusual for him) and considerations of public opinion — specifically his concern that he would be assailed for calling off a plan to get rid of Castro — to overcome his innate suspicion."

Obviously, these ancillary political and psychological factors are not symptoms of groupthink. But they may have reinforced the group norms conducive to concurrence-seeking and thus could be regarded in the same general category as biased leadership practices — that is, as conditions that foster groupthink.

Passions at Work

Dick Dabney

The other day I was in an office downtown, looking out the picture window toward the Washington Monument and the slow-sliding Potomac, which glinted in the sunlight like a knife blade. I was talking to an old friend, a GS-16 making more than $50,000 a year. As usual, he was fed up with his job and, as usual, didn't see anything he could do about it.

"Working in the bureaucracy," he was saying, "means living in hate like fish in water. But what's the alternative?"

His side door opened on to the office of a GS-18, his boss. Now, as murmuring came from there, he lowered his voice.

"You go from hating the dungeon master," he said, "to hating the system, to hating everything." He lowered his voice even more.

"There's this thing I've caught myself doing at the end of every phone conversation. Just as I hang up, I snarl, 'And *up yours!*' I mean *every* conversation — whether it's with my wife, or psychiatrist, or whoever. Each time shaving it closer. By now, I'm microseconds away from the time when somebody could hear me. But what in the hell are you going to do?"

A buzzer went off. My friend hurried into the GS-18's office. I sat there, watching the red-white-and-blue flags whipping in the wind blowing off the river, and trying not to listen to what was going on next door. Somebody was shouting, a man with a high-pitched voice like that of Don Knotts. My friend's answers, if there were any, were so muted I could not hear them.

"What do you mean, you can't explain it? . . . Hell, that's no excuse. I mean, the *Secretary* was there, for Christ's sake, and there weren't even any cocktail napkins out. Here I am letting you run the division and you haven't even got the sense to put out the napkins. Can you stand there and tell me what I'm going to do with you? Jesus Christ. I don't know what your mother taught you when you were growing up. Probably wiped her mouth on her goddamned sleeve. You disgust me. Get out of here."

When my friend came back into his office, he glanced at me and saw that I'd heard. An unless I miss my guess, I'll not see him again soon, for he's not without a sense of shame.

As I was leaving, he shook my hand firmly and told me in a deep, executive voice that we would have to get together soon. After the door closed behind him, I lingered next to it for a moment—and, sure enough, heard him say: "And *up yours!*"

Abridged and reprinted from *The Washingtonian*, March 1981, copyright © 1981. Reproduced by permission.

Afterward, I kept turning over in my mind a remark made to me earlier by Dr. Elliot Liebow, a cultural anthropologist. "Most people," he said, "would be ashamed for their children to see them at work."

Three decades ago the sociologist C. Wright Mills wrote that white-collar workers spent most of their energies on the job feigning goodwill and repressing hostility.

Mills was customarily dismissed as a leftist who sought to disparage his culture rather than to study it in any objective way. Liebow, however, chief of the Work and American Life division of the National Institute of Mental Health, cannot be dismissed as a man with an ax to grind. What's more, when he speaks of the psychic torture of the white-collar world, he tends to include among those adversely affected not only low-level workers but also middle and upper management and professionals working in corporations.

But Liebow, like many mental-health professionals, knows that this subject is politically loaded—knows that, although hate in the office is a psychic reality of our time, acknowledging its existence is treason against the free-enterprise system. This, he says, is why the NIMH routinely turns down all research proposals on the subject as being "antimanagement."

An employee's normality, after all, is defined by management — which is to say that the industrial psychologists who prescribe proper behavior customarily play for the house. Thus, most of the studies done on the debilitating conditions of modern work are more concerned with shoehorning employees into the system than they are with alleviating distress. Such studies tend to take the gratuitous psychic stresses of work as a "given," the way my friend the GS-16 did. For cultural historians, however, the radically unhealthy conditions of office work not only are new but also smack of perversion. Moreover, it is by no means clear that people can "adjust" to them, any more than they can adjust to high doses of radiation.

When I asked Dr. Avery Andrews, a medieval historian at George Washington University, to compare the life of the modern office worker with that of the medieval serf, he said the serf had been better off, no question about it.

"Not only was he freer," he said, "but his life had more dignity to it. To a serf in, say, 1100, the closeness of supervision such as that experienced in a modern office was unknown. Tradition, rather than somebody standing over his shoulder, told him what crops to plant and when to harvest them. Then too, what the lord of the manor wanted from him was simple — for instance, so many bushels of potatoes — and not some kind of complicated psychic response. And because the lord's authority was established by tradition, whatever hatred the serf may have felt toward that authority was sporadic and quick to fade — not the settled, brooding, gut-wracking thing that poisons the lives of so many workers today.

"But the modern worker, having been brought up in a democracy, tends to regard all authority as arbitrary, and to resent it. At the same time, because his very identity is defined by his work, he's afraid to express that resentment. This is because of ambition, which drives him toward achieving a position not given him by birth, and because of fear of being fired, which would not only hurt him economically but also reduce him to the status of nonperson. The serf, on the other hand, could never be promoted or dislodged, saw the lord maybe only a couple of times a year, and wasn't servant to the whim of somebody staring at him eight hours a day in an office. And, had he foreseen such a prospect, he would have regarded it as a vision of hell.

"The trouble with saying something like this," Andrews concluded, "is that it gets you labeled as a hippie or Communist."

That's true. Most of the literature on the unhealthy psychic conditions of modern work either tends to be devoid of concern for the human victims or appears parenthetically in diatribes against American life as a whole. The official culture takes the position that work is virtuous and that there must be something wrong with anyone who can't "fit in." The counterculture rages back that the nine-to-five routine is degrading and that those who participate in it are contemptible. But many American workers feel themselves caught somewhere in between; they know that something is wrong with the more gratuitous aspects of work but see no way out.

Instead, they seek out goods and services that they hope will alleviate their distress — psychotherapy, religion, alcohol, tranquilizers. But the cause of the trouble in the first place is often looked on as immutable and hence not worthy of study.

Recently, however, there have been some interesting efforts made toward understanding the pathological conditions of modern office work. These have been undertaken by psychoanalysts, sociologists, social psychologists, and cultural anthropologists — some of these operating without any knowledge of the others' work. Outstanding among them are Douglas LaBier, Michael Maccoby, Leonard Pearlin, Elliot Liebow, Otto Kernberg, Carmi Schooler, Clarice Radabaugh, and Morton Lieberman.

Because this work is being undertaken in separate studies, each of the scientists contributing to it would probably want to disclaim any endorsement of the general outline that emerges here — one that seems to confirm Andrews's statement that the typical white-collar worker is worse off than the medieval serf.

Typically, and with all exceptions noted, there seem to be two, coexisting systems of authority in offices: the rational one that gets the business done — whereby, say, the president dictates a letter to his secretary, who types it and gives it to a clerk who mails it — and a second, irrational system of dominance and submission having nothing to do with business — whereby, for instance, the president might ask the secretary humiliating questions about her sex life.

Of course, the rational system itself may engender ill will — the ordinary clashes attendant on getting the job done. But in the hidden, paralleling psychic system — often inadequately described by industrial psychologists as a "dependency system" — hatred becomes a way of life, the webbing of a net strung according to patterns closely akin to those of sadomasochism. . . .

The hidden pattern often found in the "psychostructure" of American offices is characterized by a sadomasochistic control that goes far beyond the rational needs of the organization — a control that is typically enforced not by pyrotechnical dressings down of the sort I overheard but by a series of small, highly charged humiliations. Thus, new employees are tested to determine whether they want to "play" — become subject to heavier bondage and, in turn, receive tacit permission to inflict a similar sadistic dominance on those below. One speaks here, then, of a kind of "fear ladder," which Norman Mailer in 1948 prophesied would come to characterize American life in the second half of the twentieth century.

By "sadism," however, one does not mean the desire to inflict pain on others but that deeper and more infantile itch to be God, to be in total control of another human being — an itch often accompanied by the desire to be controlled oneself.

This definition of sadism was first popularized by Erich Fromm, who held that the healthy unfolding of human character is progress from dependency to autonomy, and from irrational selfishness to reason, altruism, and the flowering of creativity. To him, psychopathology was essentially regressive, an infantile attempt to recreate the illusion of total safety and omnipotence through passivity, narcissism, and sadism.

Fromm did not write extensively on the psychosocial conditions of work, although he did leave behind a number of suggestive passages, such as that on the meaning of the little smile the post-office clerk has at the corner of his mouth when he closes the window at precisely 5:30 — not because he is ignorant of the fact that the last two people waiting in line have been there for an hour but because he *knows* it. In any case, two of Fromm's students, Douglas LaBier and Michael Maccoby, have taken up where he left off.

LaBier recently circulated, privately, a study called "Passions at Work," the report of an investigation into whether "work and career development . . . interact with the forces of human character in ways which stimulate psychopathology." This study was conducted among "the lower, middle, and upper levels of work and management of ten organizations in the federal government," including "managers and non-managers, men and women, . . . administrative, scientific, technical, legal, policy-making, legislative, and regulatory personnel." . . .

Not only are sadomasochistic patterns woven deeply into many Washington offices, LaBier found, but the psychostructure of bureaucracy itself actually seems to attract and reward irrationality and destructiveness, and to bring out those qualities among workers who were not that way to begin with. Like Maccoby, whose studies have focused on executives in high-technology corporations, LaBier found that modern bureaucracies elevate "qualities of the head," such as intellectual innovation, technological expertise, and the ability to manipulate others while feeling nothing, above "qualities of the heart," such as compassion, idealism, courage, and the capacity to love. The people most likely to experience emotional distress, he found, are those another era might have considered "normal" — people unable to surrender qualities of the heart to the psychotic demands of work.

Normal people, LaBier found, often tend to be victims in the dark underworld of office politics and as a result develop a number of symptoms of emotional distress: chronic anxiety, depression, erratic behavior on the job, hostile behavior at home. Characteristically, the victims studied often came to the conclusion that something was wrong with *them*, and it sometimes took a lot of counseling before they could be made to entertain the notion that something might be wrong with the job.

In private conversation, LaBier speaks of this as "the SS syndrome" and points out that, presumably, there were men working in the extermination camps who were disturbed by what they saw and, convinced that there was something wrong with them, went to psychiatrists; just as there were others who were looked upon by the industrial psychologists of Nazi Germany as "healthy, stable people."

There are a lot of "healthy, stable people" among modern office workers, too. Many of these, LaBier found, belong to a second large category of workers, whom he calls "power seekers." These people, ideally suited to rise, either lack the qualities of heart to begin with or have learned how to live as "crustaceans"—hard on the outside, soft within, "a body looking for a backbone." Moreover, although frequently living constricted, destructive lives, these power seekers do not have the sense that anything is wrong with them, develop little of the emotional distress that leads the "victims" to seek counseling, and are far less likely to end up in psychiatric treatment.

LaBier divides power seekers into two subcategories: masochists and sadists — or, in his words, "ass-kissers" and "ass-kickers." For both, life outside the office has become largely irrelevant.

For instance, he describes one conspicuously successful young ass-kisser, a bureaucrat in his early thirties who lived in a one-room apartment, to which he came home late from work each night, to fall asleep on an army cot while watching the *Tonight* show. There was nothing else in the apartment but a clock-radio and some cardboard boxes full of belongings. This man's wife had left him several years before, taking their children, but he felt no sense of loss and got up each morning eager to hurry to the office, where life was lived out in dominance-submission games, and where he was consistently being promoted for being a good boy.

The sadists, he found, often justify their drivenness, and their harsh behavior toward others, on the basis of "public service" — important programs that only ass-kicking can push through. In such an environment, LaBier found, "accomplishment" is often illusory. "It appears that at the highest levels of the bureaucracy what is valued most is the ability to appear and act tough; to put down others and humiliate them; to constantly test others; and to produce a flurry of activity upon demand. . . . Although the atmosphere created is one in which it appears that something important and powerful is being done, one finds, in some settings, that there is little substance or consequence to all the activity."

One of his subjects told him: "When you take a good look at things, you see that the work is not really all that important, and that what you're really after is power — exciting power. It's crazy, but nobody seems to recognize it."

The truth, of course, is that many millions of workers do recognize it and seek to stay somewhere off to the side of the bondage games that often make up the core of working reality. But this is not always possible; for while the "pencil-pushers" — those who have specialized skills such as accounting or operating a television camera — can often avoid the games if they want to, if they are willing to live without any hope of ever rising to the top, the "people-pushers" — those whose jobs consist primarily of manipulating others — may be obliged to play or get out. This is perhaps because their literal jobs are seen as requiring the same skills that the bondage games do. In other words, the sadomasochistic net often *is* the chain of command.

Because of this, as Elliot Liebow has pointed out, playing the interlocking games that make up the system may offer considerable rewards. An employee willing to become totally dominated by a sadistic boss — no matter how subtly such domination is carried out — takes on value that goes far beyond being able to get a job done. The psychic payoffs are similar to those obtainable on the short term at any sadomasochistic bar, whereby one who feels powerless when confronted by the vastness of the world can put the quietus to anxiety by coming to be like God—dominating the actions, gestures, tones of voice, and facial expressions of another person. True, these are perverse satisfactions. But that is what we are talking about. Moreover, the person being dominated is not without satisfaction, for to be totally under the rule of another—the further under the better—is to shed guilt and reachieve the paradise of childhood, too.

Real knowledge of the kicks to be had is perhaps limited to those who experience them. But most employees know that the more they are willing to degrade themselves, the more job security they have. Thus, those whose policy it is to stay outside the game structure are often tempted to play anyway. With that temptation comes self-loathing and an intense contempt for an organization that offers the employee only two choices: failure or castration. And so rage at work is by no means limited to the rat-games players and is never fully discharged within the office itself, even by them. The social effects of this are devastating.

Rage kills. Each year, tens of thousands of Americans have strokes or heart attacks that are the direct result of carrying around a hatred from which they could not escape, whether for considerations of practicality or of honor. Tens of thousands of others develop high blood pressure, ulcers, heart disease, chronic anxiety states. Many others suffer emotional breakdowns.

Moreover, rage, which is never fully sated at the office, tends to spill over into the home, expressing itself in abusiveness toward spouses and children, alcoholism, or a stoic emotional withdrawal that's really about nine parts shame. Thus, for millions of Americans, "living a normal life" becomes a heroic task. For, as Liebow points out, "powerlessness corrupts," and it is supremely difficult to come home and assume an adult's role in the family circle after one has played at being a child all day.

Efforts to deal with such hell may take a number of forms. Those who decide that the trouble is with them, rather than with the work, are typical, and hence Americans by the millions may seek out one or several of the estimated 250 methods of psychotherapy currently being practiced in this country—methods whose "cure rate" is about the same as that experienced by persons who have had no treatment at all. In the last thirty years, one form of therapy has vied with another over who is going to be in charge of damage-control.

"I make about $250,000 a year out of people who are going ape-shit on the job," a Washington psychiatrist recently told me, "and help maybe one in twenty. But even that one is likely to keep coming back. Because he is going to go on believing—in some cases, *has* to believe —that the causes are back in his childhood, or in some weird private thinking he's doing.

"All I can offer is first aid — a place where the guy can spit out some of the rage that's choking him and where he can be reassured that he's not going crazy. But how could there *be* any cure for somebody who works in an Osterizer? Of course, every week sees some promoter hustling a would-be answer — mud therapy, scream therapy, est, transactional analysis. To say nothing of the literal gurus to whom people flock for about the same reasons they come to us. Many people get into trouble in the first place by acting like children — weak, passive, and confused, and without enough backbone to stand up for their own dignity at work — so it isn't surprising that they look for someplace where they can be *cured* as children, without being obliged to grow up."

Others, who either despair of getting out of the game or don't want to, decide to play it as skillfully as possible, and these are the consumers of assertiveness-training seminars and books on power in the office. Still others, who won't or can't play, drop out into the counterculture or flip out into madness — often raging with the paranoid conviction that some crafty group — capitalists, Jews, or aliens from deep space — is behind the psychic hell that modern work has become.

Most American workers, however, when under stress of this kind, don't drop out, follow a guru, or seek psychiatric help. Instead, they try to cope with the situation with the resources at hand. This raises the question of which kinds of coping efforts are the most effective.

This question, as it happens, has been systematically investigated for close to a decade now by sociologist Leonard I. Pearlin. The results have been published piecemeal in the *American Journal of Sociology,* the *Journal of Health and Social Behavior,* and elsewhere. Pearlin's is an ongoing study, based on in-depth interviews with 2,300 men and women between 18 and 65 in metropolitan Chicago. Pearlin and his coworkers identified four major "role areas" — marriage, parenting, household economics, and occupation — and set out to study how people try to cope with "life strains" arising out of each.

In doing so, Pearlin and his colleagues concerned themselves both with "psychological set" (the person's position when confronted by stress-producing situations) and "coping responses" (what the person actually *did* to try to come to terms with unsatisfactory experiences in each of the role areas).

Examples of psychological set include such built-in attitudes as freedom from self-recrimination, the presence of favorable attitudes toward oneself, and the settled conviction that one's life is under one's own control. Coping responses consisted of the ability to remind oneself that others had it even tougher, to hope that things would turn out all right in the long run, to ignore things that could not be helped, and to be able to put up with the negative aspects of a situation in order to receive the positive rewards.

In the first three role areas — marriage, parenting, and household economics — it was found that the psychological set worked better in some cases and the coping responses in others, and that a wide variety of responses from which to choose usually augured well for the eventual success of those trying to cope.

In the fourth area, occupation, nothing seemed to work: not the right attitudes, not the right responses, not anything.

"In occupation, finally," Pearlin found, "stress hinges much more closely on psychological resources than on specific responses, although . . . *neither has an appreciable part in buffering the stressful effect of job strains* [my italics]." The only kind of response that was even marginally effective over the broad spectrum of persons studied was leaving one's personality behind when one went to work. Or, as Pearlin put it: "Stress is less likely to result when people disengage themselves from involvement."

Pearlin's study is large, carefully framed, abstrusely expressed, and massively documented, and one does damage to its essential meaning by synopsizing it here in such shorthand fashion. However, it seems important to do so, because his work not only tends to confirm that of LaBier and Liebow but also raises more clearly the question of whether the present psychological structure of work is really "part of the human condition" — something that people en masse could adapt to, if they only knew how — or whether it is so radically unnatural that a social system founded on it — as ours is — can be said to have anything but a short life expectancy.

After all, the mental hospitals, welfare rolls, and countercultures, which take in the casualties of work, are not self-supporting and cannot continue to expand forever. Moreover, there is a hidden, gargantuan cost in nonproductivity that inevitably results when workers are more interested in the psychotic byplay than they are in work itself — when, in fact, they have come to resent work and need to be watched every minute to see that they are doing their jobs. Watchers cost money. And Liebow estimates that "half the people in any office are cops."

Because many Americans see their country through the lens of their work experience, it seems likely that the conditions just described breed indifference to the welfare of this nation — and one has the sense of political consequences not far down the line. American work, manifestly, is changing American character, and it is by no means clear that the democratic institutions designed for a free society are appropriate today. And at the time our Constitution was written, 90 percent of American workers were free — owned their farms or shops, answered to nobody, and rose or fell according to their character, intelligence, and enterprise.

Today, however, 95 percent of the work force consists of employees — people who make their living by doing as they are told. And among office workers the virtues that count are not those possessed by Americans of two centuries ago. Instead, they're obedience, false affability, manipulativeness, guile, and, perhaps above all, spinelessness — the itch to dish out and to endure humiliation that has nothing to do with the rational demands of work. (Blue-collar workers, on the other hand, are nearer to the world of the serf; what's expected from them is essentially material in nature — for instance, so many car doors hung in an hour — and has nothing to do with whether they have the right expressions on their faces.) The question is whether institutions designed for free and self-respecting Americans are appropriate now.

I write as a cultural historian, and I know I have raised more questions than I have answered. But this is plain: I have not been talking here about evil management and innocent, oppressed workers in a heartless profit system — but about a malignant psychic system that saps the urge for profit or excellence, one in which those oppressed include management and one in which those oppressed are complicit.

I return at last to my friend the GS-16. You see, what makes it no longer possible for us to be friends isn't just that I overheard his boss mouth-whipping him obscenely, but that it was manifest, from a certain glint in his eyes as he emerged from his punishment, that he had enjoyed it. He can never forgive me for knowing that. And, after all, what can you say to enjoyment? This is a free country, isn't it?

Inside the Third Reich

Albert Speer

Hitler had no humor. He left joking to others, although he could laugh loudly, abandonedly, sometimes literally writhing with laughter. Often he would wipe tears from his eyes during such spasms. He liked laughing, but it was always laughter at the expense of others.

Goebbels was skilled at entertaining Hitler with jokes while at the same time demolishing any rivals in the internal struggle for power. "You know," he once related, "the Hitler Youth asked us to issue a press release for the twenty-fifth birthday of its staff chief, Lauter-

Reprinted with permission of Macmillan Publishing Co., Inc. from *Inside the Third Reich* by Albert Speer. Copyright © 1969 by Verlag Ullstein GMBH. Copyright © 1970 by Macmillan Publishing Co., Inc.

bacher. So I sent along a draft of the text to the effect that he had celebrated this birthday 'enjoying full physical and mental vigor.' We heard no more from him." Hitler doubled up with laughter, and Goebbels had achieved his end of cutting the conceited youth leader down to size.

To the dinner guests in Berlin, Hitler repeatedly talked about his youth, emphasizing the strictness of his upbringing. "My father often dealt me hard blows. Moreover, I think that was necessary and helped me." Wilhelm Frick, the Minister of the Interior, interjected in his bleating voice: "As we can see today, it certainly did you good, *mein Führer.*" A numb, horrified silence around the table. Frick tried to save the situation, "I mean, *mein Führer,* that is why you have come so far." Goebbels, who considered Frick a hopeless fool, commented sarcastically: "I would guess you never received a beating in your youth, Frick."

Walter Funk, who was both Minister of Economics and president of the Reichsbank, told stories about the outlandish pranks that his vice president, Brinkmann, had gone on performing for months, until it was finally realized that he was mentally ill. In telling such stories Funk not only wanted to amuse Hitler but to inform him in this casual way of events which would sooner or later reach his ears. Brinkmann, it seemed, had invited the cleaning women and messenger boys of the Reichsbank to a grand dinner in the ballroom of the Hotel Bristol, one of the best hotels in Berlin, where he played the violin for them. This sort of thing rather fitted in with the regime's propaganda of all Germans forming one "folk community." But as everyone at the table laughed, Funk continued: "Recently he stood in front of the Ministry of Economics on Unter den Linden, took a large package of newly printed banknotes from his briefcase — as you know, the notes bear my signature — and gave them out to passers-by, saying: 'Who wants some of the new Funks?'"[1] Shortly afterward, Funk continued, the poor man's insanity had become plain for all to see. He called together all the employees of the Reichsbank. "Everyone older than fifty to the left side, the younger employees to the right." Then, to one man on the right side: "'How old are you?' — 'Forty-nine, sir.' — 'You go to the left too. Well now, all on the left side are dismissed at once, and what is more with a double pension.'"

Hitler's eyes filled with tears of laughter. When he had recovered, he launched into a monologue on how hard it sometimes is to recognize a madman. In this roundabout way Funk was also accomplishing another end. Hitler did not yet know that the Reischbank vice president in his irresponsible state had given Goering a check for several million marks. Goering cashed the check without a qualm. Later on, of course, Goering vehemently objected to the thesis that Brinkmann did not know what he was doing. Funk could expect him to present this point of view to Hitler. Experience had shown that the person who first managed to suggest a particular version of an affair to Hitler had virtually won his point, for Hitler never liked to alter a view he had once expressed. Even so, Funk had difficulties recovering those millions of marks from Goering. . . .

Many jokes were carefully prepared, tied up as they were with actual events, so that Hitler was kept abreast of interparty developments under the guise of foolery. Again, Goebbels was far better at this than all the others, and Hitler gave him further encouragement by showing that he was very much amused.

An old party member, Eugen Hadamowski, had obtained a key position as Reichssendeleiter (Head of Broadcasting for the Reich), but now he was longing to be promoted to Leiter des Reichsrundfunks (Head of the Reich Radio System). The Propaganda Minister, who had another candidate, was afraid that Hitler might back Hadamowski because he had skillfully organized the public address systems for the election campaigns before 1933. He had Hanke, state secretary in the Propaganda Ministry, send for the man and officially informed him that Hitler had just appointed him Reichsintendant (General Director) for radio. At the table Hitler was given an account of how Hadamowski had gone wild with joy at this news. The description was, no doubt, highly colored and exaggerated, so that Hitler took the whole affair as a great joke. Next day Goebbels had a few copies of a newspaper printed reporting on the sham appointment and praising the new appointee in excessive terms. He outlined the article for Hitler, with all its ridiculous phrases, and acted out Hadamowski's rapture upon reading these things about himself. Once more Hitler and the whole table with him was convulsed. That same day Hanke asked the newly appointed Reichsintendant to make a speech into a dead microphone, and once again there was endless merriment at Hitler's table when the story was told. After this, Goebbels no longer had to worry that Hitler would intervene in favor of Hadamowski. It was a diabolic game; the ridiculed man did not have the slightest opportunity to defend himself and probably never realized that the practical joke was carefully plotted to make him unacceptable to Hitler. No one could even know whether what Goebbels was describing was true or whether he was giving his imagination free rein.

From one point of view, Hitler was the real dupe of these intrigues. As far as I could observe, Hitler was in fact no match for Goebbels in such matters; with his more direct temperament he did not understand this sort of cunning. But it certainly should have given one pause that Hitler allowed this nasty game to go on and even encouraged it. One word of displeasure would certainly have stopped this sort of thing for a long while to come.

I often asked myself whether Hitler was open to influence. He surely could be swayed by those who knew how to manage him. Hitler was mistrustful, to be sure. But he was so in a cruder sense, it often seemed to me; for he did not see through clever chess moves or subtle manipulation of his opinions. He had apparently no sense for methodical deceit. Among the masters of that art were Goering, Goebbels, Bormann, and, within limits, Himmler. Since those who spoke out in candid terms on the important questions usually could not make Hitler change his mind, the cunning men naturally gained more and more power.

NOTE

1. A pun in German; *Funken* = sparks. —*Translators' note.*

Humor in a Machine Shop: An Interpretation of Symbolic Action

Richard J. Boland, Jr. and Raymond Hoffman

THE MACHINE SHOP

The basis for this study is a small, privately owned machine shop. Such shops are found in almost every town that has an industrial or agricultural base, but are especially prevalent in the midwest where they provide custom tooled steel parts to nearby manufacturing firms. A typical shop size ranges from 10 to 50 machinists, working with large lathes, surface grinders, drill presses and other automatic machines to transform tubes and bars of steel into a wide variety of finished products.

The shop we observed works primarily with steel tubing (from ½" to 12" outer diameter) producing component parts (mostly steel bushings) for agricultural and earth moving equipment manufacturers. As a job shop, almost no request is too small and their customers and order sizes range from the single individual to the largest industrial firms. This shop (M shop) has 20 machinists in 15,000 square feet of

Abridged from "Humor in a Machine Shop: An Interpretation of Symbolic Action" by Richard J. Boland, Jr. and Raymond Hoffman forthcoming in *Organizational Symbolism* by Louis Pondy, Peter Frost, Gareth Morgan, and Thomas Dandridge (eds.). Reprinted by special permission of the authors.

floorspace. It has concrete floors and walls, 18 to 24 foot ceilings, and overhead conduits connecting the machines. Approximately 20 percent of the shop is used for stockpiling raw steel in racks 12 feet high. Overhead cranes move the required steel stock in bundles up to 6,000 pounds to the appropriate machining areas. A given order may require a dozen or more separate machining operations.

Like most machine shops, M is characterized by noise, dirt and constant threat of injury. Machine operations and steel handling create a loud whining and clanging, and the nature of the steel and the machines gives a pervasive sense of grease, oil and dust. There is a strong element of danger in the work. Lathes rotate the steel tubing at a high speed and a stationary cutting tool is applied to the softer steel stock. The result is heat, with the machined steel turning blue hot and peeling off at the tool's edge in coiled ribbons that can cause immediate third-degree burns. Other machines create equal amounts of hot steel discharge in the form of chips and shavings.

No matter how "boring" or "monotonous" a job in the shop may seem, no matter how simple and routine an operation may appear to an observer, there is an element of danger that always exists. There's an old saying that puts it well: "Take the machine for granted and it'll take your hand; pay attention and you'll be a whole man." The machines may take off an arm or hand, or severely cut an individual, while the steel itself may fall from its stacked piles and crush a foot, ankle, leg or arm. If a loose piece of clothing or long hair gets caught in a machine, the individual himself is quickly pulled in. Most injuries take place when the individual stops respecting or paying full attention to the machine. The older the machinist, the lower the accident rate. Minor accidents may be humorous to the other workers, evoking an "I told you so" look on the face. But nobody likes to get burned by blue-hot steel shavings that stick to the skin. Most machinists realize that at best the machine is a double-edged sword, capable of being controlled to an extent, but also capable of inflicting unexpected injury to its operator.

The steel itself is important in creating the atmosphere of the machine shop. Virtually everything the men work with is steel in one form or another. Steel tubing is the raw material. High carbon steel tools cut and shape the tubing on steel lathes and drill presses. Steel drums store the finished pieces and work in process. Steel is the scrap, and even work boots are lined with steel. Machinists live in a steel world for eight to ten hours every day. They make the steel take a certain form, and yet the steel shapes them. A machinist's hands become strong and thick with calluses from all the cuts, slivers, and burns he receives. Nonetheless, to a machinist, his hands are a prized possession. He is proud of them, no matter what they look like to other people. The machinist is physically altered by the process of shaping the steel, and comes to respect its inert strength. It is the "immovable object" that he struggles with.

There is also an important cognitive component to being a machinist. Steel as a raw material has a wide range of hardness, tensile strength, and malleability. The machines and tools have varied rates of material feed, cutting speed and steel removal, and a specific job order may demand tolerances of plus or minus five ten-thousandths of an inch. Being a machinist includes developing the special ability to take these standard specifications plus other, more subtle aspects of a particular piece of steel, machine, and tool into account in producing the desired result.

The machinists at M shop range in age from late fifties to late teens, and shop experience ranges from thirty-five years to no experience at all. A hierarchy exists within the shop based on experience with machines. One exception to this is the foreman, who, at forty years of age, finds himself at the top of the formal hierarchical structure even though he has less experience than several of the machinists. The foreman does not take his position as implying that he is the most experienced, however, and often calls on the advice of older machinists in problem situations. Several other hierarchies exist in the social world of M shop, including ones based on strength and intelligence.

M shop was founded in the summer of 1972. At first, much of the work was subcontracted, but in the fall of 1973 the shop began full service operation with three machinists and one owner/manager. From that point through August of 1974 the second author worked in the shop as an apprentice. He continued to work as an apprentice machinist during summers and holidays for the next five years, including the most recent summer of observation. During this time, the shop had grown to twenty full-time machinists and he has continued to be an accepted, though intermittent, member of the work force. The examples of humor discussed here are based on recorded observations, but they are elaborated with recollections of the five preceding years of work experience.

OBSERVATIONS

We do not pretend to have developed a taxonomy of all the instances of humor that were observed, but some natural headings would include language jokes, physical jokes, and machine jokes. In this paper we will deal only with physical and machine jokes as they are the easiest to relate specifically to the work place. Language jokes, especially at lunchtime and breaks, run the full spectrum of an individual's social life, including hobbies, family, personal history, etc.

Taking them into account is beyond our ability here. We would argue, however, that our narrowing to these specific behaviors is to study a particular language — a bodily and object-mediated one — not to ignore language.

Purely physical jokes include one or more individuals in direct or indirect contact with another. For example, each machinist has a rag tucked into his back pocket for use in wiping himself, the steel, or the machine. Taking his rag, without his notice, is a common and effective joke — especially when he reaches to clean a hand full of grease. Or, because lidded steel drums are put on a dolly for movement to the next machine operation, replacing a full drum with an empty one can cause the individual to fall flat on his face when he gives the heave ho. Another frequent physical joke is the goose. A broom handle or steel tube, not so delicately placed, will bring any machinist up short. Many of the physical jokes play on the desire to keep clean in the dirty shop environment. A rag wet with machine coolant or grease set on a chair or lobbed across the shop onto a clean shirt back is one example, and dropping large pieces of steel into a vat of coolant or cleaning fluid and splashing those around it is another.

Physical humor is also evident in mimicry. While the shop is in full production with all men at their machines, an extended sequence of mimicked jokes are taking place. Imitating unique physical gestures or characteristics of those stationed at other machines or walking in the aisles is a frequent form of humor. Besides the parody of unique physical gestures or abnormalities of others, mimicry often has sexual or intellectual overtones. Other machinists are often portrayed as either sexually incompetent or as sexually perverted, using bars of steel or pieces of the machine as mock sex objects to pantomime another's missing or insatiable appetites. The pantomimes may also refer to another's mental powers, as in "you are looking (acting) so stupidly."

The other major category of humor relates to the machines themselves. These are primarily jokes played on an individual through his machine. Each machinist will spend approximately 60 percent of his time on one particular machine. He will come to see the machine as his and will often give it a name, paint a unique decoration on it, and in general come to have an intimate understanding of its unique operating characteristics. Because of this relationship, the machine is an ideal medium for pulling jokes. It is an important element in establishing the individual's identity as a machinist, and therefore a powerful medium for pulling jokes about the definition of self. "Blueing" is a popular trick in which an indelible steel marking ink is rubbed on the handles or knobs of a machine. This is especially funny when the individual touches his face or clothes after grabbing the "blued" knob or handle. The natural blackened color of the knobs and handles makes this "blueing" difficult to detect. In a similar vein, the hose which sprays a fine stream of coolant over the raw steel as it is being machined can be adjusted to spray at high pressure directly onto the machine operator. Other machine jokes include removing fuses or gears from a machine, thus making them inoperable, or reversing the direction in which a machine rotates. Slightly more adventurous jokes include the outright removal of key operating parts from another's machine, or recalibrating the measurement instruments he uses for checking the narrow tolerances.

These machine tricks are best when pulled while a machinist is in the middle of a production run but has turned off and left his machine for a few minutes. When he returns, the trick pullers are watching for his reaction when the machine doesn't start, runs backwards, soaks him with coolant, or when he discovers he has "blueing" on his hands, and has just touched his face. One joke that requires a running machine is the cannon trick. Here, the running machine becomes an amusing toy for the machinist. By plugging one end of the steel tubing with a rubber ball, the air pressure is built up until a cannonlike explosion blows it out. . . .

We take the position that the instances of humor observed in M shop are seen as being funny by the individuals involved to the extent that each individual finds in "getting the joke," that two incongruous frames of reference for interpreting the self are meaningfully resolved. The problems of self-definition that this humor is dealing with are inferred from the frames of reference the jokes juxtapose. While this is ultimately each individual's unique experience in "getting the joke," we will summarize what appears to us to be the most conspicuous frames involved.

Each worker, over time, establishes a strong self-identity in the shop. In these self-identities, the definition of the individual as a worker is our primary concern, but this is deeply intertwined with other, more personal aspects of their life and we cannot separate them. The self-definition includes such things as his manner and type of dress, morning ritual of arrival, dressing, having coffee, checking his machine, etc. It also includes his identity as a machinist—the level of skills and capabilities he asserts. We see these self-identities as structured in sets of hierarchies. Humor plays both an initiating and reversing role in these nested sets of hierarchically structured self-definitions. It initiates structure by affirming an individual's place, and it also reverses structure when played on an individual's previously established identity. For instance, a new worker will have jokes played on him so he learns his place, but once established, the jokes are played to reverse his place. The ambiguity of self confirmed by humor allows for movement through the established hierarchies. While humor serves to celebrate an individual's existing identity, it also asserts its fragility and ultimate equivocality. The machinist who prides himself on being the cleanest in M shop, with a pressed uniform and scrubbed hands, is great for a wet rag, blueing, or coolant hose trick. Of course, this particular machinist defines himself by many of the structured hierarchies of the shop. He is also seen as one of the best joke pullers and one of the most difficult to pull one on. While this may or may not add to the reversal effect of a joke played on him, it does provide for multiple frames of reference that can be used as a basis for "getting the joke."

Other examples of humor used to reverse the established order are found at the lunch table. Some men will bring exactly the same lunch every day (salami on white bread, two carrots, two celery sticks, one packet of twinkies). They eat these items in the same order every day, and a good joke is to divert their attention, so that they eat their food in a different order. One man went so far as to arrange with another worker's wife to pack a different lunch for her husband as part of the trick. (He refused to eat it.)

This use of jokes to deny an asserted self-identity is a major theme of the mimicry mentioned earlier. The individual's position in the hierarchies of sexual prowess, physical strength, intelligence, or skilled machinist is a basis for much of the mimicry. The joker is saying "you're not so smart (strong, skilled)." The machine jokes (removing parts, changing adjustments, etc.) are also reversing the individual's position, but, like the lunch jokes, have a ritual interruption component also. That is, each machinist develops a highly rigid, sequenced set of actions for setting up his machine or for running a particular job. Any joke pulled on him while he is in the middle of this sequence will force him to go back to the beginning and start over again. This starting over again is an integral part of "getting the joke" and emphasizes the disparity of the several frames that must be involved.

There is an important sense in which the joke must "fit" the existing hierarchy. In order to pull a joke, an individual must himself be well established in the relevant hierarchy. For instance, a new apprentice cannot really pull a joke on anyone. Once he *is* seen as fit for pulling jokes, he only plays certain kinds, rag jokes or dirty and clean jokes, but not machine jokes. Only the machinists pull machine jokes. On the other hand, then, jokes are primarily directed against an individual's self-identity, but on the other, the joke is asserting or confirming the identity of the joke puller. . . .

A General Strategy for Getting Out of Traps

Samuel A. Culbert

THE MODEL

The model portrays a strategy for gaining greater control of our organization life, a strategy that entails a process of consciousness-raising and self-directed resocialization. In theory, this process can be broken down into five sequential stages, each of which involves a separate consciousness-raising activity. In practice, of course, these five stages can be intermingled and used out of sequence. Where possible, however, the stages should be followed in sequence because the insights developed at one stage provide the beginning points for consciousness-raising at the next stage. Learning at each stage depends on our developing skills and receiving peer group support.

Consciousness-raising can best be accomplished by focusing on a single area of organization concerns and working our way through each of the five stages of the model. Maintaining focus on a single area at a time requires discipline because insights in one area inevitably spark insights in others. Overall, the consciousness-raising process can be likened to eating an artichoke. One starts with the less meaty leaves on the periphery and progressively spirals in toward the more meaty leaves closer to the heart. Unlike eating an artichoke, however, we don't reach the heart, that is, gain control over our organization life; we merely get closer. Each insight paves the way for a meatier realization.

Experience in using this model has shown that a preliminary overview of all five stages facilitates a deeper understanding of each stage. That is the purpose of this chapter. . . .

STAGE 1: RECOGNIZING WHAT'S "OFF"

Consciousness-raising begins with a gut experience. We develop a vague awareness that something in our organization life is "off," although we can't quite put our fingers on exactly what it is. Such feelings of incoherence are frequent occurrences in our organization life, but usually we try to forget about them. However, if we want our consciousness raised, we've got to be ready to pay attention to what seems minor. Closer scrutiny will usually show much more beneath the surface than we saw originally.

Our vague feelings of incoherence serve as clues to identifying discrepancies between our nature and the expectations of the organization system. Such discrepancies usually fall into one of two categories. The first is when the organization seems to expect something that is unnatural for us or inconsistent with our best interests. The second is when we do what comes naturally and learn afterward that it was deemed inappropriate by the system.

Transforming feelings of incoherence into a more precise statement of discrepancies requires some concepts and some emotional support. The concepts will help us pinpoint where we and the organization are in conflict, and the support will help us resist our tendency to shoulder all the blame for these conflicts.

STAGE 2: UNDERSTANDING OURSELVES AND THE ORGANIZATION

Being able to specify discrepancies may make us feel that we can now proceed to solve our problems with the organization and put our minds at ease. Usually, this proves to be a short-sighted strategy. We need to treat discrepancies for what they are, symptoms rather than problems. In practice, taking our conflicts with the organization at face value and "resolving" them can be the surest way to keep from seeing the fundamental ills of the system as we currently live it.

Treating discrepancies as symptoms, on the other hand, helps us to understand aspects of ourselves and the organization that we had not previously recognized. We have a chance to probe beneath the discrepancy by asking ourselves what human qualities and what organization attributes can produce the conflicts we're experiencing.

Transforming discrepancies into new understanding requires skills to think divergently and support to resist our inclinations to think convergently. Divergent thinking keeps us focused on the fact that a discrepancy is a symptom of some lack in basic understanding. The support we get will help us resist our impulses to converge on a solution that prematurely puts our anxieties to rest.

STAGE 3: UNDERSTANDING OUR RELATIONSHIP WITH THE ORGANIZATION

Greater understanding of ourselves and of the organization system helps us to recognize alternatives that suit our interests and to resist external attempts to control us. We sense a new personal freedom. However, getting carried away by this "freedom" proves to be another short-term strategy for gaining control. It puts us underground, "working" the system. But eventually, those who however unwittingly influence and control us will discover that we've eluded them, and we'll be back playing cat and dog again.

In order to really improve things, we'll need, at some point, to focus directly on our relationship with the organization. The new understanding we developed in Stage 2, about ourselves and the organization, can now be transformed into a more thorough understanding of the assumptions that link us to the organization system. This requires that we learn about our conditioning in the organization and that we get assistance in doing this from people we trust. Some of our biases are so ingrained we will require tough-minded challenging to break through to them.

STAGE 4: MOVING TOWARD A MORE NATURAL LIFE IN THE ORGANIZATION

Increased understanding of ourselves, the organization, and our relationship with the organization will give us a new sense of power; we can now formulate the types of relationships that will give us greater control over our organization life. But while we can envision more optimal relationships, we do not yet know all that we need to know in order to see whether we can formulate alternatives that express our self-interests and yet appear practical from the standpoint of organization goals.

Transforming understanding of ourselves, the organization, and the assumptions that link us to the organization into practical alternatives also requires new skills and support. We need skills in identifying tensions between assumptions the organization makes about us and the person we're discovering ourselves to be. We need support to help us reflect on personal priorities before getting caught up in our attempts to renegotiate our relationship with the organization.

STAGE 5: AFFECTING THE ORGANIZATION LIVES OF OTHERS

Being able to envision practical alternatives gives us a great deal of control over our organization life. We derive a new sense of independence from knowing that our options are no longer limited to the best ideas that others have for us. However, as long as others in the organization are still out of control, their spontaneous actions will set off forces that oppose the mutually beneficial directions we may try to take.

Making suggestions that change and improve the organization system requires that we be mindful of the personal realities of all the people affected. To adopt a strategy where we impose our improvements on others runs counter to our reasons for wanting change in the first place. We need to think about change as if we were statesmen concerned with the well-being of all the people. We need support from a peer group that recognizes what we're trying to accomplish and that can help us maintain our focus at times when it's difficult for us to observe the effects our efforts are having.

REFLECTION

This model is applicable to most nontechnical aspects of organization life. It is one attempt to reverse the machinery of a runaway system that influences us without our knowing it.

Gaining control eventually means probing all critical areas of organization life. However, the best place to start is with the area that is currently causing the greatest discomfort. This is where you've got the energy to maintain your focus. Of course, the first area will require the greatest concentration because you'll not only be learning specific things about your organization life but you'll also be acquiring the analytic skills necessary for consciousness-raising. Thus, you can expect a cumulative effect that enables gains made in one area to shorten the work needed in another. Nevertheless, consciousness-raising is a continuing process that requires returning over and over again to the same areas. . . . We're now at a point where we can develop more confidence in our grasp of this model by following an example through each stage of consciousness-raising.

Example

The following experiment was carried out by a group of European engineers and their wives. It grew out of their distress and sense of helplessness over the personnel practices that governed relocations to company headquarters in the United States. At the end of the experiment, they were asserting themselves and suggesting improvements of a quality seldom expressed at their company level.

Each of the thirteen engineers involved was beginning a one-and-a-half to two-year training assignment in the United States, spoke English, and were men. Most had first- or second-level supervisory experience. All were married. Their ages ranged from thirty to forty-five, and they had between three and twenty-five years' experience with the company. The typical person was about thirty-three, had been with the company five years, and had two children. Initially, these engineers met to discuss adjustment problems created by their recent transfer. But when they became familiar with the consciousness-raising process, they decided to expand the scope of their discussions. They began meeting regularly, one entire day a month, and went on meeting for a year and a half.

As we have learned, the first stage of consciousness-raising uses feelings of incoherence to identify discrepancies, and this requires support and time for catharsis. In this instance, the engineers needed to overcome a feeling that "If I were just a little more adequate, I wouldn't have all these adjustment problems." They also needed time to release pent-up feelings of anger and frustration over the specific problems they'd been experiencing.

There was resentment with the company in general, and early discussions revealed problems and discrepancies in nearly every aspect of their work life. Some engineers complained that they had not been consulted when the transfer was planned for them, and some felt that not knowing the career consequences of turning it down forced them to move at inconvenient times for their family. Some resented that their wives were expected to leave good jobs without permits to work in the United States.

There was also resentment with the personnel department, which was charged with helping families relocate. The engineers complained that the neighborhoods chosen for their relocation suited the company's image rather than their own styles and preferences; that unfair policies dictated what they were allowed to ship at company expense; and that they had lost money as a result of the compensation formula that was supposed to provide them with a standard of living comparable with what they had in Europe and commensurate with what people in the United States earn for performing similar jobs.

There was resentment against the departments to which they had been reassigned. Some complained of bosses who were only understanding of relocation pressures as long as they put in a productive eight-hour day. Some complained that their expertise was disregarded because U.S. engineering practices were considered the best in the world.

The engineers resented their families because they were expected to make friends for their wives and were held accountable for problems that their children encountered at school. Some complained that their families treated the U.S. assignment as if it were a long vacation and were putting pressures on them to sightsee on weekends, when they needed time to rest and recoup from the pressures of the week.

The engineers resented the managers who made the decisions for international relocations. They didn't like the idea that they were considered a part of a mobile work force that could be picked up and moved every few years. Some felt misled by the promises of rapid advancement that had been made when they were hired.

Overall, each of the engineers seemed to be suffering the pains of culture shock, because even the smallest problems seemed to be causing them high levels of concern and anxiety. Moreover, although each engineer complained of something different, listening to one another's complaints caused them to realize that various problems had similar causes.

The engineers soon realized that for their support group to be complete their wives would have to be included. Not only were the women deeply affected by relocation pressures but they were an essential part of the family's resources for coping with adjustment problems. At the end of the second meeting, the men decided to expand their group to include their wives. This type of unprecedented involvement in company matters, however, seemed to present additional adjustment pressures for two wives, and they declined to participate.

Once a list of discrepancies was identified, the group could turn their attention to the second stage of the consciousness-raising model. A period of divergent analysis produced many insights and clarifications about the actual workings of the organization system. The engineers' insights included discovering that they believed that the company knew what's best for them; that they were afraid to turn down a transfer; that they were excessively dependent on the advice they get from higher level managers; that they felt the technical expertise they had developed in Europe was damn good and often superior to the methods used in the United States; that the longer they work for the company, becoming more technically specialized, the less desirable they become on the open job market; that being transferred caused them to feel insecure and marginal, like a guest who should follow the customs of his host; and that, in general, they didn't have the information they needed to manage their organization life intelligently.

Divergent analysis clarified their view of the organization system. The engineers discovered that policies regarding transfer allowances and compensation were not open for discussion, despite the image the personnel department tried to create; that people were controlled by never being sure of the consequences of saying no to a managerial request; that while people were encouraged to explore differences openly, they had better not be caught differing with their bosses in public; that a fail-safe system was emphasized, where the rewards for being right were seldom high enough to offset the punishments for being wrong; that they couldn't count on self-perspectives being solicited or considered when decisions were made about them; that families were treated as if they were mere appendages to the husband; and that the company's desire to put forth a conservative image often invaded their personal lives.

Strengthened by the divergent analysis of discrepancies, the engineers and their wives decided to collect some additional information about the actual way the system works and the assumptions made about them. They focused on the transfer process, because it was the primary source of their current anxieties, and on the personnel department that administered these transfers. They decided to interview a representative sampling of those involved in transfer decisions. In order to cover themselves organizationally, they advised the personnel director of their plan. Because they were not asking for his permission, it would have taken more energy than it was worth for him to object.

The engineers and their wives were surprised at the results of their interviews. They discovered that despite the reassurances that management gave them about the transfer process, their feelings of uneasiness were well founded. Before a transfer was offered, the proposed move was passed up the line, level by level, to a vice-president. If blessed by him, the word went out to the personnel department, which asked the man about his interests. By this time, all managers concerned with the man's career are convinced that the transfer is a good idea. If the man refuses, the reasons for his refusal go back up the line to "a very disappointed" vice-president. The engineers concluded that it's misleading to assume that an immediate supervisor, representative of the personnel department, or any other company manager can present them with even-handed advice. They realized that each person in this chain had to answer many questions if a proposed transfer was refused.

Most families felt that they were not advised about all the benefits that were due them. The interviews determined, contrary to some of their suspicions, that the personnel department was not getting cost-effectiveness credit for saving money on unused transfer allowances. While personnel representatives didn't tell people about all the benefits to which they were entitled, they did this out of fear that a superior might come down hard on them if the company were exploited by a transferring family. As the personnel director frankly admitted, "Most line managers, as well as myself, have a tendency to formulate policies that protect against the two percent who are inclined to test the rules. I guess we sometimes overprotect the company."

Many other realizations crystallized as group members discussed what they had learned from their interviews. However, the main point was established: the engineers and their wives obtained perspectives that added to what they were able to induce from their own experience. Combined with what they had formerly realized, they were able to construct a better picture of the assumptions made about them and the actual way the organization worked. The fact that they chose to investigate transfers is secondary to the fact that they investigated an organization process.

Combining the information received from facing feelings of incoherence, identifying discrepancies, using divergent analysis, and interviewing others gave the engineers and their wives a more realistic picture of their relationships to the organization. At this point, they were involved in the third stage of consciousness-raising, and they began to comprehend more fully the vulnerabilities and costs involved in paternalistic liaisons like the ones they had formed with the company. They had traded understanding themselves and the organization for promises of protection and security. They discovered that company terms like career track, maturing process, and professional development were cover-ups for moving people around to meet corporate needs. Recognizing that transfers were motivated at least as much by company needs as by their own needs for training and development, they learned what they needed to know to make demands and to direct company resources toward their own personal and professional objectives. If a so-called training assignment was not teaching them much, they realized it was their responsibility to make the trade-off more equitable. Consciousness-raising was exposing assumptions that blocked the self-management of their lives.

The engineers and their wives were also surprised to discover that the more they learned about how the system worked, and the assumptions made about the people who comprise the system, the fewer villains they found. Increased knowledge led them to realize that no one was doing them in intentionally. For example, they could no longer reason that the personnel department was simply trying to make their own jobs easier at the expense of transferring families. If anything, the personnel department was in a worse box, for they were expected to have an answer for every question, and their answers were supposed to be consistent with any number of company policies built on erroneous and inconsistent assumptions about the human qualities of the people involved.

While each stage of consciousness-raising had its own immediate effects, providing the engineers and wives with increasingly accurate pictures of reality, there was a bigger payoff. This came in the fourth stage of consciousness-raising, when they used what they had learned to envision alternatives. Among the specific problems that transferring families had with personnel procedures was the almost inconsequential one in which a family of music buffs was refused an allowance to ship some records to the United States. The family reasoned that because they had not used two of their three-crate allowance for books, they were entitled to ship at least two crates of records. The personnel representatives handling this request reasoned that this was not possible, because if he granted them permission to do this, others would demand the right to ship records in addition to books.

At first glance, it seemed like this couple was making a big deal out of nothing. Someone else might reason, ''The hell with personnel. I'll ship the records at my own expense and tack on an extra twenty-dollar cab fare to my moving expenses." But to this couple, their problem seemed to hold symbolic importance, although they couldn't initially figure out why. In fact, when I first asked them why it was so important, they looked sheepish and self-doubting.

But as the consciousness-raising progressed, their problem became the group's rallying point, and when its meaning and solution became evident, the group's sign of success. Wrapped up in this problem were all the assumptions an organization system makes when treating workers like children. Only if you assume you are a child, can you, as a matter of course, think of asking permission for something as inconsequential as substituting records for books. When the group discovered that the company leaders and the personnel director really intended to make transfers as easy as possible without much concern for costs, they were able to see numerous problems stemming from the same kind of discrepancy.

As the engineers and their wives discovered more about themselves, they learned that they often chided and complained like kids who don't get their way or when they felt trapped by a seemingly irrational company policy. The consciousness-raising process eventually led them to see that the entire transfer process was built on assumptions that they were children who must be monitored and closely supervised. The incident about the records would never have taken place if the existing procedure did not begin by telling people what they were entitled to take.

Envisioning alternatives became a relatively easy task once the group spotted inconsistencies between the organization's assumptions and expectations and what they believed to be their true nature. Until they discovered this difference in assumptions, each of their counterproposals merely perpetuated their dependence. Once they were able to articulate that they'd like to be treated like adults, it was relatively easy for them to envision alternatives. If prior to consciousness-raising someone had asked the engineers whether or not they were being treated and acted like adults, I'd guess only a few would have noticed that they were not. The tendency to believe that we are like our ideals is one of the most troublesome barriers to envisioning alternatives to current practices.

Reflection

In contrast to the pictures of reality acquired during socialization, the process of envisioning alternatives is mainly conscious, compatible with self-interests, and based on the lessons of our own experience. This time around, we shape our own reality, and if we get in trouble with the system, we'll have to take our lumps. But the lumps we take replace the lumps we've been taking all along without knowing it.

Newly envisioned alternatives stimulate an inner need either to change the organization system or to renegotiate our relationship with it. If the system fails to change or is intolerant of the changes we want to make, then we have a decision to make. At the extremes, we can either leave or live in discontent. Ultimately, no system is ideal for all the people who live in it. Some adaptation is always necessary; that's the nature of man's social contract. We'll have to reach our decision to stay or leave by weighing our priorities for change against our alternatives outside the organization. But we also must realize there is no Camelot; certain compromises are always necessary, and explicating our compromises allows us to take responsibility for our organization life.

Deciding whether or not there's a match between the alternatives we formulate and the goals of the system is a crucial step. We must not waste time deluding ourselves that we can make irreconcilables fit. We must know when we can modify our proposal in a way that makes no appreciable difference to us. This relies on our developing a thorough knowledge of the actual system. And, of course, we must also see when there's a ready fit. For example, the engineers and their wives formally proposed that personnel change their policies to treat them like responsible adults. They suggested that personnel ask transferring families what they need to take and what assistance they might like to have in making their transfer comfortable. Then if a request seemed excessive, the personnel representative could inquire further. A task force set up to consider their suggestion recommended that it be embodied in an experiment. Management expects this experiment to save the company money by people no longer shipping things they're entitled to, but don't particularly need, by reduced managerial aggravation, and by quicker adjustments to a new culture for the families involved. And the families are getting what they want: more control and autonomy in their relocation.

Even in instances such as the above, where benefits to the organization are readily apparent, there may be resistance. This is due to people with power assuming that each small step we take toward greater freedom and self-management means less control for them. They may not fear the particular step being negotiated as much as the step we'll want to take next. . . .

CONCLUSION: THE IMPORTANCE
OF BEING OURSELVES

Why would a Ph.D. chemist spend years trying to invent a new toothpaste flavor? Why would an administrator spend his work life putting other people's plans into action? Why would a manager put in long hours away from home to earn money for stockholders he's never met? These people are not that different from us; in fact, they are us. Our commitment to the goals of the organizations for which we work exceeds the money we receive for our efforts. We are committed to our jobs because of the opportunities that they provide us with to do something personally meaningful with our lives. We seek work that allows us to develop and expand our capabilities, and form associations that give a deep human dimension to our lives. Working to invent a new toothpaste flavor, to put the ideas of others into action, to earn money for stockholders are all vehicles for accomplishing something more important. Yet it's so easy to lose perspective and think these are our goals.

We have lived too long with the assumption that organizations are accountable only to their owners. They also should be accountable to us, the people who comprise organizations. We have staked our lives on their ability to provide us with meaningful and challenging work. We must not be unduly intimidated by the numbers of people who are worrying exclusively about rates of return on invested capital, performance effectiveness, or whatever, as if these constituted all there was to evaluating the organization's output. We can't afford to put our fates exclusively in the hands of people who don't relate to the greater meaning our work holds for us.

If we can't count on them, then we've got to count on ourselves! Each of us needs a personal frame of reference that gives focus and commitment to our projects and helps us see when our activities are out of sync with personal priorities. We know organization life is a compromise; we don't need to hear that one again. But we want to lead our lives with our compromises explicit. We want to know when we're in danger of sacrificing something that must not be compromised or when we're sacrificing more than we're receiving in exchange.

When we approach the organization with our own frame of reference, we run the risk of having such a narrow focus that all we get is what we expect. Creating an open-ended focus that still allows us to extract personal relevance from the infinitude of what's taking place depends on the types of questions we ask ourselves. When our questions are convergent, then our organization world becomes a closed system. But when our questions are phrased divergently, then we open ourselves to surprises, new meaning, and learning.

Asking the right kinds of questions, developing a frame of reference that allows us to be our own organization man, gets us to the point where we can declare ourselves and make our own special peace with the organization world, if only to revise it at another time. Making peace is not the same as copping out or retiring on the job. It means developing our own focus and pursuing it as long as it makes sense to us. During a candid discussion on career development, I heard a fifty-year-old manager with a solid record of organization service say to the big boss, "I don't want to be president. I don't even want to be a division head or an associate head. I'm no longer all that concerned with status. I don't have all the money that I could use, but I have all I need. I just want to be challenged." Then he turned down a promotion to manage a very large operation in a technical area in which he had years of experience, and volunteered to manage a small and little-understood aspect of the company's business. It was an impressive moment.

But learning how to live with the divergent questions necessary for developing this kind of perspective is not all that easy. In the divergent thinking sessions I've led with management groups, I've never seen one go by without somebody becoming quite upset with the process. In a typical instance, a normally rational advertising manager stood up, red in the face, shouting, "I can't see where all this is going to get us," as if he was sure it was going to sweep us right down the tubes. And this was only ten minutes into an all-day meeting. A few minutes of gentle inquiry were all that was necessary to set him straight. It turned out that he wasn't even angry; he was anxious. Because he couldn't identify anything that could be making him anxious, he assumed he was angry, and seized upon a reason to explode. He had the right event, just the wrong emotion. In focusing divergently, we were violating a thought structure from which he normally derived security. As this became explicit, others admitted to their own uneasiness, and normal color returned to his face. The advertising manager then settled back and became a keen contributor.

Meeting organization life with a divergent focus requires support. Throughout this book I've emphasized the role a support group plays in helping us do this. Everyone I've ever seen make substantial progress has had the support of a group. People who lack understanding of how to get group support, or who exercise extreme discipline and aren't able to blow their cool, like the advertising manager blew his, do not get the support they need to aggressively seek out greater consciousness.

Perhaps the biggest obstacle to making organization life more consistent with our needs and interests lies in the difficulty people have in being themselves and holding candid discussions about the human elements in their work life. Even so-called human development experts are reluctant to approach human concerns directly. We have learned that it's easier to get an audience when we begin talking about new ways to improve productivity or increase work group effectiveness. We've taken this tack as a foot-in-the-door to getting people to talk about the personal and social qualities of their life in the organization. We reason that planners cannot think too long about productivity goals without thinking about the people involved. We reason that work groups can't talk too long about decision making and communications without discussing personal and interpersonal needs. But while our reasoning is logical enough, we often lose out in practice. We consistently underestimate the resistance people marshal when it comes time to exhibit and talk about the human and personal issues of their organization life. Too often our tactics wind up merely supporting the status quo!

Thus, I have my doubts about any strategy for organization change that indirectly approaches the human elements of organization life. I also have my doubts about any strategy that allows people at the top to plan for people on the bottom, or any strategy that features people at any level critiquing others, but not themselves.

More than anything else, I believe the quality of our organization life depends on the level of humanity and naturalness we're personally willing to discover and exhibit. We can't reasonably expect to exhibit more candor to others than we are willing to accept in ourselves. Self-candor begins with self-acceptance. We need to accept who we discover ourselves to be, and open-endedly inquire whether or not there's more. No doubt we'll uncover some crucial gaps between our ideals and our reality. Acknowledging these gaps and divergently reflecting on their meaning take us to the next frontier of self-understanding and expression.

8

THE COMPULSION TO PERFORM

Charley: It was a very nice funeral. . . .

Linda: I can't understand it. At this time especially. First time in thirty-five years we were just about free and clear. He only needed a little salary. He was even finished with the dentist.

Charley: No man only needs a little salary.

—*Arthur Miller*

Much of the work of organizational behaviorists has one common objective: to increase the performance of employees. Treatments of such topics as motivation, compensation, training, attitudes, leadership and supervision, to name a few, commonly focus on how more input and hence more output can be induced (some might say squeezed) out of individual workers. More generally it appears that the institutions that socialize our young people (e.g., schools, churches, universities) are, in important ways, directed to the same outcomes — preparing people who are oriented to performing in modern organizations or who are at least willing to tolerate the discipline of the workplace. Given the number of people who are currently chanting about the decline of the work ethic, it is tempting to conclude that these efforts are not succeeding.

On the other hand, we are more concerned that these efforts might be *too* successful. We fear that many individuals are so fully indoctrinated with the work values and routines that psychologically they are not free to make reasonable choices about how much work to do, how hard to work, and how central a role to let work play in their lives. The title of this section — the compulsion to perform — stems from this concern. The virtues of performing work roles are so deeply ingrained in people and the costs of commitments to work and careers are so little considered, that individuals appear to play work roles compulsively without considering how they might allocate their time and energies in a more fully satisfying manner. The readings in this section focus on this compulsion and on some of the costs people pay as a result of the irresistible impulse to perform.

The first selection is from *Confessions of a Workaholic* by Wayne Oates. By comparing the "motivation" to work with an alcoholic's drive to drink, Oates provides a useful orientation for viewing the addictive nature of work.

(In this regard, Lefkowitz's discussion of the problems of "Life Without Work" in Section 5 may be interpreted as analogous to withdrawal of a drug from an addict.)

Most of the selections in this section deal directly with the costs to the individual worker. "Cat's in the Cradle" by Harry Chapin demonstrates that these consequences extend to other people outside the workplace.

The next five selections reveal how the pressures to perform are experienced by people who play various roles in organizations. In "Wheels" (Arthur Hailey) we see how the demands for performance induce an assistant plant manager to compromise his values and the interests of a foreman. Ann Marie Cunningham provides a vivid account of the influence of maintaining hectic schedules on one's total life in "The Time Pressured Life." The short article "The Organization Man, Cont'd" reveals that the workaholic pattern continues to be descriptive of the lives of a large number of high-level executives, while the article "Best Gift for a Secretary" by Ellen Goodman shows how the pressures to perform are transmitted to individuals at lower levels in the hierarchy. The selection from Arthur Miller's classic *Death of a Salesman* emphasizes the consequences of a reason for the withdrawal of work which has received far too little attention: obsolescence. This process is often more brutal than retirement because it has few of the humane, social institutions that make retirement a somewhat graceful process. In contrast to obsolescence, retirement is an expected event for which organizations can plan and which they can handle through routine procedures. As a result, any sense of personal failure can often be submerged by gifts, parties, and speeches. However, there are few such procedures for handling the individual such as Willy Loman, whom the organization defines as obsolete.

Many of the issues raised by the compulsion to perform are treated in the mainstream business literature under the heading of stress. The fact that stress has become the word that serves as the most popular label for these problems is revealing because of what it connotes. For the most part stress is an individually oriented concept; as such it leads us to try to get people to adjust to systems rather than adjusting systems to people. Moreover, many of the topics included under treatments of stress (and more recently "burnout") have often been included in discussions of anxiety, neurosis, and other terms, which have more pathological connotations. In a society dominated by a compulsion to perform, experiencing stress and being perceived by oneself and by others as able to cope with it can be indices of importance and sources of ego gratification. The same cannot be said when the underlying processes are described as anxiety or neurosis. We urge the reader to consider the last two articles in this section, "What Stress Can Do to You" and "Executive Stress May Not Be All Bad," using both sets of connotations — those suggested by stress and those suggested by the more pathologically oriented terms.

Workaholics: This Land of Ours Has to Have Them

Wayne Oates

WORKAHOLISM: THE ORGANIZATION MAN'S NECESSITY

The organizational life of business, industry, or the church tends to call for the workaholic. One asks whether this syndrome of effort-riddenness is not spawned by a bureaucratic culture. There are certain identifiable cultural factors in alcoholic addiction and drug addiction which produce an "alcoholic culture" or a "drug culture," and my point here is that this is true of work addiction also. One kind of person that an organization must have is the man or woman who has *no* value that is not subordinated to the "good of the organization." He idolizes his outfit. If he celebrates his wedding anniversary, he feels he has to do it in such a way as to be good public relations for the organization. If he takes a vacation, it must be used in a way to make progress for the company, the school, or the plant.

Furthermore, this man does not work a given number of hours. He is always on call for the company. As William H. Whyte describes him and his kind, "they are never at leisure than when they are at leisure." This person is one who "is so completely involved in his work that he cannot distinguish between work and the rest of his life—and he is happy that he cannot."[1] This is rarely a salaried man who works so many days a month and year for his income, nor the nine-to-five man who when he finishes his daily stint forgets about work until his shift comes up again. This is a person who works around the clock. Let us take a look at his typical day.

He awakens at a specific time each morning without being called or without an alarm. He lies in bed for a few minutes and arranges in his mind every known detail of the schedule for that day. He ritualistically dresses and eats breakfast. He then moves through a day in which every moment is scheduled, except the time of leaving the office. At the end of the day—usually after everyone else has gone home—he never heads for home until he has gathered materials for work at night. He eats his dinner, and his work is the main topic of the conversation at the table. He then retreats to his workroom to

Specified excerpts abridged from pp. 14–19, 57–69 in *Confessions of a Workaholic: The Facts about Work Addiction* by Wayne Oates (World Publishing Company). Copyright © 1971 by Wayne Oates. Reprinted by permission of Harper & Row, Publishers, Inc.

make the best of the remaining hours of the day. He retires and spends the time just before he drops off to sleep in trying once again to solve the problems that defied solution during the day, rehearsing accounts of conflicts he has had with other people during the day, and experiencing considerable anxiety about the amount of work he has to do the next day, week, or month.

I recall a businessman telling me of an experience which changed his whole life. He decided that he was going to quit taking work home at night. He first did so by staying at the office until he finished, gradually reducing the length of time he stayed at the office. Then he disciplined himself to have all his work done by 5:30 P.M. He tells of the first evening he went home when the rest of the office force did. He stood outside the office building and watched each one go by on his way home. Then he went through an "almost physical agony" as he resisted the temptation to go back upstairs to work or to get his briefcase to take work home. He finally made a break for home and has neither worked late nor taken work home since.

My central point in this section is: the organization *needs* a few workaholics to prosper as an organization. Culture as we have it calls for this kind of devotee to his work — workaholics who live by a sweephand watch and dream of ways to give more time than twenty-four hours each day.

WORKAHOLISM IN THE NINE-TO-FIVE MAN

The impression I have left thus far would seem to suggest that the work addict is an upper-middle-class and lower-upper-class phenomenon. He is not. The recent concern about "law and order" has called attention to the wages of policemen and firemen. Because of their relatively low pay these persons are forced to take additional jobs as security policemen, night watchmen, fire wardens, etc., for private companies in order to supplement their income.

The same need is felt also by public school teachers, and even university and college professors. I recently found one schoolteacher who worked in the evenings as a motel clerk, a job in which he could be paid extra and still have time to grade papers and prepare for classes the next day. During the Christmas holidays, he, being overweight, served as a Santa Claus in a nearby department store. These are persons with fixed-hour schedules who nevertheless moonlight in order to make additional money.

At first, the basic factor in overwork by people on fixed-schedule jobs seems to be purely financial. They need to make more money, which is not forthcoming from the public budgets out of which their initial salaries are paid. Usually they are in a type of work where labor unions, and thus strikes for higher wages, etc., are taboo. Consequently the need for more income can only be met by taking extra work. On the surface, this seems to be *the* reason for moonlighting. However, closer inspection reveals other more subtle factors.

One of them is social prestige. These persons want their families to have what other families have, notably education. They and their wives both work in order to send their children to college. They themselves had to work long hours in order to get a college education. They do not want their sons and daughters to have to work as they did but to be able to give *all* their time to study. They want to have two cars so their wives can get around as they wish and so the children can have "wheels." They want to move to a better neighborhood so their children will have a chance to better themselves through the prestige of the kinds of friends they associate with, and marry.

As we probe underneath these social factors, we find the element of competition. In the Ten Commandments, we are told not to be covetous, but tradition approves all forms of competition. The ambiguous condition of the workaholic is that he works hard to get the things and the place in society that other men envy. At the same time he isolates himself from the very people whose approval he thinks he can get by outdoing them. The salty brine of competition is exciting to swim in, cooling to the skin as one revels in it, but does not satisfy the thirst for companionship and communion with others. As Samuel Johnson said in 1775, "That is the happiest conversation where there is no competition, no vanity, but a calm, quiet interchange of sentiments."

As we probe underneath the competitive factor, we find other causes of overwork. We find men who no longer can *see* the results of their labors. Even the assembly worker on the line does not *see* the total design of what he is doing. He has to assume that by doing his particular operation he has accomplished a great deal. The assembly line has removed the artisan from our culture; rarely today can one man in business for himself create enough pieces of furniture, jewelry, pottery, etc., to earn a living by direct sale of what he produces. There is a poignancy in the situation of a man who cannot invest his identity in the *substantive things he produces* rather than in the intangible of money. He has trouble communicating to his family the *worthwhileness* of what he is doing because he cannot show them the fruits of his hands except in the form of money. He cannot teach them his skill, but can only prove his manhood by bringing money home. It is little wonder that he seeks to work more and more in order to bring more and more money home. Yet all he gets as his reward is loneliness. Money creates a mythology of power in his family's mind; it also isolates him from them. He cannot easily teach his own children how to work, or communicate with his wife about what *his* work is really like. Little wonder that he solves the problem by returning to work! When he is gone and at work, he feels that they understand a *little*. When he is at home with *nothing to do*, they have no place for him because they have organized their lives on the assumption of his absence.

AGE AND WORKAHOLISM

One of the things that our culture is doing for us and to us at the same time is enabling us to live longer. Even a full generation ago retirement for people of certain social classes was unknown. Social security has changed all this.

The middle-aged person approaching retirement begins to feel the pangs of his workaholism just when he has earned enough money to have the right to a certain amount of leisure because he doesn't know how to use that leisure. Also, unwillingness to spend money for recreational or creative purposes may actually express the fear of spending money without doing a sufficient amount of work to punish oneself for it. For example, one doctor told me that when he went on vacation he always borrowed the money because he would have to punish himself with work to pay it back, and this was just penance for the pleasure of not working!

The middle-aged person, furthermore, often feels the need to redouble his efforts in order to get ready for retirement. He continues to do repetitious tasks in order to have something in reserve for a "rainy day." He then may become severely depressed. Fortunately, excellent methods of treatment for "middle-aged depressions" are available, and a professional person can be of real assistance to someone who is suffering in this way. They have the "know-how" to help him decide things he hitherto has had no support in deciding. They can even intervene directly and decide a few things for him, such as specific changes in his work habits. Thus, although middle-aged depression is very painful, it can often lead the middle-aged work addict to do what he should have done in the first place without becoming depressed and feeling guilty about it: interrupt his routine of work, do something for a while that he really enjoys doing, and stop driving himself like a slave.

Today culture has created the possibility of more leisure time for us through a shorter work week. As a people, we have more of this world's goods at an earlier age. We are lengthening life; we can retire. Yet we have not escaped the compulsion about work that defies external efforts to make life easier. We have not found the answer to the covetousness that makes men compete with each other in their work all out of proportion to their needs. We have not found the secret of rest in the midst of plenty, renewal in the midst of work, and companionship in the atmosphere of loneliness that tarrying too long at the job produces. Our culture produces the workaholic. We need to attend to the nature of a society that needs such slaves to work, and at the same time to struggle against our individual compulsions to work.

MAJOR TYPES OF WORKAHOLICS

Previously we have been talking about *one* kind of workaholic, the dyed-in-the-wool kind. Careful observation of a business organization, a hospital staff, the military, a church organization, or a school reveals a *variety* of different types of workaholics. Therefore, we must describe and classify these various types.

The Dyed-in-the-Wool Workaholic

This man or woman has several characteristics as you see him or her in action on the job. First, whatever kind of skill and/or profession he practices, *he is a "professional" at it*. He takes the standards of excellent performance more than seriously; these are well nigh his total personal ethical code, if not tantamount to a religion for him. He will not touch an assignment lightly or halfway. To him there is no such thing as giving an assignment "a lick and a promise." He leaves his own professional stamp on a job if he accepts responsibility for it at all. A noncompulsive professional will be able to settle for a less than perfect result. The workaholic *has* to get 100 percent results.

Already you are beginning to see that the dyed-in-the-wool workaholic is a real *perfectionist*. He is merciless in his demands upon himself for thoroughness, mastery, and peak performance. Every operation for a workaholic physician is a dramatic, command performance. Every transaction of a businessman workaholic must be meticulously planned, forcefully accomplished, and followed up for a specific appraisal of the results. The workaholic minister is impeccable in his preparation and delivery of sermons and performs over and above pastoral service to people in distress. The work-addicted salesman will feel double pride in taking care of his personal customers, accounts, and so on.

Another characteristic of this kind of work addict is his *vigorous intolerance of incompetence* in those who work with him. His relationships with his fellow workers will be cordial, relaxed, and even warm until someone starts blundering—according to his estimate. Then the workaholic is hard, even impossible, to live with at all. He is apparently without qualms as to the consequences of telling off both high and low if he thinks they are doing a sloppy job.

This perfectionism and corresponding intolerance creates a parallel relationship to the peer group of the workaholic and to his superiors, or the authority structure. The peer group tends to isolate the workaholic because of his unquestioned competence which makes them feel that he is in a class to himself. Yet, when the real dirty work has to be done, they elect him to do it. They hate his guts but know that he will get the grimier jobs done. For example, he is an ideal candidate to become a union steward. He often is the unofficial and unpaid ombudsman for the organization. Because of his "eccentricity credit" — i.e., his earned right to be different, due to sheer accomplishment, and because of his job security and aggressiveness — his peers say "let him do it." All of them may consider themselves as Moses, appointed to the supreme leadership, but they think of the work addict as Aaron who does their talking for them when the going gets rough. In these conditions lie some clues for breaking the power of work addiction.

On the other hand, the executives feel ambivalent about the workaholic. They *need* him when a program is to be put into action. Yet they fear him. Their authority is an imputed, constituted, official authority. In the long run it has the last word. But they fear the workaholic because his authority is more personal, functional, and earned. In the day-to-day operation of the plant, the company, the school, or the church, the workaholic's presence must always be taken into account in many major and minor decisions. A project can be adopted on paper, but it is the workaholic who must translate it into a working, day-to-day, functional reality. In most organizations there is quite a collection of these workaholics. The typical administrator is ambivalent toward them because they are both a blessing and a problem to him. They are a blessing because they get the job done; they are a problem because they have the prestige to buck the boss with some impunity.

A fourth characteristic of the "dyed-in-the-wool" workaholic is his *overcommitment* to the institution, business, or organization for which he works. I have often speculated that some men and women replace their fathers, mothers, or siblings with the institutions they work for. It is not by chance, for example, that a school is called *alma mater*, "our mother."

A final characteristic of the dyed-in-the-wool workaholic is that he usually is both talented to begin with and has acquired a set of highly marketable skills. He is much in demand. If he has no effective internal way of rating his priorities, he is likely to take on more and more over and above his prescribed activities. Thus he collides with himself in the face of the many demands laid upon him: he is a perfectionist but he commits himself to so many people for the use of his skills that he cannot do his job well. This results in an anxiety depression amounting to panic. His sleep is more and more curtailed by the sheer problems of scheduling and by his effort to prepare for his responsibilities when he should be sleeping. The morass of contradictory demands is too deep for him to extricate himself from, and something has to be done by others to rescue him. His life has become unmanageable.

The Converted Workaholic

A second type of workaholic is the arrested or converted workaholic. He comes from the population just described. He is a "professional," but he has taken seriously the nonprofessional's way of life. The professional man is by nature a round-the-clock man. The nonprofessional is, if he is a farmer, a "sun-up-to-sun-down" man; if he is an industrial or white-collar nonprofessional, he is a "seven-to-three" or "nine-to-five" man. Also, these nonprofessionals guard their free time jealously. If they use some of it, they have to be paid time and a half; if they work very much overtime, they have to be paid double time.

Therefore, the professional who is a converted workaholic requires exceptional pay when people make his five-day week into a seven-, eight-, or nine-day one — but he will do the extra work if paid for it. Also, for the normal day's work, he sets a hypothetical limit and stays within it. For example, it took several illnesses for my body to get the message through to my brain that I was a compulsiver worker. Once it did, I decided that I would not travel past midnight, that I would not accept engagements that required my participation morning, afternoon, *and* evening in any one day. I decided that I would go to work at a specific time each day and come home at a specific time.

This sounds simple enough, but it is not that easy. Men and women sometimes take extra work for prestige reasons. A doctor chooses to work six months in a prestigious clinic as an expert in a particular procedure, teaching it to that staff. A professor is called as a consultant on a new project for a government agency or another nation. A minister is asked to do a national television series for his denomination. Too often these jobs pay off in honor, prestige, publicity, with money a secondary consideration. We might conclude that it is men's egos — not overwork — that kills them!

The element of omnipotence sneaks into the workaholic's thinking. He fantasizes that *he* is the *only* person who can respond to these requests. If for any reason he turns such an opportunity down, however, he may discover that he was fifth or sixth on the list! And if he waits and observes news notices, he will certainly discover that other people followed him on the list. . . .

We come now to the person who is new on his job, is in the "starvation period" of his profession, or is at the lowest pay echelons in his organization. This man overworks out of real necessity, not for inner psychic reasons, not for prestige reasons. He may have reasonable job security but large amounts of economic anxiety. It is not a part of this person's basic personality to work incessantly. As his practice becomes established or when his salary rises to a more adequate level, he corrects his course easily and lives more sensibly, letting work recede to a normal place in his value system. Nonetheless, he is a candidate for compulsive work addiction. The prestige system of his organization or profession, the prestige needs of his wife, the kind of neighborhood he lives in all serve to determine his habits. Not the least significant factor is the kind of older colleagues he has as advisers and models for his behavior. Younger men tend to pattern their standards of living, work habits, and approach to life on older professionals. Administrators of schools, hospitals, churches, and professional societies seem to be unaware of this element in their work patterns.

Sometimes the situational workaholic is a person whose job security is minimal. He may be new in a company that has periodic layoffs, and the last to come is the first to go. He may be in a trial period with his organization, such as under three-year nontenure contract on a university faculty. In overperforming to achieve security, he is often preparing the inner ground for compulsive overwork later on. . . .

The Pseudo-Workaholic

[Another] type of workaholic is one who has many of the characteristics of a true dyed-in-the-wool workaholic, but these are superficial. They are specific competitive accommodations to the pecking order of the organization. This person does his work in order to move from one echelon in the power structure to another. His orientation to work is not a production orientation, as in the case of the dyed-in-the-wool workaholic; his is a power orientation. He does all the right things to insure promotion. These include having a very active social life which obligates the "right people" to reciprocate his hospitality. It involves doing favors in abundance for power figures in the organization. Thus the pattern of "I've scratched your back, now scratch mine" is set in motion. The focus of interest in choosing things to do on the job is to follow the in group. If the in group is thrust out of power for any reason, he shifts, without apparent embarrassment over the inconsistency, to the new in group although their position and function on major issues is diametrically opposed. This cannot be understood unless it is seen that this man responds consistently to power and not to issues. He is opportunistic in this respect, but can be counted on to respond this way.

The pseudo-workaholic may be spotted by the lack of perfectionism in his work. He makes many brilliant starts in what he does, but when the prestige of having made a dazzling beginning wears off, the long pull of the carry-through is odious to him. He is likely to leave one project for another very soon. The pseudo-workaholic changes jobs often. He is strictly an image man, not a performance man. Laurence Peter and Raymond Hull state it well when they say *"an ounce of image is worth a pound of performance."*[2]

The real commitment of the pseudo-workaholic is to the prestige and power the organization offers *him*. He draws his name *from* the institution; he does not give his name *to* the institution. The institution is strictly a means and in no sense an end in itself. There is no attachment to or affection for the organization. In psychoanalytic jargon, the pseudo-workaholic is narcissistic. As Browning said of one of his characters, this person is deeply in love with himself and probably will win the match!

The pseudo-workaholic, furthermore, moves vigorously and actively until he reaches the limits of the prestige system. Then his real character emerges. He is basically a playboy who, as Laurence Peter and Raymond Hull say, has been promoted *beyond* the level of his competence and *to* the level of his *in*competence! These men, in their painfully humorous book, lay bare the "Peter Principle" that "for each individual, for *you,* for *me,* the final promotion is from a level of competence to a level of incompetence."[3] The real work "is accomplished by those who have not yet reached their level of incompetence."[4] . . .

The Escapist Posing as a Workaholic

I would not be true to the facts in describing the different types of workaholics if I did not make note of a very common phenomenon: the person who simply stays on the job — or in the place of work — rather than go home. I noticed this first when I was a page in the United States Senate and discovered there were a few senators who slept in their offices regularly! I will admit that this is extreme, but in a variety of organizations in which I have worked and in a large number of those I have observed, this species of worker exists, even if there are but few of them. A chaotic marriage is the cause for some of these situations. The marriage in which in-laws live in the home is another. I saw one case in which *both* sets of in-laws lived in the home. In other instances, the worker simply enjoyed the company of the people he worked with more than he did that of the people at home. For this person work was a substitute home.

Occasionally, I have seen single persons make the real mistake of expecting their job to substitute for *all* other relationships. Of course, we have a whole subculture of persons in the Roman Catholic Church who operate on this as an articulate, ordered set of values. But when it occurs without such cultural support and institutional moorings, the effects can be very frustrating, unsatisfying, and confusing.

These persons are not, ordinarily, workaholics in the sense of being compulsive workers. For them work is an escape, and this is very different from a compulsion.

SOME GUIDING PRINCIPLES ON THE JOB

It is one thing to curse the power-and-light company, and another to light a candle. I think it is time to light a candle. I have done my share of the other. Some principles of health for a group of workers in a bureaucratic situation are as follows:

First, a man or woman should fear like a plague the fate of being given a new position that calls for skills in which he is not interested, for which he has not been trained, and which do not afford him basic job satisfaction. The usual reason for going into such work is not ordinarily financial. Rather it is prestige and power. These are like salt water. Salt water does all the things fresh water does — it is wet and cool, it washes, etc. — except the one thing we need water most to do — quench thirst. Power without work satisfaction is the same: it just makes you want more.

Second, the man on the job should decide what he can best do and do it with singleminded devotion. A devout people would call this being at peace in the intention of God for our lives. Regardless of what one's image in other people's eyes may be, this should be what he strives for.

Third, health in relation to work may require that the worker reappraise his family relationships and decide that he is going to exercise leadership in his own home. An ancient Christian source suggests, for example, that the person who accepts a position of responsibility in the church must first have demonstrated effective leadership in his own home. The worker cannot continue to be intimidated by the prestige needs and money drives of his wife and children. He must lead them.

Fourth, the worker needs to begin developing a sense of humor if he does not already have one. The rollicking sense of humor with which Laurence Peter and Raymond Hull tell in a serious jest about how incompetency in an organization rises, like cream, to the top, and there sours, is a wholesome example of what I mean.

NOTES

1. *The Organization Man* (New York: Doubleday, 1957), p. 164.
2. *The Peter Principle* (New York: Bantam Books, 1969), p. 121.
3. Ibid., p. 8.
4. Ibid., p. 10.

Cat's in the Cradle

Harry Chapin

My child arrived just the other day;
he came to the world in the usual way.
But there were planes to catch and bills to pay;
he learned to walk while I was away.
And he was talkin' 'fore I knew it,
and as he grew he'd say,
"I'm gonna be like you, Dad,
you know I'm gonna be like you."

And the cat's in the cradle and the silver spoon,
little boy blue and the man in the moon.
"When you comin' home Dad?"
"I don't know when, but we'll get together then,
you know we'll have a good time then."

My son turned ten just the other day;
he said, "Thanks for the ball, Dad,
come on let's play.
Can you teach me to throw?"
I said, "Not today, I got a lot to do."
He said, "That's okay."
But his smile never dimmed, it said,
"I'm gonna be like him, yeah,
you know I'm gonna be like him."

Chorus

Well he came from college just the other day;
so much like a man I just had to say,
"Son, I'm proud of you, can you sit for a while?"
He shook his head and he said with a smile,
"What I'd really like, Dad,
is to borrow the car keys;
see you later, can I have them please?"

Chorus

I've long since retired,
my son's moved away;
I called him up just the other day.
I said, "I'd like to see you if you don't mind."
He said, "I'd love to Dad, if I could find the time.
You see, my new job's a hassle and the kids have the flu,
but it's sure nice talkin' to you, Dad,
it's been sure nice talkin' to you."
As I hung up the phone,
it occurred to me,
he'd grown up just like me;
my boy was just like me.

Chorus

Wheels

Arthur Hailey

At a car assembly plant north of the Fisher Freeway, Matt Zaleski, assistant plant manager and a graying veteran of the auto industry, was glad that today was Wednedsay.

Not that the day would be free from urgent problems and exercises in survival — no day ever was. Tonight, like any night, he would go homeward wearily, feeling older than his fifty-three years and convinced he had spent another day of his life inside a pressure cooker. Matt Zaleski sometimes wished he could summon back the energy he had had as a young man, either when he was new to auto production or as an Air Force bombardier in World War II. He also thought sometimes, looking back, that the years of war — even though he was in Europe in the thick of things, with an impressive combat record— were less crisis-filled than his civil occupation now.

Already, in the few minutes he had been in his glass-paneled office on a mezzanine above the assembly plant floor, even while removing his coat, he had skimmed through a red-tabbed memo on the desk —a union grievance which he realized immediately could cause a plant-wide walkout if it wasn't dealt with properly and promptly. There was undoubtedly still more to worry about in an adjoining pile of papers — other headaches, including critical material shortages (there were always some, each day), or quality control demands, or machinery failures, or some new conundrum which no one had thought of before, any or all of which could halt the assembly line and stop production.

Zaleski threw his stocky figure into the chair at his gray metal desk, moving in short, jerky movements, as he always had. He heard the chair protest — a reminder of his growing overweight and the big belly he carried around nowadays. He thought ashamedly; he could never squeeze it now into the cramped nose dome of a B-17. He wished that worry would take off pounds; instead, it seemed to put them on, especially since Freda died and loneliness at night drove him to the refrigerator, nibbling, for lack of something else to do.

But at least today was Wednesday.

First things first. He hit the intercom switch for the general office; his secretary wasn't in yet. A timekeeper answered.

"I want Parkland and the union committeeman," the assistant plant manager commanded. "Get them in here fast."

Parkland was a foreman. And outside they would be well aware which union committeeman he meant because they would know about the red-tabbed memo on his desk. In a plant, bad news traveled like burning gasoline.

The pile of papers — still untouched, though he would have to get to them soon — reminded Zaleski he had been thinking gloomily of the many causes which could halt an assembly line.

Halting the line, stopping production for whatever reason, was like a sword in the side to Matt Zaleski. The function of his job, his personal *raison d'être*, was to keep the line moving, with finished cars being driven off the end at the rate of one car a minute, no matter how the trick was done or if, at times, he felt like a juggler with fifteen balls in the air at once. Senior management wasn't interested in the juggling act, or excuses either. Results were what counted: quotas, daily production, manufacturing costs. But if the line stopped he heard about it soon enough. Each single minute of lost time meant that an entire car didn't get produced, and the loss would never be made up. Thus, even a two- or three-minute stoppage cost thousands of dollars because, while an assembly line stood still, wages and other costs went rollicking on.

But at least today was Wednesday.

The intercom clicked. "They're on their way, Mr. Zaleski."

He acknowledged curtly.

The reason Matt Zaleski liked Wednesday was simple. Wednesday was two days removed from Monday, and Friday was two more days away.

Mondays and Fridays in auto plants were management's most harrowing days because of absenteeism. Each Monday, more hourly paid employees failed to report for work than on any other normal weekday; Friday ran a close second. It happened because after paychecks were handed out, usually on Thursday, many workers began a long boozy or drugged weekend, and afterward, Monday was a day for catching up on sleep or nursing hangovers.

Thus, on Mondays and Fridays, other problems were eclipsed by one enormous problem of keeping production going despite a critical shortage of people. Men were moved around like marbles in a game of Chinese checkers. Some were removed from tasks they were accustomed to and given jobs they had never done before. A worker who normally tightened wheel nuts might find himself fitting front fenders, often with the briefest of instruction or sometimes none at all. Others, pulled in hastily from labor pools or less skilled duties — such as loading trucks or sweeping — would be put to work wherever gaps remained. Sometimes they caught on quickly in their temporary roles; at other times they might spend an entire shift installing heater hose clamps, or something similar — upside down.

The result was inevitable. Many of Monday's and Friday's cars were shoddily put together, with built-in legacies of trouble for their owners, and those in the know avoided them like contaminated meat. A few big city dealers, aware of the problem and with influence at factories because of volume sales, insisted that cars for more valued customers be built on Tuesday, Wednesday, or Thursday, and customers who knew the ropes sometimes went to big dealers with this objective. Cars for company executives and their friends were invariably scheduled for one of the midweek days.

The door of the assistant plant manager's office flung open abruptly. The foreman he had sent for, Parkland, strode in, not bothering to knock.

Parkland was a broad-shouldered, big-boned man in his late thirties, about fifteen years younger than Matt Zaleski. He might have been a football fullback if he had gone to college, and, unlike many foremen nowadays, looked as if he could handle authority. He also looked, at the moment, as if he expected trouble and was prepared to meet it. The foreman's face was glowering. There was a darkening bruise, Zaleski noted, beneath his right cheekbone.

Ignoring the mode of entry, Zaleski motioned him to a chair. "Take the weight off your feet, then simmer down."

They faced each other across the desk.

"I'm willing to hear your version of what happened," the assistant plant chief said, "but don't waste time because the way this reads" — he fingered the red-tabbed grievance report — "you've cooked us all a hot potato."

"The hell I cooked it!" Parkland glared at his superior; above the bruise his face flushed red. "I fired a guy because he slugged me. What's more, I'm gonna make it stick, and if you've got any guts or justice you'd better back me up."

Matt Zaleski raised his voice to the bull roar he had learned on a factory floor. "Knock off that goddam nonsense, right now!" He had no intention of letting this get out of hand. More reasonably, he growled, "I said simmer down, and meant it. When the time comes I'll decide who to back and why. And there'll be no more crap from you about guts and justice. Understand?"

Their eyes locked together. Parkland's dropped first.

"All right, Frank," Matt said. "Let's start over, and this time give it to me straight, from the beginning."

He had known Frank Parkland a long time. The foreman's record was good and he was usually fair with men who worked under him. It had taken something exceptional to get him as riled as this.

"There was a job out of position," Parkland said. "It was steering column bolts, and there was this kid doing it; he's new, I guess. He was crowding the next guy. I wanted the job put back."

Zaleski nodded. It happened often enough. A worker with a specific assignment took a few seconds longer than he should on each operation. As successive cars moved by on the assembly line, his position gradually changed, so that soon he was intruding on the area of the next operation. When a foreman saw it happen he made it his business to help the worker back to his correct, original place.

Zaleski said impatiently, "Get on with it."

Before they could continue, the office door opened again and the union committeeman came in. He was a small, pink-faced man, with thick-lensed glasses and a fussy manner. His name was Illas and, until a union election a few months ago, had been an assembly line worker himself.

"Good morning," the union man said to Zaleski. He nodded curtly to Parkland, without speaking.

Matt Zaleski waved the newcomer to a chair. "We're just getting to the meat."

"You could save a lot of time," Illas said, "if you read the grievance report."

"I've read it. But sometimes I like to hear the other side." Zaleski motioned Parkland to go on.

"All I did," the foreman said, "was call another guy over and say, 'Help me get this man's job back in position.' "

"And I say you're a liar!" The union man hunched forward accusingly; now he swung toward Zaleski. "What he really said was 'get this *boy's* job back.' And it so happened that the person he was speaking of, and calling, 'boy,' was one of our black brothers to whom that word is a very offensive term."

"Oh, for God's sake!" Parkland's voice combined anger with disgust. "D'you think I don't know that? D'you think I haven't been around here long enough to know better than to use that word that way?"

"But you *did* use it, didn't you?"

"Maybe, just maybe, I did. I'm not saying yes, because I don't remember, and that's the truth. But if it happened, there was nothing meant. It was a slip, that's all."

The union man shrugged. "That's your story now."

"It's no story, you son-of-a-bitch!"

Illas stood up. "Mr. Zaleski, I'm here officially, representing the United Auto Workers. If that's the kind of language . . ."

"There'll be no more of it," the assistant plant manager said. "Sit down, please, and while we're on the subject, I suggest you be less free yourself with the word 'liar.'"

Parkland slammed a beefy fist in frustration on the desk top. "I said it was no story, and it isn't. What's more, the guy I was talking about didn't even give a thought to what I said, at least before all the fuss was made."

"That's not the way *he* tells it," Illas said.

"Maybe not now," Parkland appealed to Zaleski. "Listen, Matt, the guy who was out of position is just a kid. A black kid, maybe seventeen. I've got nothing against him; he's slow, but he was doing his job. I've got a kid brother his age. I go home, I say, 'Where's the boy?' Nobody thinks twice about it. That's the way it was with this thing until this other guy, Newkirk, cut in."

Illas persisted, "But you're admitting you used the word 'boy.'"

Matt Zaleski said wearily, "Okay, okay, he used it. Let's all concede that."

Zaleski was holding himself in, as he always had to do when racial issues erupted in the plant. His own prejudices were deep-rooted and largely anti-black, and he had learned them in the heavily Polish suburb of Wyandotte where he was born. There, the families of Polish origin looked on Negroes with contempt, as shiftless and troublemakers. In return, the black people hated Poles, and even nowadays, throughout Detroit, the ancient enmities persisted. Zaleski, through necessity, had learned to curb his instinct; you couldn't run a plant with as much black labor as this one and let your prejudices show, at least not often. Just now, after the last remark of Illas, Matt Zaleski had been tempted to inject: *So what if he did call him "boy"? What the hell difference does it make? When a foreman tells him to, let the bastard get back to work.* But Zaleski knew it would be repeated and maybe cause more trouble than before. Instead, he growled, "What matters is what came after."

"Well," Parkland said, "I thought we'd never get to that. We almost had the job back in place, then this heavyweight, Newkirk, showed up."

"He's another black brother," Illas said.

"Newkirk'd been working down the line. He didn't even hear what happened; somebody else told him. He came up, called me a racist pig, and slugged me." The foreman fingered his bruised face which had swollen even more since he came in.

Zaleski asked sharply, "Did you hit him back?"

"No."

"I'm glad you showed a little sense."

"I had sense, all right," Parkland said. "I fired Newkirk. On the spot. Nobody slugs a foreman around here and gets away with it."

"We'll see about that," Illas said. "A lot depends on circumstances and provocation."

Matt Zaleski thrust a hand through his hair; there were days when he marveled that there was any left. This whole stinking situation was something which McKernon, the plant manager, should handle, but McKernon wasn't here. He was ten miles away at staff headquarters, attending a conference about the new Orion, a super-secret car the plant would be producing soon. Sometimes it seemed to Matt Zaleski as if McKernon had already begun his retirement, officially six months away.

Matt Zaleski was holding the baby now, as he had before, and it was a lousy deal. Zaleski wasn't even going to succeed McKernon, and he knew it. He'd already been called in and shown the official assessment of himself, the assessment which appeared in a loose-leaf, leather-bound book which sat permanently on the desk of the Vice-President, Manufacturing. The book was there so that the vice-president could turn its pages whenever new appointments or promotions were considered. The entry for Matt Zaleski, along with his photo and other details, read: "This individual is well placed at his present level of management."

Everybody in the company who mattered knew that the formal, unctuous statement was a "kiss off." What it really meant was: *This man has gone as high as he's going. He will probably serve his time out in his present spot, but will receive no more promotions.*

The rules said that whoever received that deadly summation on his docket had to be told; he was entitled to that much, and it was the reason Matt Zaleski had known for the past several months that he would never rise beyond his present role of assistant manager. Initially the news had been a bitter disappointment, but now that he had grown used to the idea, he also knew why: He was old shoe, the hind end of a disappearing breed which management and boards of directors didn't want any more in the top critical posts. Zaleski had risen by a route which few senior plant people followed nowadays — factory worker, inspector, foreman, superintendent, assistant plant manager. He hadn't had an engineering degree to start, having been a high school dropout before World War II. But after the war he had armed himself with a degree, using night school and GI credits, and after that had started climbing, being ambitious, as most of his generation were who had survived *Festung Europa* and other perils. But, as Zaleski recognized later, he had lost too much time; his real start came too late. The strong comers, the top echelon material of the auto companies — then as now — were the bright youngsters who arrived fresh and eager through the direct college-to-front office route.

But that was no reason why McKernon, who was still plant boss, should sidestep this entire situation, even if unintentionally. The assistant manager hesitated. He would be within his rights to send for McKernon and could do it here and now by picking up a phone.

Two things stopped him. One, he admitted to himself, was pride; Zaleski knew he could handle this as well as McKernon, if not better. The other: His instinct told him there simply wasn't time.

Abruptly, Zaleski asked Illas, "What's the union asking?"

"Well, I've talked with the president of our local . . ."

"Let's save all that," Zaleski said. "We both know we have to start somewhere, so what is it you want?"

"Very well," the committeeman said. "We insist on three things. First, immediate reinstatement of Brother Newkirk, with compensation for time lost. Second, an apology for both men involved. Third, Parkland has to be removed from his post as foreman."

Parkland, who had slumped back in his chair, shot upright. "By Christ! You don't want much." He inquired sarcastically, "As a matter of interest, am I supposed to apologize before I'm fired, or after?"

"The apology would be an official one from the company," Illas answered. "Whether you had the decency to add your own would be up to you."

"I'll say it'd be up to me. Just don't anyone hold their breath waiting."

Matt Zaleski snapped, "If you'd held your own breath a little longer, we wouldn't be in this mess."

"Are you trying to tell me you'll go along with all that?" The foreman motioned angrily to Illas.

"I'm not telling anybody anything yet. I'm trying to think, and I need more information than has come from you two." Zaleski reached behind him for a telephone. Interposing his body between the phone and the other two, he dialed a number and waited.

When the man he wanted answered, Zaleski asked simply, "How are things down there?"

The voice at the other end spoke softly. "Matt?"

"Yeah."

In the background behind the other's guarded response, Zaleski could hear a cacophony of noise from the factory floor. He always marveled how men could live with that noise every day of their working lives. Even in the years he had worked on an assembly line himself, before removal to an office shielded him from most of the din, he had never grown used to it.

His informant said, "The situation's real bad, Matt."

"How bad?"

"The hopheads are in the saddle. Don't quote me."

"I never do," the assistant plant manager said. "You know that."

He had swung partially around and was aware of the other two in the office watching his face. They might guess, but couldn't know, that he was speaking to a black foreman, Stan Lathruppe, one of the half dozen men in the plant whom Matt Zaleski respected most. It was a strange, even paradoxical, relationship because, away from the plant, Lathruppe was an active militant who had once been a follower of Malcolm X. But here he took his responsibility seriously, believing that in the auto world he could achieve more for his race through reason than by anarchy. It was this second attitude which Zaleski — originally hostile to Lathruppe — had eventually come to respect.

Unfortunately for the company, in the present state of race relations, it had comparatively few black foremen or managers. There ought to be more, many more, and everybody knew it, but right now many of the black workers didn't want responsibility, or were afraid of it because of young militants in their ranks, or simply weren't ready. Sometimes Matt Zaleski, in his less prejudiced moments, thought that if the industry's top brass had looked ahead a few years, the way senior executives were supposed to do, and had launched a meaningful training program for black workers in the 1940s and '50s, there would be more Stan Lathruppes now. It was everybody's loss that there were not.

Zaleski asked, "What's being planned?"

"I think a walkout."

"When?"

"Probably at break time. It could be before, but I don't believe so."

The black foreman's voice was so low Zaleski had to strain to hear. He knew the other man's problem, added to by the fact that the telephone he was using was alongside the assembly line where others were working. Lathruppe was already labeled a "white nigger" by some fellow blacks who resented even their own race when in authority, and it made no difference that the charge was untrue. Except for a couple more questions, Zaleski had no intention of making Stan Lathruppe's life more difficult.

He asked, "Is there any reason for the delay?"

"Yes. The hopheads want to take the whole plant out."

"Is word going around?"

"So fast you'd think we still used jungle drums."

"Has anyone pointed out the whole thing's illegal?"

"You got any more jokes like that?" Lathruppe said.

"No." Zaleski sighed. "But thanks." He hung up.

So his first instinct had been right. There wasn't any time to spare, and hadn't been from the beginning, because a racial labor dispute always burned with a short fuse. Now, if a walkout happened, it could take days to settle and get everybody back at work; and even if only black workers became involved, and maybe not all of them, the effect would still be enough to halt production. Matt Zaleski's job was to keep production going.

As if Parkland had read his thoughts, the foreman urged, "Matt, don't let them push you! So a few may walk off the job, and we'll have trouble. But a principle's worth standing up for, sometimes, isn't it?"

"Sometimes," Zaleski said. "The trick is to know which principle, and when."

"Being fair is a good way to start," Parkland said, "and fairness works two ways—up and down." He leaned forward over the desk, speaking earnestly to Matt Zaleski, glancing now and then to the union committeeman, Illas. "Okay, I've been tough with guys on the line because I've had to be. A foreman's in the middle, catching crap from all directions. From up here, Matt, you and your people are on our necks every day for production, production, more production; and if it isn't you it's Quality Control who say, build 'em better, even though you're building faster. Then there are those who are working, doing the jobs — including some like Newkirk, and others — and a foreman has to cope with them, along with the union as well if he puts a foot wrong, and sometimes when he doesn't. So it's a tough business, and I've been tough; it's the way to survive. But I've been fair, too. I've never treated a guy who worked for me differently because he was black, and I'm no plantation overseer with a whip. As for what we're talking about now, all I did — so I'm told — is call a black man 'boy.' I didn't ask him to pick cotton, or ride Jim Crow, or shine shoes, or any other thing that's supposed to go with that word. What I did was help him with his job. And I'll say another thing: if I did call him 'boy'—so help me, by a slip!—I'll say I'm sorry for that, because I am. But not to Newkirk. Brother Newkirk stays fired. Because if he doesn't, if he gets away with slugging a foreman without reason, you can stuff a surrender flag up your ass and wave goodbye to any discipline around this place from this day on. That's what I mean when I say be fair."

"You've got a point or two there." Zaleski said. Ironically, he thought, Frank Parkland *had* been fair with black workers, maybe fairer than a good many others around the plant. He asked Illas, "How do you feel about all that?"

The union man looked blandly through his thick-lensed glasses. "I've already stated the union's position, Mr. Zaleski."

"So if I turn you down, if I decide to back up Frank the way he just said I should, what then?"

Illas said stiffly, "We'd be obliged to go through further grievance procedure."

"Okay." The assistant plant manager nodded. "That's your privilege. Except, if we go through a full grievance drill it can mean thirty days or more. In the meantime, does everybody keep working?"

"Naturally. The collective bargaining agreement specifies . . ."

Zaleski flared, "I don't need you to tell me what the agreement says! It says everybody stays on the job while we negotiate. But right now a good many of your men are getting ready to walk off their jobs in violation of the contract."

For the first time, Illas looked uneasy. "The UAW does not condone illegal strikes."

"Goddamit, then! Stop this one!"

"If what you say is true, I'll talk to some of our people."

"Talking won't do any good. You know it, and I know it." Zaleski eyed the union committeeman whose pink face had paled slightly; obviously Illas didn't relish the thought of arguing with some of the black militants in their present mood.

The union—as Matt Zaleski was shrewdly aware—was in a tight dilemma in situations of this kind. If the union failed to support its black militants at all, the militants would charge union leaders with racial prejudice and being "management lackeys." Yet if the union went too far with its support, it could find itself in an untenable position legally, as party to a wildcat strike. Illegal strikes were anathema to UAW leaders like Woodcock, Fraser, Greathouse, Bannon, and others, who had built reputations for tough negotiating, but also for honoring agreements once made, and settling grievances through due process. Wildcatting debased the union's word and undermined its bargaining strength.

"They're not going to thank you at Solidarity House if we let this thing get away from us," Matt Zaleski persisted. "There's only one thing can stop a walkout, and that's for us to make a decision here, then go down on the floor and announce it."

Illas said, "That depends on the decision." But it was plain that the union man was weighing Zaleski's words.

Matt Zaleski had already decided what the ruling had to be, and he knew that nobody would like it entirely, including himself. He thought sourly: these were lousy times, when a man had to shove his convictions in his pocket along with pride—at least, if he figured to keep an automobile plant running.

He announced brusquely, "Nobody gets fired. Newkirk goes back to his job, but from now on he uses his fists for working, nothing else." The assistant plant manager fixed his eyes on Illas. "I want it clearly understood by you and by Newkirk—one more time, he's out. And before he goes back, I'll talk to him myself."

"He'll be paid for lost time?" The union man had a slight smile of triumph.

"Is he still at the plant?"

"Yes."

Zaleski hesitated, then nodded reluctantly. "Okay, providing he finishes the shift. But there'll be no more talk about anybody replacing Frank." He swung to face Parkland. "And you'll do what you said you would—talk to the young guy. Tell him what was said was a mistake."

"An apology is what it's known as," Illas said.

Frank Parkland glared at them both. "Of all the crummy, sleazy backdowns!"

"Take it easy!" Zaleski warned.

"Like hell I'll take it easy!" The burly foreman was on his feet, towering over the assistant plant manager. He spat words across the desk between them. "You're the one taking it easy—the easy out because you're too much a goddam coward to stand up for what you know is right."

His face flushing deep red, Zaleski roared, "I don't have to take that from you! That'll be enough! You hear?"

"I hear." Contempt filled Parkland's voice and eyes. "But I don't like what I hear, or what I smell."

"In that case, maybe you'd like to be fired!"

"Maybe," the foreman said. "Maybe the air'd be cleaner some place else."

There was a silence between them, then Zaleski growled, "It's no cleaner. Some days it stinks everywhere."

The Time Pressured Life

Ann Marie Cunningham

Today's symbol of success is a schedule simmering with pressure. Carrying diaries jammed months ahead with commitments, we regiment our time — lunching for contracts, dining for contacts, reading only for business. Dripping with crocodile tears, successful men and their growing number of female colleagues brag about their surfeit of duties, their lack of time.

Thus, committed time translates easily into status, and "no time" is a sure sign that someone is doing something important. Once luxury was status, leisure was status, but nowadays overextension, not even overachievement, is the ironic equivalent of the Good Life.

As women rise to executive and professional status, they become as time-pressured as men. But man-time and woman-time are still far from equal. Woman-time generally means trying to integrate professional and personal life, while man-time traditionally involves using the personal as a support system for the professional. Pressure to "improve each shining hour" by devoting it to work is hard enough on men; it is monstrous for women.

For roughly 25 years, the thinking in sociology ran that the more social roles we had, the more strain we suffered because each role carried obligations. Then in 1974, as more women entered the working world, Sam D. Sieber, a sociologist at Columbia University, noticed that the more roles we had, the more benefits, not just duties, we accrued. Sieber pointed out that privileges — meaning liberties or freedoms — are "part and parcel of every social role." The more roles you have, the more privileges you enjoy; quite simply, "more is more." One role's privileges become a kind of capital that can be reinvested — one job, one introduction, leads to others, "handsomely compensating," according to Sieber, "for the possible burden of multiple role obligations."

Among the advantages that go along with "more is more," Sieber points out, is the opportunity of placing social eggs in many baskets. With many roles, you may be spread thin but you have social security. Should you fail in one role, the others will buffer you. As you acquire more roles, you become more valuable to the people who know you in each role. Because you're valuable, and also less avail-

---

Abridged and reprinted from *Savvy*, December 1980. Reproduced by permission.

able, they will probably slacken their demands on you. Appreciated and even competed for, you will find your self-confidence ballooning. "Getting around" may leave you drained, but neither bored nor boring. Sieber would be surprised if we "did not often find that the tension engendered by conflict overload was totally overshadowed by the rewards" of many roles. He pointed out that demands for equality from women and minority groups seem to include "a desire for access to the profits and pleasures of role accumulation."

But, ultimately, more may not be more; there's the question of quality. How we choose to spend our time, which roles we adopt, means deciding on a set of values. If the prestigious life is spent as a pressured and divided human assembly line, then the heart of the American dream is dark indeed. From Sieber's description, all is not rosy in the multiroled world. There are distinct *sub rosa* tints of greed and predation. Your privileges may include connections, invitations, friends, lovers — "and by no means least, graft, bribes and payola." You will have to practice a fair amount of fancy footwork and quick exits to balance the demands of one set of "role partners" against another. Such privileges may mean liberties but they hardly seem freeing.

How does time pressure really affect women's lives? As they live lives more like those of men, are they adopting the very values of male society they formerly criticized? Are women being trained to ignore their traditional concerns? Because executive and professional women are recent arrivals on the sociological scene, no one knows how they go about balancing solid achievement and personal satisfaction. Behind the façade of the competent Superwoman, what is the life like, hour by hour, day by day?

Savvy asked fifteen successful women, aged 32 to 57—married and single, with and without children — to write dispatches from the front. These players of many roles were to keep track of their daily schedules from the alarm clock's ring to bedtime. *Savvy*'s study meant to examine the quality of the lives of this vanguard group, women on the edge of time, who have achieved the female version of the American Dream. Accordingly, the participants were asked to log what they thought about and how they felt while carrying out the day's tasks. What did these women—who included a White House special assistant, a company president, and a management consultant earning "low six figures"—think they had? And what do they really have?

Allowing for individual differences, the logs give a general impression of constant activity, of virtual enslavement to schedule. True to Sieber's notion of the effects of role accumulation, every woman reported happiness and satisfaction with her personal and professional lot. But those days of austere, machine-like productivity create the suspicion that there are pitfalls in time-pressured terrain.

The participants were subject to a scale of time pressures, culminating in a high of virtually around the clock for two mothers with three small children each. But nonstop schedules were not unique to mothers. "When I arrive at work, I get on a merry-go-round," said Helen Klein, a single copywriter who works for a large agency. "Sometime before bedtime, I'm thrown off. Next morning, I pick myself up and get on the merry-go-round again." The logs offer evidence that women have surpassed even male whirling: The average high-level male executive works a 60-hour week. But Barbara Taylor, who is married, childless, and a partner in Cullen and Taylor, Ltd., a public relations firm that specializes in travel and, ironically, leisure accounts, reported "100 hours of work out of 122 logged — definitely workaholic." Having accepted the notion that time pressure gives importance and direction to life, have these women been sold a bill of goods? An inability to stop trying to beat the clock is not so much the price, as the stark reality of the way we live now — the nightmare side of the American Dream.

The idea that a slippery devil like time can be managed is peculiarly Western. "Remember that Time is money," Benjamin Franklin, our most pragmatic Founding Father, admonished in 1748, in *Advice to a Young Tradesman;* but it wasn't until more than 100 years later that the "science" of time management was born in the factories of the industrial revolution.

Until 150 years ago, human schedules coincided with daylight hours and the annual cycle of the seasons. Then, in the mid-nineteenth century, electric light and heat allowed work to continue 24 hours a day, 365 days a year. In 1875, a lawyer's son named Frederick W. Taylor arrived at one of the new factories in Philadelphia as an apprentice. Poor eyesight had forced him to abandon plans to go to Harvard. But Taylor, an ascetic, energetic man who eschewed stimulants of all kinds, set great store by self-discipline as a means of developing "character." His "character" stood him in good stead as he rose from machine-shop laborer to chief engineer in a Philadelphia steel plant.

There he noticed that workers, under the mistaken impression that working rapidly today would lead to layoffs tmorrow because there would be no work left, were "soldiering," or working as slowly as possible. As an antidote, Taylor introduced, in 1881, what he called "scientific management." He argued that it was the way both management and labor could get what they wanted: high wages and production, combined with low labor costs.

Taylor's method was to select "a first class man," the most energetic worker, and then break his job down into as many simple, elementary movements as possible, discarding useless motions and selecting the most effective. He would then reconstruct the job and train the worker in the most efficient way of doing it.

Neither organized labor nor management believed him. At Bethlehem Steel, where Taylor was consulting, workers threatened his children, his wife and his life. Unions — and a young socialist named Upton Sinclair — were convinced that Taylor "gave about a 61 percent increase in wages, and got a 362 percent increase in work." Management did not appreciate Taylor either, because he blamed low production and soldiering on their lack of planning. When Taylor tried to reorganize the sprawling Army and Navy bureaucracies, their concerted opposition and the unions' resentment led to a blistering Congressional investigation of his methods.

A bruised Taylor survived to lecture at Harvard and to publish *Principles of Scientific Management*, which has been in print since its publication in 1911. Ultimately Taylorism flourished and led to the development of mass production techniques, which contributed to the great gains made by industrial production in the 1920s.

In 1973, Alan Lakein, who became a time management specialist when his computer business failed, took time management techniques one step further and applied them to personal life. In *How to Get Control of Your Time and Your Life,* Lakein urged readers to develop a "master plan for life," to rank each day's tasks *A, B,* or *C* in order of importance, and to concentrate only on accomplishing *A*'s. To fight the boredom inevitable in a life resembling Drucker's well-run factory, Lakein advised scheduling one exciting activity per day. He also suggested a wall sign bearing "Lakein's question": "What is the best use of my time right now?"

Lakein followed his own advice. The result sounded like a life spent in blinkers: He never watched television, talked over the phone rather than face to face, and seldom read beyond the first two paragraphs of a newspaper story. To gain more time, he slept less. Before finally dropping off, he programmed his unconscious mind to mull over an unsolved problem.

Lakein's book sold 150,000 copies in hardcover and there are 1,810,000 paperbacks currently in print. Like Taylor, Lakein used to lecture widely, but he has had no known address for more than a year. No one knows why he has disappeared. "We can only assume," said a sales manager at his paperback publisher, "that he found a better way to spend his time."

Despite his defection, Lakein remains the grand master of time management. Lesser gurus, often former workaholic women, sell time management to its new female audience with the zeal of the converted.

Does the training they offer work? When I told freelance time consultant Denise Racine that I planned to poll women who had heard her presentation at a conference, she said, "I can tell you what you will find. Changing the way you organize your time means changing habits, which is hard. Most women try everything I suggest and give up quickly. The trick is to do only one or two little things." A month after the conference, some women had done just one thing—had bought answering machines and had begun closing their office doors to work alone for an hour each day. But an equal number responded, "I haven't had time to get organized," and another third never called back, presumably having relegated my message to the C rank.

No time manager has great secrets for sale: Everyone advises that you plan ahead and do first things first. A chill lingers ominously around time management literature, however, because of its Taylorist emphasis on self-discipline. You're encouraged to think of yourself as a well-oiled machine, programmed with the proper software, and to speak always in the future tense. The purpose of the present—even if spent in sleep—is to think of the future. To time managers and their converts, life looks like an hourglass, whose two bulbs represent the fading past and the looming future. The tiny connecting neck is all that remains of the present.

The women who kept time logs for *Savvy's* study performed triumphs of time management, even though only two had attended formal seminars. Their logs held few surprises: They were well aware of how they spent their time. Careful planning, often years in advance, had enabled them to accumulate roles. Barbara Taylor, partner in her own public relations firm, summed up the mindset of the logs: "We're used to thinking ahead, not registering how we're reacting to what's going on now." Perhaps inevitably, two of these model planners had trouble envisioning a log that recorded how they felt. They were "not sure what you mean by emotions."

These women think ahead, rise early (7:00 A.M. at the latest), and know at what time of day they work best. Alice Haemmerli, vice president of Chase Manhattan Bank, N.A., currently dealing with projects involving China's economy, spent four years in France and found her planning "entirely at odds with the culture. It was a constant source of irritation." She liked to work on her doctoral thesis in the mornings, when she was freshest, and devote the afternoon to shopping. However, since all shops closed from 1 to 4 P.M. Haemmerli continued working through the hours when she would have preferred to do something "less intellectually demanding." While the French ate big lunches and napped, Haemmerli chose to work with an eye on the future. Ellen Futter, a lawyer who became acting president of Barnard College last August, had a job so new that she could not plan. Forced to live in the present, she was finding the experience painful: "I like to know what the day is going to look like."

Three women, schedules drawn tight as harp strings, were almost consumed by work. Financial consultant Virginia Gobats usually unwinds in front of Mary Tyler Moore reruns at 2:30 A.M., and wakes at 6:30 A.M. Her work involves "doing the same thing for hours and hours on end." She was so worried by her boring log that she lined up a substitute. Gladys Dobelle, who runs her own public affairs public relations agency, said her log did not communicate "the frenetic quality of my life. I never see the light at the end of the tunnel; I always feel I've left something unfinished." When we met at 10:00 A.M., Dobelle had already laid out her clothes for the next day and explained that she had "seven of everything" to keep her wardrobe simple. A management consultant, who insisted on remaining anonymous because of her company's emphasis on low visibility, didn't get to bed again until 39½ hours after her alarm first rang.

These women represent the extreme end of the time-pressure scale, where no seam separates work from life. Gobats said she felt worried if her business day did not start on time. She is not alone: Johanna Hawkins, a copywriter at Foote, Cone & Belding, commented, "Most people in advertising prefer a busy schedule. They get depressed otherwise."

In politically powerful Washington, D.C., nonstop schedules may seem especially attractive. But subtract names like Brzezinski and issues like the fate of the ERA from the log belonging to Sarah Weddington, Carter's special assistant in charge of women's concerns, and her workhorse schedule is as flat as Dobelle's or Gobat's. Because the center-of-empire feeling that pervades Washington encourages workaholic habits, many private offices there actively encourage their employees to end the day promptly at 5:00 P.M. One such company lured Suzanne Woolsey, mother of three boys, aged 7, 5 and 3. She left a job as associate director of the Federal Office of Management and Budget and is now a management consultant at Coopers & Lybrand, an accounting firm. Much of Woolsey's log records pleasure and relief over her new, easier schedule: "If you have an important job in government, leaving the office before 6:30 or 7:00 P.M. is considered lack of commitment." Woolsey sleeps as little as Gobats, but for different reasons. She wasn't sure whether to begin her log with the midnight feed or when she dressed for work.

Not surprisingly, several husbands had schedules as demanding as their wives. Consequently, some husbands seemed quite peripheral to their spouses' lives: One woman didn't mention her husband until her log's third page. Others scheduled their husbands in: Ellen Futter reserves Friday night. Barbara Taylor, married one year to a professional fund raiser, frequently reflected, "How lucky I am!" to have a stable personal life. She described a dinner with her husband, their first night alone in two weeks. He outlined his timetable for the previous two days: breakfast in New York, lunch in Los Angeles, dinner in San Diego, breakfast in Chicago, lunch in Baltimore, and finally dinner in New York with his wife.

Two women, a journalist and a company president, lived with men who had less demanding schedules than they did and were willing to play supporting roles. The husband of *New York Times* science reporter Jane E. Brody was checking the galleys of her 500-page book against the original manuscript. He was also willing to comb through several years of her weekly columns to select those suitable for collection in another book. He generally volunteered when she needed this sort of help—"I'm not good at asking," she explained. Carole Herrscher, the president and controlling partner of a Houston-based firm that makes a quarter of a million dollars annually manufacturing chemicals for the oil pipeline industry, regularly checked with her fiancé, Chuck, on business problems. In her log she consistently misspelled his name as "Check."

Only two women, both married, reported sex (with their husbands, once each). One described it as "hug therapy," the other as a "matinée." While reticence may have been a factor in the low incidence of reported lovemaking, a management consultant pointed out that "fatigue is also a strong urge"—strong enough to cancel out the sexual one in those who work late and rise early. If the logs are accurate, many women who are hardly isolated from men are ignoring a source of replenishment and comfort.

A monthly period is every woman's reminder of the biological deadline — a factor that prompts women to think about the future more than men. Some married women had decided that the demands of their careers precluded children, but two single women agreed that they were prey to panic on the subject.

One goblin can never be vanquished: There were a surprising number of intimations of mortality in the logs. Alice Haemmerli cried one evening at the thought of her mother's death a year earlier. Ann Gaillard, a divorced account executive with two children, ended her log-keeping abruptly when her mother died. Jane Brody returned a phone call, heard about the death of an old friend and felt "vulnerable and scared. Can't stand to hear about any more deaths and fatal illnesses. Too many in one year." Mary Didie, a pediatrician, saw four patients and felt "lucky" when she compared them to her own three children.

Gloria Morris, a Houston freelance writer who also teaches, had been seriously ill in 1977 and had to take a day off to rest during her log-keeping. Morris's close brush with death had gotten her cracking; she is as busy as any corporate executive. "When you don't have much time, you don't waste it." Now she uses a flow chart of five parallel bars to keep abreast of roles she's acquired since her illness — freelance writing, teaching at two local universities, advising student publications, involvement in a local organization for women in communications, and personal life. Keeping the *Savvy* log made her realize how much she relies on her flow chart. "There's a pleasure in plotting. You feel less buffeted." But she thought about other things besides leaping new hurdles. Some women recorded the weather; Morris was the only one who commented on the scenery, and who booked a regular dinner "to press the flesh" with close female friends.

Asked what they would do if faced with the prospect of imminent death, these women generally preferred to keep on keeping on. Only two restless souls said that, given just six months to live, they would definitely quit their jobs. Helen Klein said, "I probably wouldn't believe I had only six months. Only if I had a death sentence would I stop." Fueled by coffee, exercised as regularly as race horses, these women feel "proud I can swing it."

Yet they lead rather austere lives. The logs suggest that while opportunities for women have burgeoned, quality of lives has declined. To do what we love best, we have sacrificed many simple pleasures, including sleep, privacy, friends, nest-building, pets, home-cooked food and in some cases, children. No log-keeper had time simply to sit and think — which sometimes was the very thing she was paid to do. Some had no time to spend their money in enjoyable ways. Others were obliged to pay heavily for housekeepers, surrogate wives and a plethora of other time-saving services. "Home" is stripped down to a place "that works"; "wardrobe," to clothes that function.

Having done well in school, we can't break the habit of living in dormitories and wearing school uniforms. Indeed, Gladys Dobelle's log described her stripped-down-to-work life as boarding school: "Stuck with old-fashioned, 'use-Sunday-night-to-get-ready-for-Monday.' " Perennially good girls, we are always doing for others — the children or the corporation. This is traditional feminine behavior, but nowadays it earns salaries and status.

The time logs excerpted here illustrate four good girls who have fallen into the traps of time pressure. Often, a multirole life becomes a soap opera, which Carole Herrscher's log strongly resembles. Before she met her fiancé, she relied heavily on her staff for companionship — and she ruefully confessed that she is paying now. She devotes two days to smoothing others' feathers, sorting out internecine squabbles among her staff. Herrscher's life is a cliff-hanger: In the aftermath of her 4:00 A.M. conference with Chuck, what will the next installment bring?

While Herrscher wonders who she has to pay off to get out of her serial, *New York Times* science reporter and personal health columnist Jane E. Brody, 39, glows with a good girl's rewards. Slim and rosy-cheeked from frequent exercise, she is the apple of editors' eyes because she writes prolifically and finishes on time. Once she was a procrastinator, but writing about the way stress eats at the heart and stomach made her work hard to avoid last-minute panic. "If you get your work done, your free time — sex, food, anything — feels like a wonderful reward. I go on vacation very very easily," she said. "My goal now is to get pieces written early in order to have free weekends. If I succeed, only my husband knows about my extra time."

Brody does admit to anxiety in the face of big, unfamiliar freelance writing projects, which she tries to do only for "good reasons — either the subject appeals to me or it opens new markets." As the principal wage earner in her household — her husband, a lyricist, does most of the chores their ten-room house and eleven-year-old twin sons entail — Brody cannot afford to slow down in her career. "I don't want to be dependent on anything in my life, and that includes *The New York Times.*"

She had just completed a 500-page book on nutrition, a year-and-a-half project for which she set a strict schedule, writing from 5:00 A.M. to 6:30 A.M. weekday mornings and weekends. She does elaborate cooking for dinner parties, and because she abhors sitting still and finds chores a relief after writing, she goes without a dishwasher and is considering not repairing the clothes dryer.

While Brody's efficiency and productivity are undeniable, she sounds suspiciously like one of her own columns on the healthful life. She acknowledged that she censored herself during her log-keeping: "It puts you on good behavior because you don't want to put down that you went crazy." Indeed, although her emotions column is fairly sparse, she said that the evening after her log ended, she exploded at her family. "After 10 P.M. I had no cope left."

Unlike Brody, Mary Didie feels out of shape, and her cheeks are pale. Her list of professional responsibilities alone is exhausting. It includes an acting directorship of the pediatric outpatient clinic at New York Hospital, where she is also an assistant attending physician; an assistant professorship at Cornell University Medical College and a private practice. She puts in a 9:00 A.M. to 7:00 P.M. working day, for which her base salary is $35,000 — "a man would earn at least $7,000 more."

At home, Didie and her husband, who works full time as a project engineer at *The New York Daily News,* have three children under the age of 5. Her babies were scheduled to arrive during periods of her training when she was either not on call for hospital night duty, or "when I would inconvenience the least number of people."

Unlike his older brother and sister, Didie's youngest child, now 13 months old, played havoc with his mother's careful clockwork. He is dysrhythmic: His waking and feeding times change from day to day. Because he is still nursing, Didie's lunch, which she normally doesn't have until 3:00 P.M., consists of a yogurt she eats at her desk while she expresses her milk. This she freezes for her son. While this sounds like an extreme scheduling sacrifice — an assembly-line mother — it is Didie's way of making a direct and irreplaceably personal gift to her son. Though her schedule could be essayed only by a woman who needs very little sleep, her emotions are consistent and of a piece with her experiences.

In the process of wringing everything she wants from life, Didie has somewhat wrung herself out. She knows her life has narrowed — "my conversation isn't what it used to be" — but "I have to say that I'm happy." She laughs frequently over her hair-raising schedule — "What would my mother say?" — and appreciated her *Savvy* interview as "another set of ears" to hear about it. As a teacher, a doctor and a mother, Mary Didie does for other people all her many waking hours, but she knows that what she does makes a vital difference.

The most time-pressured log belongs to the most financially successful woman, a married, childless management consultant. Her log graphically depicts how the added burden of travel taxes mind, body and relationships in a multiroled life.

On the eve of a recent European trip, our management consultant is stoic: "Having revisited this situation for possibly the fifth time, I resign myself to an exhausting week." Her perennial anxiety is "where the energy is going to come from. The unknown is always just how tired I'm going to get."

Small wonder: She spends much of the trip battling jet lag and plane delays. Yet she succeeds in making her time-serving life even harder. On her return, she is determined to stay up so she won't spend her first day home asleep. She finally goes to bed when she's been up "some 21 hours." Before her trip she had a single exhausting workout on Nautilus machines and then no exercise the rest of the week, relying on caffeine to keep awake for the clients and unwinding in front of television.

Both this woman and her husband travel so much that they must preclude all but spontaneous, last-minute recreation. Over dinner, after the wife's week-long absence, they planned ahead, as usual, and discussed the goods and services they needed to keep themselves going: "our upcoming vacation, the weekend house we are trying to

buy, the meeting with our accountant tomorrow, the type of tele-
phone-answering machine we ought to get, and some documents my
husband would like me to have my secretary mail for him." The consultant and her husband are not eager to have children because "we
are used to the freedom that we have."

If this sort of enslavement to schedule spells freedom and the
Good Life, then time management deals only with a topical rash, not
the underlying malady. The management consultant's log is the portrait of a girl so dutiful that she no longer has a life of her own—even
though she maintains that she is "doing what I love best." Surely we
—for in all these women I see a mirror image—should stop once in a
while—if only to enjoy the fruits of our labor.

As women take on many roles, we gain the considerable satisfaction of calling ourselves professionals or executives. We feel included
in more parts of society. But we lose time—and perhaps the inclination—to think about what exactly we are doing. We work hard, but
our work, may add up to killing time. Forced to emphasize productivity, we avoid that nasty worry about whether doing a lot equals
achievement, whether "having it all" may mean losing it all.

As there are good reasons why time management doesn't work,
there are also good reasons why it shouldn't. Philosopher Amelie Ok-
senberg Rorty writes, "Women who must juggle the demands of
many different sorts of lives tend to become efficient, and so become
competent, rather than original."

In *The Partners*, novelist and practicing attorney Louis Auchincloss,
has given us a model in Felicia Currier, a beautiful and intelligent
lawyer whose speedy mind darts to "the dead center of any tangle of
circumstances." She never works evenings or weekends, yet does as
well at her firm as her workaholic husband, whose long hours are
spent birthing stale memos. "A law firm is only a tool to make a
happy life," Felicia tells Marc, sensing that his "dark cloud of indus-
triousness" has nothing to do with his "professional ambition or love
of the law."

Time is all we have. We each choose different tools to build our
lives, but surely the Good Life is nourished and replenished by time
spent contemplating beauty, the landscape, ideas, dreams; enjoying
children, friendship, sex; working for what we believe in.

Time-pressured lives are competent and productive. But they don't
foster satisfaction; only more work, requiring more dutifulness. If we
can stop being drudges, if we can run our own lives, we will accomplish a great deal. And should we fail to accomplish a great deal,
perhaps we won't even care. For ultimately, time isn't money or
status; time is life itself.

Savvy, December 1980

A Case for Inefficiency

By Anne Marie Cunningham

Bertrand Russell thought that four hours of work a day was plenty for anyone. William Faulkner regretted it was possible to do more: "One of the saddest things is that the only thing a man can do for eight hours a day is work. You can't eat eight hours a day, nor drink eight hours a day, nor make love eight hours a day—all you can do is work."

Most great hunches and major breakthroughs seem to have popped into people's heads when they weren't working—when they were staring into space, goofing off or even sleeping. Stanislaw Ulam, the Polish expatriate physicist who, with Edward Teller, hit on the design for the hydrogen bomb in 1951, was considered spectacularly lazy by his colleagues at Los Alamos. While everyone else worked around the clock to win the Cold War, he never appeared at the lab before ten and was gone by four. When other scientists went hiking in the New Mexican mountains, he remained at the foot of the trail and watched through binoculars.

James D. Watson, one of the three unravelers of the structure of DNA, was too lazy a doctoral candidate to take chemistry or physics. He was drawn to science by the partying at conventions, and went to Cambridge, England, where he hooked up with Francis Crick and Maurice Wilkins, to learn biochemistry. The three were well matched: Crick girl-watched incessantly and subscribed only to *Vogue.* At the height of the race with Linus Pauling to decode DNA, Wilkins disappeared regularly for fencing lessons. Watson spent afternoons on the tennis court, showing up at the lab "for only a few minutes of minor fiddling before dashing away to have sherry with the girls at Pop's." He pondered DNA at the movies, where he spent almost every evening.

Savvy, December 1980

A Lot Can Happen in an Hour

By Beth Greer Youdin

At times an hour can seem like an eternity, but did you ever notice how quickly a lunch hour slips by? There's hardly a chance to sip a Bloody Mary and pick at a Quiche Lorraine before you've got to get back to work. If cramming cocktails, quiche and coffee into that interval seems hard, consider how many other events can occur before sixty minutes pass.

During a New Yorker's rushed lunch at Lutece, ten cars are stolen, twelve people are born and eight die in this city. By the time espresso is served, the sanitation department has disposed of 2 million pounds of garbage.

In the hour it takes for the hunger-inhibiting factor of tobacco to wear off after smoking one cigarette, 460,000 McDonald's hamburgers are eaten and over 26,000 Cokes are guzzled.

During an hour-long soap opera on television, 20 women are beaten, 124 people get divorced and 30 people call the VD Hotline in the real world.

While 700,000 shares of stock are traded on the American Stock Exchange each hour, almost as many U.S. Treasury notes are printed and Parker Brothers prints $392,000 in Monopoly money.

New Yorkers have the unique distinction of having used over 8 million kilowatt hours of electricity in just one hour this past summer. And in the hour it takes for a human sperm to reach an egg, 420,000 New Yorkers have pushed their way into the subway.

According to Pierre Franey, the 60-Minute Gourmet, you can prepare *Crevettes Jardinier* (shrimp and vegetables cognac), *Riz Persillé* (parsleyed rice) and *Tomates Grillées* (broiled tomatoes) in the time it takes for one catering-service employee to prepare 200 hors d'oeuvres, or a Dunkin' Donut employee to make 480 cake-style doughnuts.

In an hour, you can sit around and lose 42 brain cells or you can walk three miles and burn 300 calories.

You can earn 1½ cents an hour by placing $1,000 in the bank in a two-and-one-half-year savings plan.

Speaking of gains, in 1978 General Motors made a net profit of $400,456 an hour,* and F.W. Woolworth's made $14,874 an hour.* At a $30,000 salary you, on the other hand, earned only $3.42 an hour.*

In the hour it takes a postal employee to sort 1,200 letters by hand, you could die from exposure in the waters of the Arctic Circle, take the College Board Achievement Test in any subject, swallow 60 times, hand-pick fifteen pounds of cotton or travel a third of the way to London by Concorde jet.

And, while all this happens, a mayfly is born, meets a mate, probably has a baby or two, and dies.

*Based on a 365-day year and a 24-hour day.

Vancouver Sun, 29 January 1981.

Whistle stops anger office staff

BOISE, Idaho (AP)—Seven times a day, someone blows a whistle at the Idaho health and welfare office. The secretaries have to stop and fill out a form saying what they're doing at that moment.

Administrators in the state department of health and welfare say it's a good way to check office efficiency, part of a drive to eliminate three secretarial positions in an economy move.

Secretaries call it insulting, degrading and disruptive.

The procedure began on Monday. That was when Theo Murdock, chief of the state's welfare division instructed aides to blow the whistle—literally—on the secretarial staff. He said the "random moment time study" would enable him to judge how the secretaries spend time on the job.

Murdock said he has been ordered by Gov. John Evans to cut the budget by $110,000. This means three secretaries have to go.

Efficient or not, the secretaries say they don't like the whistle stops.

"It's insulting to my intelligence the way they go about these things," said one of them, Lois Moreland.

Complained Angie Stelling: "Yesterday morning, there wasn't a single whistle. They all blew in the afternoon and everybody was sitting on pins and needles afraid to take a break or go to the bathroom."

Murdock, however, said he doesn't expect even the most dedicated secretary not to take a coffee break once in a while. "That's part of the working day. If none of those showed up, I would be concerned."

But the biggest objections appeared to be aimed at the chief whistle blower, Robert Jensen.

"They're paying him a good salary to lay off three of our people," said Lois Moreland.

The study is due to end in mid-February.

The Organization Man, Cont'd

From Dodsworth on, the figure of the businessman self-alienated from the wider life has been held up to Americans as a somewhat tragic figure.

Little seems to have changed in the quarter-century since William H. Whyte Jr. wrote those words about corporate executives in his classic "The Organization Man." A new study by Heidrick and Struggles, a large executive-search firm, says that today's top executives have been forced into the same single-minded, workaholic patterns as their predecessors. They work long and hard, putting in an average of 57.5 hours a week. Many, in fact, make no distinction between work and pleasure. And a large majority will uproot their families for a more rewarding job in some other part of the country. "The findings of this study fly in the face of those who would portray the route to the top as easier than it really is," says Michigan State University management Prof. Eugene E. Jennings.

The survey focused on executives who were promoted to posts ranging from vice president to chief executive officer by their companies in 1979 or who were hired by other companies to fill equivalent positions. The typical senior executive, the study found, is white, male (only 1.1 percent of the respondents were women, just 1.2 percent were members of ethnic minorities), Protestant and 48 years old. One in four has an M.B.A. degree and 11 percent have a degree of some sort from Harvard. The executive's annual pay last year was $134,500, enough to keep him ahead of inflation. But less than half the 1,501 respondents said that money was the chief attraction, and 70 per cent maintained that they took the new job because it was more challenging.

Lingering too, is the image of the good corporate wife, subordinating her own career interests to her husband's. Only one spouse in ten held a full-time job outside the home, and 18 percent of those had refused a promotion or another job in the last two years—most often because it would have conflicted with their partners' career. But the marital stress implied in the statistics apparently wasn't terminal: 84 percent of the corporate achievers were still married to their first spouses, compared with just 53 percent nationwide.

Best Gift for Secretary: An Electrocardiogram

Ellen Goodman

They used to say it with flowers or celebrate it with a somewhat liquid lunch. National Secretaries Week was always good for at least a token of appreciation. But the way the figures add up now, the best thing a boss can do for a secretary this week is cough up for her cardiogram.

"Stress and the Secretary" has become the hottest new syndrome on the heart circuit.

It seems that it isn't those Daring Young Women in their Dress for Success Suits who are following men down the cardiovascular trail to ruin. Nor is it the female professionals who are winning their equal place in intensive care units.

It is powerlessness and not power that corrupts women's hearts. And clerical workers are the number one victims.

In the prestigious Framingham study, Dr. Suzanne Haynes, an epidemiologist with the U.S. National Heart, Lung and Blood Institute, found that working women as a whole have no higher rate of heart disease than housewives. But women employed in clerical and sales occupations do. Their coronary disease rates are twice that of other women.

"This is not something to ignore," says Dr. Haynes, "since such a high percent of women work at clerical jobs." In fact, 35 percent of all working women hold these jobs.

When Dr. Haynes looked into their private lives, she found the women at greatest risk—with a one in five chance of heart disease—were clerical workers with blue-collar husbands, and three or more children. When she then looked at their work lives, she discovered that the ones who actually developed heart disease were those with nonsupportive bosses who hadn't changed jobs very often and who had trouble letting their anger out.

In short, being frustrated, dead-ended, without a feeling of control over your life is bad for your health.

The irony in all the various and sundry heart statistics is that we now have a weird portrait of the Cardiovascular Fun Couple of the

Office. The Type A Boss and his secretary. The male heart disease stereotype is, after all, the Type A aggressive man who always needs to be in control, who lives with a great sense of time urgency . . . and is likely to be a white-collar boss.

"The Type A man is trying to be in control. But given the way most businesses are organized there are, in fact, few ways for them to be in control of their jobs," says Dr. Haynes. The only thing the Type A boss can be in control of is his secretary who in turn feels . . . well, you get the picture. He's not only getting heart disease, he's giving it.

Now then, as if all this weren't enough to send you out for the annual three-martini lunch, clerical workers are increasingly working for a new Type A boss: the computer.

These days fewer women are sitting in front of bosses with notepads and more are sitting in front of video display terminals. Word processors, data processors, microprocessors . . . these are the demanding, time-conscious, new automatons of automation. According to the IBM Word Processing Plan, "In the office of 1985 . . . there are no secretaries." Just pools of processors.

There is nothing intrinsically evil about computers. I am writing this on a VDT and if you try to take it away from me, I will break your arm. But as Working Women, the national association of office workers, puts it in their release this week, automation is increasingly producing clerical jobs that are deskilled, downgraded, dead-ended and dissatisfying.

As Karen Nussbaum of the Cleveland office described it, the office of the future may well be the factory of the past. Work on computers is often reduced to simple, repetitive, monotonous tasks. Workers are often expected to produce more for no more pay, and there are also reports of a disturbing trend to processing speed-ups and piece-rate pay, and a feeling among clerical workers that their jobs are computer-controlled.

"It's not the machine, but the way it's used by employers," says Working Women's research director, Judith Gregory. Too often, automation's most important product is stress.

Groups like Working Women are trying to get clerical workers to organize in what they call "a race against time" so that computers will become their tools instead of their supervisors.

But in the meantime, if you are 1) a female clerical worker, 2) with a blue-collar husband, 3) with three or more children, 4) in a dead-end job, 5) without any way to express anger, 6) with a Type A boss, 7) or a Type A computer controlling your work day . . . YOU BETTER START JOGGING.

Death of a Salesman

Arthur Miller

From the right, Willy Loman, the Salesman, enters, carrying two large sample cases. The flute plays on. He hears but is not aware of it. He is past sixty years of age, dressed quietly. Even as he crosses the stage to the doorway of the house, his exhaustion is apparent. He unlocks the door, comes into the kitchen, and thankfully lets his burden down, feeling the soreness of his palms. A word-sigh escapes his lips — it might be "Oh, boy, oh, boy." He closes the door, then carries his case out into the living room, through the draped kitchen doorway.

Linda, his wife, has stirred in her bed at the right. She gets out and puts on a robe, listening. Most often jovial, she has developed an iron repression of her exceptions to Willy's behavior — she more than loves him, she admires him, as though his mercurial nature, his temper, his massive dreams and little cruelties, served her only as sharp reminders of the turbulent longings within him, longings which she shares but lacks the temperament to utter and follow to their end.

LINDA, *hearing Willy outside the bedroom, calls with some trepidation:* Willy!

WILLY: It's all right. I came back.

LINDA: Why? What happened? *Slight pause.* Did something happen, Willy?

WILLY: No, nothing happened.

LINDA: You didn't smash the car, did you?

WILLY: *with casual irritation:* I said nothing happened. Didn't you hear me?

LINDA: Don't you feel well?

WILLY: I'm tired to the death. *The flute has faded away. He sits on the bed beside her, a little numb.* I couldn't make it. I just couldn't make it, Linda.

LINDA, *very carefully, delicately:* Where were you all day? You look terrible.

WILLY: I got as far as a little above Yonkers. I stopped for a cup of coffee. Maybe it was the coffee.

LINDA: What?

WILLY, *after a pause:* I suddenly couldn't drive any more. The car kept going off onto the shoulder, y'know?

LINDA, *helpfully:* Oh. Maybe it was the steering again. I don't think Angelo knows the Studebaker.

WILLY: No, it's me, it's me. Suddenly I realize I'm goin' sixty miles an hour and I don't remember the last five minutes. I'm—I can't seem to —keep my mind to it.

LINDA: Maybe it's your glasses. You never went for your new glasses.

WILLY: No, I see everything. I came back ten miles an hour. It took me nearly four hours from Yonkers.

LINDA, *resigned:* Well, you'll just have to take a rest, Willy, you can't continue this way.

WILLY: I just got back from Florida.

LINDA: But you didn't rest your mind. Your mind is overactive, and the mind is what counts, dear.

WILLY: I'll start out in the morning. Maybe I'll feel better in the morning. *She is taking off his shoes.* These goddam arch supports are killing me.

LINDA: Take an aspirin. Should I get you an aspirin? It'll soothe you.

WILLY, *with wonder:* I was driving along, you understand? And I was fine. I was even observing the scenery. You can imagine, me looking at scenery, on the road every week of my life. But it's so beautiful up there, Linda, the trees are so thick, and the sun is warm. I opened the windshield and just let the warm air bathe over me. And then all of a sudden I'm goin' off the road! I'm tellin' ya, I absolutely forgot I was driving. If I'd've gone the other way over the white line I might've killed somebody. So I went on again — and five minutes later I'm dreamin' again, and I nearly —*He presses two fingers against his eyes.* I have such thoughts, I have such strange thoughts.

LINDA: Willy, dear. Talk to them again. There's no reason why you can't work in New York.

WILLY: They don't need me in New York, I'm the New England man. I'm vital in New England.

LINDA: But you're sixty years old. They can't expect you to keep traveling every week.

WILLY: I'll have to send a wire to Portland. I'm supposed to see Brown and Morrison tomorrow morning at ten o'clock to show the line. Goddammit, I could sell them! *He starts putting on his jacket.*

LINDA, *taking the jacket from him:* Why don't you go down to the place tomorrow and tell Howard you've simply got to work in New York? You're too accommodating, dear.

WILLY: If old man Wagner was alive I'd a been in charge of New York now! That man was a prince; he was a masterful man. But that boy of his, that Howard, he don't appreciate. When I went north the first time, the Wagner Company didn't know where New England was!

LINDA: Why don't you tell those things to Howard, dear?

WILLY, *encouraged:* I will, I definitely will. Is there any cheese?

LINDA: I'll make you a sandwich.

WILLY: No, go to sleep. I'll take some milk. I'll be up right away. . . .

[*Editor's note:* The scene shifts to Howard Wagner's office the following day.]

WILLY: Pst! Pst!

HOWARD: Hello, Willy, come in.

WILLY: Like to have a little talk with you, Howard.

HOWARD: Sorry to keep you waiting. I'll be with you in a minute.

WILLY: What's that, Howard?

HOWARD: Didn't you ever see one of these? Wire recorder.

WILLY: Oh. Can we talk a minute?

HOWARD: Records things. Just got delivery yesterday. Been driving me crazy, the most terrific machine I ever saw in my life. I was up all night with it.

WILLY: What do you do with it?

HOWARD: I bought it for dictation, but you can do anything with it. Listen to this. I had it home last night. Listen to what I picked up. The first one is my daughter. Get this. *He flicks the switch and "Roll out the Barrel" is heard being whistled.* Listen to that kid whistle.

WILLY: That is lifelike, isn't it?

HOWARD: Seven years old. Get that tone.

WILLY: Ts, ts. Like to ask a little favor if you . . .

The whistling breaks off, and the voice of Howard's daughter is heard.

HIS DAUGHTER: "Now you, Daddy."

HOWARD: She's crazy for me! *Again the same song is whistled.* That's me! Ha! *He winks.*

WILLY: You're very good!

The whistling breaks off again. The machine runs silent for a moment.

HOWARD: Sh! Get this now, this is my son.

HIS SON: "The capital of Alabama is Montgomery; the capital of Arizona is Phoenix; the capital of Arkansas is Little Rock; the capital of California is Sacramento . . ." *and on, and on.*

HOWARD, *holding up five fingers:* Five years old, Willy!

WILLY: He'll make an announcer some day!

HIS SON, *continuing:* "The capital . . ."

HOWARD: Get that—alphabetical order! *The machine breaks off suddenly.* Wait a minute. The maid kicked the plug out.

WILLY: It certainly is a—

HOWARD: Sh, for God's sake!

HIS SON: "It's nine o'clock, Bulova watch time. So I have to go to sleep."

WILLY: That really is—

HOWARD: Wait a minute! The next is my wife.

They wait.

HOWARD'S VOICE: "Go on, say something." *Pause.* "Well, you gonna talk?"

HIS WIFE: "I can't think of anything."

HOWARD'S VOICE: "Well, talk—it's turning."

HIS WIFE, *shyly, beaten:* "Hello." *Silence.* "Oh, Howard, I can't talk into this . . ."

HOWARD, *snapping the machine off:* That was my wife.

WILLY: That is a wonderful machine. Can we—

HOWARD: I tell you, Willy, I'm gonna take my camera, and my bandsaw, and all my hobbies, and out they go. This is the most fascinating relaxation I ever found.

WILLY: I think I'll get one myself.

HOWARD: Sure, they're only a hundred and a half. You can't do without it. Supposing you wanna hear Jack Benny, see? But you can't be at home at that hour. So you tell the maid to turn the radio on when Jack Benny comes on, and this automatically goes on with the radio . . .

WILLY: And when you come home you . . .

HOWARD: You can come home twelve o'clock, one o'clock, any time you like, and you get yourself a Coke and sit yourself down, throw the switch, and there's Jack Benny's program in the middle of the night!

WILLY: I'm definitely going to get one. Because lots of time I'm on the road, and I think to myself, what I must be missing on the radio!

HOWARD: Don't you have a radio in the car?

WILLY: Well, yeah, but who ever thinks of turning it on?

HOWARD: Say, aren't you supposed to be in Boston?

WILLY: That's what I want to talk to you about, Howard. You got a minute? *He draws a chair in from the wing.*

HOWARD: What happened? What're you doing here?

WILLY: Well . . .

HOWARD: You didn't crack up again, did you?

WILLY: Oh, no. No . . .

HOWARD: Geez, you had me worried there for a minute. What's the trouble?

WILLY: Well, tell you the truth, Howard. I've come to the decision that I'd rather not travel any more.

HOWARD: Not travel! Well, what'll you do?

WILLY: Remember, Christmas time, when you had the party here? You said you'd try to think of some spot for me here in town.

HOWARD: With us?

WILLY: Well, sure,

HOWARD: Oh, yeah, yeah. I remember. Well, I couldn't think of anything for you, Willy.

WILLY: I tell ya, Howard. The kids are all grown up, y'know. I don't need much any more. If I could take home—well, sixty-five dollars a week, I could swing it.

HOWARD: Yeah, but Willy, see I—

WILLY: I tell ya why, Howard. Speaking frankly and between the two of us, y'know—I'm just a little tired.

HOWARD: Oh, I could understand that, Willy. But you're a road man, Willy, and we do a road business. We've only got a half-dozen salesmen on the floor here.

WILLY: God knows, Howard, I never asked a favor of any man. But I was with the firm when your father used to carry you in here in his arms.

HOWARD: I know that, Willy, but—

WILLY: Your father came to me the day you were born and asked me what I thought of the name of Howard, may he rest in peace.

HOWARD: I appreciate that, Willy, but there just is no spot here for you. If I had a spot I'd slam you right in, but I just don't have a single solitary spot.

He looks for his lighter. Willy has picked it up and gives it to him. Pause.

WILLY, *with increasing anger:* Howard, all I need to set my table is fifty dollars a week.

HOWARD: But where am I going to put you, kid?

WILLY: Look, it isn't a question of whether I can sell merchandise, is it?

HOWARD: No, but it's a business, kid, and everybody's gotta pull his own weight.

WILLY, *desperately:* Just let me tell you a story, Howard—

HOWARD: 'Cause you gotta admit, business is business.

WILLY, *angrily:* Business is definitely business, but just listen for a minute. You don't understand this. When I was a boy — eighteen, nineteen—I was already on the road. And there was a question in my mind as to whether selling had a future for me. Because in those days I had a yearning to go to Alaska. See, there were three gold strikes in one month in Alaska, and I felt like going out. Just for the ride, you might say.

HOWARD, *barely interested:* Don't say.

WILLY: Oh, yeah, my father lived many years in Alaska. He was an adventurous man. We've got quite a little streak of self-reliance in our family. I thought I'd go out with my older brother and try to locate him, and maybe settle in the North with the old man. And I was almost decided to go, when I met a salesman in the Parker House. His name was Dave Singleman. And he was eighty-four years old, and he'd drummed merchandise in thirty-one states. And old Dave, he'd go up to his room, y'understand, put on his green velvet slippers —I'll never forget—and pick up his phone and call the buyers, and without ever leaving his room, at the age of eighty-four, he made his living. And when I saw that, I realized that selling was the greatest career a man could want. 'Cause what could be more satisfying than to be able to go, at the age of eighty-four, into twenty or thirty different cities, and pick up a phone, and be remembered and loved and helped by so many different people? Do you know? when he died— and by the way he died the death of a salesman, in his green velvet slippers in the smoker of the New York, New Haven and Hartford, going into Boston—when he died, hundreds of salesmen and buyers were at his funeral. Things were sad on a lotta trains for months after that. *He stands up. Howard has not looked at him.* In those days there was personality in it, Howard. There was respect, and comradeship, and gratitude in it. Today, it's all cut and dried, and there's no chance for bringing friendship to bear—or personality. You see what I mean? They don't know me any more.

HOWARD, *moving away, to the right:* That's just the thing, Willy.

WILLY: If I had forty dollars a week—that's all I'd need. Forty dollars, Howard.

HOWARD: Kid, I can't take blood from a stone, I—

WILLY, *desperation is on him now:* Howard, the year Al Smith was nominated, your father came to me and—

HOWARD, *starting to go off:* I've got to see some people, kid.

WILLY, *stopping him:* I'm talking about your father! There were promises made across this desk! You mustn't tell me you've got people to see—I put thirty-four years into this firm, Howard, and now I can't pay my insurance! You can't eat the orange and throw the peel away—a man is not a piece of fruit! *After a pause:* Now pay attention. Your father—in 1928 I had a big year. I averaged a hundred and seventy dollars a week in commissions.

HOWARD, *impatiently:* Now, Willy, you never averaged—

WILLY, *banging his hand on the desk:* I averaged a hundred and seventy dollars a week in the year of 1928! And your father came to me—or rather, I was in the office here—it was right over this desk—and he put his hand on my shoulder—

HOWARD, *getting up:* You'll have to excuse me, Willy, I gotta see some people. Pull yourself together. *Going out:* I'll be back in a little while.

On Howard's exit, the light on his chair grows very bright and strange.

WILLY: Pull myself together! What the hell did I say to him? My God, I was yelling at him! How could I! *Willy breaks off, staring at the light, which occupies the chair, animating it. He approaches this chair, standing across the desk from it.* Frank, Frank, don't you remember what you told me that time? How you put your hand on my shoulder, and Frank . . . *He leans on the desk and as he speaks the dead man's name he accidentally switches on the recorder, and instantly*

HOWARD'S SON: ". . . of New York is Albany. The capital of Ohio is Cincinnati, the capital of Rhode Island is . . ." *The recitation continues.*

WILLY, *leaping away with fright, shouting:* Ha! Howard! Howard! Howard!

HOWARD, *rushing in:* What happened?

WILLY, *pointing at the machine, which continues nasally, childishly, with the capital cities:* Shut it off! Shut it off!

HOWARD, *pulling the plug out:* Look, Willy. . . .

WILLY, *pressing his hands to his eyes:* I gotta get myself some coffee. I'll get some coffee . . .

Willy starts to walk out. Howard stops him.

HOWARD, *rolling up the cord:* Willy, look . . .

WILLY: I'll go to Boston.

HOWARD: Willy, you can't go to Boston for us.

WILLY: Why can't I go?

HOWARD: I don't want you to represent us. I've been meaning to tell you for a long time now.

WILLY: Howard, are you firing me?

HOWARD: I think you need a good long rest, Willy.

WILLY: Howard —

HOWARD: And when you feel better, come back, and we'll see if we can work something out.

WILLY: But I gotta earn money, Howard. I'm in no position to —

HOWARD: Where are your sons? Why don't your sons give you a hand?

WILLY: They're working on a very big deal.

HOWARD: This is no time for false pride, Willy. You go to your sons and you tell them that you're tired. You've got two great boys, haven't you?

WILLY: Oh, no question, no question, but in the meantime . . .

HOWARD: Then that's that, heh?

WILLY: All right, I'll go to Boston tomorrow.

HOWARD: No, no.

WILLY: I can't throw myself on my sons. I'm not a cripple!

HOWARD: Look, kid, I'm busy this morning.

WILLY, *grasping Howard's arm:* Howard, you've got to let me go to Boston!

HOWARD, *hard, keeping himself under control:* I've got a line of people to see this morning. Sit down, take five minutes, and pull yourself together, and then go home, will ya? I need the office, Willy. *He starts to go, turns, remembering the recorder, starts to push off the table holding the recorder.* Oh, yeah. Whenever you can this week, stop by and drop off the samples. You'll feel better, Willy, and then come back and we'll talk. Pull yourself together, kid, there's people outside. . . .

REQUIEM

[*Editors' note:* Biff & Happy are Willy's sons. Charley is a neighbor.]

CHARLEY: It's getting dark, Linda.

Linda doesn't react. She stares at the grave.

BIFF: How about it, Mom? Better get some rest, heh? They'll be closing the gate soon.

Linda makes no move. Pause.

HAPPY, *deeply angered:* He had no right to do that. There was no necessity for it. We would've helped him.

CHARLEY, *grunting:* Hmmm.

BIFF: Come along, Mom.

LINDA: Why didn't anybody come?

CHARLEY: It was a very nice funeral.

LINDA: But where are all the people he knew? Maybe they blame him.

CHARLEY: Naa. It's a rough world, Linda. They wouldn't blame him.

LINDA: I can't understand it. At this time especially. First time in thirty-five years we were just about free and clear. He only needed a little salary. He was even finished with the dentist.

CHARLEY: No man only needs a little salary.

LINDA: I can't understand it.

BIFF: There were a lot of nice days. When he'd come home from a trip; or on Sundays, making the stoop; finishing the cellar; putting on the new porch; when he built the extra bathroom; and put up the garage. You know something, Charley, there's more of him in that front stoop than in all the sales he ever made.

CHARLEY: Yeah. He was a happy man with a batch of cement.

LINDA: He was so wonderful with his hands.

BIFF: He had the wrong dreams. All, all, wrong.

HAPPY, *almost ready to fight Biff:* Don't say that!

BIFF: He never knew who he was.

CHARLEY, *stopping Happy's movement and reply. To Biff:* Nobody dast blame this man. You don't understand: Willy was a salesman. And for a salesman, there is no rock bottom to the life. He don't put a bolt to a nut, he don't tell you the law or give you medicine. He's a man way out there in the blue, riding on a smile and a shoeshine. And when they start not smiling back — that's an earthquake. And then you get yourself a couple of spots on your hat, and you're finished. Nobody dast blame this man. A salesman is got to dream, boy. It comes with the territory.

BIFF: Charley, the man didn't know who he was.

HAPPY, *infuriated:* Don't say that!

BIFF: Why don't you come with me, Happy?

HAPPY: I'm not licked that easily. I'm staying right in this city, and I'm gonna beat this racket! *He looks at Biff, his chin set.* The Loman Brothers!

BIFF: I know who I am, kid.

HAPPY: All right, boy. I'm gonna show you and everybody else that Willy Loman did not die in vain. He had a good dream. It's the only dream you can have—to come out number one man. He fought it out here, and this is where I'm gonna win it for him.

BIFF, *with a hopeless glance at Happy, bends toward his mother:* Let's go, Mom.

LINDA: I'll be with you in a minute. Go on, Charley. *He hesitates.* I want to, just for a minute. I never had a chance to say good-by.

Charley moves away, followed by Happy. Biff remains a slight distance up and left of Linda. She sits there, summoning herself. The flute begins, not far away, playing behind her speech.

LINDA: Forgive me, dear. I can't cry. I don't know what it is, but I can't cry. I don't understand it. Why did you ever do that? Help me, Willy, I can't cry. It seems to me that you're just on another trip. I keep expecting you. Willy, dear, I can't cry. Why did you do it? I search and search and I search, and I can't understand it, Willy. I made the last payment on the house today. Today, dear. And there'll be nobody home. *A sob rises in her throat.* We're free and clear. *Sobbing more fully, released:* We're free. *Biff comes slowly toward her.* We're free . . . We're free . . .

Biff lifts her to her feet and moves out up right with her in his arms. Linda sobs quietly. Bernard and Charley come together and follow them, followed by Happy. Only the music of the flute is left on the darkening stage as over the house the hard towers of the apartment buildings rise into sharp focus, and The Curtain Falls

What Stress Can Do to You

Walter McQuade

It has long been a matter of common intuition that bottled-up anger can crack the bottle, prolonged strain can make people sick. This old folklore now has considerable scientific support. Working independently, several groups of medical researchers—both physicians and psychologists — have collected impressive evidence that emotional factors are primarily responsible for many of the chronic dis-

Fortune, Walter McQuade, copyright © 1972 Time Inc. All rights reserved.

eases that have been hitting American males hard in middle age, notably the big one, heart disease. Challenging medical dogma, these doctors deny that fatty diet, cigarette smoking, and lack of proper exercise pose the main perils to men in their working prime. Much more important, they say, is stress. Stress might be defined as the body's involuntary reactions to the demanding life that we Americans choose — or that chooses us.

These reactions are rooted deep in the prehistory of the human species. Early man survived in a brutal world because, along with an elaborate brain, he had the mechanisms of instantaneous, unthinking physical response when in danger. Picture a primitive man, many thousands of years ago, lying in the sun in front of his cave after the hunt, digesting. Suddenly, he felt the cool shadow of a predatory carnivore, stalking. Without thinking, he reacted with a mighty surge of bodily resources. Into his blood flashed adrenal secretions that mustered strength in the form of both sugar and stored fats to his muscles and brain, instantly mobilizing full energy, and stimulating pulse, respiration, and blood pressure. His digestive processes turned off at once so that no energy was diverted from meeting the threat. His coagulation chemistry immediately prepared to resist wounds with quick clotting. Red cells poured from the spleen into the stepped-up blood circulation to help the respiratory system take in oxygen and cast off carbon dioxide as this ancestral man clubbed at the prowling beast, or scuttled safely back into his cave.

A COOL MEMO FROM A V.P.

Today, say stress researchers, a man in a business suit still reacts, within his skin, in much the same chemical way. He does so although today's threat is more likely to be in the abstract, for example, a cool memo from a vice president of the corporation: "The chairman wants a study of the savings possible in merging your division with warehousing and relocating to South Carolina."

Flash go the hormones into the blood; up goes the pulse beat—but the manager who receives the memo can neither fight physically nor flee. Instead his first tendency is to stall, which only induces guilt, before he plunges into a battle fought with no tangible weapons heavier than paper clips. Under his forced calm builds repressed rage without any adequate target—except himself.

If he is the kind of hard-driving, competitive perfectionist whom many corporations prize, and if this kind of stress pattern is chronic, the stress experts will tell you that he is a prime candidate for an early coronary (an even likelier candidate than American men in general, whose chances of having a heart attack before age sixty are one in five). If not a coronary, it may be migraine, ulcers, asthma, ulcerative colitis, or even the kind of scalp itch James V. Forrestal developed as he began to give way to interior pressure. Or perhaps a collision on the road — stressed people are more accident-prone.

Chronic strain is so common that there are conventional ways of fighting back. Millions of pills repose in desk drawers, ready to foster calmness or energy. The trouble with them, say the doctors, is that after the calm or the uplift there usually comes a period of depression. Martinis may be better, although they too involve dangers. Some people under stress try to vent their repressed anger in polite violence at a driving range or bowling alley, or by chopping wood or throwing themselves at ocean waves breaking on the beach. But the violent exercisers had better be careful of contracting another common stress symptom, low back pain.

Marriages have to accept a lot of stress, both in hurtful words and yet another symptom, temporary impotence. If a man coming under job stress has been on an anticholesterol diet he had better stay on it, but the competitive strain on him will be upping his serum cholesterol, whatever he eats. In broad terms, man the victorious predator now preys internally on himself.

LOST CONSOLATIONS

. . . Particularly destructive of the individual's sense of security have been the side effects of one of the industrial world's most precious products — social mobility. This bright trophy of our times has its deeply etched dark side. Social mobility has weakened the sense of belonging to a class, the sense of having a place in the social order. More important, social mobility implies that success depends on merit alone, and to the extent that a society believes in such correlation, individual bread-winners are thrust into an endless competition in which losing or lagging can be interpreted as a sign of personal inadequacy. . . .

DISCOVERING THE UBIQUITOUS

A pioneer investigator into the implications of stress was Dr. Hans Selye, a Canadian who has become the world's acknowledged authority on his subject. Selye, now sixty-four, defines stress as the nonspecific response of the body to any demand made on it. He maintains that stress went unstudied in detail for centuries simply because it had always been so common. "Stress is ubiquitous, and it is hard to *discover* something ubiquitous."

Selye recalls that an intimation of his future specialty came to him in his youth. "I was a second-year medical student in Prague in 1926 when my professor brought in five patients for the students to diagnose — one with cancer, one with gastric ulcer, etc. It struck me that the professor never spoke about what was common to them all, only about what were the specifics of the diagnosis. All these patients had lost weight, lost energy, and lost their appetites."

Ten years later, as an assistant professor at McGill in Montreal, Selye observed that various kinds of insults to the bodies and nervous systems of laboratory animals had lasting effects in making them vulnerable to subsequent stress. "I was trying to isolate a hormone in the laboratory. I was working with extracts of cow ovaries and injecting them into rats. All of them, when later subjected to stress, had the same reaction—adrenal overaction, duodenal and gastric ulcers, and shrinking thymus, spleen, and lymph nodes. The worse the stress, the stronger the reaction. Then I tried injecting other materials, even simple dirt. I even tried electric shock, and got the same results." When he tried inducing fear and rage, results were again similar.

WHEN ALL THE RATS DIED

One of Selye's most significant breakthroughs came when he realized he could take two similar groups of rats and predispose one group to heart disease, uncommon in animals, by injecting an excess of sodium and certain types of hormones. Then he would expose both groups of rats to stress. None of the control group suffered. *All* the rats in the predisposed group died of heart disease.

In time, Selye came to the conviction that the endocrine glands, particularly the adrenals, were the body's prime reactors to stress. "They are the only organs which do not shrink under stress; they thrive and enlarge. If you remove them, and subject an animal to stress, it can't live. But if you then inject extract of cattle adrenals, stress resistance will vary in direct proportion to the amount of the injection, and can even be put back to normal."

Selye explains that when the brain signals the attack of a stressor—which could be either a predatory beast or a threatening memorandum — the adrenal and pituitary glands produce the hormones ACTH, cortisone, and cortisol, which stimulate protective bodily reactions. If the stress is a fresh wound, the blood rushes irritants to seal it off; if the stress is a broken bone, swelling occurs around the break. The proinflammatory hormones are balanced by anti-inflammatory hormones, which prevent the body from reacting so strongly that the reaction causes more harm than the invasion.

ENERGY THAT CAN'T BE REPLENISHED

So the initial reaction to any kind of stress is alarm. It is followed by an instantaneous rallying of the body's defenses. The fight is on—even if the body, in effect, is just fighting the mind. If the threat recedes or is overcome, stability returns. But if the attack is prolonged, deterioration sets in, as the defense system gradually wears down. Selye calls this process the General Adaptation Syndrome, and it is recognized in the field as a brilliant concept.

Stress is not only a killer, Selye teaches, but also a drastic aging force. Different men have different hereditary capacities to withstand stress, but once each man's "adaptation energy" has been expended, there is no way yet known to replenish it. Selye believes that some time in the future it may be possible to produce from the tissues of young animals a substance that could replenish human stress energy. "But that is for the Jules Verne future — soft research, like soft news, that *may* happen."

Selye likens each man's supply of life energy to deep deposits of oil; once the man has summoned it up and burned it in the form of adaptation energy, it is gone — and so, soon, is he. If he picks a high-stress career, he spends his portion fast and ages fast. "There are two ages," says Selye, "one which is chronological, an absolute, and the other which is biologic and is your effective age. It is astonishing how the two can differ. . . .

A QUEERLY CONTEMPORARY QUALITY

Stress research in the U.S. centers on heart disease, and for good reason. Cardiovascular ailments such as coronary heart disease now take an appalling annual toll in lives of American men in vigorous middle age. Of the 700,000 people who died from coronary heart disease in the U.S. last year, almost 200,000 were under sixty-five.

Yet until this century heart disease was virtually unknown anywhere in the world, and as late as the 1920s it was still fairly rare in the U.S. Dr. Paul Dudley White, the eminent cardiologist, recalls that in the first two years after he set up his practice in 1912 he saw only three or four coronary patients. The queerly contemporary quality of heart disease cannot be attributed to the ignorance of earlier doctors. As far back as the time of Hippocrates, most afflictions were described well enough to be recognizable today from surviving records. A convincing description of heart disease, however, was not entered in medical records until late in the eighteenth century.

Some of the most important research on the effects of occupational stress in the U.S. has been carried out by the University of Michigan's Institute for Social Research, and the experts there are not impressed with the conventional medical wisdom regarding coronaries. Professor John R. P. French, Jr., an austere and plainspoken psychologist at the institute, says that the known risk factors do not come close to accounting for the incidence of the disease. He maintains that "if you could perfectly control cholesterol, blood pressure, smoking, glucose level, serum uric acid, and so on, you would have controlled only about one-fourth of the coronary heart disease." There is little solid evidence, he adds, "to show that programs of exercise substantially reduce the incidence of coronary heart disease or substantially reduce some of the risk factors."

To a great extent, argues French, the problem is the job. "The stresses of today's organizations can pose serious threats to the physical and psychological well-being of organization members. When a man dies or becomes disabled by a heart attack, the organization may be as much to blame as is the man and his family." A nationwide survey directed by French's colleague Robert L. Kahn found evidence of widespread occupational stress in the U.S. The results indicated that 35 percent of the employees had complaints about job ambiguity, meaning a lack of clarity about the scope and responsibilities of the work they were supposed to be doing. Nearly half—48 percent—often found themselves trapped in situations of conflict on the job, caught in the middle between people who wanted different things from them. Some 45 percent of the sample complained of overload, either more work than they would possibly finish during an ordinary working day, or more than they could do well enough to preserve their "self-esteem."

Other occupational stresses found by the survey included insecurity associated with having to venture outside normal job boundaries; difficult bosses or subordinates; worry over carrying responsibility for other people; the lack of a feeling of participation in decisions governing their jobs — a malaise, adds Dr. French, that distinctly lowers productivity.

Management jobs carry higher risks than most. In a detailed study done for NASA at the Goddard Space Flight Center, the investigators from Ann Arbor found that administrators were much more subject to stress than engineers or scientists. Responsibility for people, French explains, always causes more stress than responsibilities for things — equipment, budgets, etc. The rise in serum cholesterol, blood sugar, and blood pressure among ground managers is much greater during manned space flights than during flights of unmanned satellites. Whatever their assignment, the administrators at Goddard, as a group, had higher pulse rates and blood pressure, and smoked more, than the engineers or scientists. Medical records revealed that administrators also had suffered almost three times as many heart attacks as either the scientists or the engineers.

THE CORONARY TYPE

In any occupation, though, people vary a great deal in the amounts of stress they can handle. Some researchers at the institute hope psychologists will be able to work out methods of screening employees for their tolerance of stress. There may even prove to be physiological methods of selection. Dr. French and his associates have discovered a direct correlation between "achievement orientation" and high readings of uric acid in the blood—regarded in the past principally as a sign of susceptibility to gout. "High serum uric acid persons," French reported, "tend not to see the external environment as a source of pressure. [They] tend to master their external environment, while high cholesterol persons are typified by the perception that the external environment is mastering them."

It is not a new observation that some people are more subject to stress than others. Sir William Osler lived too early to see many coronary cases, but he left a shrewd description of the angina type. "It is not the delicate, neurotic person who is prone to angina," he commented, "but the robust, the vigorous in mind and body, the keen and ambitious man, the indicator of whose engine is always at 'full speed ahead' . . . the well set man of from forty-five to fifty-five years of age, with military bearing, iron gray hair, and florid complexion."

This Osler quotation is a favorite of two California cardiologists, Meyer Friedman and Ray H. Rosenman, who are among the country's leading students of stress. In the past seventeen years they and their staff at the Harold Brunn Institute of Mount Zion Hospital in San Francisco have spent thousands of hours and hundreds of thousands of research dollars building up an impressive case that behavior patterns and stress are principal culprits in the high incidence of coronary heart attacks among middle-aged Americans—and that personality differences are of vital importance.

Until 1955, Friedman and Rosenman were conventional cardiologists, doing research in the standard heart risk factors: serum cholesterol, cigarette smoking, blood pressure, diet, and obesity. They also gave half their time to practice, however, and, says Friedman, "We finally began to look at the individuals. They were signaling us. More than 90 percent showed signs of struggle. An upholsterer came in to redo our waiting room, and pointed out that the only place the chairs were worn was at the front edge."

In studying reactions to stress, Friedman and Rosenman gradually came to the conviction that people can be divided into two major types, which they designate A and B. Type A, the coronary-prone type, is characterized by intense drive, aggressiveness, ambition, competitiveness, pressure for getting things done, and the habit of pitting himself against the clock. He also exhibits visible restlessness. Type B may be equally serious, but is more easygoing in manner, seldom becomes impatient, and takes more time to enjoy leisure. He does not feel driven by the clock. He is not preoccupied with social achievement, is less competitive, and even speaks in a more modulated style. Most people are mixtures of Type A and Type B characteristics, but a trained interviewer can spot one pattern or the other as predominant.

A RATHER GRIM CHUCKLE

The extreme Type A is a tremendously hard worker, a perfectionist, filled with brisk self-confidence, decisiveness, resolution. He never evades. He is the man who, while waiting in the office of his cardiologist or dentist, is on the telephone making business calls. His wife is certain he drives himself too hard, and she may be a little in awe of him. The world is a deadly serious game, and he is out to amass points enough to win.

He speaks in staccato, and has a tendency to end his sentences in a rush. He frequently sighs faintly between words, but never in anxiety, because that state is strange to him. He is seldom out sick. He rarely goes to doctors, almost never to psychiatrists. He is unlikely to get an ulcer. He is rarely interested in money except as a token of a game, but the higher he climbs, the more he considers himself underpaid.

On the debit side, he is often a little hard to get along with. His chuckle is rather grim. He does not drive people who work under him as hard as he drives himself, but he has little time to waste with them. He wants their respect, not their affection. Yet in some ways he is more sensitive than the milder Type B. He hates to fire anyone and will go to great lengths to avoid it. Sometimes the only way he can resolve such a situation is by mounting a crisis. If he himself has ever been fired, it was probably after a personality clash.

Type A, surprisingly, probably goes to bed earlier most nights than Type B, who will get interested in something irrelevant to his career and sit up late, or simply socialize. Type A is precisely on time for appointments and expects the same from other people. He smokes cigarettes, never a pipe. Headwaiters learn not to keep him waiting for a table reservation; if they do, they lose him. They like him because he doesn't linger over his meals, and doesn't complain about quality. He will usually salt the meal before he tastes it. He's never sent a bottle of wine back in his life. Driving a car, Type A is not reckless, but does reveal anger when a slower driver ahead delays him.

Type A's are not much for exercise; they claim they have too little time for it. When they do play golf, it is fast through. They never return late from vacation. Their desk tops are clean when they leave the office at the end of each day.

AN UNRECOGNIZED SICKNESS

But in the competition for the top jobs in their companies, says Dr. Friedman, A's often lose out to B's. They lose because they are too competitive. They are so obsessed with the office that they have attention for nothing else, including their families. They make decisions too fast — in minutes, rather than days — and so may make serious business mistakes. They are intoxicated by numerical competition: how many units were sold in Phoenix, how many miles were traveled last month. Also, says Friedman, Type A's frequently have about them an "existential" miasma of hostility, which makes others nervous.

Type B's differ little in background or ability from A's, and may be quietly urgent, but they are more reasonable men. Unlike Type A, Type B is hard to needle into anger. Friedman says, "A's have no respect for B's, but the smart B uses an A. The great salesmen are A's. The corporation presidents are usually B's."

What is most tragic of all in this picture of hopeful, driving, distorting energy is that the Type A's are from two to three times more likely than the Type B's to get coronary heart disease in middle age. In all of Sinclair Lewis' pitiless characterizations of the go-getting American businessman of another era, there is nothing so devastating as these doctors' cool, clinical statistics. Says Rosenman about the Type A condition: "It is a sickness, although it is not yet recognized as such."

The test program that Friedman and Rosenman offer as their strongest body of evidence was undertaken in 1960 with substantial backing from the National Institutes of Health. A total of 3,500 male subjects aged thirty-nine to fifty-nine, with no known history of heart disease, were interviewed and classified as Type A or Type B. Then came complete physical examinations, which are still being performed on a regular basis as the program continues to accumulate data. So far, 257 of the test group — who are roughly half A's and half B's — have developed coronary heart disease. Seventy percent of the victims have been Type A's.

Even more emphatic is the picture that emerged when A's and B's were evaluated with respect to the generally accepted risk factors for heart trouble. As a group the A's had higher cholesterol levels than the B's. But it was found that even A's whom the conventional wisdom would have rated safer in blood pressure, parental history, or any combination of the usual risk factors were more likely to develop coronary heart disease. Conversely, B's could show adverse ratings in blood pressure and other factors and still be relatively safe. Dr. Rosenman reported that any B whose level of cholesterol and other fatty acids was within normal limits "had complete immunity to coronary heart disease, irrespective of his high-fat, cholesterol diet, family history, or his habits of smoking or his lack of exercising."

What creates a Type B or Type A? These cardiologists do not profess to know the complete answer yet. But to them it is obvious that both heredity and environment are involved. A's are naturally attracted toward careers of aggressiveness and deadline pressure. American life today, Friedman and Rosenman observe, offers plenty of these. What Type A's need but cannot easily achieve is restraint, says Dr. Friedman, who himself suffered a heart attack in 1967.

The medical debate that the Brunn Institute and the other stress researchers have joined is a bitter one, with deeply entrenched positions. The most emphatic opponents of the stress theory are those nutrition experts who, over the past twenty years, have virtually convinced the nation that a diet high in saturated fat and cholesterol is responsible for the epidemic of heart trouble. One pointed criticism that opponents make against the Friedman-Rosenman studies is that their method of classifying individuals into Type A or Type B is subjective, relying heavily on signs of tension as observed by the interviewer. The two cardiologists do not deny this, but point out that a good deal of all medical analysis is subjective. Their independent appraisals of Type A's or Type B's agree, they say, at least as much as doctors' readings of identical X-ray films. Says Rosenman: "Most epidemiologists are incapable of thinking of anything that cannot be qualified. There are no positive links between diet or exercise and heart disease, either. A migraine is subjective, too."

LAST WORDS OF A GREAT MAN

Studies of stress and its effects are now under way around the world. In 1950 Hans Selye's pioneering work was the sole technical treatise published on stress; last year there were close to 6,000 separate reports on stress research. At the Brunn Institute, Dr. Rosenman says, "we can't keep up with the requests from all over the world to train people here." During recent years, courts of law in the U.S., in a highly significant switch, have begun to favor plaintiffs seeking compensation for damage related to heart attacks caused by alleged stress on the job.

Now that even cardiologists are beginning to believe heart disease can be traced to unrelenting competitiveness and baffled fury, will a wave of concern over stress sweep over this hypochondriacal country, to match the widespread interest in jogging and polyunsaturated oils? Quite likely. There is nothing more fascinating to the layman than folklore finally validated by reputable scientists. A murmur of assent rises faintly from the past. When the great Pasteur lay in terminal illness, in 1895, he reflected once again on his long scientific disagreement with Claude Bernard. Pasteur's dying words were: "Bernard was right. The microbe is nothing, the terrain is everything."

Executive Stress May Not Be All Bad

In recent years, popular literature and medical journals alike have cited corporate stress as the root of executive ills ranging from alcoholism and nervous breakdowns to heart attacks and divorce. In response, companies have increasingly sought ways to reduce the amount of stress they place on their executives. Now, a backlash seems to be developing. More and more medical experts studying the matter insist that the perils of executive stress have been blown out of proportion. They argue that companies may be losing sight of the fact that too little stress can be as harmful as too much.

To be sure, stressful situations do elevate blood pressure, and relentless stress is bound to be harmful. But the new proponents of stress believe that a measure of it gives some executives the energy to be the achievers they believe they must be. "High-powered executives need this stimulation that we call stress," says Rosalind A. Forbes, a specialist in stress management and founder of Forbes Associates in New York City. "They're adrenalin freaks."

The Alcoholic Myth

Forbes and other experts are now marshaling evidence to restore stress's good name. Executives "thrive on stress," says Reginald B. Cherry, a physician and director of the Houstonian Preventive Medicine Center in Houston. Cherry questions the popular belief that the pressure of high-level corporate positions inevitably leads to heart attacks. As proof, he cites a 1974 study by Metropolitan Life Insurance Co. that found that the presidents and vice-presidents of the 500 largest industrial companies had 40% fewer fatal heart attacks than middle managers of those companies. In fact, says Cherry, stress is only one of 13 coronary risk factors, including blood fat levels and smoking, and he ranks it only about 10th on the list.

Charles E. Thompson, founder and director of professional services for the Thompson Medical Center in Chicago, disputes the notion that the stress of executive jobs produces a high incidence of alcoholism. Out of 17,000 executives examined by the center in the last 23 years, Thompson says, only three were true alcoholics. He explains that while 99% of executives drink, 90% drink only one to two ounces of alcohol a day.

Interviews with top executives support the notion that many of them know how to take stress in stride. John H. Vogel, chairman of the National Bank of North America, for example, starts his business day at 6 A.M. and does not stop until after a dinner engagement. "The hours are tough on a typical person," he says, but quickly adds, "I don't think you can get to the top unless you can handle stress." Roy A. Anderson, chairman of Lockheed Corp., says he does "not particularly enjoy stress," but he adds: "Some degree of stress is a motivator. If the job's too soft, you lose your mental acuity." And John H. Zimmerman, vice-president of employee relations for Firestone Tire & Rubber Co., who faces an April 21 contract deadline with the United Rubber Workers, declares: "Stress is what you make of it, and that can be the difference between coping and collapsing."

This attitude not only holds for corporate executives but also for high-level managers of all kinds. "It's important to me to be in a high-pressure environment," says Dallas Cowboys coach Thomas W. Landry, who has flourished under the rigors of professional football coaching for more than 20 years. When the heat is off, he says, "I'm already looking forward to the next time."

Indeed, a positive reaction to stress may well be a key ingredient to any executive's successful performance. "It becomes an asset for managers, because it helps them to do a better job," says consultant Forbes. For example, to improve their performance on the field as game time approaches, coach Landry builds up the amount of stress his players are under. Edmund T. Pratt Jr., chairman of Pfizer Inc., contends that "stress in the sense of challenge is important to getting a job done."

Theoretical Problem

Too little stress can have just the reverse effect. "In offices where there is not enough stress due to a lack of job challenge," says consultant Forbes, "fatigue, increase in accidents, and insomnia are reported along with other symptoms [usually] related to too much stress." Deborah C. Chamberlain, assistant professor of organizational behavior at Southern Methodist University's Edwin C. Cox School of Business, says that the lack of stress helps explain complaints of boredom by telephone operators during off-peak periods and by airline pilots during instrument flying. "Those problems are really due to lack of stimulation," she says. "And stress is a stimulant."

As a result, some companies are starting to recognize that reducing executive job-related stress may not be in their best interests. "The top management in our company is under a tremendous amount of pressure, but we don't have any alcoholism or anything else because they can't cope with stress," says Jimmy R. Gray, vice-president of personnel and administration at the Drilco Div. of Smith International Inc. As a result, Drilco has discontinued its stress management program, which used a combination of biofeedback and exercise techniques to reduce stress. And a Southwest manufacturing company stopped its stress management program, open to anyone in the company who had a feeling of too much stress, because "we had more blue-collar workers getting involved than executives," says a company official. "We weren't getting our money's worth out of it."

Of course, executive stress may primarily be a theoretical problem, too, because most managers in stressful fields or stressful positions are innately able to cope. Experts say that persons who work in high-stress professions, such as advertising, expect tight deadlines and other pressures and are therefore prepared to handle them on a daily basis. Generally, such executives have a high opinion of themselves, are flexible in their approach to life, and are not easily frustrated—personality traits that contribute to their success as executives as well as to their ability to handle great amounts of stress. "The successful executive learns very early to handle stress well," declares Thompson of the Thompson Medical Center. "If a company has to reduce stress for an executive, it has the wrong executive."

Old-Fashioned Solutions

In fact, when an executive finds his job too stressful, the best solution may well be to change jobs. Chicago's Thompson, for example, calls some other popular solutions, such as meditation and biofeedback, "a lot of garbage."

Gerard E. Fisher, president of the Center for Organization Development in Rochester, N.Y., insists that longer vacations and exercise rooms are a "great cover-up," because they help executives to dissipate the symptoms of too much stress without eliminating the source. Fisher adds that stress that is harmful to some managers may be healthy for others. "Stress is a neutral term," he says. "Some people have taken the word and made it negative."

Such attitudes raise the question of whether companies are wasting valuable executive time worrying about stress when they cannot do anything about it. Declares Cherry: "Executives are often bored with these stress programs because they already know how to deal with stress."

9

HAZARDS

"I find it's a company that preaches safety but doesn't practice it. Their biggest excuse is they're always in the process of fixing things."

—Rachel Scott

We are all accustomed to newspaper and television stories about the heavy toll extracted by accidents at work and illnesses caused by exposure to hazardous materials in the work environment. Periodically we see statistical summaries of occupational accidents, disabilities, and deaths. Since these events are removed from the lives of most of us, they tend to make little lasting impression. After all, Workman's Compensation and OSHA were created to insure that justice is done on the one hand and that dangerous working conditions are corrected on the other. To be sure, our perceptions of the latter agency are diluted by news stories of the misdirected bureaucratic zeal with which its efforts are sometimes addressed to trivial conditions in the work environment, correction of which is annoying and expensive to employers.

We think it is important, however, that our look at organizational reality include first a brief summary of the cost to society of health and safety problems and some graphic illustrations of these costs to the individuals concerned. The selection by Sayles and Strauss presents the former and notes that the workplace is in fact becoming more, not less, hazardous. The two selections from Rachel Scott's *Muscles and Blood,* "Automobiles" and "Oil," bring the statistics to life through accounts of the experiences of individuals in two of our major industries. Management's attitudes toward the individuals affected, and the conditions responsible for the accidents, are illuminating.

We are accustomed to think of job hazards as limited to blue-collar work. Executives and white-collar people do occasionally slip on freshly waxed floors, bruise their fingers while closing a file drawer, or inadvertently cut themselves on a letter opener. But their work certainly is removed from the dangers of heavy, high-speed machinery, explosions, or vehicles running out of control. But the psychological environment within which white-collar employees work can be severely debilitating. "The Deep Discontent of the Working Woman" cites frightening evidence of the effects of life in large organizations on the women who inhabit them. Much emphasis is placed by academic writers on the importance of satisfying growth needs and respecting human dignity. Indeed, these are central tenets of the Quality of Work Life movement that currently is enjoying so much popularity. This article cites convincing evidence that, indeed, many female office employees are bored, feel exploited in their jobs, and would be deeply grateful for an application of quality of work life practices.

Physical and psychological hazards are not confined to blue-collar or office work. Evidence of the pervasiveness of these phenomena is found in the excerpt from Dave Meggyesy's "Out of Their League" which exposes us to some of the less visible and less savory aspects of intercollegiate and professional football and in "The Underlife of Cabdriving: A Study in Exploitation and Punishment" by James M. Henslin.

Our next reading turns to another hazard of life in organizations. It is widely known that profound restructuring of our economy is well under way. Employment in manufacturing has been declining for some years. New technologies and even new industries are on the rise. Obsolete plants in the former North Central industrial hub are increasingly being located in the Southern and Southwestern sunbelt. As a consequence, more and more employees are being subjected to the trauma of plant closing, job loss, and the necessity of mid-life occupational change or relocation. Arthur Shostak's article, "The Human Cost of Plant Closings," explores these issues and raises a number of very real questions that must be addressed by our organizational society.

The reader is invited to contrast the readings in this section with other materials on work life quality, job enrichment, participative management, and employee development.

Safety and Occupational Health

Leonard R. Sayles and George Strauss

SCOPE OF THE PROBLEM

A decade ago there was considerable optimism about "curing" industry's safety problems. Between 1926 and 1956, the accident frequency rate in manufacturing had declined by about 50 percent. But by the beginning of this decade, accidents were occuring 26.77 percent more frequently than a decade earlier. Further, we have recently learned that a number of terrible diseases are associated with industrial and mining processes — for example, black lung, cancer, and asbestosis.[1] The scope of this growing challenge to management can be inferred from these annual statistics for the United States:

Reprinted from *Managing Human Resources*, 2nd ed., by Leonard R. Sayles and George Strauss, copyright © 1981, Prentice-Hall, by permission.

- 3 million (1 out of 8) workers become ill or are injured
- 2 million workers are disabled
- 14,000 deaths occur in work accidents
- 100,000 deaths occur from occupationally caused illnesses
- 400,000 new cases of disabling illness occur
- These illnesses and injuries cost $9 billion, including 45 million man-days of work lost

Shocking as these figures are, they understate industry's true costs from health and safety problems. Worker productivity suffers as a result of fear of accidents and resentment over uncorrected hazards. Companies pay high insurance premiums to cover their liabilities for accidents. Injuries mean reduced productivity and possible break-in and training costs for substitute employees. Some authorities have estimated that for serious accidents there may be $4 of indirect costs associated with every dollar of direct costs.

Obviously, some accidents just happen. In a world filled with moving vehicles, rotating equipment, exotic chemicals, and tall buildings, injuries are bound to occur. We have all read about how dangerous the average home is, and most of us have seen friends take needless chances in the routines of everyday living.[2] However, we should certainly not be content to permit a "that's life" attitude to excuse a problem of the magnitude of the current one. Furthermore, the law requires that management pay close attention to its safety and health records, and violations are costly.

Notes

1. One of the more gruesome accounts of unsolved safety problems in industry is provided by Rachel Scott, *Muscle and Blood* (New York: Dutton, 1974).

2. One of the authors sustained his most serious work-related injury while leaning against a wall in a steel chair while only two of the legs were on the floor. A slight shift in weight and the chair slipped, throwing the surprised occupant to the concrete floor.

Chicago Tribune, 13 October 1978.

Every 40 minutes, a worker is killed on the job...

By TERRY BROWN

Globe-Democrat-Chicago Tribune
News Service

CHICAGO—About every 40 minutes last year, an accident claimed the life of a worker on the job. Every 14 seconds, a worker was injured.

If all those work accidents could have been prevented, every corporate shareholder in the nation could have received a special $800 dividend, or every employee a $4-a-week raise.

That may seem a crass way to look at lost human lives and maimed limbs, but the Chicago-based National Safety Council believes such figures may help dramatize the horrendous waste of preventable accidents.

During the public service organization's annual convention in Chicago last week, Vincent L. Tofany, NSC president, discussed in an interview what he calls the "grim story of the economics of safety." He stressed that:

—Accidents impose a tremendous economic burden on the nation and contribute to such fundamental problems as inflation and lower productivity.

—Government intervention in the safety area has added to the costs of accidents, while doing little to improve the health and safety of the American worker.

Automobiles

Rachel Scott

Most companies find, as Chrysler apparently does, that it is more profitable to plan for disability and to compensate the sick and maimed workers than it is to install safety measures to protect them. It is hard to believe that companies can be so callous, so brutal as to

follow such a policy. Yet whether it is the brutality of choice or inad-
vertence, indifference or ignorance, brutality is what the evidence indicates. The daily stories are remarkable for their similarities.

The story of Brian Flannigan, for example. Flannigan was a young
man working at the Ford Rouge foundry during the summer of 1969
to earn money to return in the fall to Notre Dame, where he was
enrolled in the School of Architecture. "I was working on a crankshaft
table," said Flannigan. "The mold would come down the conveyor in
halves. My job was to pick it up and put it on the conveyor which
goes over our heads. The conveyors were old and had a tendency to
jerk and halt, which would cause the dollies to wiggle and swing.
Parts would fall off. It happened eight or ten times. We complained to
everybody — to our committeeman on the shift, the millwright, the
foreman. Our basic complaint was there was nothing above our heads
to protect us.

"That Friday night it emptied two molds, which came down on top
of me. Knocked me out. The guys on the table took me to the medical
office. Because I might have a back injury they sent me to central
medical. They took some X-rays. Basically they didn't think anything
was wrong. They gave me some Darvon because I had a headache
and sent me back over to the job. They gave me a light duty slip. The
foreman tried to put me back on the job. I went and got my committeeman. He went to see the general foreman. He let me go home only
because he knew me — he knew that I was hurt.

"I went home, woke up the next day and could not move. Sunday
was the same way. My mother drove me back to central medical. For
a two-week period they gave me Darvon. At no time did they ever
take cervical X-rays. They would poke me a few times — had me come
in every day for about two weeks and then every third day. Finally
Dr. Johnson said it was his position it was psychosomatic. They sent
me to Ford Hospital to have two neurologists look at me because I
was losing feeling on the left side of my hand. Their position was,
why wasn't Ford treating me?

"I went to my family doctor and he sent me to Grace Hospital for
X-rays. He called me the next day, said 'Your neck is broken in three
places.'"

By this time Flannigan had been off work eight weeks. Because he
had not been receiving compensation benefits, he contacted lawyer
Ron Glotta. Glotta was amazed to find that Ford was not only withholding payments, it had not even filed the accident form required by
state law — in effect denying that the accident had occurred.

"Generally what would happen in a case like that," said Glotta,
"the attorney makes more money the longer the case sits, because
more benefits accrue, and you only get a fee out of the accrued

benefits. But it was such a drastic case that I wrote a letter for a Rule Five hearing, which is that Ford Motor violated the act and is therefore subject to some kind of punishment . . . In a situation where a guy receives a definite injury on the job, they are required to provide a Form 100 to the state indicating an industrial injury. If they don't, that's a violation of the law. Ford Motor is notorious, particularly the Rouge plant. They never send in Form 100s. One of the guys out there, one of the attorneys for Ford Motor, said, 'If we send in Form 100s for every injury out there, we'd just be doing paperwork all the time.'"

They so seldom file, said Glotta, that "there probably aren't five filed with the state in the last ten years — other than, I suppose, in those cases where the guy dies there, or loses an arm, or something like that, you know, something so dramatic. A lot of workmen's compensation cases are that a guy's back gives out. And their position is, well, it could have given out anywhere. But Brian was standing there; a rather heavy item fell about ten feet and hit his back. He was clearly disabled; he was having serious problems; no medical care had been provided to him. No indication from the Ford Motor Company that they were liable for it. In fact, they said it was arthritis, or he was faking, or something.

"In order to start paying benefits you've got to send in a Form 100. But for all the other injuries, for which they dispute benefits anyway, they never sent in a Form 100. The reason for the Form 100 is then the state can explain to the man what his rights are and everything. And if they send in the Form 100, all sorts of problems have been solved for the worker's attorney. Number one, there's clear notice. Because the way a workmen's comp trial is, the guy comes in and says, 'I injured myself when I did this or that.'

"'Did you tell anybody?'

"'Yes, I went to the foreman and told him. He sent me to first aid, and they treated me, sent me back to work and I couldn't do the work and eventually I left and then I was fired.'

"That's the process of a comp case. Now if they sent in a Form 100, when he goes and says he injured himself by making a lift at work, then they've eliminated a whole legal issue that they always litigate: *notice*. Because when they send in the form, they indicate that he *told* them. But [without a Form 100] what happens in a trial, the worker says it and then the foreman comes in and says, 'No, I don't remember him ever telling me his back hurt.' Then the first aid person comes in and says, 'No, there's no note in here that he said his back hurt.'

"But you know, nobody down at the comp department really believes in that notice provision anyway. Because everybody knows the company is lying. And everybody knows that when a guy hurts his back, all the foremen know it, all of the first aid people know he hurt his back. So if the man says he told his foreman, everybody agrees that he probably did. Because you don't go walking around half-crippled and have the foreman just ignore it."

Again, the point of not sending in the Form 100s is economic. "If they were conscientious on the Form 100 situation," said Glotta, "it would cost them a lot of money, so they are purposely not anxious about that. And the national safety figures are compiled out of Michigan off the Form 100s, and the Form 100s are never sent in on any kind of regular basis." The company tries to get the injured worker on the group insurance plan, which may pay as well or often better than compensation. "They'll immediately pay group insurance," Glotta said. "They'll say, 'Here, take ninety dollars a week and don't fight the workmen's comp.' The guy figures he's going to get back to work anyway. And most guys do. After three or four weeks they go back to work. But a year later they have more trouble with their backs, they're off three or four weeks, and a year later they have more trouble. Each time it's been made nonindustrial. Now at one point or another it's going to become so bad he can't work anymore. At that point, if each time a Form 100 had been filed and he'd been paid workmen's comp, he would immediately get his workmen's comp and he would get it for the rest of his life. Instead, what he has is litigation."

In the Flannigan case, Glotta forced Ford into filing the Form 100, and Flannigan began to collect his compensation benefits—sixty-nine dollars a week. "You can't survive on that much," Flannigan said. "I'm lucky I can live on sixty-nine dollars a week, but most people can't." Flannigan also filed for unemployment compensation but was denied benefits. "He's entitled to both, you know, theoretically," Glotta said. "Because the comp act says you're disabled from doing the work that you were doing at the time of the injury. Unemployment, you have to be ready and available for work, but only any work that you're able to do. But they beat him on the unemployment case, and the reason is clear. They don't want guys collecting both benefits, because he has to stay on a sustenance level. If a guy were collecting both benefits, he'd be doing fairly well."

So that's the system. First, don't bother to keep the plant safe, because it's cheaper to pay off the crippled worker. Second, don't pay the man too much, on the theory that if there's money in it, he'd rather be crippled than work. It is a system based wholly on economics—in effect, on man's worth as a machine.

Zoltan Ferency, a Lansing compensation attorney, who was a former deputy director of the Michigan workmen's compensation administration and was a Democratic candidate for governor of Michigan, pointed out that the basic premise of the law is false, because people want and need to work. "The typical thing that happens," he told me, "is, the guy goes to work, or the girl goes to work, that day and the trauma happens. It's only then that the whole impact hits—the loss of job, loss of well-being. Hits them all at once. He has to go home and explain to his wife and kids, 'I am no longer able to work for a living.' Unless you're in this business, you don't understand what a feeling it is to be a worker and not be working. Until it happens, even the man doesn't understand it—the Puritan ethic. I've had cases where a man loses his potency, his manhood. You become a useless person."

These are strains on the person that can be expected in the best of circumstances even if the company immediately and voluntarily begins to pay him compensation. But often simply trying to get that compensation becomes a major problem, dragging on in many cases for years, focusing the man's attention morbidly on his disability. During this time he is at the mercy of his lawyers, who may or may not have his best interests at heart, and of his employer or the employer's insurance company, which may be withholding his payments in an attempt to pressure him into settlement or returning to work.

In Detroit there are law firms that commonly convince their clients to press for settlement rather than proceed with litigation, regardless of the merits of the case, because the lawyer makes more money that way. "As soon as you get volume," Ferency said, "sheer economics tells you that settling a thousand cases at fifteen percent is more than litigating two hundred and fifty at thirty percent. Lawyers will deal off one case against another."

In the Detroit compensation courts, it is a common sight to see a docket listing fifteen or twenty cases, all from Chrysler or Ford, all represented by one attorney, who will attempt to settle all the cases in one session, bargaining with company lawyers, trading a thousand dollars off Mrs. Hugh's amputated leg for an extra thousand on Mr. Frye's broken back. And their clients, grateful for the few thousand lump sum settlement—probably more money than they've ever seen at one time before—may never know that they may have been entitled to twice or three or four times that amount, or more.[1]

The Johnson, Carter, and Flannigan stories are varieties of a tale that is replayed constantly in the auto shops. It is a story of basic conflict between the worker and his work, causing the countable injuries—the amputated fingers, broken bones, back injuries, and such—but also the more hidden but equally devastating effects on workers who may never appear in the workmen's compensation docket.

NOTE

1. Johnson and Carter refer to cases discussed in an earlier chapter of the original book (Eds.).

Oil: Dealing with Men as Cattle

Rachel Scott

One safety hazard the union had complained about was an area where a "mule" hauling four cars, each carrying fifty-five-gallon drums, came down a ramp, then had to turn and go up another ramp. "You have no control of that mule coming down the ramp," said Bailey. "You just have to ride it out." Bailey said he showed the area to a federal inspector, but the company man said when conditions were bad they cut down the number of cars. The inspector did not cite it as a hazard. A few weeks later, Joe Mondile, a Mobil worker, was walking up the ramp as a mule coming down the ramp slipped on oil, jackknifed and hit him.

"My back was turned," said Mondile later. "It didn't make any sound and it pinned me against the wall. It twirled me around. Then I seen the drums against my chest. The wagon is what got my leg." The muscles of his chest were ripped away from the rib cage and a long gouge was torn in one leg.

When he was hit, Mondile landed in a puddle of water. There had been a leak in the pipe at that spot for two years. "Two years employees have been writing slips on that leak," said Mondile. "Within half an hour after they put me in the ambulance and took me away, they had a pipe fitter over there to fix that leak.

"I find it's a company that preaches safety but doesn't practice it. Their biggest excuse is they're always in the process of fixing things. If it's production it gets fixed. If you want something done for safety, it's 'No manpower.' They could use another thousand men for a year — that's just for cleaning up and repairs. There's too much overtime, and a lack of maintenance and housekeeping and a 'I don't give a damn' attitude as far as management is concerned. How many barrels of oil have been refined today and that's all they're interested in."

Mondile was forty-nine and had worked at Mobil for twenty-five years. He took the job because "it had security," he said. "That's a big thing when you're a family man. Good benefits. A married man with children thinks about these things."

Union president Dick Meyer said the union had difficulty getting men in the plant to cooperate during the OSHA inspection. "Some people know their unit like they know their wife, I guess, but a lot of places we couldn't get anybody that would talk. The history of the oil industry is your grandfather worked there, your father worked there.

For years it was a good plant. We used to hate to miss a day. All that stuff changed in the fifties.'' The average age of Paulsboro plant workers was fifty-five, he said, and most of the men continued to believe that the company was looking after them. ''I think if they'd cut 'em a dollar an hour, they'd say thank you,'' he said.

''They win safety awards pretty near all the time,'' said Meyer. Like many plants, he said Mobil kept its lost-time accident rate down by bringing injured workers back into the plant. ''One time my leg swelled up from a jackhammer. They sent me to a doctor. He put it in a cast. They brought me in there. There was a man named Green that got burned pretty bad. I saw him one night — he was crying. They brought him in there in an ambulance so they wouldn't get that lost time. That's been going on for twenty years. I can't tell you how many people's been coming in there in pain.''

It's easy for the workers to talk about accidents that are readily recognized as hazards, but they generally are not nearly as familiar with the chemical exposures. ''In the ketone area where ammonia is,'' Meyer went on, ''people started falling out—and you wonder what's happening. When people were starting to die in their forties and fifties, that's when I started to get concerned.''

One chemical hazard common to oil refineries is hydrogen sulfide gas. The gas is a by-product of the refining of oil, produced by the combination of sulfur in the crude oil with hydrogen. Pipe fitters at Mobil consider it a major hazard, with good reason.

Don Fuller, a Mobil pipe fitter, had worked for the company thirty-two years at the time he was gassed.

''The day it happened, I'll never forget,'' he said.

''I was kidding Eddie, my boss. He had his arm wrapped around me. He said, 'Guess what, Don?'

''I wrapped my arm around him. I said, 'Guess what, Eddie? My wife told me how much she loved me this morning. I want to see her tonight.' I said, 'Don't hurt me. It's my wedding anniversary.'

''He said, 'Look up there — that's where you're going to be working.'

''I said, 'Oh, no, Eddie, you don't mean we're going to be working on that gas line—that hydrogen sulfide?'

''He said, 'It's all right, it's been cleared.'

''I said, 'All right, Ed.'

''There were about five men in our gang. For some unlucky reason, I climbed the stairs first. The next guy that came around the railing saw me and screamed. They thought I was dead.''

Fuller was taken unconscious to the hospital. He remained unconscious. ''One doctor, Snider, my wife said, he stayed there the longest. He'd say, 'If only he'd come to,' and he'd look and feel and then he'd go out. He said, 'If only he'll come to screaming and fighting, everything's going to be all right.' He said, 'If he comes to like a baby and just lays there,' he said, 'he won't be no good.'

"So she said it was the twenty-seventh hour. She said, 'You opened your eyes and started screaming and fighting. She said, 'They had to tie you down.'"

At first Fuller didn't know who he was or where he was, and even after two weeks he thought it was 1955, not 1972. Eventually, with his doctor's help, he regained most of his memory, though he began to forget people's names. "When I see a man on the street I've known thirty-two years I go through everything trying to remember his name. I get embarrassed, so I duck in a store. Damage has been done somewhere."

Headaches were Fuller's biggest complaint. "One night lying in the hospital, I'd swear somebody stabbed me right in the head. Ever since then it's headache after headache. I keep a record every day — date, headache, date, headache, date, severe headache, date, pretty good, date, headache, all the way through. I say to my wife, 'Get my belt and tie it around my head tight as you can.' 'I will not, you'll kill yourself.' I say, 'Betty, I get relief.' But I can't get any relief from it."

Joe Duca was another Mobil pipe fitter. He worked for the refinery forty years and told me he had been gassed with hydrogen sulfide several times.

"Each time I got hurt and fell off the scaffold. The last time was three and a half years ago. Seven years prior to that me and seven other fellows were gassed. I fell on a steam line six feet below. Five of the other guys did too. One guy got his neck all messed up — Joe English — because he fell on the cement.

"This last time we were taking a pipeline apart. We knew the hydrogen sulfide was there. The safety man came around and checked and said it was safe to work. But they didn't order us no gas masks.

"When we took the flange apart and put the blank in, it was okay. But maybe somebody neglected to check the other end. When we finished the job, I took the blank out. I was alone on top of the scaffold. I don't remember what happened. I just passed out.

"For three weeks I was just like a dead person. I couldn't make my voice come out like I wanted, say things I wanted to say. Even now sometimes I can't remember things. I forget awful quick. There's more to that than I can say. I'm still going to the doctor and taking pills for my nerves and my head. And I have a lot of noise in my ears — like a generator — all the time. My head sometimes doesn't feel good. I get headaches. Another thing, sometimes I get dizzy, too. I can't balance myself. I get in a sweat, like, and I know it's coming and have to sit down.

"After that last gassing they wanted me to work. I worked about a week and a half. My nerves got so shot they took me back to the hospital for two weeks. After that they told me I better take my pension.

"I hope somebody puts something in there that wises the company up. So they show some concern for the men. It used to be like a family, now it's dog eat dog."

Les Jandoli, a Camden, New Jersey, attorney, handled about thirty compensation cases a year from the Mobil plant. "The problem down there is they have a very weak union," he said. "Mobil discourages men from filing claims. I've seen letters from supervisors: 'If you continue to lose work you may be let go.' After thirty-two years. A fellow came in last week, he'd been off nineteen days over and above what they allowed for sick leave and they threatened to fire him. It's happened time and time again.

"A lot of men develop lung problems down there. All the pipes are wrapped in asbestos. Pipe fitters, welders, et cetera, are submitting themselves to a hazardous condition. The men are not willing to strike for better working conditions, not willing to put their jobs on the line for each other. Gloucester County was a farm area — now, they're making a nice standard of living which their fathers and grandfathers never did."

The company thinking, Jandoli explained, was this: "They're paying the men and that's all their responsibility extends to. They feel as long as they do pay the men, their responsibility is over. They are so used to dealing with men as cattle, when the men do raise issues, they can't cope with it."

Jandoli added, "Mobil isn't by any stretch of the imagination a bad employer."

The Deep Discontent of the Working Woman

The popular image of working women is that of swinging white-collar careerists who juggle challenging jobs, cultural interests, and romance. But to the 80 percent of all working women who are not professionals but who hold factory, service, or clerical jobs, reality is strikingly different, as a Senate committee will learn on January 31.

According to a study by the National Commission on Working Women (NCWW), the average woman worker is a lonely person in a dead-end job, seething with frustration over her lot. Home and children only deepen her dissatisfaction, because they raise problems of housework and child care. With the number of women at work rising to 48.4 percent in 1977 from less than 40 percent in 1960 — and projected to rise to 60 percent in the next decade — Congress is beginning to take heed.

Child Care

The Senate Human Resources Committee, headed by Senator Harrison Williams (D-N.J.), will hear a parade of witnesses testify on a broad range of women-related concerns in the hearings, which start on January 31 and lead off with depressing evidence unearthed by the NCWW. Separately, Senator Alan Cranston (D-Calif.) will open hearings on February 5 on a child care bill he introduced. Cranston thinks that chances for passage of the bill, which would lay the groundwork for federal aid for child care, have vastly improved since the last go-around in 1974, when such a bill never made it to a vote. "People used to say women would be drawn away from the family if offered child care help," says a Cranston aide. "It is clear by now that they are going to work anyway."

The Williams hearings will feature such headline stars as Bella Abzug, who was recently fired by Carter as chairperson of his Advisory Committee on Women. But the presentation that could most affect the future of women and men will be that of W. Willard Wirtz, former Labor Secretary, chairman of the National Manpower Institute, and, in this case, witness for the NCWW.

Wirtz will tell senators the preliminary results of a survey of 150,000 women who responded to questionnaires that the NCWW placed in women's magazines and union publications last September. Not only was the response so overwhelming that computers have still not completed tabulations, but several thousand women wrote unsolicited letters detailing their grievances. "Imagine people so isolated and upset that they will write to a post office box for solace, and you have an idea of the women we touched," says an NCWW staffer.

Some of the NCWW's findings about ordinary women workers:

- Forty percent felt that their jobs were boring and did not utilize their skills, and nearly half said they had no chance to train for better jobs. One-third reported receiving no counseling about other jobs or training. Because of failure to advance and what they had been told about women's capabilities, one in four said they lacked the self-confidence to get ahead. Among those who had problems with their jobs, 60 percent named as their primary problem their lack of opportunity to advance.
- Fifty-five percent had no leisure time and 39 percent had no time to pursue education. Presumably their after-work hours were devoted to housework. A study by the University of Michigan's Institute for Social Research found that on days when the wife works, only 5 percent of husbands spent as much as three and one half hours on home chores. Only 14 percent of women in the commission survey could say that job and family life did not interfere with each other.
- Among women with young children who already had jobs and presumably had made some arrangement for child care, almost one-third said they needed additional child care help. Wirtz will say that when the data on child care are finally tabulated, he expects to see a "much higher" figure for women who are not working, but who wish to.

More vivid than the survey results were the letters. "I'm on sick leave from my job, and my problems are directly related to having to work, run a household, and care for children," complained a Michigan woman, who said that she and many of her coworkers are "tired, don't have time to express ourselves."

Single parents, said a New York woman, experience "great frustration" in advancing because of educational deficiencies, then find that they cannot remedy this lack. "I have tried to attend school at night while working full time and raising my children," the New Yorker wrote, "but have been forced to postpone my education until the time when my children are older." A Massachusetts woman wrote that "retirement income is a function of earnings, and this is where the working woman is hurt. . . . The day I stop working is the day that my home of 30 years goes on the market. It frightens me."

Neither Wirtz nor Williams predicts that women workers will take to the streets in rage. But as their frustration is translated increasingly into political and legal action, they are likely to seek changes in such areas as counseling, training, and child care help that could be costly to employers or society and prompt some painful readjustment.

The Wall Street Journal, 11 December 1980.

Smiles of Flight Attendants Mask Hostility, Fatigue and Bodily Pain

By SUSAN HARRIGAN

Staff Reporter of The Wall Street Journal

The next time a flight attendant smiles at you, smile back sympathetically. The friendly skies, it seems, are a seething cauldron of stress.

Attendants suffer from so much fatigue, bodily pain and other stress symptoms that at the end of many a day, they don't feel able to deal with emergencies, according to a study by the Aviation Safety Institute, a nonprofit research group. The study drew on detailed records kept by 30 flight attendants—27 women and three men —over a two month period.

Constant travelers mightn't be surprised to learn that attendants don't always feel terrific. Some other findings of the study, however, are less predictable.

Stressful Routes

For one thing, your smiling attendant actually may feel hostile toward you if you are on a southwesterly or northeasterly flight. Attendants' pulse rates and other stress indicators rise on such flights, according to the study, which couldn't find "plausible explanations" for the phenomena.

Flight attendants say such flights are more stressful because passengers on them are "higher-strung." Southwesterners tend to be "hustling" types who drink a lot and call stewardesses "baby," says Jean Bombach, an Eastern Airlines attendant. "You're always trying to shake that anyhow, and when somebody's blatant about it, you really get turned off," she says.

Northeasterners, by contrast, aren't "laid back" enough when they fly, attendants say. "They want everything (served to them) in the Northeast," Mrs. Bombach says. "You have to make sure they don't take the seats with them when they leave."

A little in-flight turbulence actually calms jumpy flight attendants, according to the study, which can't explain that finding, either. But Mrs. Bombach says, "It feels like being rocked— back-to-the-womb security."

Wisdom of the Elders

Mature years help, too. In general, older flight attendants report less fatigue than younger ones do, the study found. It hypothesizes that younger attendants tend to rush off to see the sights during layovers, while older and wiser ones rest up. Enid Grigg, an Eastern attendant for 14 years, says older attendants tend to fly the same routes continually and "know how to deal with passengers' hostility when it crops up."

And, in a finding sure to strike a sympathetic chord among fellow travelers, the study revealed that flight attendants suffer from "mild malnutrition." They don't eat enough on flights, partly because they don't have time, but mostly because they don't want to swallow "plastic food," as many of them call airline meals.

"It seems to me that the food is mostly fillers," one flight attendant says. "All the stuff congeals after a while, and the meat turns blue or various shades of purple and green. After you've seen that, you can't eat it."

Out of Their League

Dave Meggyesy

When a player is injured, he is sent to the team physician, who is usually more concerned with getting the athlete back into action than anything else. This reversal of priorities leads to unbelievable abuses. One of the most common is to "shoot" a player before a game to numb a painful injured area that would normally keep him out of action. He can play, but in so doing he can also get new injuries in that part of his body where he has no feeling.

When I spoke to a group of athletes at the University of California in the spring of 1970, Jim Calkins, cocaptain of the Cal football team, told me that the coaching staff and the team physician had put him on anabolic steroids. Both assured him such drugs would make him bigger and stronger, and this is true. But they didn't bother to tell him that there are potentially dangerous side-effects. "I gained a lot of weight like they told me I would, but after a month or so, those steroids really began to mess me up," Jim told me. "I went to the team physician and he admitted that there are possible dangers. I had complete faith in the coaches and medical staff before this, and I felt betrayed." And well he might, because steroids are known to have caused atrophied testes, blunting of sex drives, damage to liver and glands, and some physicians believe that they are the causal agent for cancer of the prostate. And they are widely used.

The violent and brutal player that television viewers marvel over on Saturdays and Sundays is often a synthetic product. When I got to the National Football League, I saw players taking not only steroids, but also amphetamines and barbiturates at an astonishing rate. Most NFL trainers do more dealing in these drugs than the average junky. I was glad when Houston Ridge, the San Diego Chargers' veteran defensive tackle, filed a huge suit last spring against his club, charging them with conspiracy and malpractice in the use of drugs. He charged that steroids, amphetamines, barbiturates and the like were used "not for purpose of treatment and cure, but for the purpose of stimulating mind and body so he (the player) would perform more violently as a professional . . ."

I don't mean that players are given drugs against their will. Like Calkins, most players have complete trust in their coaches and team doctors and in the pattern of authority they represent. Associated with this is the atmosphere of suspicion which surrounds any injured player unless his injury is a visible one, like a broken bone. Coaches constantly question the validity of a player's complaints, and give him the silent treatment when he has a "suspicious" injury. The coaches don't say, "We think you're faking, don't you want to play football?" They simply stop talking to a player and the message comes across very clearly. Most players want and need coaches' approval, especially when they are injured and can't perform, and it really tears them up when the coach won't even speak to them. This is especially true in college where the players are young and usually identify closely with the coach. After a few days of this treatment, many players become frantic. They will plead with the team physician to shoot them up so they can play. The player will totally disregard the risk of permanent injury.

Coaches love to recount examples of players who have played with serious injuries. Ben's[1] favorite story was about Jim Ringo. According to Ben, Ringo played one game his senior year with infected boils covering both legs. Ben would emphasize that both Ringo's legs were covered with pus and blood when he came into the locker room at half time. According to Ben, Ringo did not once speak of the pain. He simply bandaged the draining boils, put on a clean pair of pants and went back out to play a great second half. It's like the fictional American soldier played by John Wayne who fights on with crippling, fatal wounds. In the Catch-22 world of football, as in war, this passes for reasonable behavior. . . .

I must admit to mixed feelings about the athletic department's willingness to keep guys out of trouble since they kept me out of jail once when the police had a warrant out for my arrest, because of my collection of over fifty-five parking tickets. They handled the matter so well that I not only avoided jail or a fine, but I didn't even pay the original fines. I remember standing before the judge trying to look humble and contrite. I knew the athletic department had already worked things out because it was Ben who had told me when to show up in court. But the judge began to lecture me in a stern monotone: "The total for these tickets and accumulated fines is over $800 and you could spend up to six months in jail. Just because you are a football player, don't think you can get away with this kind of thing." He kept on for about five minutes, and I began to have visions of myself sitting in jail wondering how the hell I was going to get $800. Suddenly the judge looked up, half smiled, and asked, "Are you guys going to have a good football team this year?" I heaved a sigh of relief; everything was all right. "We have a real dedicated bunch of guys," I told him with all the boyish modesty I could summon, "and I think we can go all the way." "I'm glad to hear that," he said. "All of us down here follow the team closely and are pulling for you." He quickly switched back to his judge's face and voice, informed me I was being fined $10 for court costs and called the next case.

I was elated at getting off so easily, especially after the temporary scare the judge had given me. But I was also thinking about how the judge had treated other people in court that morning. The shabbily dressed defendants, many of them black, were given the harshest penalties while the more affluent looking, like me, usually paid no more than a nominal fine. With my background it was easy to identify with the poor defendants, for I knew if I was not a college football star, I would be in the same boat.

Taking care of $800 worth of parking tickets, of course, was trivial compared to the effort and expense the athletic department had to put out for many players. This sort of thing makes you see yourself as pretty important. With all the wheeling and dealing the athletic department does on your behalf, you get the feeling you're immune from normal responsibilities — which is possibly why some athletes act like animals all the time.

After years of this special treatment, ball players begin to lose sight of the fact that this immunity is only temporary. For those who don't make it to the pros, it usually expires along with their college reputation. There are few more pathetic sights than a former college football hero walking around campus unnoticed. The same university that used to fix his grades, bail him out of jail and give him money under the table has now turned its back on him. You see a lot of guys whose life actually stopped after their last college game. They hang on by becoming insurance salesmen and the like, selling their former image as a football player. . . .

[*Eds. Note:* The author now relates his pro football experiences.]

At eleven o'clock we had to be in our rooms in bed with the lights out. I'd lie in my bed with my door about six inches open to hear the coach coming by for bed check. He'd open the door, shine the flashlight directly in your eyes to make sure you were in bed, and mumble "Good night." Players never mess around with bed check because they realize if they're ever reported to the head coach for missing bed check they face — at least under Winner[2] — an automatic $500 fine.

A guy would be in the bathroom taking a dump or brushing his teeth and you'd hear the coach open the door and holler to him, "Get to bed now, it's after eleven o'clock." But what really pissed me off in this enforced infantilization were the times I hadn't been able to reach the one phone in the dorm to call my family until close to 11:00. I'd be talking with Stacy and the coach would come down and yell "Hang up now and get to bed." It was worse than absurd. The guys being bed-checked were adults, pulling down an average of about $25,000 a year. Many of them are stockbrokers off season; a few have Ph.D. degrees. But you find yourself reacting like a kid. Some nights when I was really digging a book, I'd turn off the light when I heard the coach coming up the hall and pretend to be sleeping when he opened my door. He'd check the other rooms and when he left the floor, I'd put on the light and continue reading like a guilty kid who sneaks a book under the covers with a flashlight after his parents have told him to go to sleep.

The 1969 season was the first one that I was able to rent a house near the training camp and have Stacy and the kids with me; but the coaches still insisted I had to be in bed in the dormitory at eleven o'clock. This meant I'd drive over to the house after dinner and spend an hour and a half or so playing with the kids, then rush back in time for the eight o'clock meeting. After that, I could drive back and be with Stacy until 10:45 when I'd have to run to the dorm and be in the sack when the coach came around for bed check.

In pro football, as in high school and college, the only way the coaches can establish their authority is to treat their players as boys. After I'd decided to retire, I was talking to "Chip" Oliver, the Oakland Raider linebacker who'd also quit at the peak of his career. We were talking in the Bay Area commune where he's now living and one of his comments struck me as right on. He said he'd told Al Davis, general manager of the Raiders, that he still liked football and would happily come back to play again if the coaches would treat him like a man. We smiled because we both knew this meant permanent retirement as long as he stuck to this demand. . . .

My contract made it financially important to me to play as many defensive plays as possible during the regular season. At the same time, the team, including myself, was attempting to win a division championship. So, where I was able to pick up a particular tip on the opposition, I was confronted with the dilemma of whether or not to share it with the other linebackers. Coaches constantly talk about team spirit but I've always wondered how the hell there can be team spirit if I know that the more other linebackers screw up, the more I'll be able to play, and the more I play, the more money I make. Owners keep writing contracts with performance clauses such as the one I had, though these can only work to create divisiveness on the team, for these clauses create a situation where the amount of money a player gets is dependent on how badly his teammates at his position play. A second-string player who will not get his bonus unless he plays at least 40 percent of the plays will not be upset if the guy ahead of him screws up badly. The owners introduced these bonuses with the idea that they would extract better performances from the players and result in more victories. In reality, just the opposite usually happens. Rumors began to spread around the league during the 1969 season that receivers who had bonus clauses for the number of passes they caught were paying kickbacks to the quarterbacks.

This dual level of competition is built into pro football. On one hand, the player is competing against his opponent, the guy across from him, and wants to do a good job to further the club's success. At the same time, I was constantly aware that my every move would be on movie film and would be scrutinized closely by the coaching staff the following Monday when they decided between me and my competitors on the team for the starting role. This competition involved not only linebackers, but also halfbacks that I had to cover in practice: if they looked good it meant that I wasn't doing my job and that could get me demoted to second team.

Players bullshit the press on how they help the various rookies. I have rarely seen this happen—certainly I received no help at all when I was a rookie. Quite the contrary, rookies generally received constant abuse from the vets, designed to intimidate them and break their confidence. The new player must not only prove himself on the field, he must also prove he can take their harassment. It's survival of the fittest from beginning to end. . . .

The only thing I had going for me after my return from the Virgin Islands was being enrolled in graduate school at Washington University. I began my studies again, yet felt the university setting added less and less meaning to my life. Though I'd done a lot of thinking about who I was, I never seemed able to know my real feelings about many things. There was, in short, much ambivalence in my life. Then, in the last week of March '69 I attended a five-day workshop at Esalen Institute led by Seymour Carter. My experience at Esalen was, to make an understatement, significant. I saw very acutely the contradiction between the feelings I had during my experiences at Esalen and the experiences I had working within my craft, which was football. Since high school, I had been using the mask of "football player" to confront the world. It was both my main line of defense and my main source of gaining approval and recognition. I also realized, paradoxically, how cut off and removed I was from my body. I knew my body more thoroughly than most men are ever able to, but I had used it and thought of it as a machine, a thing that had to be well oiled, well fed, and well taken care of, to do a specific job. My five days at Esalen left me with an immensely good feeling. I had glimpsed a bit of myself and realized that the "me" behind the face guard was alive and well and could feel and think.

NOTES

1. Ben Schwartzwalder, former coach at Syracuse University — *Eds.*
2. Charlie Winner, former St. Louis Cardinals coach — *Eds.*

The New York Times, 12 May 1981.

Homosexuality Causes Sports Tremors

By NEIL AMDUR

Four years after David Kopay became the first pro football player to admit publicly his sexual preference for men, he is still unable to land a coaching position.

"I was very excited at having written my book and the favorable response it received," said Kopay, who played in the National Football League for 10 years with five teams, wrote "The David Kopay Story," and now works at his uncle's linoleum and hardware store in Hollywood, Calif. "But I've been frustrated at finding a niche for myself. I'm disappointed at not having had any coaching opportunities. I've constantly been told forget it, there's no chance. I hadn't counted on this."

Homosexuality is the most sensitive issue in the sports marketplace, more delicate than drugs, more controversial than violence.

The Underlife of Cabdriving: A Study in Exploitation and Punishment

James M. Henslin

What is the work of the cab driver like? Many people appear to have the idea that a cabbie's work is carefree. He hops into his cab, picks up passengers at various locations, and delivers them to their destinations. In the meantime he meets interesting people from all walks of life, enjoys good conversation, and collects sizeable tips — roaming

Reprinted by permission of the publisher from *Varieties of Occupational Experience,* by P. L. Stewart and M. G. Cantor (eds.), pp. 67–79. © Schenkman Publishing Co., Inc., 1974. This is a revised version of a paper read at the annual meeting of the Midwest Sociological Society, St. Louis, Missouri, April 1970.

the city as a sort of modern vagabond on wheels.

Such a view does contain an element of truth. The cabbie indeed delivers people to places they want to go. He does meet many people, of whom some are interesting and a few are even fascinating. He does become involved in many conversations. And he does collect tips. But there is much more to the work of the cabbie. And not all of it is rewarding — or even pleasant. This paper emphasizes the punishments and exploitation to which the cabbie is subjected, the brutalizing elements which are built into his job and go hand in hand with driving a cab.

One must also understand the rewarding aspects of the cabbie's life if one is to have an accurate or balanced picture of the cabbie's world. These rewarding aspects of the occupation are also crucial in the cabbie's life. They also shape his identity, mold the way he thinks of himself, and structure the way he views the world. . . .

This analysis of the underlife of cabdriving is based on data gathered by this participant observer who drove a cab in the city of St. Louis on a part-time basis for about a year. Neither the management nor the workers knew they were being studied. A hidden tape recorder was used to record: 1) interaction among cabbies before and after work, 2) messages transmitted over the cab's radio, 3) conversations with passengers, 4) conversations with cabbies at the cab stands, and 5) crap games which these cabbies played after work. At no time were people informed that they were being studied, nor did they indicate any awareness that they had a researcher in their midst.

Why the choice of participant observation? A major goal of many sociological researchers is to understand the subject's world from *his* point of view. This purpose goes under various names in sociology, such as *verstehen*, interpretative understanding, subjective interpretation, definition of the situation, uncovering underlying "background expectancies," or investigating the "socially-sanctioned facts-of-life-that-any-bonafide-member-of-the-group-knows." . . . The assumption is that intimate familiarity with someone's world can lead to an understanding of that person's definitional process, and that we can thereby know the factors he finds important and better understand his behavior.

Those researchers who follow this goal ordinarily choose a method of research which least molests the phenomena they are studying. Participant observation is frequently chosen because it not only allows the researcher entry into the everyday world of his subjects, but also, when done correctly, minimizes disruption to interaction. Thus the researcher can have greater confidence that the data he gathers by this method is representative of the regularly occurring, ongoing interaction of the group he enters; that it is naturalistic and not an artifact of his presence. . . .

If one attempts to understand life's experiences from the perspective of the other, the researcher must "get into" the symbolic system of those he is studying. He must know what members of that group consider important in any relevant situation. When he understands how the members of a culture define their situations, the researcher knows much of what goes into the decisions they make. He then has some understanding of what influences and buttresses their life style.

In this research, I entered their world as someone who knew little about cabdriving and cab drivers. Not having previously learned to accept the cab drivers' view of reality as reality, led me to question fundamental aspects of their existence. I then sociologically analyzed parts of their world which they routinely and unquestioningly took for granted. . . .

Not only did I gain information about the world of those I was studying, but more importantly, I directly experienced that world. I was thus able to understand the events in cabbie culture from the perspective of the members of that culture. For example, I not only learned *what* a "no-go" is (a location to which a cabbie is dispatched, but where there is no passenger when he arrives), but I also learned the *meaning* of a "no-go" for the cab driver, such things as the effect of the "no-go" on his income for that shift, the frustration which seethes within him, and his feelings of futility in dealing with his world.

This paper, then, is presented from the point of view of the cab driver, and is an examination of the major areas of his life which he sees as punitive. Relevant aspects of his work setting are examined, including problematic aspects of interaction with passengers, competition among cabbies, mechanisms of social control, the cabbie's equipment, and factors which are structured into the occupation that exert control over his life situation and lead him to work hard but to live in poverty.

THE CABBIE AND HIS PASSENGERS

The cab driver is constantly on the go, being dispatched throughout the city. He transports businessmen, shoppers, tourists, workers, drunks, prostitutes, and housewives to their destinations. As he deals with these people, the cabbie regularly confronts passengers who threaten his self, his routine, and sometimes his property or even his life.

The cabbie is frequently treated as a nonperson, that is, people sometimes act as though he were not present. Passengers sometimes do not adjust their behavior for his presence — any more than they would for the steering wheel of an auto. When intimate arguments are fought out in the cab between lovers, for example, it is as though the cab driver were merely a nonhuman extension of the steering wheel, a kind of machine which guides the cab. Such interaction in all its varied aspects — the tones and loudness of voice, the words used, the subjects spoken about — takes place as though the individuals were in private, with no third person present. The effect on the cabbie of some types of nonperson treatment is a challenging of the self since others are not acknowledging his self but acting as though he did not exist.

The cabbie also regularly has passengers who in various ways challenge his control over the transaction. Some passengers berate him for not going fast enough or for missing a green light, while others withhold the tip as a sanction against something they did not like about the driver. The cabbie must also put up with persons who are "playing." (In "cabby-ese" this refers to those who call in and have a cab dispatched to a location where no one desires a cab.) Other callers are present when he arrives but refuse to enter the cab. Still others, "bucket loads," skip out without paying their fare. Other passengers demand services he is unwilling to provide, such as locating a prostitute or entering an area of the city which the driver considers to be unsafe after dark. To communicate some of the "flavor" of such problematic interactions, I shall illustrate the punitiveness of the belligerent and noncooperative passenger. In an afterwork group, a driver related the following incident:

> He picked up a passenger who said, "Take me to thirty-five." The driver asked, "Thirty-five what?" The passenger became somewhat angry and raised his voice, saying, "Just take me to thirty-five!" In exasperation, the driver said, "Well, thirty-five what?" The passenger then said, "Just start driving!" The driver began driving, and after he had driven a short while, the passenger told him to make a right turn, and the driver did so. A while later, the passenger asked, "Where in the hell do you think you're going?" The driver then said, "I don't know where I'm going." The passenger then said, "I told you to take me to thirty-five!"
>
> At this point the driver covertly placed his hand on a hammer he carried in the cab and said, "Thirty-five hundred what? You just name me the street, and I'll show you what thirty-five hundred is on any street in St. Louis!" At this, the passenger finally named his street. When they arrived at his destination, the fare was $1.55, and the passenger handed two one-dollar bills to the driver, who still had his hand on the hammer. He then tapped the driver on the shoulder, and said, "There you are, buddy. Take it easy."

In reaction to such passengers, cabbies frequently develop a veneer of hardness, an outward crust which helps deflect painful threats to the self. This veneer manifests itself in the commonly perceived belligerency of cab drivers — the shaking fist and the cursing mouth, or the "Don't-tell-me-how-to-get-there" attitude. These are part of the cabbies' attempt to maintain control over threatening passengers and a life situation over which he actually has little control.

The threat of danger is also a constant part of the cab driver's work. Each day he drives his cab he lives with the knowledge that he might be robbed or murdered. This uncertainty of safety is constantly in the back of his mind as he picks up strangers as a routine part of his job. In the privacy of the cab, with these strangers at his back, he is literally at their mercy for his very life. This fear for his own safety constantly gnaws at him, and because holdup men are disproportionately black, both black and white cabbies tend to avoid black neighborhoods and black passengers — especially at night. . . .

Since the potential of danger is always present, many warning devices have been suggested. One was to install a mechanism to flash the cab's top lights when the cab driver stepped on a button. The flashing lights would supposedly alert pedestrians, motorists, and the police. But cabbies scoffed when the device was suggested, saying that the light would also alert the robber since he would be able to see its reflection as they drove past store windows. If this happened, the robber might retaliate physically, and cabbies felt that they would be in greater danger with this device than without it.

In spite of this continual and seemingly permanent danger of robbery and murder, cabbies are prevented by law from carrying weapons, even for self-defense. Most drivers just take their chances, but some find substitute weapons:

> While we were waiting for the cabs to arrive, I noticed that one driver was carrying what looked like a small fishing tackle box. As he was putting something in this box, I saw a hammer and said, "Hey, watcha got that for?" The driver replied, "Ah ha! That's it! I use that! Cops can't get you for carrying a concealed weapon. And it will do the job. I just lay it right out on the front seat."
>
> Another driver picked up the small ball peen hammer, one with a regular flat nail-driving surface on one end but with a ball instead of the nail-pulling claw on the other, and hit the flat surface against his hand and said, "Yeah, that will do the job." The first driver took the hammer, gestured to the end with the ball, and said, "No. Hit 'em with this other end. It'll go way in."

Some drivers are not satisfied with weapons such as hammers or tire tools, and they run the risk of being arrested on a felony charge for carrying a gun. Cabbies, however, generally feel utter futility and defenselessness in the face of this danger. This is well expressed by the driver who said: "You got ten guns—that don't do a fucking thing when . . . son-of-a-bitch puts that fucking thing in the back of your neck, there's not a fucking thing you can do."

COMPETITION AND CONFLICT

Besides problems with passengers, cabbies also are problematic to one another. The major reason for this is the intense competitiveness of cabdriving. Each cabbie, if he is to survive financially, directly competes with all other cab drivers in the city — both those from rival companies and drivers from his own company.

Intracompany competition regularly takes the simple but legitimate form of beating other drivers to a stand or getting one's own bid for "open" orders accepted by being faster at the mike than others. At other times competition with coworkers takes the more deviant form of being dissimulative when bidding for "open" orders, that is, lying about one's location in order to be eligible for the order. A more deviant form of intracompany competition, however, is "scooping" (stealing orders). It is possible to "scoop" or steal an order because all drivers can hear via their cab radio the location to which a driver is being dispatched. By also knowing the location of the stand from which the driver is being dispatched, a second driver can approximate the time it will take the first driver to arrive at the order. If he figures that he can get there first and still have enough time to pick up the passenger and be out of sight when the dispatched driver arrives, scooping is within his realm of possible action. The dispatched driver is then confronted with a "no-go." Since "no-goes" are punitive, scooping is a technique by which cabbies sometimes "pay back" or "get even with" other cabbies. Its use as a sanction is illustrated by the cabbie who said, "He's a son-of-a-bitch! Every chance I get, I scoop him!"

Intercompany competition is always keen, but it sometimes changes to conflict. Beatings, tire slashings, and other violence during periods of strikes and rate disputes are well known. However, even during "times of peace" the "truce" is uneasy and regularly threatens to erupt in violence. For example, after work one Metro driver related:

> I was drivin' in Forest Park, and these three women flagged me down. I pulled over, and as they was gettin' in the cab I saw this Red Top Cab come beatin' down the road and the last woman wasn't in yet and she said, "Look! There's our cab now!" Red Top is an air-conditioned cab, and so they wanted to ride with him. The women got out, and I said, "You better pay me somethin' for my stoppin' or else this bastard's gonna get his windshield knocked in." One woman gave me a dollar, and I left.

SOCIAL CONTROL THROUGH SARCASM, CENSURE, AND THREATS

While he is on the job the cabbie needs to deal not only with problematic passengers and competitive coworkers, but he must also drive for an extremely punitive management. Management regularly uses biting verbal techniques in order to keep cabbies in line. For example, in the early morning hours some drivers park at stands with the motors running and their radios on, and then lie down on the front seat and sleep, keeping mentally "tuned" for their stand to be called. When their stand is called they sometimes awaken in time to answer the call, but they frequently respond more slowly than usual, or are perhaps a bit sluggish in their speech. The following, which took place at 4:45 A.M., illustrates the dispatcher's generous use of (1) sarcasm, (2) censure, and (3) threats:

DISPATCHER: "DeBaliviere Delmar." (The dispatcher is calling a "stand," places where drivers park to await orders.)

CABBIE: ((Gives his cab number and stand.))[1]

DISPATCHER: "5560 Waterman."

CABBIE: ((Probably says, "Clear," meaning that he understood the order.))

DISPATCHER: (1) *"Did I disturb you, junior?"*

CABBIE: ((. . .))

DISPATCHER: "Well I'm glad to hear that."

CABBIE: ((. . .))

DISPATCHER: (2) *"Then quit laying down,* (3) *or you won't get the order."*

To understand the punitory nature of this combined sarcasm, censure, and threats, keep in mind first of all that this occurs *publicly.* These statements are being broadcast to all drivers, making the violator's positive reference group knowledgeable of the problem. Secondly, the regular dispatcher on the shift I usually worked was a woman. This means that males, who are already being ordered about by anyone who has the price of a cab, must undergo scorn or berating by a female in the "audible presence" of their fellow drivers.

Cabbies have not found an effective recourse to this ill treatment. Some drivers attempt to "get even" with dispatchers by "tying up the air." They keep the button on their microphones depressed in order to make it difficult for the dispatcher to give out orders. Not only is this action seldom successful, but were a cabbie to succeed in "tying up the air," he would also be penalizing his fellow cabbies by preventing them from receiving orders. He would end up being punitive toward those with whom he strongly identifies. With neither a legitimate nor an effective recourse open to get back at a dispatcher with whom he is having problems, a driver will sometimes withdraw — sitting in his cab, but angrily refusing to answer his radio. This, of course, is also a most ineffective sanction because he ends up harming himself, further lowering his already depressed income.

THE CABBIE AND HIS EQUIPMENT

In analyzing negative aspects of cabdriving, I wish to broadly apply the concept of punishment. The common sense idea of punishment refers to more than just persons as punitive agents. People frequently apply the term punishment not only to persons who are either purposely or inadvertently punishing to them, but also to experiences with material objects in which they feel that they are in some way humiliated, degraded or frustrated. We shall now examine this broader approach to understanding punishment and cab drivers, looking at objects which are punishing to cabbies.

The cab is obviously of extreme importance to the cab driver. He is so strongly identified with this vehicle that his name is but a diminutive of it — "cabbie." Moreover, . . . the cabbie's vehicle is a sort of armed weapon with which he approaches a hostile world. However, even his cab, with its equipment, is in many ways inimical to the cabbie.

Although the cab driver is supposed to "check out" his cab before he begins driving, he soon finds that factors militate against doing so. First of all, checking the cab for mechanical problems means that the cabbie loses time when he could be taking his first order. Secondly, he soon learns to avoid the garage men who repair the cabs since they become surly and sarcastic when they see anyone bringing a cab to the garage. The garage men are salaried, so cabs needing repairs represent only additional work for them. Finally, since cabs sitting in the garage also represent a loss of income to management, there is little encouragement from this sector.

The typical attitude is that as long as the cab moves when the accelerator is pressed it should be on the road. These cabs are on the go twenty-four hours a day, with one driver turning a cab in at the end of his twelve-hour shift and another driver immediately taking it out again. When a motor burns out, another is merely shoved into the old chassis. With the combination of not checking the cabs and running them continuously, cabs, at least in the city of St. Louis, are some of the most unsafe vehicles on the road.

A dysfunctional consequence is that it is not uncommon for a cabbie to find himself without such "niceties" as signal lights and properly working brakes. Additionally, with the condition of the cabs on the road, breakdowns are not infrequent. When a breakdown occurs, the cabbie is stuck. He must await "Metro Safety," whom the dispatcher sends to either make on-the-road repairs or to tow the cab away. Even such a small item as a flat tire means a breakdown for the cabbie since it is the practice of Metro Cab Company to send drivers out with neither a spare tire nor tire-changing tools.

His cab can also prove physically dangerous to the cabbie. The air intake of the cab is unfortunately located in front of the vehicle. In bumper-to-bumper traffic it directly sucks in the exhaust of the car in front. Those who live in urban settings all experience short periods of such exposure when they drive in rush hour traffic, but the cabbie is frequently in such situations for extended periods of time. In protest against the location of the mounting of the air vent, one Chicago cabbie refused to return his taxi to the garage. For this defiant act, however, he was summarily fired.[2]

The other major part of a cabbie's equipment, his radio, is also a punitive source for the driver. He sometimes receives an electric shock, especially when he is perspiring and resting his arm on the cab's door as he presses the button on his microphone. His radio is also likely to "go bad" at any moment, and to do so without warning. The new driver soon learns by painful experience that a variety of factors will cause his transmission to be too fuzzy or too weak for the dispatcher to receive, such as having too little water in the cab battery, parking too close to the curb, not warming up the radio, and even driving in a low area of the city. These occupational factors are ordinarily learned only through frustrating personal experience.

Radio silence is also threatening to the cab driver. When his radio is silent, the cabbie does not know whether anything is being broadcast or whether his radio is malfunctioning. He can check the source of radio silence by pressing the button on his mike and listening for a click to indicate working order, or he can call the dispatcher. These checks, however, tell him only if his radio is working *at that moment*. Should there continue to be silence, as happens during slack periods, the driver is again made uncomfortable, thinking that he might not be receiving orders which are being broadcast. In periods of radio silence drivers nervously respond to this tension, as indicated by the dispatcher saying such things as, "There's nothing wrong with your radio, Driver. I just don't have any orders." But this only gives a momentary reassurance since his radio can begin malfunctioning at any time, without warning.

HARD WORK AND POVERTY

In the midst of these varied problems, the cabbie works hard to make a buck. Sometimes even the weather and climate appear to conspire against him. In summer the cabbie swelters in heat since none of the rental cabs are air-conditioned. It is only when his cab is moving that he has air circulating to cool him. In winter, on the other hand, he not only suffers from heaters which are less than adequate, but he must climb in and out of his cab as he searches for a house number or picks up a package. Consequently, he cannot wear clothing adequate for the situation, and he is either too warm in heavy clothing or too cold in lighter clothing.

Cabdriving does not even allow normal release of bladder tension. If he is to make any money at all, the cabbie must be constantly listening to his radio, and doing so does not give him time to urinate. If he takes time out to use the restroom of a gas station or restaurant (to use a dark street is to invite arrest), he runs the risk of missing orders and lowering his income. On the other hand, if he takes time to relieve his bladder after he has received an order, it takes longer to arrive at the order and greatly increases the chances of a "no-go." And, of course, after he picks up the passenger, it would be both humiliating and awkward to, in effect, "ask permission" of his passenger to go to the bathroom! Consequently, bladder tension is a routine part of the cabbie's job.

Another physical need which cabdriving cuts into is sleep. St. Louis cabbies work an eleven- or twelve-hour day, six days a week. Since this is required to make a living, and the cabbie must also allow for driving time to and from work, the cabbie must either cut down his sleep or cut down on the amount of time he spends in nonwork activities such as his family or recreation. Judging from the haggardly tired appearance marking these cabbies, most seem to make the choice of cutting down on sleep.

Although they work full time, usually six days a week, eleven or twelve hours each day, cabbies in St. Louis still live in poverty. One cabbie, for example, goes to the City Hospital when he is sick since there he can receive the free treatment which the city provides for indigents. This full-time working man considers himself to be so poor that he is in need of public welfare. I have also seen a cabbie begging other drivers for a dollar with which to buy breakfast, and another cabbie who did not know where he was going to sleep that night after work. In a single issue of *Taxi Union News* (March 1967), which focuses primarily on cabbies in Chicago, it was reported that food and clothing had been given to one cabbie who along with eight children had been burned out of his home. Another cabbie had been put out of his home by the landlord. Still another cabbie had been placed in an industrial plant and his "family of five children were put back into their apartment after the furnishings had been placed in the street."

Above rental and gasoline expenses, St. Louis cabbies average approximately fifteen to eighteen dollars per twelve-hour shift. From this pittance they must put away money for income taxes, which are not withheld since cabbies are "independent entrepreneurs." Nor do they even receive a check from which to withhold taxes. If they desire basic social security coverage, cabbies must pay at the higher "self-employed" rate since they are technically not employees of the company. Through this loophole in the law, their "employer" contributes nothing. In effect, cabbies are day laborers who end up with a variable but small amount of cash at the end of each working day. Cabbies struggle for existence without the benefits American workers have learned to take for granted: they do not enjoy employer-contributed pension plans, paid sick leaves, hospitalization, holidays, vacations, or even social security. Nor do they even have job security, but are subservient to the employment whims of management. Not surprisingly, this leads to a life situation which prevents cab drivers from planning ahead, giving them little security for either the present or the future.

There are indeed not many unionized occupations today where poverty characterizes workers who labor sixty-six to seventy-two hours per week under the punitive and degrading conditions I have outlined. How can this possibly be? How can a group of men be unionized and yet be so blatantly exploited?[3]

Cabbies themselves have not been in a good bargaining position. Alternative means of transportation are usually readily available, and if their collective demands bring too great an increase in fares, they may run out of passengers. More than this is involved, however. The major source of exploitation appears to be the capitalistic system under which these men labor. Management, regardless of any high-sounding ideological phraseology to the contrary concerning service to the public, has but one purpose — and that is profit. In order to turn the greatest profit, costs must be cut. Management, as we have seen, drastically cuts the amount it spends on the maintenance of its cabs. Safety features, also expensive, are almost nonexistent. But the major source of cutting costs centers around the remuneration cabbies receive. By paying them little, management cuts its costs and remains competitive. By keeping them poverty-stricken and in physical need, management attempts to assure itself of a certain type of labor — a fawning, self-ingratiating type which is grateful for every "favor" it receives.

Central to management maintaining its dictatorial dominancy is the cooptation of the unions. Management has been able to manipulate cabbie unions to the point that union officials frequently appear to represent management more than they do workers. For example, management is able to successfully and regularly manipulate work rules to the detriment of workers. As a case in point, we can note "down time" refunds. During "down time" a driver is supposed to be refunded his cab rental for the period during which his cab is inoperable, being reimbursed about seventy-five cents an hour. This reimbursement is merely a negation of the amount which he would otherwise have had to pay during that period for an operable cab. It is not remuneration from management; nor does it represent a profit. Yet the cabbie ordinarily has to fight *as an individual* to get even this cancellation of rental fees.

When the interests of management and union officials coincide, it is ordinarily at the direct cost and detriment of cabbies. Collusion between the two does not appear to be uncommon, as one would infer from what took place in San Francisco in 1970. At that time a more dissident element of a major cabbie union attempted to vote its candidates into power. The establishment of the union refused to recognize the motion and hastily adjourned the meeting. In the following weeks the management of this cab company fired a dozen or so of its cabbies which of course included the dissident group who had attempted to gain control over the union.[4]

The nationally noted cab strike of 1970 in the city of New York was not, as commonly thought, an attempt to gain higher wages for cab drivers. It was, rather, a successful attempt to gain a higher fare structure for *employers*. Moreover, while higher profits were gained for the employer, wage *cuts* were "gained" for the cabbies. After the union's fifteen-day strike, taxi fares went up from 45 cents for the first sixth of a mile to 60 cents for the first fifth of a mile, and from 10 cents for each additional one-third mile to 10 cents for each additional one-fifth mile. "Waiting time" charges were also increased at about the same proportion. But the drivers' commission on the total fare was actually reduced by 10 cents for each trip: 10 cents per trip is subtracted from the total bookings and held in "escrow" for "benefits" which no one has seen. Additionally, the commissions of "new" drivers were further reduced from 49 percent of "new" bookings to 42 percent. . . .

CONCLUSION

If from my presentation the reader comes to the conclusion that almost everything about cabdriving appears to be punitive, this is not too far from the truth. Although there are indeed compensations to this occupation, the cabbie is enmeshed in a hostile, exploiting, threatening, and punitive world. Some of the punitive and exploitative aspects of cabdriving are willfully inflicted on the cabbie, but most are built into the structure of cabdriving. The source of this exploitation and punishment does not arise primarily from individuals, such as passengers, managers, and fellow cabbies, but it originates especially from the structuring of the profit system within which the cabbie works.

In order to understand man, one must study the structure which helps determine the elements present in his world, and the situations or contexts within which man lives out his life. Cabdriving is structured such that it is exploitative to cabbies. This centers especially around its capitalistic context and focuses specifically on the nature of cabbies' shift work and the forms and amounts of remuneration which he receives. These men live a hard, exploited life — a life in which they are filled with frustration and in which they are continually manipulated by both their physical and social environments. It is difficult to escape the view that cabbies are captives within an extremely exploitative and punishing system. It is probably not that the men directing the system are invidious. It is, rather, that the system itself is invidious, pitting man against man for the sake of profit. . . .

If sociologists desire to understand the everyday or common-sense experience of man, interaction in occupations should be a focal point since they demand such a huge part of the waking hours of people in our society. Man's everyday experiences in his occupations greatly structure his perception of the world. If, for example, we are to understand such a common thing in our society as why cabbies feel they are punished, we must understand both the structure of the occupation and the cabbie's reaction to or perception of his place in that structure.

NOTES

1. The cabbie's response to the dispatcher cannot be heard by other drivers. The double parentheses indicate these responses. Where the responses are patterned, I have indicated the typical response, placing it within the double parentheses.

2. It should be noted that in this case Yellow Cab Company was forced to pay the "offender" ten months' back wages. This decision was won through arbitration, and the union claimed that because of it they now had "greater protection and a higher degree of job security than ever before." (For details, see *Taxi Union News*, 3, January and April 1967.)

3. This situation may be different in other parts of the country, such as New York where the number of cabs allowed on the street is limited and where the demand for cabs is exceptionally high. New York cabbies are also exploited, however. See the relevant item in the conclusion to this paper.

4. My thanks to George Toussaint for this information.

The Human Cost of Plant Closings

Arthur Shostak

Union members are by now all too familiar with the tremendous social and economic consequences of a plant closing. Yet when they look to academia for help in sorting out the antidotes, for ways to ease the pain, for remedies to heal the hurt, they are likely to be seriously disappointed.

The necessary research work has still not been done. Our library of materials is paltry and inadequate. We do know some helpful things, however, and with the assistance of the trade union movement this subject could soon get the research attention it deserves.

Our case studies of plant closings were largely done in the 1960s, and are still quite sound. The difference in being unemployed in the 1960s and being unemployed in the 1980s appears a matter of degree, rather than one of kind.

Here are some of the highlights of what we found in the 1960s in the aftermath of plant closings:

- Social Hardships — People were reluctant to move, and geographic mobility was low. Relocating represented an incredible challenge for the individual. They were not only reluctant to move from the frost belt to the sun belt, for example, but were unwilling to move even a few hundred miles. We soon secured anecdotal data about what it cost people to be weekend husbands, to be without family, to leave familiar settings for a savage-appearing new city.

  In the 1960s we had considerable failure to regain steady and satisfactory employment after plant closings. Men and women who readily found jobs showed up disproportionately later as frequent job changers, discontented and restless. Large numbers of reemployed workers suffered real losses from previous levels of economic attainment. If they had been working for $7 an hour, they were soon working for $4.50 or $5.25. And many of the others laid off with them struggled to survive protracted unemployment.

- Health Problems — Health research is difficult. You've got to talk people in the home or the factory into giving urine samples, take blood from them, measure blood pressure, and do a lot of things that appear not so much for their benefit as for the benefit of "ivory tower" research needs. That's tough. Thus the little research we got from the 1960s indicated high uric acid levels, increased cholesterol, elevations in blood pressure, and elevations

Abridged and reprinted from *AFL-CIO American Federationist,* August 1980. Reproduced by permission.

in pulse rate among the suddenly unemployed. We also found the rich man's disease of gout, which, in fact, was no longer exclusively a rich man's disease. We connected data on plant closings to heart disease, hypertension, and pervasive tension. At the bottom of all of this we found an increase in drinking — hard drinking — and we found a tragic increase in self-destruction and inexplicably fatal accidents.

At a reductionist level of analysis, each of us is a social system. As such we promote an equilibrium, a pattern of habitual behavior and attitudes. There are certain times of day when all of us like our morning coffee. You may prefer to brush your teeth before or after breakfast; you probably take a particular route to work every day. All of us like to minimize stress through such repeatable behaviors. One of the major consequences of plant closing, then, is that it shatters habitual worklife patterns.

There's a terrible story about Russian troops moving through the remains of Berlin at the end of World War II. They are supposed to have found at the Civil Service headquarters of the shattered Third Reich civil servants at their desks preparing requisitions for next year's paper clips, rubber bands, note pads and that sort of thing. I don't know if it's true, but I've been told that certain elderly Berlin postal workers continued to walk their mail rounds after the city was destroyed, even though they had no mail to deliver, because it helped fill out the day and it made sense to them — delivering nonexistent mail to bombed-out addresses, the better to cling to routine and help time pass in a meaningful, familiar way.

That is the kind of deep-reaching psychological attachment to worklife habits that can get shattered in the aftermath of a plant closing.

- Reduced Social Interaction — People begin to withdraw into themselves in the aftermath of a plant shutdown. They begin to withdraw from family contacts; many begin to withdraw from union meetings and even from a passive interest in union matters.
- Political Alienation — A worker caught in a plant closing can become bitter in every direction. They feel betrayed and sold out, and he or she may demand to know where organized labor has been all that time. Where was COPE? And how did it come down this way?
- Openness to Economic Radicalism — Sociologists have noted a new openness to economic radicalism among workers when capitalism gets them in the neck; one is receptive to hearing something radical and even revolutionary in the aftermath of a plant closing, the research suggests.

That's about the sum of what we know from the case studies of plant closings in the 1960s. There are some new research strategies now in the 1980s, one of which focuses on closings as a type of separation experience, a trauma with about six phases.

In the opening phase, a plant is "up and going." You may hear we used to have 8,700 on the payroll, and now we've got 1,800; we used to have 9,000 now we have 3,000, but the plant's still "up and going."

That's a preclosing state of affairs, and in preclosing time you may get what workers perceive as company blackmail: "we need more productivity." In this preclosing phase some workers will urge the union to take the issue to the mayor, government, or the press. Employees know when a closedown is coming. Certain kinds of strategic stock materials are not being reordered; certain kinds of maintenance are not being done; farming out of contracts is increasing. So, a proactivist set of possibilities exists in the preclosing phase.

Then comes the news of the closedown over the loudspeaker, in the mail, or in a general auditorium session. Some are stunned; others say, "I told you so." The cynics may rise to power in the local union; the optimists are likely to fall in stature.

Then is the phase of unemployment itself, the search for a new job, and a new definition of "success," as a wage-earner. This "success" becomes highly individual. We might look at the job-seeker's new job and think it second rate; but that's not legitimate—only the individual can tell us whether it's second rate or not, and why, and we must learn to listen and suspend our judgment.

The next and last phase is the rehired worker's adjustment to the new job, a stage that is often overlooked by researchers, union leaders, and counselors. Not only is the job new, but the worker has the equivalent of a new family and a new community. Once you get a new job, your family may be altered by that event and its aftermath.

A psychologist told me recently about his practice, which now includes an increasing number of plant closing cases. One of his clients, for example, came off traditional factory work and found a job driving a panel truck. This gave him independence and autonomy, removed him from supervision, put him out in the open air, allowed him to choose his own coffee breaks, and to go to his favorite diner. It was all wonderful, except for one minor problem: he was now employed as an exterminator, complete with a can and a hose, and his wife now said that at the end of the day, he stunk. He hadn't smelled badly before; he had always been clean, even fastidious.

So, what did our reemployed worker have now? A different wife and a different family, because of an odor problem unadvertised and unavoidably part of his otherwise desirable new job.

In our 1980s research we should focus on certain problems regretfully unexplored in the 1960s material, such as the sense of self-punishing personal guilt that may come with plant closings. In the book *The Hidden Injuries of Class*, Richard Sennett and Jonathon Cobb explain that America encourages us to hold ourselves responsible for what happens to us, the better to exonerate its social order: "It isn't capitalism. It isn't federal favoritism to regions. It isn't corporate board decisions. It's probably some flaw in you and me that explains our plight. We picked the wrong plant to work in; we picked the wrong industry to identify with; we didn't get out in time; people told us 10 years ago we should leave. The handwriting was on the wall."

When all that nonsense comes together, a laid-off worker can derive a profound sense of guilt from it, a notion that he or she has let the family down. This sense of guilt for those caught in plant closings is something humanists and capitalists alike should worry about.

Another problem for new research attention is that individuals involved in plant closings often suffer from diminished attention span. If a local union meeting has an agenda that puts something else on ahead of the subject of a shutdown's impact, you are likely to discover 35 minutes into the meeting that people are wandering out of the hall. People involved in a plant shutdown have little patience for any other topic. It had better come early in the meeting's agenda.

Then there is the widespread feeling of loneliness, especially in the sense of abandonment, that often accompanies a factory shutdown. If there is guilt, if there is self-blame, then loneliness and abandonment on top of it can be hard for many ex-workers to handle.

In the 1980s we've begun to find evidence of the notion that "they've done it to me again." "They," those incredibly vague "others," include the government, Congress, union staffers — somebody. The worker begins to pull from memory a host of past failures: "I should have gone to get that associate degree" or "I should have taken that training program" or "When I was offered the stewardship, I should have said 'yes'." And so on. Such an individual may begin to wallow in "I-should-haves," and in much self-blame, all at a great cost to mental well-being.

Since the critical success of Gail Sheehy's book, *Passages*, we've begun to give a lot of attention to middle age crisis. Beginning at about age 40, social events begin to shift away from weddings, bar mitzvahs, and baptisms to the funerals of friends and acquaintances. And that shift is easily exacerbated by plant closings. Middle-aged unemployed adults begin to think of themselves as over-the-hill; plant closings invite a morbidity in one's mind set, a new sense of personal frailty, a heightened recognition of the uncertainties of life and, the allure of a stress-resolving death.

Work gives many people the indispensable leverage they need to contain self-destructive habits and behaviors. Certain people who used to drink to excess get a job and sober up; the pressure that comes from knowing alcoholism isn't accepted on the job is enough to help keep them from further drinking, at least during working hours. Similarly, people who are chronic gamblers, or on occasion abuse a spouse or a child may control the situation through the discipline of their employment: after a plant closing, however, they may find the loss of a job severely weakens the control mechanisms they so desperately need.

For these reasons we may see more and more men whose anxiety on losing their jobs appears disproportionate, as it is, after all, "only a job." But, such men may understand that this loss could mean a return to alcoholism or to gambling, or to other comparable terrors, even if they've been sober and self-regulating for many years. And that specter, for them, is the end, the sentence of a living death, a fate being forced back into their lives by the reverberating disaster of a plant closing.

When we focus our research on family life one of the things that worries us is the possibility of "cabin fever." Blue-collar wives do not welcome having the male hanging around home, particularly during conventional working hours. And when a male displaced by a plant closing does stay home, cabin fever is highly predictable . . . as when an exasperated unemployed worker says: "It isn't anything that she's said or done; it's the way she puts the coffee on the table in the morning." His wife, in turn, may say: "I don't know what the hell he's talking about. He hasn't been the same for three months, since the plant closed. There's nothing that I can do that can make a difference, even a little difference. And when I put a cheaper cut of meat on the table, he almost destroyed the kitchen. I thought I was doing good; he behaved like I was destroying him."

Finally, one of the major 1980s research frontiers may concern how men and women relate in their sexuality. Many working class women seem to have absorbed new attitudes in the sexual realm, and their sexual agendas are different today from the 1960s; they expect their husbands to be better lovers, and their lovers to be more sensitive than before, and both husbands and lovers to be more open to their female sexuality than was true in earlier decades. In good times, all of this could be a fine prescription. In a recession, however, especially one combined with plant layoffs, it can prove a prescription for interpersonal disaster: men who are cut off from work may have self-esteem hurt by the loss of the central role in the male life, that of the primary breadwinner, and it also hurts self-esteem in the bedroom.

Given all these historic, ongoing, and readily anticipated social problems, what are some possible reforms worth research attention?

- Social Impact Legislation: Harry Levinson, a leading industrial psychologist, identified the presence of the "psychological contract" some years ago while doing research on a Kansas utility company and its workers. The "psychological contract" is never put in writing, but it assures an injured worker a claim on the company for another post in the company compatible with the worker's remaining capabilities. This is one way we get factory gatekeepers, watchmen and messengers, many of whom are former employees who have been crippled in work-related accidents, and even sometimes in a nonwork-related accident. This pledge of readjusted work is a tradition, a "psychological contract" that we might add to social impact legislation. Employers might pledge to provide new jobs and compensation, under the "psychological contract," to cover counseling costs entailed in helping workers recover any emotional and social well-being undermined by a plant closing.
- Career and Community Continuation Teams: You cannot adequately help workers in a plant closing unless you also help the larger surrounding community. The federal government should therefore have, on a stand-by basis, several career and community aid teams of economists, counselors, psychologists, job-location and job-retraining experts, all trained in crisis theory and intervention techniques.
- Rehabilitation for the Reemployed: People who are rehired should not fade out of our concern.

First, many rehired workers become sensitive to the idea that the new employer expects them to be obligated for the job. The rehired workers may soon resent a new foreman, a new regimen, a new set of expectations that makes it seem the new boss is lording it over the new worker. And the new worker may determine not to put up with this. A troubled person, a troubled union member, a person under a lot of stress, is a very real possibility here, though no one ever intended this, and few intervene in time to avert avoidable trouble.

Another thing we find is loss of morale: some reemployed workers may privately say: "For 27 years I worked for one employer, and I gave him everything. I was there on time, accepted overtime with a smile, never stole a thing. I put suggestions in the suggestion box. I'm not going to do any of that again; I'm not going to do one little part of that again. They fooled me the last time. They're not going to get anything from me this time but eight hours of regular output, and they damn well better accept that because it's all they've got coming this time around."

The last kind of reaction for which postrehiring counseling would seem necessary involves the gunshy new worker. This individual comes in expecting his new work place to close, even though the plant is in a great industry, is healthy, has a Dun & Bradstreet rating of AAA plus—but, if this worker has known disaster, he is sure that if something can go wrong for this company, it will. The presence of such a person can bring the local workforce stress, trouble, bad vibes. Such workers need remedial counseling, concerned "outsiders" who can help notice this troubled worker and help guide him or her to a source of counseling help.

In sum, then, plant closings are still far too under-researched. We in academic work are going to need labor's help if this subject is soon going to get the research attention that its quotient of human problems deserves. Only as organized labor reaches out to concerned researchers at colleges and universities will we really have any chance of it soon happening.

In every locale with a major plant, there are at least a few academics nearby who will respond to labor's request. At first, of course, they will be astonished that you've asked; they will be pleased; then they will ask how can they help. America needs the case studies they can do—and workers need them.

The subject grows daily too important to continue without this research. The impact of plant closings can be lessened, provided some fresh lessons are soon drawn from collaborative labor-academic research into this topic—possibly the most important domestic issue of the 1980s.

10

ORGANIZATION

"I feel that in the beginning stages of this program someone made a mistake, and refused to admit that mistake . . . he simply covered up, you know . . . They had no time to start over . . ."

—Mr. Vandivier

Recent years have seen a number of instances of the decline of organizations that long have been important to our society. The effectiveness of an organization is a "bottom-line measure." It is a term used to summarize the overall success of the organization in acquiring, transforming, and using resources to establish favorable reactions with its important constituents. Of course, bottom-line measures often interfere with understanding underlying dynamic processes. So it has been with effectiveness.

Almost all books on management, whether they are written by presidents, accountants, economists, engineers, or behavioral scientists, place the goal of organizational effectiveness (or some related goal such as efficiency) at the core of their analysis. Most writers stress some set of rational designs, decisions, controls, policies, models, and so on, which organizations use or ought to use in the pursuit of effectiveness. However correct these ideas may be as normative approaches, they provide only limited insight into what organizations actually do in their efforts to achieve "effectiveness" and provide little insight into the social processes that are major determinants of effectiveness.

Frequently, writers have failed to realize that "organizational effectiveness" is more than a pervasive goal of almost all organizations; it is also a constraint upon how organizational members use resources. Members most frequently define, justify, and defend their decisions and actions in terms of "effectiveness." Our first selection, "Organizational Psychology and the World Series," by Edwin A. Locke, a distinguished organizational psychologist, illustrates one formula for the pursuit of effectiveness. Although it is written very much with tongue in cheek, we have encountered many managers to whom the question is just that simple.

Of course, it is a mistake to conclude that the explicit concern with effectiveness leads directly to well-run organizations which are well managed and achieve their goals. There are many aspects of organizations that can go astray. Reward systems are one such component. In "On the Folly of Rewarding A, While Hoping for B," Steven Kerr examines some of the dysfunctions of reward systems. The article has been widely reprinted. Some readers take strong exception to the fact that Kerr does not offer solutions to the problems he raises. We include the article because we have found it provocative and one that leads to many stimulating discussions.

Often it is assumed that the causes of ineffectiveness lie in the behaviors of lower-level members of the organizational hierarchy. However, the actions of people at the top are frequently far less compatible with effectiveness than we assume. "The Vega" from James Patrick Wright's "On a Clear Day You Can See General Motors" provides, in the author's words, ". . . a classic case of management ineptitude."

Readers familiar with the history of General Motors will recall that Alfred P. Sloan's design for the GM organization restricted the role of corporate headquarters to broad policy, long-range planning, and general financial control of the operating divisions such as Pontiac, Chevrolet, or Cadillac. Within broad parameters design, production, and marketing of the several product lines were to be the responsibility of these operating divisions. Over the years, however, more and more of the operating decisions were withdrawn from the divisions and centralized at corporate level, to be debated at great length by a complex array of committees. Further, corporate decisions increasingly were based primarily on financial advice without due regard for production or market considerations. Wright maintains that this trend, together with extensive political maneuvering among the top corporate officials, led to the Vega fiasco (see "Loyalty — Team Play — The System" in Section 2). Recent events indicate that mismanagement in the automobile industry has by no means been unique to this incident or to General Motors.

"Air Force A-7D Brake Problem" is another case study of corporate mismanagement, in this instance by lower-level managers. The selection concerns an extended attempt to cover up a mistake made early in the design process. The case also is an illustration of how far responsible and competent employees can be pushed by the organization before they rebel and "blow the whistle." We have included a news story, "Who Blows the Whistle on Big Corporations?", to give the reader further insight on individuals who jeopardize their future employment prospects by this course of action.

"Industrial Espionage" (Paul Mixson) and "How Computer Criminals Get Rich Quick" (Sharon Rutenberg) are short accounts of but two forms of white-collar crime that plague organizations of all kinds and make the firing line on which they operate more risky and complex. For further information on these topics see Harold Wilensky, *Organizational Intelligence* (New York: Basic Books, Inc., 1967), or Gilbert Geis and Ezra Stotland (eds.), *White-Collar Crime: Theory and Research* (Beverly Hills, CA: Sage Publications, 1980).

Our final selection, the report by Tom Alexander, noting that it took a crisis before U.S. Borax discovered how much slack existed in its operation, indicates how far an organization can deviate from effective behavior without top management even being aware of it. The stimulus for greater effectiveness in this case is a crisis rather than the rational behavior of management at any level.

Clearly, the selections in this section give only a glimpse of some of the processes that influence the effectiveness of organizations. Most of these processes have been given little attention by students of management, who have sought to understand effectiveness through traditional economic, management and behavioral science models. We hope that the direct look at the behavior of organizations themselves provides the reader with a greater understanding of the actual dynamics of processes that influence organizational effectiveness.

Organizational Psychology and the World Series

Edwin A. Locke

As scientists we should not be closed to any source of information which bears upon the validity of our theories. For example, consider what we can learn from the victory of the Yankees in the World Series:

1. authoritarian management can be quite effective, providing it is both smart and rich;
2. lack of group cohesion (intragroup conflict) does not inhibit short-term success, providing the members have talent and do their jobs;
3. intragroup conflict is unpleasant and may lead to high turnover;
4. on the other hand, if enough money is offered to stay, it may not.

What more do you need to know to run a successful organization?

On the Folly of Rewarding A, While Hoping for B

Steven Kerr

Illustrations are presented from society in general, and from organizations in particular, of reward systems that "pay off" for one behavior even though the rewarder hopes dearly for another. Portions of the reward systems of a manufacturing company and an insurance firm are examined and the consequences discussed.

Whether dealing with monkeys, rats, or human beings, it is hardly controversial to state that most organisms seek information concerning what activities are rewarded, and then seek to do (or at least pretend to do) those things, often to the virtual exclusion of activities not rewarded. The extent to which this occurs of course will depend on the perceived attractiveness of the rewards offered, but neither operant nor expectancy theorists would quarrel with the essence of this notion.

Nevertheless, numerous examples exist of reward systems that are fouled up in that behaviors which are rewarded are those which the rewarder is trying to *discourage*, while the behavior he desires is not being rewarded at all.

In an effort to understand and explain this phenomenon, this paper presents examples from society, from organizations in general, and from profit-making firms in particular. Data from a manufacturing company and information from an insurance firm are examined to demonstrate the consequences of such reward systems for the organizations involved, and possible reasons why such reward systems continue to exist are considered.

SOCIETAL EXAMPLES

Politics

Official goals are "purposely vague and general and do not indicate . . . the host of decisions that must be made among alternative ways of achieving official goals and the priority of multiple goals . . ." (8, p. 66). They usually may be relied on to offend absolutely no one, and in

Reprinted from *The Academy of Management Journal* (December 1975), pp. 769–783. Reproduced by permission of the publisher and author.

this sense can be considered high acceptance, low-quality goals. An example might be "build better schools." Operative goals are higher in quality but lower in acceptance, since they specify where the money will come from, what alternative goals will be ignored, etc.

The American citizenry supposedly wants its candidates for public office to set forth operative goals, making their proposed programs "perfectly clear," specifying sources and uses of funds, etc. However, since operative goals are lower in acceptance, and since aspirants to public office need acceptance (from at least 50.1 percent of the people), most politicians prefer to speak only of official goals, at least until after the election. They of course would agree to speak at the operative level if "punished" for not doing so. The electorate could do this by refusing to support candidates who do not speak at the operative level.

Instead, however, the American voter typically punishes (withholds support from) candidates who frankly discuss where the money will come from, rewards politicians who speak only of official goals, but hopes that candidates (despite the reward system) will discuss the issues operatively. It is academic whether it was moral for Nixon, for example, to refuse to discuss his 1968 "secret plan" to end the Vietnam War, his 1972 operative goals concerning the lifting of price controls, the reshuffling of his cabinet, etc. The point is that the reward system made such refusal rational.

It seems worth mentioning that no manuscript can adequately define what is "moral" and what is not. However, examination of costs and benefits, combined with knowledge of what motivates a particular individual, often will suffice to determine what for him is "rational."[1] If the reward system is so designed that it is irrational to be moral, this does not necessarily mean that immorality will result. But is this not asking for trouble?

War

If some oversimplification may be permitted, let it be assumed that the primary goal of the organization (Pentagon, Luftwaffe, or whatever) is to win. Let it be assumed further that the primary goal of most individuals on the front lines is to get home alive. Then there appears to be an important conflict in goals — personally rational behavior by those at the bottom will endanger goal attainment by those at the top.

But not necessarily! It depends on how the reward system is set up. The Vietnam War was indeed a study of disobedience and rebellion, with terms such as "fragging" (killing one's own commanding officer) and "search and evade" becoming part of the military vocabulary. The difference in subordinates' acceptance of authority between World War II and Vietnam is reported to be considerable, and vet-

erans of the Second World War often have been quoted as being outraged at the mutinous actions of many American soldiers in Vietnam.

Consider, however, some critical differences in the reward system
in use during the two conflicts. What did the GI in World War II
want? To go home. And when did he get to go home? When the war
was won! If he disobeyed the orders to clean out the trenches and
take the hills, the war would not be won and he would not go home.
Furthermore, what were his chances of attaining his goal (getting
home alive) if he obeyed the orders compared to his chances if he did
not? What is being suggested is that the rational soldier in World War
II, *whether patriotic or not,* probably found it expedient to obey.

Consider the reward system in use in Vietnam. What did the man
at the bottom want? To go home. And when did he get to go home?
When his tour of duty was over! This was the case *whether or not* the
war was won. Furthermore, concerning the relative chance of getting home alive by obeying orders compared to the chance if they
were disobeyed, it is worth noting that a mutineer in Vietnam was
far more likely to be assigned rest and rehabilitation (on the assumption that fatigue was the cause) than he was to suffer any negative consequence.

In his description of the "zone of indifference," Barnard stated that
"a person can and will accept a communication as authoritative only
when . . . at the time of his decision, he believes it to be compatible
with his personal interests as a whole" (1, p. 165). In light of the reward system used in Vietnam, would it not have been personally irrational for some orders to have been obeyed? Was not the military
implementing a system which *rewarded* disobedience, while *hoping*
that soldiers (despite the reward system) would obey orders?

Medicine

Theoretically, a physician can make either of two types of error,
and intuitively one seems as bad as the other. A doctor can pronounce
a patient sick when he is actually well, thus causing him needless
anxiety and expense, curtailment of enjoyable foods and activities,
and even physical danger by subjecting him to needless medication and surgery. Alternately, a doctor can label a sick person well,
and thus avoid treating what may be a serious, even fatal ailment. It
might be natural to conclude that physicians seek to minimize both
types of error.

Such a conclusion would be wrong.[2] It is estimated that numerous
Americans are presently afflicted with iatrogenic (physician *caused*)
illnesses (9). This occurs when the doctor is approached by someone
complaining of a few stray symptoms. The doctor classifies and or-
ganizes these symptoms, gives them a name, and obligingly tells the
patient what further symptoms may be expected. This information

often acts as a self-fulfilling prophecy, with the result that from that day on the patient for all practical purposes is sick.

Why does this happen? Why are physicians so reluctant to sustain a type 2 error (pronouncing a sick person well) that they will tolerate many type 1 errors? Again, a look at the reward system is needed. The punishments for a type 2 error are real: guilt, embarrassment, and the threat of lawsuit and scandal. On the other hand, a type 1 error (labeling a well person sick) "is sometimes seen as sound clinical practice, indicating a healthy conservative approach to medicine" (9, p. 69). Type 1 errors also are likely to generate increased income and a stream of steady customers who, being well in a limited physiological sense, will not embarrass the doctor by dying abruptly.

Fellow physicians and the general public therefore are really *rewarding* type 1 errors and at the same time *hoping* fervently that doctors will try not to make them.

GENERAL ORGANIZATIONAL EXAMPLES

Rehabilitation Centers and Orphanages

In terms of the prime beneficiary classification (2, p. 42) organizations such as these are supposed to exist for the "public-in-contact," that is, clients. The orphanage therefore theoretically is interested in placing as many children as possible in good homes. However, often orphanages surround themselves with so many rules concerning adoption that it is nearly impossible to pry a child out of the place. Orphanages may deny adoption unless the applicants are a married couple, both of the same religion as the child, without history of emotional or vocational instability, with a specified minimum income and a private room for the child, etc.

If the primary goal is to place children in good homes, then the rules ought to constitute means toward that goal. Goal displacement results when these "means become ends-in-themselves that displace the original goals" (2, p. 229).

To some extent these rules are required by law. But the influence of the reward system on the orphanage's management should not be ignored. Consider, for example, that the:

1. Number of children enrolled often is the most important determinant of the size of the allocated budget.
2. Number of children under the director's care also will affect the size of his staff.
3. Total organizational size will determine largely the director's prestige at the annual conventions, in the community, etc.

Therefore, to the extent that staff size, total budget, and personal prestige are valued by the orphanage's executive personnel, it becomes rational for them to make it difficult for children to be adopted.

After all, who wants to be the director of the smallest orphanage in the state?

If the reward system errs in the opposite direction, paying off only for placements, extensive goal displacement again is likely to result. A common example of vocational rehabilitation in many states, for example, consists of placing someone in a job for which he has little interest and few qualifications, for two months or so, and then "rehabilitating" him again in another position. Such behavior is quite consistent with the prevailing reward system, which pays off for the number of individuals placed in any position for 60 days or more. Rehabilitation counselors also confess to competing with one another to place relatively skilled clients, sometimes ignoring persons with few skills who would be harder to place. Extensively disabled clients find that counselors often prefer to work with those whose disabilities are less severe.[3]

Universities

Society *hopes* that teachers will not neglect their teaching responsibilities but *rewards* them almost entirely for research and publications. This is most true at the large and prestigious universities. Clichés such as "good research and good teaching go together" notwithstanding, professors often find that they must choose between teaching and research-oriented activities when allocating their time. Rewards for good teaching usually are limited to outstanding teacher awards, which are given to only a small percentage of good teachers and which usually bestow little money and fleeting prestige. Punishments for poor teaching also are rare.

Rewards for research and publications, on the other hand, and punishments for failure to accomplish these, are commonly administered by universities at which teachers are employed. Furthermore, publication-oriented résumés usually will be well received at other universities, whereas teaching credentials, harder to document and quantify, are much less transferable. Consequently it is rational for university teachers to concentrate on research, even if to the detriment of teaching and at the expense of their students.

By the same token, it is rational for students to act based upon the goal displacement which has occurred within universities concerning what they are rewarded for. If it is assumed that a primary goal of a university is to transfer knowledge from teacher to student, then grades become identifiable as a means toward that goal, serving as motivational, control, and feedback devices to expedite the knowledge transfer. Instead, however, the grades themselves have become much more important for entrance to graduate school, successful employment, tuition refunds, parental respect, etc., than the knowledge or lack of knowledge they are supposed to signify.

It therefore should come as no surprise that information has surfaced in recent years concerning fraternity files for examinations, term paper writing services, organized cheating at the service academies, and the like. Such activities constitute a personally rational response to a reward system which pays off for grades rather than knowledge.

BUSINESS RELATED EXAMPLES

Ecology

Assume that the president of XYZ Corporation is confronted with the following alternatives:

1. Spend $11 million for antipollution equipment to keep from poisoning fish in the river adjacent to the plant; or
2. Do nothing, in violation of the law, and assume a one in ten chance of being caught, with a resultant $1 million fine plus the necessity of buying the equipment.

Under this not unrealistic set of choices it requires no linear program to determine that XYZ Corporation can maximize its probabilities by flouting the law. Add the fact that XYZ's president is probably being rewarded (by creditors, stockholders, and other salient parts of his task environment) according to criteria totally unrelated to the number of fish poisoned, and his probable course of action becomes clear.

Evaluation of Training

It is axiomatic that those who care about a firm's well-being should insist that the organization get fair value for its expenditures. Yet it is commonly known that firms seldom bother to evaluate a new GRID, MBO, job enrichment program, or whatever, to see if the company is getting its money's worth. Why? Certainly it is not because people have not pointed out that this situation exists; numerous practitioner-oriented articles are written each year to just this point.

The individuals (whether in personnel, manpower planning, or wherever) who normally would be responsible for conducting such evaluations are the same ones often charged with introducing the change effort in the first place. Having convinced top management to spend the money, they usually are quite animated afterwards in collecting rigorous vignettes and anecdotes about how successful the program was. The last thing many desire is a formal, systematic, and revealing evaluation. Although members of top management may actually *hope* for such systematic evaluation, their reward systems continue to *reward* ignorance in this area. And if the personnel department abdicates its responsibility, who is to step into the breach? The change agent himself? Hardly! He is likely to be too busy collecting anecdotal "evidence" of his own, for use with his next client.

Miscellaneous

Many additional examples could be cited of systems which in fact are rewarding behaviors other than those supposedly desired by the rewarder. A few of these are described briefly below.

Most coaches disdain to discuss individual accomplishments, preferring to speak of teamwork, proper attitude, and a one-for-all spirit. Usually, however, rewards are distributed according to individual performance. The college basketball player who feeds his teammates instead of shooting will not compile impressive scoring statistics and is less likely to be drafted by the pros. The ballplayer who hits to right field to advance the runners will win neither the batting nor home run titles, and will be offered smaller raises. It therefore is rational for players to think of themselves first, and the team second.

In business organizations where rewards are dispensed for unit performance or for individual goals achieved, without regard for overall effectiveness, similar attitudes often are observed. Under most Management by Objectives (MBO) systems, goals in areas where quantification is difficult often go unspecified. The organization therefore often is in a position where it *hopes* for employee effort in the areas of team building, interpersonal relations, creativity, etc., but it formally *rewards* none of these. In cases where promotions and raises are formally tied to MBO, the system itself contains a paradox in that it "asks employees to set challenging, risky goals, only to face smaller paychecks and possibly damaged careers if these goals are not accomplished" (5, p. 40).

It is *hoped* that administrators will pay attention to long-run costs and opportunities and will institute programs which will bear fruit later on. However, many organizational reward systems pay off for short-run sales and earnings only. Under such circumstances it is personally rational for officials to sacrifice long-term growth and profit (by selling of equipment and property, or by stifling research and development) for short-term advantages. This probably is most pertinent in the public sector, with the result that many public officials are unwilling to implement programs which will not show benefits by election time.

As a final, clear-cut example of a fouled-up reward system, consider the cost-plus contract or its next of kin, the allocation of next year's budget as a direct function of this year's expenditures. It probably is conceivable that those who award such budgets and contracts really hope for economy and prudence in spending. It is obvious, however, that adopting the proverb "to him who spends shall more be given," rewards not economy, but spending itself.

TWO COMPANIES' EXPERIENCES

A Manufacturing Organization

A midwest manufacturer of industrial goods had been troubled for some time by aspects of its organizational climate it believed dysfunctional. For research purposes, interviews were conducted with many employees and a questionnaire was administered on a companywide basis, including plants and offices in several American and Canadian locations. The company strongly encouraged employee participation in the survey, and made available time and space during the workday for completion of the instrument. All employees in attendance during the day of the survey completed the questionnaire. All instruments were collected directly by the researcher, who personally administered each session. Since no one employed by the firm handled the questionnaires, and since respondent names were not asked for, it seems likely that the pledge of anonymity given was believed.

A modified version of the Expect Approval scale (7) was included as part of the questionnaire. The instrument asked respondents to indicate the degree of approval or disapproval they could expect if they performed each of the described actions. A seven-point Likert scale was used, with one indicating that the action would probably bring strong disapproval and seven signifying likely strong approval.

Although normative data for this scale from studies of other organizations are unavailable, it is possible to examine fruitfully the data obtained from this survey in several ways. First, it may be worth noting that the questionnaire data corresponded closely to information gathered through interviews. Furthermore, as can be seen from the results summarized in Table 1, sizable differences between various work units, and between employees at different job levels within the same work unit, were obtained. This suggests that response bias effects (socially desirability in particular loomed as a potential concern) are not likely to be severe.

Most importantly, comparisons between scores obtained on the Expect Approval scale and a statement of problems which were the reason for the survey revealed that the same behaviors which managers in each division thought dysfunctional were those which lower level employees claimed were rewarded. As compared to job levels 1 to 8 in Division B (see Table 1), those in Division A claimed a much higher acceptance by management of "conforming" activities. Between 31 and 37 percent of Division A employees at levels 1-8 stated that going along with the majority, agreeing with the boss, and staying on everyone's good side brought approval; only once (level 5-8 responses to one of the three items) did a majority suggest that such actions would generate disapproval.

Table 1
Summary of Two Divisions' Data Relevant to Conforming and
Risk-Avoidance Behaviors (Extent to Which Subjects Expect Approval)

Dimension	Item	Division and Sample	Total Responses	Percentage of Workers Responding		
				1, 2, or 3 Disapproval	4	5, 6, or 7 Approval
Risk Avoidance	Making a risky decision based on the best information available at the time, but which turns out wrong.	A, levels 1-4 (lowest)	127	61	25	14
		A, levels 5-8	172	46	31	23
		A, levels 9 and above	17	41	30	30
		B, levels 1-4 (lowest)	31	58	26	16
		B, levels 5-8	19	42	42	16
		B, levels 9 and above	10	50	20	30
	Setting extremely high and challenging standards and goals, and then narrowly failing to make them.	A, levels 1-4	122	47	28	25
		A, levels 5-8	168	33	26	41
		A, levels 9+	17	24	6	70
		B, levels 1-4	31	48	23	29
		B, levels 5-8	18	17	33	50
		B, levels 9+	10	30	0	70
	Setting goals which are extremely easy to make and then making them.	A, levels 1-4	124	35	30	35
		A, levels 5-8	171	47	27	26
		A, levels 9+	17	70	24	6
		B, levels 1-4	31	58	26	16
		B, levels 5-8	19	63	16	21
		B, levels 9+	10	80	0	20
Conformity	Being a "yes man" and always agreeing with the boss.	A, levels 1-4	126	46	17	37
		A, levels 5-8	180	54	14	31
		A, levels 9+	17	88	12	0
		B, levels 1-4	32	53	28	19
		B, levels 5-8	19	68	21	11
		B, levels 9+	10	80	10	10

Table 1 (continued)

Division and Sample	Total Responses	Percentage of Workers Responding		
		1, 2, or 3 Disapproval	4	5, 6, or 7 Approval
Always going along with the majority. A, levels 1-4	125	40	25	35
A, levels 5-8	173	47	21	32
A, levels 9+	17	70	12	18
B, levels 1-4	31	61	23	16
B, levels 5-8	19	68	11	21
B, levels 9+	10	80	10	10
Being careful to stay on the good side of everyone, so that everyone agrees that you are a great guy. A, levels 1-4	124	45	18	37
A, levels 5-8	173	45	22	33
A, levels 9+	17	64	6	30
B, levels 1-4	31	54	23	23
B, levels 5-8	19	73	11	16
B, levels 9+	10	80	10	10

Furthermore, responses from Division A workers at levels 1-4 indicate that behaviors geared toward risk avoidance were as likely to be rewarded as to be punished. Only at job levels 9 and above was it apparent that the reward system was positively reinforcing behaviors desired by top management. Overall, the same "tendencies toward conservatism and apple-polishing at the lower levels" which divisional management had complained about during the interviews were those claimed by subordinates to be the most rational course of action in light of the existing reward system. Management apparently was not getting the behaviors it was *hoping* for, but it certainly was getting the behaviors it was perceived by subordinates to be *rewarding*.

An Insurance Firm

The Group Health Claims Division of a large eastern insurance company provides another rich illustration of a reward system which reinforces behaviors not desired by top management.

Attempting to measure and reward accuracy in paying surgical claims, the firm systematically keeps track of the number of returned checks and letters of complaint received from policyholders. However, underpayments are likely to provoke cries of outrage from the insured, while overpayments often are accepted in courteous silence. Since it often is impossible to tell from the physician's statement which of two surgical procedures, with different allowable benefits, was performed, and since writing for clarifications will interfere with other standards used by the firm concerning "percentage of claims paid within two days of receipt," the new hire in more than one claims section is soon acquainted with the informal norm: "When in doubt, pay it out!"

The situation would be even worse were it not for the fact that other features of the firm's reward system tend to neutralize those described. For example, annual "merit" increases are given to all employees, in one of the following three amounts:

1. If the worker is "outstanding" (a select category, into which no more than two employees per section may be placed): 5 percent
2. If the worker is "above average" (normally all workers not "outstanding" are so rated): 4 percent
3. If the worker commits gross acts of negligence and irresponsibility for which he might be discharged in many other companies: 3 percent

Now, since (a) the difference between the 5 percent theoretically attainable through hard work and the 4 percent attainable merely by living until the review date is small and (b) since insurance firms seldom dispense much of a salary increase in cash (rather, the worker's insurance benefits increase, causing him to be further overinsured), many employees are rather indifferent to the possibility of obtaining the extra one percent reward and therefore tend to ignore the norm concerning indiscriminant payments.

However, most employees are not indifferent to the rule which states that, should absences or latenesses total three or more in any six-month period, the entire 4 or 5 percent due at the next "merit" review must be forfeited. In this sense the firm may be described as *hoping* for performance, while *rewarding* attendance. What it gets, of course, is attendance. (If the absence-lateness rule appears to the reader to be stringent, it really is not. The company counts "times" rather than "days" absent, and a ten-day absence therefore counts the same as one lasting two days. A worker in danger of accumulating a third absence within six months merely has to remain ill (away from work) during his second absence until his first absence is more than six months old. The limiting factor is that at some point his salary ceases, and his sickness benefits take over. This usually is sufficient to get the younger workers to return, but for those with 20 or more years' service, the company provides sickness benefits of 90 percent of normal salary, tax-free! Therefore . . .)

CAUSES

Extremely diverse instances of systems which reward behavior A although the rewarder apparently hopes for behavior B have been given. These are useful to illustrate the breadth and magnitude of the phenomenon, but the diversity increases the difficulty of determining commonalities and establishing causes. However, four general factors may be pertinent to an explanation of why fouled-up reward systems seem to be so prevalent.

Fascination with an "Objective" Criterion

It has been mentioned elsewhere that:

> Most "objective" measures of productivity are objective only in that their subjective elements are a) determined in advance, rather than coming into play at the time of the formal evaluation, and b) well concealed on the rating instrument itself. Thus industrial firms seeking to devise objective rating systems first decide, in an arbitrary manner, what dimensions are to be rated, . . . usually including some items having little to do with organizational effectiveness while excluding others that do. Only then does Personnel Division churn out official-looking documents on which all dimensions chosen to be rated are assigned point values, categories, or whatever (6, p. 92).

Nonetheless, many individuals seek to establish simple, quantifiable standards against which to measure and reward performance. Such efforts may be successful in highly predictable areas within an organization, but are likely to cause goal displacement when applied anywhere else. Overconcern with attendance and lateness in the insurance firm and with number of people placed in the vocational rehabilitation division may have been largely responsible for the problems described in those organizations.

Overemphasis on Highly Visible Behaviors

Difficulties often stem from the fact that some parts of the task are highly visible while other parts are not. For example, publications are easier to demonstrate than teaching, and scoring baskets and hitting home runs are more readily observable than feeding teammates and advancing base runners. Similarly, the adverse consequences of pronouncing a sick person well are more visible than those sustained by labeling a well person sick. Team-building and creativity are other examples of behaviors which may not be rewarded simply because they are hard to observe.

Hypocrisy

In some of the instances described the rewarder may have been getting the desired behavior, notwithstanding claims that the behavior was not desired. This may be true, for example, of management's attitude toward apple-polishing in the manufacturing firm (a behavior which subordinates felt was rewarded, despite management's avowed dislike of the practice). This also may explain politicians' unwillingness to revise the penalties for disobedience of ecology laws, and the failure of top management to devise reward systems which would cause systematic evaluation of training and development programs.

Emphasis on Morality or Equity Rather than Efficiency

Sometimes consideration of other factors prevents the establishment of a system which rewards behaviors desired by the rewarder. The felt obligation of many Americans to vote for one candidate or another, for example, may impair their ability to withhold support from politicians who refuse to discuss the issues. Similarly, the concern for spreading the risk and cost of wartime military service may outweigh the advantage to be obtained by committing personnel to combat until the war is over.

It should be noted that only with respect to the first two causes are reward systems really paying off for other than desired behaviors. In the case of the third and fourth causes the system *is* rewarding behaviors desired by the rewarder, and the systems are fouled up only from the standpoints of those who believe the rewarder's public statements (cause 3), or those who seek to maximize efficiency rather than other outcomes (cause 4).

CONCLUSIONS

Modern organization theory requires a recognition that the members of organizations and society possess divergent goals and motives. It therefore is unlikely that managers and their subordinates will seek the same outcomes. Three possible remedies for this potential problem are suggested.

Selection

It is theoretically possible for organizations to employ only those individuals whose goals and motives are wholly consonant with those of management. In such cases the same behaviors judged by subordinates to be rational would be perceived by management as desirable. State-of-the-art reviews of selection techniques, however, provide scant grounds for hope that such an approach would be successful (for example, see 12).

Training

Another theoretical alternative is for the organization to admit those employees whose goals are not consonant with those of management and then, through training, socialization, or whatever, alter employee goals to make them consonant. However, research on the effectiveness of such training programs, though limited, provides further grounds for pessimism (for example, see 3).

Altering the Reward System

What would have been the result if:

1. Nixon had been assured by his advisors that he could not win re-election except by discussing the issues in detail?
2. Physicians' conduct was subjected to regular examination by review boards for type 1 errors (calling healthy people ill) and to penalties (fines, censure, etc.) for errors of either type?
3. The president of XYZ Corporation had to choose between (a) spending $11 million dollars for antipollution equipment, and (b) incurring a fifty-fifty chance of going to jail for five years?

Managers who complain that their workers are not motivated might do well to consider the possibility that they have installed reward systems which are paying off for behaviors other than those they are seeking. This, in part, is what happened in Vietnam, and this is what regularly frustrates societal efforts to bring about honest politicians, civic-minded managers, etc. This certainly is what happened in both the manufacturing and the insurance companies.

A first step for such managers might be to find out what behaviors currently are being rewarded. Perhaps an instrument similar to that used in the manufacturing firm could be useful for this purpose. Chances are excellent that these managers will be surprised by what they find — that their firms are not rewarding what they assume they are. In fact, such undesirable behavior by organizational members as they have observed may be explained largely by the reward systems in use.

This is not to say that all organizational behavior is determined by formal rewards and punishments. Certainly it is true that in the absence of formal reinforcement some soldiers will be patriotic, some presidents will be ecology minded, and some orphanage directors will care about children. The point, however, is that in such cases the rewarder is not *causing* the behaviors desired but is only a fortunate bystander. For an organization to *act* upon its members, the formal reward system should positively reinforce desired behaviors, not constitute an obstacle to be overcome.

It might be wise to underscore the obvious fact that there is nothing really new in what has been said. In both theory and practice these matters have been mentioned before. Thus in many states Good Samaritan laws have been installed to protect doctors who stop to assist a stricken motorist. In states without such laws it is commonplace for doctors to refuse to stop, for fear of involvement in a subsequent lawsuit. In college basketball additional penalties have been instituted against players who foul their opponents deliberately. It has long been argued by Milton Friedman and others that penalties should be altered so as to make it irrational to disobey the ecology laws, and so on.

By altering the reward system the organization escapes the necessity of selecting only desirable people or of trying to alter undesirable ones. In Skinnerian terms (as described in 11, p. 704), "As for responsibility and goodness — as commonly defined — no one . . . would want or need them. They refer to a man's behaving well despite the absence of positive reinforcement that is obviously sufficient to explain it. Where such reinforcement exists, 'no one needs goodness.'"

NOTES

1. In Simon's (10, pp. 76 – 77) terms, a decision is "subjectively rational" if it maximizes an individual's valued outcomes so far as his knowledge permits. A decision is "personally rational" if it is oriented toward the individual's goals.

2. In one study (4) of 14,867 films for signs of tuberculosis, 1,216 positive readings turned out to be clinically negative; only 24 negative readings proved clinically active, a ratio of 50 to 1.

3. Personal interviews conducted during 1972 – 1973.

REFERENCES

1. Barnard, Chester I. *The Functions of the Executive* (Cambridge, Mass.: Harvard University Press, 1964).

2. Blau, Peter M., and W. Richard Scott. *Formal Organizations* (San Francisco: Chandler, 1962).

3. Fiedler, Fred E. "Predicting the Effects of Leadership Training and Experience from the Contingency Model," *Journal of Applied Psychology,* Vol. 56 (1972), 114 – 119.

4. Garland, L. H. "Studies of the Accuracy of Diagnostic Procedures," *American Journal Roentgenological, Radium Therapy Nuclear Medicine*, Vol. 82 (1959), 25 – 38.

5. Kerr, Steven. "Some Modifications in MBO as an OD Strategy," *Academy of Management Proceedings*, 1973, pp. 39 – 42.

6. Kerr, Steven. "What Price Objectivity?" *American Sociologist*, Vol. 8 (1973), 92 – 93.

7. Litwin, G. H., and R. A. Stringer, Jr. *Motivation and Organizational Climate* (Boston: Harvard University Press, 1968).

8. Perrow, Charles. "The Analysis of Goals in Complex Organizations," in A. Etzioni (Ed.), *Readings on Modern Organizations* (Englewood Cliffs, N.J.: Prentice-Hall, 1969).

9. Scheff, Thomas J. "Decision Rules, Types of Error, and Their Consequences in Medical Diagnosis," in F. Massarik and P. Ratoosh (Eds.), *Mathematical Explorations in Behavioral Science* (Homewood, Ill.: Irwin, 1965).

10. Simon, Herbert A. *Administrative Behavior* (New York: Free Press, 1957).

11. Swanson, G. E. "Review Symposium: Beyond Freedom and Dignity," *American Journal of Sociology,* Vol. 78 (1972), 702–705.

12. Webster, E. *Decision Making in the Employment Interview* (Montreal: Industrial Relations Center, McGill University, 1964).

The Province, 3 June 1981.

Labor Threatens Woodward's War over Shutdown

By Don Hunter

Threats of "open war" on the B.C. labor scene and a boycott of Woodward's stores were made Tuesday in the wake of an abrupt announcement by Woodward's that saw the whole staff of its food distribution warehouse in Richmond laid off as one shift was ending and before the next one could begin.

Woodward's official Peter Richardson in a meeting Monday afternoon told the 70-80 employees—some with up to 23 years' service—that the entire operation had been sold to Johnston Terminals and that they should right then "pick up your termination packages...and leave the property."

Day shift workers were paid overtime for attending the meeting and those on the afternoon shift got paid for the 7½ hours they would have worked.

Richardson told them Woodward's plans to buy warehouse and distribution services from the new owners.

B.C. Federation of Labor boss Jim Kinnaird called the Woodward's move "just plain sleazy" and in a hurriedly-called news conference on Tuesday threatened a province-wide boycott of Woodward's unless the company moved to find alternative employment for the suddenly jobless. Kinnaird also called on provincial labor minister Jack Heinrich to get involved.

Woodward's spokesman Bill Brown defended his company's move and the no-notice announcement of job termination.

He rejected Kinnaird's claim of "shabby" treatment of the employees (whom the union said number 86 but Brown said comprised 63 full-time and 10 part-time workers).

Brown, who said the move was an economic one that would mean "substantial savings for Woodward's," said Kinnaird had failed to mention the fact that severance pay was given at the rate of one week's wages for every year worked, that all workers got two weeks pay in lieu of notice, that a number of them (those aged 45 and with 10 years' service) would still qualify for company pension at age 65, and that medical coverage continued through June 30 and dental coverage beyond that.

He denied the union-busting charge, saying the company was simply moving from one organized shop to another —Johnson Terminal employees are Teamsters.

Abridged and reprinted by permission of the *Vancouver Province* (Canada).

The Vega

James Patrick Wright

On October 3, 1968, Chairman James M. Roche told an audience of dignitaries, reporters and employees that in two years GM would introduce a new subcompact car designed for American tastes and developed to counterattack the growing trend toward foreign cars. It was a bold announcement for a corporation which usually refuses to talk about future products for fear of hurting the sales of those already in dealer showrooms. (Current Chairman Thomas Murphy's announcement to shareholders in May of '75 that GM would build a sub-subcompact car, the Chevette, in 1976 was the only similar departure from tradition since Roche's speech in 1968.) And Roche went one step further. He predicted that the car, code-named the XP-887 and later named the Vega, would weigh less than 2,000 pounds, be priced at the level of the Volkswagen Beetle — less than $1,800 then — and feature the most automated assembly process known to American automotive technology.

A study of the conception and gestation of the Vega reveals not a lesson in scientific marketing and development, but rather a classic case of management ineptitude.

In the early and mid-1960s, Chevrolet and Pontiac Divisions, conscious of the growing appeal of smaller, foreign-built cars, were working separately on futuristic small cars. At Pontiac we developed our small car mindful that Chevy would probably get first crack at such a new market. But we wanted our own version just in case we got lucky and either beat Chevy into the market or were allowed to come in quickly afterward. The Chevrolet staff also was fast at work on its mini-car. Ed Cole, who was executive vice-president of Operating Staffs, was working on his own small-car project using the corporate engineering and design staffs. He took this program with him into the president's office in 1967. When the corporation started talking seriously about a mini-car, Cole's version was chosen. It was chosen mainly because of Cole's corporate position and the forcefulness of his personality and salesmanship. The proposals from Chevy and Pontiac were rejected. Pontiac eventually was entirely cut out of the small-car development meetings. The new mini-car was Cole's baby, and it was to be given to Chevrolet to sell.

Abridged and reprinted from *On A Clear Day You Can See General Motors* by J. Patrick Wright, published by Wright Enterprises © 1979. Reproduced by permission.

While the early announcement of the Vega was a break with GM tradition, so was the manner of its development. The guiding corporate precept of centralized policymaking and decentralized decision making was totally and purposefully ignored. GM tradition dictated that the Fourteenth Floor would decide that a new market, such as small cars, should be developed (policy) and then would assign the responsibility for producing a car for that market to one of the five car divisions (operations). However, with the Vega, not only did corporate management make the decision to enter the mini-car market, it also decided to develop the car itself. This was to pave the way for many of the Vega's troubles. It was a corporate car, not a divisional car. Ed Cole was the chief engineer, and Bill Mitchell, the vice-president of the Design Staff, was the chief stylist. It was being put together by people at least one step removed from the marketplace. There was no system of checks and balances. The divisions reported to the Fourteenth Floor. But the Fourteenth Floor reported only to itself.

When Roche announced the car, his information came from statistical abstractions. Not one prototype had been built or tested. There was no model to point to because the car existed only in financial statistics and blueprints derived from a consensus of the existing subcompact cars, all of them foreign and some of them built by GM overseas. The engineering blueprints were costed out by the central financial staff in conjunction with the Chevrolet finance staff. Their work was to be proven shoddy and haphazard. All of this information provided a weight and price class for the car that became the foundation for the chairman's startling small car announcement. Shortly thereafter, the first prototype was delivered from the central staff to Chevrolet.

The first indication that this was an unwise way to build a GM car was not long in coming. Chevrolet engineers took the prototype Vega to the GM test track in Milford, Michigan. After eight miles, the front of the Vega broke off. The front end of the car separated from the rest of the vehicle. It must have set a record for the shortest time taken for a new car to fall apart. The car was sent to Chevy engineering where the front end was beefed up. Already the small, svelte American answer to foreign car craftsmanship was putting on weight—20 pounds in understructure to hold the front end intact. Thus began a fattening process of the "less-than-2,000-pound" mini-car that would take it to ponderous proportions in weight and price compared to the original car described at the opening of the new GM building in New York City.

From the first day I stepped into the Chevrolet division, in 1969, it was obvious that the Vega was in real trouble. General Motors was pinning its image and prestige on this car, and there was practically no interest in it in the division. We were to start building the car in little more than a year, and nobody wanted anything to do with it. The Vega was an orphan. Chevy's engineering staff was disgruntled because it felt it had proposed a much better car (and it had) than the one it was given by the corporate management. It was going through the motions of preparing the car for production, and that was all. Engineers are a very proud group. They take immense interest and pride in their creations, but they are very disinclined to accept the work of somebody else. This was not their car, so they did not want to work on it.

Other complaints were surfacing about the car from inside the division. While it looked similar to the Fiat 124, the division executives felt it could have been more contemporary European with a greater use of glass. Work that was proceeding on the car revealed that the central staff had completely misgauged the weight and cost of the car they designed. Simple items, such as side door crash protection beams, were left out of the original drawings even though they were in the plans for all future GM cars. To be a viable product on the road, the Vega was going to arrive on the market heavier and costlier than the company's target because it was already close to 200 pounds heavier than planned, and production costs were running way above estimates. These miscalculated costs were pervasive: The estimated body costs were wrong; the chassis costs were wrong; and the tooling costs were wrong. So it was obvious that the Vega was going to miss the market in weight and cost, and it was feared that Chevrolet people who didn't want the "corporate car" were going to bear the blame from the public.

The biggest objection from the division, specifically the engineering staff, was reserved for the Vega engine. In their own small-car program, Chevy's engineers developed a neat, little, short-stroke, four-cylinder engine with a cross-flow hemispherical cylinder head. It was made of cast iron and fit easily into the subcompact car body. The Engineering Policy group, however, discarded this engine along with the Chevy-designed mini-car in favor of the engine pushed by Cole and the corporate engineering staff which featured an aluminum cylinder block with a cast-iron head.

The industry had fooled around for a couple of decades with aluminum engines. Each of the auto companies at one time or another had an aluminum engine, GM most recently in the early 1960s. And each in turn rejected their aluminum engines primarily because they cost too much to build. The lure of aluminum is its weight. It is one-third as heavy as iron. If this much weight can be taken out of the engine, it means more weight can be taken out of the car's structure which supports the engine weight—suspension systems can be made lighter and brakes can be made smaller. Weight is all-important in building small cars, to keep them small, lower in cost, and light in fuel consumption.

The disadvantages of aluminum compared with iron are that it does not wear as well and is distorted easier during the heat of operation. To improve the wearing characteristics of aluminum engines in the past, iron sleeves were put into each cylinder and used with standard aluminum pistons. The costs of doing this in a small engine exceeded the cost saving from the lower-weight material. So aluminum engines for smaller cars were generally rejected. The heat distortion problems of aluminum engines have never been fully solved.

Reynolds Aluminum Co., however, kept working on the various problems with these engines and, in the late '60s, developed a longer wearing material—aluminum with a 17 percent silicone content—for the die-cast engine block. This proved compatible with iron-coated aluminum pistons and was a fairly simple production process. Ed Cole fell in love with it, even though this method was still more costly than the time-proven cast-iron engine process. He was hooked on the Reynolds idea. In addition, the corporation engineers decided that the aluminum engine needed a longer piston stroke, and a bigger, iron cylinder head. The longer stroke (distance traveled by the piston) approach was chosen to better control engine emissions. And the iron head was needed to withstand the pressure of combustion.

Now during the '60s, the auto industry became enamored of short-stroke, high-speed engines for their compactness and performance. Chevy's engineers felt that emission problems could be worked out within the framework of such a short-stroke design for the Vega. But the corporate engineers, instead, went the route of a longer stroke engine which was traditionally less polluting. So while they were going for an innovative production process in using aluminum, they were relying on an old basic design for the engine. What resulted was a relatively large, noisy, top-heavy combination of aluminum and iron which cost far too much to build, looked like it had been taken off a 1920 farm tractor and weighed more than the cast-iron engine Chevy had proposed, or the foreign-built, four-cylinder iron engine the Ford Pinto was to use. Chevy engineers were ashamed of the engine. With the start of engine production rapidly approaching there were still several major engineering problems to be solved such as excessive wear of the valve lifters and the camshaft. Yet Chevy engineers were almost totally disinterested in the car.

The most important problem for me with the Vega, therefore, was to motivate the hell out of the division to get this car into as good a shape as we could before introduction. So we made the final development of the Vega the first project of the new Planning Committee and gave it top priority with the revised marketing department. Then I told each and every staff of the division: "It does not matter now that you had an argument over the nature of this car and lost. Like it or not, we are going to be building and selling this car. Any way you look at it, this car is going into the market as a Chevrolet. We can't put a little notice in the glove box saying, 'We didn't design this car, Central Staff did.' It's a Chevrolet, and we are going to be responsible to the public for how good a car we build and sell."

The reaction was surprisingly positive. A genuine effort was constructed in the division to put life and spirit into the Vega project. As the Lordstown, Ohio, assembly plant was converted to Vega production, we also introduced an intense program for quality control with the target of making the first cars off the assembly line the best quality cars, from a manufacturing standpoint, ever built. As the starting date approached we put tens of additional inspectors and workers on the line and introduced a computerized quality control program in which each car was inspected as it came off the line and, if necessary, repaired. As the defects in workmanship showed up during inspections, they were typed on a keyboard on the spot and immediately displayed on a screen in the area where the defective work was being done. This quickly told workers where the defective work was occurring, that a problem had developed. Generally this information stopped the defect after only a handful of cars had been built, where previously the defect often went uncured until later after as many as four weeks' worth of defective cars had been assembled and sometimes even sold to customers. We also test drove the first 2,000 Vegas built and a sizeable proportion of the others thereafter. The corporation gave us strong support in approving the additional manpower and expenses we needed to improve the quality of these cars. I was able when the car was introduced to brag that it was the best quality car we'd ever introduced. I'm thankful no one asked me if I thought it was the best designed and engineered car ever introduced.

The marketing problems with the Vega were substantial. By late winter 1969, it was well known in the corporation that the car was far above its original estimates in weight and cost. The Fourteenth Floor was pretty damn shook up about this. The big question was: "How the hell can we promote a car that is going to be bigger and cost more than any car in the market in which it is supposed to compete?" Mr. Roche said the market target was the small foreign cars and the price would be in "the ball park" of the VW Beetle. How could we explain the variance from that?

Tom Staudt and his staff attacked this problem vigorously. They initiated a raft of background tests and evaluations to determine how the car was going to be perceived and, thus, how we should sell it. They tested the car as a stripped-down model and as a fully equipped luxury model. They researched a long list of potential names. In all they spent more than half-a-million dollars in marketing research. The Chevrolet Planning Committee discussed and explored all aspects of the mini-car. The marketing people made recommendations for selling the car based on its higher price and heavier size. They advised that we abandon the cheap end of the mini-car market, spend a few more dollars on trim and appointments and sell it as a premium small car. Since, as yet, a name for the car had not been chosen — we were still using the code name XP-887 — they advised that we call the car the Gemini.

Specifically, the marketing people argued that since the cost of the car was going to be too high to price it head on with the Beetle or others like the Toyota Corolla, we should add about $12-15 more cost to the car in chrome stripping, interior trim and a larger tire size to give it a real quality, semi-luxury motif. Then we should sell it for the higher price we were going to need to make any money on the car. The recommendation struck a familiar chord at GM. The corporation has always been very good at selling its cars as the "best version" in a specific market class. Moving customers into more expensive cars, and selling the best quality product in each market was a concept at the heart of Sloan's marketing philosophy from the time Chevy was reorganized in the 1920s to better compete with Ford. We presented this recommendation to the Engineering Policy Committee and received its enthusiastic but tentative approval to develop a plusher mini-car than the others in the market.

Naming the car was a matter of serious concern for both Staudt and me. A good name can "make" a marketing program simply because of the image it conjures in the customer's mind. A bad name can make marketing a new product a difficult chore. The studies that we conducted showed that one name stood head and shoulders above every one — Gemini. It had a kind of magic not found often in car names. Since the NASA space program was constantly in the public eye, the name Gemini was instantly familiar and it sort of imparted some of the aura of excitement around the space program to our car. What's more, we learned from the tests that the public instantly identified the phonics of it. When pronounced, it almost said "G-M-ini." At the bottom of the list of preferred names was Vega, which had very little automotive connotation to it. It sounded like a disease or a fungus. But modern, scientific marketing tests notwithstanding, Ed Cole liked the name Vega and so did top corporate management who threw our test results out the window and named the mini-car the Vega. We were told that corporate management was afraid that we would overdo the GM association by using the name Gemini.

That was a tough battle to lose. But an even bigger and totally unexpected loss came a short time later, just before the public introduction of the Vega on September 10, 1970, when the Pricing Review Committee on the Fourteenth Floor completely countermanded the tentative okay from the Engineering Policy Group giving us approval to upgrade the Vega. While they kept our recommended selling price, they took out most of the additional interior and exterior trim we'd added and knocked back the standard tire for the car by one size. The saving on the tire change was about $3 a car, but the loss in appearance, ride, and fuel economy to the customer was much more than that. If customers wanted a plush Vega, they were going to have to pay for it through the optional equipment route. They were not going to get it as part of the basic car package.

The Pricing Review people obviously wanted to extract the last dime of profit from the car even if it meant hurting the car's image and our marketing program. The incredible thing to me was that the members of this group were almost exactly the same people who sat on the Engineering Policy Group. What they were giving us with one hand they were taking away with the other. In a sense they were contradicting themselves. I still can't figure how they could do that. And I never did get a satisfactory answer to my questions about it. I guess in the final analysis the corporation was more cost-profit oriented than it was product-marketing oriented.

Ford management, which earlier announced the base Pinto price as $1,919, I suspect to give us an indication of what they thought the price level should be, must have been gleeful when we introduced a plain-Jane Vega with a basic sticker price of $2,091. This put the car $172 higher than the base Pinto, $311 more than the VW standard Beetle and $192 more than the Super Beetle. It was literally priced out of the market. It weighed 382 pounds more than the Beetle and 161 pounds more than the Pinto. We had earlier forecast that 400,000 Vegas would be sold our first year, taking 100,000 of those sales from VW. But I was now privately suspecting that our targets were too high.

The timing of the price announcement for our 1971 cars couldn't have come at a worse time for me. The media got hold of them in time for a lunch I was hosting in connection with our national new-car press preview. As general manager of Chevy, I was called on to explain the unexplainable. How could we call our car "competitive" when it weighed almost 400 pounds more, and was priced more than $300 above the intended foreign competitor? What happened to the car Mr. Roche announced two years earlier? It was an embarrassing experience for me and highlighted a problem I had all through the publicity buildup for the Vega. While I was convinced that we at Chevy were doing our best with the car that was given to us, I was called upon by the corporation to tout the car far beyond my own personal convictions about it. There was a moral conflict in this. In press releases, I was praising the name Vega when I knew it was one of the worst we could have chosen. And now I was justifying the price and weight of the car when I knew well that a better designed and engineered car would have weighed less and cost less to build. The realization that hundreds of thousands of jobs, the health of the national economy and my job depended on the sales of Chevy cars gave some justification for this and similar actions hyping some of our products. But this conflict never did resolve itself fully in my mind and was one of the many factors that precipitated my departure from the company.

At this particular press conference, however, I said that the new car was different and more American than the Beetle and that, viewed in this context, the price and weight were fully justified. I said with a clear conscience that it was a quality car, which it was because we road-tested the first 2,000 off the assembly line and spent millions of dollars to reinspect and repair each vehicle. The press was not happy with my answer, however. One particular exchange sticks in my mind. In reply to a question on whether the Vega was in the "ball park" with the Beetle, as Mr. Roche had promised, I answered, "When you consider the car we are talking about, equipped as it is, I think it is in the ball park." I thought to myself: "Well, now I've worked around that problem pretty well."

Then Dan Fisher of the *Los Angeles Times* fired off the zinger. "Would your boss accept a ball-park estimate of your anticipated expense budget at Chevrolet for the next year that was a plus or minus 25 percent?"

The question struck right at the heart of the problem with this car. The Vega has missed its mark in almost every respect because it was poorly managed from the very beginning. In the past we all knew of management foul-ups, but this knowledge was kept internally. With this car, however, management incompetence was out in the open for everyone to see.

I cringed at the question, then rattled off an answer telling Fisher that he missed the point, that the Vega represented good value for the money to be spent. All of which was true. But we still didn't have an answer for the imported car popularity which their increasing sales figures later proved.

After lunch, I went back to my Chevrolet office and thought, "What a helluva lousy way to kick off a new car." But these problems were purely academic by midnight when the United Auto Workers struck General Motors. The 24,000 Vegas we had on dealer lots or in transit were all we were going to see for two-and-a-half months. The strike ashcanned the '71 Vega for all intents and purposes. Our dealers didn't get an adequate supply of the cars until well after January 1, 1971. In the 1971 model year we sold only 245,000 of the mini-cars, compared with Ford's Pinto sales of 316,700. GM lost money on the Vega that year.

We regrouped and decided to make a second major effort with the car for the 1972 model year which began in September of 1971. There were several things in our favor. President Nixon's economic actions on August 15, 1971, abolishing the 7 percent excise tax and putting a surtax on imported-car sales — which were then taking 20 percent of all car sales in the U.S. — made us competitive with the Beetle and its foreign friends. The decision to let the dollar fluctuate vis-à-vis other currencies soon resulted in the upward revaluation of the German *deutsche mark* and the Japanese *yen*, which eventually gave the Vega a pricing advantage over the foreigners. We were also able to take about $20 of cost out by using lighter-gauged steel in a few places on the car. And there was still plenty of public interest in the automated assembly line at Lordstown, which had giant Unimates spot welding our cars, and a seemingly happy work force which was cranking out almost 100 cars an hour. The Vega design was intended to last for at least five model years, so we had very little new to do to the car except bring it up to the 1972 safety and pollution standards. We got off to a strong start for the 1972 model year, with substantial stocks of cars in the hands of our dealers. It looked like the Vega would get off the ground (albeit a year late), challenge the Pinto and take a swift kick at the imports. That was too hasty an assessment.

On October 1, 1971, a most unfortunate occurrence took place. The corporation transferred the last three car assembly plants under our jurisdiction to the GM Assembly Division (GMAD). It completed a management move giving the tough GMAD almost complete control over the company's assembly operations. The rationale for the move was that one assembly division in the place of several produced a more efficient and coordinated production operation. The plants we lost control of were the Ypsilanti, Michigan, Nova plant; the St. Louis Chevelle and Impala plant; and the Lordstown Vega plant. Chevrolet now had control only over its Flint, Mich. truck assembly plant.

When each car division assembly plant was turned over to GMAD, so was the accompanying Fisher Body Plant (traditionally in GM, Fisher Body Division had built all car bodies and transferred them to nearby assembly plants where the body was joined to the rest of the car). In each case previously, a GMAD takeover resulted in huge union squabbles and many local strikes. The combining of each body plant and assembly plant under one management, where there had been two, eliminated the need for two separate union locals which had dealt with the two separate managements. So problems developed as two union local leaderships tried to out-muscle each other for representation of the new, single local.

Once this matter was settled, the new leadership began to bargain with GMAD for a single local contract where there had been two. In these negotiations, the union tried to incorporate the features of the old contracts which were best for the workers, and the company tried to incorporate the features that were best for itself. Natural eruptions resulted. In addition, GMAD had a tough reputation among unionists for trying to eliminate jobs and extract more work from each worker. This technique was evident practically from the day GMAD took over the Lordstown plant, when it fired 700 workers, many employed in quality control areas. The division also took out the computer quality-defect feedback system. The company said the move by GMAD was just to eliminate extra jobs that had been created to ease through the problems of starting up an entirely new assembly process. They said that no one was being asked to work any harder. But the union people didn't buy that reasoning one bit. They are no dummies. They can count. And they knew that when you took 700 people off the assembly line, you were going to work the butts off the ones who remained. The UAW balked. GMAD remained firm on its firings; the union wasn't going to tell GM how to run its operations.

The brewing trouble in Lordstown attracted national news media attention, especially after a couple of reporters touring Lordstown noticed a few long-haired youths on the line and in the union halls. The stories started flying fast and furiously out of this little central Ohio town that a monumental sociological struggle was taking place as the young, militant workers rebelled against the mindless system of mass production. This struggle was called "the Lordstown Syndrome." It captured the imagination of young Americans, the very people to whom we were trying to sell new Vegas. The stories completely misplayed the situation. Sure, young workers were rebelling against the system in America. But not at Lordstown. What was taking place was a classical confrontation of union and management over the oldest issue in the history of auto-labor relations—a work speed-up. The company was trying to do the same job with fewer workers, and the workers were refusing to go along. In February of 1972, UAW's Lordstown local struck the Lordstown assembly plant, and a bitter three-week work stoppage resulted. The second start-up of the Vega was halted only months after it began.

In the battle between the company and the UAW, which was being waged in the press, once-happy workers at the Lordstown plant charged that the company was so productivity conscious that the workers were being forced to push cars along the line that were little more than "pieces of junk." The company countered that the workers were sabotaging the cars. That feud left the unfortunate conclusion in the minds of consumers that both sides felt the Vega was of poor quality. That impression gained the status of fact when the company was forced to recall 132,000 cars for defective carburetors, which had caused fires.

Later, when the heat distortion problems inherent in aluminum engines surfaced, Vega engines started to burn out when excessive thermal expansion forced water out of the cooling system. Once the water was forced out, the engine's ability to cool was impaired. The little engines overheated and eventually were severely damaged or completely burnt out.

These problems led to the recall of thousands more Vegas with engine trouble. Chevrolet, trying to overcome the engine's poor public image, later introduced a 60,000-mile warranty which was a very costly burden to the division and the corporation.

By the end of the Lordstown strike, the once bright little mini-car from GM was held in disrepute by a growing segment of the market. The combination of the Lordstown strike, its erroneous "young-worker-against-the-system" theme and the real and apparent quality problems the car was experiencing just about ruined its image and our marketing program. The strike ended, but the 1972 Vega was shot. Consequently, two years after its dramatic introductions, the Vega was in deep trouble. The recall campaigns of themselves may have been weathered. But the combination of quality-sociological-labor problems was too much for the car and the company. We went back to the drawing board to correct our quality problems and prepare another marketing program. This was launched with the introduction of the 1973 models, and by the 1974 model year the Vega was finally selling close to the Pinto, largely on the sheer strength of the Chevrolet dealer force.

Nevertheless, the decision to turn over the Vega plant to GMAD was devastating to our program for the car. A year later might have been a much better time. And the car itself, like the camel which was a horse designed by a committee, arrived on the scene vastly different than planned in weight and cost, primarily because it was designed on the Fourteenth Floor, far removed from the practical demands of the marketplace. I hope the Vega lesson was learned well by GM management and that the knowledge gleaned from this lesson is applied in the development of future products. As for the Vega, it was discontinued at the end of the 1977 model year.

Air Force A-7D Brake Problem

MR. VANDIVIER. In the early part of 1967, the B. F. Goodrich Wheel & Brake Plant at Troy, Ohio, received an order from the Ling-Temco-Vought Co. of Dallas, Tex., to supply wheels and brakes for the A-7D aircraft, built by LTV for the Air Force.

The tests on the wheels and brakes were to be conducted in accordance with the requirements of military specification Mil – W – 5013G as prepared and issued by the U.S. Air Force and to the requirements set forth by LTV Specification Document 204 – 16 – 37D.

The wheels were successfully tested to the specified requirements, but the brake, manufactured by Goodrich under BEG part No. 2 – 1162 – 3, was unable to meet the required tests.

The laboratory tests specified for the brake were divided into two categories: dynamic brake tests and static brake tests.

The dynamic brake tests basically consisted of 45 simulated normal energy stops, 5 overload energy stops and one worn-brake maximum energy stop, sometimes called a rejected take-off, or RTO.

These simulated stops were to be conducted on one brake assembly with no change in brake lining to be allowed during the test.

In addition, a maximum energy brake stop (or RTO) was to be conducted on a brake containing new linings and still another series of tests called a turnaround capability test was to be performed.

The turnaround capability test consisted of a series of taxis, simulated takeoffs, flight periods and landings, and time schedule for the turnaround test was supplied by LTV to coincide with conditions under which the A–7D brake might operate on a typical mission.

Generally speaking, the brake successfully passed all the static brake tests, but the brake could not and did not pass any of the dynamic tests I have just described with the exception of the new brake maximum energy stop.

During the first few attempts to qualify the brake to the dynamic tests, the brake ran out of lining material after a few stops had been completed and the tests were terminated. Attempts were made to secure a lining material that would hold up during the grueling 51-stop test, but to no avail.

Although I had been aware for several months that great difficulty was being experienced with the A–7D brake, it was not until April 11, 1968, almost a full year after qualification testing had begun, that I

From the Hearing before the Subcommittee on Economy in Government of the Joint Economic Committee of the Congress of the United States, Ninety-first Congress, August 13, 1969.

became aware of how these tests were being conducted.

The 13th attempt at qualification was being conducted under B. F. Goodrich Internal Test No. T–1867.

On the morning of April 11, Richard Gloor, who was the test engineer assigned to the A–7D project, came to me and told me he had discovered that some time during the previous 24 hours, instrumentation used to record brake pressure had *deliberately* been miscalibrated so that while the instrumentation showed that a pressure of 1,000 pounds per square inch had been used to conduct brake stops No. 46 and 47 (two overload energy stops) 1,100 p.s.i. had actually been applied to the brakes. Maximum pressure available on the A–7D is 1,000 p.s.i.

Mr. Gloor further told me he had questioned instrumentation personnel about the miscalibration and had been told they were asked to do so by Searle Lawson, a design engineer on the A–7D.

CHAIRMAN PROXMIRE. Is this the gentleman who is with you now, Mr. Vandivier?

MR. VANDIVIER. That is correct. I subsequently questioned Lawson who admitted he had ordered the instruments miscalibrated at the direction of a superior.

Upon examining the log sheets kept by laboratory personnel I found that other violations of the test specifications had occurred.

For example, after some of the overload stops, the brake had been disassembled and the three stators or stationary members of the brake had been taken to the plant toolroom for rework and during an earlier part of the test, the position of elements within the brake had been reversed in order to more evenly distribute the lining wear.

Additionally, instead of braking the dynamometer to a complete stop as required by military specifications, pressure was released when the wheel and brake speed had decelerated to 10 miles per hour.

The reason for this, I was later told, was that the brakes were experiencing severe vibrations near the end of the stops, causing excessive lining wear and general deterioration of the brake.

All of these incidents were in clear violation of military specifications and general industry practice.

I reported these violations to the test lab supervisor, Mr. Ralph Gretzinger, who reprimanded instrumentation personnel and stated that under no circumstance would intentional miscalibration of instruments be tolerated.

As for the other discrepancies noted in test procedures, he said he was aware they were happening but that as far as he was concerned the tests could not, in view of the way they were being conducted, be classified as qualification tests.

Later that same day, the worn-brake, maximum energy stop was conducted on the brake. The brake was landed at a speed of 161 m.p.h. and the pressure was applied. The dynamometer rolled a distance of 16,800 *feet* before coming to rest. The elapsed stopping *time was 141 seconds.* By computation, this stop time shows the aircraft would have traveled over 3 miles before stopping.

Within a few days, a typewritten copy of the test logs of test T−1867 was sent to LTV in order to assure LTV that a qualified brake was almost ready for delivery.

Virtually every entry in this so-called copy of the test logs was drastically altered. As an example, the stop time for the worn brake maximum energy stop was changed from 141 seconds to a mere 46.8 seconds.

On May 2, 1968 the 14th attempt to qualify the brakes was begun, and Mr. Lawson told me that he had been informed by both Mr. Robert Sink, projects manager at Goodrich — I am sorry, Mr. Sink is project manager — and Mr. Russell Van Horn, projects manager at Goodrich, that "Regardless of what the brake does on test, we're going to qualify it."

CHAIRMAN PROXMIRE. What was that?

MR. VANDIVIER. The statement was, "Regardless of what the brake does on test, we're going to qualify it."

He also said that the latest instructions he had received were to the effect that if the data from this latest test turned out worse than did test T−1867, then we would write our report based on T−1867.

CHAIRMAN PROXMIRE. The statement was made by whom?

MR. VANDIVIER. Mr. Lawson told me this statement was made to him by Mr. Robert Sink, project manager and Mr. Russell Van Horn, projects manager.

During this latest and final attempt to qualify the four rotor brake, the same illegal procedures were used as had been used on attempt No. 13. Again after 30 stops had been completed, the positions of the friction members of the brake were reversed in order to more evenly distribute wear.

After each stop, the wheel was removed from the brake and the accumulated dust was blown out.

During each stop, pressure was released when the deceleration had reached 10 miles per hour.

By these and other irregular procedures the brake was nursed along until the 45 normal energy stops had been completed but by this time the friction surfaces of the brakes were almost bare, that is, there was virtually no lining left on the brake.

This lack of lining material introduced another problem.

The pistons which actuate the brake by forcing the friction surfaces together were almost at the end of their allowable travel and it was feared that during the overload stops the pistons might actually pop out of their sockets within the brake, allowing brake fluid to spray the hot surfaces, resulting in fire.

Therefore, a metal spacer was inserted in the brake between the pressure plate and the piston housing.

This spacer served to make up for the lack of friction material and to keep the pistons in place.

In order to provide room for the spacer, the adjuster assemblies were removed from the brake.

The five overload stops were conducted without the adjuster assemblies and with the spacer in place.

After stop number 48 — the third overload stop — temperatures in the brake were so high that the fuse plug, a safety device which allows air to escape from the tire to prevent blowout, melted and allowed the tire to deflate.

The same thing happened after stop number 49 — the fourth overload stop. Both of these occurrences were highly irregular and in direct conflict with the performance criteria of the military requirements.

CHAIRMAN PROXMIRE. I understand you have a picture of this that might help us see it.

MR. VANDIVIER. Yes.

CHAIRMAN PROXMIRE. Do you want to show that to us now?

MR. VANDIVIER. I was going to show it here just a little bit later.

CHAIRMAN PROXMIRE. Go ahead.

MR. VANDIVIER. For the worn brake maximum energy stop the adjusters were replaced in the brake and a different spacer was used between the pressure plate and the piston housing.

Now I have a copy, a picture of this brake just before it went on the maximum energy test, and here you may see at the top is the additional spacer that has been added in order to get sufficient braking action on the brake.

CHAIRMAN PROXMIRE. Who took that picture?

MR. VANDIVIER. That was taken with a Polaroid camera. I am not sure —

CHAIRMAN PROXMIRE. I think it is only fair to the committee, Mr. Conable and the committee, to ask you about it later. You go ahead and we will ask questions.

MR. VANDIVIER. All right.

In addition to these highly questionable practices, a turnaround capability test, or simulated mission test, was conducted incorrectly due to a human error. When the error was later discovered, no corrections were made.

While these tests were being conducted, I was asked by Mr. Lawson to begin writing a qualification report for the brake. I flatly refused and told Mr. Gretzinger, the lab supervisor, who was my superior, that I could not write such a report because the brake had not been qualified.

He agreed and he said that no one in the laboratory was going to issue such a report unless a brake was actually qualified in accordance with the specification and using standard operating procedures.

He said that he would speak to his own supervisor, the manager of the technical services section, Mr. Russell Line, and get the matter settled at once.

He consulted Mr. Line and assured me that both had concurred in the decision not to write a qualification report.

I explained to Lawson that I had been told not to write the report, and that the only way such a report could be written was to falsify test data.

Mr. Lawson said he was well aware of what was required, but that he had been ordered to get a report written, regardless of how or what had to be done.

He stated if I would not write the report he would have to, and he asked if I would help him gather the test data and draw up the various engineering curves and graphic displays which are normally included in a report.

I asked Mr. Gretzinger, my superior, if this was all right and he agreed as long as I was only assisting in the preparation of the data, it would be permissible.

Both Lawson and I worked on the elaborate curves and logs in the report for nearly a month. During this time we both frankly discussed the moral aspects of what we were doing and we agreed that our actions were unethical and probably illegal.

Several times during that month I discussed the A–7D testing with Mr. Line, and asked him to consult his superiors in Akron, in order to prevent a false qualification report from being issued.

Mr. Line declined to do so and advised me that it would be wise to just do my work and keep quiet.

I told him of the extensive irregularities during testing and suggested that the brake was actually dangerous and if allowed to be installed on an aircraft, might cause an accident.

Mr. Line said he thought I was worrying too much about things which did not really concern me and advised me to just "do what you're told."

About the first of June—

CHAIRMAN PROXMIRE. You skipped one line here.

MR. VANDIVIER. Yes.

CHAIRMAN PROXMIRE. You said "I asked him"—

MR. VANDIVIER. Yes. I asked Mr. Line if his conscience would hurt him if such a thing caused the death of a pilot and this is when he replied I was worrying about too many things that did not concern me and advised me to "do what you're told."

About the first of June 1968, Mr. Gretzinger asked if I were finished with the graphic data and said he had been advised by the chief engineer, Mr. H. C. Sunderman, that when the data was finished it was to be delivered to him—Sunderman—and he would instruct someone in the engineering department to actually write the report.

Accordingly, when I had finished with the data, I gave it to Mr. Gretzinger who immediately took it from the room. Within a few minutes, he was back and was obviously angry.

He said that Mr. Sunderman had told him no one in the engineering department had time to write the report and that we would have to do it ourselves.

At this point, Mr. Line came into the room demanding to know "What the hell is going on." Mr. Gretzinger explained the situation again and said he would not allow such a report to be issued by the lab.

Mr. Line then turned to me and said he was "sick of hearing about this damned report. Write the——thing and shut up about it."

CHAIRMAN PROXMIRE. Let me ask you, you had this in quotes. Did you make a note of this at the time?

MR. VANDIVIER. Yes.

CHAIRMAN PROXMIRE. Do you have your notes with you?

MR. VANDIVIER. No. I have notes with me, yes. I am not sure if I have this note or not, but I have notes with me.

CHAIRMAN PROXMIRE. All right.

MR. VANDIVIER. When he had left, Mr. Gretzinger and I discussed the position we were in and Mr. Gretzinger said that we both should have resigned a long time ago. He added that there was little to do now except write the report.

Accordingly, I wrote the report, but in the conclusion, I stated that the brake had "not" met either the intent or the requirements of the specifications and was therefore "not" qualified.

When the final report was typewritten and ready for publication, the two "nots" in the conclusion had been eliminated, thereby changing the entire meaning of the conclusion.

I would like to point out at this time the various discrepancies between the military standards and procedures and the qualification tests actually conducted:

1. Brake pressure was cut on all stops at 10 miles per hour and the wheel allowed to coast to a stop.

2. The five overload stops were conducted with a spacer between the pressure plate and the piston housing.

3. The lining carriers used for the test were specially made with an additional 0.030 of an inch lining material. This was done to assure sufficient lining material on the carriers.

4. Stators in the brake were physically reversed after stop 30 and remained in those positions throughout the test.

Mr. Chairman, the next two sentences of my printed statement contain a typographical error, words have been omitted and I would like to insert those in at this time.

5. The worn brake RTO was conducted with an additional pressure plate between the original pressure plate and piston housing. This was done because allowable piston travel had been exceeded and without the additional pressure plate the brakes could not have been applied.

6. Prior to the worn brake RTO (maximum energy stop), the inside diameter of the lining carriers was increased by 0.120 of an inch to alleviate the severe shrinkage of the lining carriers on the torque tube caused by overheating.

7. On stops 48 and 49 (overload stops 3 and 4) the fuse plug eutectic material — material designed to melt at a specified temperature — melted, allowing the tire to deflate.

8. The torque plate and keyway inserts for the wheel had their drive surfaces chromeplated, because of extreme wear. This was not a production process on this brake.

9. Before the start of the tests and at teardowns the keyway inserts were sprayed with molybdenum disulfate (a lubricant).

10. After every stop the wheel and tire assembly were removed from the brake, the brake was blown out with high-velocity air and the keyway inserts and heat shield were wiped clean.

11. After stops Nos. 10, 20, 30, 40, 45, and 50 the brake was disassembled and the expansion slots in the lining carriers were cleaned of excess lining material and opened. Excess materials removed from between the segments in the rotors and the lugs and links on the rotors were cleaned and radiused by machining processes. This in a sense is equivalent to a minor overhaul in the brake linings.

In addition there were at least four other major irregularities in the test procedure.

These, gentlemen, are only irregularities which occurred during the testing. As for the report itself more than 80 false entries were made in the body of the report and in the logs.

Many, many of the elaborate engineering curves attached to the report were complete and total fabrications, based not on what had actually occurred, but on information which would fool both LTV and the Air Force.

I have already mentioned that the turn-around capability test which was supposed to determine what temperatures might be experienced by the brake during a typical flight mission, had been misconducted through a human error on the part of the test lab operator.

Rather than rerun this very important test, which would have taken only some 6 hours to complete, it was decided to manufacture the data.

This we did, and the result was some very convincing graphic curves. These curves were supposed to demonstrate to LTV and the Air Force exactly what the temperatures in the brakes had been during each minute of the simulated mission.

They were completely false and based only on data which would be acceptable to the customers.

I could spend the entire day here discussing the various elaborate falsifications that went into this report but I feel that, by now, the picture is clear.

The report was finally issued on June 5, 1968, and almost immediately, flight tests on the brake were begun at Edwards Air Force Base in California.

Mr. Lawson was sent by Goodrich to witness these tests and when he returned, he described various mishaps which had occurred during the flight tests and he expressed the opinion to me that the brake was dangerous.

The same afternoon, I contacted my attorney and after describing the situation to him, asked for his advice.

He advised me that, while I was technically not guilty of committing a fraud, I was certainly part of a conspiracy to defraud.

He further suggested a meeting with U.S. Attorney Roger Makely in Dayton, Ohio.

I agreed to this and my attorney said he would arrange an appointment with the Federal attorney.

I discussed my attorney's appraisal of our situation with Mr. Lawson, but I did not, at this time, tell him of the forthcoming visit with Mr. Makely.

Mr. Lawson said he would like to consult with my attorney and I agreed to arrange this.

Shortly thereafter, Mr. Lawson went to the Dallas offices of LTV and, while he was gone, my attorney called and said that, upon advice of the U.S. attorney, he had arranged an interview with the Dayton office of the FBI.

I related the details of the A-7D qualification to Mr. Joseph Hathaway, of the FBI.

He asked if I could get Mr. Lawson to confirm my story and I replied that I felt Mr. Lawson would surely do this.

Upon Mr. Lawson's return from Dallas, I asked him if he still wished to consult my attorney and he answered "I most certainly do."

Mr. Lawson and I went to the attorney's office, and Mr. Lawson was persuaded to speak to the FBI.

I wish to emphasize that at no time prior to Mr. Lawson's decision to speak to the FBI was he aware that I had already done so. His decision and mine were both the result of our individual actions.

Mr. Lawson related his own story to Mr. Hathaway, who advised us to keep our jobs and to tell no one that we had been to see him.

I might add here that he advised us that an investigation would be made.

About this time the Air Force demanded that Goodrich produce its raw data from the tests.

This Goodrich refused to do, claiming that the raw data was proprietary information.

Goodrich management decided that, since pressure was being applied by the Air Force, a conference should be arranged with LTV management and engineering staff.

A preconference meeting was set for Goodrich personnel in order to go over the questionable points in the report.

On Saturday, July 27, 1968, Mr. Robert Sink, Mr. Lawson, Mr. John Warren — A–7D project engineer — and I met and went over the discrepant items contained in the qualification report.

Each point was discussed at great length and a list of approximately 40 separate discrepancies was compiled.

These, we were told by Mr. Sink, would be revealed to LTV personnel the following week.

However, by the time of the meeting with LTV, only a few days later, the list of discrepancies had been cut by Mr. Sink from 43 items to a mere three.

Mr. Chairman, during this meeting Mr. Lawson took from the blackboard at the Goodrich conference room word for word listing of all these discrepancies. This contains the 43 items I have just mentioned.

I would like to enter this into the record, and also enter the subsequent list of three major discrepancies which later came out of this meeting.

CHAIRMAN PROXMIRE. Do you have copies of those documents?

MR. VANDIVIER. Yes, I do have.

MR. VANDIVIER. The following 2-month period was one of a constant running battle with LTV and the Air Force, during which time the Air Force refused final approval of the qualification report and demanded a confrontation with Goodrich about supplying raw data.

On October 8, another meeting was held, again with Mr. Sink, Mr. Lawson, Mr. Warren, and myself present.

This was only 1 day prior to a meeting with Air Force personnel and Mr. Sink said he had called the meeting "so that we are all coordinated and tell the same story."

Mr. Sink said that LTV personnel would be present at the meeting with the Air Force and our policy would be to "Let LTV carry the ball." Mr. Sink appeared to be especially concerned because Mr. Bruce Tremblay, the Air Force engineer most intimate with A–7D brake, would be present at the meeting and it was felt at B. F. Goodrich that Mr. Tremblay was already suspicious.

Mr. Sink warned us that "Mr. Tremblay will probably be at his antagonistic best."

He added that the Air Force had wanted to meet at the Goodrich plant, but that we — Goodrich — couldn't risk having them that close to the raw data.

"We don't want those guys in the plant," Mr. Sink said.

What happened at the meeting with the Air Force, I do not know. I did not attend.

On October 18, I submitted my resignation to Goodrich effective November 1.

I would like to read that resignation. This is addressed to Russel Line, manager of technical services:

> In May of this year I was directed to participate in the preparation of qualification report for the A7D, 26031. As you are aware this report contained numerous deliberate and wilful misrepresentations which according to legal counsel constitutes fraud and therefore exposes both myself and others to criminal charges of conspiracy to defraud. In view of this fact, I must terminate my employment with the B. F. Goodrich Company effective November 1, 1968. I regret that this decision must be made, but I am sure that you will agree that events of the past seven months have created an atmosphere of deceit and distrust in which it is impossible to work effectively and productively.

On October 25 I was told that my resignation was to be accepted immediately, and within 20 minutes I had left the Goodrich Co.

Gentlemen, I am well aware that the B. F. Goodrich Co. is a well known and well respected firm with an almost impeccable reputation.

I am equally aware that the charges I have made are serious.

However, everything I have said to you is completely true and I can prove my statements with documentary evidence.

The unfortunate part of a situation such as this is that, invariably, many innocent persons are made to suffer along with the guilty.

Therefore, I should like to emphasize that three people whom I have mentioned here are, I feel, completely blameless and were implicated in this situation through no fault of their own.

Mr. Ralph Gretzinger from the very start fought this situation and tried very hard to use his influence to stop the issuance of the false report.

Mr. Richard Gloor, in his own handwriting, listed the irregularities occurring during the test and was outspoken in his opposition to the report.

This list was shown to B. F. Goodrich management.

Mr. Lawson, of course, was in a position similar to mine and the fact that he voluntarily disclosed the details of the A–7D test program to the FBI and GAO should stand upon its own merits. Thank you.

CHAIRMAN PROXMIRE. Thank you, Mr. Vandivier.

Mr. Lawson, you have heard the statement as read and I take it you have had a chance to see the full statement?

MR. LAWSON. No, I have not.

CHAIRMAN PROXMIRE. You have not?

MR. LAWSON. No, I have not.

CHAIRMAN PROXMIRE. The statement you have just heard read by Mr. Vandivier, do you agree with it fully or in part or do you disagree and can you tell us your reaction to it?

MR. LAWSON. The factual data that Mr. Vandivier has presented is correct, to the best of my knowledge.

CHAIRMAN PROXMIRE. There is no statement that you heard him read with which you would disagree in any part?

MR. LAWSON. I really don't know. I haven't read the complete text.

CHAIRMAN PROXMIRE. Would you disagree with any part of what you heard him read right now in your presence?

MR. LAWSON. No. I don't believe there is.

CHAIRMAN PROXMIRE. Now I would like to ask you, Mr. Vandivier, you gave us a picture which we may want to ask other witnesses about, so I want to qualify that picture. As far as we know, it is a picture which you say was taken of the brake that was tested?

MR. VANDIVIER. That is correct.

CHAIRMAN PROXMIRE. But we would like to make sure that we qualify that, because it is going to be used later.

Now would you describe again, tell us how you came to have that, when the picture was taken and so forth?

MR. VANDIVIER. Yes. This was taken just approximately an hour and a half or 2 hours before the worn brake RTO was conducted. This was for the qualification test, and I asked the plant photographer if he would take a Polaroid picture of this for me. He did so, and I took the Polaroid shot and I had it enlarged. I have a certification on this. I had the original Polaroid negative. I have the negatives that the photographer used.

CHAIRMAN PROXMIRE. Wil you give us the date, the time that was taken, if you have that?

MR. VANDIVIER. If you will give me just a moment, I can.

CHAIRMAN PROXMIRE. Meanwhile, may I ask Mr. Lawson, while Mr. Vandivier is looking up that, if you can confirm that this is in fact the picture of the A–7D brake that was undergoing qualification?

MR. LAWSON. Yes, it appears to be.

CHAIRMAN PROXMIRE. It appears to be?

MR. LAWSON. I would say it is.

CHAIRMAN PROXMIRE. It is. All right. Well, you can supply that a little later for the record, Mr. Vandivier.

MR. VANDIVIER. All right.

CHAIRMAN PROXMIRE. Let me ask you this. You say you worked for Goodrich for 6 years?

MR. VANDIVIER. That is correct.

CHAIRMAN PROXMIRE. What was your previous employment before you were hired by Goodrich?

MR. VANDIVIER. I worked for the Food Machinery and Chemical Corp. at their Newport, Ind. plant.

CHAIRMAN PROXMIRE. Technical writer is a professional position that requires considerable competence and ability. What experience did you have that would qualify you to be a technical writer?

MR. VANDIVIER. I had none.

CHAIRMAN PROXMIRE. Did you immediately go into this or did they give you a training course?

MR. VANDIVIER. No. I had no training course. I kind of worked into the job, I guess. It was —

CHAIRMAN PROXMIRE. You were not hired to be a technical —

MR. VANDIVIER. No, I was actually hired as an instrumentation technician, and Goodrich engaged in a mass changeover of instrumentation techniques, and they wanted degreed people for this kind of work so I was switched over to the technical writing section.

CHAIRMAN PROXMIRE. How long did you work as a technical writer?

MR. VANDIVIER. Approximately 3 years.

CHAIRMAN PROXMIRE. Three years. How many reports did you prepare for B. F. Goodrich?

MR. VANDIVIER. At least 100, possibly 150.

CHAIRMAN PROXMIRE. Were any of these reports questioned in any way?

MR. VANDIVIER. No, they were not.

CHAIRMAN PROXMIRE. Were they accepted? Did you get any reaction at all favorable or unfavorable in these reports that you wrote?

MR. VANDIVIER. Occasionally we would get a question from the manufacturer about a wording or a clarification, and these would be supplied.

CHAIRMAN PROXMIRE. Was there any question as to the accuracy or competence of the report?

MR. VANDIVIER. No, none whatsoever.

CHAIRMAN PROXMIRE. Were you criticized at any time that the reports were not adequate?

MR. VANDIVIER. No; I was not.

CHAIRMAN PROXMIRE. In your statement, you say "Accordingly I wrote the report but in the conclusion I stated that the brake had 'not' met either the intent or the requirement of the specification and therefore was 'not' qualified." Then you add "When the final report was typewritten and ready for publication the two 'nots' in the conclusion had been eliminated, thereby changing the entire meaning of the conclusion."

Now it seems to me that you have testified before this that you and Mr. Lawson constructed this report based on your instructions from your superiors, and that this report was false in many ways that you knew, and that the report seemed to qualify the brakes, at least that was the impression I got, and yet you concluded, and I quote, "I stated the brake had not met either the intent or the requirement of the specifications and therefore was not qualified."

Doesn't it seem on the basis of your testimony that this is somewhat inconsistent? In other words, you had written a report that would qualify the brake and then you come in with a one-sentence conclusion in which you say it was not qualified? Do you see what I am getting at?

MR. VANDIVIER. Yes. Mr. Chairman, this was probably one final gesture of defiance. I was so aggravated and sick at having to write this thing. I knew the words "not" would be taken out, but I put them in to show that, I do not know, that they had bent me to their will but they had not broken me yet. It was a foolish thing perhaps to do, but it was showing that I still had a little spirit left. At least this is how I felt.

CHAIRMAN PROXMIRE. What did you think your superiors at B. F. Goodrich would do when they found the "not qualified" in your report, when you had been told to show the brake qualified?

MR. VANDIVIER. I knew it would be changed probably without question. I was not worried if you are trying — I was not worried at being called on the carpet for this. I knew they would just merely change it.

CHAIRMAN PROXMIRE. Was this the only time in the 3 years you worked as a technical writer with Goodrich the only time that you made false entries into a report of manufacture?

MR. VANDIVIER. Yes, it was.

CHAIRMAN PROXMIRE. So as far as you know B. F. Goodrich's record is clean in every other respect with your experience?

MR. VANDIVIER. With me —

CHAIRMAN PROXMIRE. With this single incidence being an exception?

MR. VANDIVIER. That is right; that is correct.

CHAIRMAN PROXMIRE. They had never before asked you to do this?

MR. VANDIVIER. No.

CHAIRMAN PROXMIRE. Do you know of any other technical writer you worked with, in which Goodrich had instructed them to take this kind of action?

MR. VANDIVIER. If they had done this, I would know nothing of it. I could not say.

CHAIRMAN PROXMIRE. This was the only incident?

MR. VANDIVIER. Yes, as far as I know, the only incident which I was asked to do this.

CHAIRMAN PROXMIRE. What was the normal procedure at Goodrich when a brake failed to meet all of the requirements or when normal procedures were not followed?

MR. VANDIVIER. If for some reason or other the normal procedure was not followed or the brake simply could not meet a particular requirement, the report was written and a deviation was requested from the manufacturer, which in other words is a request to allow him to accept the brake with these noted deviations from the procedure.

I might add that there are many times that a brake just could not meet a certain requirement specified by the manufacturer, and it was always the customary procedure to ask for a deviation, and many times it was granted or some sort of a compromise was reached between the manufacturer and Goodrich.

CHAIRMAN PROXMIRE. I cannot understand what was going through the minds of Goodrich's management the way you have told the story. I cannot see what they have to gain by passing on a brake that would not meet qualifications. Somewhere along the line this is going to be shown as an unqualified brake. As you pointed out, it might be under disastrous circumstances, but in any event Goodrich would suffer and suffer badly by passing on a brake to LTV or the Air Force that was not going to work. What is their motivation?

MR. VANDIVIER. I cannot tell you what their motivation is. I can tell you what I feel was behind this.

CHAIRMAN PROXMIRE. All right.

MR. VANDIVIER. I feel in the beginning stages of this program someone made a mistake, and refused to admit that mistake, and in order to hide his stupidity or his ignorance, or his pride, or whatever it was, he simply covered up, you know, with more false statements, false information, and at the time it came time to deliver this brake, Goodrich was so far down the road there was nothing else to do.

They had no time to start over, I think it was a matter not of company policy but of company politics. I think that probably three or four persons within the Goodrich organization at Troy were responsible for this. I do not believe for a moment that the corporate officials in Akron knew that this was going on.

Who Blows the Whistle on Big Corporations?

What breed of cat is the whistle blower—that embarrassing employee who tells the emperor, and the proper authorities—that the corporation isn't wearing any clothes?

If whistle blowers attending the First National Seminar on Individual Rights in the Corporation, and research presented to that gathering, are typical, they are not the breed that might at first be expected.

Whistle blowers are "neither neurotic, nor misfits, nor malcontents," Andrew Hacker, professor of political science at The City University of New York, told the gathering at the Roosevelt Hotel in that city. Faced with loyalty to their employers and loyalty to their moral principles they chose the latter, he said.

Whistle blowers who told their stories at the conference pictured themselves as conservative persons who did what they had done for reasons of loyalty to the higher goals of the corporations that employed them or of the nation of which they are citizens. They included a Harvard graduate, a nuclear physicist and a corporate attorney who described himself as a "former union buster." Most admitted having voted for former President Richard M. Nixon not once but twice.

Dan Gellert, an Eastern Air Lines pilot who went public with design problems of the Lockheed L10-11 after his attempts to inform the airline's management of the defects got nowhere and subsequently won a $1.6 million judgment against the corporation, defended his actions as an example of professionalism.

"Our responsibilities (as pilots) to our passengers, our crews and aircraft supercede red ink on a balance sheet," Gellert contended. "If they do not, you are not a professional," he added.

Joseph Rose, the corporate attorney who exposed the Associated Milk Producers' efforts to bribe government officials, said that unless a fundamental change takes place in how corporate officials approach their responsibilities, whistle blowing will go on. "Unless you have someone to come forward in times of crisis, this society is in deep trouble," he said.

Ironically, whistle blowers at the conference did not back the idea that legislation should be enacted that would make their activities easier. They said that despite admitting that those who refuse to play the game risk being ostracized by fellow employees and/or being retaliated against by management.

Because the whistle blower faces a bleak future and a present in which "he is strictly on his own," said Peter Faulkner, a nuclear physicist who told Congress about defects in construction of nuclear power plants, "a high quality whistle blower" will be guaranteed. If his or her way were softened employees might become "a bit trigger happy," Faulkner said. After all is said or done, the whistle blower's strength of character will bring him through, he added.

—PM

Industrial Espionage

Paul Mixson

Some time in the last few months you met an industrial spy. At his deceptively casual request you passed on to him highly valuable information about your company, its policies, and its prospects for the future. That spy turned around and used that information to do your firm serious, possibly irreparable damage. Chances are, however, you never knew what happened or how. Loose lips sink more than ships.

Take the case of the junior executive of an engineering company engaged in offshore support work for the North Sea oil industry. All he did was tell a casual acquaintance that he was busy renting temporary quarters at a dozen different sites in a particular remote, obscure part of Scotland. The information was quickly passed to a third party who valued it highly, to whom that piece of Scotland was not at all remote or obscure.

Transparent in the young manager's cheery account of his assignment was his firm's intention to create a substantial permanent installation. Knowing the corporate plan, a land developer bought the only attractive piece of land in the area. When the company was ready to make a formal move, it would end up paying several million dollars more for the land than originally budgeted. Pity.

Acts of industrial espionage are rarely the stuff of pulp novels or television's "Executive Suite"; hardly ever Watergate-type break-ins or classic cloak-and-dagger. Corporate spying, in the main, is the petty pilferage of information. One man in Australia, a professional industrial "secret agent," employs a network of stewards and air hostesses to gather tidbits of information overheard in the first class compartment of international flights. He makes $1 million a year selling those tidbits.

Reprinted from *MBA Magazine*, March 1977.

Stephen Barlay, British author of *The Secrets Business,* is one of the world's leading authorities on the illicit traffic in corporate information. "Industrial espionage is particularly a big problem for junior executives," says Barlay. "No one ever properly warns them about it. They are thrown into a new world with their first executive job, and their most natural reaction is to show off a bit to demonstrate their knowledge.

"Companies can't expect them to stop talking business in public places, but they *should* expect the new executive to choose carefully where and to whom he speaks."

A further problem is that many senior executives don't believe corporate spying is all that widespread. Says Barlay, "They've seen too many films. They believe that all such operations are merely fiction. If they've once seen such a situation as a fictitious presentation, it becomes terribly hard for them to believe that it's true."

One financial executive in charge of an American mutual fund's vast investments heard that some people in his circle had their offices debugged. Purely as a status symbol, he ordered an expert "sweep" of his Wall Street offices. Much to his astonishment, a bug was indeed found in an expensive electric clock given to him by an old college friend two years previously. The friend had made a fortune, taking advantage of confidential information.

The story did not end there, however. The engaging bugging expert advised the executive on how to take his revenge. For three months the executive staged fake phone calls to his broker for the benefit of his unseen audience, giving terrible investment advice. Hoping that his "mistakes" were copied by his listeners, he would loudly bemoan to the broker his own "losses."

The bait promptly swallowed, the unfortunate, erstwhile friend was ruined in a month. The strategy was continued for another 60 days to make certain that everybody who might have been involved with the bugging would suffer the same fate.

The large profits that come from information on investment plans or real estate transactions draw the industrial spy as sugar draws the bee. But almost any confidential information has its use. Industries — like electronics and chemicals — that depend upon sophisticated advertising and marketing strategies are obvious targets. Research and development projects are almost as tantalizing. Barlay, based in energy-starved Britain, is aware of a booming trade in company secrets about the electric vehicles now under development, particularly storage cell technology, but even he can't tell who is buying.

Industries like automobile companies that have regular model changes are targets, as is virtually any industrial operation with information or plans that could hurt the competition.

Sagging profits and increasing competition, says Barlay, are clear proxies for industrial spying. He claims shipbuilding—because of the continued increase in Japanese facilities against reduced shipyard profits—is infested with spies as never before.

"Gadgets," says Barlay, "play only a minor role. The best way to obtain information is to simply chat someone up over a drink. You get even more information by taking an executive out to lunch and still more over dinner with a show thrown in. Friendly chat is a better information source than any bug."

"Economic intelligence," argues Barlay, "is a terribly respectable profession. Spying is not. But are they really different? The only way to distinguish between gathering information and being a spy is how you obtain the information."

After extensive experience in the field, Barlay believes that the manner in which you get information must be compatible with your use of it. For example, if you pick up information casually at a cocktail party under the cover of, say, a journalist, disguising your real intent to pick up secrets, then you are an industrial spy.

A classic example of picking up free information occurred at a Detroit cocktail party some years ago. A Chrysler executive heard that Ford's chief photographer was in Paris at the time when ad campaigns were always in preparation. Some checking disclosed that Ford's forthcoming campaign would show new American-made models in front of international landmarks.

Chrysler promptly coopted Ford's strategy not by plagiarizing it but by placing Chrysler cars in front of American landmarks, assuming that the average consumer could identify more readily with American sites. A little patriotism turned profitable. Who said patriotism and profits don't mix?

Dummy recruitment ads are another fertile source of information. Here a bogus interviewer is really a spy, pumping applicants for information about their jobs and their company. Applicants are under pressure to cooperate in order to make a favorable impression.

Such information doesn't have to be complete. It merely directs the spy to further research. Applicants talk freely about who is dissatisfied with his job and the general lines along which a company is moving, and occasionally they drop a really salable piece of information on the company's immediate planning.

No business survives without customers. Barlay says that the practice of buying such information is widespread. The difficulty in controlling it is that very few laws exist to protect companies from spies, or to punish those that buy purloined information.

The absence of penalty leads to some bizarre situations. The case of two junior executives in service to competing investment houses comes to mind. These two rogues would meet periodically and exchange confidential information about their companies. Then each would slowly feed the information to superiors.

The bosses were so glad to receive inside information that they continually promoted the two men.

"In the final analysis," warns Barlay, "the whole question of industrial espionage is a moral one. There are few laws, and even definitions of right conduct here are vague and subjective. There is always the terrible temptation to indulge in it, to buy information from professionals without asking how they obtained it, and then get recognized or even promoted by equally lax — or jaded — superiors."

If you want to avoid compromising your company's secrets to spies, Barlay offers several pointers to junior executives:

- Keep your mouth shut outside the office. Do talk business but carefully choose what you talk about, with whom you discuss it, and where you talk about it. Particularly avoid discussing your company and what is new about it. Instead, turn such conversations to topics of general interest about the whole industry.
- Be especially careful in public places or gatherings where the competition is present.
- Watch what papers you throw away. If they involve new plans or techniques it is best to shred them. There are extensive networks of industrial spies who make outstanding livings cleaning offices and sifting the rubbish.
- Secretaries are especially vulnerable since they get to see all plans. The higher your position becomes, the more care you should take in picking her and watching her habits, especially if she takes on expensive living styles.
- Do not leave things lying around your office when you leave it. There was one case when a spy made an appointment and during the interview — brazenly and in the open — photographed confidential information on the executive's desk and then threw his camera out the window to a waiting confederate. There was nothing the company could do but buy the film back at a high price.
- International conferences are always suspect. They are a mecca for industrial spies. Be especially careful of conversation in such gatherings.
- If you deal with Iron Curtain countries it is always a safe assumption that they want information and the more confidential the better. Keep the commissar and his agents at arm's length.
- Never let a visitor with whom you have an appointment walk in or out of your factory or office unescorted. This is the most important advice. Reports Barlay: "I had an appointment where the security checks to get in were the strictest I've ever run across, but when I finished my interview the junior executive I

was talking to let me walk out alone. I could have wandered through the whole plant, even though they had a special visitor's route, and when caught could have simply claimed I was lost. There would have been nothing they could do."

Industrial espionage exists, and according to most authorities in corporate security it is a booming, lively business. Some is conventional cloak-and-dagger work. But most lives off the minutiae and gossip of cocktail parties and two-hour lunches. Most is inadvertent, and you can go a long way toward protecting your company if you exercise simple caution and common sense.

But if you decide to take the risky road of promoting your career by trafficking in the business of secrets, remember you were warned. You'll be dealing with professionals, usually ruthless, and you may find yourself trapped by your own duplicity.

How Computer Criminals Get Rich Quick

Sharon Rutenberg

It's easier than robbing a bank. The chances of getting caught are low. Even housewives and children are doing it.

The temptation is obvious: Just sit down for 10 minutes at a computer terminal—at work, school or in your own bedroom—and double a lifetime's earnings.

As a result, computer crime is becoming a billion dollar headache for banks and business.

"Each instance of bank embezzlement without a computer averages $23,500. With a computer, $430,000," said Paul Nolan, FBI special agent in the white collar crime section.

A masked robber walks off the street into a bank and steals an average $3,200 with a 95 percent capture rate, FBI statistics show. Bank robberies account for $12-$15 million per year, computer security pioneer Robert Jacobson said.

Stan Rifkin, a computer security consultant, stole $10.2 million in 1978 by transferring funds from Los Angeles' Security Pacific National

"How Computer Criminals Get Rich Quick," as it appeared in the *Vancouver Sun* (Canada), April 4, 1981. Reprinted by permission of United Press International.

Bank to his Zurich bank account after gaining access to the day's code for authorizing transfers. He was sentenced to eight years in federal prison.

"This one fellow all by himself—no mask, no gun—stole as much money as all the bank robbers," Jacobson said.

Nolan said computer crime is not a major problem and is manageable from a law enforcement point of view.

But the Computer and Business Equipment Manufacturers Association, a trade organization, is concerned about reports computer crime is becoming rampant and will cause "economic chaos in the 1980s," spokesman Jeff Wood said.

"We just don't subscribe to that theory. We think that's overblowing the situation," Wood said. "We think the incidence of actual computer crime . . . is not nearly as great as tends to be purported."

Alarming Increase

However, computer security consultants are alarmed at the increase of computer abuse. Expert Robert Campbell said "the problem could reach $40 billion in annual loss." European authorities say computer crime is the fastest growing element of the crime problem.

"As a computer literacy grows, in some decades from now everybody will have computer literacy from grade school to high school. And that will make the computer abuse and computer crime an even more frightening affair," said Carl Hammer, Sperry Univac director of computer sciences.

"It will be flourishing unless management wakes up and does something about it. I hate to say it, but I see a particularly rosy future for it."

A 14-year-old student at Manhattan's exclusive Dalton High School used a school computer terminal to dial into GTE Datanet, which was connected to Canadian Datapak. The student claimed he gained access to host computers at 19 Canadian companies. Prosecutors said the student caused considerable damage to one firm's computer systems by destroying or modifying data.

Child prodigy Jerry Schneider developed his own extensive telecommunication system at the age of 10. Nine years later, he posed as a magazine writer and spent six months researching the telephone company's equipment ordering system in Los Angeles. He was sent to jail for stealing more than $1 million in telephone equipment.

An officer at Wells Fargo Bank's Beverly Hills, Calif., branch allegedly embezzled $21.3 million by juggling accounts for 10 minutes every five days for more than two years. The bank named operations officer L. Ben Lewis and Muhammad Ali Professional Sports Inc. and its top officers as conspirators in a civil suit over the losses.

Three former employees of Coca-Cola Co. of Miami were charged with using the company's computer system to steal an estimated $500,000 in Coke products. They were charged with grand theft and burglary.

An Internal Revenue Service employee was prosecuted for using a computer terminal to change addresses on tax refund checks and send them to her relatives.

A woman employed at a Social Security Administration office in Baltimore authorized payments of large checks to several of her friends who were in collusion with her.

Brian Catlin and Christopher Adams, both 17-year-old students at Fremd High School in suburban Palatine, Ill., shut down Chicago's DePaul University computer system last Sept. 17-19 — enrollment week — as a challenge. They were charged with theft of services.

Ten years ago, computer crime meant placing bombs to destroy computer files and information. Now computer thieves lurk in the woodwork of business.

A profile of computer abusers shows they are amateurs, 18-30 years old, who don't want to hurt anyone, but are disgruntled with employers, fascinated with challenge and game-playing and fear unanticipated detection and exposure, computer crime expert Don Parker said.

Many are "computer freaks" — college graduates to whom computers are their whole life. They tend to be bright and aggressive, the type a corporation would want in an executive position.

"Just the sort you'd like to have working for you," Jacobson said. "We are being done in by a lot smarter people."

The amount of money to be made is startling.

The average white collar worker can expect to earn about $1 million in his lifetime — working from age 25 to 65 at an average yearly salary of $25,000, Hammer said.

"There's obviously a great temptation to double your income if you can work on this terminal for a couple of hours and make $2 million. To double your lifetime earning in 10 minutes is not an unreasonable temptation," he said.

FBI Categories

The most popular target for computer thieves is the banking industry — where the commodity is money. Next, in order, are government, education and manufacturing.

The FBI categorizes computer crime into five groups — and not all involve money transactions. Computer thieves also can steal goods and services, college degrees and title to property.

The agency's breakdown:

- System deceit, or unauthorized transaction.

     If a college student about to flunk out finds out the university registrar's authorized entry code, he can "magically" change his grades and receive a bachelor's degree.
- System alteration.

     In a simple procedure requiring only computer terminal access, a bank teller can withdraw money from a customer's account and deposit the money in her boyfriend's account.

     A programmer computing interest in a savings account recently had the fractions deposited to his own account, rather than rounding them to the nearest whole cent. For instance, a 15 percent interest on $1,111.11 is $166.6665. The fractions, or mils, could add up to millions of dollars.
- Physical destruction.

     Culprits can blow up the computer system or make it do something wrong. A disgruntled U.S. Defense Department employee programmed the computer to stop generating payroll checks so many days after he left.

     In the DePaul University case, the students were playing with computers for the fun of it. It was a challenge. They left messages that they had gained access and even tried to hold the computer ransom.
- Theft of information.

     Here are the industrial espionage cases. People steal from within. They sell trade secrets to give the company's competitor an advantage.

     In the competitive business of selling business forms — with almost uniform products — a dishonest employee in charge of data processing sold a competitor the company's customer purchase list, virtually putting his firm out of business.

     In another case, Encyclopedia Britannica employees offered to sell a million-name list to brokers.
- Time theft, or use of computer.

     Computers are a great strength for businesses and a powerful advantage to help them operate more efficiently, but they have created a new group of hazards.

     The substitution of paper with computers has resulted in a sophisticated technological crime — manipulation of a computer program.

"As the number of computers grows, the potential for abuse grows. There is no way to prevent computer crime as long as humans are involved with machines," Wood said.

Computer crime can be committed from the inside or outside. But many believe the problem lies at home — with their own employees.

"It's people who commit the crimes. Management must simply look at the people," Hammer said. "It's usually the people on the inside. That's the easiest way to do it."

Honest people in data processing are absolutely floored by the notion that some of their colleagues might be dishonest," Jacobson said.

Jacobson said the answer is not in an attempt to try to figure out who to trust, but to build systems to minimize temptation.

"A manager who allows a slack condition to exist has to take some responsibility for the ruined life if someone succumbs to temptation, commits a crime and gets caught. We have some obligation to our employees to protect them against overwhelming temptation.

"It would never occur to anyone to put a barrel near the front door filled with $100 bills with a sign, 'Don't take it.' The victim is part of the problem if he's failed to take reasonable steps to secure the system."

Companies are now looking for ways to tighten security on their precious computer systems.

"Prudent business management says: "I have to protect this asset just like any asset in the business," Jacobson said.

Companies are encouraged by the experts to safeguard against penetration of their systems by physical control of both computers and terminals and built-in protection in the computer programs.

First, they should make sure computer terminal areas are physically secured—either with door locks or by making sure unauthorized people are not permitted in the areas.

The security experts also suggest companies confine access to the password, or entry code, restrict from computer facilities an employee about to be terminated, make sure those allowed access have prior approval, use badges, and monitor terminals with closed-circuit television.

How the Tenderfeet Toughened Up U.S. Borax

Tom Alexander

Over the past few months, an extraordinary drama of labor-management conflict has been playing itself out in the California desert. A company got shoved a little too hard and shoved back. As a result, its white-collar employees found themselves toiling away in a singularly hellish mine and refinery in the middle of the Mojave.

Reprinted from material originally appearing in the December 1974 issue of *Fortune* Magazine by special permission; © 1974 Time Inc.

The mine in question produces about 60 percent of the free world's borax and is owned by U.S. Borax & Chemical Corp., a subsidiary of the giant British mining company, Rio Tinto Zinc. While just about everybody associates the company's product with old-fashioned cleansing agents, Death Valley Days, and twenty-mule teams, it turns out that borax—otherwise known as sodium borate—is one of those all-around whizzer chemicals of the new industrial age. A lot of borax still goes into soap, but it also finds its way into everything from agriculture to atomic energy (where it controls the rate of nuclear reactions). The biggest use of all, though, is in making certain kinds of glass, including glass fiber.

Well before its contract with the International Longshoremen's and Warehousemen's Union expired last June, U.S. Borax was in an odd kind of trouble: largely because of the huge increase in demand for glass-fiber insulation, the world wanted more borax than Borax could provide. At the same time, the company was discovering that its automated plant, two miles north of the tiny town of Boron, was apparently incapable of producing as much borax as it was designed to. When demand surged last year, the managers of the plant tried to go to full production but were seldom able to exceed about 80 percent of the nominal capacity. Instead of increasing, in fact, plant output had been dropping for the last year. So customers were put on allocation, shipments were delayed, and by last June, the borax stockpiles had dwindled to nothing.

YOU DARE NOT LET IT COOL

The company's president, Carl Randolph, now says that because of the inventory bind, Borax entered the negotiations all prepared to buy a costly settlement from the I.L.W.U. locals that represent the hourly workers at Boron and at a smaller plant in Wilmington, California. Initially, the union demands included an immediate 25 percent boost in hourly pay—which then averaged $5.02. The company countered by offering a 10 percent immediate increase and 7 percent rises in each of the two subsequent years. But what put management's back up were union demands that would infringe upon management prerogatives; for example, the Boron local wanted to review new construction projects with an eye to doing the work themselves. U.S. Borax was planning a $60 million refinery-expansion program, aimed at increasing output by a third. The company wanted the new construction done by outside contractors and decided that it would take a strike rather than give in to this and other union demands. Management resolved, however, to try to keep the two plants operating with supervisory personnel plus salaried employees brought in from elsewhere.

The problem with that idea was that Borax is not really all that big a company. While an annual sales figure of more than $130 million is scarcely trivial, the company has only about 2,000 employees. Nearly 1,200 of these were members of the striking I.L.W.U. locals. The rest are mainly white-collar people — managers, secretaries, clerks, salesmen, computer specialists, engineers, and scientific researchers — hardly the kind of people that one would judge to possess the requisite skills and toughness to operate a borax mine and a technically complex refining plant in a mid-Mojave summer.

Furthermore, once you get a borax refinery in operation, you have to keep it going twenty-four hours a day. The basic refining process consists mainly of dumping crushed ore into hot water, which extracts the soluble borax from the insoluble clay. Then the concentrated solution is piped to various parts of the plant to be turned into various kinds of borax products. Once the solution is in the pipelines, you dare not let it cool, or else the borax will crystallize and solidify inside the pipes.

BAGGIES IN THE GAS TANKS

The drifts of borax were symptomatic of the complex troubles at Boron. Some company men say that one of the problems was that the plant was ill-designed in the first place. But foremen and managers contend that a major source of trouble was worker intransigence, slowdowns, and a lot of outright sabotage, including the plastic Baggies that someone dropped into the fuel tanks of trucks and earth-moving machines. In any case, everybody agrees that labor relations had been deteriorating for a number of years. In its effort to get production up, the company had kept hiring more men. But the newcomers, no matter how eager, soon came under pressure from older hands to slow down.

Over the years, the powdery fallout had accumulated waist-deep throughout many portions of the mine and plant, with drifts running much higher. Plant workers were confined to narrow paths shoveled through the Lower Slobbovian whiteness. Foremen, under pressure to increase production, neglected day-to-day cleanup chores, and in any case could usually count on foot-dragging when they ordered workers to shovel borax. The foremen felt all but powerless in the face of this resistance because of the many regulations and guarantees of job security that had crept into the union contracts over the years.

It's little wonder, then, that the foremen's eyes gleamed when the white-collar men stepped off the planes. The job assignments were made by refinery manager Ken Barnhill without much attention to normal company rank or occupation. "We used the Army system," said Barnhill, "and tried not to let a man's background influence his placement." Inevitably, however, the new men's inexperience meant that they wound up with most of the grubby laboring jobs — the toting, oiling, refueling, and the eternal shoveling and cleaning. The more skilled and technical tasks were done by the foremen and resident supervisors. Once the makeshift crew had mastered the routine of keeping the plant running, the foremen seized the opportunity to set the newcomers to digging the plant out from under all that borax. Shovels were handed out and when the men asked where they should start digging, the foremen replied, "Anywhere."

After looking over its roster, the company concluded that at best it could muster only about 450 able-bodied people to run the two plants that normally employ over 1,400. The 450 included the plant supervisors, virtually the entire sales and research staffs, together with clerks, managers, and so forth, all the way up to vice presidents.

A week or two prior to the expiration of the union contract, the prospective strikebreakers were given a chance to volunteer for the duty, although few were under much illusion that there was anything particularly voluntary about it. Aside from the obvious fact that unless the plants kept going, the salesmen would have nothing to sell and the managers nothing to manage, the only inducements were peer pressure and unverified rumors that the company would pay its salaried scabs $60 a day as a bonus. Ultimately such a bonus was declared, but only after the strike was already under way.

In view of the company's intentions, management seems to have been oddly surprised by the violence that ensued. Within minutes after the walkout on midnight of June 14, several hundred I.L.W.U. men massed outside the Boron plant gates. A group of strikers broke through the gates, roughing up several plant guards. Railroad cars, an automobile, and a small building were burned.

The white-collar "volunteers" assembled early the next day in U.S. Borax's Los Angeles parking garage to be bused to Fox Field Airport. From there they were flown in company planes to the plant's airstrip where they confronted — many of them for the first time — the vast whiteness of an operating borax mine.

It must have been a sobering sight. Automated the refinery may be, but it is scarcely any paragon of industrial efficiency or cleanliness. It's an eighty-acre complex of furnaces, calciners, centrifuges, vibrators, scrubbers, and baggers, all interconnected by an overhead network of what must be some kind of the leakiest conveyors ever built. Day and night, the plant — and the sagebrush for miles downwind — are dusted with a warm, unremitting outfall of borax, white as snow, fine as flour, and gritty as sand.

In the presence of moisture, the stuff dissolves and recrystallizes in solid lumps. Without constant application of brooms, shovels, sledgehammers, and sometimes even dynamite, the machines and furnaces clog up and stop working. All the more delicate pieces of machinery are labeled "Do Not Beat."

At the same time, though, the presence of all those great big vehicles and other machines standing idle aroused small-boy instincts in the shovelers. They discovered that if they wanted to jump into some mechanical monster and try to run it, why, there was no one to discourage them. Soon, the plant and the mine were aswarm with bucket loaders and Lectra Haul dump trucks careening around with dangerous enthusiasm.

For the first two and a half months of the strike, most of the out-of-towners worked eighteen days straight and then got four days off to return home. Aside from their "R. and R.," they virtually never left the heavily guarded plant compound — no one had any enthusiasm for crossing the sporadically violent line of picketers. The company had scattered cots throughout the plant — in rented trailers, offices, conference rooms, even the ladies' rest rooms. A cafeteria was set up in a large storeroom, manned by one of the catering services that specialize in feeding on-location motion-picture crews. The strikebreakers ate well; steak and lobster appeared regularly on the menu. Twice a week — on Wednesdays and Saturdays — each man was issued precisely two cans of beer. Work clothes and boots, snacks, and other items were handed out free in a "goody room," as it was called. It bore a sign: "Through these doors pass the best damn scabs in the world."

They worked twelve-hour shifts, ate, and tumbled into bed. Throughout the night, helicopters with spotlights flew round and round the plant perimeter.

GLOOM IN THE SONIC BOOM CAPITAL

Beyond that perimeter was a grimmer world, without steaks and lobsters and $60 bonuses. Since the mine opened in 1926, it has existed in a tight but infrequently abrasive symbiosis with the small town that was swept together on the desert floor for the miners to live in. Boron, as it is now called, is a tough town in a tough place. More than a thousand of its inhabitants work—*used to work*, that is—at the mine and refinery. In a quest for other distinction, the Boron Chamber of Commerce has claimed for the town the title "Sonic Boom Capital of the World," but even that comes courtesy of the test pilots of Edwards Air Force Base, thirty miles away, who try out experimental aircraft overhead.

The town's average wage earner has been working at the Borax mine for about fifteen years, and some families have three generations employed there. Many of the families came there years ago from the coal fields in Kentucky, West Virginia, and Oklahoma, bringing with them the coal miner's traditional refractoriness.

For the first thirty years, the borax deposits were worked through conventional underground mining techniques, calling upon the special skills and psychological immunities of the coal miners. The raw ore was shipped by rail to the refining plant in Wilmington. In 1957, however, the company elected to convert the underground mine to an open pit. Among other economies, this would permit utilization of the 40 to 50 percent of ore that is normally wasted in the form of pillars to hold up the roof of an underground mine. The borax emerges from open-pit operations mixed with a lot of contaminating clay, so Borax built the refining plant near the rim of the pit.

The change in mining techniques and the coming of the refinery specialists from outside naturally disturbed the restive, captive population of Boron. Miners and their descendants saw their skills rendered beside the point as the machines stripped away the hundred-foot-thick overburden to expose the gleaming borax lode riddled with the ants'-nest handiwork of old shafts and chambers. Many of the higher-paid men proved less adept with the new machines than younger men and outsiders; they often wound up in lowlier jobs and worried for their future.

Isolated together with their troubled work force and under little competitive pressure, the plant managers made some attempts to placate their men over the years. They established special pay categories for the displaced workers, paying them at their old rate even when they worked in lower categories. Such special treating, of course, only antagonized the other workers. In addition, the company accumulated all kinds of overmanned shop practices and featherbedding. Skilled laborers, plumbers and electricians admit to sitting idly for hours, waiting for a laborer to finish preparatory work under union rules.

Over the years, the insecurities, jealousies, and militance fermented. In 1964 the plant workers voted to switch from the A.F.L.-C.I.O. International Chemical Workers Union to the more radical I.L.W.U. Four years later, the union's tough negotiations plus a violent strike ended with the company's buckling under and the workers getting pretty much what they demanded.

The success in 1968 and subsequent gains in 1970 encouraged the I.L.W.U. locals at Boron and Wilmington to ask for more this year. Since the company had a big backlog of orders, and virtually no reserves of refined borax, the timing seemed highly favorable.

Once the strike was under way, however, confidence began to evaporate. The locals had accumulated nothing in the way of strike funds and as the payless weeks went by, workers' savings disappeared. Some got part-time jobs, some had working wives, some got food stamps. Other I.L.W.U. locals contributed a little. Banks and finance companies extended loan contracts on cars and furniture, but unpaid bills accumulated, and utilities shut off services.

The social fabric of the close-knit little town began unraveling. Plant managers and foremen crossed the picket lines each morning and evening, setting neighbor against neighbor, and in some cases, foreman father against union son. The foremen's cars were regularly stoned and occasionally shot at, families received threatening phone calls, windows were broken, one or two houses were bombed. A few union men broke ranks and returned to work. The house trailer of one was firebombed when no one was home. A bundle of dynamite was thrown under another returnee's house when the family *was* at home, but the fuse went out and the family was spared.

"THEY CAN'T BE PRODUCING MUCH"

In mid-August, the Wilmington local voted to accept the company's terms and go back to work, but the Boron local held on. Local 30's leaders told the members that if only they stuck it out, they could bring U.S. Borax to its knees. The leaders claimed they were being kept informed about what was going on in the plant by people who were crossing the picket lines. The leaders told the workers that the plant, which could be seen belching its familiar clouds of dust and sending out its strings of railroad cars, was really producing only 15 percent of normal output. This estimate was backed up, it is said, by one union member who was allowed into the plant to collect his tools. When he emerged, he told his fellow strikers, "They can't be producing much borax in there. The place is *clean*."

In fact, however, the plant had rarely ever done so well. The skimpy, undertrained work force of 325 scabs (not counting about fifty hired guards and helicopter pilots) was regularly shipping out more borax than the normal work force of more than a thousand. Prior to the strike, the plant had averaged about 3,100 tons of borax a day; during the strike months of July and September, output averaged around 3,600 tons a day, and on a few days reached an all-time record of 4,000 tons. Production dropped off a little in August because several days of heavy rain hobbled operations in the pit and a storm knocked out the electric power. All told, the plants' managers calculated that output per man-hour averaged between two and three times that of the prestrike force.

As the implications of this began to sink in, U.S. Borax management gained a new perspective on their old labor practices. Company

President Randolph traces many of the problems to the company's posture in the 1968 strike. "It was easy to make concessions that seemed small at the time, but they grew into major problems. We only realized the magnitude of it after we began operating with the temporary people—and began producing more than we had before."

Plant managers ascribed the high output to the strong motivation of the salaried men. "They didn't need any supervision," marveled mine superintendent Lowell Page. "They would just run the mine until they knew they had enough to keep the refinery going, and then they'd look around for additional jobs to do." Randolph traces the high motivation to anger over union violence. "It created a cause for them to rally around."

A STIFFENING STAND

One of the implications, of course, was that the Boron facility should be able to get along with a lot fewer people — 750 to 800 instead of more than a thousand. After they had learned the ropes, many members of the tiny force of scabs wondered how the regular workers had occupied their time. One of those who wondered was Al Ertel, who left his regular job as a computer-systems designer in Los Angeles and served as an oiler at the Boron plant. "I'd like to be here when there were eight or nine hundred hourly workers in this place," he said. "They'd be crawling all over each other."

U.S. Borax began taking a stiffer stand in its labor negotiations. In August the company offered to up the pay boost from 10 to 11 percent. In return, however, it demanded a number of major concessions. They included reserving to the company the right to contract out not only new capital construction, but also a lot of major repairs and other work. The company also demanded that new job categories be created, consolidating several old ones. For example, a new "millwright" category would include former mechanics, welders, and pipefitters. The union negotiating committee predictably refused the offer, though it did reduce its wage-increase demand from 25 to 20 percent.

A month later, Borax addressed a letter to the strikers, warning them that it would begin hiring permanent replacements to fill the jobs of employees who were not back at work by September 23. Twenty-four employees returned by the deadline, despite a lot of intimidation and some violence by militant union members. The frustration of those who stayed out manifested itself in a major escalation of violence. On the morning of September 23, strikers lined the roads to the plant, stoning every car going in or out, and injuring several people.

DESERT CARAVANS

But two developments put the seal on the strike's outcome. The first was the refusal of various A.F.L.-C.I.O. craft unions that were slated to perform the contract work at Boron to agree to observe the I.L.W.U. picket lines. The second was the unexpectedly large response to the company's prominent help-wanted ads in several California cities. Unemployment in the state was then averaging around 7.5 percent, and within days after the ads appeared in late September, hundreds of eager applicants showed up, despite the traditional reluctance of many people to cross a union's picket line. The company claimed that the newly hired workers often turned out to be far more willing hands than the old ones. It suddenly saw that it had within its grasp not only the chance to reduce its plant manpower but, if it chose, to rid itself of all its ingrained Boron labor troubles and start afresh.

The newcomers commuted in from such towns as Mojave, Barstow, and Lancaster, thirty to fifty miles away. Every morning and evening, they gathered into hundred-car convoys. Guarded by police cars, led by a helicopter, the caravans made their way across the hostile desert.

By then, the union had begun to cave in. It had reduced its wage-increase demand to a face-saving 13 percent. Among the remaining sticking points was the issue of amnesty. The company had made clear its intention of firing or suspending about ten individuals who had been identified in acts of violence. The union wanted the company to drop all charges and disciplinary action.

U.S. Borax refused to make even this concession. In its final offer, possibly made to convince the National Labor Relations Board that it was still bargaining in good faith, the company said it would take back all strikers except those under discipline. Most of the supervisors and the now-toughened tenderfeet in the Boron plant hoped that the union would turn down the offer.

A SIGH HEARD ALL OVER

The union met on the night of October 7. After a quick show of hands, the leaders ruled that no formal vote would be taken, the effect of this being that the company offer was rejected. When the news reached the plant the next morning, "the sigh of relief," as one man put it, "could be heard all over the place." The company immediately began large-scale hiring from cities as far away as San Diego and Tucson.

On October 24, the union finally voted 332 to 86 to go back to work, accepting all the company's terms. By that time, though, 250 people had already been hired. And since the company was by then contemplating a workforce reduction of another 200 to 300, a substantial proportion of Boron's breadwinners would be looking for work in a bad and worsening job market. Many owned houses that they would have a hard time selling if they decided to move; for a long time to come, no doubt, most of the newly hired plant workers would rather commute a long way than move to a resentful community where life would be uncomfortable at best and possibly dangerous. So, it appeared that the dusty plant and the little town would continue in uneasy coexistence side by side—one in improved health, the other sorely ailing, both wiser than they were before.

EPILOGUE

The material presented in this book provides, we feel, an interesting view of life and death in organizations. It is different in many ways from what is encountered in academic treatments of formal organization. One might question why material such as is described in this book is not dealt with typically in teaching and research within the organizational behavior and management field. We have concluded that this is so in part because scholars in these fields treat the material as aberrational, as something which doesn't fit the traditional or conventional views of formal organization. The material is thus ignored or discarded. We feel that to the extent such material is not seriously examined for its potential contribution to the field, so our current academic perspectives on organizations are incomplete.

Clearly, organizations and their members survive and prosper in the midst of and, at times, apparently because of conflict-ridden, manipulative, spontaneous and even serendipitous behaviors and processes. Equally clear from a reading of the material in this book is the inference that organizations and their members suffer, are injured and, on occasion, die under the same sets of conditions and events. The principles, models and ideals described in some organizational behavior and management texts may in fact cushion the extremes of failure, pain and decline in organizations. We feel they succeed only partially, and often not at all, because of their development in ignorance of, or without reference to, the kinds of behaviors and situations presented in this book.

We are reminded of the story of the somewhat inebriated young man who, one dark night, was found peering at the ground around a lighted lamppost by a passing patroller. When the officer of the law asked him what he was doing, he replied he was looking for his car keys. "Where did you lose them?" the patroller inquired. "Over there, around the corner," replied the man. "Then why look here?" asked the cop, somewhat surprised. "Because there's a light here and I can't see anything there at all."

Perhaps we need to look around the corner in our search for a deeper understanding of organization. There may be organizational phenomena "over there" which are being described consistently by others but which we don't regard typically as sources of light, and so we perceive only a dark corner, if we see anything there at all.

We have found our own thinking greatly stimulated and our own models of organization much in need of revision as a result of our encounter with the material in this book. We suspect there is in such literature a rich source of questions to be explored, ideas to be investigated and challenges to be met in building new models to better describe and explain formal organization.

Perhaps our visitor to Earth from planet Utopia, arriving ten years from now, will take back documents from academia and documents from periodicals, newspapers and other sources which reflect a steady flow of ideas and applications between the theoretical and the so-called "real world" of organizational behavior. We look forward to such a development!